BEHIND THE CAMERA

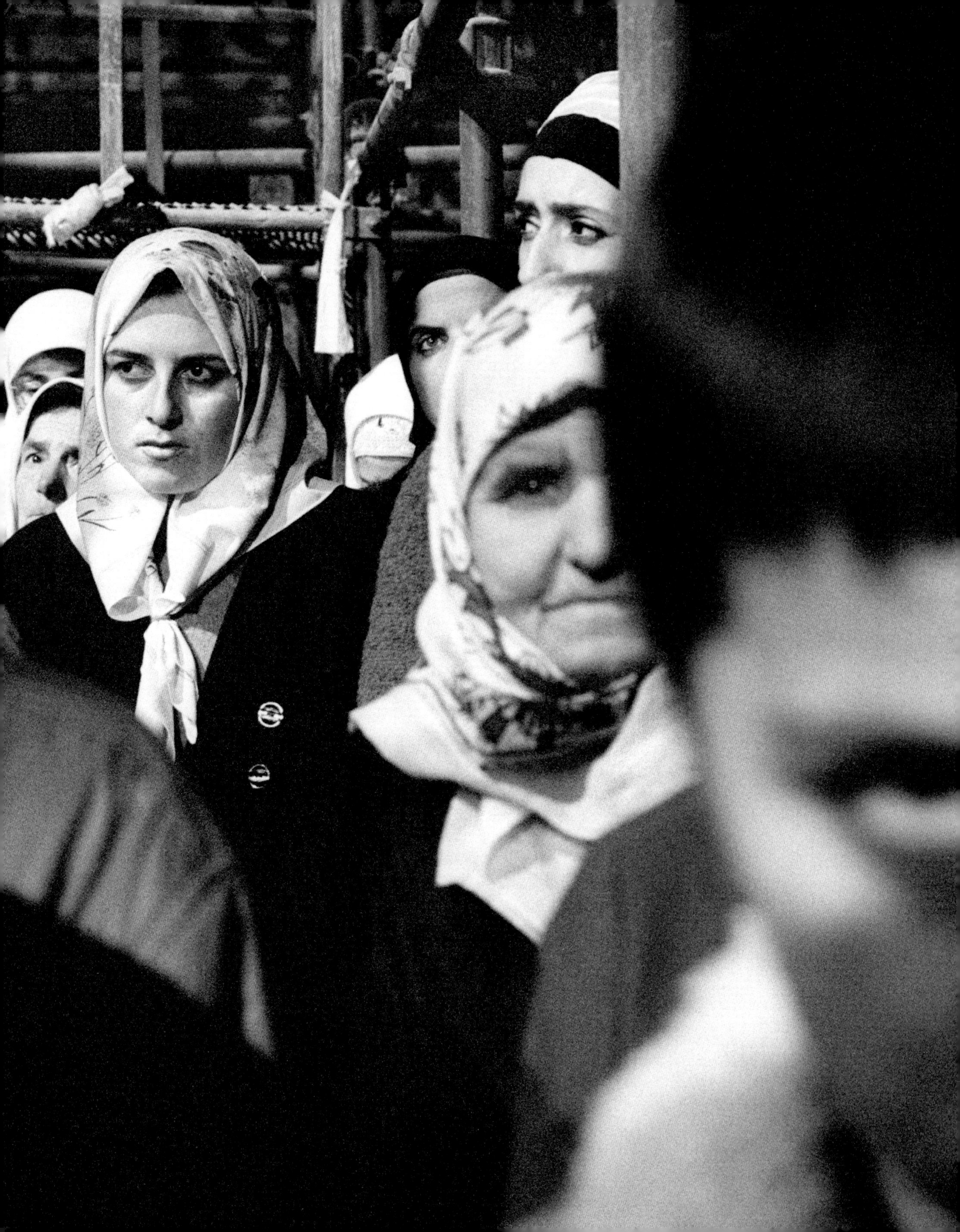

BEHIND THE CAMERA

CREATIVE TECHNIQUES OF 100 GREAT PHOTOGRAPHERS

PAUL LOWE

PRESTEL
MUNICH • LONDON • NEW YORK

Previous page
People worshipping during the first prayers at Begova Dzamija mosque in Sarajevo, Bosnia, after its reopening following the civil war.

Prestel Verlag, Munich · London · New York 2016
A member of Verlagsgruppe Random House GmbH
Neumarkter Strasse 28 · 81673 Munich

Prestel Publishing Ltd.
14-17 Wells Street
London W1T 3PD

Prestel Publishing
900 Broadway, Suite 603
New York, NY 10003

www.prestel.com

This book was produced by
Quintessence Editions Ltd.
The Old Brewery
6 Blundell Street
London N7 9BH

Project Editor	Sophie Blackman
Editor	Fiona Plowman
Designer	Josse Pickard
Picture Researcher	Jo Walton
Proofreader	Sarah Yates
Indexer	Ruth Ellis
Production Manager	Anna Pauletti
Editorial Director	Ruth Patrick
Publisher	Philip Cooper

Library of Congress Control Number: 2016941558

ISBN: 978-3-7913-8279-1

10 9 8 7 6 5 4 3 2 1

Color reproduction by Bright Arts, Hong Kong.
Printed in China by C&C Offset Printing Co., LTD.

Contents

Foreword by Simon Norfolk

I happened to be in Paris on the night of the terrorist attacks at the Bataclan concert hall and the Stade de France in 2015. The other guests in the restaurant received anxious text messages from faraway families and I felt obliged to nip down there to see what was going on—it's my job isn't it? The streets were weirdly deserted, and there were no cabs, so I jumped on a Vélib' hire bike and dashed across town. No battery in my phone, my only tactic was to chase fire engines, and at one point I ended up in Les Halles where the police thought the attackers were hiding. A battalion of SWAT police units—dressed like armoured insects and bristling with weapons and shields—scouted the streets. I followed behind them accompanied by at least a dozen random passers-by, all photographing with their mobile phones held in the air. For some reason, homeward-bound drunks, interested locals, and the morbidly curious had transformed themselves into CNN news crews. In front of us, the police were prepared for serious violence; behind was a shoal of lads (they were all lads) in T-shirts and jeans hoping for scraps like those tiny fish that follow behind big sharks, casually live-streaming to Facebook and Periscope. And me on a hire bike. I didn't know why any of us were there. We were either totally wasting our time (the terrorists were elsewhere) or we were about to become sponges for absorbing stray bullets. I wondered why they thought they were suddenly pro photographers. They'd left the house that evening looking for a fun Friday night out and now here they were, writing The First Draft of History, an eager world awaiting their dispatch—at least that's what they thought. And was I that different? Why was I trying to be a part of this? Why does anybody take pictures? We're all doing it now, billions a day, and a small number of those are mine. For twenty-five years photography has been paying my mortgage but I still don't know why. I felt foolish and superfluous at Les Halles and I gave up and cycled home through empty streets.

The closest answer I can give to the question of why I take pictures is a metaphor. For me, taking a picture is like the ignition point in a combustion engine; ingredients (petrol vapour, air) are brought together in masterful engineering, compressed in one exquisitely timed moment, and jolted into producing brilliant sparks and power. At the genesis of a successful photograph all the preceding effort comes together in one focused moment: the research time tracking down that specialist academic, the hard slog up that hill to get to the location before the light shifts, the clever gimmick dreamed up to make the story tell itself in a new and intriguing way, the silvery metaphor that wraps the whole idea, and then the weather plays along and you didn't forget to charge the battery on that bit of kit and, and, and. And when all of this is compressed together into the same fraction of a second and reaches its ignition point . . . well, the sense of satisfaction is overwhelming. It's. The. Best.

It happens so rarely, but when it's right I feel like it's a privilege to be allowed to do this as a job. Miraculous. Like Wordsworth wrote, "Bliss was it in that dawn to be alive."

Some photographers see themselves as hunters, prowling and sniping down the streets, but that's not me, I'm a gatherer. I often think I'm not a real photographer at all because in that moment of coalescence, the pictures seem to simply fall out of the camera. All I have to do is go out and gather them up, bring them home like lost kittens. All the work is done before the picture-making moment. I imagine a theoretical mathematician feels the same when they get down to the bottom right-hand corner of the blackboard and the final calculation produces a eureka moment when they know it works. Perhaps this is why I rarely review my old photographs, why I get so little satisfaction from being told my work is any good, why I have folders of unpublished projects, why I'd rather others designed my books or hung my shows. Or wrote forewords to books. All that afterwards stuff isn't a fraction as good as going out and making those magic sparks.

It's not all a bed of roses, of course. The successes are overwhelmed by the failures and the not-quites 999:1, and some of the things I've seen along the way have been terrifying and/or truly horrible. However, I think the reason I'm still making pictures and I'm not bored or I don't feel more bitter about the things I've seen, or why I haven't gone crazy or just given up and swapped to what my mother still calls "a proper job," is because I switch on the evening news and some lying politician is telling their lies or some pseudo expert is mouthing something stupid, some moron is being lionized and, hey presto!, I'm furious again and I'm online trying to buy a plane ticket, I'm packing a bag, making my apologies to Mrs. Norfolk, and once again thinking about how to bring it all together into sparks.

Introduction

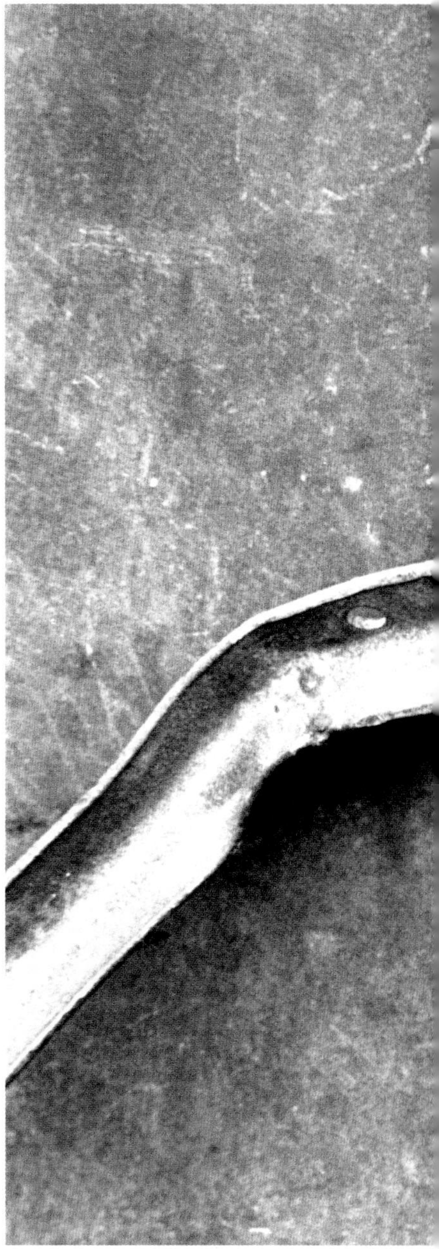

The photographic image, although still in its infancy compared to other forms of artistic expression, so completely permeates our lives that it is hard to imagine how the world could be described and interpreted without it. This book offers unique insights into how photographers think and feel about their practice, and how they relate it to their understanding of the physical and conceptual world. Each photographer featured within these pages has an original and personal vision, and he or she has used the formal aspects of the medium not only to describe the world, but also to explore, interpret, and ask questions about it.

The performative image

The act of photography can be regarded as a form of performance—whether it is the collaborative "dance" that takes place between photographer and subject in a portrait session, the athletic gymnastics of the street photographer, or the theatricality of the landscape photographer using a large-format view camera on a tripod and viewing the image from under a black cloth. The taking of a photograph can be likened to improvised theater, with a multitude of decisions being made in real time about how and what to photograph. This can include the formal composition of the image as the photographer moves around the subject, with minute changes in distance and space significantly impacting the final form of the image that will appear within the frame. In this way, the photograph can be regarded as a performative space. Furthermore, the performance of taking the image involves a choreography between the photographer, the subject, and the environment. On looking at the image, the audience or viewer is invited to reflect on what could have occurred in the

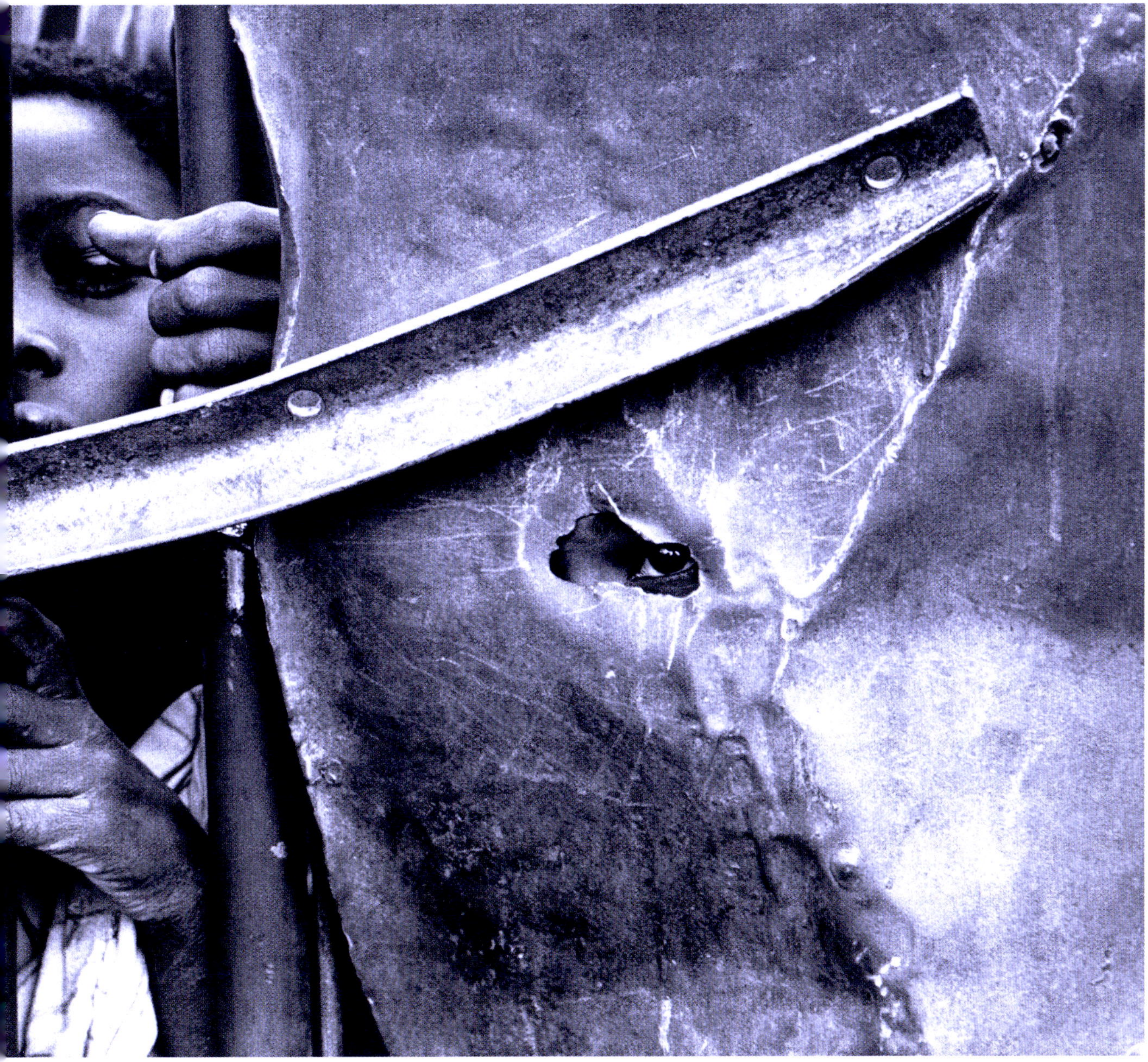

The relationship between the subject and the photographer is central to your photographic practice; the direct gaze of these young Somalian refugees peering through the gate of a feeding center addresses the viewer directly (1992).

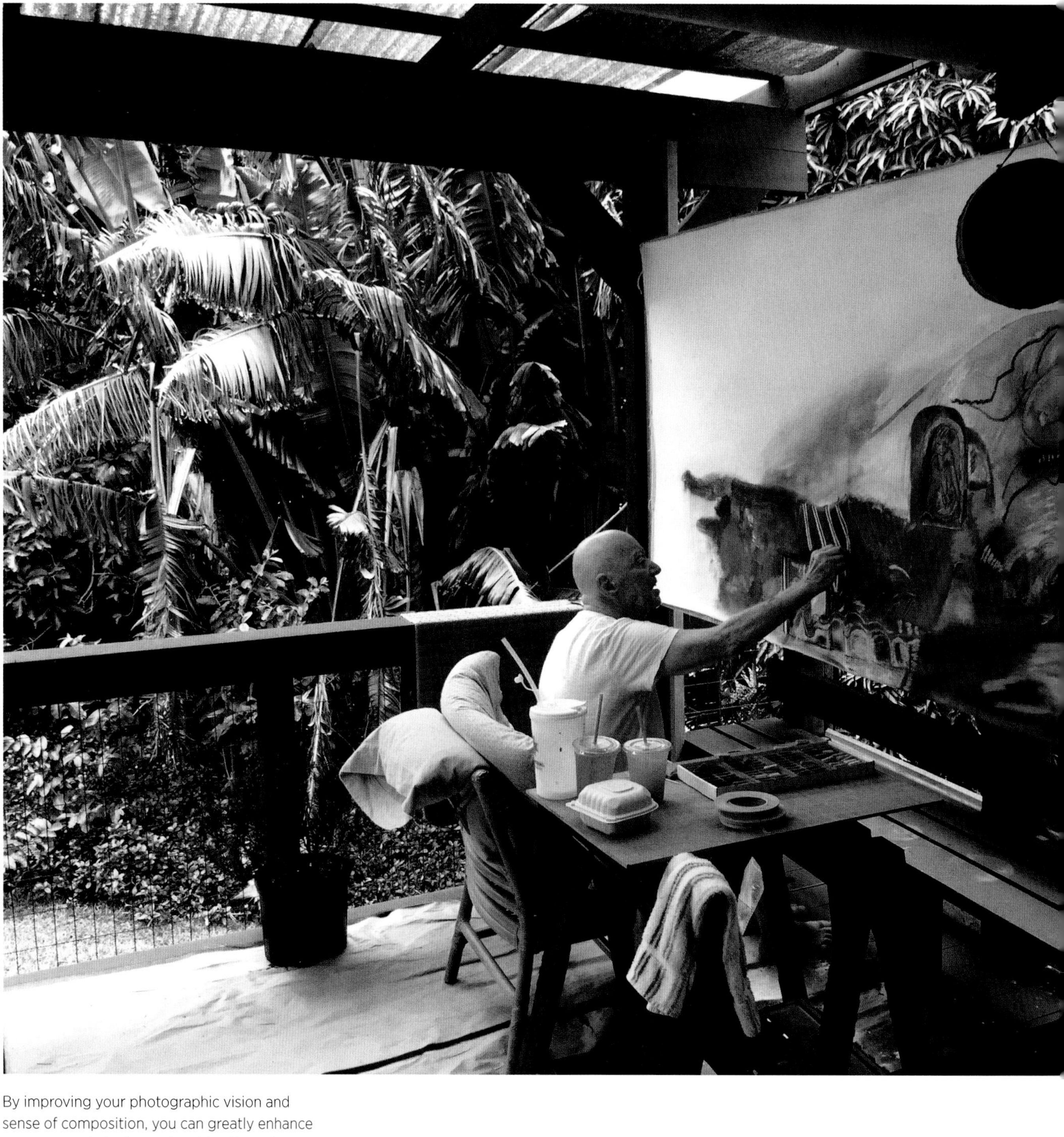

By improving your photographic vision and sense of composition, you can greatly enhance your personal photographs of family and friends. This quietly observed moment of the photographer's father, an artist, was shot on a camera phone during a visit to his home (2015).

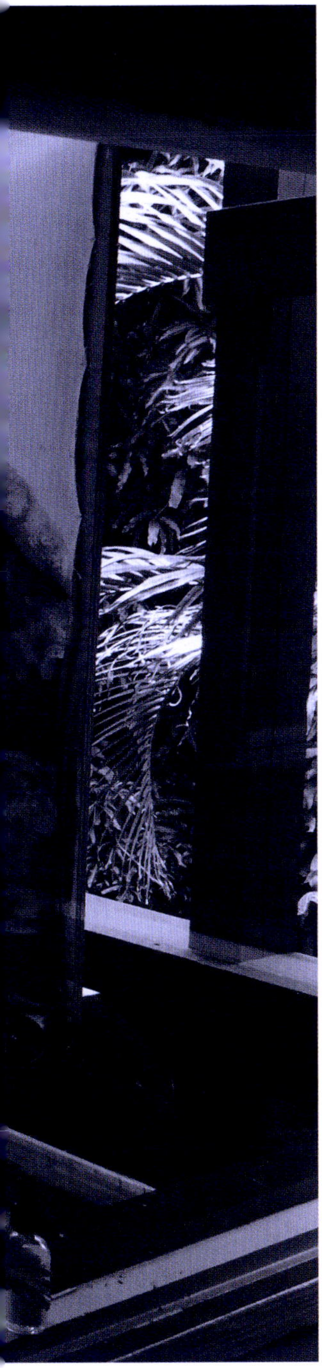

moments before and after the photograph was taken, which contributes to an imaginative reading of the image. The viewer is thereby encouraged to actively participate in generating their own meaning for the image, rather than allowing the meaning to be given to them solely by its author. No matter how much the photographer attempts to predetermine or control the interpretation of an image, it is only when the viewer brings their unique personal engagement to it that the meaning is finally determined. One of the great joys of looking carefully at photographs is discovering new insight or meaning in an image you have already spent hours poring over; the potential for new interpretation can be almost endless. Spend time with the images presented in this book and really look hard at them, asking yourself how they work, how they are constructed, and how they offer up their meaning. Interrogate them for technical lessons, but also appreciate them for the diverse ways in which they use composition and form to contribute to the interpretation of their content. Use these images as inspiration for your own work. As an exercise, try to go out for a day and make photographs in the style of another photographer; reinterpreting the work of others is an excellent way of developing your own unique vision.

The photobook

Throughout the following pages, key photobooks produced by the photographer concerned are discussed. Use the photobooks described as an entry point into the work of each photographer, and then build out from them to deepen your understanding of the medium itself. Although photographs are disseminated via a range of media, including exhibitions, magazines, slideshows, and the internet, the photobook is potentially the most effective way for the photographer to present and disseminate his or her work in a coherent and discrete format. It allows the photographer to organize and sequence his or her work in a complex narrative or structure and combine it, where appropriate, with textual information that interacts with images and adds to their meaning.

The photobook offers a haptic experience whereby the material and tactile qualities of its format can enhance the viewer's experience of the work. Its size, flexibility, and material durability also enable it to be shared and widely distributed. Many of the books mentioned here deploy structural and physical qualities that seek to engage the viewer in a more nuanced and complex way, inviting them to engage more actively with a particular photographer's ideas. A sustained engagement with a range of photobooks is one of the best ways of developing photographic vision, whether you are delving deep into a particular genre or photographer, taking a historical cross section of practice, or merely collecting a set of your favorite image-makers.

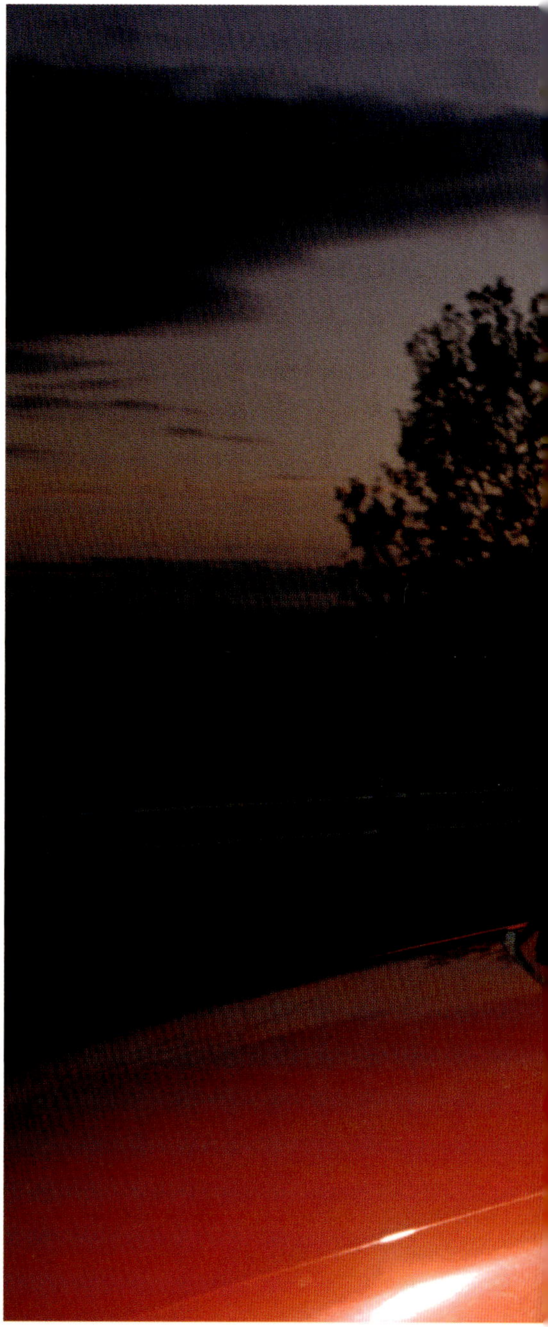

The continuity of practice

Many questions and ideas have recurred throughout the history of photography. Each photographer responds to them in his or her own personal way, adding new insights and interpretations that define the development of the medium. Throughout this book links between photographers can be traced, demonstrating how they regularly engage in conscious critical dialog with their own work, with the work of others, and with how those works operate in context. Few photographers operate entirely in isolation; most are developing and challenging concepts and ideas from others.

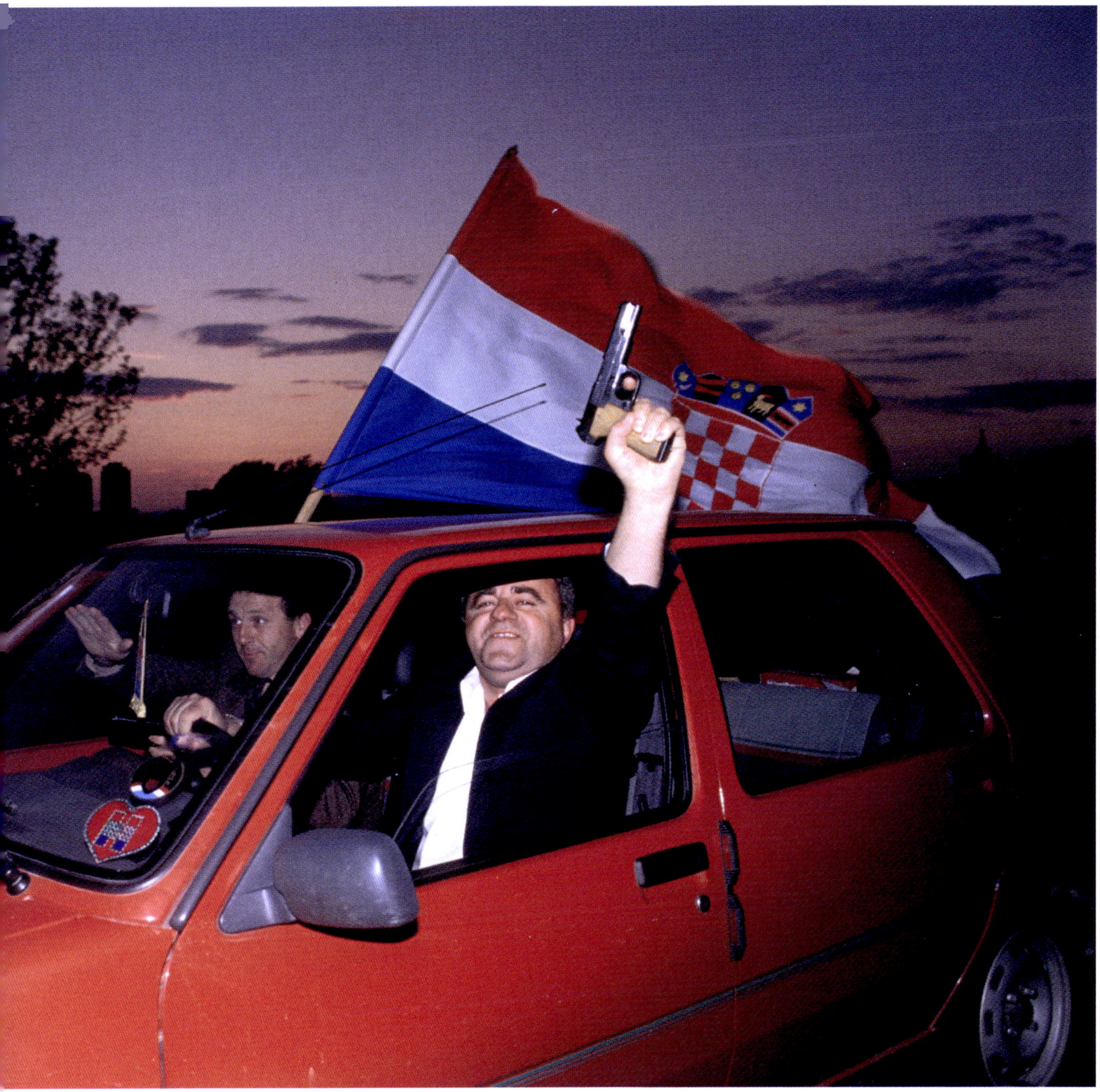

For this shot of Croatians celebrating their country's independence (1991), the exposure was set for the sky in the background, and then the flash was set for the same aperture. This balanced the foreground light with that of the background and retained the detail in the sunset.

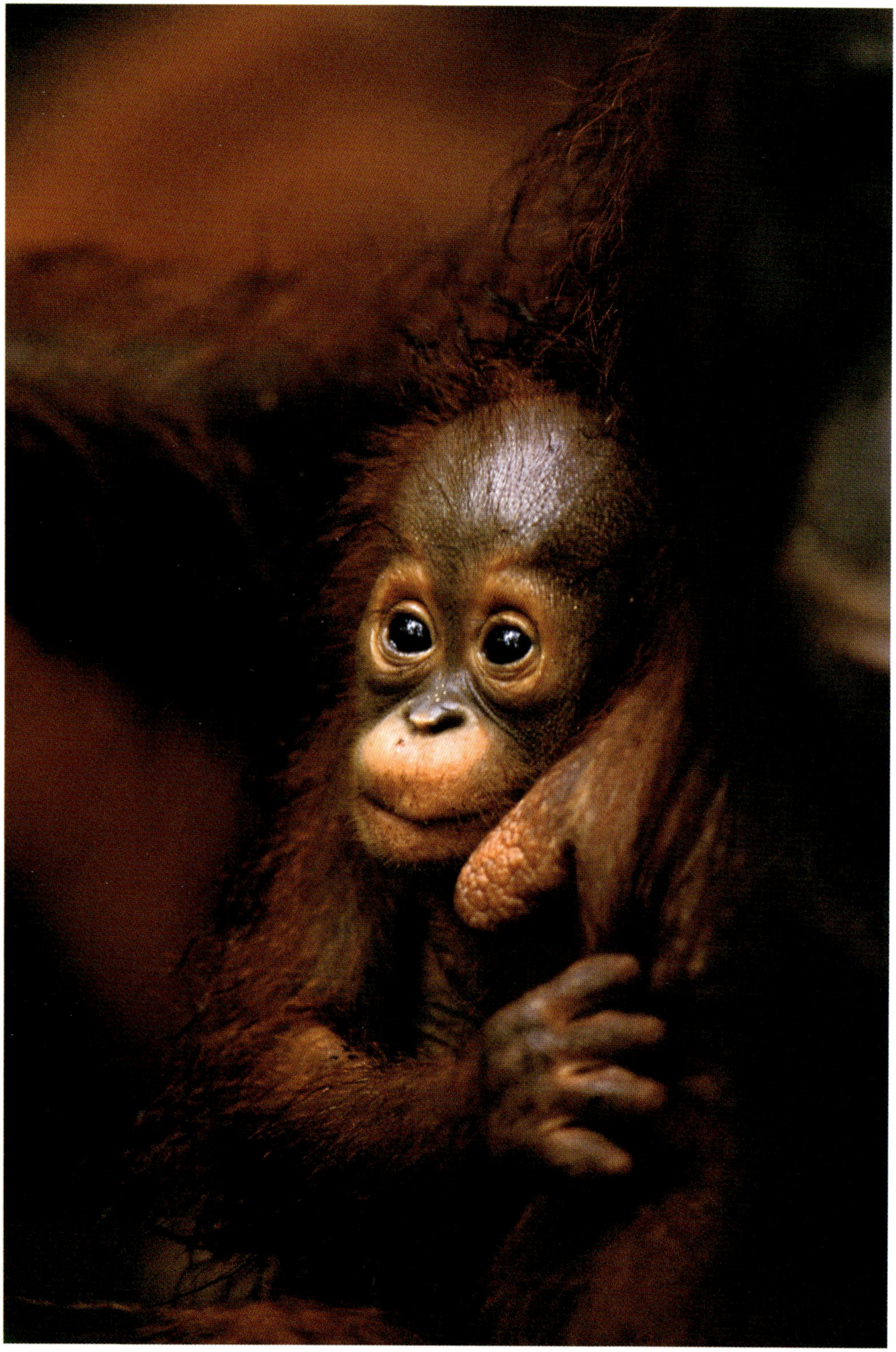

(Left) By tightly framing the infant orangutan by using a short telephoto lens, the harmony of the color palette is maintained, concentrating all of the viewer's attention on the eyes (2000).
(Right) What you leave out of the frame is as important as what you include. This photograph of a funeral during the Bosnian conflict (1992) focuses on the contrast between the rose and the soldier's uniform; the emotion of the moment is concentrated and conveyed symbolically.
(Bottom right) Shooting in low light can have unpredictable results, but the subtle qualities of the light in this Japanese bar were preserved by resisting the temptation to use flash and by holding the camera as steadily as possible (1994).

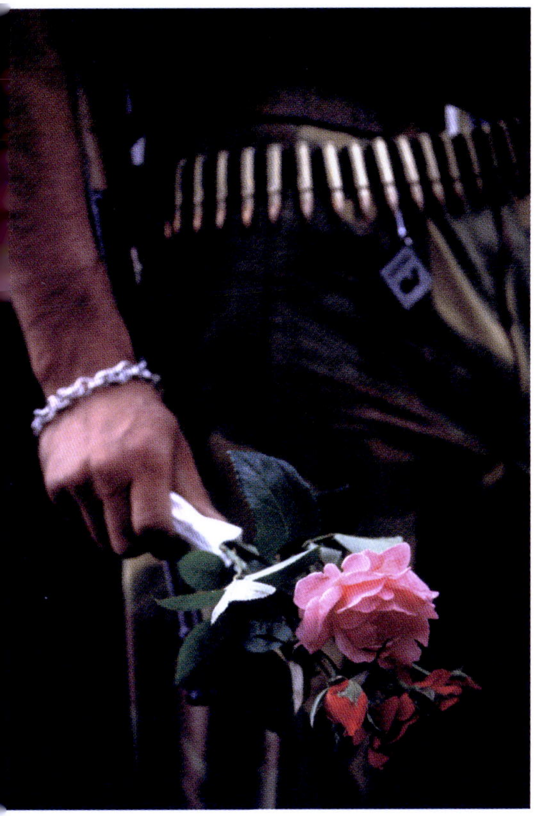

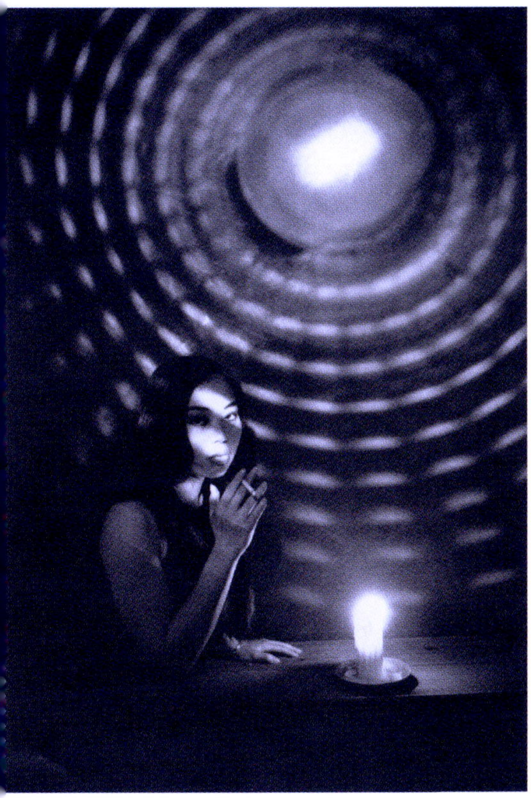

Photographers operating at the highest levels of practice are deeply aware of complications and contradictions within the medium, and consciously explore the relationship between form and content, and how it relates to the meaning of the final image. Photographers do not engage in this process in isolation, however. They interact and discuss their work with colleagues, friends, and mentors. They are often highly sensitive to the history of the medium, cross-referencing their work with that of earlier photographers and carrying on themes investigated by a previous generation. The ongoing road trip of visually describing America, for example, can be traced from Timothy H. O'Sullivan (see p.48), through Walker Evans (see p.78), Robert Frank (see p.186), Lee Friedlander (see p.194), and Robert Adams (see p.52), to William Eggleston (see p.100), and Joel Sternfeld (see p.54). Each has taken on the baton of representation in a continuing relay race in which each generation engages with how a particular set of formal concerns can be deployed to explore the changing social, political, and natural landscape. The influence of key editors and educators in this process must also be acknowledged. The inspiration of the photographer and teacher Alexey Brodovitch, for example, can be seen across a range of photographic practice, linking Tony Ray-Jones (see p.190), Lisette Model (see p.116), Garry Winogrand (see p.192), and many more. These connections and collaborations are fascinating to follow, and this book attempts to show how recurring questions of representation, themes, and ideas permeate the essence of the medium. An awareness of history helps to situate your own work in the context of others, and discovering connections between photographers creates a deeper awareness of the process of photography.

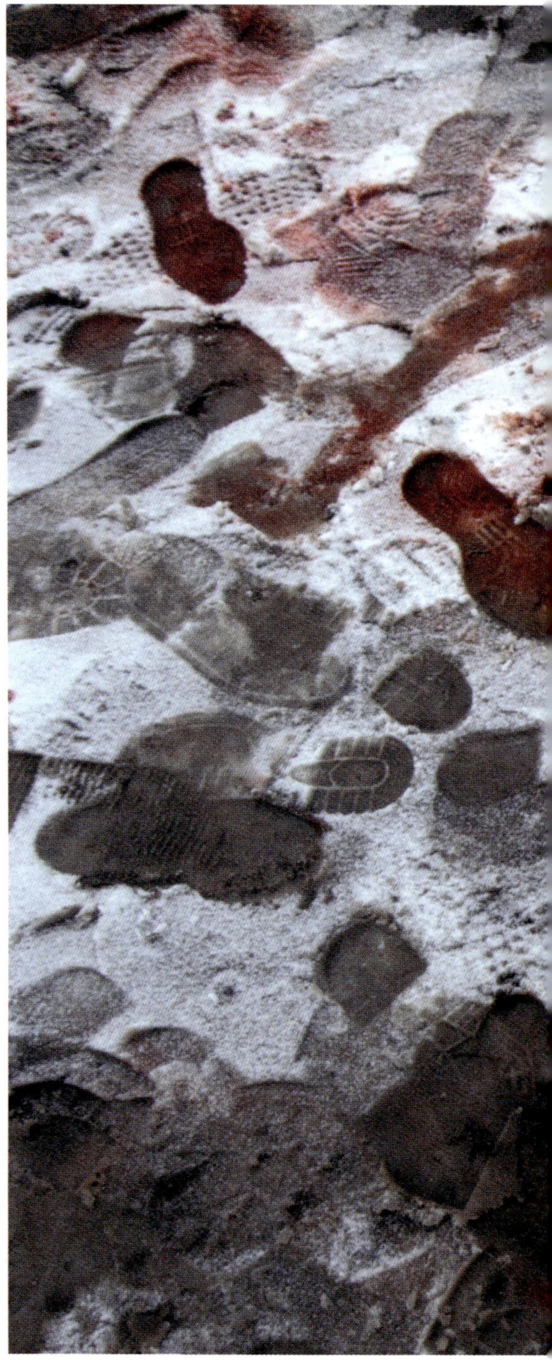

Selecting 100 photographers means excluding hundreds more, and the photographers chosen here are in no way intended to be a definitive list of the world's greatest image-makers. Instead, the intention has been to suggest a range of methodologies and approaches, a broad historical sweep that explores photography's technological and esthetic development, and a sense of the global reach of the medium. Many of those featured, such as Henri Cartier-Bresson (see p.260) or Ansel Adams (see p.50), are well known, but newer, less established names are included as well, for example Laura Pannack (see p.156) and Dougie Wallace (see p.202). The themes that structure the book are an attempt to codify a range of visual approaches to engaging with the world through the camera, offering a fresh interpretation and categorization of the traditional genres of landscape, portrait, still life, street photography, fashion, reportage, and so on. The idea of genres is useful to help classify different styles and approaches, but there is considerable overlap between them, and many photographers operate across a range of fields. Exploring the practical details of making a photograph can greatly intensify interpretation and understanding, and this book seeks to offer insight into the methods and ideas of the practitioner. It provides a starting point to follow up on the photographers featured and to explore their work in more detail, using them and the themes presented as a way into the extraordinarily rich history of the medium. Each entry includes a short biography of the photographer, an extended discussion of a specific image, and a series of tips organized around twelve areas, each identified by an icon, and covering a range of methodological and technical concepts and skills, which are explained over the next few pages.

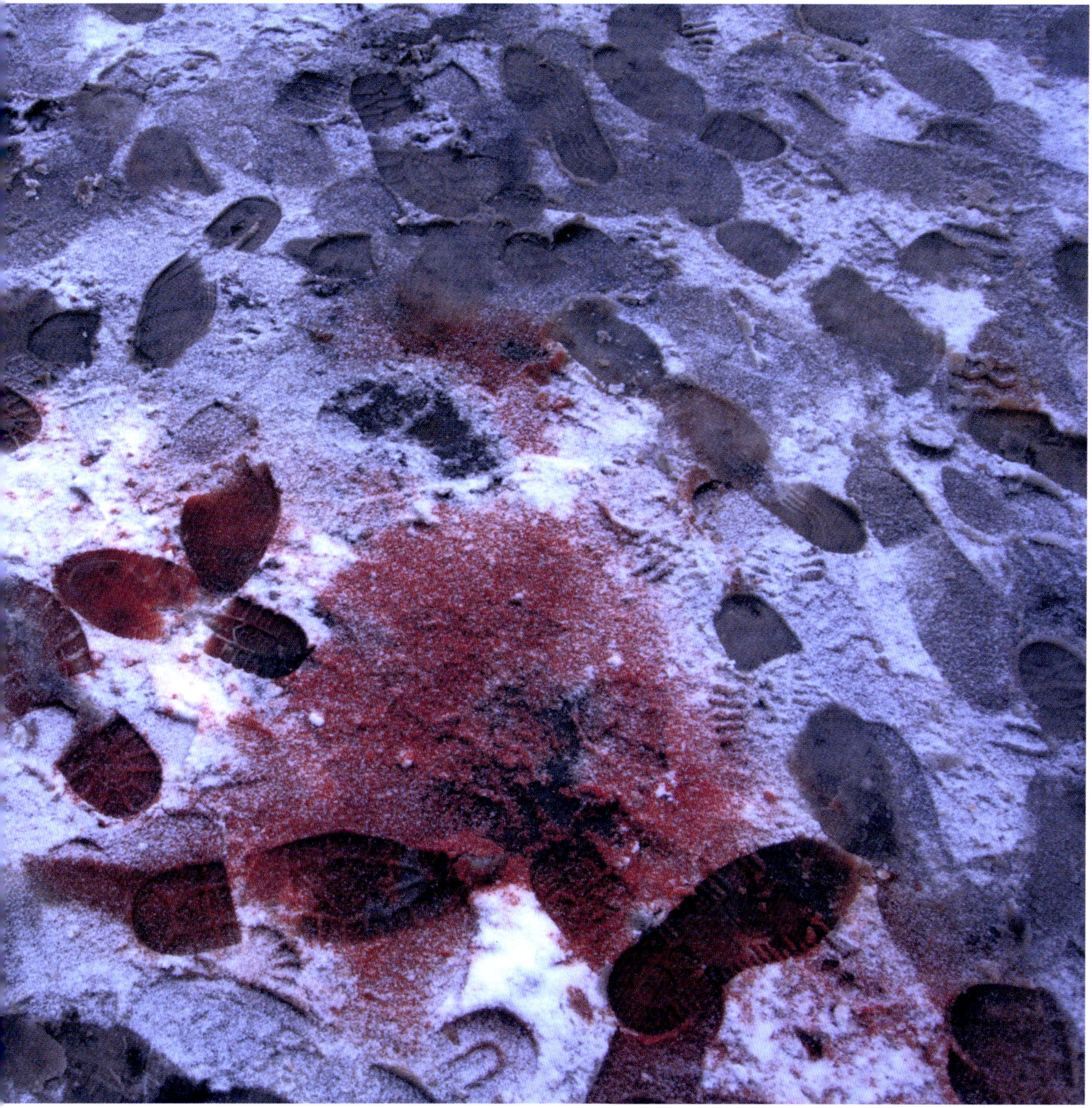

Photography is intimately linked to time. The layers of snow, blood, and footsteps in this image of the aftermath of an attack on civilians during the Chechen war (1994) act as a visual trace of the traumatic event, requiring the viewer to imagine the horror of what happened there.

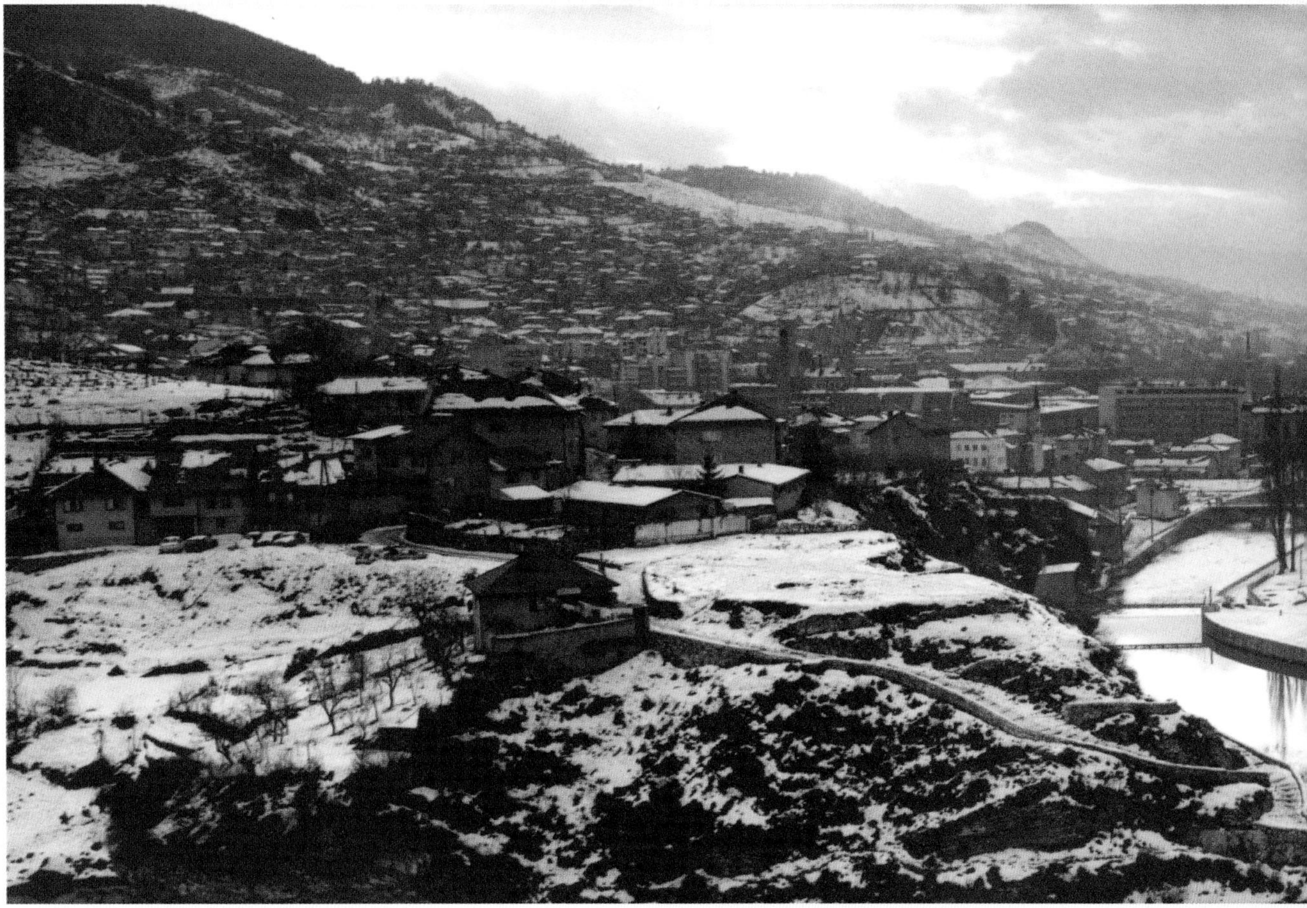

This photograph of Sarajevo taken during the siege in 1994 was shot on a specialist panoramic camera, a 6 x 17 cm Fuji. Many digital cameras provide a panoramic mode or, alternatively, you can shoot a series of overlapping images and stitch them together in post-production.

Key to creative tips and techniques icons

Each entry in this book is accompanied by a series of technical and creative tips that are organized under the following themes: camera, color and tone, composition, digital, exposure, flash, lens, lighting, location, method, processing, and subject. Each theme is accompanied by a corresponding icon and an explanation of each of the themes follows.

- **Camera** (see p.19)
- **Color/Tone** (see p.21)
- **Composition** (see p.23)
- **Digital** (see p.24)
- **Exposure** (see p.26)
- **Flash** (see p.28)
- **Lens** (see p.30)
- **Lighting** (see p.32)
- **Location** (see p.35)
- **Method** (see p.36)
- **Processing** (see p.38
- **Subject** (see p.41)

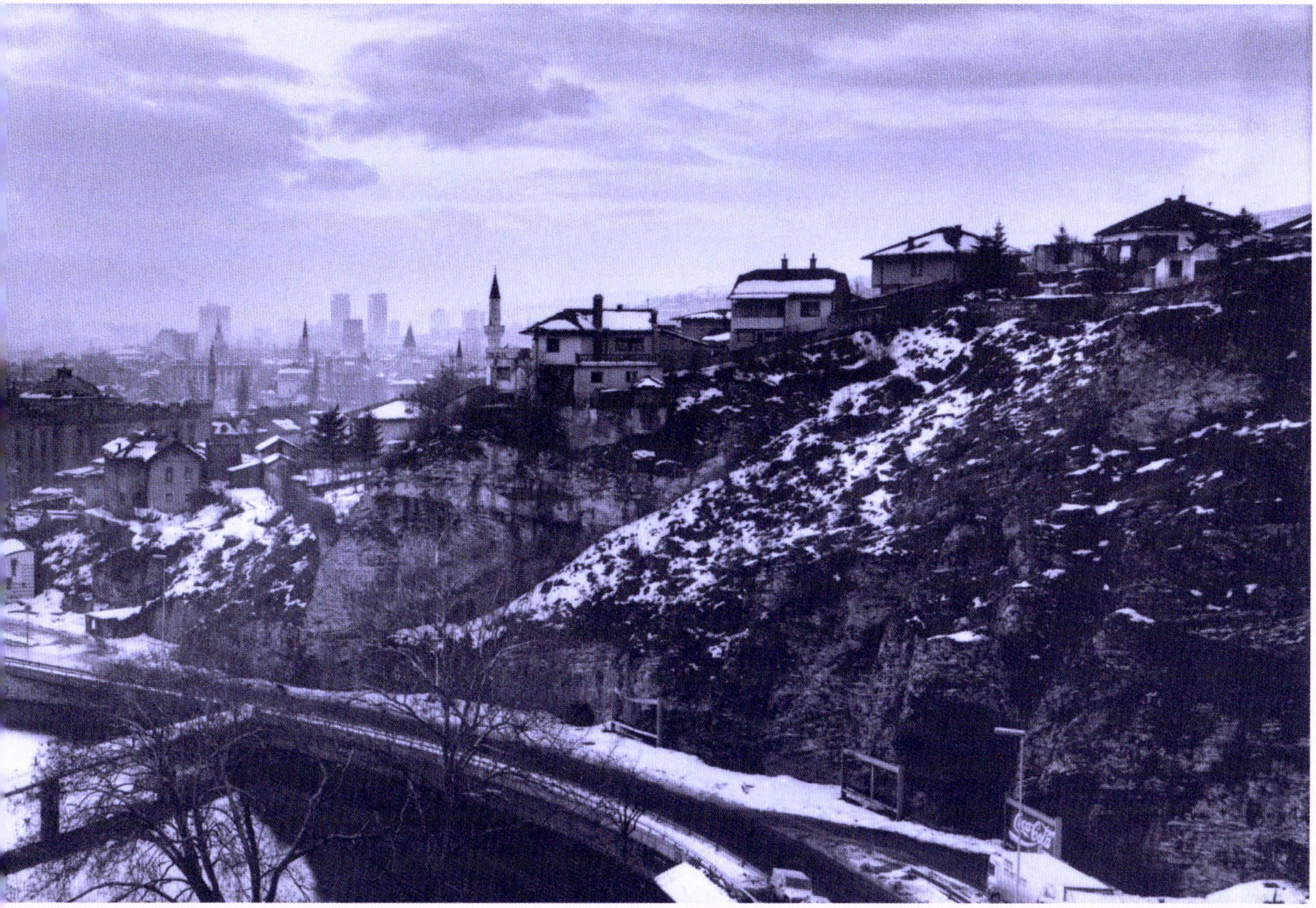

Camera

In one sense, all cameras, whether film or digital, are the same; they all have a lens and a light-sensitive surface on which the image is recorded. However, different formats and types of camera do have specific advantages and disadvantages that make them more or less suitable for particular genres of photography.

Single-lens reflex (SLR)

The SLR is the most flexible and adaptable of all cameras, as it can be used with a wide range of lenses, including zooms. It also delivers images of high quality. It is a great all-round camera that can be used effectively for almost every genre.

Rangefinder

Rangefinder cameras such as the Leica are excellent for street photography and for working in intimate situations, because they are small, quiet, and unobtrusive. The direct viewfinder gives a clear view and is excellent for fast-moving subjects as you can see beyond the edges of the frame to predict elements coming into the composition. They work best with lenses in the standard to medium wide-angle range.

Medium-format cameras

Medium-format cameras are heavier and more cumbersome than SLRs, but give higher-quality images because the film or sensor is significantly larger. They are excellent for landscape, portrait, and studio work, especially when used on a tripod. The 6 x 6 or 6 x 7 cm formats give a certain sense of weight and presence to the final image.

Large-format cameras

Large-format cameras, also known as view cameras, take a huge negative in single sheets, typically either 5 x 4 or 10 x 8 inches. This gives exceptional quality; a contact print made directly from the negative onto the paper gives an extraordinary level of detail and tonal values. Large-format cameras also have the ability to move the lens in relation to the film plane, allowing for distortions to be corrected in the camera. This is particularly useful for architectural and landscape work.

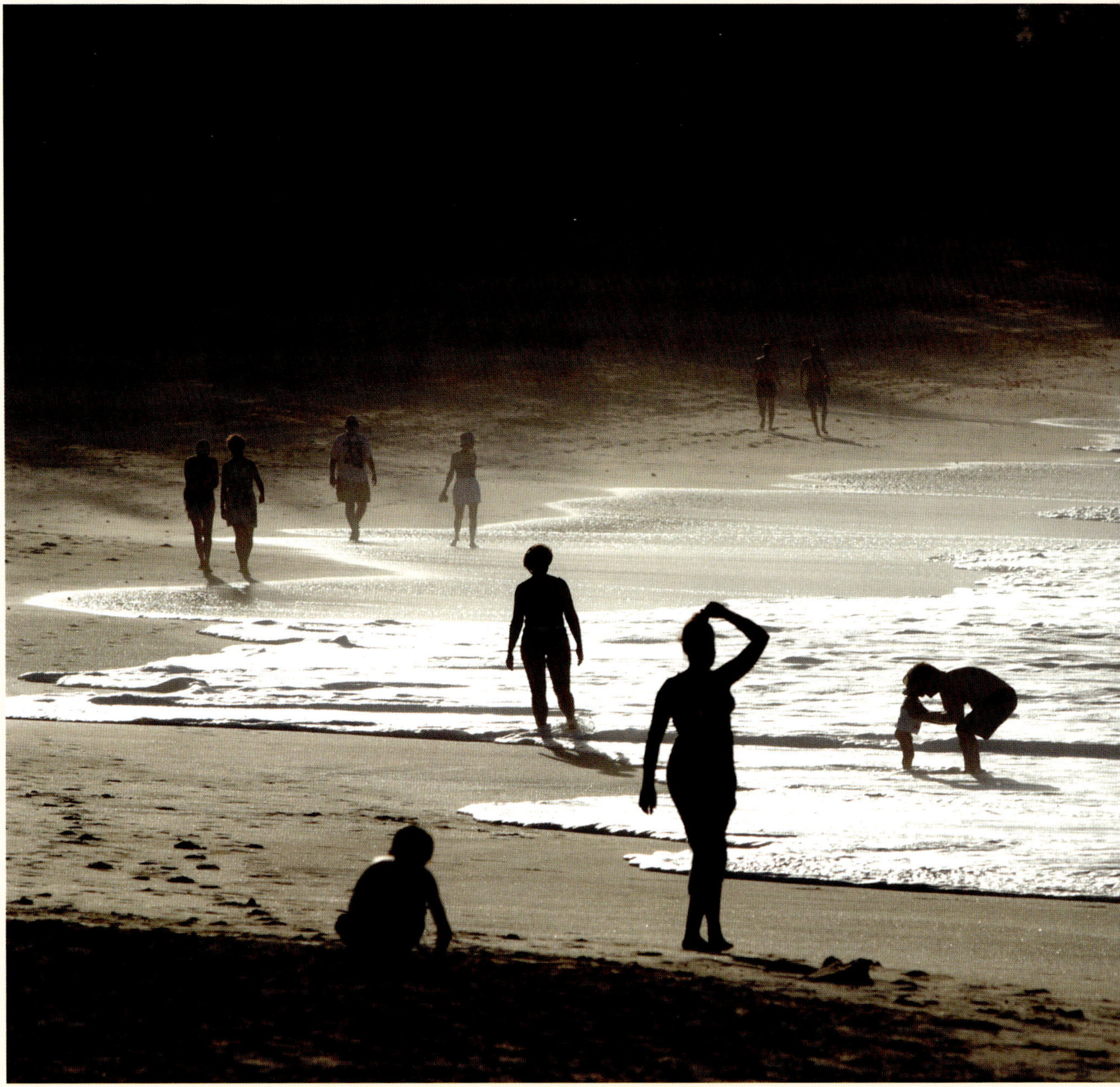

Shooting against the light has created an almost monochromatic effect in this beach photograph (2005), with the late-afternoon light suffusing the shadows and the highlights with warmth. The telephoto lens has also compressed the perspective.

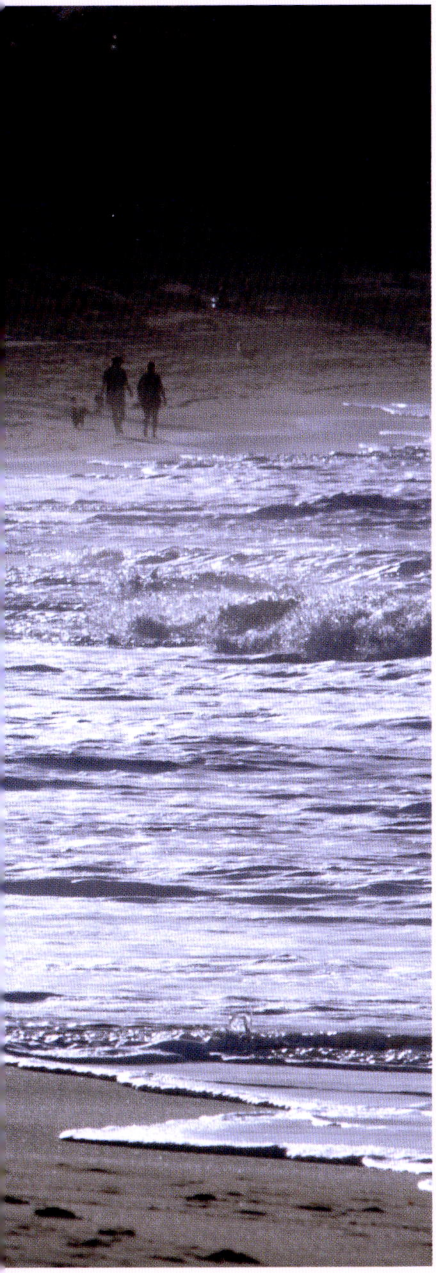

Color/Tone

Whether shooting in color or black and white, understanding how light affects a photograph is fundamental. Mastering a range of different types of light and using light creatively to contribute to the final photograph are key to expressing your individual vision as a photographer.

Color versus black and white

Black and white creates a more analytical and abstract feel, emphasizing forms and giving a sense of timelessness. Color tends to be more visceral, and clearly adds an extra level of pure description. Choosing the appropriate color or exposure range to match the feel of the final image's color and tone can have a significant emotional or psychological effect. Shooting in overcast light creates a soft, muted range of colors, with low saturation and a high level of detail, as all tones will be recorded, whereas working in the late afternoon gives warm, rich, saturated colors, with deep blacks and detailed highlights. In black and white, the light has a similar effect. Flash can be used to make colors pop, creating a hyperreal effect. Some photographers favor particular kinds of light, shooting mainly in high- or low-contrast situations to give images a consistent feel and color palette. However, gaining a feel for working across a range of light intensities and understanding how they change colors in a scene are vital. By shooting at different times of day or night and in different situations, indoors and outdoors, you can develop your visual memory of how color changes the atmosphere of an image.

Color of light

Different types of light, both natural and artificial, will have varying color temperatures. Midday light is desaturated and relatively blue in temperature, and can look "washed out." Many photographers avoid shooting during the middle of the day, especially if they are working in color, and instead try to get up for the dawn light or work in late afternoon, when the sun is at an angle to the earth and produces a light that, although still quite hard, is very directional, warmer in color, and more interesting. In the early morning, strong shadows cast across a scene can create dramatic effects; these shadows change completely again in the afternoon. Use these shadows as part of your composition. Indoors, the light from a single, bare light bulb will be very warm, almost orange; it will also be harsh, as it is a small light source; a table lamp can be used to light only the subject, throwing the rest of the room into darkness. Fluorescent light is generally soft, but be aware that it gives off a green light, although negative films and digital cameras cope with it quite well. Be careful, however, if you have window light and fluorescent light in the same scene, as they are very different in color and it can be difficult to balance the two.

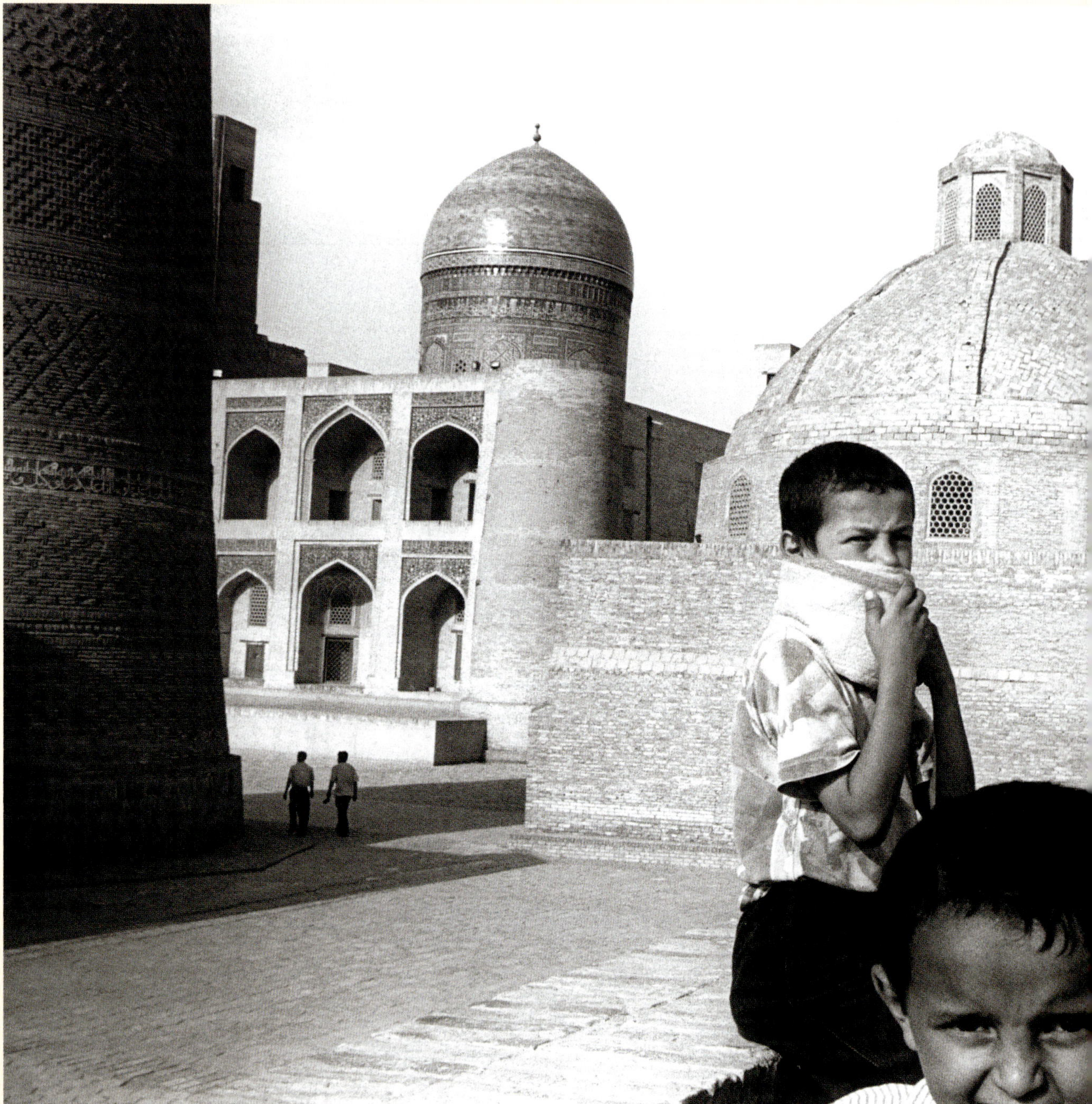

This shot of the ancient city of Bukhara in Uzbekistan (2002) captured a moment when the light and activity on the street combined with the geometry of the buildings to create a balanced composition. The small figure of the man on the right could be seen as a punctuation mark, returning the eye to the frame's center.

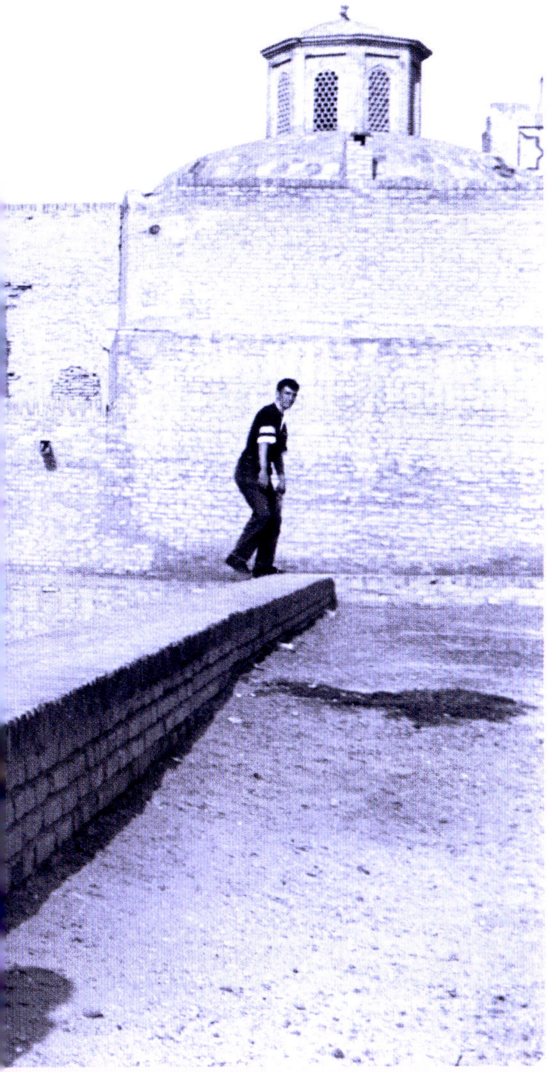

Composition

There are many so-called "rules" of composition that can help in making strong, interesting images, but do not forget that rules are meant to be broken. Always remember first what you are trying to say with your image, then think of how to say it using the formal techniques available to you to get across the content of the picture.

Learning how the camera sees

We have to learn how the camera sees, because a photograph does not reproduce a scene in the same way as the human eye does. The camera records only part of the larger scene, reducing it to two dimensions, framing it, and stopping the moment in time. When we look at a scene our eye selects only certain elements and ignores the rest. A camera, on the other hand, sees all the detail. Elements that we don't notice can become dominant when seen in a print. Be very aware of the frame itself; when we look with our eyes we don't have a frame, so we have to learn how the frame works. A simple technique is to use your hands to make a rectangle through which to view a scene. The way elements inside the frame interact with the frame itself is paramount; some images use the frame much like a picture frame, surrounding the subject and "holding" it in space; others dynamically intersect the frame and the frame cuts through elements of the image, cropping into them, creating energy and drama. The best way to learn about elements that make a two-dimensional image interesting is to look at many different types of pictures, not only photographs but artworks too, as every artist has to deal with the organization of space within the frame. The more images you look at carefully, the more you will have in your "memory bank" to help you improve the composition of your own pictures.

Rule of thirds

This method of composition has been used as far back as ancient Greece. It divides the frame into thirds, both horizontally and vertically, which gives six points of intersection between them. If you place elements of your composition along these lines and points, the image will appear well composed. For landscapes, the horizon line is often placed along one of these axes. Note, however, that if this is the only way you compose your images they will become repetitive. Using the rule of thirds your pictures will normally appear "balanced," another important aspect of composition. Balance can also mean working with the visual "weight" of elements of your composition, for example, a small dark object positioned in the corner of the frame will balance against a large light area in the rest of it, or vice versa.

Digital

Digital cameras are now of such high quality that they can generate files that are the equal of film, with medium-format digital backs able to deliver resolution that rivals that of large-format cameras. Digital has many obvious advantages in terms of speed, turnaround, and cost, as film and processing are expensive. The rise in digital cameras has led photographers to explore shooting in extremely low-light conditions, as the sensitivity of the digital sensors generally exceeds that of film. The ability to check your image instantly is a great advantage, especially if you also use the histogram to check the exposure. However, it is sometimes useful to switch off the screen on the back of the camera and shoot blind to help develop your eye and your instincts rather than always relying on the camera. For the best-quality result, always try to shoot RAW files if you want to use the images for publication or exhibition. You can generate a jpeg afterward, but RAW is the equivalent of a digital negative from film.

Camera phones

The main advantage of the camera in your phone is its presence in your pocket—the camera you will use the most is the one you have with you the most. Modern smartphones have cameras with better resolution than digital cameras of a generation ago. They are perfect for daily photography, especially if the intention is to publish images on-screen and online. Professional photographers use phones extensively, not only for personal diary shots but also on assignment, when the discreet nature of the phone allows them to shoot without calling attention to themselves. Using a phone can get you professional results, but it also allows you to blend into the crowd.

Practical tips

Hold the phone like you would a camera, using both hands: this will reduce camera shake and make composition easier. You can use the large screen of the phone like the ground glass of a view camera; it gives a clear view of the subject. Generally, it is best to avoid using the digital zoom on phones, as the quality is poor; it is better to move closer to the subject. Similarly, the built-in flash is usually harsh and unforgiving, so avoid it in most cases. To aid composition, turn on the camera grid, which will help you get images straight; it is also a useful guide for the classic rule-of-thirds composition. Auto HDR is a good feature to use, as it will help get the best results in difficult lighting conditions. Take advantage of the small size and light weight of the phone by holding it up high and down low to get different viewpoints. You can use the volume controls on the phone headset as a shutter release if needed. Try out some of the many apps available that automatically add effects to images and you can recreate a range of styles at the touch of a finger.

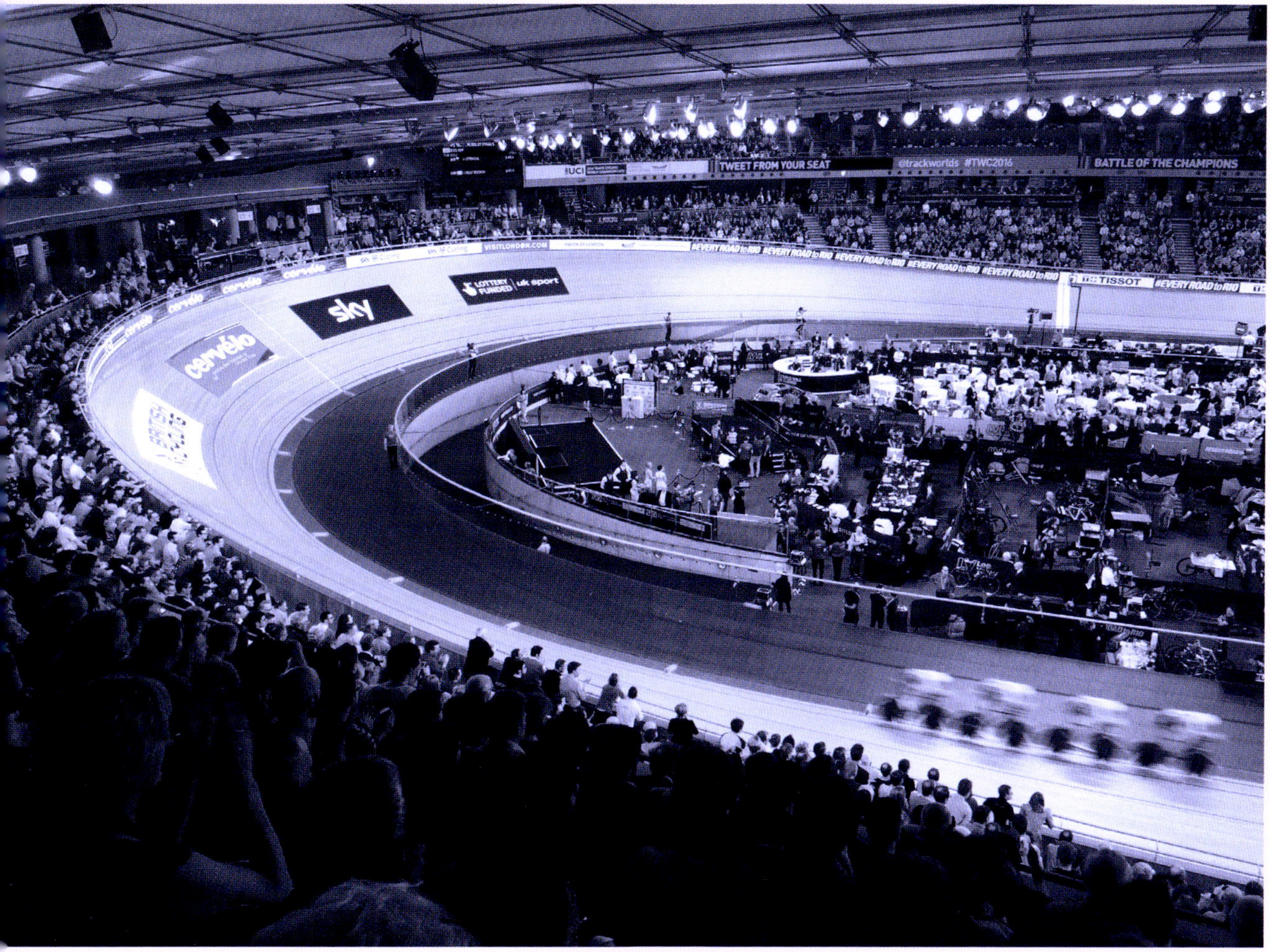

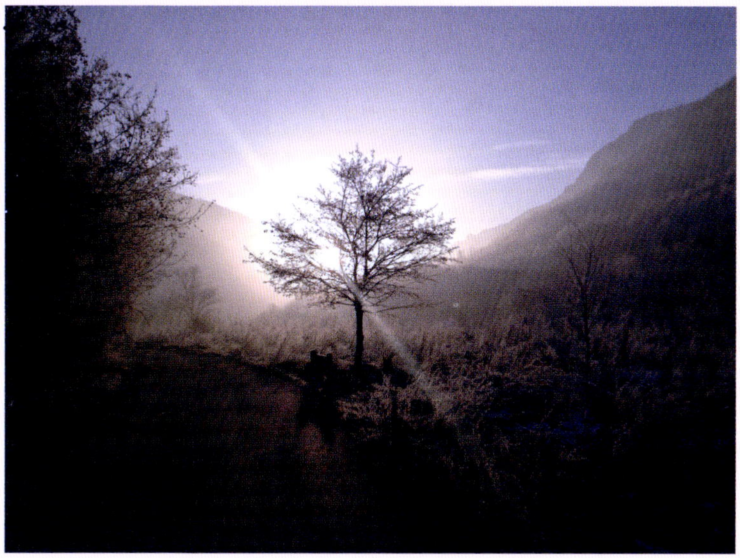

(Above) The burst setting on camera phones can be very useful when shooting fast-moving subjects. For this shot of track cycling (2015) a sequence of ten frames was made in quick succession, so that the one in which the riders were in the best position in the frame could be selected. **(Right)** Shooting against the light can create flare, but in this image, taken on an early morning run (2015), a diagonal streak of light adds movement to the composition.

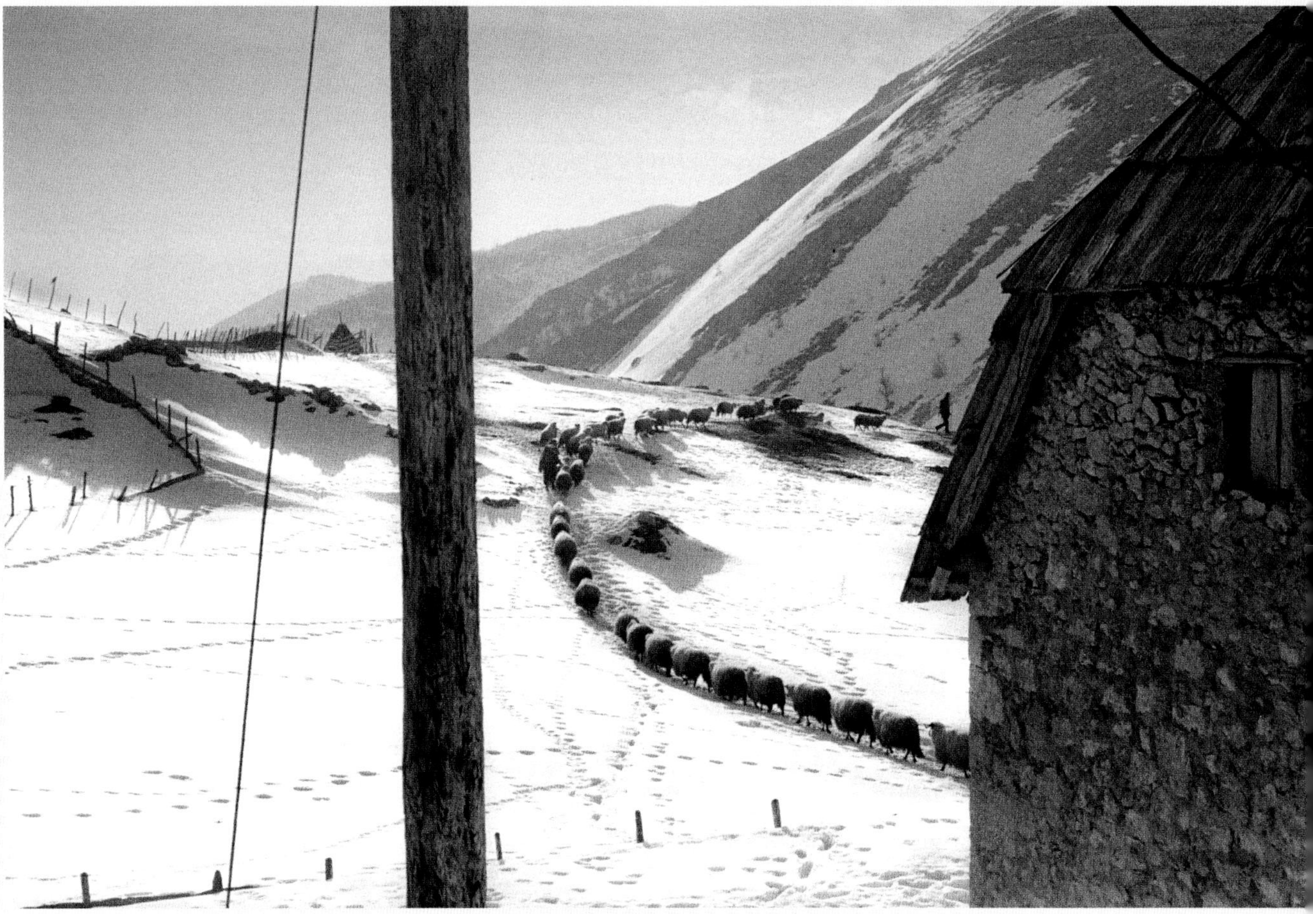

Exposure

An understanding of how to creatively expose your images with more control will contribute significantly to your ability to express your ideas in photographs.

Average exposures

The meter in the camera is very accurate, but it is designed to take an average reading from a scene and make an exposure that will contain an average set of values. This is based on what is known as "18 percent gray," referring to a tone that is suitable for most situations. However, this can lead to all pictures being exposed in the same way, which takes control away from photographer. Whether shooting on film or on a digital sensor, there is a limited range of exposure, or dynamic range, within which detail can be recorded. Although the dynamic range is getting longer as sensors improve, outside of this range, nothing will show on the final image: in the highlights, the image will be totally white; in the shadows, it will be completely black. When the difference between the brightest and darkest areas is so large that a single exposure cannot capture them both, you have to decide whether to hold detail in the shadows and lose detail in the highlights, or vice versa. An average exposure will put this range in the middle of the possible range, so that anything three to four stops above or below will not show any detail. This usually makes an acceptable image, but it can be a little bland and flat. If you choose to move this range up or down, by under- or overexposing the film, you can take control of the exposure to make a more interesting image.

Bracketing and exposure

When faced with difficult light, make a series of exposures at 1/2 or 1/3 stop intervals either side of the basic exposure,

Left) Underexposing the hotograph will hold detail in ne highlights when shooting ubjects with a lot of bright areas. owever, when shooting snowy cenes, such as this mountainous illage in Bosnia (2000), slightly verexposing the photograph om the reading given by the amera will keep the snow white. racketing can be useful in etermining the precise level of ver- or underexposure to use.
Right) For this sunset photograph 2005) the exposure was based n the skyline, so that the image ept the saturation needed. If ne exposure had been set on the oreground, all the atmosphere ould have been lost and the image ould have missed all the subtle olors in the sky.

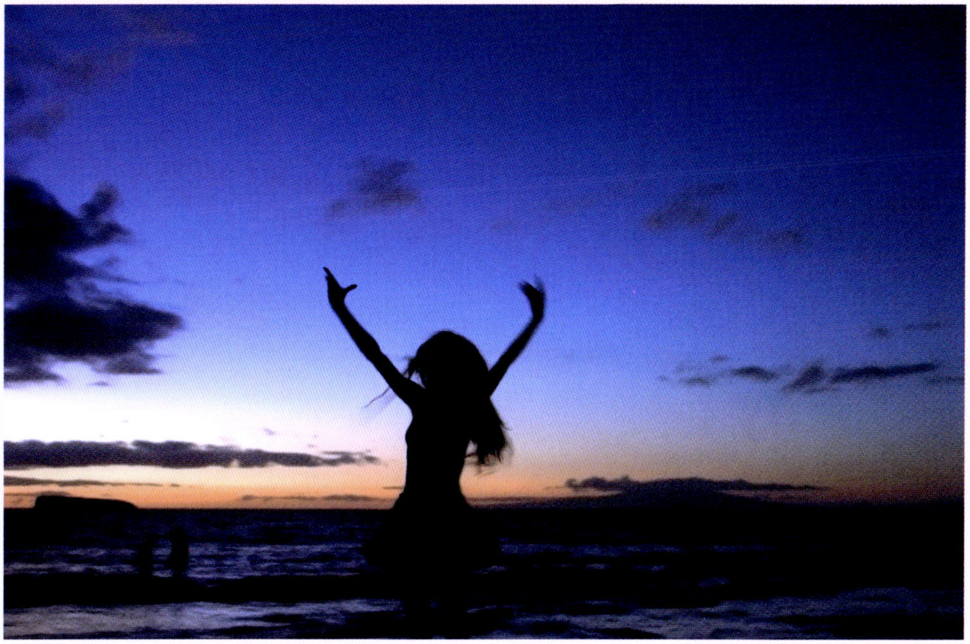

hen choose the best one. This is known as "bracketing" and nany cameras today have a program that can be set to do his automatically. You can deliberately over- or underexpose scene to make it more interesting. Sunsets and shots against ne light usually look better underexposed, as this increases the aturation of colors, whereas overexposure has the opposite ffect, making colors washed out and less intense. You can make high-key image that is light and bright by overexposing or a ow-key image that is dark and dramatic by underexposing. n everyday scene can be transformed by careful exposure.

xposure testing

ake a series of everyday objects—for example, fruit, a bowl, or book—and position them on a table near to a window so that ney are lit by side light. Then put your camera on a tripod in ront of the table and take an average exposure reading with an exposure time of 1/4 of a second. Take one photograph of this scene at the average reading; now stop down the lens four stops and take another photograph. Then make more exposures, each time opening up one stop, until you are four stops over the original exposure. If you reach the limits of the aperture on your lens, change the shutter speed one stop. Look at the images and notice how changing the exposure affects the tones, particularly the highlights and shadows. You can do this for a scene outside as well; choose a sunny day and find a scene with a good range of highlights and shadows. Observe how, as the image is under- or overexposed, the shadows fill up and become black whereas more detail is held in the highlights; or alternatively how highlights "blow out" and go completely white, with more detail visible in the shadows. Try to use this new understanding of exposure creatively, underexposing or overexposing the image to get the result you desire.

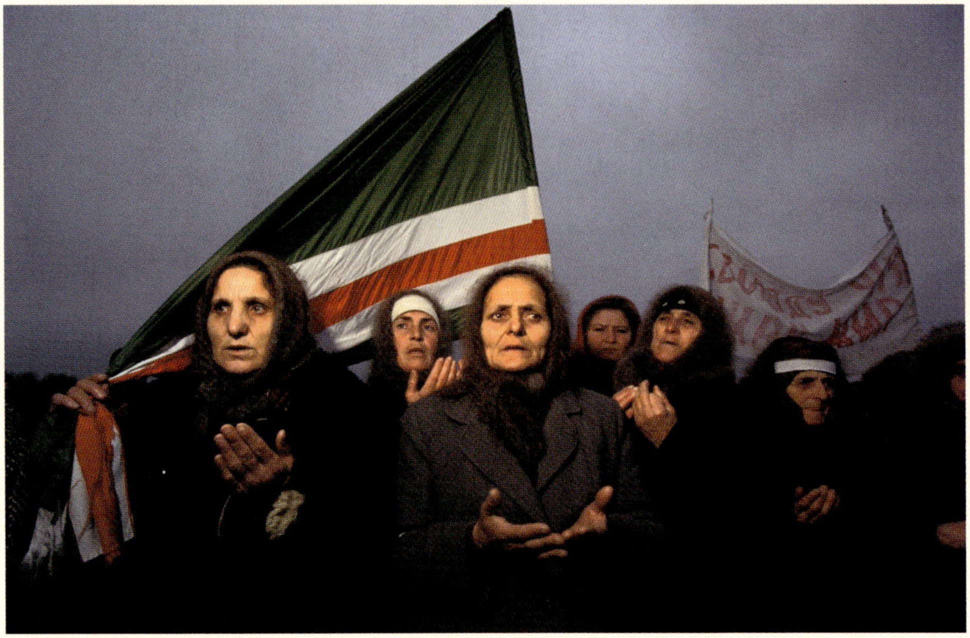

(Left) The flash was held off the camera to create a directional light on the faces of these Chechen women on a peaceful protest (1994). A warm-up gel was also used on the head of the flash to prevent the skin tones from looking too cold and blue.
(Right) Fill flash was used on this image of a fully grown male orangutan (2001), shot on a telephoto lens. Without the flash, the animal's skin and eyes would have looked dark and lifeless. The flash has lifted the highlights and put a catch light in the eyes.

Flash

Sunshine in your pocket might be one way of describing the usefulness of flash; however, it is also the key to understanding how to use it effectively. Like natural sunlight, flash can be used to give a hard, direct and directional light or a soft, gentle overall illumination. Many cameras now have a built-in flash but this can only light the subject frontally. Ideally you can use a separate flashgun, either mounted on the camera hot shoe or used off camera connected by a TTL cord or infrared trigger.

Direct flash and fill flash

The most obvious way to use flash is to mount it directly on the camera, but this can be the worst way to use it unless absolutely necessary. Direct flash gives hard edges, creates high contrast, flattens out subjects, and causes red eye. It should only be used when there is no other alternative, for example in a tight situation where you have to fight with other photographers for space or when the subject is very far away. The other situation in which direct flash is useful is when it is used as a fill light to reduce the contrast in a backlit subject such as someone standing with their back to the sun. The technique for this is to set the flash to around 2½ stops below the ambient light, depending on how strong you want the fill-in to be. This means that if your light reading for the scene in general is, say, 1/250th at f11, the flash output should be set at f5.6, f8, or f9. It is best to experiment with this until you get a ratio between the flash and the daylight that you like. Most modern cameras and flashes work with TTL (through-the-lens metering) and the power of the flash is easily adjustable.

This technique can also be used in the opposite way, where the flash is more powerful than the available light and acts as the main light. This can make day into night or it can be used in the evening to make a dramatic image. The technique is to take the overall reading, say 1/60ths at f11, and then use the flash at f11 but with the shutter speed set to 1/250ths; this will make the background two stops darker than the foreground that will be lit by the flash. Alternatively, in the evening, to balance the flash and the available light in the same ratio, for example, set the overall reading to 1/15ths at f5.6, and set the flash to f5.6 as well; this will balance the background with the foreground.

If at all possible the best approach is to get the flash off the camera on a cord and use it from the side, holding the flash

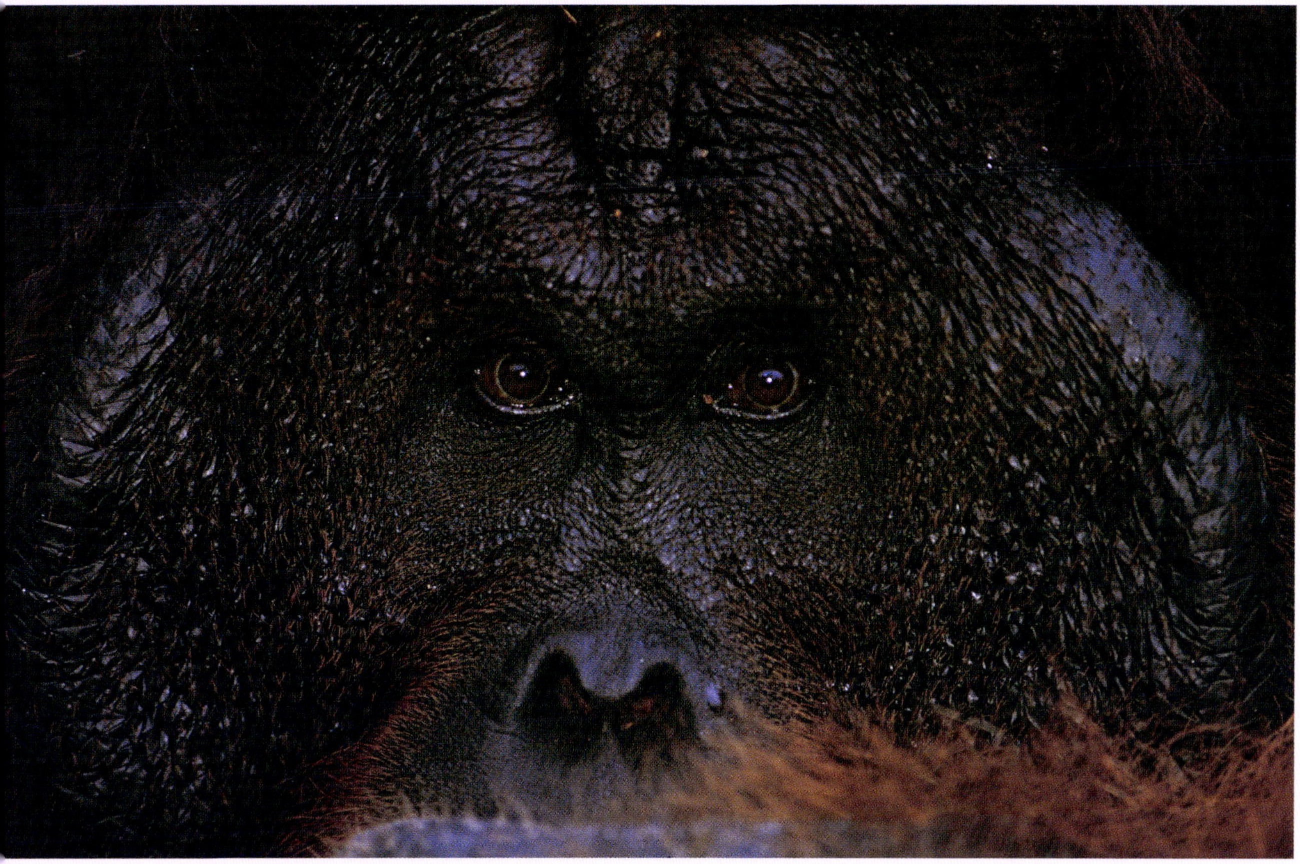

ı one hand and the camera in the other. The flash can be irected at the subject from the side at an angle of 45–90 egrees. This gives a more interesting and directional light that vill add considerable depth to the final image.

Balancing flash and bounce flash

nother technique similar to fill flash is to balance the flash to ne available light indoors. This means taking an overall light eading and using the flash to fill the foreground and letting long exposure fill the background. For example, if your light eading is 1/15ths at f5.6, you would set the flash to f5.6 and let light the front of the scene. Again, experiment with different xposure times from one second to 1/30th of a second to get ne effect you want. Longer exposure times will give a "flash lur" effect, where the subject is frozen by the flash whereas ne background is blurred and moving. This can make very ramatic and interesting pictures. The best way to practice nis technique is to go to a nightclub or disco and shoot lots of ictures with different settings; point light source—for example, potlights—will leave long trails of light that can look very trange and interesting in the image.

The other principal way to use flash is to bounce it off the ceiling or walls of the room you are shooting in. This gives a soft, overall light that fills the whole space. It can be a little flat and low in contrast, but it is flattering. Most modern cameras with TTL work well this way; older automatic flashes tend to need to be given a little more exposure than normal, so open up the aperture ½ a stop. If you are shooting color, be aware that the flash will take on the color of the surface it is bounced off; beware of green walls!

Many photographers use accessories such as a bounce card, which is a small reflective piece of plastic put on the flash head to reflect a little light forwards, as well as upward, towards the ceiling. Other gadgets, for example the omni-bounce or LumiQuest, act as diffusers on the head of the flash to soften it and simulate bounce flash when the room is too large or outdoors. Again, experiment with different accessories to find one that you like. Many flashes give out light that is rather cold; it is often a good idea to apply a thin layer of very pale orange gel over the flash head to warm it up a little bit, especially if you mix the flash with ambient light indoors, as this tends to be warm, too.

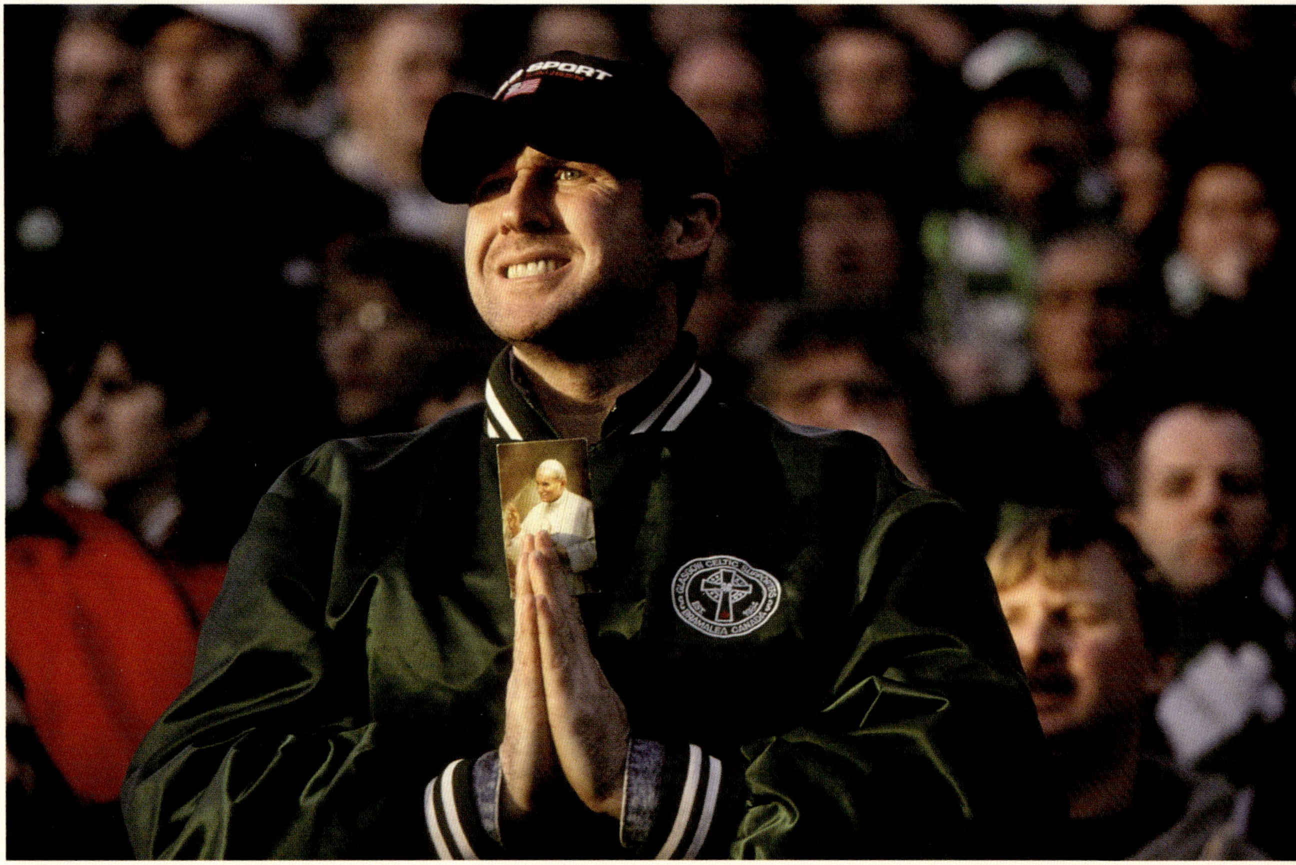

Lens

Lenses can bring a radically different perspective to a scene, but they can also dominate it if they are used without care. The ideal starting point is to ask yourself what you are trying to say in your photograph and what is the best way to say it. This will help you to decide what lenses to use in any given situation. It will also help you to determine what lenses to use in general.

Working with lenses

If you are a sports photographer, you will need a full range of lenses from long telephotos to extreme wide-angles; a news photographer will probably need almost as many to cover every eventuality, but a documentary photographer might use a very small range of lenses. Many documentary photographers working on long-term projects in intimate situations use very few lenses, mostly the 35mm, with a 50mm and a 28mm when they need to shoot a little more tightly or when space is limited. For example, Henri Cartier-Bresson (see p.260) shot almost all of his masterpieces with only a 50mm lens. There is a pattern that is common among many photographers in that they start out working with very few lenses, simply a standard and a wide-angle or short zoom; then, as they can afford more lenses, they buy a full range and use the extremes of focal lengths. As time goes on, they tend to return to more normal lenses and end up shooting most of their pictures in the range of 28–70mm.

Extreme lenses

The advantage of extreme lenses is that they distort the world in ways the human eye does not. An extreme wide-angle lens can include a lot of information or make the foreground appear huge in comparison to the background; a long telephoto can

Left) A telephoto lens is perfect or picking faces out of a crowd, llowing you to stand back and not ıtimidate your subject. This Celtic ootball fan is lost in the moment, raying for his team to win (2000). Right) A wide-angle lens, such as 24mm, enables you to get close, utting the viewer inside the action, s in this shot of children playing on sculpture in Kazakhstan (1990).

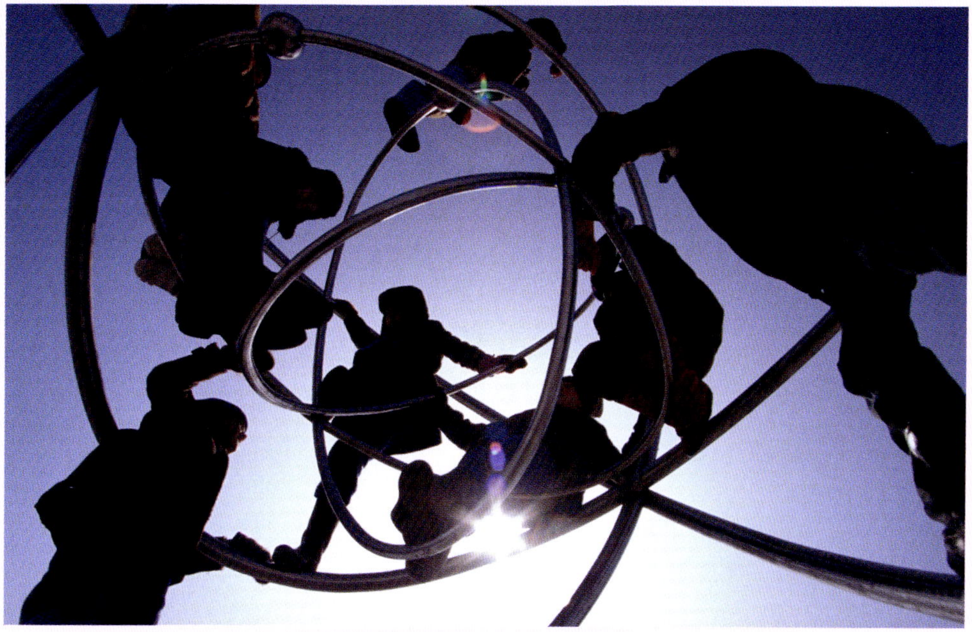

ompress an image and bring distant objects apparently close o one another. This can help to make the subject appear more nteresting, but unfortunately, too many photographers use nese lenses indiscriminately, so that their images actually ecome repetitive and dull. When this happens, the equipment s winning over the story and form is defeating content. Wide-ngle lenses over 24mm have a tendency to distort the image oo, especially at the edge of the frame—over-elongated heads re common—and can simply be too distracting, especially vhen used to shoot verticals. There are few situations that are o cramped that you cannot step back a few feet, rather than sing a wider lens. It is also hard to control so much space in the nage with an extreme wide-angle lens. Long lenses do more nan simply let you photograph things that are far away. hey can also be used on subjects that are relatively near to "fill ne frame" and seek out details. The lack of depth of field can be used to isolate the subject from the background and make it stand out more, or the compression that a telephoto lens gives can be used to relate the foreground to something far away in the background that would not have been visible with a wide-angle.

Standard lens

Many people dismiss the 50mm standard lens as dull, but if it is employed effectively it can be a very useful lens, because its point of view is very similar to that of the human eye. It therefore makes very natural-looking images with no distortion. It can relate foreground and background together, and is useful when you want to orchestrate an image as it allows you to stand back a little but still include the whole scene. For these reasons, it was a favorite of Henri Cartier-Bresson, because it allowed him to remain discreet and unobserved.

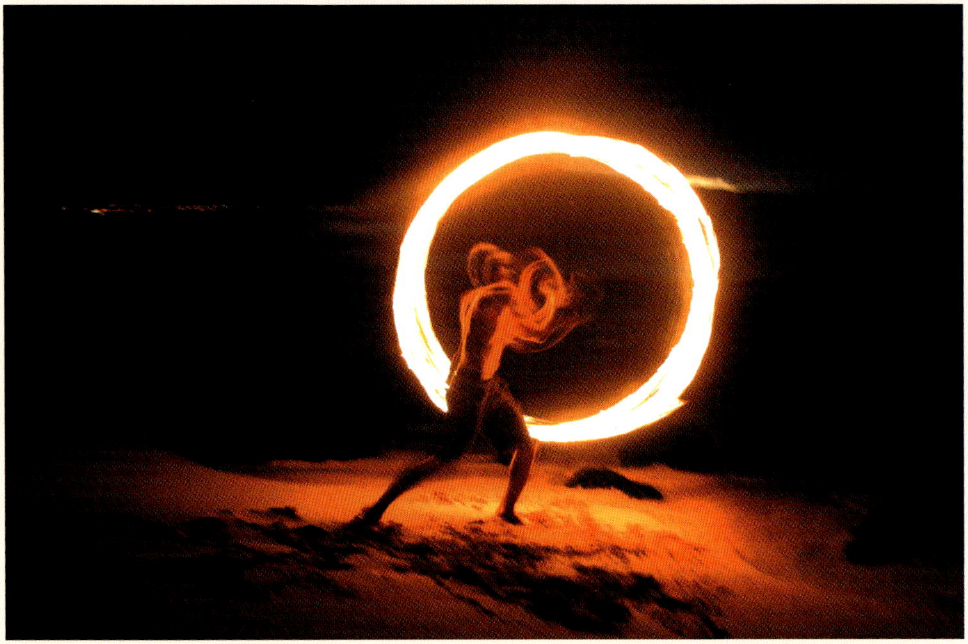

(Left) The long shutter speed of a second was used to capture the light trails of this Hawaiian fire dancer; the flame illuminates the beach and the dancer's body (2005
(Right) In this photograph, taken in a refugee camp in Somalia during the famine there (1992), a momentary break in the clouds on an overcast day suddenly created a halo of shadows around the stricken boy, highlighting the way the world watches these events unfold but does not intervene effectively.

Lighting

Light is what really makes photographs, so you must think about light and how it affects the image. The quality of light in a photograph is one of the most important elements you can use creatively to get across your message. A distinctive feeling for the use of light is what marks out the exceptional photographer.

Quality of light

Light can be described in several ways—hard or soft, directional or diffused, high or low contrast, cold or warm—and each aspect of the quality of light affects the photograph. Really look at the light in the situation you are shooting and make it work for you; move around the subject to get the best light, and look for shafts of light cutting across scenes, creating strong contrast between areas of light and shade. This technique, known as *chiaroscuro*, can give great depth, making an image almost three-dimensional. The smaller the light source and the further away from the subject it is, the harder the light that it produces will be. Conversely, the larger the light source and the closer it is to the subject, the softer and more diffuse the light will be. Weather also affects the light. Full sun, because it is a long way away from the subject and seemingly relatively small, will give a very hard light, with distinct shadows, sharp, well-defined edges, and high contrast. The difference between highlights and shadows will be several stops, often beyond the ability of the camera to record everything. When the sky is overcast, the sun's light will be diffused and the whole sky is effectively the light source, which is huge. The light will be soft and the shadows less distinct and less contrasty—the contrast range between highlights and shadows will be small, and the camera will be capable of recording all the detail in the scene.

Shooting after the sun has risen or set will also make images that are low in contrast but lit by a very warm light; these images can be very beautiful and peaceful with a soft light. Sunshine in the middle of the day will usually give a very harsh and ugly light, as it is coming directly from above, throwing shadows directly down. It makes faces, in particular, very difficu

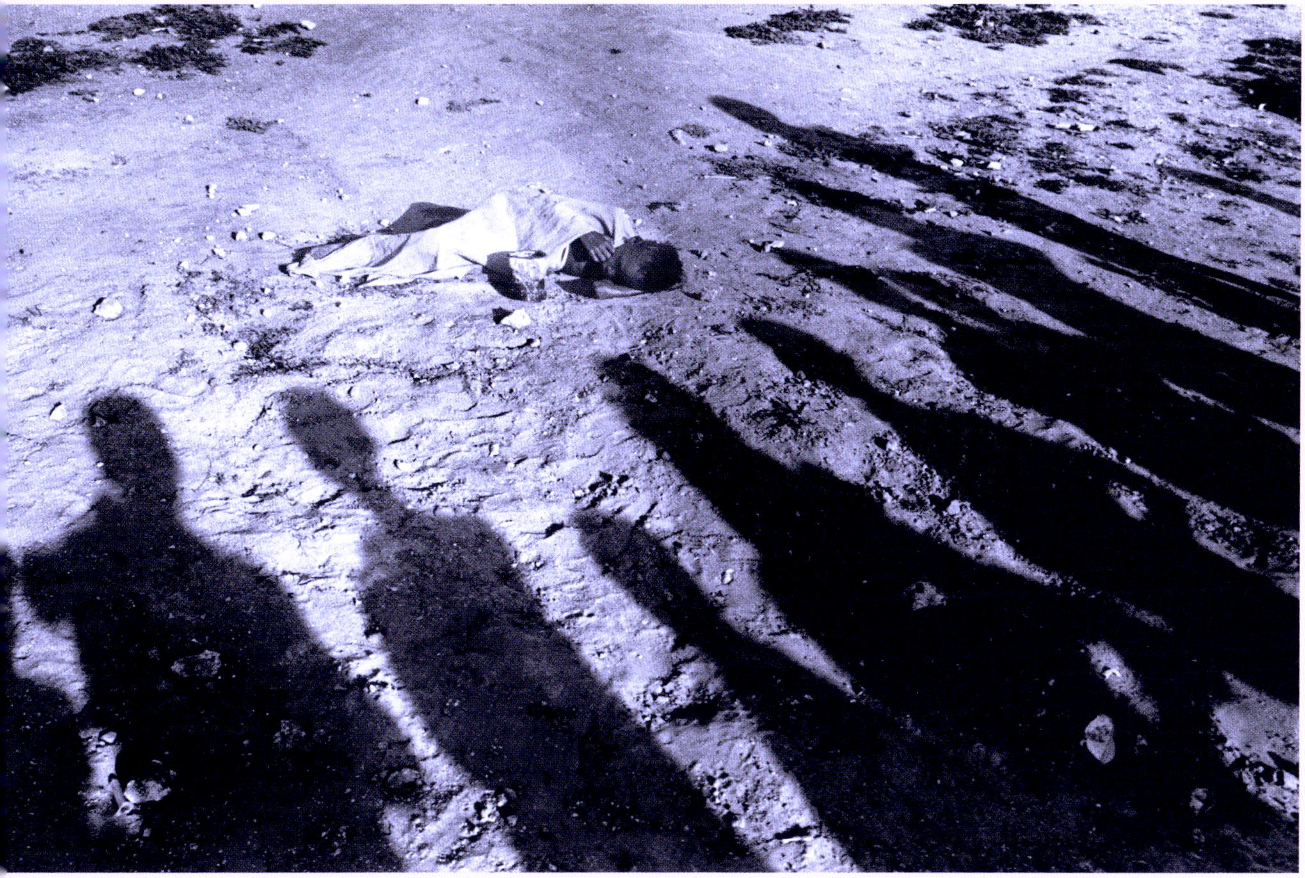

o shoot, as it will throw deep shadows in people's eyes and ınder their noses. Fill flash can help balance this out. Window ight is often very beautiful, as it is relatively soft yet directional; t is very good for showing the relief in a subject as it models it ery well, giving an almost three-dimensional quality.

)bserving light

'ou can learn a lot about light by looking at paintings, ›specially those by Old Masters such as Rembrandt and :aravaggio, as well as closely watching films to work out how he cinematographer has controlled the light to get an effect. 'ry photographing the same scene at different times of day and n different light conditions and see how it changes. Having the atience to wait for the right light or understanding when that ight will come is a key skill for a good photographer.

;hooting in low light

)ne of the areas that has advanced the most through the ntroduction of digital cameras is the ability to shoot in very low-light situations and still achieve reasonable results. Sensors now have incredible sensitivity, allowing ISO speeds of up to 12,800 or even more. Although there is a lot of digital noise at these high sensitivities, if it means getting the picture in situations with almost no light it can be acceptable. Combining this with a fast lens such as a 35mm f1.4 means that effectively you can shoot scenes in which the naked eye cannot see any detail, but the camera sensor can. For example, the screen of a mobile phone will give off enough light to illuminate a face and a moonlit landscape can look as if it was shot in the middle of the day. Experiment with your camera to find the sweet spot of compromise between the level of noise versus your ability to hold the camera steady. A tripod is also a worthwhile investment; purchase one that is sturdy but reasonably light. Not only will it assist with using slow shutter speeds to give you greater depth of field or the ability to shoot with longer shutter speeds in low light, but it will also slow down your photography and make you concentrate on each frame with more intensity.

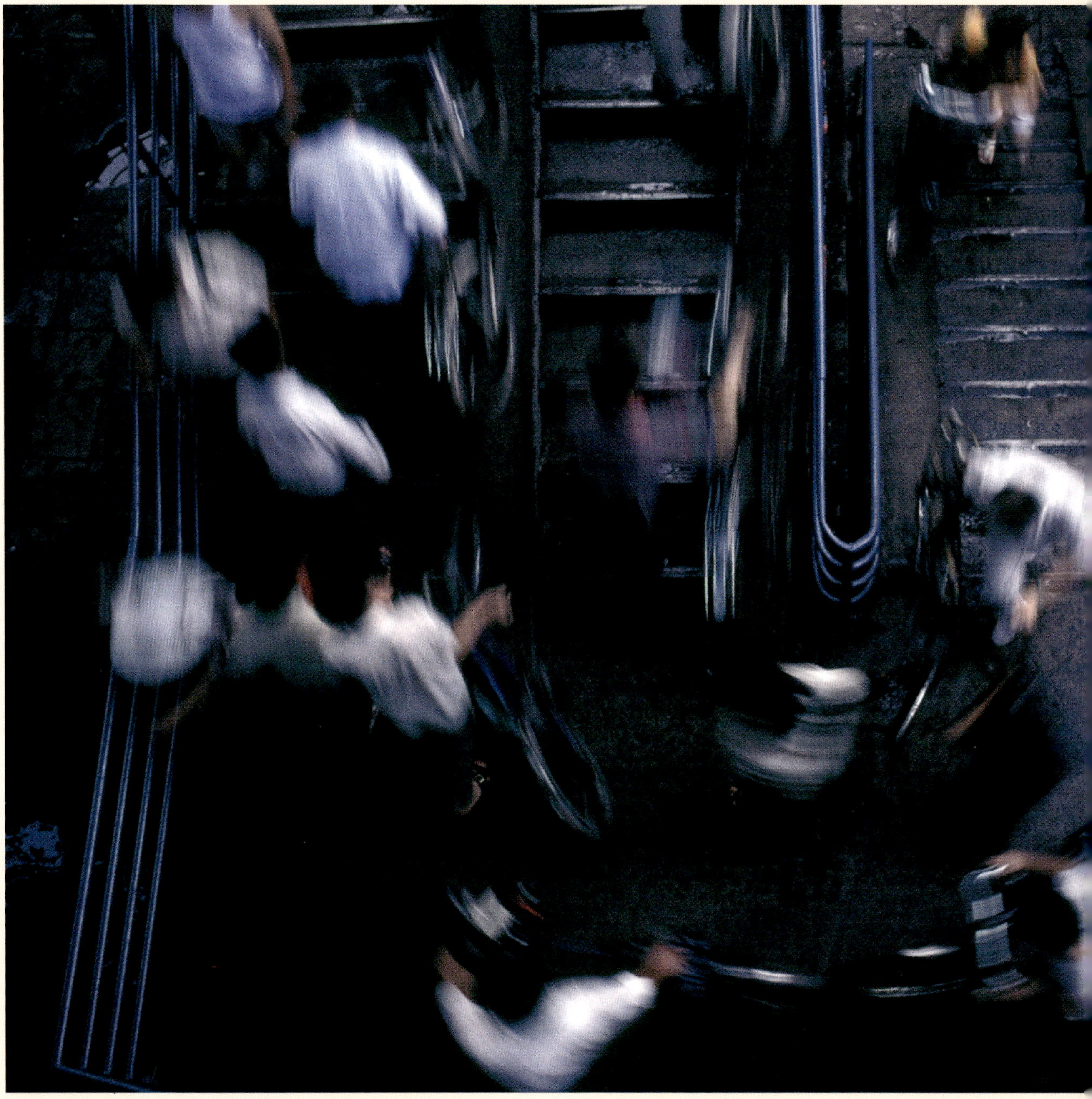

Rush hour in Shanghai (2004) provided a perfect opportunity to illustrate the pace and energy of the crowded city. Shooting from above brings out patterns and flow in the scene.

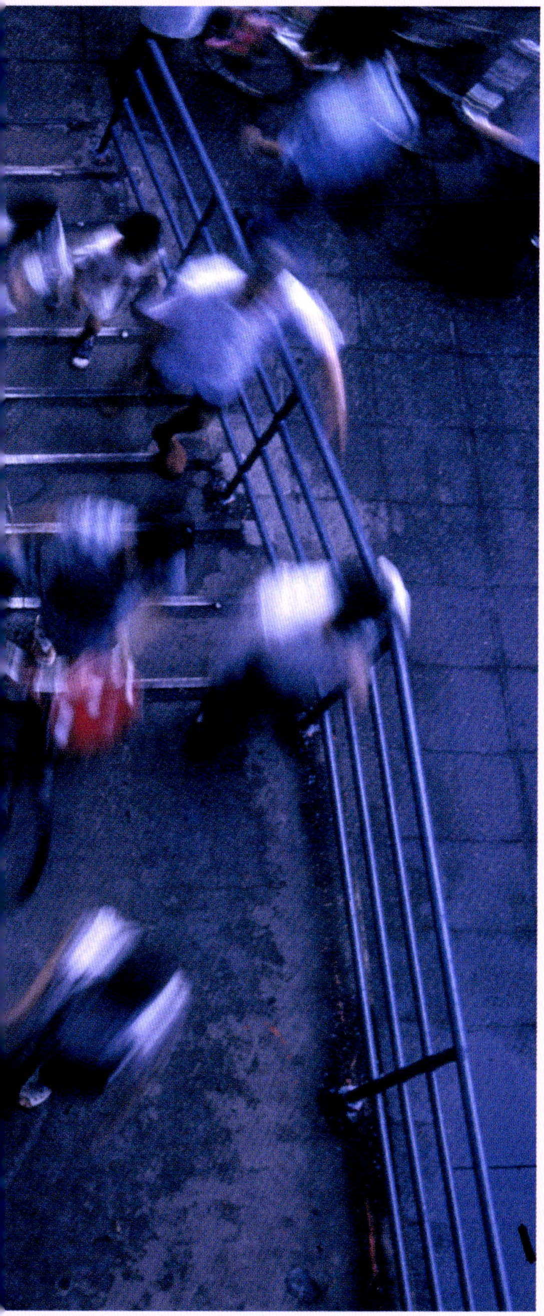

Location

Developing a sense of what makes a photographically interesting location is vital. It demands the ability to visualize how a scene will look through a given focal length lens and to be able to predict at a location how the light will change depending on the time of day and quality of light, as its color temperature and harshness are affected by time of day. Bright sunlight, an overcast day, and evening sun are all very different; the photographer has to imagine how he or she wants the final image to look and then decide on the best kind of light to achieve the end result.

Time management

Planning your day so that you are located at the right place at the right time requires careful scheduling and management of your time. For example, a landscape photographer might get up well before dawn, shoot a location till early morning, sleep during the middle of the day, then return to shoot before sunset and possibly work on into the night. For a street photographer, the hunt for a location where the combination of light, street furniture, buildings, and movement of people is suitable can involve repeatedly walking around a particular area, possibly returning to a chosen spot several times to observe how the ebb and flow of human movement changes, in order to capture that spontaneous moment where everything comes together to create an extraordinary image. Similarly, for an environmental portrait photographer, recognizing the potential of a particular background that will express the character of the subject and then working out how to fit the person into that specific scene are valuable skills.

Useful apps for planning

Google Earth and Google Maps are enormously useful tools to help you plan a location shoot in advance. You can see down over the topography of the location, looking for the best angles, viewpoints, interesting features, and distinctive buildings. You can also work out what the best access points are to reach a location—for example, a beach or mountain trail. Google Earth allows you to virtually "enter" a location and explore it from near eye level, framing the landscape almost as if you were physically there with your camera. You can then take screen grabs and store them on your phone to remind yourself of the exact spot when you finally get there. You can also explore other people's geotagged photographs of the same area. There are even apps available that will help you calculate the direction and angle of the sun at any given date and time in the future, so that you can plan exactly the best time to be at a particular location in order to get the light you want. Putting yourself in the right place, at the right time, with the right light are essential components of the practice of photography.

Method

Every photographer has their own unique methodology that affects how they approach making work, whether consciously expressed or not, and certain key elements that are common to the practice of the majority of photographers can be determined. These can include the technical choices made, the photographer's viewpoint, the formal and aesthetic approach and vision of the photographer, their inspiration, the choice of subject, their research process, the nature of their collaboration or interaction with the subject, their use of symbolism and metaphor, and how they structure the narrative of their images, both individually and in sequence

Image elements

Those elements within the control of the photographer include the camera format, with each type from the rangefinder to the view camera having its own unique signature "voice" that changes the relationship between the photographer and subject; the choice of lens (in the photograph on the right a medium-wide angle, which relates the foreground and background to each other, giving the image depth and an almost three-dimensional quality); the film type (black and white versus color, or Tri-X with its characteristic granular, gritty grain as opposed to a slower film such as Plus-X with a more fluid transition of tones); and the different sensitivity settings in a digital camera that lead to increased levels of "noise" as the image quality is degraded.

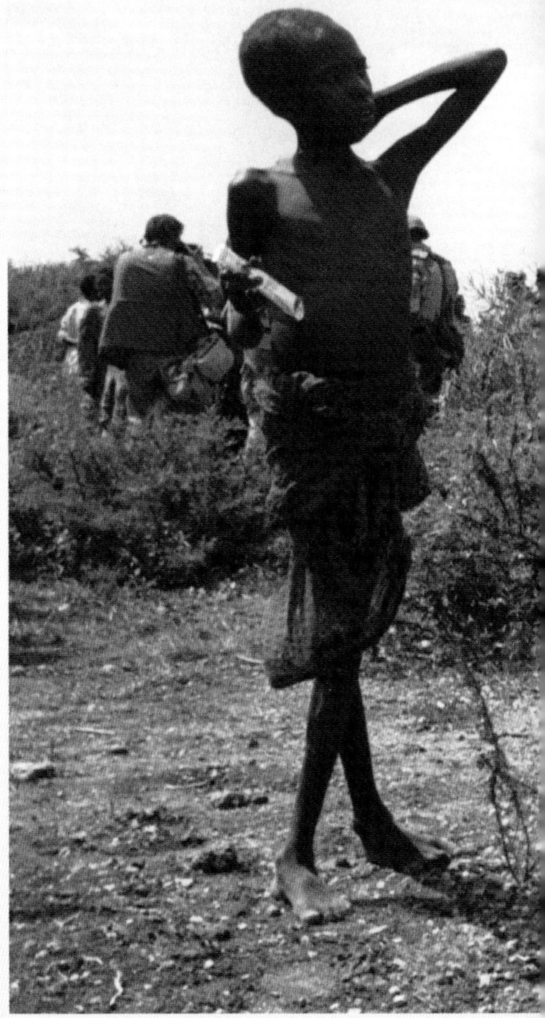

Research

For some photographers, extensive research into the subject they are dealing with is absolutely central to their practice, as a detailed understanding of the issues they are engaged with is required to give their images the depth and resonance needed. Others prefer to work more spontaneously, allowing the world to offer up serendipitous moments, whereas others may undertake a project in which the photography itself is the research process, exploring how the technical aspects of the medium can be developed, for example.

Personal vision

Developing a unique, individual visual signature is an important part of the process of becoming a photographer. Some practitioners, like Henri Cartier-Bresson (see p.260), shot almost all of their work in a distinctive style, so that wherever they went, their images had the same unique visual qualities. However others, such as Walker Evans (see p.78) in his exploration of vernacular America, adapted their formal strategy to the demands of the individual project, although they frequently kept the overall theme of their work consistent.

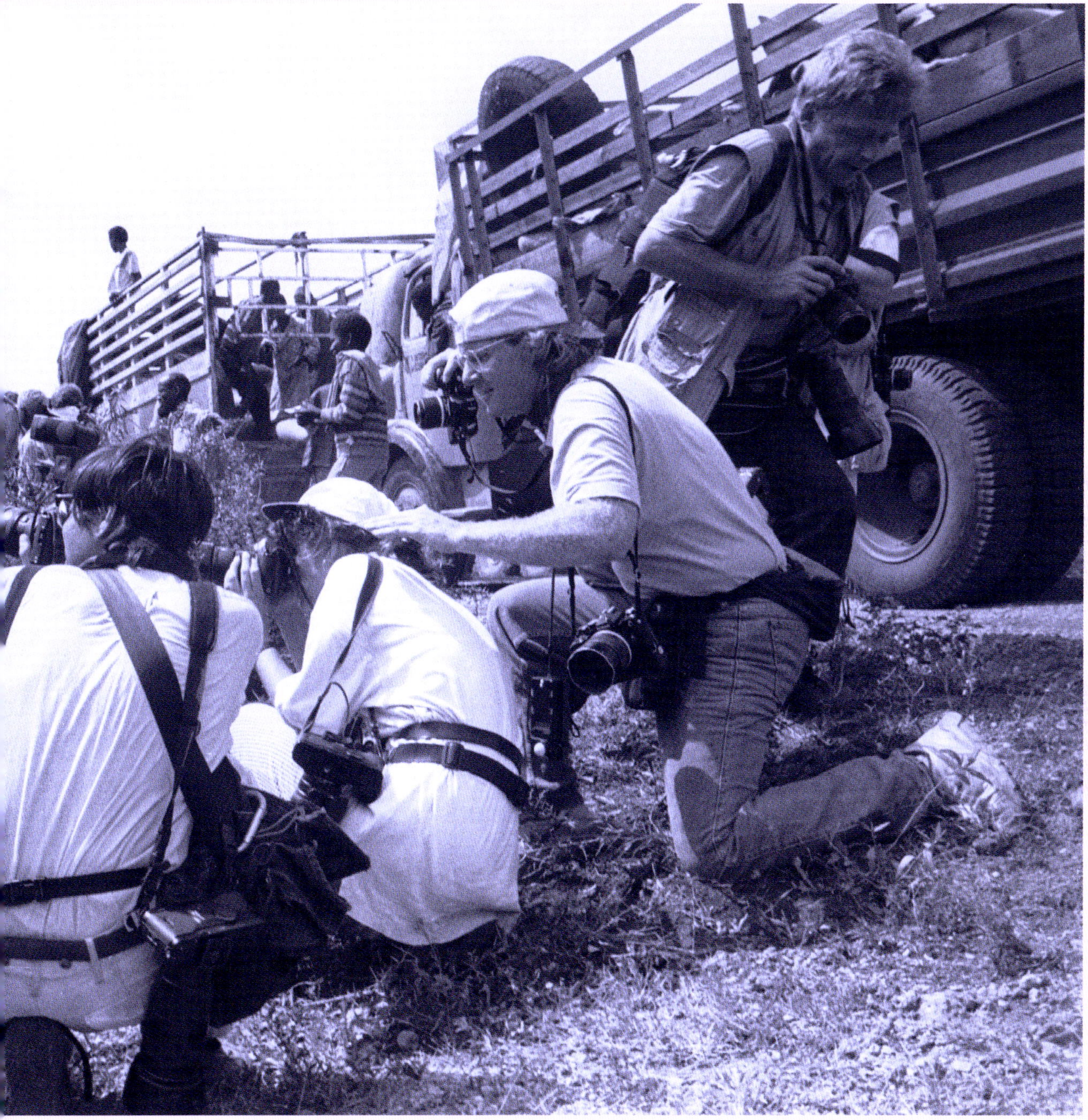

When we look at news images, it is easy to forget that photographers are not invisible. In fact, they are as much protagonists in the situation as the people they are reporting on (1992).

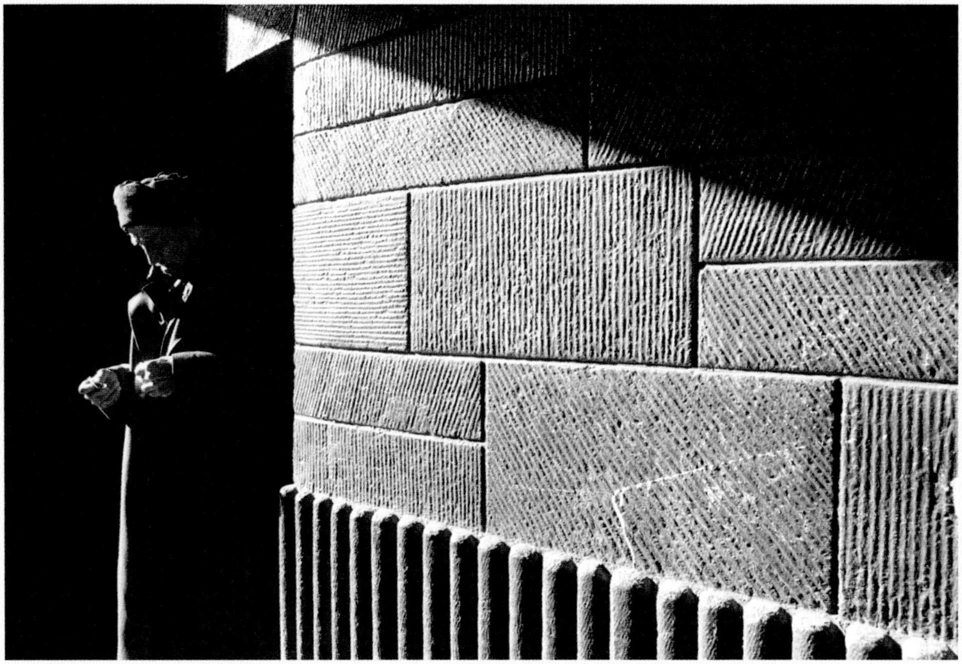

(Left) In order to keep shadows and highlights intense in this photograph taken on the streets of Sarajevo (1993), the man's face had to be carefully dodged to lighten it and make his features visible.
(Right) By burning in the highlights you can add drama to the sky. This image shows the scale of the tragedy during the famine in Somalia (1992).

Processing

Editing is a crucial stage in the creation of a successful photograph, especially once you start working on larger projects or photo essays. It is therefore extremely important that you become familiar with editing your own work and understanding some of the essential elements involved in this process.

Normally the photographer or a photo agency representing a photographer will carry out the first broad edit, narrowing down the choice from possibly hundreds of pictures. This is sometimes called the rough edit. At this stage, you should take an initial look at all your material, marking or noting anything that seems to be interesting and eliminating anything that has obviously not worked, either technically or visually.

For the second edit, take a critical viewpoint, based on your awareness of the range of images you have initially selected. Some pictures will now look weaker or unsatisfactory compared to others. A useful method of editing at this stage is to group all the similar kinds of images together—for example, portraits, details, landscapes, establishing shots, and so on. When you isolate these groups, it becomes very apparent which are the stronger shots. Remove the less successful pictures until you are left with a small but strong selection in each group. Sometimes there may be several effective pictures that are making the same point, but eventually a difficult decision will have to be made to choose the one or two that seem to do the job best.

The final edit is the hardest, and the one in which you have to be extremely self-critical. You should aim to include here only those photographs that you would be happy to see published or presented to an audience. If you have any doubts about an image, leave it out.

Post-processing

Perfectly acceptable results can be obtained from modern digital cameras by shooting in jpeg and simply taking the image as it is generated by the camera. For real control of the process,

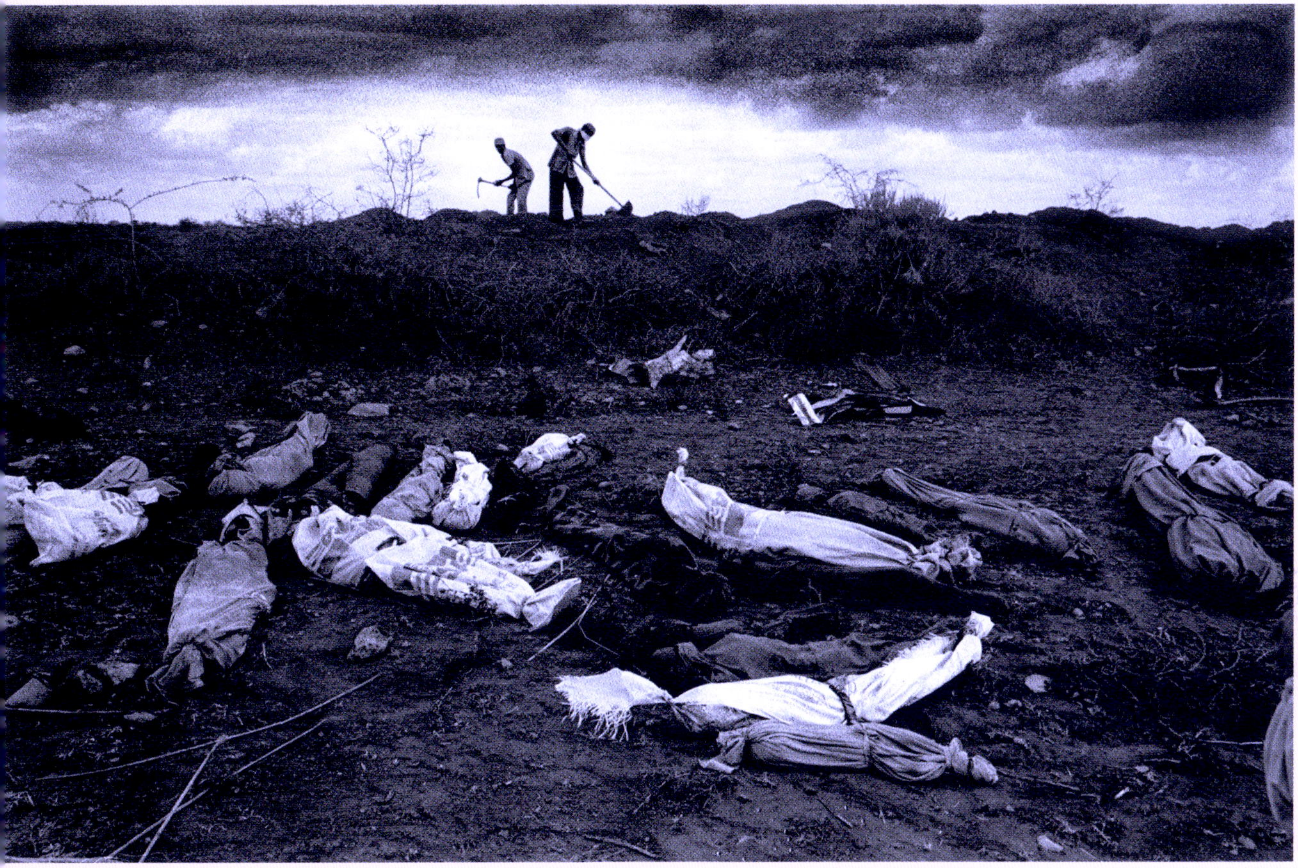

however, it is much better to shoot in RAW format. This means that you will need to acquire image editing software to process the RAW files, but it will give you much more control over the final image. It is definitely worth investing time in learning how to properly use the controls in a program such as Photoshop; as with only using the program mode on the camera, using the automatic presets in the editing program will give acceptable results, but it will not not allow the fine control that can make or break a final image. Although it is beyond the scope of this book, developing a consistent workflow to process your images and calibrate your computer monitor is vital if you want to achieve reliable and consistent results from digital files, as viewing them on screen can be very different to the final print if everything is not matching up. Be very careful with using dodging and burning tools and sharpness filters. Although they can seem fine viewed on a computer screen, the effect can look very obvious and clumsy in a final print. Less is generally more, unless you are very highly skilled.

If possible, it is still a very useful exercise to learn how to print in the traditional analog darkroom. This experience will give you a much better sense of how tones in the negative transfer to the final print, as well as an enhanced appreciation of what a good print actually looks like. Similarly, going to exhibitions and carefully studying the prints is a worthwhile investment in time so that you can understand better what a genuinely great print looks like. The quality from modern inkjet or pigment printers that you can use yourself is exceptional, but they are expensive to run. It can actually be more cost effective to go to a professional lab that can help get the very best from your files. They can also advise on the most appropriate printing process for the results you want. Developing a relationship with a good printer can really help take the final image to another level of quality and expression. A reliable lab will be able to interpret your files, and create a stunning final print. You will discover that holding a beautiful print is a very different experience to viewing an image on a screen.

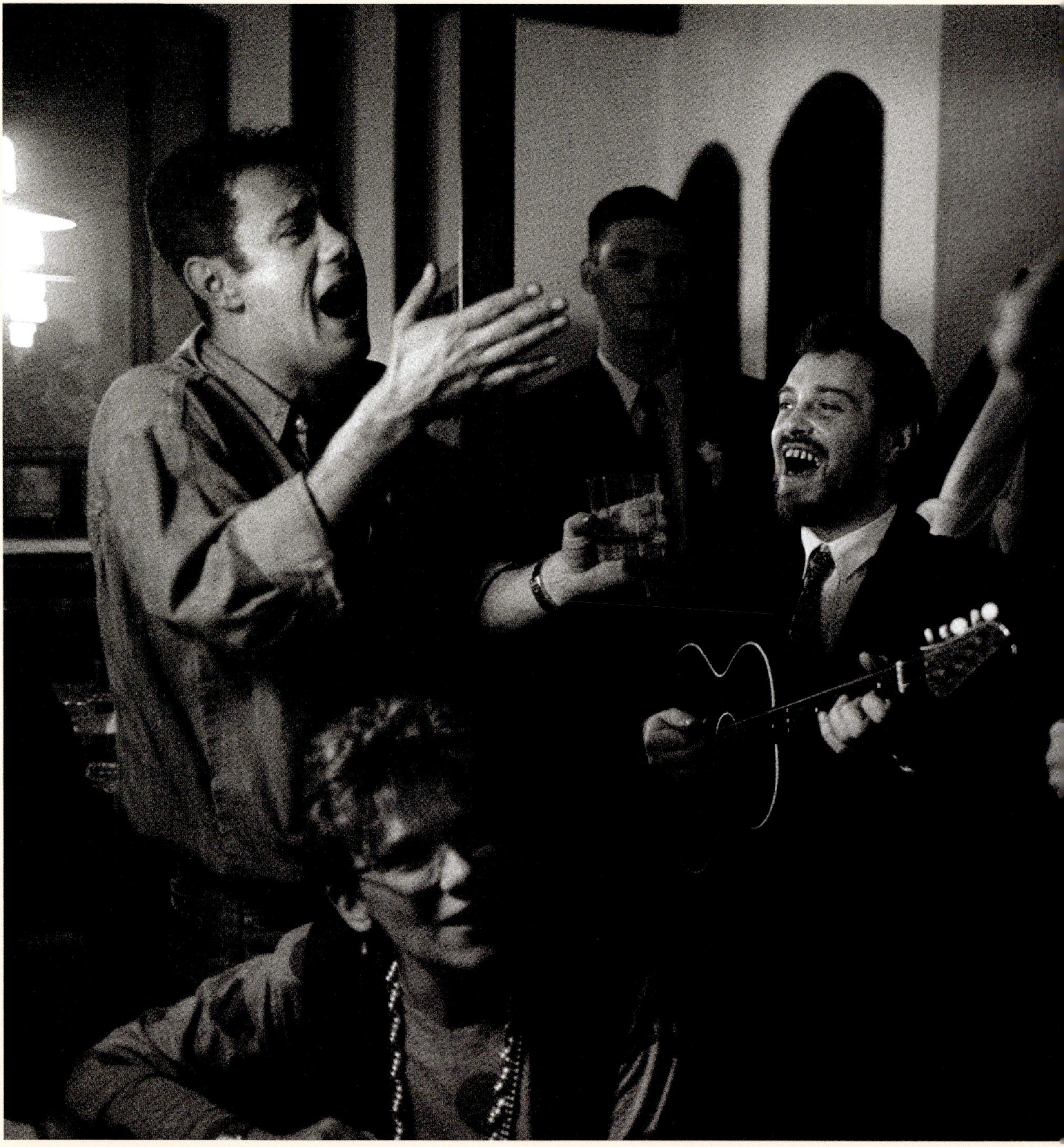

Having a camera with you at all times means you can take advantage of situations as they occur, as with this shot of a Balkan wedding party that spontaneously erupted into song (1996).

Subject

Finding a theme or subject to focus on defines the work of many of the greatest photographers; they have systematically investigated and explored the possibilities of a subject, idea, location, or issue in depth. This could be a journalistic or documentary-inspired project or one led more by an examination of esthetic or formal qualities. Regardless of his or her individual inspiration, a sustained engagement with a particular field allows the photographer to discover something unique, personal, and original. There is an extraordinary amount of work that exists only because of the dedication and commitment of the photographer to that idea, often in the face of adversity including lack of funds and public interest, but driven fundamentally by the individual's passion and involvement. Finding your own particular theme that you can occupy and own is one of the key moments in developing your own individual vision.

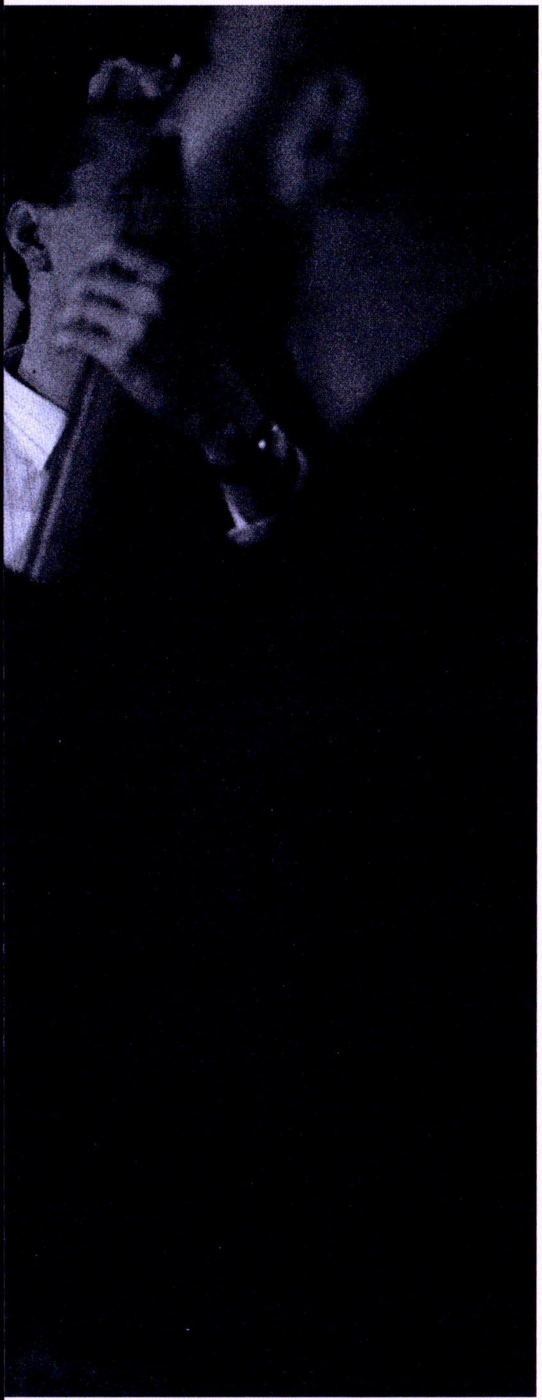

Photographic subjects

To paraphrase Garry Winogrand (see p.192), a photographer needs a strong sense of what the world will look like when photographed—the ability to visualize a scene and imagine how it will convert to the flat plane of the photographic image. Being able to identify subject matter that has visual potential demands close attention to the world, along with an imaginative leap that can find value even in the banal, everyday, and ordinary, not only in the exotic and visually striking. This could include an urban landscape, a particular type or category of person, or a forensic still life; in all cases the photographer has to recognize the hidden potential of the subject that can be revealed by the camera.

Working with people

Some photographers start taking pictures of people as soon as they meet them, feeling that the energy of the immediate encounter is an invaluable moment that cannot be missed. Others prefer to spend a considerable amount of time with the subject without even taking their camera out, slowly getting to know the person and winning their confidence. Some photographers talk incessantly to their subjects, whereas others hardly say a word. There is no single formula for success; however, an awareness of your own presence in the particular situation, no matter how loud or quiet, is highly significant. Think about the impact you are having on the situation you intend to shoot and be very aware of the personal boundaries and rights of the people you are working with. Body language is hugely important, too: it can reveal a lot about the person in the final photograph, as well as be a valuable sign to you, the photographer, as to whether or not they are happy to cooperate with you.

Place

A sense of place is a fundamental concern of photography. The ability of the camera to record the detail of a landscape has always been one of the defining characteristics of the medium. Photographers recognize the temporal, historical, and spatial complexity of the landscape before them, which they shape and give meaning to, often alluding to the impact of human activity on the world. The landscape thus becomes more than a topography: it is transformed into a space of memory, allusion, metaphor, association, and remembrance. Photographs of landscapes become an intervention where, by careful framing and timing, the photographer makes connections between separate elements in the image. This process necessitates the active engagement of the viewer, who must search the scene for clues to the history of the place depicted. The landscape photograph can therefore be interpreted as a palimpsest, a layering of time across the topography of space. Photographers in this genre have traditionally used cameras with negative sizes of 5 × 4 or even 10 × 8 inches, or their digital medium-format equivalents. This allows for virtually grain-free images that can withstand extreme enlargements. As such, they allow tiny elements of the image to become the most salient features, inviting the viewer to pore over them in an almost forensic manner. When enlarged for display in an exhibition, they fill the field of vision. This detail draws the viewer in to actively scan the image and engage with it. The focus is on the viewer deciphering the meaning of the image through a detailed exploration of the surface of the photograph and a simultaneous imaginative reading of its topography.

Francis Frith

Traveler's Boat at Ibrim *c.* 1857

In this photograph, taken from the book *Sinai and Palestine* (*c.* 1863), Francis Frith plays on the repetitive forms of the boat's triangular sails reflected in the River Nile, and the riverbank in the foreground. This area was flooded after the construction of the Aswan Dam, from 1898 to 1902, so the image has historical as well as esthetic value. Frith traveled to the Middle East on three occasions, initially to Egypt in 1856, and then later to Jerusalem, Syria, and Lebanon. On his final visit, in the summer of 1859, he explored further south, to Nubia, than any photographer had previously. He took with him on his travels a specially designed wicker carriage that acted as both darkroom and sleeping chamber. In his life story, written when he was sixty-three, Frith recounted fighting "an awful midnight battle to the very point of surrender with a deadly pack of hungry, wild dogs" and being captured by bandits. Dressed in Arab costume, Frith traveled to Akaba by camel, meeting "desert princes and rival sheikhs, blazing with jewel-hilted swords." He worked with very large plate glass cameras that took 16 x 20-inch glass plates, using the wet-collodion process, an extraordinary achievement considering the difficulties of operating in the heat and dust of Africa; he was often forced to develop negatives in tombs, temples, and caves. The huge size of the plates meant that the negatives were able to record extremely fine detail, and the prints from 19th-century images are breathtaking in their beauty. Frith was adept at using human figures to accentuate the scale of the vistas he photographed, and gave considerable attention to getting clear, unobstructed viewpoints. He noted the "difficulty of getting a view satisfactorily in the camera: foregrounds are especially perverse; distance too near or too far." Like many of his contemporaries, Frith sold albums of original prints to fund his travels and those that still exist are highly collectable today.

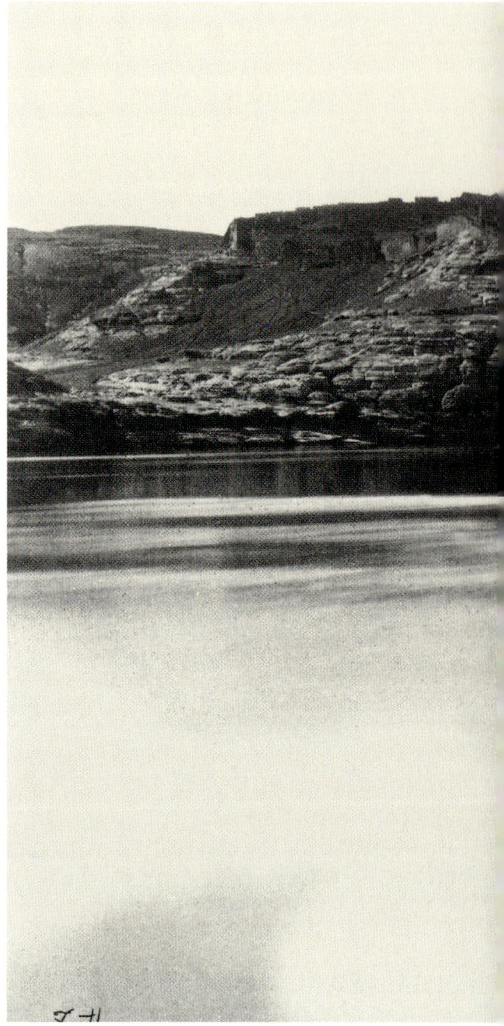

"Oh what pictures we would make if we could command our point of views."

Francis Frith

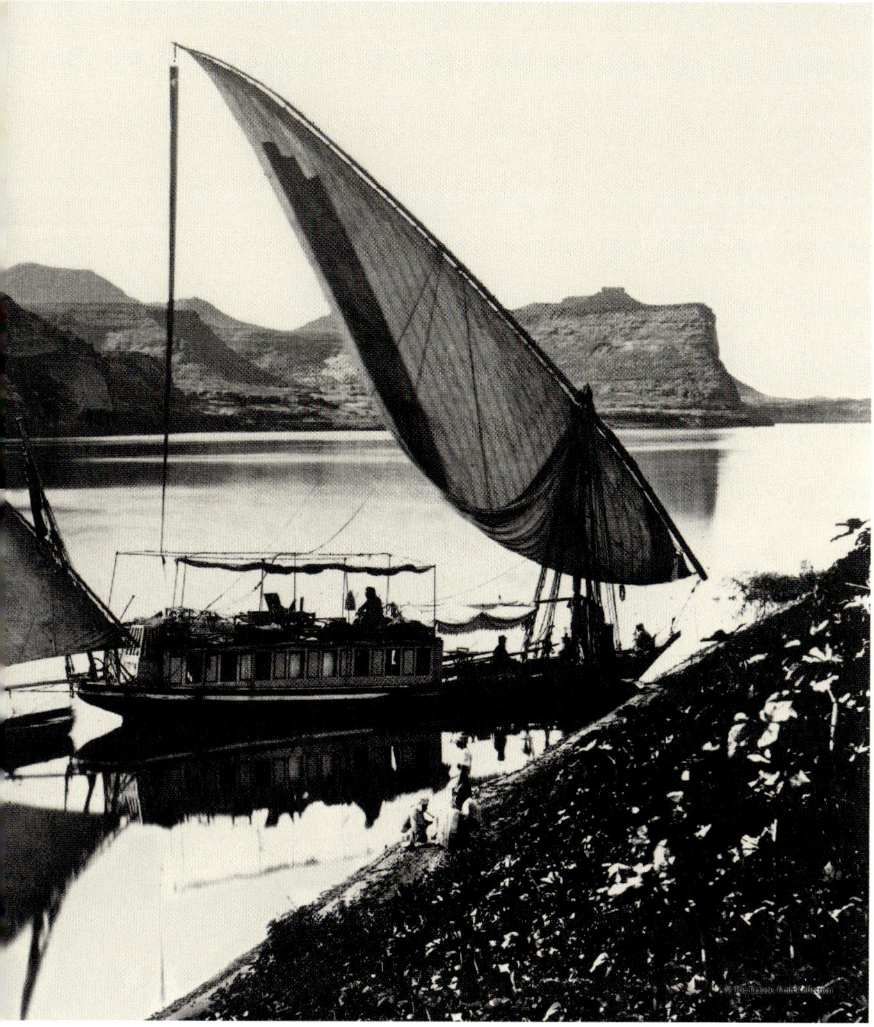

ancis Frith (British, 1822–98) was a pioneer early travel and landscape photography who unded a business selling postcards that lasted ell into the 20th century. He was a highly ccessful entrepreneur, who sold his grocery Jsiness in Liverpool in 1855 for £200,000, which the equivalent today of over £15,000,000. This ealth allowed him to devote himself to his own notography. He journeyed extensively in Europe d the Middle East, making trips from which produced prints for sale through the agent omas Agnew & Sons, and he worked with James Virtue to publish albums of his images, making him one of the earliest photographers to produce work commercially. In 1859 he set up Frith & Co. in Reigate, Surrey, as the world's first specialist photographic publisher. He then undertook the hugely ambitious task of photographing every town and village in the United Kingdom. Within a few years, thousands of shops across the country were selling his postcards. A Frith & Co. catalog issued in 1886 lists thousands of views of the British Isles, as well as photographs of Europe, China, Japan, the United States, and Canada. By 1970, Frith's collection contained over a third of a million pictures of 7,000 cities, towns, and villages.

Creative tips and techniques

The wet-collodion process entailed coating the glass plate with chemicals before making the exposure, and then quickly developing it to fix the image afterward. The wet-collodion process was sensitive only to blue light; therefore clouds do not register, as their color spectrum is too close to that of a blue sky. To record skies with tonal detail, the photographer often made two exposures, one for the sky and one for the land, and then combined them into a single print. This is still a useful technique digitally, if you have extremes of contrast between sky and landscape.

From the 1850s to the 1890s most photographs were printed using the albumen process, whereby paper is coated with a solution made from egg whites and salt, and then dipped in silver nitrate to make the surface sensitive to UV light. The paper is usually contact printed against the negative and then fixed to make the final photograph. The contact-printing process does not involve any enlargement of the negative and so captures all the detail of the image, resulting in a final photograph with incredible detail and smooth tonal values from dark to light.

To recreate the look of 19th-century photographic techniques digitally, you must work carefully with Photoshop to convert color images to black and white. To simulate the lack of sensitivity to the color spectrum other than blue, use channel mixers to remove all colors except blue. Skin tones of non-white people, or a sunburnt white face, will darken, and the detail will be lost from the skies. Use duotone controls to add tone, or software such as the Topaz range of preset filters.

Timothy O'Sullivan & Mark Klett

Green River Buttes/Castle Rock, Green River, WY
1872/1979

In the 1860s and 1870s, the US government initiated four major expeditions to survey the vast resources of the American West. The expeditions consisted of scientists, cartographers, and photographers, including Timothy O'Sullivan. Tasked with simply recording the geological terrain of these newly colonized lands, they surpassed their brief and produced images that have defined the landscape of the West in the imagination ever since.

A century later, Mark Klett and his team researched and returned to the locations of many of these iconic images to determine how the landscape had changed due to human activity. When O'Sullivan initially photographed this location, it was beautiful yet barren, as the West was still to be colonized and developed. A hundred years later, the vista was covered by tract houses and telephone lines, symbols of the impact of human activity on the natural landscape. Klett's project was not simply an exploration of the physical landscape, but also of the photographic techniques of the earlier surveyors. The Rephotographic Survey team used large-format film cameras to replicate the original glass-plate apparatus of the 19th century, and by the end of the journey in 1979 they had covered thousands of miles into the far-flung corners of Arizona, California, Colorado, Idaho, New Mexico, Nevada, Utah, and Wyoming, returning to the sites of more than 120 historic photographs. Klett found the journey to be a spiritual one as well as a physical one, arguing that "so much of what we know, and what we think we know, about the land has first passed through someone's lens. The interesting thing is to make use of this history, not merely to be absorbed into it."

> "Place and people are made familiar to us by means of the camera in the hands of skilful operators, who...take care to lose no good chance to scour the country in search of new fields for photographic labor." Timothy O'Sullivan

Timothy O'Sullivan (American, 1840–82) was one of the 19th century's most significant photographers, and his documentation of the US Civil War and the exploration of the West have influenced countless photographers. The Rephotographic Survey Project was set up by **Mark Klett** (American, 1952–) in 1977 to investigate how the iconic landscapes of the American West changed over the previous century. With a team of co-researchers Klett returned to the exact sites of photographs made in the 19th century as part of the exploration of and expansion into the West, and made new photographs from the same position and with similar equipment to that of the early pioneers. They repeated the process decades later, adding multimedia resources, for the "Third View" project. It is a fascinating study of not simply the physical landscape, but also the cultural and social values attached to it. Klett sums up the ethos of the Survey: "most people assume that landscape photographs are about rocks or trees or space. But I believe their real meaning concerns our essential connection to place, to each other, and, most important, to time."

Creative tips and techniques

This project is intimately bound up with one of the central features of the still photograph: its relationship to time. Klett explains that most of his pictures were based on the question: how long is a "moment" in time? Working in sites of what he calls "high image density" such as Yosemite National Park, where hundreds of photographers have made images over time, he notes that photographs show the same landscape with only slight variations in position and framing. He observes that although the pictures look different, the landscape itself has hardly changed at all. He stresses that the photographs in the survey are not to be seen in isolation, but as part of a more complex set of relations to other images, such that they should be regarded as overlapping layers in time.

In the follow-up project to the Rephotographic Survey, "Third View," the team returned twenty years later to many of the same sites to make new views. This time they expanded the process by using digital media, and collecting audio and video recordings, interviews, artefacts, and site-related imagery, including virtual reality panoramas. This allowed for a richer, more multivalent engagement with the subject, and facilitated new ways to present the work.

Follow Klett's lead and carry out a rephotographic survey of a location near you. Pick a scenic spot, local landmark, or historic site and research photographs taken there over the last 150 years. Try to find as many images of the same location as you can, and then go to the location and reshoot them from the same camera positions. You can then collate the work to create a timeline of how the place has changed over the years.

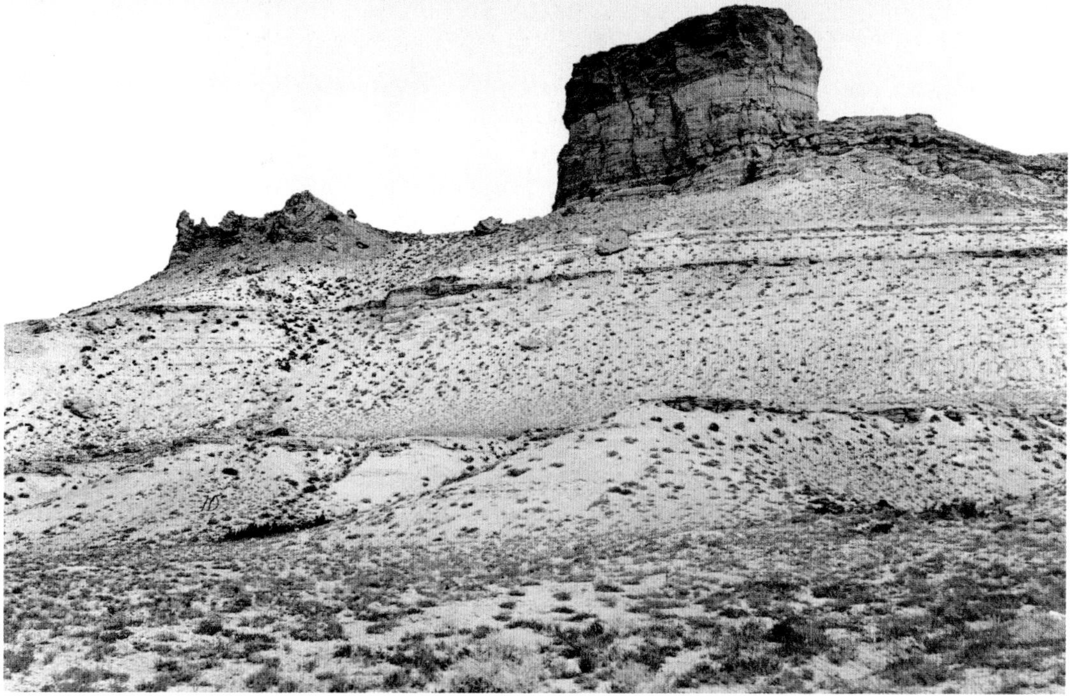

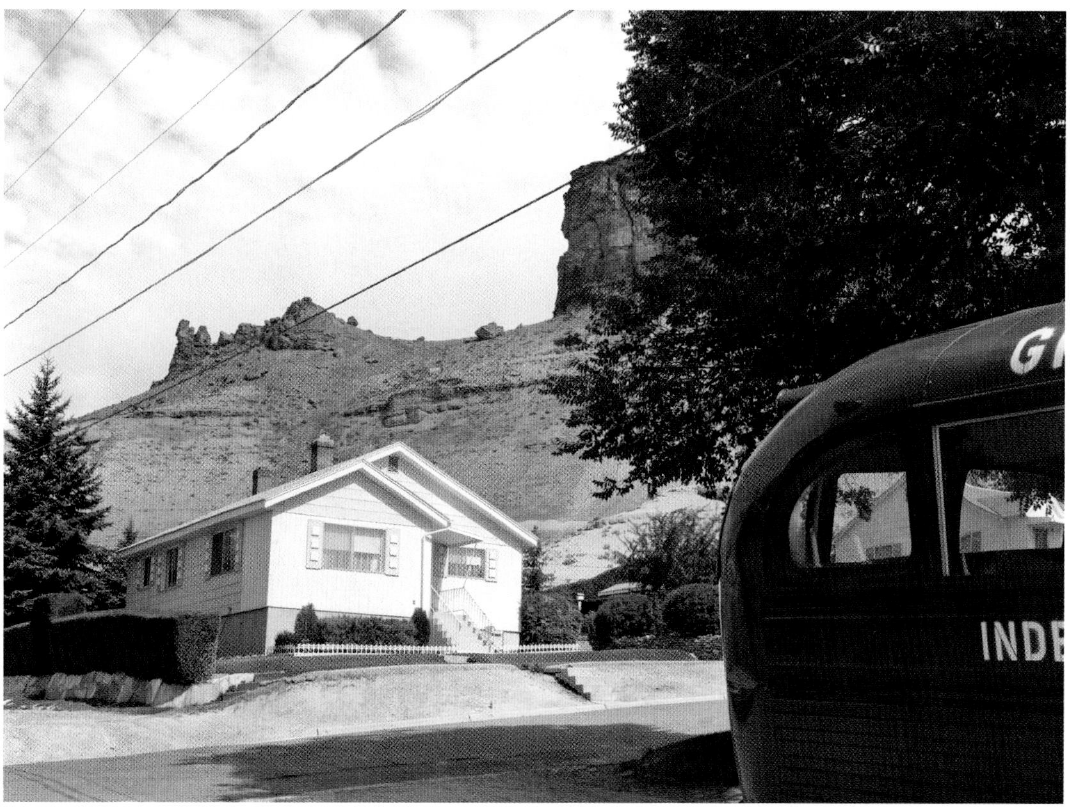
INDE

Ansel Adams

Clearing Winter Storm, Yosemite Valley *c.* 1935

Ansel Adams worked mostly in black and white, and did not seek to create realistic documents of nature, but rather attempted to evoke an emotional sense of engagement with the experience of sublime beauty. His dramatic vistas of remote valleys and mountains, suffused with the light of the sun breaking through the clouds, created a representation of the magnificence of nature that was often more powerful than the real thing.

Adams lived in the Yosemite Valley for ten years from 1937, and knew its geography intimately, which meant he knew exactly where to position himself to find the perfect composition, making use of weather and the direction of light, stating that "a good photograph is knowing where to stand." This is apparent in this image, where he waited for the moment immediately after a storm to shoot, ensuring that the light dusting of snow on the landscape would bring out all the detail of the topography of the scene. The photograph leads the eye through the valley, using the darker areas of the foreground to channel the viewer toward the sunlit areas of the center, and in particular to the vertical line of the waterfall caught by the sun. He has exposed the negative perfectly to capture all the tonal detail from black to white and through a full range of grays.

"Sometimes I do get to places just when God's ready to have somebody click the shutter."

Ansel Adams

Ansel Adams (American, 1902–84) was a hyper-active child, who was expelled from several schools for poor behavior and was educated by his family and private tutors from the age of twelve. This restlessness was initially focused on the piano, which gave him self-discipline and an attention to detail, but after a trip to Yosemite National Park in 1916 he began to experiment with photography, which rapidly became his passion. In 1916 he joined the influential environmental organization the Sierra Club, founded by legendary conservationist John Muir in 1892. Adams's association with the Club and the preservation of wilderness areas were central to his career. He became friends with Paul Strand (see p.120) and Edward Weston (see p.98), with whom he founded the influential group f/64, referring to the minimum aperture of a lens that gives the greatest depth of field. Adams was a master of the technical and esthetic aspects of photography; he was a dedicated craftsman who worked tirelessly both on his photography and on campaigning to protect the environment, in particular Yosemite and the other national parks.

Creative tips and techniques

Adams worked with a large-format 10 x 8 plate camera that took single sheets of film, which allowed him very precise control over the development and processing of each negative. Along with photographer Fred Archer, he developed the idea of the "zone system," a method for the exposure and development of black-and-white photography, which has ten zones of density, from pure black to pure white with a subtle gradation of tones of gray in between. He used roman numerals for the scale of the system, so that 0 represents black, V middle gray, and X pure white. One zone is the equivalent of one stop of exposure on the camera. The meter in the camera usually tries to average out the light in a scene to an exposure based on zone V, but can easily be fooled if the scene is very dark or very light—for example, a black cat in the snow or a white bird against a night sky. Using the zone system to predetermine the tonal range of the scene by manually controlling the exposure allows the photographer much greater control of the final image. To use it, select an area of the scene, meter it, and then adjust the exposure by the difference between the zone you want in the final image and zone V.

Adams was intimately familiar with the geography of the American landscapes he worked in, and so could reliably predict where the sun would fall at any given time of day on a specific location. He was also aware of how the weather could affect the image, knowing that the moments after a storm when the sun breaks through the clouds, for example, often make for strong contrasts and a high level of detail in the clouds, as in this particular photograph.

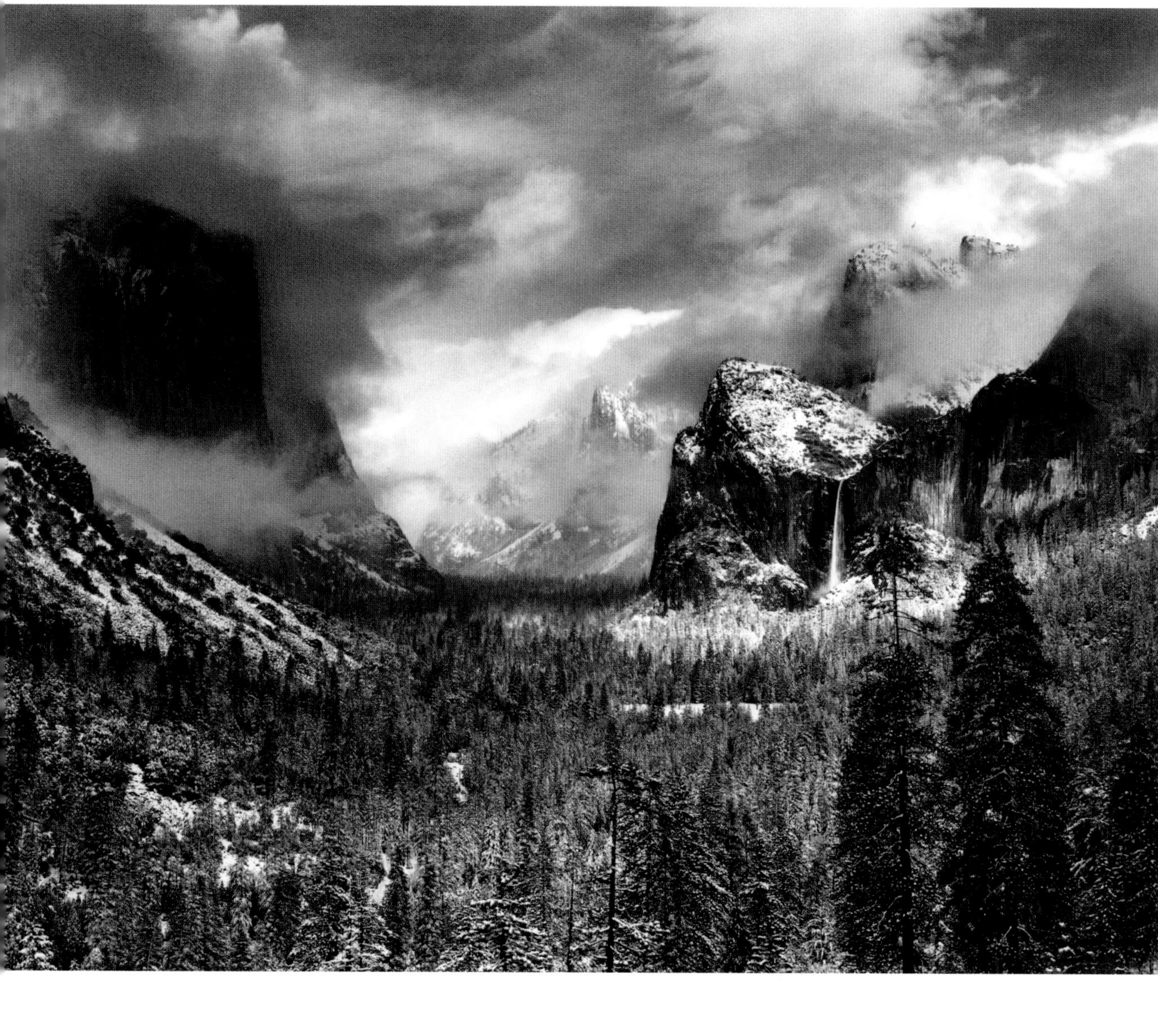

Robert Adams

Colorado Springs, Colorado 1968

This photograph comes from a series that Robert Adams made in the early 1970s, which later became his first major book. Published in 1974, *The New West* marked a shift in the photographic repres-entation of the American landscape. Adams worked along the edges of the sprawling, ever-growing American cities and towns around Denver, Colorado, where he explored how urbanism was defacing the landscape. His subject matter was ordinary and banal—tract homes, shopping malls, and concrete churches—and he often photographed them in the bright light of the middle of the day. His exhibition prints were relatively small (6 x 6 in./15 x 15 cm) and were printed in a high-key fashion to distil the intensity of the sunlight. Adams once commented of the image: "Nabokov said there's no light like Colorado's, except in central Russia. And you can see it in this picture. It's absolutely sublime." Adams has primarily been concerned with the transition from nature to urbanism and has focused on the boundaries and collisions between the city and the land. His work has a spare formalism combined with a deep emotional sensitivity to the conflict between humanity and nature.

"One does not for long wrestle a view camera in the wind and heat and cold just to illustrate a philosophy. The thing that keeps you scrambling over the rocks, risking snakes and swatting at the flies is the view."
Robert Adams

Robert Adams (American, 1937–) initially worked as a professor of English literature before turning full time to photography in the mid-1970s. He is one of the most eloquent writers on photography, as well as one of the most significant documentarians of the American landscape. Adams's visual heritage can be traced back to the 19th-century photographers of the American West, in particular Timothy O'Sullivan (see p.48), William Henry Jackson, and Carleton Watkins. He was part of the seminal exhibition "New Topographics: Photographs of a Man-Altered Landscape," curated by William Jenkins at the International Museum of Photography at George Eastman House in 1975. The show was a landmark in defining a stripped-back, unromantic view of the landscape. Adams has published dozens of books, including *Beauty in Photography* (1981), *To Make It Home* (1989), *Listening to the River*, and *Why People Photograph* (both 1994). He has won many awards for his work, including a Guggenheim Fellowship in photography in 1973 and 1980, and he received a MacArthur Fellowship in 1994.

Creative tips and techniques

Adams worked with a variety of formats, from a 6 x 7 Pentax and a 10 x 8 view camera to, in this instance, a 6 x 6 Rolleiflex medium-format camera. The square format of this image allows Adams to emphasize the repetition of a series of square and rectangular shapes within the frame, which is contrasted with the manicured sweep of the path across the lawn to the front door. The figure inside the house seems trapped in isolation, alienated from the world outside in the security of her tract home. Look for patterns and repeating shapes in your compositions.

Adams is very skilled in making the most of the harsh light of the American West. Rather than romanticizing it by shooting early in the morning or late in the afternoon when the light is at an angle, he often works during the middle of the day when the light is overhead, creating hard shadows and a sense of the burning light of the hot sun. Challenge yourself by going out in difficult light conditions to experiment with how to deal with less than ideal situations.

Adams's work invites us to explore how even the most mundane and banal location can still have significant visual potential. His photographs create a tension between the subject, which is often a commentary on man's degradation of the natural environment, and the form of the image, which is often a meditation on the esthetics of light and structure. As an exercise, go to the outskirts or suburbs of a city, and explore the forms and shapes of buildings and landscapes, looking for those moments when light and form combine to illuminate even the most unprepossessing of subjects.

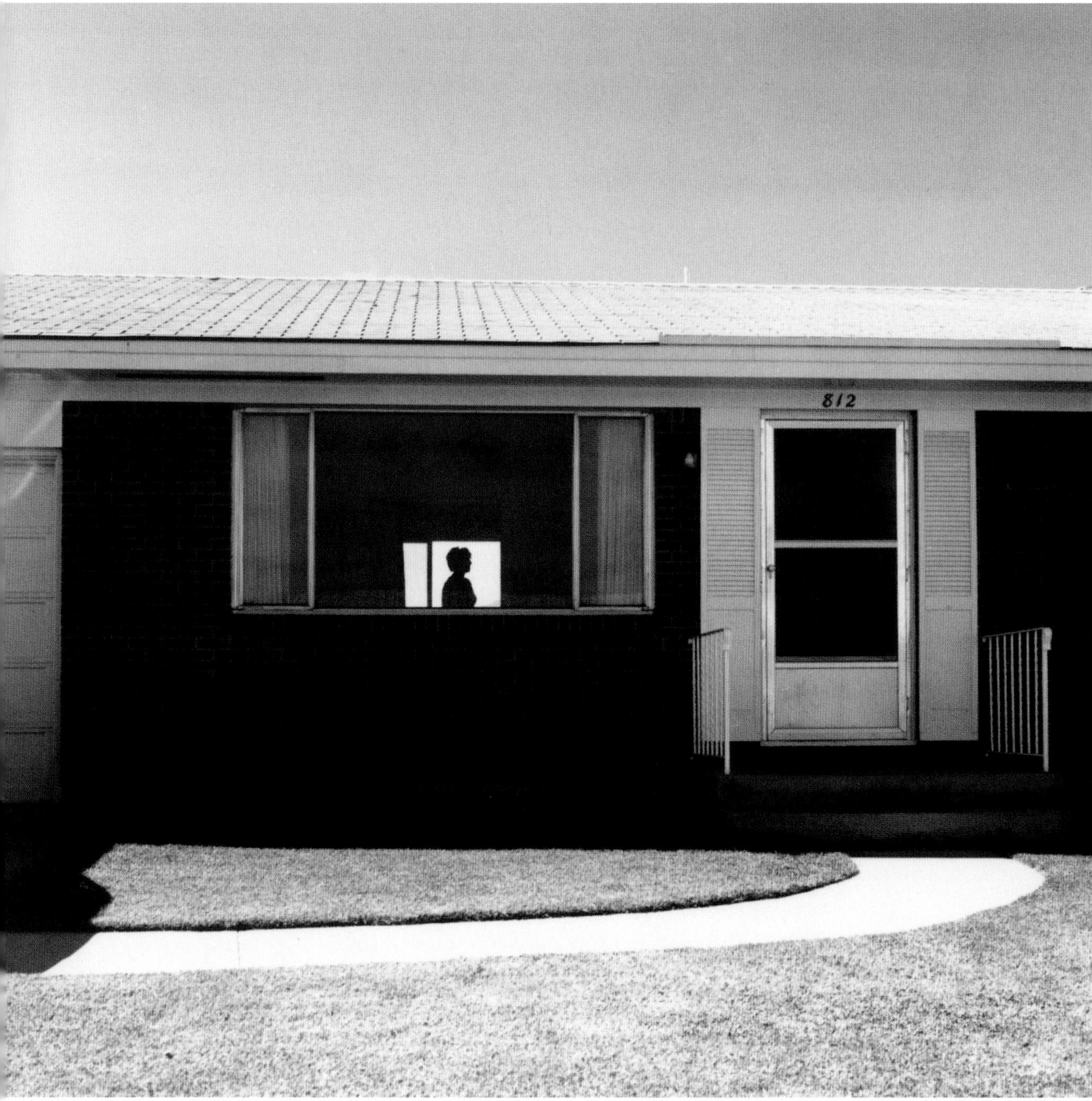
812

Joel Sternfeld

"Photography has a certain verisimilitude; it has gained a currency as truthful—but photographs have always been convincing lies."

Joel Sternfeld

Joel Sternfeld (American, 1944–), Stephen Shore, and Joel Meyerowitz (see p.60) emerged in the late 1970s and early 1980s as the most significant documenters of the US landscape in color. Taking inspiration from the pioneering work of William Eggleston (see p.100), they eschewed the then dominant tradition of working in black and white, and were drawn to the banalities, oddities, and beauty of the everyday topography of the United States. Sternfeld maintains that his work "has been about ideas of utopia and dystopia. I think that's what gives America interest. It's many things all at once. It's such a complicated society." He is acutely aware of the hidden meanings in the landscape; for *On This Site: Landscape in Memoriam* (1997) he photographed places in the United States where significant historic events had taken place, including the assassination of Martin Luther King Jr, and explored the palpable sense of history in each location.

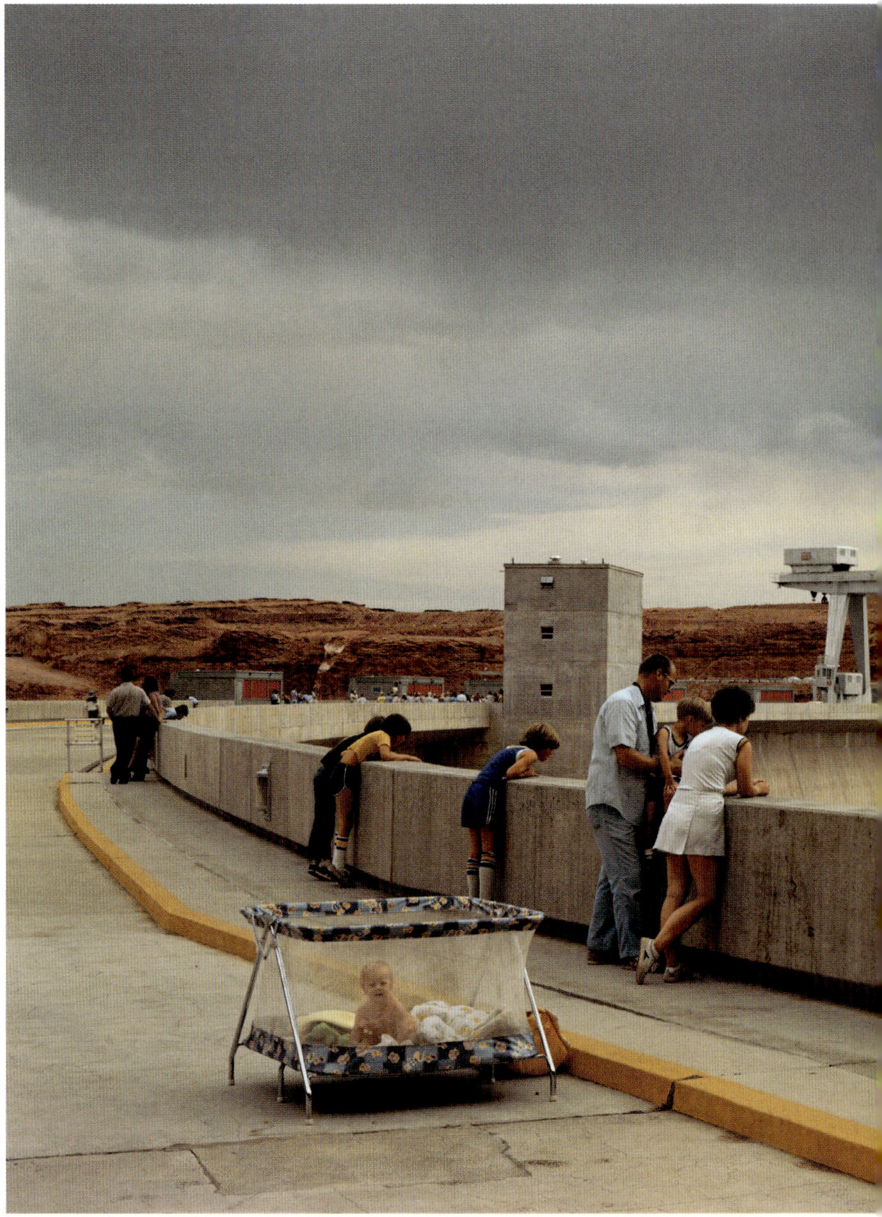

Creative tips and techniques

Sternfeld is highly aware of the contradictions inherent in the selective vision of the medium of photography. While appearing to offer an authentic representation of reality, every photograph is the result of a calculated series of decisions about how to frame the scene. He points out that photography has always been capable of manipulation and every image that is put out into the world is an interpretation. In this sense photographs have always been authored: "I could get my camera and point it at two people and not point it at the homeless third person to the right of the frame, or not include the murder that's going on to the left of the frame. You take 35 degrees out of 360 degrees and call it a photo. There's an infinite number of ways you can do this." Be aware that what

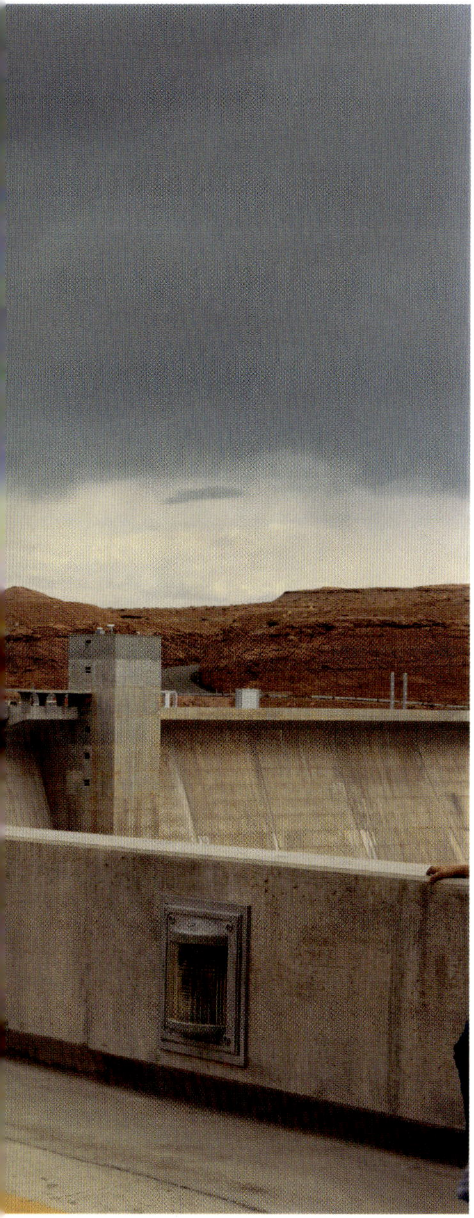

Glen Canyon Dam, Page, Arizona, August 1983 1983

This photograph is from Joel Sternfeld's book *American Prospects* (1987), which records a road trip he took across the United States following in the visual tradition of photographers Walker Evans (p.78) and Robert Frank (p.186). Sternfeld traveled across the country in a Volkswagen camper van, photographing with a large-format, 10 x 8 view camera on a tripod. He is a master at observing the contradictions and dark humor inherent in American life, particularly in the suburbs where the national desire for order conflicts with its longing to make a connection with nature. In this photograph, taken on the Glen Canyon Dam—a symbol of humanity's domination of nature—the baby in the crib appears like some alien life form cocooned in a life-support system, crying out for help while its parents gaze out across the vista behind it. Sternfeld explains that he is interested in the landscape for what it "reveals about the human moment, past, and the present human moment. I mean this is the surface of the earth, and what we do with it tells us an awful lot about ourselves." He wrote that the inspiration for the work was "of someone who grew up with a vision of classical regional America and the order it seemed to contain, to find beauty and harmony in an increasingly uniform, technological, and disturbing America."

ou chose to leave out of the frame is as nportant as what you choose to keep in.

Sternfeld is acutely tuned into the nuances and subtleties of colors and ow they can convey meaning as well as ormal beauty. This image is composed of ariations on browns, yellows, and earth ones, and the flat, overcast light gives the nage a radiant quality. Even the clothes f the people in the photograph are harmonious, with the yellow and blue of the boys' shirts echoing the patterns on the baby's crib. Try to work with images that use a limited palette to explore how small variations of tone and color can build up the image.

Sternfeld looks for locations that say something profound about the nature of American life. Some of these, like this dam, are markers of human technological intervention into the landscape. Others, such as his poignant *Exhausted Renegade Elephant* (1982), were the result of chance collisions with strange yet meaningful events while on the road. By building a plan for a body of work that takes you to key locations where you can make pictures, you will create a scaffolding for a project but still be open to chance encounters that are at the heart of the photographic moment.

John Davies

Agecroft power station, Salford 1983, from "The British Landscape 1979–2006"

John Davies was influenced by the American New Topographics movement and sought to apply its esthetic of objective but precise description of the landscape to his work. His images are classically composed, with sweeping vistas full of the detail that large-format cameras are capable of recording. In this photograph, which depicts the industrial landscape of northern England, the tiny figures playing the British national sport of soccer are dwarfed by the monumental structures of the power station cooling towers, symbolic of the rise and fall of British industry. In the left-hand corner, a tiny horse references the rural history of the countryside. The image has multiple layers that lead the eye around and through the landscape, reading it as if it were a map.

Davies's photographs are often shot from a high viewpoint, laying out the terrain as if in a geological slice through the strata of history. He explains: "I try to look for the best view to show features in context, and aim to get the maximum detail from my photographs." The process of economic growth and decline is embedded within the fabric of his images; as he notes, he is attempting to "create a narrative by image sequences to tell visual stories about process, change and transformation." Although each of his photographs can be viewed in isolation, the cumulative effect of describing the process of change becomes a powerful statement on the impact of man on the landscape and on the social fabric of society. He describes it as a "body of work using image as metaphor and an historical topographic survey, viewed from an independent contemporary perspective, of the remains of massive industrial and population growth and the impact of subsequent de-industrialization, shrinkage, regeneration, and experiments in planning new communities."

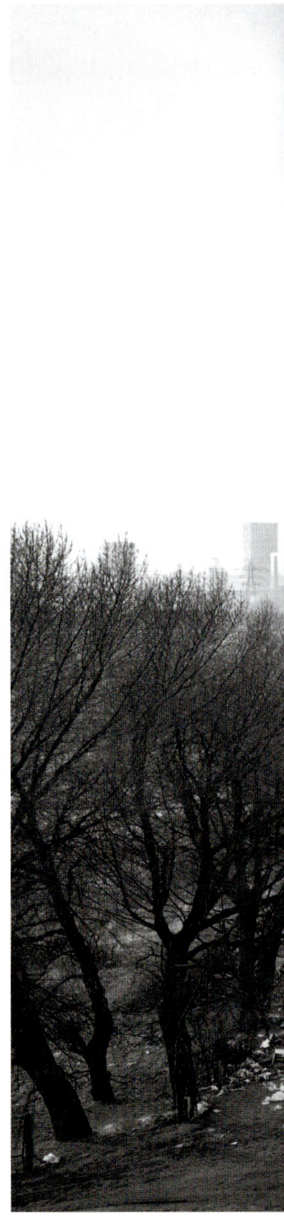

Creative tips and techniques

Davies is concerned with how the landscape can be made to narrate its history, and he uses the features of the terrain to generate meaning about larger social and economic forces. Think of a landscape not only aesthetically, but also in terms of what the vista can make the viewer feel and think. By combining natural and man-made elements in the same frame, Davies creates a debate about the nature of our relationship to the physical landscape.

The images in "The British Landscape" series are filled with detail and every part of the frame is carefully considered. When Davies composes photographs, he looks for interesting aspects around the edges. Try to shoot for a period of time in which you concentrate on building up your compositions from the outside edges of the frame inward, rather than from the center outward.

The landscapes Davies documents are not conventionally esthetic, as they are populated with features of Britain's industrial legacy. However, his formal approach and attention to nuances of detail mean that the photographs do have a strong sense of esthetic structure. Davies

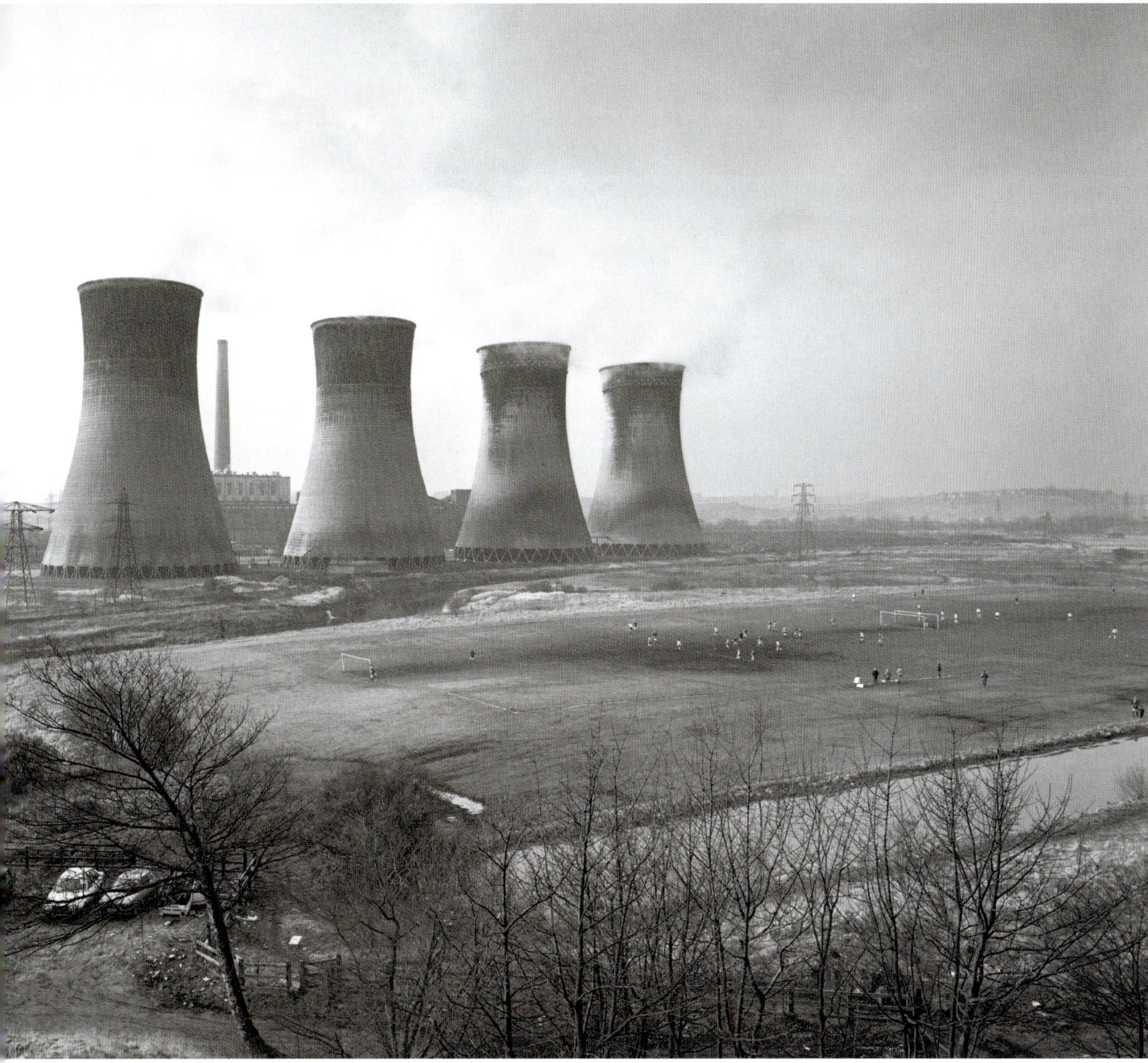

using the conventions of large-format, lack-and-white photography in the radition of American photographer Ansel dams to subvert expectations of what is suitable subject for the camera. In this nage, for example, the subtle gradations f gray tones in the cooling towers are sually pleasing, yet they signify the ccretion of dirt and toxins from years of olluting the atmosphere that the tiny gures below are breathing daily.

"We are collectively responsible for shaping the landscape we occupy and in turn the landscape shapes us ..." John Davies

John Davies (British, 1949–) is one of Britain's leading chroniclers of the landscape and is interested in exploring the impact of human activity on the topography of the countryside. He was born in County Durham, in northern England, and grew up in both farming and coal-mining communities. He seeks, in his words, "to raise questions about our collective responsibility in shaping the environments in which we live." His extensive work "The British Landscape," made between 1979 and 2006, documented the impact of long-term economic changes on the post-Industrial Revolution terrain. His project "Metropoli" explored the urban landscapes of the major cities of the north of England, whereas "Ground Control" examined the disposal and privatization of public open space. Images from the latter series appeared in Anna Minton's book *Ground Control* (2012).

Paul Graham

Untitled 1984, from "Troubled Land"

This photograph is from the series "Troubled Land" (1984–86), which, together with *Beyond Caring* (1986), a photo book recording the experience of unemployment offices in Margaret Thatcher's Britain, marked Paul Graham as one of the most important photographers of his generation. "Troubled Land" deals with the social and political landscapes of Northern Ireland and how the conflict is embedded in the very fabric of the streets, towns, villages, and fields of the province. Graham had become frustrated with the mainstream depiction of riots, bombs, sectarian marches, and soldiers patrolling the streets; making this image was a breakthrough for him in the project, as it showed how a distanced viewpoint could set the Troubles into the context of the social landscape in which they were taking place. He was approached on the street by a British Army patrol who interrogated him, warning him not to take any more photographs. As they left, he made this image of them leaving the area. At first glance, it appears to be a nondescript suburban roundabout that could be anywhere in Britain. Yet a closer examination reveals telling and subtle details of the scene that locate it clearly in Belfast: the pro-IRA (Irish Republic Army) graffiti on the metal fence, the broken kerbstones used by rioters as missiles, and the smashed streetlights signify this as the arena for nightly battles with the RUC (Royal Ulster Constabulary) and the British Army. The tiny figure of the soldier running across the frame completes the narrative. The image has a sense of stillness, as if caught in time, an experience that is central to Graham's sensibility. As he puts it, "Normally, photography offers these frozen shards of time where the world is ossified into a singular moment. I've struggled to get away from that brittle, crystalline notion by inviting time into the work, making it a quality that you feel and experience."

"Sometimes, when I go out with a camera, I don't have a plan or even know what it is I am looking for." Paul Graham

Paul Graham (British, 1956–) emerged in the 1980s as one of the leading British color documentary photographers, along with Martin Parr (see p.102), Paul Reas, and Peter Fraser (see p.106). Although Graham's earlier projects were concerned with traditional documentary themes of conflict and poverty, his later work has expanded to a more complex engagement with the nature of the world around us, and his experiential responses to it, while still remaining rooted in the encounter with the "real." He maintains: "I am interested in more elusive and nebulous subject matter. The photography I most respect pulls something out of the ether of nothingness... you can't sum up the results in a single line."

Creative tips and techniques

Graham is constantly pushing the edges of how the camera records the world, to try to find new ways to describe it. Writing about his "A Shimmer of Possibility" project, for which he deliberately overexposed the images, he observed that by breaking the norms you can uncover "photography's unwritten rules accidentally." A particular way of representing a subject is often a matter of convention, so be prepared to bend and break the rules to see what happens.

Graham explores the formal qualities of the medium in order to investigate how they can be used to convey meaning. Talking about his series of works in the United States, he noted that, "'End of an Age" alternates between sharp and blurry photos—soft camera-shake pictures, coupled with sharp, direct flash pictures—so that deals with focus. 'American Night' has very light pictures and very dark pictures—intense light flooding in or restricted down—so that deals with exposure or... aperture. And 'Shimmer' uses stuttering single frames—action, flowing or frozen—so that tackles time or... shutter speed. So we have the three principal controls of the camera: focus, aperture, and shutter." He compares this exploration of the potential of technique to that of an artist experimenting with the material qualities of the process. Set yourself a series of experiments in which you explore the edges and limitations of shutter speed and exposure. See how, by deliberately using slow shutter speeds in order to create blur and over- and underexposure, you can create unnaturally dark and light tones, which will give you control over changing the feel and meaning of your images.

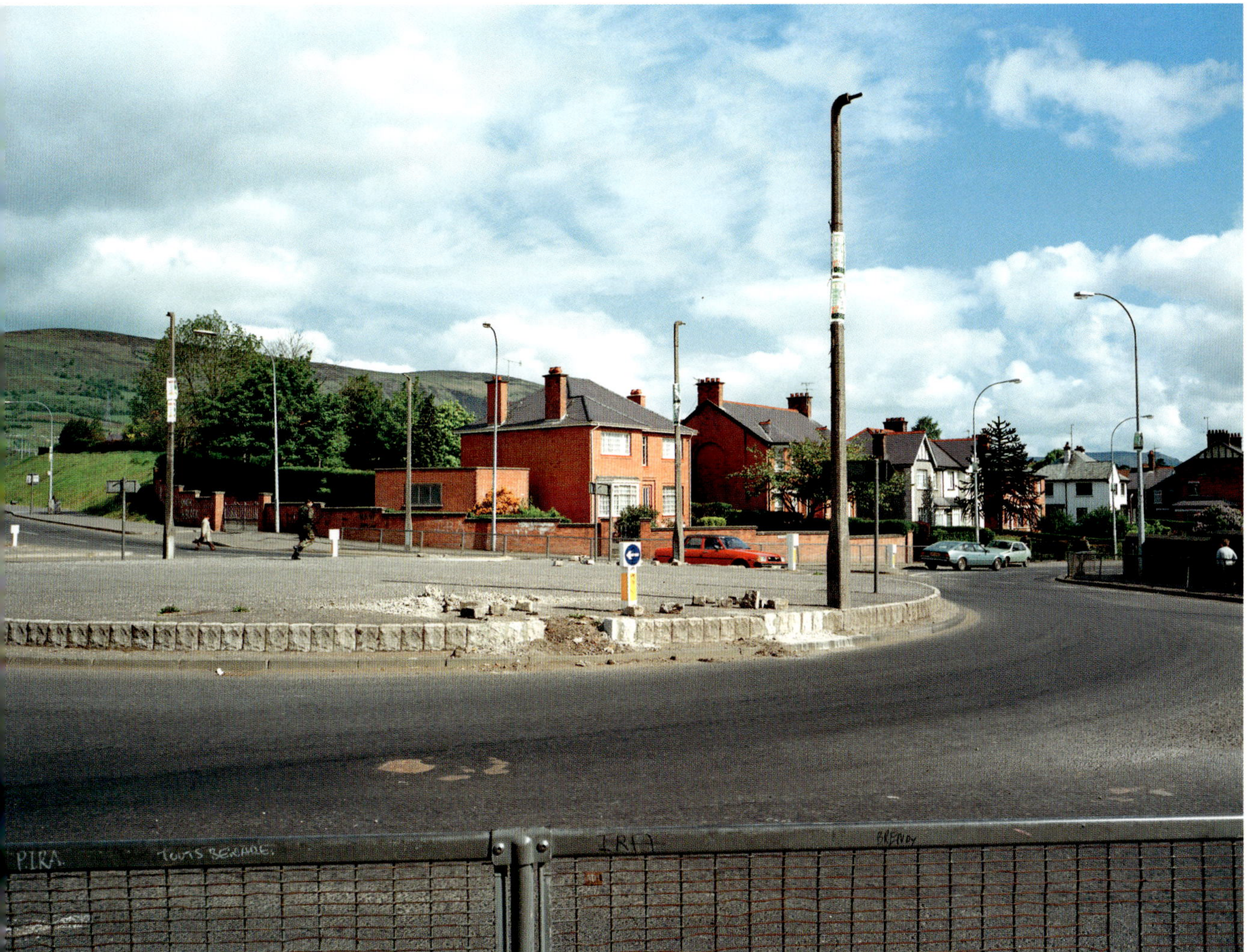
PIRA
TOUTS BEWARE

Joel Meyerowitz

"Color plays itself out along a richer band of feelings: more wavelengths, more radiance, more sensation."
Joel Meyerowitz

Joel Meyerowitz (American, 1938–) began working in the advertising industry, but after a shoot with Robert Frank (see p.186) in 1962, he was so inspired by photography that he quit his job. He became part of the street photography movement of the 1960s, along with Garry Winogrand (see p.192), Tony Ray-Jones (see p.190), and Lee Friedlander (see p.194), abandoning black-and-white film for color, using slow Kodachrome slide film to make a witty and carefully observed essay on the chaotic theater of New York's streets called "Out to Lunch." He began working with the large-format 10 x 8-inch camera, initially still in an urban setting but later exploring portraiture and the natural landscape. He is the author of numerous books, including the monumental *Aftermath: World Trade Center Archive* (2006), which documents the destruction wrought on the city of New York by the attacks of 11 September 2001.

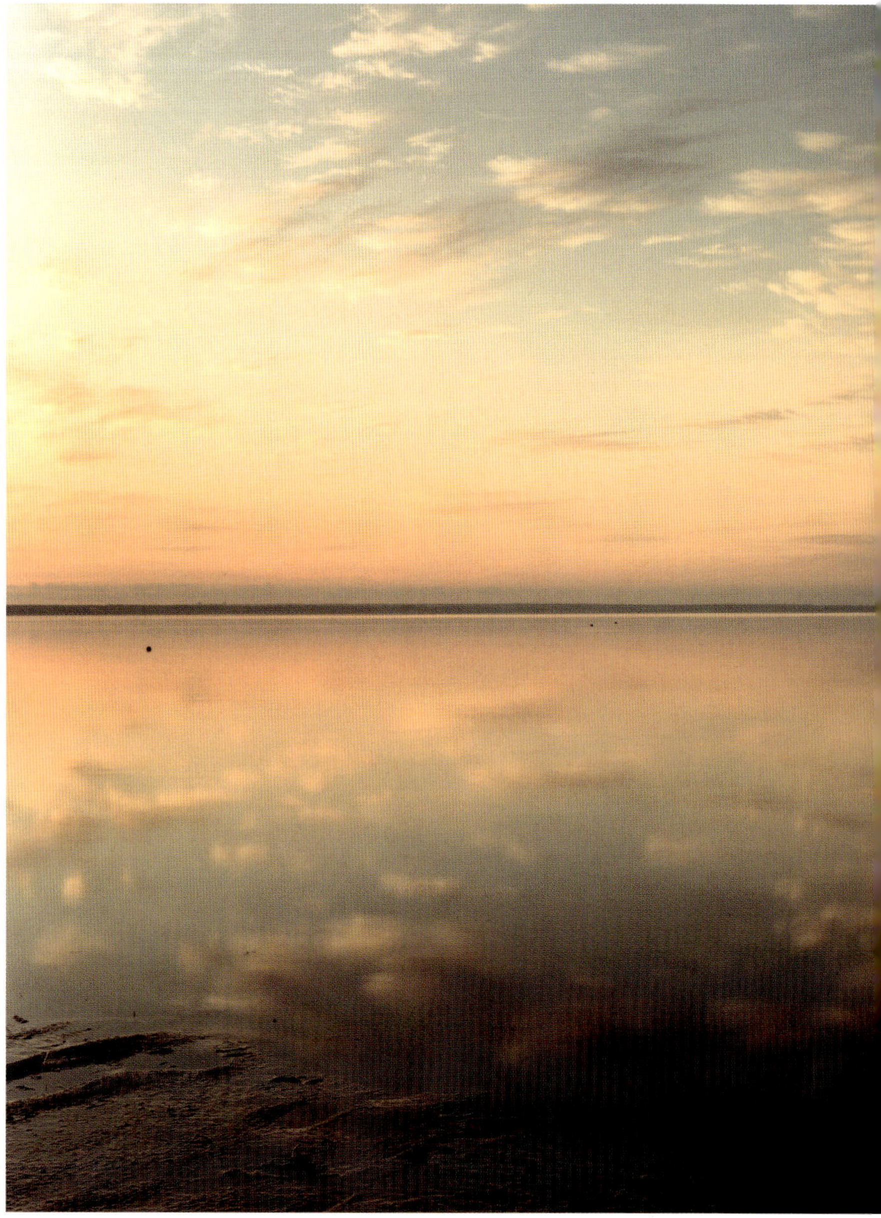

Creative tips and techniques

Meyerowitz responds instinctively to a scene. He says that as he has got older he has relied more on gut sensation than the purely "optical" point of view, and regards it as a valid and valuable way of working. He has identified a direct connection with his deep instinct before he sees what is in the frame. He says "That quickening of the intuitive 'knowing' is my guide." At times, stop thinking too much about your work and simply respond intuitively to the world that you see around you; occasionall go out without any specific agenda in minc and open yourself up to the pure quality of light around you.

Meyerowitz advises that artists should be vigilant and not listen too much to their audience or even to favorabl

Bay/sky, dawn, fall 1986

This beautifully serene image is from Joel Meyerowitz's first book, *Cape Light* (1979), which explores the quality of light on the seascapes of Cape Cod. He describes the implications of changing to color photography in his practice: "Once I changed to color full time, I had to step back 15 feet or so from the plane I normally worked on when shooting on Fifth Avenue. That change—made to give color's shallow depth of field more room to describe the entire space—caused me to reconsider what to make the frame about, and it was then that I gave up [capturing] the 'incident,' [which has long been] the basic way of working for street photographers." He realized that "by stepping back and taking in the overall image that I would need to make bigger prints with more 'description,' which, after all, is what photography does first: describe things. This led me to the 8 x 10-inch view camera with a film of such quality that it would easily let me go up to 60 inches or more in print size." Such large prints, in color, were rare at the time in photography and had a profound influence on their display. The images in *Cape Light* play off how the transition from light to dark and to light again engages with the transition from land to sea, creating photographs in which the translucent quality of light becomes the subject matter itself.

itics; he warns that, when artists try to lease the crowd, "their work flattens out." emain true to your own personal vision, ather than what you think the viewer wants see based on convention. Pandering to onvention can dilute one's unique point f view.

Meyerowitz believes that digital photography has changed audiences' xpectations of what they are seeing. He recounts how, in the early days of digital, he had an exhibition at a New York gallery of vintage 35mm photographs that had been made twenty or more years earlier. The images contained many startling "moments" that he had been quick enough to see and photograph. However, when visitors to the gallery saw these images, he heard their remarks that the scenes "must have been set up, or directed." The audience could not imagine that someone could be quick enough to see these things and actually manage to capture them on camera. Meyerowitz is also enthusiastic that the freedom of digital—as anyone with a smartphone has a camera—will inspire millions of fresh minds into considering making photographs and to use the camera in strange and unexpected ways. New visions will emerge from this pool of people.

Richard Misrach

Outdoor Dining, Bonneville Salt Flats, Utah 1992, from "Desert Canto XV: The Salt Flats"

Richard Misrach's work explores the impact of human activity on the environment, particularly in the deserts of North America, where he has made a series of works, grouped together as "Desert Cantos" (*canto* being an Italian term that refers to a subsection of a long poem). Misrach's project is partly influenced by the poetry of Ezra Pound, and critic Gerry Badger has suggested, "Misrach's goal may be said to be a search for the photographic Holy Grail, to fuse reportage with poetry."

Begun in 1979, there are now over thirty individual "cantos," or subseries, in the work, covering a wide range of concepts, ideas and subjects including fires, floods, nuclear testing, car racing, the sky, and the space shuttle launches. Each is self contained, and stands in its own right, but taken together they provide not only a deep exploration of the nature of the desert experience, but also a meditation on the nature of photography itself. The shifting visual style of each canto is also a deliberate attempt to engage the viewer, as in Pound's epic poem, "The Cantos." Visually, Misrach's cantos are often epic in scale and suffused with the clear desert light, making them esthetically powerful, as in this striking and surreal image of a restaurant where the walls seem to have disappeared. However, the subject matter of the series is also often dark and disturbing, as in "The Pit," which deals with mass graves of dead animals. This results in a powerful combination of form and content, as Misrach explains: "I've come to believe that beauty can be a very powerful conveyor of difficult ideas. It engages people when they might otherwise look away."

"The desert...may serve better as the backdrop for the problematic relationship between man and the environment."

Richard Misrach

Richard Misrach (American, 1949–) discovered the work of the classic canon of landscape photographers such as Ansel Adams (see p.50), Wynn Bullock, Edward Weston (see p.98), Harry Callahan (see p.118), and Paul Caponigro when he was a student at Berkeley, California, in 1970. Caught up in the anti-war protests of the time, he was "tear gassed and billyclubbed for taking pictures." This created a potent combination of esthetics and political commitment. He recalls: "it was that cocktail—the combination of the gritty, turbulent political historical moment mixed with the elegant, romantic fine print tradition of landscape photography—that established the poles that would inform my work.' Influenced by John Szarkowski's seminal endorsement of serious color photography in William Eggleston's *Guide* in 1976 (see p.100), he experimented with it, and considers its explosion in the late 1970s as a "pivotal moment of practice" in the history of art.

Creative tips and techniques

Misrach has worked in the deserts of the American West for decades. He is captivated by the clear, pure light and the monochromatic tones of the landscape. By establishing a theme for each of his cantos, he has been able to explore a wide range of topographies, including the sky and clouds above the land. For one canto, Misrach made a series of star trail images at night, interested in what happens when all the normal identifying elements of a place—the terrain, landmarks, and topography—are removed.

Working on a series of interrelated essays on a common theme can be an excellent way to develop a long-term project. Each one can be completed as an individual unit, but they build to a greater whole. You can keep the visual style consistent for each one or vary it to experiment with different formal strategies, as Misrach did with "Desert Cantos." This is an excellent way to work on a project that could take months or even years to complete, as it allows you to promote and market each chapter individually once it is finished, and then compile all of them together in the final complete body of work.

Misrach works with a large-format 10 x 8-inch camera that produces negatives with extra-ordinary detail and almost no grain, which allows for a seamless feel to the final prints. This means that very subtle variations in color can be experienced, as in this beautiful desert study. The image is composed of a few harmonious colors and tones, based around yellows, oranges, browns, and beige, with the bright red of the Coca-Cola trademark lettering providing a hint of color above the bar on the left of the photograph.

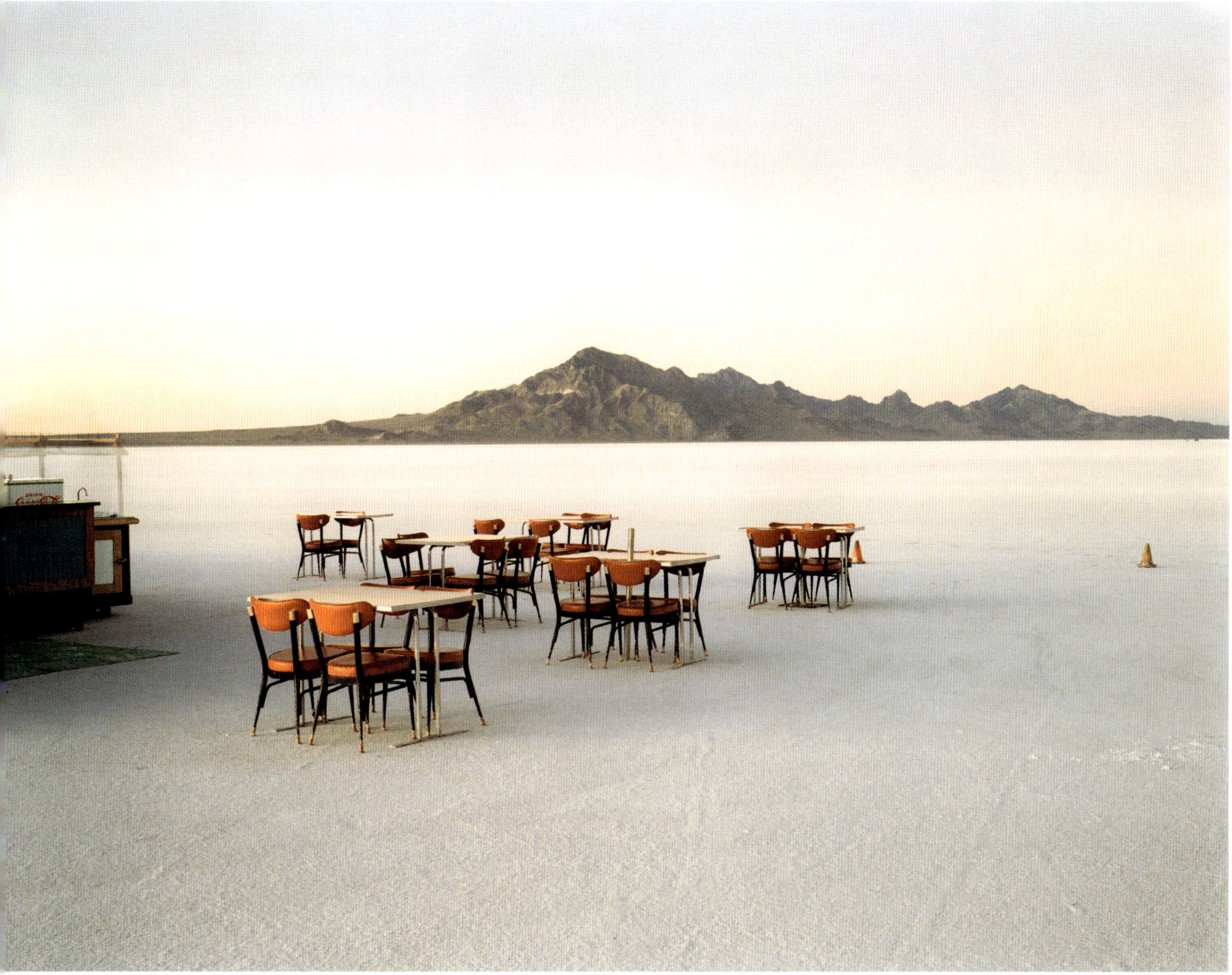

Jem Southam

"I eschew grandeur for the sake of it, preferring to revel in a subtler scale and history. But there's still an epic story to be told which exists wherever humans have made their homes."
Jem Southam

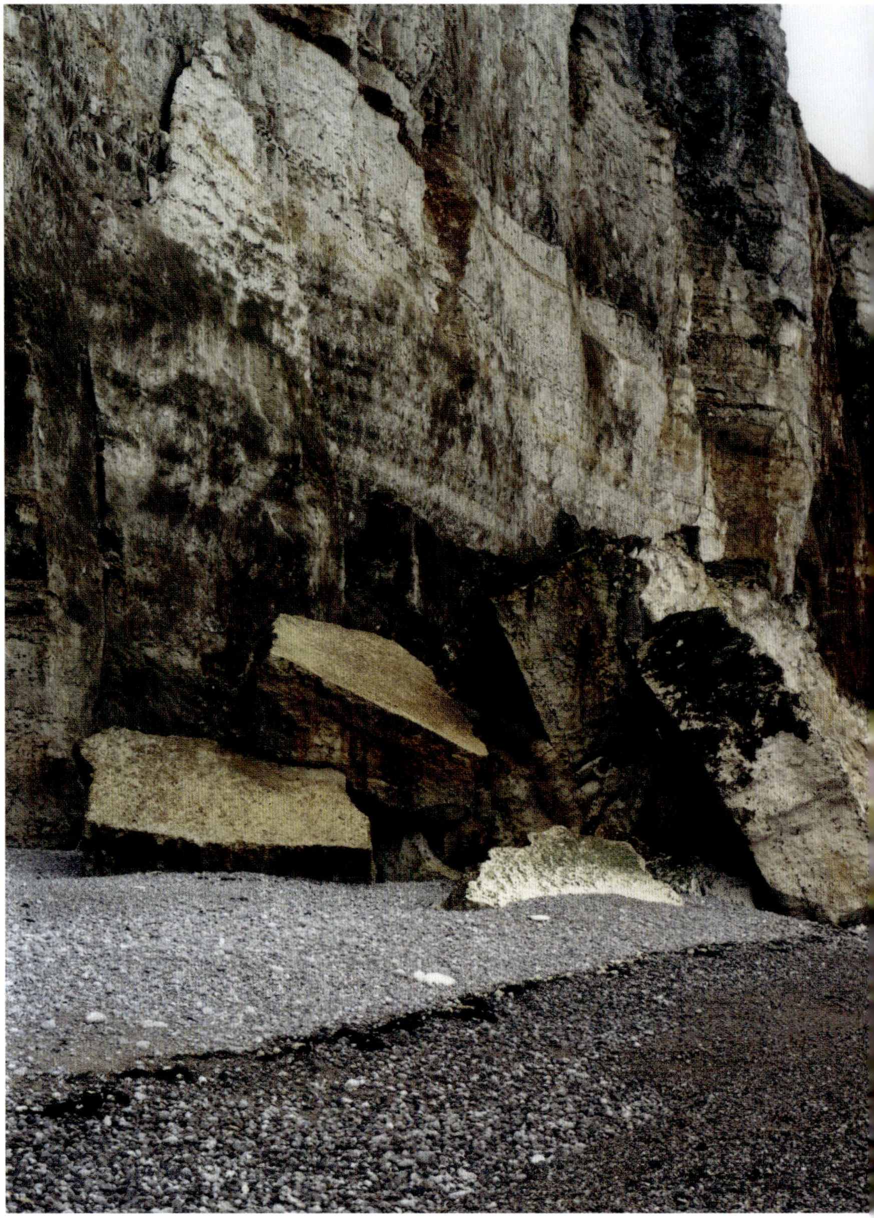

Jem Southam (British, 1950–) emerged along with Martin Parr (see p.102) and Paul Graham (see p.58) as one of Britain's leading proponents of color photography. Unlike them, he has remained rooted in a relatively restricted set of physical spaces and themes, maintaining that "standing still and paying close attention will reveal as many riches as charging around the globe." His main subject is the rural landscape of south-west England. He is fascinated by the cycles of nature, the constant oscillation between decay and renewal. He works on extended series of images of a particular place, returning to the same location repeatedly over months and years. David Evans has called him the "photographer of the slow rhythms of social time and the even slower rhythms of physical geography." Southam is currently a professor of photography at the University of Plymouth, Devon.

Creative tips and techniques

Like many landscape photographers, Southam has always preferred to work with a large-format 10 x 8 view camera, which requires a tripod and a darkcloth draped over the photographer's head in order to see the image projected onto the camera's ground glass screen. The image is inverted, because there is no mirror between the lens and the film plane as with an SLR. This makes the process of creating photographs significantly more laborious and time consuming than when using smaller cameras, but it does allow for very precise framing and composition. Southam persists with this particular approach, however, because it is so "difficult" and "enthralling." The process of making the image is therefore central to the experience rather than a barrier to it.

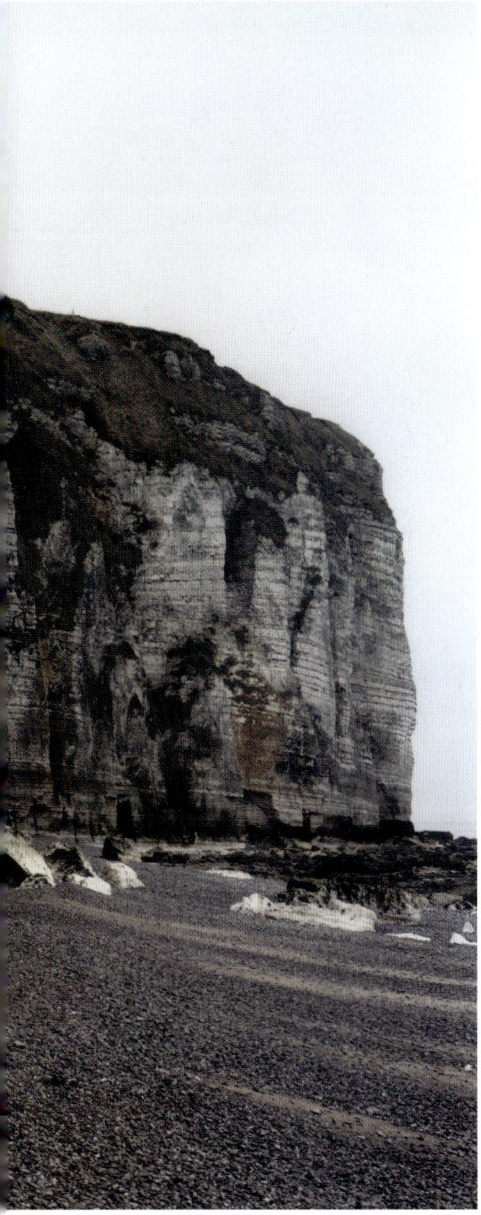

Yport 2005, from "Rockfalls"

This photograph is from a series Jem Southam made of rockfalls on the Normandy coastline, a continuation of a similar project he had worked on along the south coast of England. Although initially reluctant to take on a commission to photograph in France, a place unfamiliar to him, once he visited the coastline he was immediately captivated by it, recalling that: "Because the cliffs in Normandy faced north-west rather than south, as all the chalk cliffs I had photographed in England did, the sculptural presence of the rockfalls was quite distinct and I knew immediately I wanted to work there." The image is composed around a series of diagonal lines converging on the fallen rocks in the center of the frame, which themselves diverge from the lines running toward them. The color palette is subdued and harmonious, with the soft light of a gray day pulling together subtle variations in tones of gray, brown, and beige. At first glance, the image is simple, but the complexity of the composition, and the tones and textures of the terrain, are endlessly fascinating, fulfilling his wish to "make pictures that are complex and demand patient attention."

Southam shot the image on a Wista field camera with a 240mm wide-angle lens. As in the case of many of his images, he used a stepladder and a tall tripod to elevate his viewpoint above that of eye level, shooting from a height of approximately 9 feet (3 meters). The photograph sums up Southam's fascination with how the surface of the land can be shaped by the forces of nature and by human activity, revealing esthetic forms and shapes that are the result of happenstance rather than design. He is fascinated by locations where the processes that transform landscape are evident, often as a result of large-scale industrial activity such as mining: "landscapes which are formed by these processes are completely unplanned—they are the result of the technologies required to do the particular actions required."

Southam shoots very sparingly; during the period in which this image as made, he only exposed around fifty eets of film a year, from which he would pect to get perhaps ten photographs at he was satisfied with. Partly this is ecause he restricts his shooting days those when the light is overcast, ding that the traditional landscape otographer's preference for sunlight—articularly that just after dawn or before sunset—is too overtly romantic for his needs. He prefers fall, winter, and early spring to shoot, partly because of lighting and problems with excessive amounts of foliage, but also because of the slow, methodical, and almost meditative process by which he works, gradually developing his projects over many years. This is a very disciplined approach compared to shooting hundreds of frames a day with digital, but can be very therapeutic for your practice, so try to really make every shot count. Although Southam shoots on film, he often prints digitally from a scan of the negative. To replicate his methodical approach with a digital SLR, use a tripod and limit yourself to a small number of exposures each day you go out to shoot—say ten to twelve, which is the typical number of dark slides a photographer shooting large format would take into the field.

Simon Norfolk

"Mine was less a work of photography and more one of archeology: peeling back the layers . . ."

Simon Norfolk

Simon Norfolk (British, 1963–) is one of the key practitioners of "aftermath" photography. He deploys the landscape visually to address complex social, political, and moral issues in post-conflict situations. His method is to "take the inert and try to make that landscape reflect back to me—human struggles, political struggles, ethical struggles, to vitalize the landscape, to make it live, and tell me back the stories it has witnessed, to turn the landscape into a storyteller." An exhaustive research process, evidenced by the extraordinary depth of caption information that supports his photographs, establishes and underpins the credibility and authenticity of his work. This specificity and certainty allows him to draw inferences from the locations he depicts. As he maintains, "If you take to the landscape a knowledge of history, [that landscape] will tell you its memories."

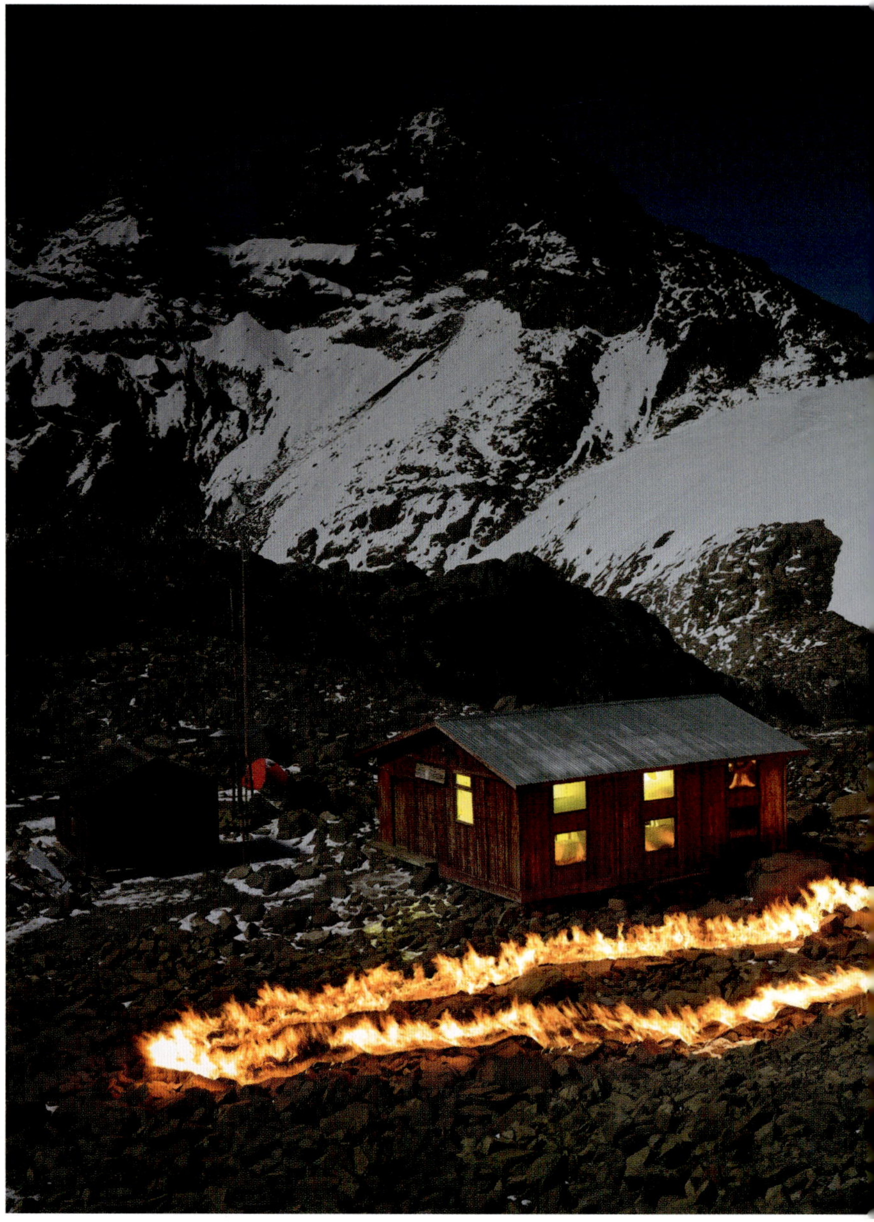

Creative tips and techniques

Norfolk spends a considerable amount of time experimenting with techniques in advance of the actual shoot, so that when he arrives at the final location he is fully prepared and knows exactly what to expect and how to get the perfect shot. He even uses Google Earth to look at locations before he goes there, so that he can work out the terrain and where the light will be fallin on any given day. Follow his advice and try out ideas for photographs in a controlled situation so that you know how to achieve any given effect.

Norfolk's image is composed broadl according to the "golden ratio" principle, with the main areas of interest positioned approximately one-third across the frame in both axes. The line of fire runs

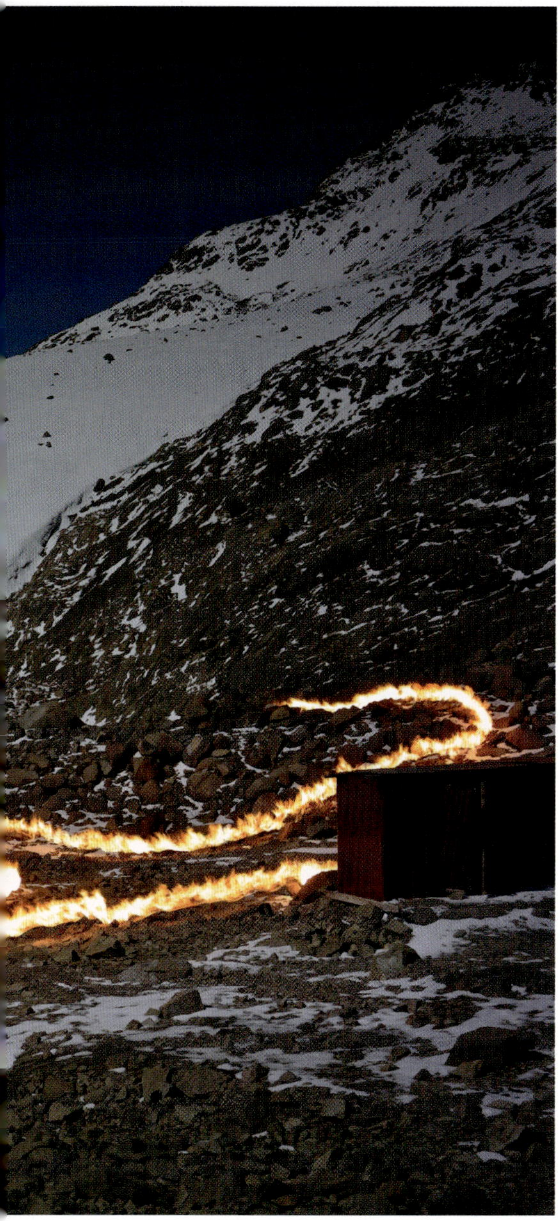

The Lewis Glacier, Mt Kenya, 1963 (A) 2014

This photograph is from a haunting series Simon Norfolk made on the subject of climate change. It indicates the extent of the depletion of the Lewis Glacier on Mount Kenya in Africa. Norfolk created the image with a very long exposure. Using a gas-soaked rag tied to the end of a pole, he created a ribbon of fire tracing the boundary of the glacier in 1963, the year in which he was born.

The image speaks of the temporality of the scene by using the very product that is charged with causing climate change to inscribe its effects on the landscape. Norfolk literally embeds the passage of time into the image, making the retreat of the glacier chillingly apparent. Norfolk calls this image a "stratograph"—a photographic description of time's "layeredness." He evocatively described the experience of the project as follows: "To be next to the ice is to feel privileged: like you are beside a colossal, sleeping giant. I imagine being close to a darted bull-elephant feels the same, and I'm reminded of a 17th-century Dutch painting of bewildered burghers contemplating a beached whalefish. Close up, one senses the immensity of the ice mass, its coiled, dormant energy and its colossal longevity. And, of course, the glacier's cold, resigned indifference. One is chilled by an overwhelming feeling of one's own smallness and transience."

Norfolk's photographs are carefully staged and composed, and draw on a series of metaphors, allegories, and symbols to construct an imaginative space into which viewers can project their own thoughts and responses. As he explains: "My strategy is to confuse the stereotypes, to shatter that preconception of the work. In that split second before the viewer rebuilds the fortress of their preconceptions, you can get inside with all kinds of subversions of symbols."

ɔward from left to right, leading the eye ːross the composition, and the final turn the trail of fire takes the eye back into e image. Note also how the lines of the e echo the shape of the mountain. To ɔply the golden ratio (also known as the le of thirds) to your own work, position ɔur main focal points on imaginary lines nning along one third of the image ı either axis, and on the intersections ətween them.

To record this shot, Norfolk used a very long exposure of up to one hour, which allowed him to create the fire trails in the image. This also allowed the light from the full moon to illuminate the landscape, giving the "day for night" effect. Using such a long exposure will also create light trails from the stars. Experiment with this technique in your own compositions in natural settings for some striking results. Take a series of shots that are under- and overexposed by several stops each side of the measured exposure, and see how the light changes across the scene. For night photography, the camera meter will often give you an exposure that is too bright—it will appear almost as if the photograph was taken in daylight—so deliberately underexposing the image to make it darker will give a realistic effect.

Space

S

The concept of a "poetics of space"—the idea that an interior scene can tell us something about the people who use that space—underlies the appeal of interiors and architectural features in photography. The study of the volume, line, and structure of a building can provide esthetic surprises, as the architect's vision is reinterpreted by that of the photographer. Like things, spaces have a presence, a personality even, that holds meaning. They intimately connect us to who we are, forming our habitat, a protective cocoon around us, as well as the sites of culture and entertainment. Spaces contain the traces of those who built them and occupy them, often long after those people have passed into memory and history. Patterns of human activity and consumption can be catalogued and documented, and the grandeur and folly of hubris encountered.

The patina of the past is a highly visible sign of the passage of time, and one that is literally written into the fabric of the space. The play of light across the features of a room describes its volume and form, creating the sense of a three-dimensional space that the viewer is invited to enter, explore, and occupy. We are invited to imagine the lives of those who have lived and died in the rooms captured by the camera. However, as always, it is in the selective eye of the photographer that much of an image's meaning is generated. By choosing a particular space and shooting in that particular moment, the photographer forges a connection to larger themes and concepts. The empty space can be a powerful reminder of the presence of humanity, and the viewer can read into its structure the social, political, and economic forces that have created it.

Frederick H. Evans

A Sea of Steps, Wells Cathedral 1903

Frederick H. Evans was meticulous in his preparations for photography. He spent days at the churches and cathedrals he visited, fastidiously observing how the light shifted and modulated to get the perfect exposure. On one shoot he even requested that church pews be removed so that he could obtain the best position. This is perhaps his greatest photograph and it, too, was the result of lengthy preparation, as he returned to Wells Cathedral in Somerset several times over a three-year period before he made the final masterpiece. So popular did the image become that marks were purportedly made in the floor of the cathedral so that others could place their tripods in exactly the same position he had.

His own words best describe the grandeur, spirituality, and sense of the passage of time encapsulated in his photograph: "The steps now rise steeply before one, and the extraordinary wear in the top portions, leading to the corridor, is now shown just as it appeals to the eye in the original subject, a veritable sea of steps; the passing over them of hundreds of footsteps during the many years the stair has served its purpose have worn them into a semblance of broken waves, low-beating on a placid shore." Evans believed in pure, unadorned process, arguing that photography is "too uniquely valuable and beautiful to be spoilt by making it imitate something else." However, he also believed that the artist should establish an emotional connection with the spaces he or she photographs, urging others to "try for a record of an emotion rather than a piece of topography."

> "One should always find in the artist's picture a revelation of beauty and grandeur beyond what the untrained eye would discover for itself."
>
> Frederick H. Evans

Frederick H. Evans (British, 1853–1943) began practicing photography in the 1880s while he was working as a bookseller in London. He counted novelist George Bernard Shaw as a friend, who remarked of his images, "the obscurest detail in the corners seems as delicately penciled by the darkness as the flood of sunshine through window or open door is penciled by the light." Evans photographed a wide range of subjects, and took photo-micrographs (close-up photographs), landscapes, and portraits. One of his notable portraits is of the illustrator and author Aubrey Beardsley adopting the pose of a famous gargoyle, known as "The Vampire," at Notre Dame Cathedral, Paris. However, it is the magnificent architectural series capturing the grandeur and spirituality of English cathedrals for which Evans is best remembered. In 1900, he was elected to the exclusive Linked Ring group of pictorial photographers, thus cementing his reputation. In 1903 he was the first British photographer invited by Alfred Stieglitz to contribute to his new journal *Camera Work*, and an entire issue of the journal was devoted to Evans's work.

Creative tips and techniques

Evans used a special double-coated film made by Sandell and Sons that had both a slow and a fast emulsion layer, meaning that it could capture the largest range of tones. He regarded the camera's ability to render precisely the scene in front of it as the defining characteristic of the medium, stating that "detail, when softly lit and allied to perfect gradation ... coupled with the perfect rendering of tone-values, of atmosphere, of gradation ... is the fundamental characteristic of our art-method." Today, the equivalent process would be to use the HDR mode in a digital camera to capture the full range of tones. He made platinum contact prints from the full-size 10 x 8 negative to achieve the maximum quality of the final image. He believed in this process so strongly that when he could no longer afford to make these prints because of the high costs involved, he effectively stopped being a photographer.

Although Evans made beautiful prints, his preferred medium for showing his work was actually the lantern slide. He felt that the projected image gave the most accurate experience of viewing the full range of tones from the original negative, arguing that "Paper, with its lack of depth, its abrupt stoppage of image at the surface, will not fully or adequately exhibit the entire value and charm of these infinitely related planes, but glass can and does when properly handled." Evans made thousands of glass slides and used them during his public performances, when he guided his audience through each view, no doubt using the projected image to enhance the sense of spirituality of light so inherent in his work, and allying that with the larger scale that projecting the images allowed.

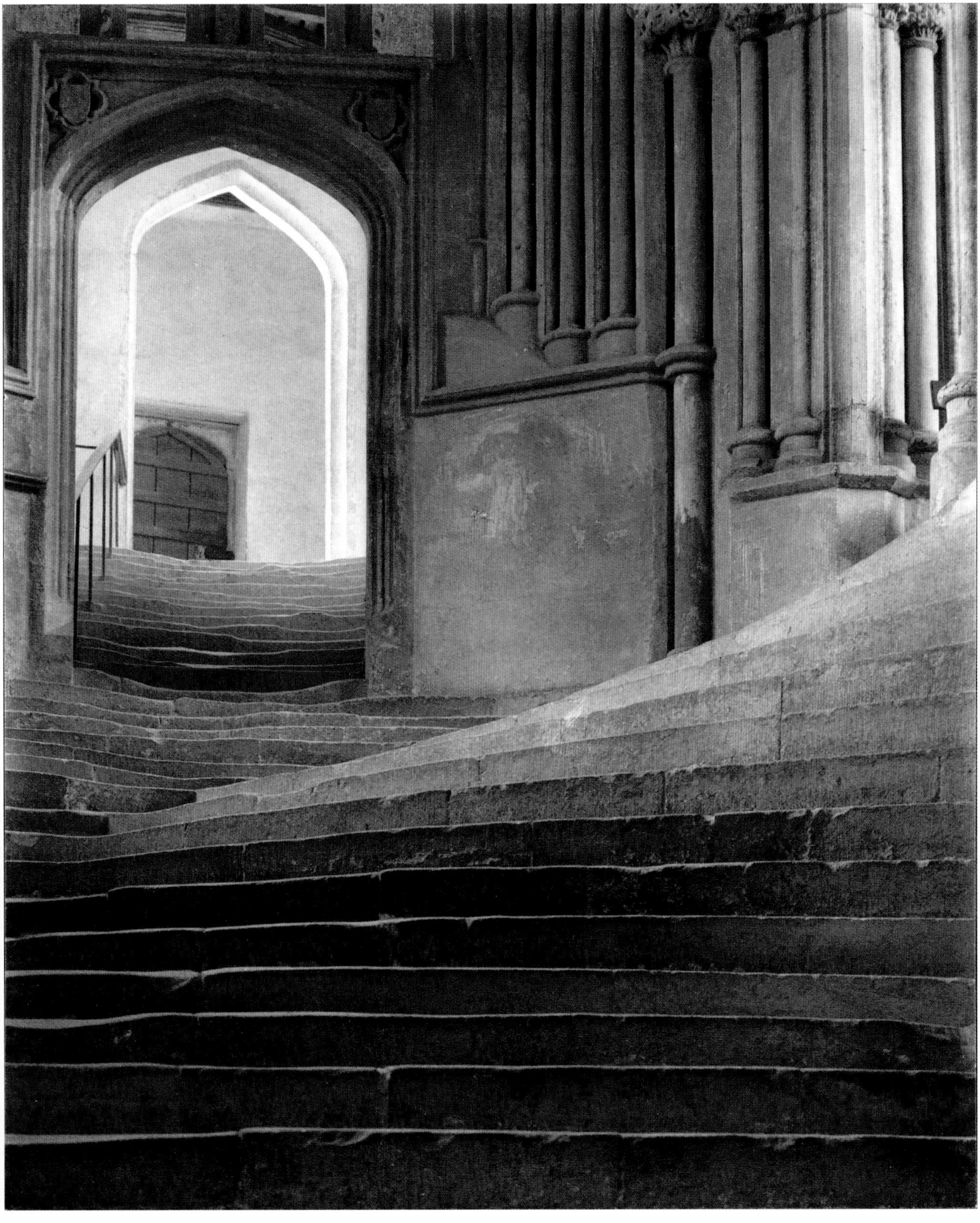

Magasin, Avenue des Gobelins 1925

Windows and shopfronts were a recurrent theme of Eugène Atget's work in Paris. Toward the end of his life, he made a series of images of the windows of the department stores along the Avenue des Gobelins that played with the contrast between the lifelike and overdressed mannequins and the architecture of the street outside. The figures appear to be trapped in a theatrical space, performing a strange set of social interactions; the head of the central mannequin is posed at an inquisitive angle as if passing comment on his neighbor. The manicured perfection of the models is in contrast with the blurred energy of the trees, and the barely discernible outlines of people passing by on the street. This combination of the real and the staged dissolves the space between imagination and reality, an area that caught the attention of the Surrealists. Photographer Berenice Abbott (see p.76), then Man Ray's assistant (see p.94), often visited Atget, and introduced him to art dealer Julien Levy, who bought almost the entire collection of negatives and prints in Atget's possession. On their return to New York, he and Abbott held an exhibition of Atget's photography at the Weyhe Gallery, and made an unsuccessful attempt to sell the archive to the Museum of Modern Art (MoMA). Ironically, forty years after its rejection of Levy's offer, MoMA agreed to purchase the collection in 1969. Abbott summed up the reaction to Atget's work: "There was a sudden flash of recognition—the shock of reality unadorned. The subjects were not sensational, but nevertheless shocking in their very familiarity. The real world, seen with wonderment and surprise, was mirrored in each print. Whatever means Atget used to project the image did not intrude between subject and observer."

"A good photograph is like a good hound dog, dumb but eloquent." Eugène Atget

Eugène Atget (French, 1857–1927) was relatively unknown during his lifetime as he worked quietly and tirelessly recording the fabric of urban Paris. However, thanks to the interest shown in his work by the Surrealists in the 1920s, in particular artist Man Ray (see p.94), his work is now seen as one of the most extraordinary documents of the quotidian beauty and meaning in the texture of the city. Photographer Berenice Abbott (see p.76), a champion of Atget's work, declared that he was "a Balzac of the camera, from whose work we can weave a large tapestry of French civilization." In 1890 the self-taught Atget opened his Paris studio, and in 1898 he began the project that would occupy him for the next thirty years, to document the streets of what he called "Old Paris." Working alone, he created a huge archive of over 10,000 large-format, glass plate negatives of the city, documenting the buildings and their architectural details. In 1920, Atget wrote: "Today this enormous artistic and documentary collection is finished; I can say I possess all of Old Paris." The French government then acquired 2,600 of Atget's plates for 10,000 francs.

Creative tips and techniques

Like many of his contemporaries in the 19th century, Atget photographed Paris with a large-format wooden bellows camera with 10 x 8 inch glass plates. He continued with this approach throughout the 1920s, even when lighter film cameras became available. Most of his prints were made as contact prints using the albumen process, and therefore have the extraordinary range of tones and detail that this technique delivers. The camera also necessitated the use of a tripod, which for a photograph like this allows for the precise arrangement of all the elements in the frame. The long exposure used also enhances the contrast between the still interior and the movement in the street outside.

Reflections are an excellent way of opening up the image and suggesting that there is a world beyond the four sides of the photographic frame. They allow you to make connections between what is in front of the camera and what is behind it, for example, suggesting a connection or contrast between the interior world behind the glass and the exterior world reflected in it. However, be careful to ensure that both what is inside and what is outside are visually interesting and relevant or the image will become a confusing, meaningless mess. Scan the frame very carefully to see where the reflections fall, and remember that the sky outside will appear as a highlight area against the darker parts of the image on the other side of the window. Atget has used this to great effect in this image; observe how the lamppost bisects the face of the mannequin, revealing only one eye staring out of the photograph at the viewer whereas the rest of the face is obscured by the brightness of the sky.

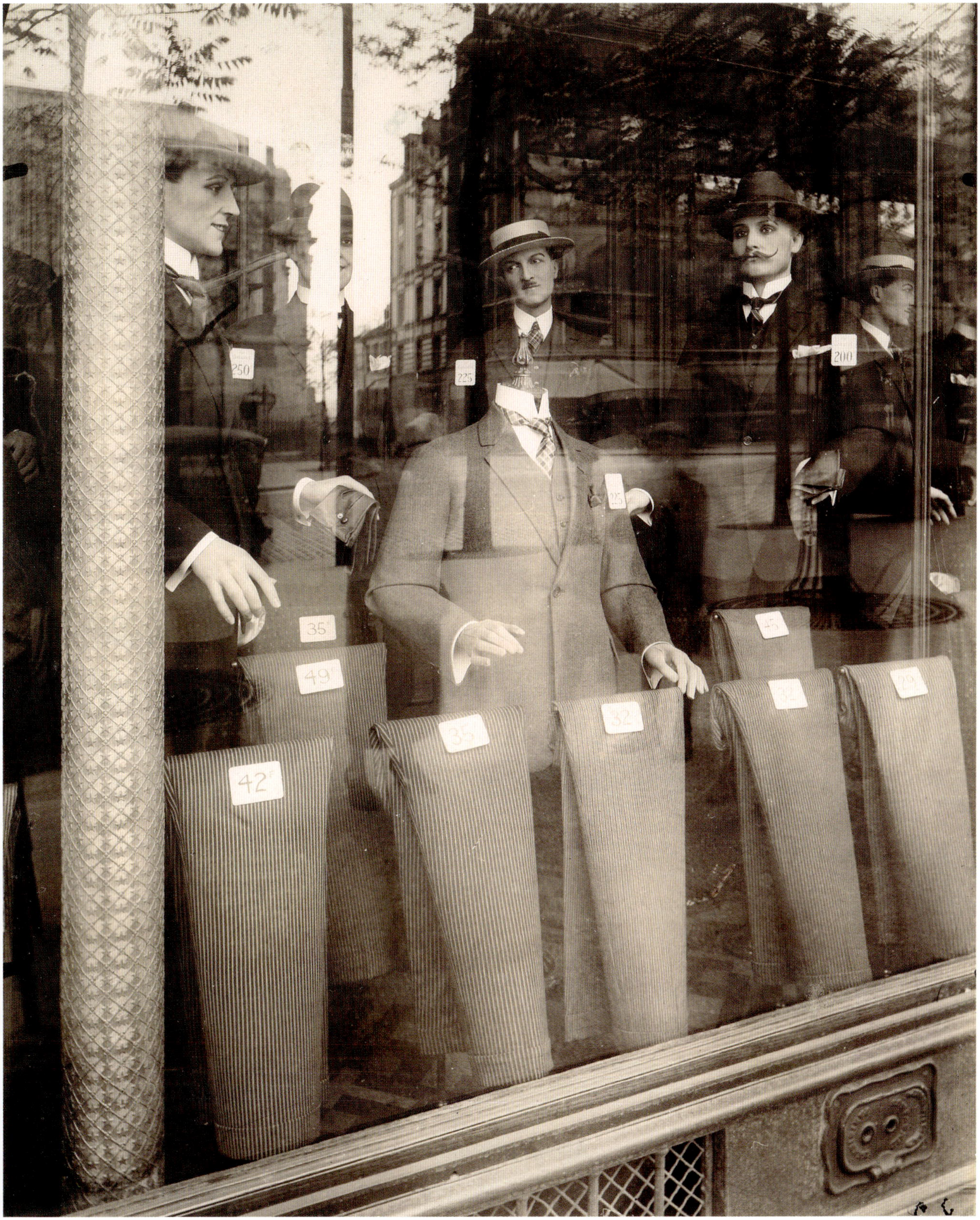
250
225
200
35
49
42
32
29

Berenice Abbott

Nightview, New York 1932

In the 1930s, Berenice Abbott embarked on a monumental study of the city of New York that was influenced by Eugène Atget's work on Paris (see p.74). However, she saw the city as a modernist entity moving into the future, rather than trying to preserve the details of its past. Funded by the Federal Art Project (FAP), she documented the architecture of the city, exploring the city's commercial, artistic, and civic values as embodied in its streets and buildings. This dramatic image, one of her most famous, captures the energy of the teeming metropolis in a way that is still as fresh and vibrant more than eighty years later. The bird's-eye view typifies her approach and she argued that a successful photograph should be a "significant document, a penetrating statement, which can be described in a very simple term—selectivity." This particular image also embodies her description of the perfect photograph: "Suppose we took a thousand negatives and made a gigantic montage: a myriad-faceted picture containing the elegances, the squalor, the curiosities, the monuments, the sad faces, the triumphant faces, the power, the irony, the strength, the decay, the past, the present, the future of a city—that would be my favorite picture." The final portfolio of 302 images was distributed by the FAP to schools, libraries and other public institutions in the metropolitan area and was widely exhibited. In 1939 it was published as the book *Changing New York*.

"What the human eye observes casually and incuriously, the eye of the camera... notes with relentless fidelity." Berenice Abbott

Berenice Abbott (American, 1898–1991) was introduced to photography by Man Ray (see p.94) for whom she worked as a darkroom assistant in Paris during the 1920s. She quickly began to take her own photographs, and recalled that "I took to photography like a duck to water. I never wanted to do anything else." She set up her own portrait studio in Paris, where she photographed Jean Cocteau, André Gide, James Joyce, and his publisher Sylvia Beach, who maintained that "To be 'done' by Man Ray and Berenice Abbott meant you were rated as somebody." Abbott also discovered the work of Atget (see p.74) in Paris, and became one of the major promoters of his work. After her return to New York in 1944, she became the photographic editor of *Science Illustrated* and she pursued the task of making scientific photographs that expressed both the beauty and structure of physical processes. She felt that "some people's ideas of scientific photography is just arty design, something pretty. That was not the idea. The idea was to interpret science sensibly, with good proportion, good balance and good lighting, so we could understand it." This position culminated in her work with the Physical Science Study committee at the Massachusetts Institute of Technology (MIT), with whom she collaborated on illustrations for a physics textbook, published in 1960, which was studied by millions of US schoolchildren.

Creative tips and techniques

Abbott shot this on a Graflex Century Universal 10 x 8 inch-field camera, which was a relatively lightweight wooden camera that was also used by Edward Weston (see p.98) and Ansel Adams (see p.50). She started using the bigger camera instead of a 35mm for the New York project, as the combination of the larger negative and the ability to use the movements of the camera to correct verticals and horizontals in the image to avoid distortion was vital to the accurate rendition of architecture. She also felt that the view camera was the best way for a beginner to learn the fundamentals of photography, arguing that "the perfect negatives needed to produce gratifying pictures from miniature films require that the photographer thoroughly understand lenses, exposure, problems of focusing, processing. This basic knowledge he will acquire more easily and better on a larger camera."

Abbott planned this image carefully, realizing that there was a very limited window of opportunity when the streets would be dark enough and the lights in the buildings still on. She also had to negotiate access to the top floor of the skyscraper to get the perfect vantage point, recalling that it was hard to get permission as "they always thought you wanted to commit suicide." She worked out that "there was only one time of the year to take it, shortly before Christmas. I started about 4:30 p.m. and didn't have much time... I knew I had no opportunity to make multiple exposures because the lights would start to go out shortly after 5:00 p.m. when the people began to go home and so it had to be correct on the first try." Such meticulous planning of lighting and camera position is vital for successful landscape and architectural photography.

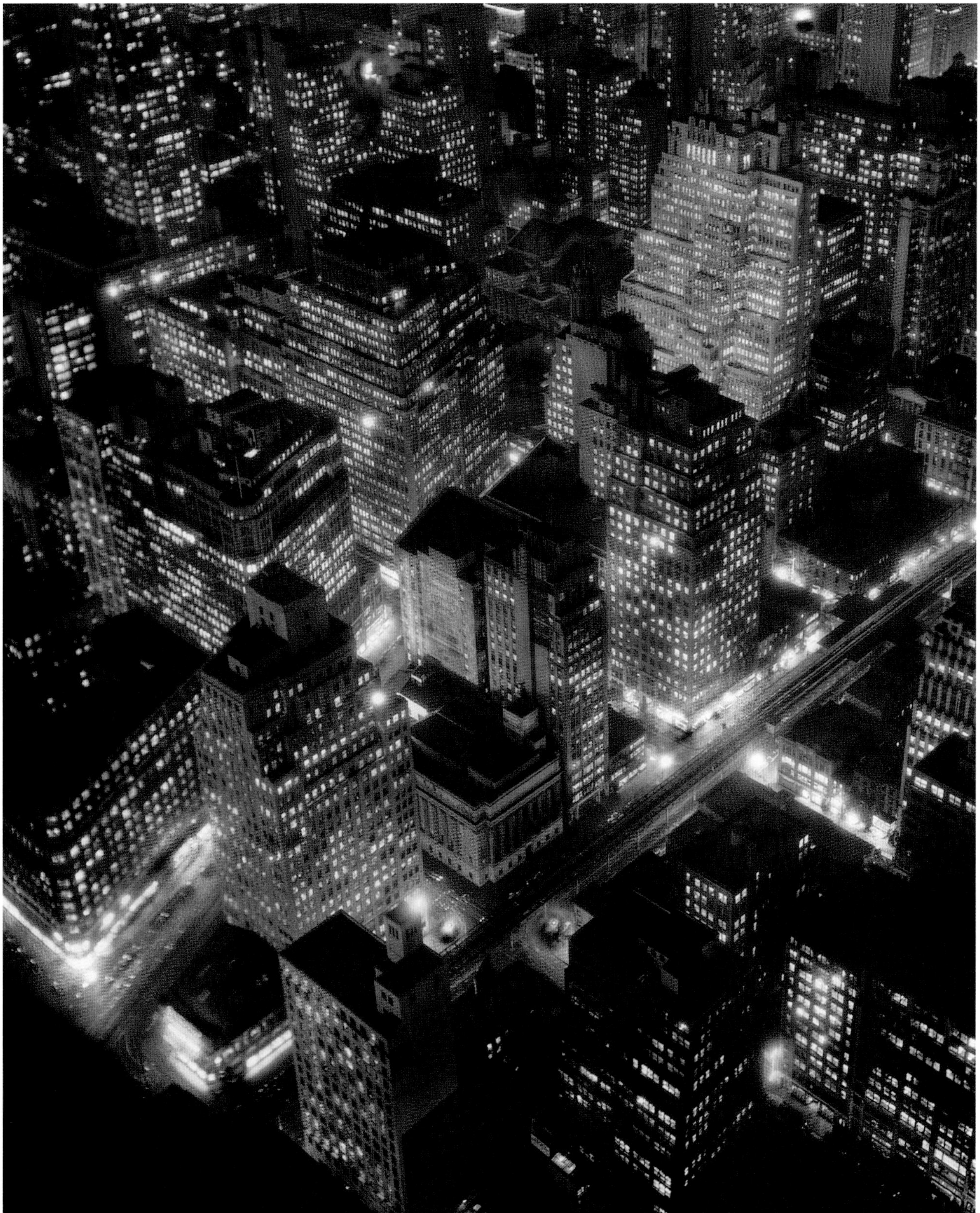

Walker Evans

Alabama farm interior (Fields family cabin) 1936

The ability of Walker Evans to find visual poetry in the vernacular is encapsulated in this study of a sharecropper family's interior wall, shot in 1936 during his work with the Farm Security Administration (FSA). The study later became part of his documentary book with writer James Agee, *Let Us Now Praise Famous Men* (1941).

The photograph is taken square on and at first glance appears to be a simple, almost flat, formal composition. On deeper inspection the composition reveals itself as a complex arrangement of lines, shapes, and forms that recall Cubist or Abstract Expressionist art. The rudimentary arrangement of the cutlery suggests some kind of shrine or secular altar to the important and essential things in life. The overall pattern is anthropomorphic and resembles a face, with the plate and can being the eyes and the utensils the mouth. Behind the utensils, the surface of the wall has a darker tone where the repeated motion of taking away and replacing items has worn away the paintwork and left traces of grease and dirt from the hands of the family members. In its subtle arrangement of gray tones the image reveals its temporality, attesting to the hundreds of times that the family has used the hanging utilitarian objects. There is a strong sense of the ongoing passage of time, of how it existed before the moment of this photographic encounter and continued after it. Time breathes from the simple objects, which themselves speak of the quiet dignity of the sharecroppers' lives. Evans's photography elevates everyday moments and scenes into a celebration of the quotidian poetry of the ordinary, evoking a response from the viewer and giving them a much deeper meaning.

"Stare. It is the way to educate your eye, and more. Stare, pry, listen, eavesdrop. Die knowing something. You are not here long." Walker Evans

Walker Evans (American, 1903–75) initially wanted to be a writer and was influenced by authors including James Joyce and Marcel Proust. After spending a year in Paris in 1926, Evans returned to the United States and began to take photographs in 1928. His first published images appeared in Hart Crane's poetry book *The Bridge* (1930). During the 1930s he worked for the FSA on a documentary photography project led by Roy Stryker, primarily shooting in the southern United States. Most of the work he made for the FSA used a large-format, 8 x 10-inch camera. Produced in collaboration with author James Agee, Evans's *Let Us Now Praise Famous Men* (1941) recorded the lives of impoverished white sharecroppers in Alabama, and is now considered a modernist documentary masterpiece. In 1938, Evans began to take photographs on the New York subway using a camera hidden in his coat. He had the first solo exhibition by a photographer at the Museum of Modern Art, New York, in 1938. In 1965 he became a professor of photography at Yale University School of Art.

Creative tips and techniques

In this shot, Evans used the flatness of the items arranged on the wall to create an almost abstract series of patterns of tones from black through pale gray to white. As you go about your day, be on the look-out for similar organizations of objects, which are often accidentally created. Experiment with the crop and composition, and use your camera to elevate the ordinary to the extraordinary.

This photograph is a study in variations in tonal values from black to gray. It uses a very subtle control of contrast to create the visual dynamism of the frame, with the dark vertical and horizontal lines of the woodwork producing a grid-like pattern with great visual energy, in spite of it being a static subject. To help you to evaluate the contrast and patterns of a scene, a useful tip is to half close your eyes and look through your eyelashes—this will reduce the level of detail in the scene you are looking at and emphasize the tonal values of the image.

To recreate the flatness of Evans's photograph, use either a standard lens or a short telephoto lens so that the perspective is slightly flattened. This will also allow you to stand at a reasonable distance from the subject.

Try using a tripod, as you will need to use a small aperture to get maximum depth of field. This will remove camera shake and allow you to make precise compositions. This will also slow down your process, and help you think more carefully about the composition. Very small and subtle changes in framing can significantly change the final image.

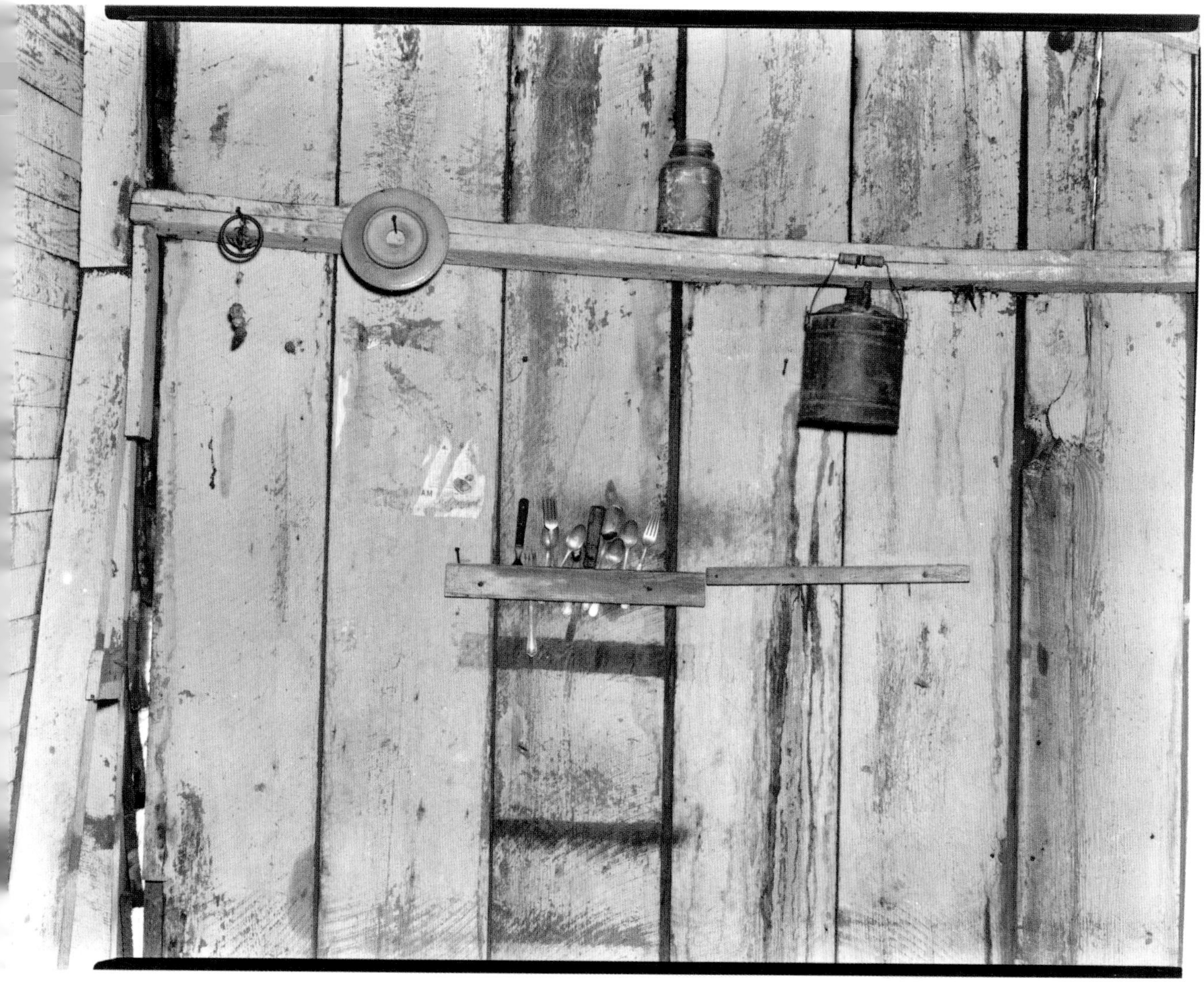

Hiroshi Sugimoto

Cabot Street Cinema 1978, from "Theaters"

In many ways, Hiroshi Sugimoto's images of American movie theater interiors—lit by the film being screened—are meditations on pure light, and how it illuminates a space, wrapping itself around the contours and internal architecture in a three-dimensional, sculptural way. They are also images that only exist because of the artist's intervention—the theater is not meant to be lit by this eerie light, emanating from the screen like some otherworldly force. Sugimoto expresses his desire for the final print to "look like a very brilliant white rectangle coming out from the screen, shining throughout the whole theater. It might seem very interesting and mysterious, even in some way religious."

He initially conceived of "Theaters" as a way of exploring a more abstract concept of how to express the surfeit of light that would create a pure white exposure. Influenced by Minimalist artists such as Carl Andre and Dan Flavin, he came up with the idea of working in cinemas, with the concept of photographing the "entire duration of a movie, so I was imagining that if I were to do that, the result might be a completely white screen. I could guess it would be, but the question is, can I prove and make real my envisioned image as a printed photograph?." Sugimoto is aware that the final artefact also has to be esthetically interesting, and he consciously chose ornate theaters from the 1920s and 1930s with rich architectural details. Sugimoto exposed each negative for the exact length of each film, from the opening to the closing credits. He often had to reshoot the theaters, because the exposures were very difficult to predict and he tray-processed the negatives in his hotel room as he went along. One intriguing aspect of the series is how different genres of film produce different final images, as the average light levels appear to differ for certain kinds of movie. Sugimoto wryly notes that "if it's an optimistic story, I usually end up with a bright screen; if it's a sad story, it's a dark screen. Occult movie? Very dark."

> "They look empty but they are full of information... It is all an illusion to the human eye." Hiroshi Sugimoto

Hiroshi Sugimoto (Japanese, 1948–) studied politics and sociology in Tokyo and then retrained as a fine artist in California, before opening a gallery specializing in Japanese art in New York. This sense of being a polymath is key to his life; he claims that "traditional values, modernist values, and contemporary art values are all part of who I am. I work as an architect, artist, traditional theater producer, and antique collector. I try to fit all this together." He sees his passion for collecting as deeply informing his practice, noting, for example, that "fossils work almost the same way as photography...as a record of history." This forms the focus of his work, in which he has explored museum interiors, seascapes, and modernist architecture.

Creative tips and techniques

Sugimoto is a master craftsman, who works to exacting standards, especially in the final printing of photographs. He uses a large-format view camera, mounted on a tripod, because it produces the most detailed negatives. However, he sees this as a major contributor to the meaning of the images, not simply an empty exercise in quality for quality's sake. He enjoys working in black and white, as it allows for silver colors and fine tones. At the same time, he wants to make something artistic and conceptual, and he respects craftsmanship. He says he would describe himself as "a postmodern-experienced pre-postmodern modernist." He argues that he has to be technically skilled so that the image will show up. He has invested considerable effort in developing a deep understanding of the technical aspects of the medium, but always relates them to the nuances of the esthetic he is seeking. He feels that this is a skill that is in danger of being lost in the digital age where the camera makes all the decisions. He notes that early photographers used to feel how the light affected the surface of the object. There are some things that the machine cannot measure and which can be gained only from studying nature.

Sugimoto works in monochrome, and has perfected the final print so that it contains all the subtle tonal detail that he relies on as an integral part of the photograph's meaning. He has developed his own style of printing after testing methods including those used by Walker Evans (see p.78) and Ansel Adams (see p.50). He studied chemicals and how to develop large-format negatives, elements that make the tones of his images so rich.

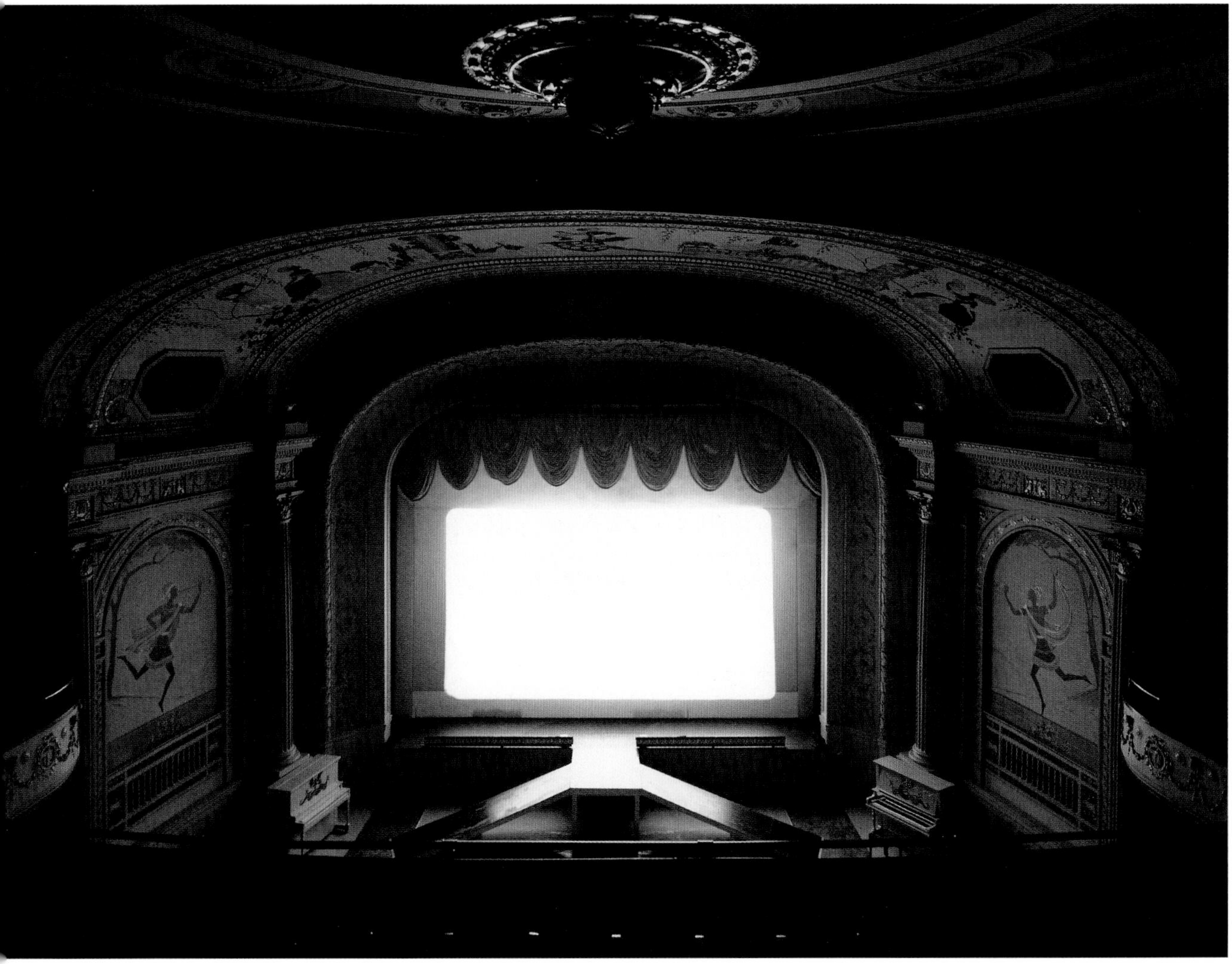

Andreas Gursky

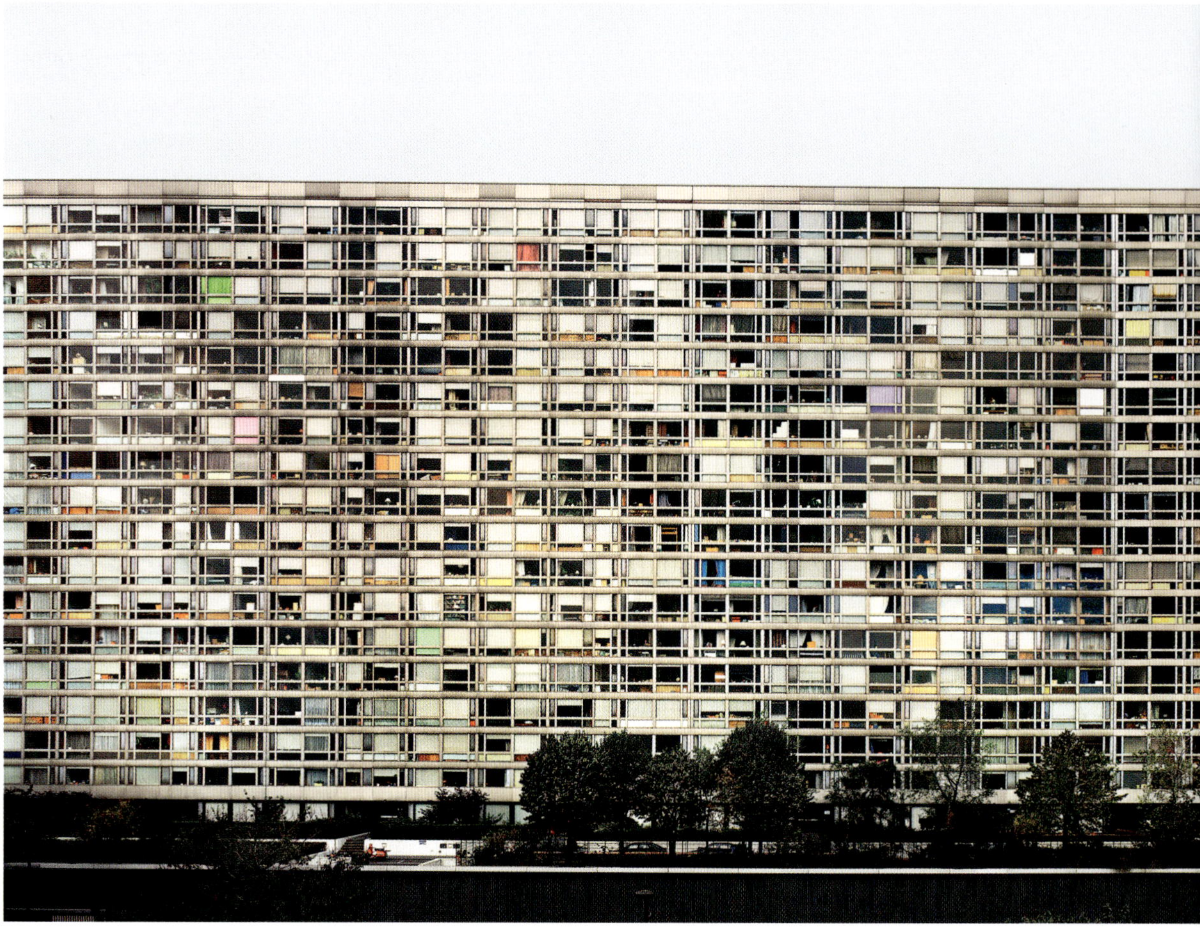

Montparnasse, Paris 1993

This monumental panorama exemplifies Gursky's vision of the modern world and his technique of producing huge digitally enhanced images that can be seen only through the medium of photography. The image is printed on an epic scale, measuring almost 6½ feet (2 meters) high and over 13 feet (4 meters) long. One print is held in the collection of London's Tate Modern, and another sold at auction in 2013 for £1,482,500. Seen on the museum wall, the photograph fills the audience's field of vision, from a distance merging into a unified whole but close up dissolving into hundreds of smaller images of individual apartment windows. The Immeuble d'habitation Maine-Montparnasse II is Paris's largest apartment building; it was designed by French modernist architect Jean Dubuisson and completed in 1964. Gursky often explores the urban environment in his work, maintaining that "to go to the center-city is to encounter the 'social truth,' to take part in the magnificent plenitude of 'reality'." To make the image, Gursky took two photographs from different positions from the vantage point of a hotel opposite, parallel to the building's flat front. In one of his first uses of digital manipulation, these two photographs were then joined together to create an image that could not be seen from a single vantage point, because of the scale of the building an because of obstructions that would have blocked the view.

Gursky cropped the ends of the building from the frame giving the sense that the façade could continue endlessly in either direction, as if all humanity could be housed in thi massive edifice. The photograph is like a gigantic ant colon where the whole makes a coherent construction, which is in turn made up of a myriad of individuals—what Gursky has dubbed an "aggregate state"—formed of separate units collected into a whole. The viewer is enticed to peer voyeuristically into each apartment, the resolution of the image allowing detailed examination of each separate livin space, like a version of Alfred Hitchcock's film *Rear Windov* (1954). The repetitive patterns of colors and rectangles enclosed within a grid echoes the structural explorations of modernist painters.

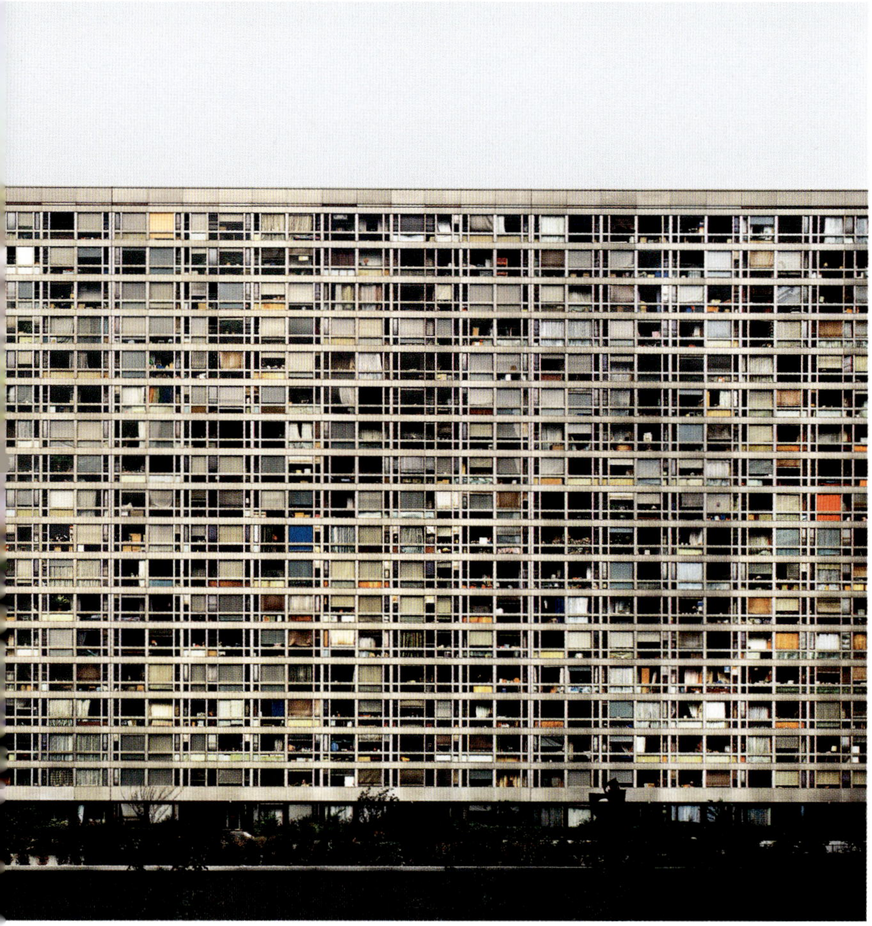

pace is very important for me but in a more abstract way, think. Maybe to try to understand not just that we are living a certain building or in a certain location, but to become ware that we are living on a planet that is going at enormous peed through the universe." Andreas Gursky

dreas Gursky (German, 1955–) emerged ong with Thomas Ruff, Candida Höfer, and omas Struth from the influential Düsseldorf hool, which came out of the Kunstakademie der the tutelage of Bernd and Hilla Becher e p.240). Gursky lives with his wife and nily in Düsseldorf, in an industrial substation nverted by Tate Modern's architects, Herzog & Meuron. His work is concerned with extracting d interpreting the patterns and rhythms generated by the modern urban experience, as he claims: "In retrospect I can see that my desire to create abstractions has become more and more radical. Art should not be delivering a report on reality, but should be looking at what's behind something." His monumental works are exhibited on a grand scale, echoing that of the modernist painters, and have become some of the most collectable and valuable photographs ever made, with his prints selling for huge sums at auction.

Creative tips and techniques

Gursky frequently positions his camera to give a flat perspective to the image, with no central point of focus, and looks for repetitive patterns around which to build his composition. His photographs often reference modern art; this one could be compared to a Jackson Pollock painting, a composition by Piet Mondrian, or one of Gerhard Richter's *Color Charts*. Gursky usually keeps some connection with the context of the subject to avoid it becoming a completely abstract composition. In your own work, look for patterns and rhythms in the scene in front of you, and frame it carefully to remove all extraneous information that does not contribute to the final image.

Creating digital composites and panoramas is relatively simple, but you need to take care to get consistent results. Many cameras have a built-in "panorama" setting, which can be useful for making quick images. However, for more control, do it manually. Ideally use a tripod, so that you can control the amount the camera moves. Position the camera in the center of the scene you want to shoot, and establish your start and end points for the final image. You can shoot horizontally or vertically, with the latter giving a higher-resolution final image. Set your camera to manual focus and exposure, and use RAW if possible to ensure that each image is consistent with the next. Take a series of shots with at least 15–25 percent overlap between each frame to allow the photostitching software to work correctly. Retake the sequence several times to allow for any mistakes. Once you have the shots, stitch them together using the photomerge tool or a panorama stitching plug in.

Robert Polidori

"I would say that the emblematic photographic image is a picture from inside a room looking out. I think this defines photography. It's the metaphor for the notion of first sight. What one saw first."

Robert Polidori

Robert Polidori (Canadian, 1951–) initially worked as an avant-garde film-maker in New York. However, as his interest in spaces and rooms grew, he began to explore how the still image could better translate his ideas about rooms, which he called "memory theaters," and he began to experiment with large-format view cameras. His first major body of work on the Palace of Versailles near Paris was published in 1991. Since then he has documented the relationship of interiors and historical memory, notably in series on Havana, Chernobyl, and New Orleans in the aftermath of Hurricane Katrina. Latterly, he has focused on panoramic explorations of what he calls "Dendritic Cities"—the phenomenon of the organic growth of housing around the centers of established cities such as Mumbai, Rio de Janeiro, and Amman.

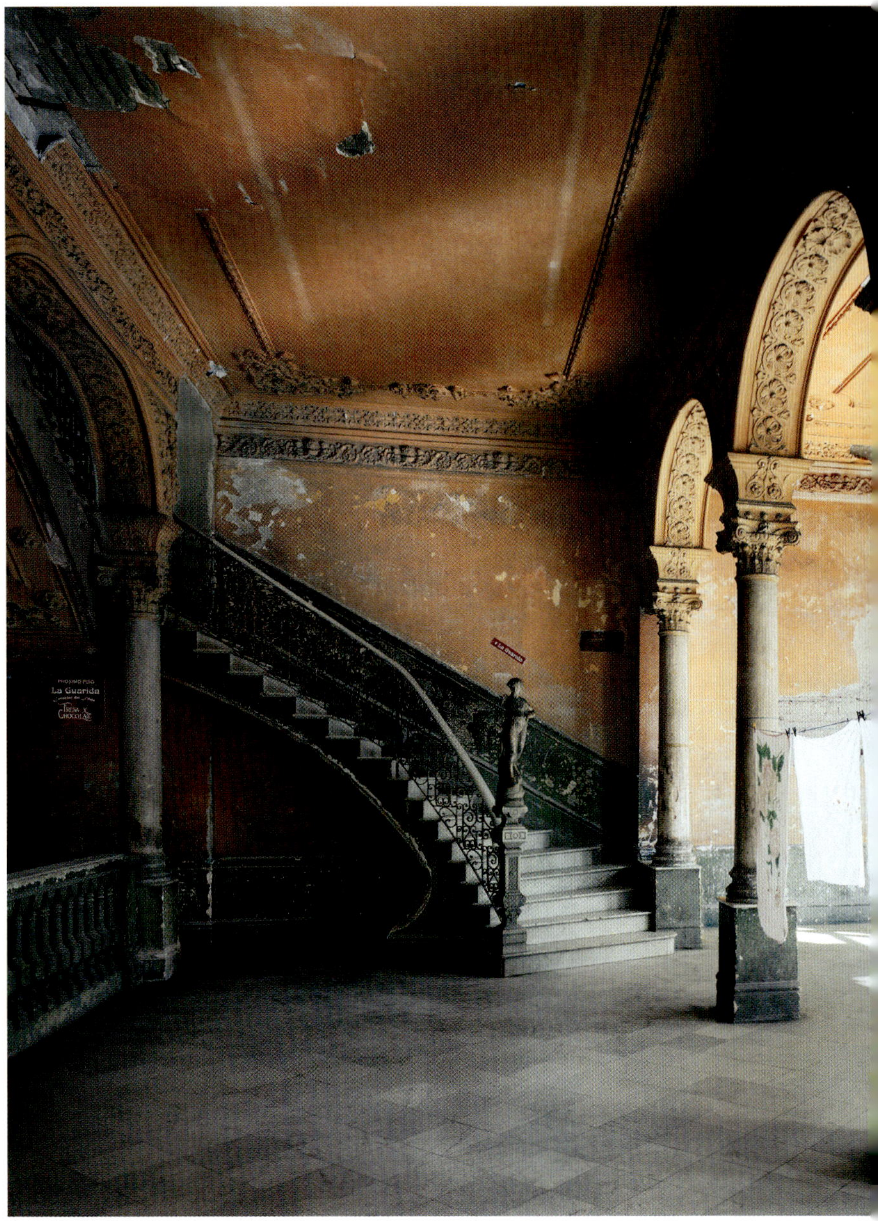

Creative tips and techniques

Polidori works with a wide-angle lens on a view camera, using a variety of sizes of sheet film including 5 x 4, 5 x 7, 8 x 10, and even 11 x 14 inches. This gives an extraordinary level of detail to each image, which he cites as being "more satisfying. They just lend themselves to better scrutiny." It also allows him to fully use the movement of the camera to avoid distortion, especial converging verticals. He regards this as using the technical aspects of the camera effectively, likening taking proper view camera manipulations to proper grammar. With a 35mm digital camera, you can enhance the resolution of your work by using the slowest ISO setting, and a tripoc To minimize the effect of converging verticals, try to keep the back of the came parallel to the horizontal lines in your imag

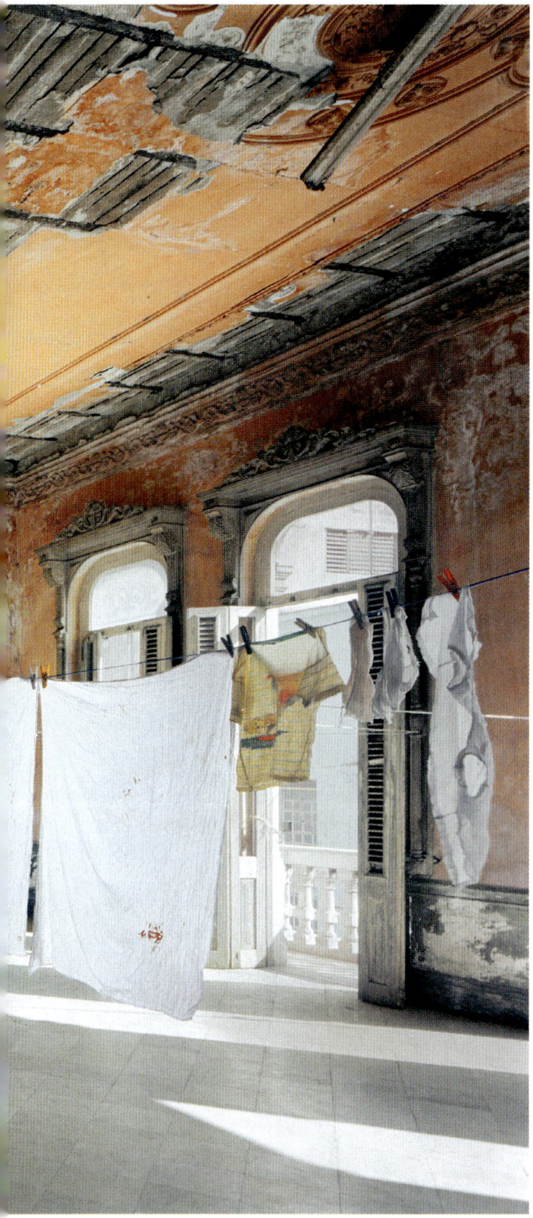

La Guarida restaurant, entrance 418 Concordia, Vedado, Havana 1997

This photograph is from a series Robert Polidori made on the city of Havana, in which he investigated the fading grandeur of the Cuban capital before it decays completely or is modernized by international investors. The image has a powerful sense of movement through it, inviting the viewer to enter the scene and then choose whether to go up the stairs to the left, or out onto the balcony to the right to survey the world outside. The composition plays on the repetition of strong verticals and diagonals to lead the eye around the frame. The color palette is harmonious, and holds the image together in the soft light from the windows. The large format allows Polidori to record all the detail of the fading paint, cornicing, and falling plasterwork, highlighting the passage of time and the fall from grace of this once magnificent interior. This room is also the entrance hallway to one of Havana's leading private "parador" restaurants, making a subtle comment on the impact of the free market on the socialist stronghold. Polidori has explored the idea of rooms as "memory theaters" and maintains that they act as "metaphors and vessels for memory—places marked by the signatures of lives past and present." He is therefore mostly drawn to interiors with a history rather than modern constructions, arguing that "the rooms that are devastated by time are the ones that have the most traces."

Polidori makes photographs that are pin sharp, with a full range of tones and packed with detail, and often prints them extremely large in exhibition. This is fundamental to how he represents the scene in front of him; he argues that "when images are soft, they just remain evocative, or in your imagination. You get a mood, and it remains on the emotional level. The viewer has to put more of him or herself into it. When there is more detail, it's like that old expression: there's no fiction stranger than reality. Reality will compose the most extreme paradoxes and contradictions and adjacencies, which can't be understood."

› get the movements of a view camera, ther invest in a wide-angle tilt-and-shift ns—a specialized piece of equipment that ows limited correction of vertical and rizontal lines—or alternatively correct the stproduction image in Photoshop using ransform'"controls.

Polidori typically uses very long exposures running into minutes with e camera on a tripod. This allows him to use slow film to record every detail and a small aperture to get maximum depth of field. In an interior such as this, you also have to carefully balance the daylight coming in from the windows with the darker shadows deep in the interior. A compromise has to be reached where enough detail is held in the image's highlights but shadows are not allowed to block up and become too dark. The camera meter will often give you an average exposure for a scene with a high contrast range like this; it will in effect be overexposed, losing the highlights. A useful technique in this situation is to bracket your exposures, taking a series of shots that are under- and overexposed by one to two stops in total, in third or half a stop increments, then choosing later the one that gives the best result. Study the shadow and highlight detail to find the combination that gives the desired effect.

Gregory Crewdson

Production Still (The Father)

2007, from "Beneath the Roses"

The elderly man sits transfixed, staring at something seemingly outside of the frame, and lit by an otherworldly light that seems to have no discernable source, isolating him in the center of this otherwise mundane domestic scene. The sense of a disruption of everyday life is central to Crewdson's work; he creates images that have a sense of timelessness, located in a mythical, idealized version of suburban America. They have a sense of foreboding—of something not being right with the world, even though they are formally very striking. He argues that his "pictures must first be beautiful, but that beauty is not enough. I strive to convey an underlying edge of anxiety, of isolation, of fear." He claims to like nondescript subjects: "You vaguely recognize my scenes as 50s, 60s, 70s, but on the whole it's outside of time." The sourcing of locations is a time-consuming and slow process: "Usually I'll drive to certain locations over and over again, over a course of months really. And then it might just be I hit it at the right time, and the right light. And then I might go to that location over and over again, and then what happens in that lag time where—the image sort of locks in—all of a sudden I see it in my mind's eye. All of a sudden... I could see the narrative. I could see the image." Crewdson's work deals with the deep unease lying below the surface of society, and he says that he is "interested in using the iconography of nature and the American landscape as surrogates or metaphors for psychological anxiety, fear or desire." To achieve this, he taps into his own psyche and claims: "All my pictures are very voyeuristic, but ultimately I'm looking at what lurks in my own interior. I make photographs because I want to answer the question of what propels me to do the things that I do. But that always remains a mystery."

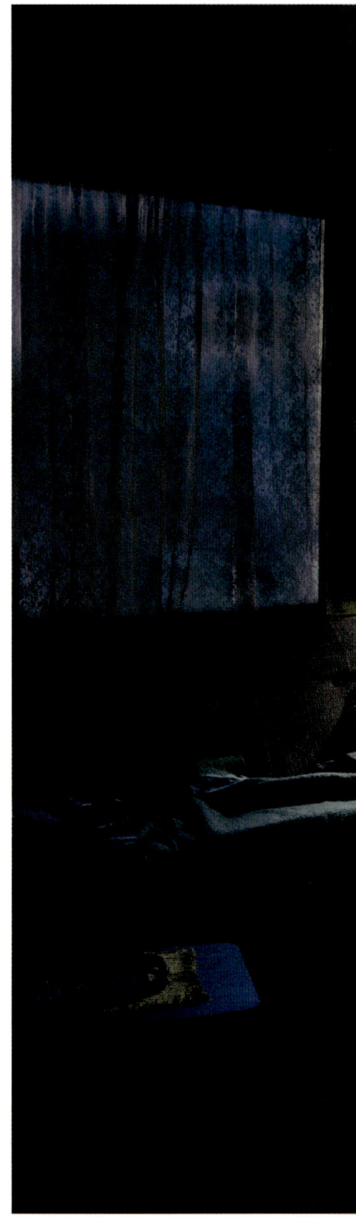

Creative tips and techniques

Crewdson has described his images as "frozen moments" in which it seems that something is happening but it is not entirely clear what. This leaves room for the viewer's imagination. He notes that although his images are seen as being about storytelling, there is very little actually happening in the pictures. He explains that he does not seek a conscious awareness of narrative and does not try to create a sense of plot. Photography is very good at suggesting that something has either just happened or is just about to happen. Look out for these "pregnant moments" in the world around you.

Crewdson usually works around dusk, with the twilight hours giving a sense of otherworldliness. There is a practical reason for working in the brief window between daylight and night-time; he is highly aware that it is a beautiful, magical hour. Also it is the only time in which you can work with the lights and daylight at the same time. He describes it as a period of transition and transformation that is about being between places. Shooting at dusk or dawn can create richly evocative images that combine natural and artificial lighting. Go out regularly at these times to

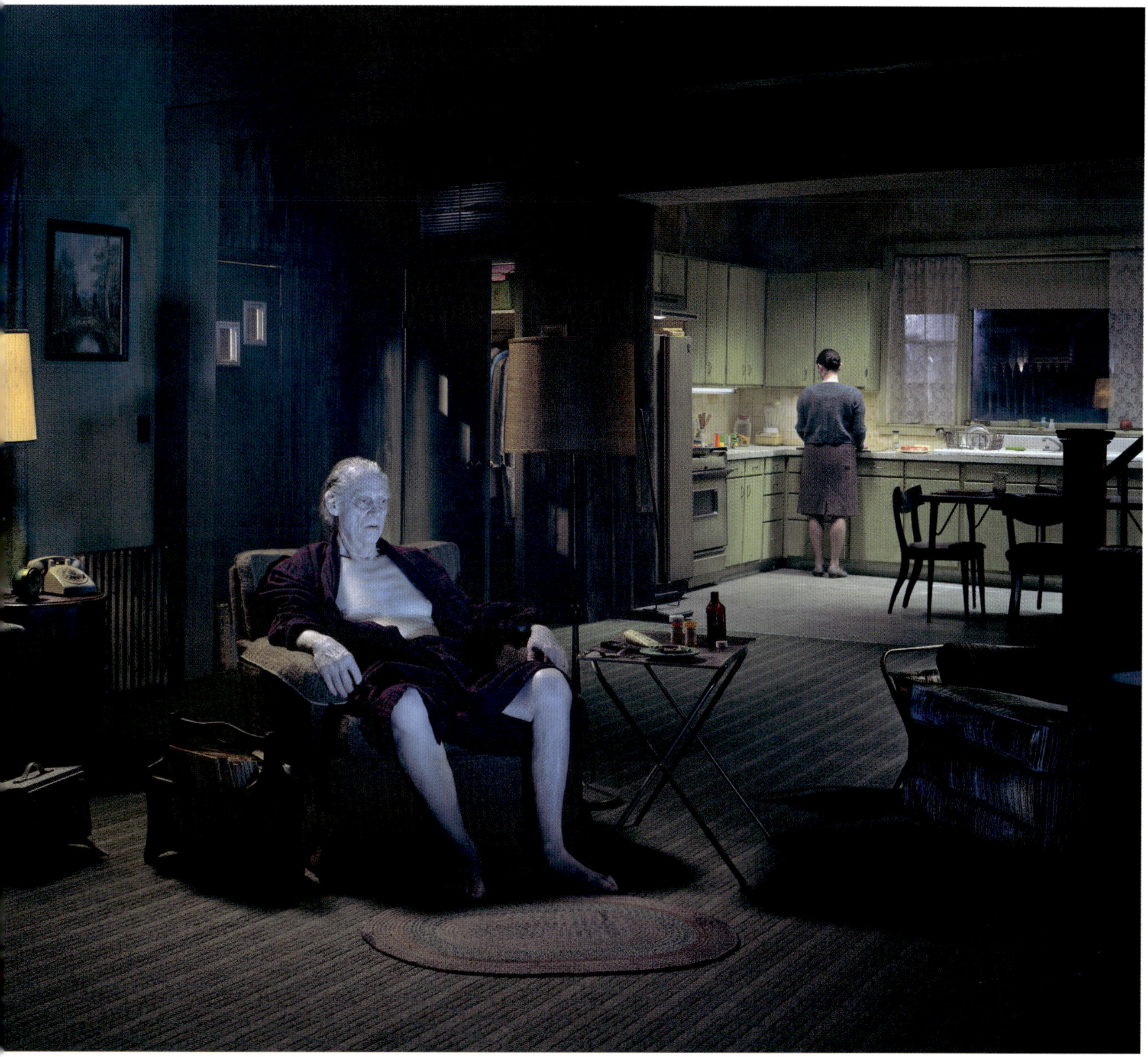

periment with how the camera records e transitions of light to dark.

Crewdson cites film-makers such as David Lynch as influences. He otes how the focus of Orson Welles's ms affects how he wants his images to ok. Being inspired by other art forms key. Analyzing how artists in other edia engage with the human condition uminates how photography works.

"It's very hard to describe what I'm looking for—something that feels both familiar and strange at the same time." Gregory Crewdson

Gregory Crewdson (American, 1962–) concentrates and refines the American social landscape into his staged tableaux. He spends months researching locations and preplanning his shoots, working with a crew of set builders, lighting assistants, and producers. Most of his work has been made in and around Massachusetts, where he spent vacations as a child with his family, and where he first began to take photographs at the age of nineteen, when he made an image of a red convertible car in front of a suburban house with a white picket fence, set against dark clouds, of which he claims "I've been making the same picture ever since." Crewdson had his first solo exhibition at the Houston Center for Photography in Texas in 1992. He joined the Yale University School of Art in 1993. He has won many awards, including the Skowhegan Medal.

Lisa Barnard

Training set, FlatWorld 2008, from "Virtual Iraq"

This theatrical space is a stage set in a warehouse in California that is used by the United States military in the training of soldiers for combat operations. It is part of an immersive virtual reality world that combines computer-generated virtual characters, objects, and effects to convincingly engage with real objects and people. The environment was designed to closely replicate the experience of soldiers serving in Iraq; smells, sounds, and images are mixed with life-sized holographic projections of potential insurgents.

Lisa Barnard became fascinated by the way in which research shapes the conduct of modern conflict. She argues that "Technology is always at the heart of innovation for the military, and it always revolves around them trying to be more efficient in the job of war. In that sense I'm not sure it has an ambivalent role; the objectives are always the same, to help Americans win battles, effectively and efficiently. It's about a few in power making money out of the suffering of others who don't have the resources or influence to defend themselves." This photograph plays on the space between reality and fiction; the set is clearly meant to signify a connection to the tangible world, but it is also obviously located in a controlled environment. As she puts it, this blurring of the boundaries of imagination and actuality leads to a slippage in our sense of what is happening: "Reality has been complicated and 'real' places, let's say on the ground in Pakistan or Afghanistan, have possibly become a simulacra or what [Jean] Baudrillard terms a 'hyper-real copy' of a real location—become almost too real, more real than the event or thing itself."

"I am much more interested in photography as a conduit for ideas, reflecting on both itself as a medium and as a document of reality." Lisa Barnard

Lisa Barnard (British, 1967–) explores the complex relationships between power, politics, and conflict, testing the limits of what can be seen and photographed. Her book *Machines in the Garden, Hyenas of the Battlefield* (2015) explores the global war on terror, whereas *Chateau Despair* (2013) chronicled the legacy of Thatcherism by examining the fabric of the British Conservative Party's former headquarters after it had been sold. She is senior lecturer in documentary photography at the University of South Wales.

Creative tips and techniques

Barnard combines images, video, text, and installations in her work to expand the vocabulary she uses to engage with the difficult ideas she tackles. She believes that her practice reflects a contemporary documentary stance, engaging with complex ideas visually, using a variety of different forms and strategies, including text and appropriated imagery. However, she clearly demonstrates that form and content must work together; the ideas must be sound and deep as well as the images resonant. Barnard says that research is the most important aspect of her practice, and she always starts with reading and listening. The visual esthetic should not feel like an afterthought, to make the work appear contemporary.

Barnard's work grows organically, and she attempts to work within her own constraints, rather than the dictates of any external market or arbiter. She explains that she does not really work on projects that have a beginning, middle, and end. She says that she makes the work she wants to and does not try to squeeze her ideas into what is a very conservative marketplace. "The photography world likes series and tangible conclusions; that doesn't sit well with me." This requires considerable self-belief and Barnard advises that you have to be tenacious and not give up. She recalls one unusual technique she employed to gain access to a situation, when she locked herself in the toilet after closing time, so that she could photograph it when it was empty. She explains that military access always takes time and mostly people try to persuade her that there is nothing of interest to photograph. She says that she in turn has learned to be quite persuasive in such situations.

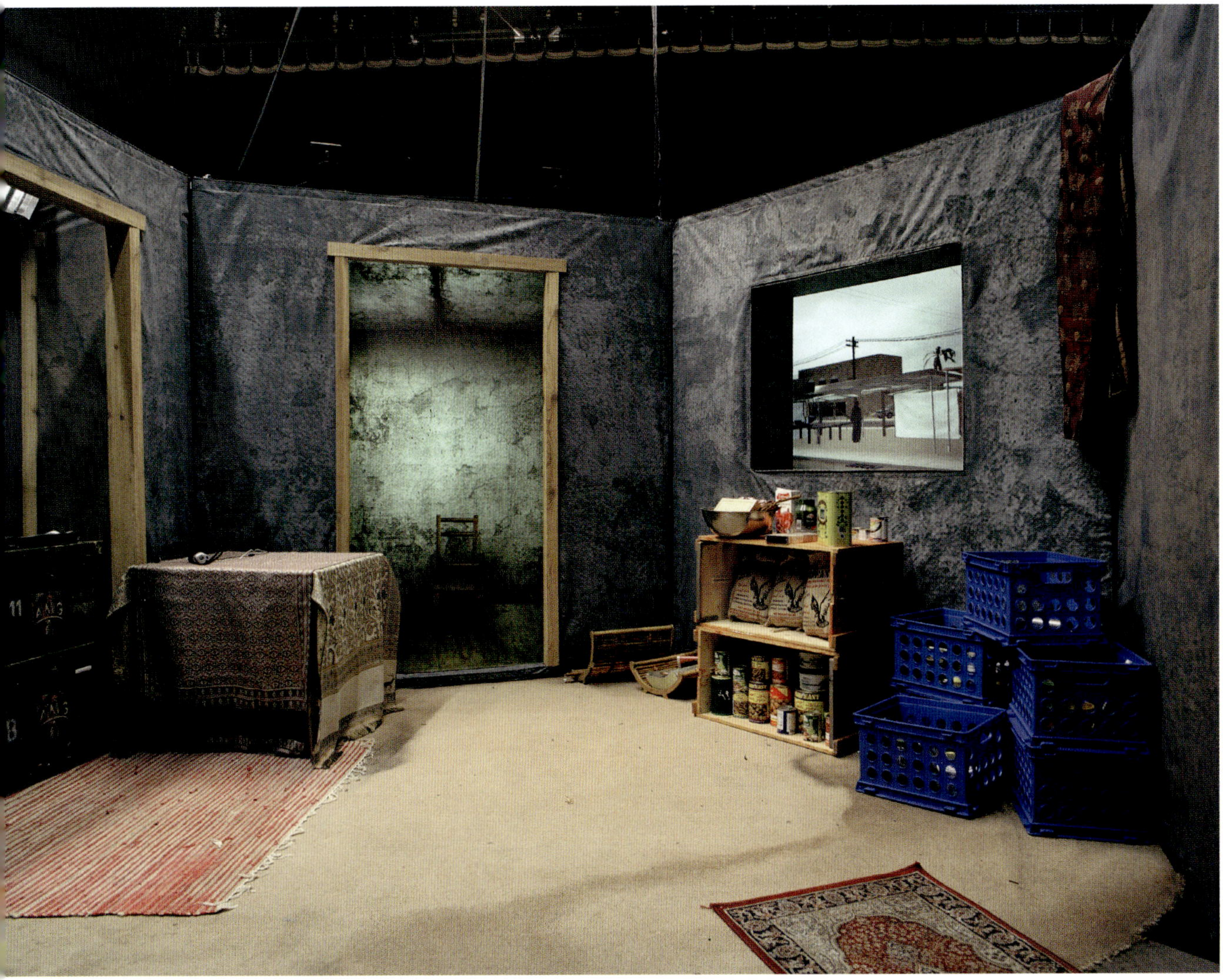

Thing

S

The thing, an object or a still life, is a recurrent theme of photography, as the photographic process lends itself to the identification of objects as worthy of attention. The material qualities of the image play an essential part in this process. Photographs have a dual “thingness:” they are depictions of things, yet they are also things in themselves. This dual materiality gives them a unique power to draw attention to the material world. The photographer first looks and then draws the viewer’s attention toward something that might otherwise have been ignored. Through this act, the photographer can transform a mundane artefact into a metaphor or symbol for something more significant. In their usual state, things exist simply as mundane objects or tools that are taken for granted. However, there are moments when this everyday ordinariness is transmuted into something extraordinary. Such moments are often generated by a disturbance or interruption, when the photographer makes a connection to a scene and things become more noticeable; the viewer then becomes aware of how that thing relates to the world. By paying attention to things and objects, the photograph can elevate them from the status of unnoticed elements into carriers of emotional and psychological meaning. This transformation can endow the thing that is being photographed with the qualities of the person who possessed it, enhancing the connection between viewer and subject through the object rather than directly through an image of the person. The image of a thing therefore operates with a different set of resonances to that of an image of a person; the emotions it generates are different, poignant, and reflective.

Man Ray

"If I'd had the nerve, I'd have become a thief or a gangster, but since I didn't, I became a photographer."
Man Ray

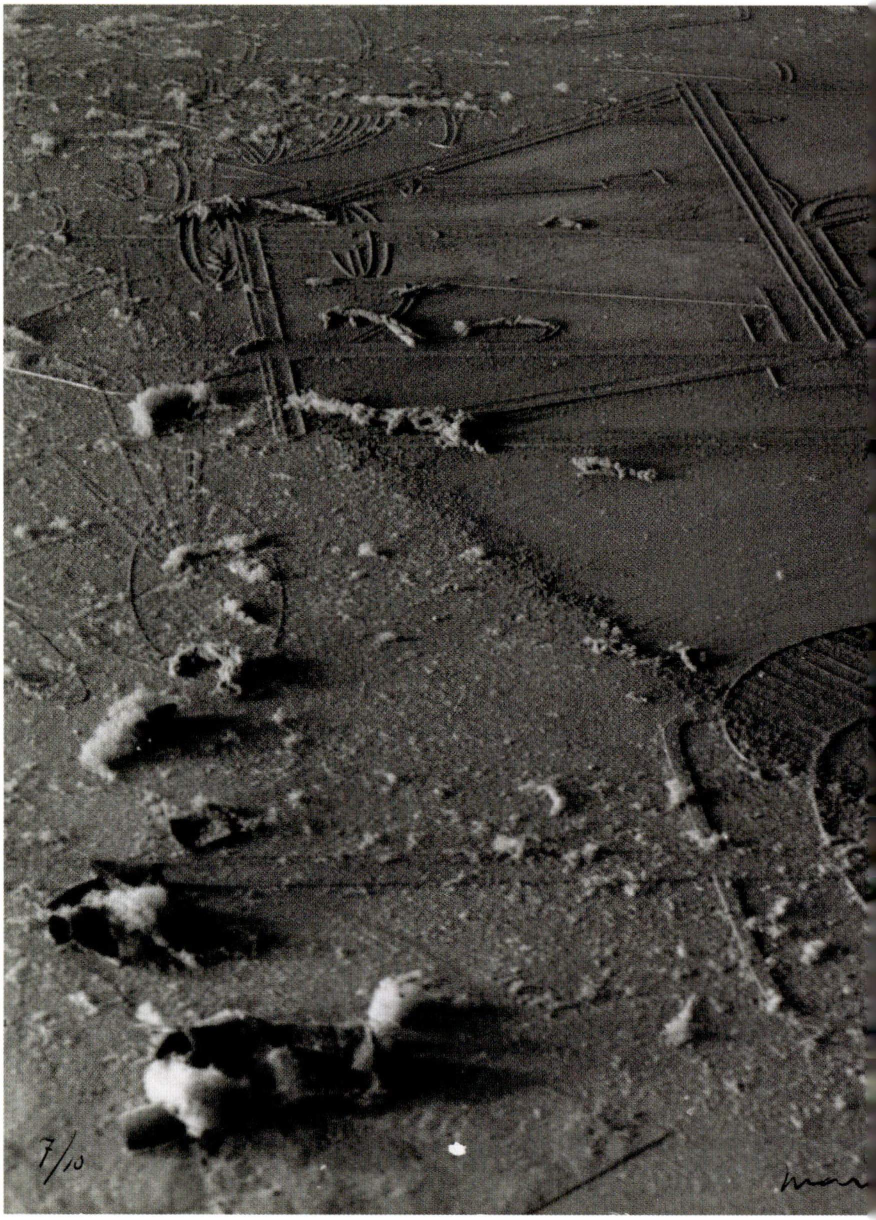

Man Ray (American, 1890–1976), who was born Emmanuel Radnitzky, worked across a range of art forms, including painting and photography, which he took up in 1918. Along with Marcel Duchamp, he was a leading proponent of Dada art. After moving to Paris in 1921, he became associated with the Surrealists. He was a highly skilled and sought-after commercial photographer as well as an artist. He developed a series of camera-less images that he dubbed "rayographs." Together with photographer Lee Miller, he pioneered the renaissance of solarization, a process that records images on the negative.

Creative tips and techniques

Man Ray felt that his experience as a painter was a valuable foundation for his photographic work. He admitted that he maintained the approach of a painter to such a degree that he was accused of trying to make a photograph look like a painting. Although he never set out to do this consciously, he said that it turned out that way because of his training. Man Ray worked across a wide range of art forms, not preferring one above another but rather accepting each for its strengths, claiming: "I paint what cannot b photographed, that which comes from the imagination or from dreams, or from a unconscious drive." He did not feel that or approach was inherently more effective than another, but rather that the medium needed to suit the message. He claimed

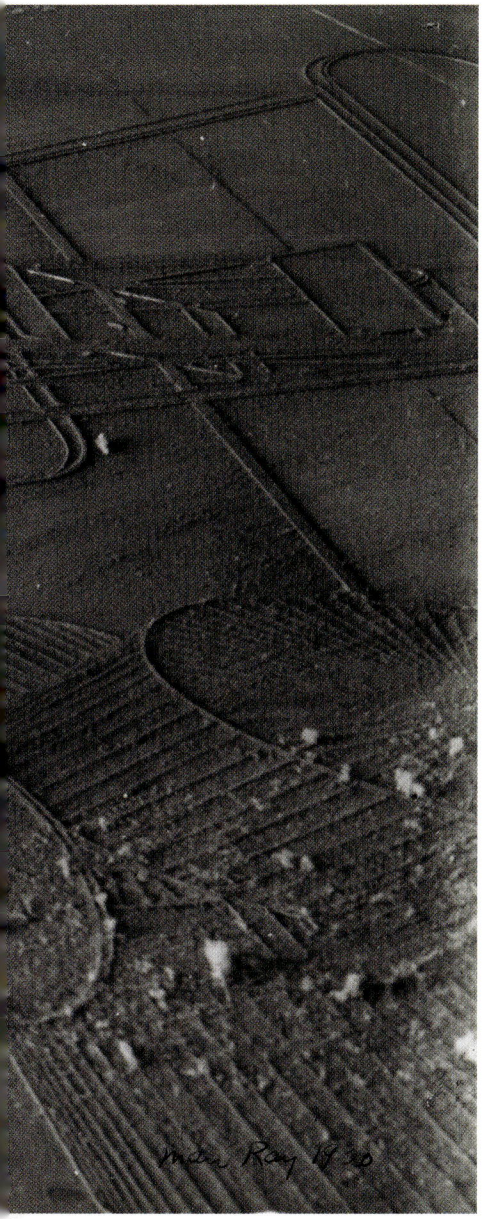

Dust Breeding 1920

In this enigmatic image, all sense of scale and distance is lost. It appears to be a surreal landscape viewed from the air, with lines inscribed across it like the geoglyphs made by the ancient Nazca civilization of Peru. The rigid forms of the lines are softened by the fluffy detritus scattered across the left side of the frame, like tumbleweed blowing across a desert.

In fact, the image shows a sheet of glass covered in dust. It forms part of Marcel Duchamp's seminal work, *The Bride Stripped Bare by Her Bachelors, Even* (1915–23). Duchamp left a sheet of glass that forms one side of the work on a table in his studio for a year; a sign was hung next to it to prevent cleaning, which read "Dust breeding. To be respected." Man Ray made this photograph of a small section of the work. The lines on the glass are traces of thin metal strips Duchamp used to delineate elements of the work. The angle of view and the cropping into the glass surface give the image the appearance of an aerial reconnaissance photograph. After the image was taken, Duchamp cleaned most of the glass, leaving one area of dust that he sealed permanently with glue. Duchamp and Man Ray thus collaborated on making an artwork out of the most mundane material, transforming the traces of neglect into one art form and then into another.

at he never shared the contempt shown painters for photography, believing at they are two media engaged in ferent paths. He was equally disdainful the apparatus, scornfully remarking, ien people asked him what camera used: "You don't ask a writer what pewriter he uses."

Man Ray was constantly exploring the edges of what the photograph can represent, pushing it to see how he could show his ideas and imagination rather than simply recording the factual world. He explained that some of the most successful artworks have been produced when their authors had no idea of creating a work of art, but were concerned with the expression of an idea. For him, the concept always came first, and then the formal strategy to execute it emerged out of the thought process. He acknowledged that there will always be some who look only at technique, asking "how," whereas those with a more curious nature will ask "why." He said that personally he "preferred inspiration to information." He also revealed how he allowed the influence of Dadaism and Surrealism to be expressed in his work, claiming that he would "photograph an idea rather than an object, a dream rather than an idea."

László Moholy-Nagy

Photogram 1926

László Moholy-Nagy explored the possibilities of camera-less image making throughout his life, arguing that "it must be stressed that the essential tool of the photographic process is not the camera but the light-sensitive layer." The photogram had its origins in early photography. In the 1830s William Henry Fox Talbot made images of plants and flowers by leaving them on sheets of light-sensitive paper out in the sun. However, Moholy-Nagy, along with Man Ray (see p.94), transformed the process from recording tangible physical objects into a new form of expression that used light itself as the fundamental determinant of the final image, dubbing the resulting cameraless images "Rayographs."

With this particular image, made with his own hand and the outline of a paintbrush, Moholy-Nagy was perhaps suggesting that photography has transcended painting and become the true expressive art form of the 20th century. He experimented with abstract compositions, using a variety of found materials, transforming everyday objects into strange and beautiful two-dimensional sculptures, in which light—enveloping and transmitting through various levels of opacity and translucency—becomes the creator of the image. Abstract in nature, the photograms play with the fact that they are made with tangible material objects, but the process of exposing them to light creates non-representational, non-figurative forms. The photogram is therefore not a copy but a transmutation of the real, and an investigation into the very nature of light. And, first and foremost, of the phenomenon of the "shaping of light."

> **"The photographer is a manipulator of light; photography is a manipulation of light."**
>
> László Moholy-Nagy

László Moholy-Nagy (Hungarian, 1895–1946) had a significant impact on the arts in Europe and the United States, both as an artist and, importantly, as an educator. He taught at the Bauhaus school in Germany in the 1920s with Walter Gropius, and later set up the influential Institute of Design in Chicago in 1939. Moholy-Nagy initially worked as a lawyer, but his bitter experiences as an officer in World War I led him toward art as a means of social activism and the improvement of society. He argued that the unique qualities of photography needed to be exploited, as "no intention exists of making photography into an art in the old sense. We definitely have to go back to the deeper responsibility of the photographer who accomplishes a work with the photographic means which could not be accomplished in the same way with other means. Therefore the existence of photography today exists less in serving individual artistic expression but rather much more in its pedagogical function." As an advocate of avant-garde photography, Moholy-Nagy was influential in art movements including Dadaism, Suprematism, and Constructivism.

Creative tips and techniques

Moholy-Nagy created many montages, which he dubbed "photoplastics." These typically used cut-outs from photographs mounted onto white backgrounds, with thin lines intersecting and connecting them. As with his rayograms and actual photography, they are graphic and high contrast, and rely on complex patterns and unusual angles to create dynamic final images.

Moholy-Nagy argued that mastery of the photogram would have a positive impact on the photographer's sense of light and composition, as it allowed for the exploration of light and structure without any constraints. He felt that the photosensitive layer is a *tabula rasa,* or blank page, on which one can make notes with light in the same way that the painter works on canvas.

There are several ways to recreate photograms digitally. One approach is to place objects on top of a backlit surface; an iPad works well for this when set to give a pure white screen. You could use a light box or make one from a sheet of glass, or even use a glass table lit from below with white tracing paper underneath it to diffuse the light. You can also simply place objects against a white background, but with this option you will not get the effect of light passing through the object from behind. Another approach is to use a flatbed scanner and scan the objects. Once you have arranged your objects, take your photographs or make the scan, and then open them up in your editing program. Select the invert filter, which will turn them into a negative. You can then adjust contrast and brightness to get the final result you want. This works in color or you can convert the image to black and white.

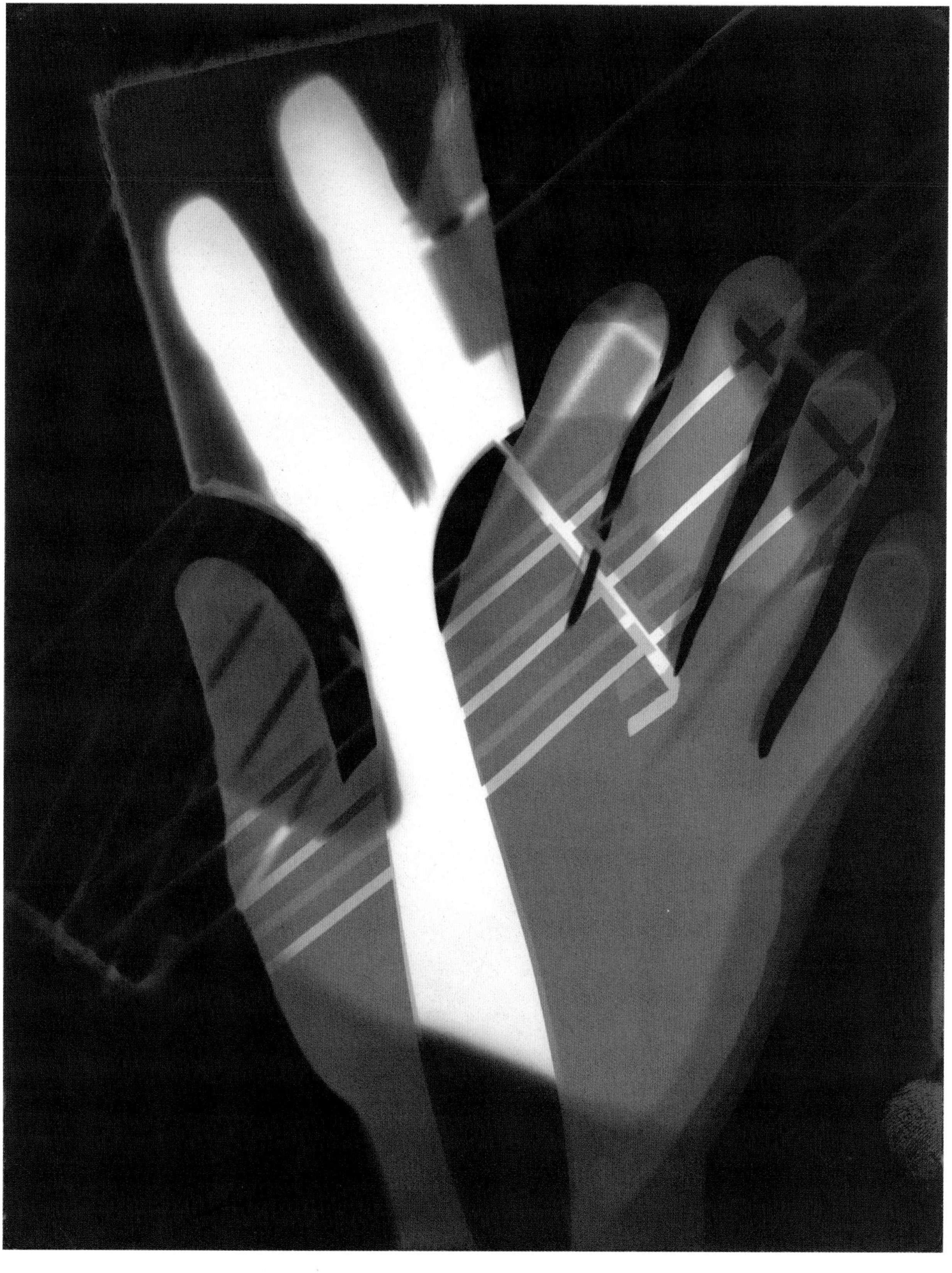

Edward Weston

Pepper #30 1930

In his work after 1922, Edward Weston concentrated on searching for the form revealed by the camera in the natural world, whether found in the nude human body, the shape of a vegetable, or the curve of a sand dune. He kept detailed notes on his investigations in his published *Daybooks*, which date from 1923 to 1934 and are an excellent resource on the artistic process and craft of photography. He photographed peppers consistently for many years, making his first exposures in 1927. This image was one of a series of more than thirty negatives he made in August 1930 and has become one of his most iconic images, with a print selling at auction in 2014 for almost $350,000.

Seeking the perfect way to light the pepper, he experimented with a large tin funnel in which he placed the vegetable, so that the light reflected all around it, giving it the intense three-dimensional quality that makes the image so extraordinary. He realized how successful the image was in elevating the simplest of objects into something meaningful: "It is a classic, completely satisfying—a pepper—but more than a pepper; abstract, in that it is completely outside subject matter. It has no psychological attributes, no human emotions are aroused: this new pepper takes one beyond the world we know in the conscious mind." The story of the creation of this image is a metaphor for the photographic experience, how the combination of years of patient devotion to the craft can ally with the simplest of things to create the pinnacle of expression. Weston was one of the supreme exponents of understanding how the camera extracts something from the world that is different to it, where the process transforms the everyday into the extraordinary.

"I have done perhaps fifty negatives of peppers: because of the endless variety in form manifestations, because of their extraordinary surface texture, because of the power, the force suggested in their amazing convolutions." Edward Weston

Edward Weston (American, 1886–1958) began his career as an adherent of Pictorialism, a style of photography emphasizing technique, soft focus, and darkroom manipulation. During a visit in 1922 to the Armco Steel Plant in Middletown, Ohio, he made a series of photographs that simply and straightforwardly depicted the complex forms of the factory's industrial chimneys and towers. He renounced the overworked Pictorialist approach in favor of a more direct vision, arguing that the "camera should be used for a recording of life, for rendering the very substance and quintessence of the thing itself, whether it be polished steel or palpitating flesh." In 1926 he began a series of images of natural forms including seashells, peppers, and cabbages, revealing their textures and sculptural form. With Ansel Adams (see p.50) and Imogen Cunningham (see p.140), Weston was one of the founders of the f/64 movement in 1932. Sadly, his career was cut short by the onset of Parkinson's disease. He spent the last years of his life collaborating with his sons on printing portfolios of his work, culminating in a show at the Smithsonian Institution, Washington, in 1956.

Creative tips and techniques

Weston worked with a large-format view camera, in this instance an Ansco 8Q10 Commercial View with a Zeiss 21mm lens. He made contact prints of the negatives and most of his actual prints are sized 9 ½ x 7 ½ in. (24 x 19 cm). He was skilled at manipulating the print, using his hands to shade the paper during the exposure to selectively darken and lighten key areas of the final image.

Weston believed that photographers should practice to the point where decisions about how to shoot become instinctive. You need to foster an innate sense of how the optical process of photography translates the three-dimensional world into a two-dimensional image, and how light can be used to bring three-dimensional depth back into it again. Set up a series of still-life objects on a table at right angles to a large window, or use an artificial light source or flash, so that the light is falling across the image. Work out the average exposure for the scene, and then make a series of exposures that do five full stops under and five full stops over this base exposure in half or third stop increments. When you have finished, arrange them in a sequence from dark to light and see how the image changes with the exposure. Repeat the process with the position of the objects to the light source changed so that the light falls frontally onto the object. The way in which light falls and your exposure of it can drastically alter the apparent depth of each object.

Weston argued that composition cannot be codified according to abstract principles. Although guides like the rule of thirds can be useful, they can become sterile. Try to respond on a more intuitive level to the world around you.

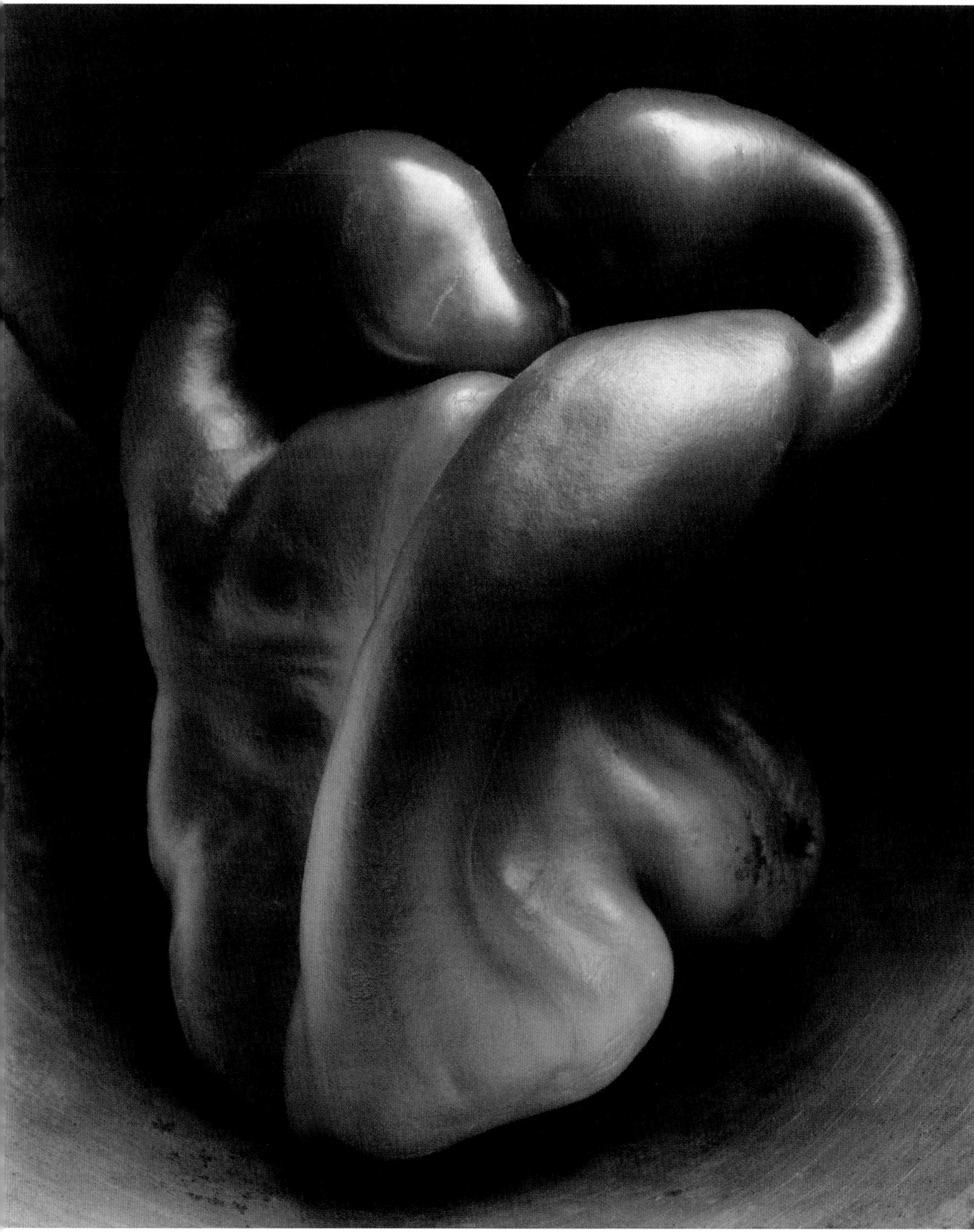

William Eggleston

Untitled (Memphis) 1970

This photograph was the cover image for William Eggleston's *Guide*, a landmark book and exhibition in 1976, which in 2012 sold for over half a million dollars in a new edition of digital prints made at a larger size than the photographer had previously worked with. The low viewpoint makes the child's tricycle appear monumental and sculptural, reminiscent of the works of sculptor Claes Oldenburg, and transforms an everyday, banal object into something extraordinary and strange. The colors of the image are those of the American flag, red, white, and blue, although the rust that defaces the tricycle is perhaps a comment on America's fading glory. The street behind is a typical suburban one, but the framing of the car between the wheels of the tricycle suggests a sense of animation, as if it may drive out and crush the toy.

Eggleston shoots voraciously, but claims to "only ever take one picture of one thing. Literally. Never two. So then that picture is taken and then the next one is waiting . . . I don't really worry if it works out or not. I figure it's not worth worrying about. There's always another picture." In this sense, the moment of contact with the world is the key feature, rather than the attempt to shoot the same scene repeatedly until the best shot is obtained. This makes the process more like a game or even a meditation, as he notes, "I had this notion of what I called a democratic way of looking around, that nothing was more or less important." Eggleston took this approach even further in his later work, sometimes not even looking through the viewfinder, a technique that he maintains "makes you much freer, so you can hold the camera up in the air as if you were 10 feet tall. You end up looking more intensely as you walk around. When it is time for you to make the photograph, it's all ready for you."

"A picture is what it is, and I've never noticed that it helps to talk about them, or answer specific questions about them."

William Eggleston

Creative tips and techniques

At first glance, Eggleston's work may seem simplistic, but as one looks more closely at his images, patterns and themes recur too frequently to be accidental. Many of his photographs are composed around a cross-shaped central form; Eggleston once claimed, perhaps facetiously, that it referred to the Confederate flag. There is, however, a strong sense of a coherent personal vision in his work, in which each image exists as a succinct distillation of the exact experience of encountering the world at that precise moment, with whatever caught Eggleston's eye or imagination, be it color, light, or form, faithfully captured within the four sides of the frame. He elevates the ordinary into the special, celebrating the fact that it is the artist's vision that makes something worthy of our attention.

Eggleston discovered the dye-transf printing process in the 1970s, and he used it extensively to make his exhibition prints. In dye transfer, separations are made for the yellow, magenta, cyan, and black layers, and then each layer is printec separately in a process similar to silk screening. This laborious method allows very precise adjustment of the color of ea layer, and produces prints with stunningly rich and saturated colors that are almost

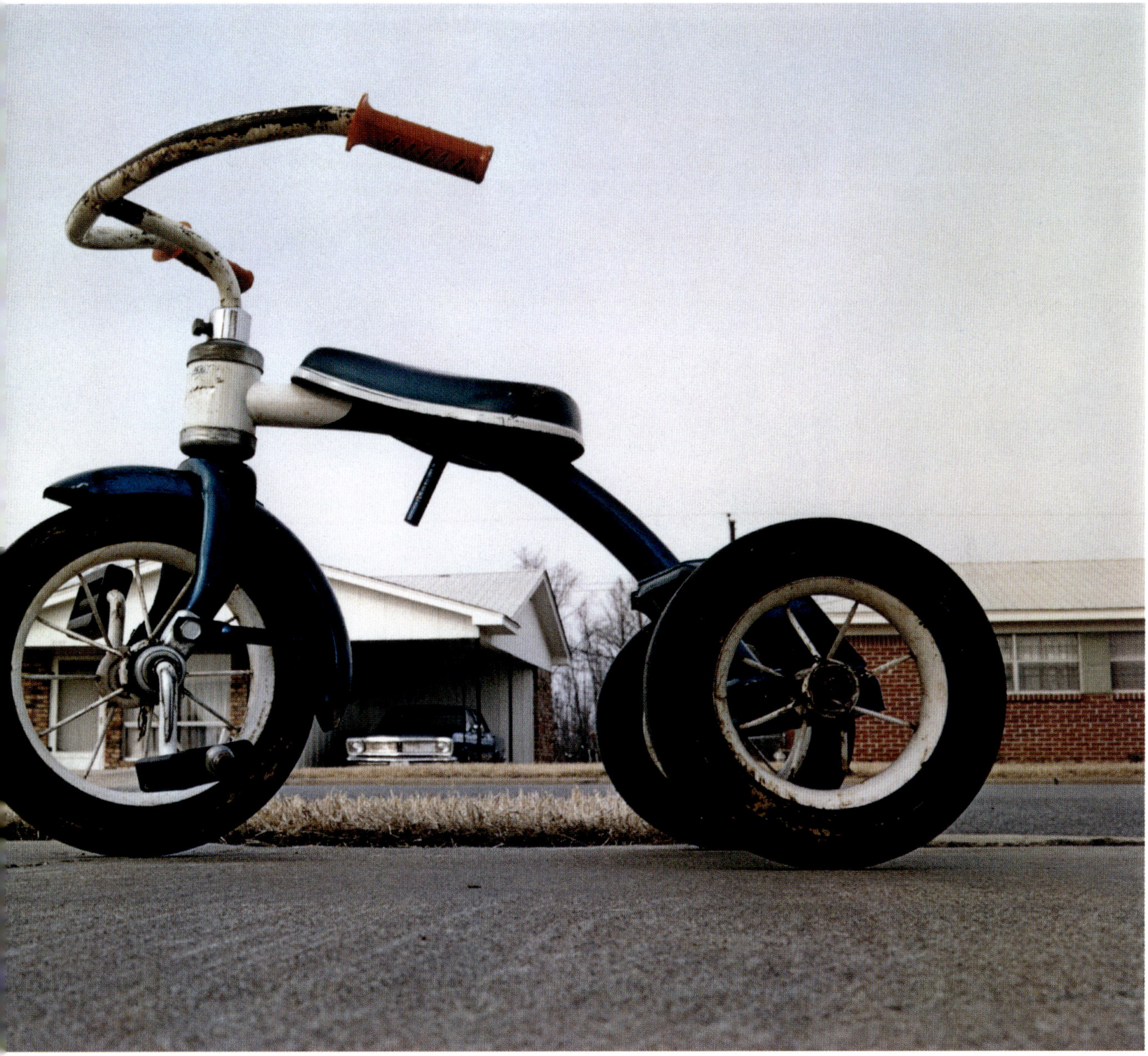

ıpossible to replicate in other printing
·ocesses. However this process is now
rely used, because Kodak discontinued
·oduction of dye-transfer materials in
·93 and all inventories of materials
ere sold to existing practitioners at
at time. To replicate this process
gitally is almost impossible, but you
ın adjust the saturation of your digital
es in post-production in order to
ıhance the colors.

William Eggleston (American, 1939–) is regarded as the godfather of serious color photography. He has had a huge influence on generations of photographers and film-makers, both in terms of his use of color and the deceptively casual esthetic he deploys. In 1976 *Guide* was the first solo show of color photographs the Museum of Modern Art in New York had ever presented. Eggleston was born in Memphis, Tennessee, on the edge of the Mississippi Delta, which has remained central to his work ever since. He bought his first camera, a Canon Rangefinder, in 1957, and began shooting color seriously in 1965. A pivotal experience for him was working in one of the first industrial photofinishing laboratories, watching hundreds of color photos flowing out of the developing machines. This exposure to the "snapshot esthetic" became key to his practice.

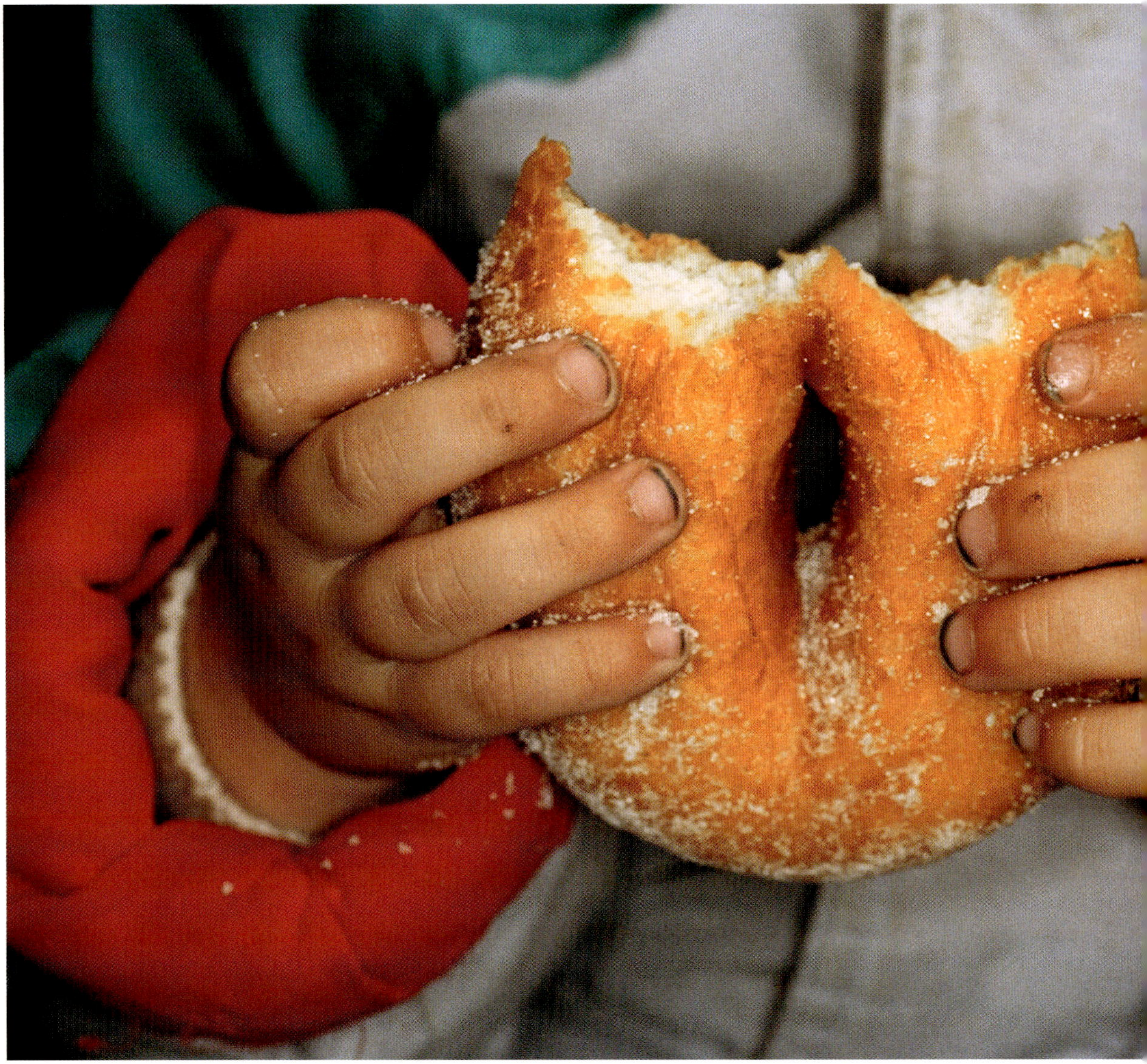

Ramsgate 1996, from "Common Sense"

Martin Parr works on extended projects that examine the world of material culture, but he is also fascinated by the medium itself, and explores a variety of formal strategies to see how they can describe the world in different ways. In his color work he initially deployed a Plaubel Makina medium-format hand-held film camera with fill in flash, as in *The Last Resort* (1986), his breakthrough project on the rundown holiday town of New Brighton near Liverpool in northern England. In the series "Common Sense," from which this image is taken, he explored how the close-up allowed him to extract telling details of the excesses of consumer culture, fast food and fashion. His use of flash and amateur film gives images super-saturated color, enhancing the brashness of the scene. Every detail is clear and the dirt under the child' fingernails contrasts with the sugary whiteness dusting the food. The color palette is simple but strong, with the blues of the coat providing a consistent background to the pop c the puffy red sleeves that echo the shape of the doughnut.

Parr's penchant for detail helps him avoid some of the criticism that he is exploiting his subjects. He is one of the few photographers who fully deploy humor as part of their visual strategy, and is happy to acknowledge the satirical edge to his work. He also revels in the ordinary and the everyday, finding a rich vein of material in situations that many other photographers ignore. Parr's work is therefore an important part of our visual history.

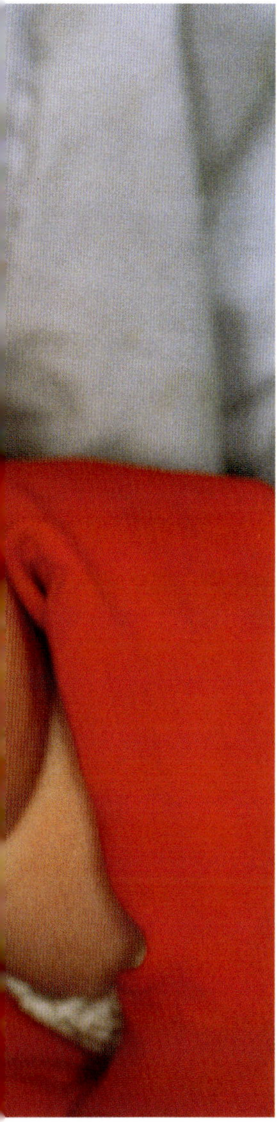

Creative tips and techniques

Parr works close to the people he photographs, often uncomfortably so. He dresses like a middle-class British tourist on vacation, in shorts and sandals, the antithesis of the "professional photographer." He does not look at the people he photographs, especially afterward; if someone objects to being photographed, he moves on.

Parr developed the technique of balancing flash with daylight to enhance the saturation and hyperreality of his images. This means he does not have to resort to Photoshop to enhance colors. For close-ups, he uses a macro lens and ring flash. When working at a greater distance, he uses a diffuser mounted onto his flashgun to soften the light, and often sets the power output of the flash to match or even exceed the exposure for the daylight. This technique can be useful to fill in dark shadows from bright sunshine, or when the subject is backlit, against a sunset, for example. To use fill-in flash in this way, take a meter reading and then set the flash to match the aperture you want to use. As the duration of the flash is so short, it will not be affected by the shutter speed. To learn this technique, go out on a sunny day, ideally with a model. Set your main exposure, say 1/250th of a second at f8, and then make a series of exposures bracketing the flash power under and over the aperture you have set. Most modern cameras and flashguns have an exposure compensation feature for the flash so you can dial in the ratio. Then do the same thing, but this time underexpose the main exposure by one stop, then two stops. This will make the flash the main light for the scene and darken the background, which can create powerful effects.

truly believe that the ordinary is much more interesting han people make out." Martin Parr

artin Parr (British, 1952–) is one of the ost prolific and influential contemporary otographers, not only because of his own tput, but also because of his work as a curator d champion of the photographic book. Parr's elong obsession has been with material culture d the impact that it has on our lives, as he otes his photography is "an observation of e Western world's middle classes and their dless quest for material abundance." Parr has explored the rituals of English life in the tradition of Tony Ray-Jones (see p.190), yet mediated by the American approach to color photography exemplified by Joel Meyerowitz (see p.60), William Eggleston (see p.100), and Stephen Shore. He is a voracious collector of photographic ephemera, especially postcards, and the bright, saturated color of the Butlin's postcards of John Hinde has had a huge influence on his later work.

Alec Soth

"I have the belief that Americana still exists. Because that's the thing, these places are still out there, these people are still out there, and that's something I'm less jaded about; it's still a rich world to be explored."

Alec Soth

Alec Soth (American, 1969–) grew up in Minneapolis, Minnesota, in the American Midwest, where he still lives. He works mostly on long-term documentary projects based around an engagement with spaces, places, and the people who inhabit them in his home state, and has published over twenty-five books including *Sleeping by the Mississippi* (2004), *Niagara* (2006), *Broken Manual* (2010), and *Songbook* (2015).

He works in the tradition of Walker Evans (see p.78), Robert Frank (see p.186), and Joel Sternfeld (see p.54). He cites Sternfeld as a major formative influence and recalls how, as a student, he took a class with him: "In one slide he pointed out his van, the van he had used to traverse America. Something clicked. I realized that was what I wanted to do. This sort of boyish wanderlust is common in America, but it was new to me."

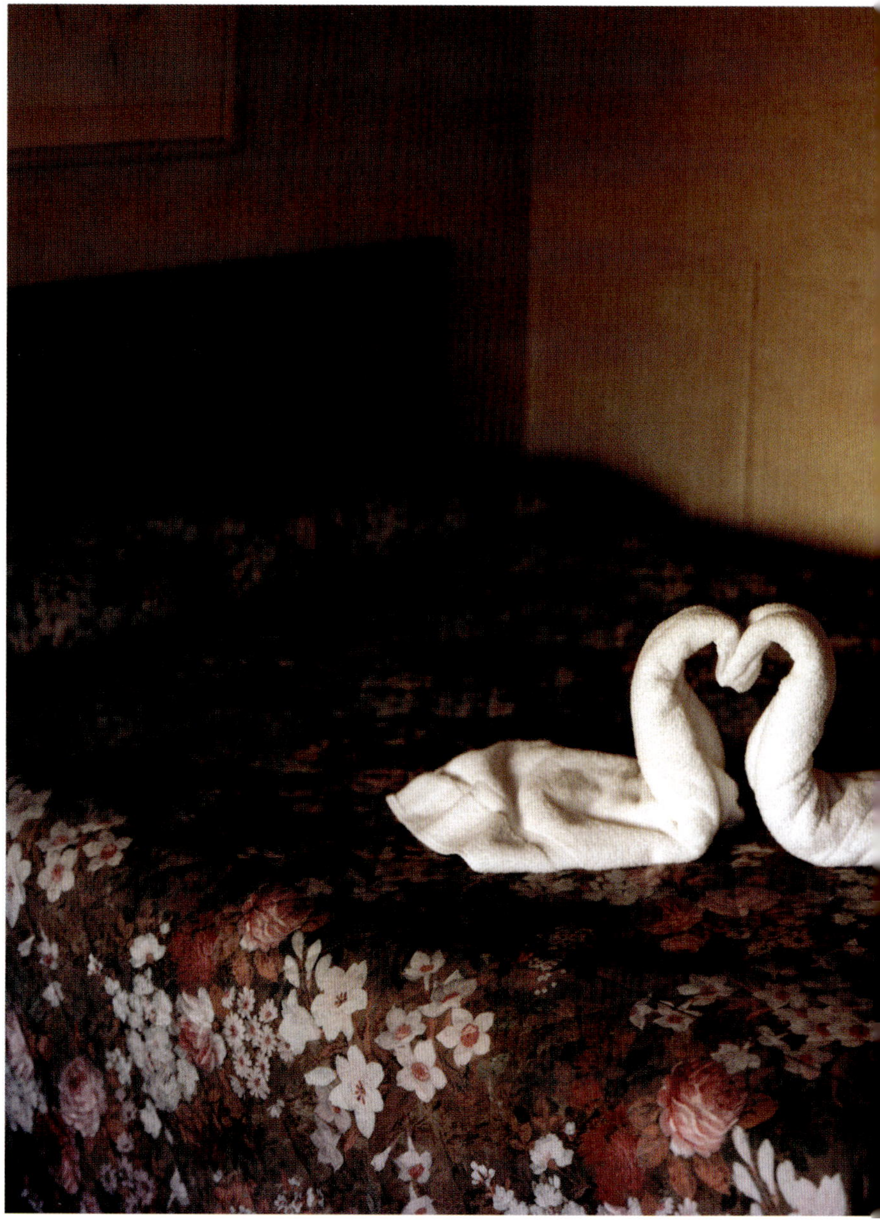

Creative tips and techniques

Soth works mostly on large-scale, long-term projects in which each image is important, but it is in the collective body of work that the real meaning resides—he is more focused on creating a body of images. Try to develop a project that is about a collection of images, where each one adds to the next, or builds upon the previous, and experiment with how sequencing and grouping together photographs can introduce a deeper meaning.

Soth notes that when he began photographing, he was trying to cram as much information into the image as possible. However, he soon realized that the opposite approach can be a more successful strategy. What is excluded from the frame is often as important, if not more

Two towels 2004, from "Niagara"

One of the key traits of the photographer is paying attention to things that others do not see and, through the process of carefully framing the world around them, extracting significant details that convey a deeper meaning. These two folded towels become lovers, tenderly kissing each other, the slightly crumpled folds adding an air of melancholy and a deep emotional charge to the image. The flower-patterned bedspread highlights our relationship to nature, but is also a wry observation of the depressing interiors common to chain hotels. The soft window light picks out the whiteness of the towels, making them glow luminously against the darker tones of the room.

Soth's work combines portraits, landscapes, interiors, and details, which he uses rhythmically in his books to develop themes and resonances, creating a poetic narrative around the subjects in which he is interested. In the book *Niagara*, for which this image is the cover, photographs of the falls are interspersed throughout the pages as a recurrent theme. Soth explores the contradictions of the place, which is at once a symbol of romance and love, but also of loneliness and despair. He explains, "What fascinated me is how this crashing waterfall is a metaphor for that crazed intensity of new love, and how it's like this force that peters out. Niagara Falls is also where a lot of people go to commit suicide." Soth works intuitively, believing that "great pictures are all about luck." He feels his way into a place, exploring its nuances and its people, seeking those moments of connection that are charged and resonant, especially with the unexpected encounter: "I'm a big believer in serendipity. The goal is to find the flow of things.'"

, than what is left in it. Try to be precise ıd discerning about everything that u include in your images. Aim for otographs that still have meaning but e stripped down to the bare essentials.

Although Soth acknowledges that the advent of digital photography s been generally positive and that he akes extensive use of social media to sseminate his work, he is also wary of the dangers of the constant changes involved. He argues that it is easy to lose oneself in the technology as it is constantly evolving, with new equipment and new processing techniques, and new forms such as video and multimedia. It's easy to get caught up in thinking that if something is not new, it isn't good. Make sure you master the basics of the camera and only experiment with new tricks if they are genuinely contributing to the message you want to convey.

Soth has sound advice for those starting out as photographers: do not expect success too soon, as it is important to let your work develop without external pressures. Rather than putting too much effort into promoting yourself, you need to build up a significant body of work in order to make an impact. That is not going to happen overnight, but only as the result of an extended period of sustained practice.

Peter Fraser

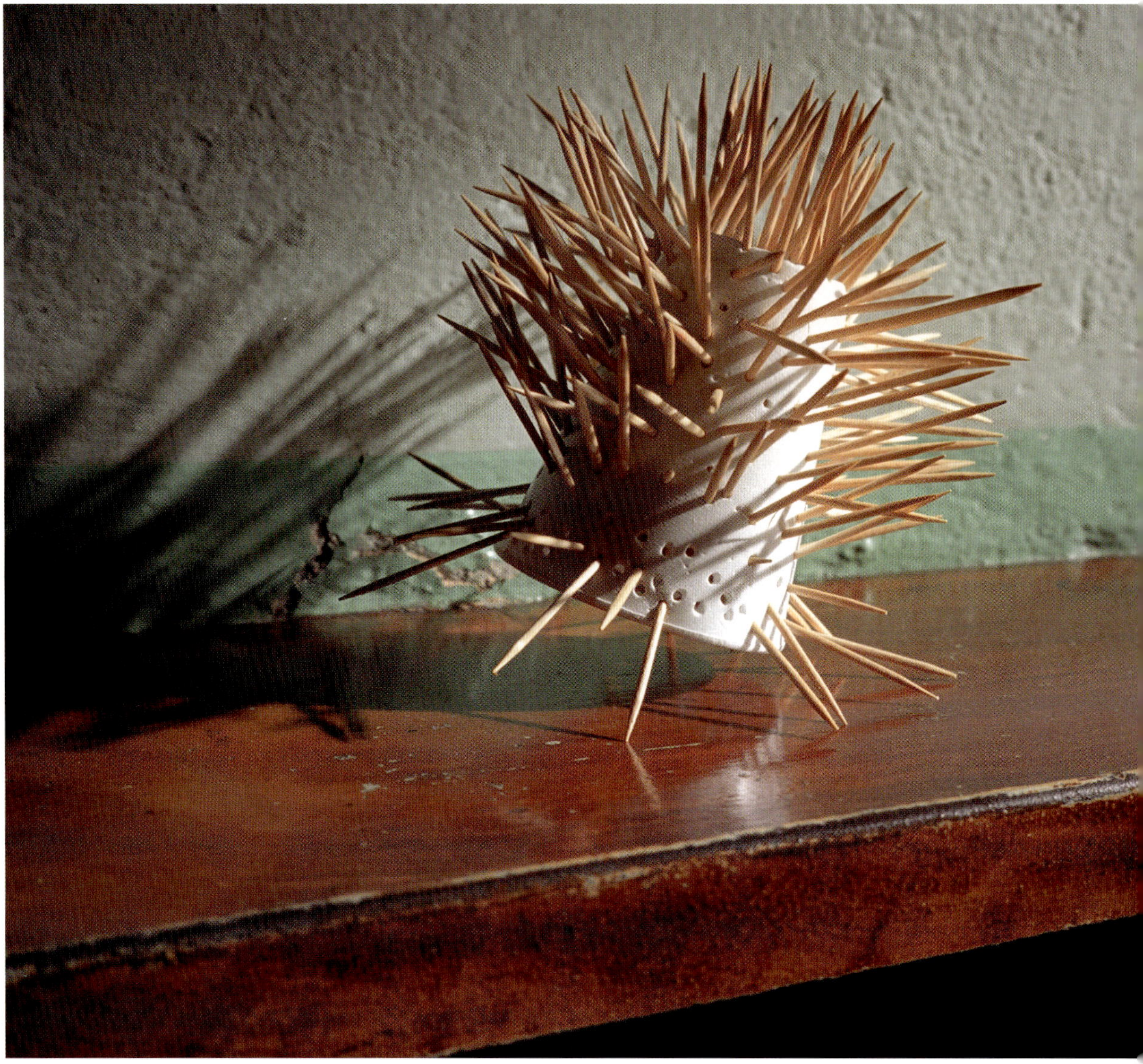

Untitled 2006

This unusual construction appears to be alive, almost as if it is crawling along the shelf like some alien Heath Robinson-like version of a hedgehog. The object is clearly the product of crafting the material world, yet the empty holes suggest that the final result is imperfect. The intense light pouring onto the scene generates a sense of movement across the frame and creates an intensity of color with a spiritual quality to it. Fraser has always been fascinated by objects, and has spent years photographing them close up: "I think small things are really important, not least because everything in the universe is made up of matter so small we can't see it with the naked eye. I almost never interfere with my subjects: there are mysterious forces at work in the world and they know, better than I do, how things should be placed." His recollection of th moment of making this photograph reveals the rewards that the simple act of looking hard at the world around you can bring. He recalls entering a church in a Welsh village during a photographic road trip: "I always find churches interesting as places of quiet where you can hear your inner voice, away from the distracting ambient noise of modern life." He sense that this was a place with potential for a powerful image, the stumbled across this bizarre sculpture, which he recognized as "an exquisite example of the brain directing the hand to change the nature of materials…[I] took several photos, unable to believe my eyes. Minutes later, I was breathing the air outside, delirious with the thrill of being alive."

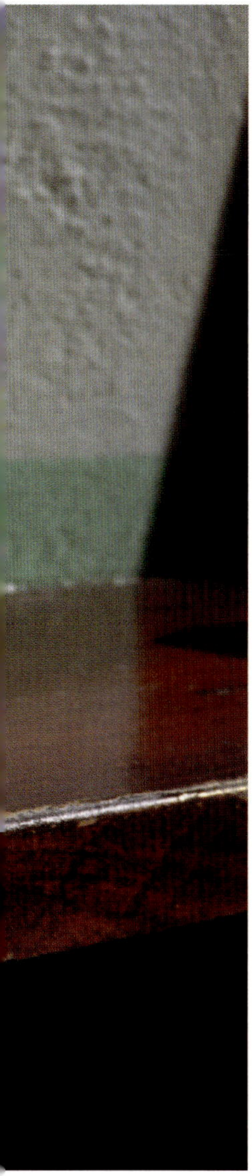

ractically everything on Earth looks the way it does because, t some point, a human brain directed a hand to change the hape and nature of materials." Peter Fraser

ter Fraser (British, 1953–) studied photography Manchester Polytechnic at the same time Martin Parr (see p.102), Brian Griffin (see 26), and Daniel Meadows, graduating in 1976. 1984 he traveled to Memphis in the United ates to spend nearly two months working with illiam Eggleston (see p.100), who gave him the nfidence to believe that he could devote himself tally to the discipline of photography and that he "could work with color photography and win new territory for it." His first major publication, *Two Blue Buckets*, won the Bill Brandt Prize in 1988. In 2013 Tate St Ives held a retrospective of Fraser's career and published a monograph of his work. He is concerned with how the material world can be interrogated to reveal subtle yet deeply suggestive meditations on the relationship of human endeavor to its environment.

Creative tips and techniques

Fraser argues that paying close attention to the world can lead to meaningful insights that surpass anything that the human imagination can produce. Much of Fraser's work is underpinned by a deep fascination with science and mathematics. The idea that in the most minute and insignificant observation can lie a profound philosophical truth is at the core of his practice.

Fraser worked with medium-format film cameras using a Plaubel Makina rangefinder, which was the classic tool for many of the 1980s generation of British color photographers, including Martin Parr (see p.102). Fraser is a meticulous and precise exponent of obtaining perfect color images, and prints his own work. However, after his 2006 series he experimented with digital pigment or inkjet printing, finding that they were able to reproduce a wider range than conventional analog prints. He also found that the exaggerated grain of the scanned negatives he was using was interfering with the final perception of the world transmitted through the print. He then began to work with digital cameras, feeling that with digital "the images were so grain free that they were filmic."

Fraser puts himself into a meditative state of mind in which he is finely tuned into the world around him. To try this approach, Fraser suggests you sit with eyes closed for twenty minutes, slow your breathing, and intently use your senses except sight to tune into your environment. Then open your eyes and photograph the first things you see. Try this in different locations and situations; it can be a powerful technique to help you find the extraordinary in the ordinary.

Faces

The human face and figure have long held a fascination for photographers and artists. We sense that we can read into the physiognomy of a subject the essence of his or her being. We are endlessly intrigued by how people look, hoping to see in their faces some hint as to their character, or simply to try to know them better. Celebrities and the unemployed, rich and poor, famous and unknown are all subjects for portraits. Some of these images are predetermined encounters, in which sitter and photographer come together to collaboratively produce an image that will express the identity of the subject. Others rely on the photographer's eye for a distinctive visage in the crowd, isolating them from the world through careful framing or the use of flash to exaggerate their appearance. A portrait photographer needs to connect with the sitter; this can be the result of personality, dialog, or intense focus. An essential skill is a feel for how a subtle change in angle or pose can make or break the final photograph. Most people truly do have a “best side,” where their face magically coheres into a photogenic image. Developing an eye through careful study of the features of people through the lens, and exploring how incremental changes in position and framing reveal the face to its best advantage, are key to the process. Light also plays a huge part in determining the feel of the portrait and can be used to enhance or exaggerate the sitter’s features. The best portraits transcend the immediate moment, making deep psychological and emotional connections between viewer and subject, so that we learn something of the human condition and of what it means to be alive.

Julia Margaret Cameron

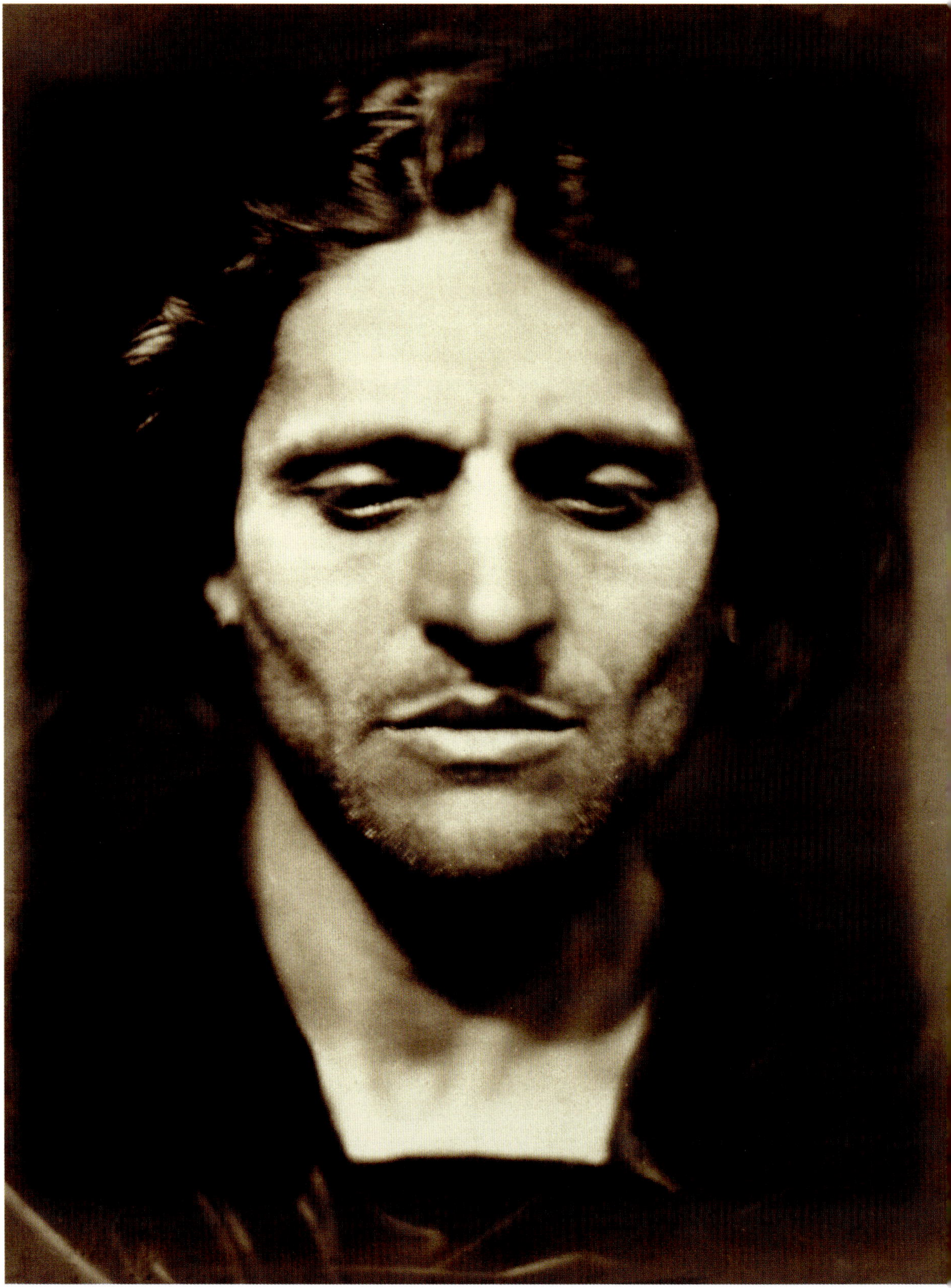

go, study from an Italian 1867

is powerful portrait is strikingly modern. The shallow depth field, dramatic lighting, and downcast eyes of the subject mbine to create a haunting sense of a man troubled by some ep dilemma. Julia Margaret Cameron wrote of how she sought capture "that roundness and fullness of form and feature, at modellng of flesh and limb, which the focus I use only n give." Her use of a shallow depth of field concentrates the ewer's attention on the textural surface of the model's face; accentuates the stubble on his chin and the intensity of his oded eyes. Cameron made albumen prints from her images, aising the flat finish that they produced as the "dull quiet surface a photograph, however rich in tone and tint it may be, that nstitutes I think the harmony of the work." The image is thought be of model Angelo Colarossi whom Cameron posed as Iago om Shakespeare's *Othello*. It is the only photograph by Cameron a professional model. Most of her images were of family and ends, and included such literary and artistic celebrities as arles Darwin, Lord Alfred Tennyson and Robert Browning.

Cameron worked with a large-format, glass plate camera and ed the wet-collodion process to make albumen prints. In 1866 e acquired a plate camera with a Jamin Rapid Rectilinear lens d a fixed aperture of f3.6; this had the shallow depth of focus at she required for the close distances at which she worked. The mera required long exposure times of three to seven minutes, d her subjects were required to remain as still as possible. She ote, "From the first moment, I handled my lens with a tender dour, and it has become to me a living thing, with voice and emory and creative vigor."

/hen I have had such men before my camera my whole soul as endeavored to do its duty towards them in recording ithfully the greatness of the inner as well as...the outer man."

ia Margaret Cameron

ia Margaret Cameron (British, 1815–79) gan to take photographs relatively late in life. December 1863, at the age of forty-eight, e received her first camera as a gift from her ughter and son-in-law. She immediately threw rself into the medium, and in a prolific period ust over ten years produced an extraordinary ies of portraits and staged photographs, rking with large plates and prints. Her rk received mixed reviews at the time, with some criticizing its patent lack of technical sophistication. Others recognized the potential threat to visionary painting in her dreamlike portraits. She frequently asked famous people to sit for her and when they did she asked them to sign her prints, which increased their value. Her work was rediscovered after Helmut Gersheim published a book on her photography in 1948. She is now regarded as one of the greatest pioneers of portrait photography.

Creative tips and techniques

Cameron used natural light in her images. Try shooting inside and using light from a window to get a similar result. First, to achieve a softer overall illumination, position the subject facing the window. Second, position your subject at an angle to the window. The lighting will be more dramatic with more definition from the shadows. In both lighting set-ups, you will achieve the rapid fall-off in light intensity that will make the background appear much darker than the subject. The face will really emerge from the image and give a more three-dimensional feel.

Cameron used a telephoto lens for her portraits, which flattens the perspective, therefore giving a more flattering effect. Using this lens allowed her to work at a comfortable distance from her subject—not so close as to be intrusive. Telephoto lenses have less depth of field, too, and she worked mostly with the lens wide open to give a shallow depth of field, emphasizing specific parts of the subject. To recreate this effect, use a telephoto lens in the 85–135mm range and shoot with the maximum aperture. As a rule, you should focus on the eyes of a portrait subject.

Cameron often composed her portraits with the subject looking directly at the camera. This can be a difficult pose because it can end up looking like a photo-booth or mug shot. However, careful use of light and shadow to bring out the features of the subject prevents this by giving the face depth and definition. Here the light comes from slightly above the subject, giving deep shadows around the eyes and nose, but Cameron has carefully controlled the angle of the light and the position of the subject to concentrate the attention onto the model's closed eyes.

Nadar

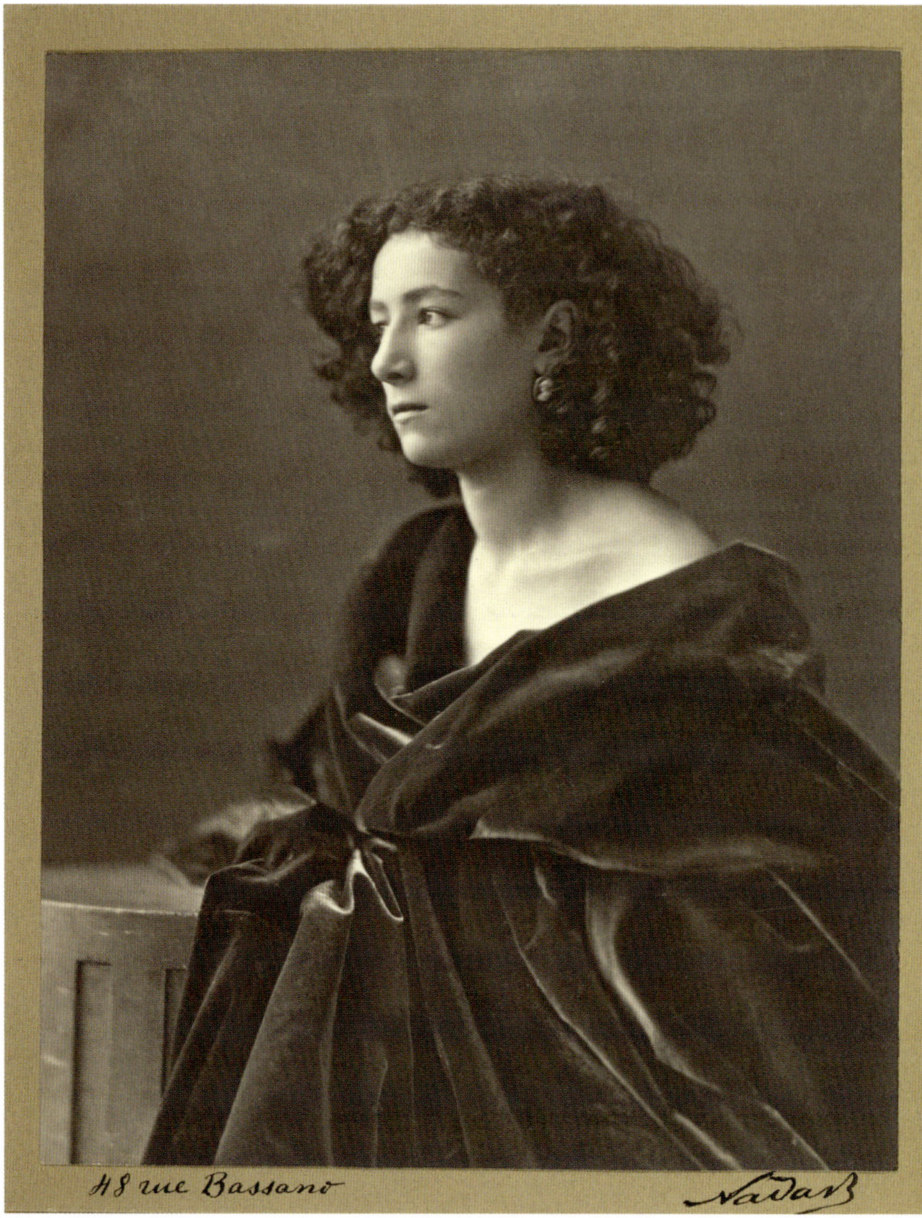

Nadar (French, 1820–1910), born Gaspard-Félix Tournachon, began his career as a caricaturist, adopting the pseudonym *tourne à dard*—the one who stings or twists the dart—which he later shortened to Nadar. He developed a sharp sense for the key features of his subjects, a talent he carried through into his photography. He had a huge personality and was a master of self-promotion. His portrait subjects included novelist Victor Hugo, painter Eugène Delacroix, and composer Franz Liszt. In 1858 he took the first ever aerial photographs from a hot air balloon. He also pioneered the use of artificial lighting in photography, which he used to photograph the catacombs and sewers beneath Paris. His famous studio was the venue for an exhibition of painting that was widely considered a failure at the time. Renoir, one of the artists involved said, "The only thing we got out of it was the label 'Impressionism,' a name I loathe."

Creative tips and techniques

Nadar was a master of using light in a controlled way to accentuate the structure of his sitter's face. He used strong side lighting to bring out the contours, highlight key details, and give his images a three-dimensional sense. To help you develop this feeling for the light, position a model near a window so that they are at 90 degrees to the light falling from it. Get them to turn their head left and right, and tilt it up and down, and watch carefully how the light falls across their face. The classic lighting for portraits is known as 45/45, which means that the light source is at a 45-degree angle to the subject and 45 degrees above them. Make a series of exposures in different positions to explore how subtle changes can make a huge difference to the final image as the contrast between light and shade change across the eyes, nose, and cheeks. You can try adding a reflector—a white sheet or white polystyrene will do—opposite the light source to fill in the shadows and lessen the contrast. Try using the hands as part of the composition. This can look forced, but experiment with a variety of positions—resting the chin on the hand, holding the cheek, framing or even covering the face with the hands.

Sarah Bernhardt/Self-portrait 1859/1865

This portrait of actress Sarah Bernhardt (far left) typifies Nadar's approach. He rejected the overwrought settings and frozen poses commonly used by other portrait photographers of his era, who constructed elaborate sets with painted backdrops and used costumes to accentuate the character of their subjects. Instead, he preferred a simple plain backdrop, dark clothes, and a tight framing to concentrate all attention on the subject's face. The large-format 8 x 10-inch camera he used completely captured the detail of his subject's face. He often used a three-quarter pose and framed only the head and shoulders, but he also used the sitter's hands to add movement to the composition, as in this photograph: Bernhardt's hands form the bottom of a triangle with her face, and the highlights of the draped fabric across her shoulders add extra visual interest. Nadar was highly skilled at using light and often modified the natural light he favored with a range of reflectors, screens, and mirrors to bring out the features of his subjects.

Nadar's larger-than-life personality also played a vital role in the performative nature of his sittings, with his humor and stories putting his subjects at ease. He became almost as famous as the celebrities he photographed. His red hair was his trademark, and he carried the theme through wearing red robes, making his studio red inside and out and advertising it with his name in huge red gaslit letters across the front of the building that drew in the crowds, as he described: "These visitors, from all classes, unknown or even famous, were more than welcome, providing us free stock models quite ready for the new experience."

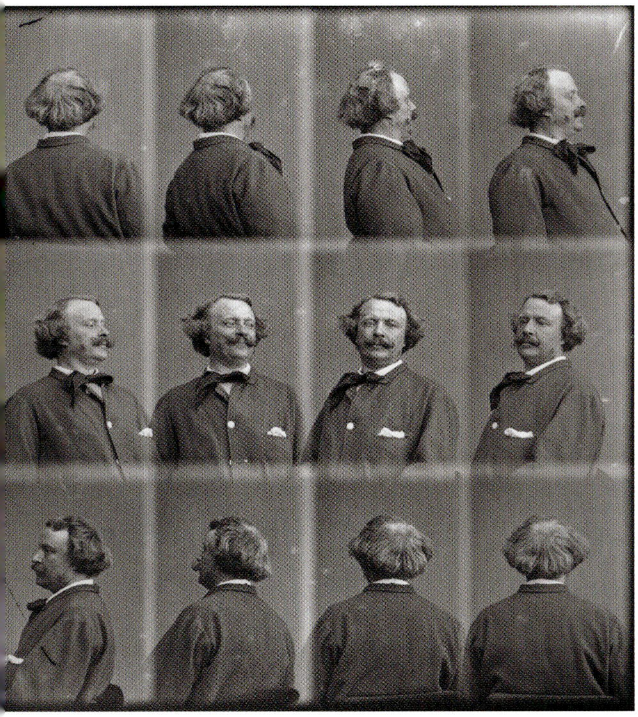

Most people have a particular angle from which they look the most otogenic. Nadar's skills as a cartoonist eant he was able to find the best position bring out distinctive features. Follow e guide of the 360-degree self-portrait made of himself (above) and set up a odel looking straight at the camera. Look rough the lens and ask the model to owly move their head left and then right in all increments, and take a photograph of each position. Ask them to look slightly up and down in each position too. As you look through the camera, try to sense when they look their best. You should find that shooting one side of the face from a particular angle gives a more flattering result. Usually, shooting from above the subject will reduce double chins and be more forgiving. A short telephoto lens will compress the features to avoid the nose appearing overly large.

"To produce an intimate likeness rather than a banal portrait, the result of mere chance, you must put yourself at once in communion with the sitter, size up his thoughts and his very character." Nadar

Lisette Model

Woman with veil, San Francisco 1949

Lisette Model made this photograph when she was invited by the f64 group to teach a class at the San Francisco School of Fine Arts. The influence of German Expressionist painters, including Otto Dix and Max Beckmann, can clearly be seen in this photograph of a finely attired woman who is past her prime. Model shared their interest in exaggerated characters, although she tempered it with a more affectionate humor and sensitivity. The photograph is a study in texture, with the fur, fabric, and lace contrasting with the wrinkled and drawn skin of the woman, suggesting a faded sense of grandeur and glamor. Model had a keen eye for what she called "specialist personalities," and she was drawn to those on the edges of society, whether rich or poor. She commented that the "camera is an instrument of detection. We photograph not only what we know, but also what we don't know."

Model's own childhood was troubled, and it is possible that she channelled some of this trauma into her work and her teaching. She claimed, "my vulnerability is my shield," and advised her protégés to carry their own experiences into their work and "photograph from your guts." She wanted her students to make pictures of subjects they really cared about, advising, "Never take a picture of anything you are not passionately interested in." She fervently believed that the act of photographing itself had a pedagogic function and maintained, when asked what she wanted to prove by her photographs: "The answer is, I don't want to prove anything. They prove to me, and I am the one who gets the lesson."

"I am a passionate lover of the snapshot, because of all photographic images it comes closest to truth..."

Lisette Model

Lisette Model (American, 1901–83) was one of the generation of European photographers who went to the United States to escape the Nazi threat. She was one of the great street photographers and also one of the most influential educators, counting Bruce Weber, Larry Fink, and Diane Arbus among her protégés. She studied music with Arnold Schönberg in her native Vienna, before moving to Paris in 1933, where her younger sister, Olga, introduced her to the camera. Her candid portraits of eccentrics sunning themselves on the Promenade des Anglais in Nice, taken in 1934, showed a precocious talent for picking out characters. She and her husband moved to New York in 1938, where she came to attention as part of the first photographic exhibition of the Museum of Modern Art. Alexey Brodovitch assigned her to photograph Coney Island for *Harper's Bazaar*, where she made one of her most famous images of a woman bather. Over the next decade she made a series of visual essays on New York. In the 1950s she began to teach at Columbia University's New School of Social Research.

Creative tips and techniques

Model learnt to photograph using a Rolleiflex medium-format camera. The Rolleiflex is a twin-lens reflex camera: this means that you look down onto the viewfinder, which is separate from the lens that takes the photograph. Unlike a single-lens reflex camera or rangefinder, such as most modern 35mm cameras, the Rolleiflex gives the photographer a different relationship to the subject, as the camera does not need to be brought up to the eye to frame and shoot. The Rolleiflex has no mirror, either, which makes it very quiet. Model could thus unobtrusively make her photographs without seeming to be taking pictures. Some 35mm digital cameras have a viewing screen at the back that can be tilted up so that it can be viewed from above. This will allow you to deploy Model's surreptitious technique.

Model often cropped her images, changing the format from square to rectangular, and enlarging the subject within the frame to exclude background detail. This also allowed her to shoot further away from the subject but still fill the frame in the final print, with the larger Rolleiflex negative retaining more quality than that of a 35mm camera. She learnt from Alexey Brodovitch how to tilt the frame to create visual energy. Look closely at this image and you can see that the street and bench are at an angle to the horizontal; the woman must, in fact, been leaning heavily to the left, but Model has straightened her up.

The Rolleiflex has a depth of field that is shallower than that of a 35mm camera. Model used this to make her subjects stand out more from the background, which was often out of focus. You can recreate this effect by using a short telephoto lens.

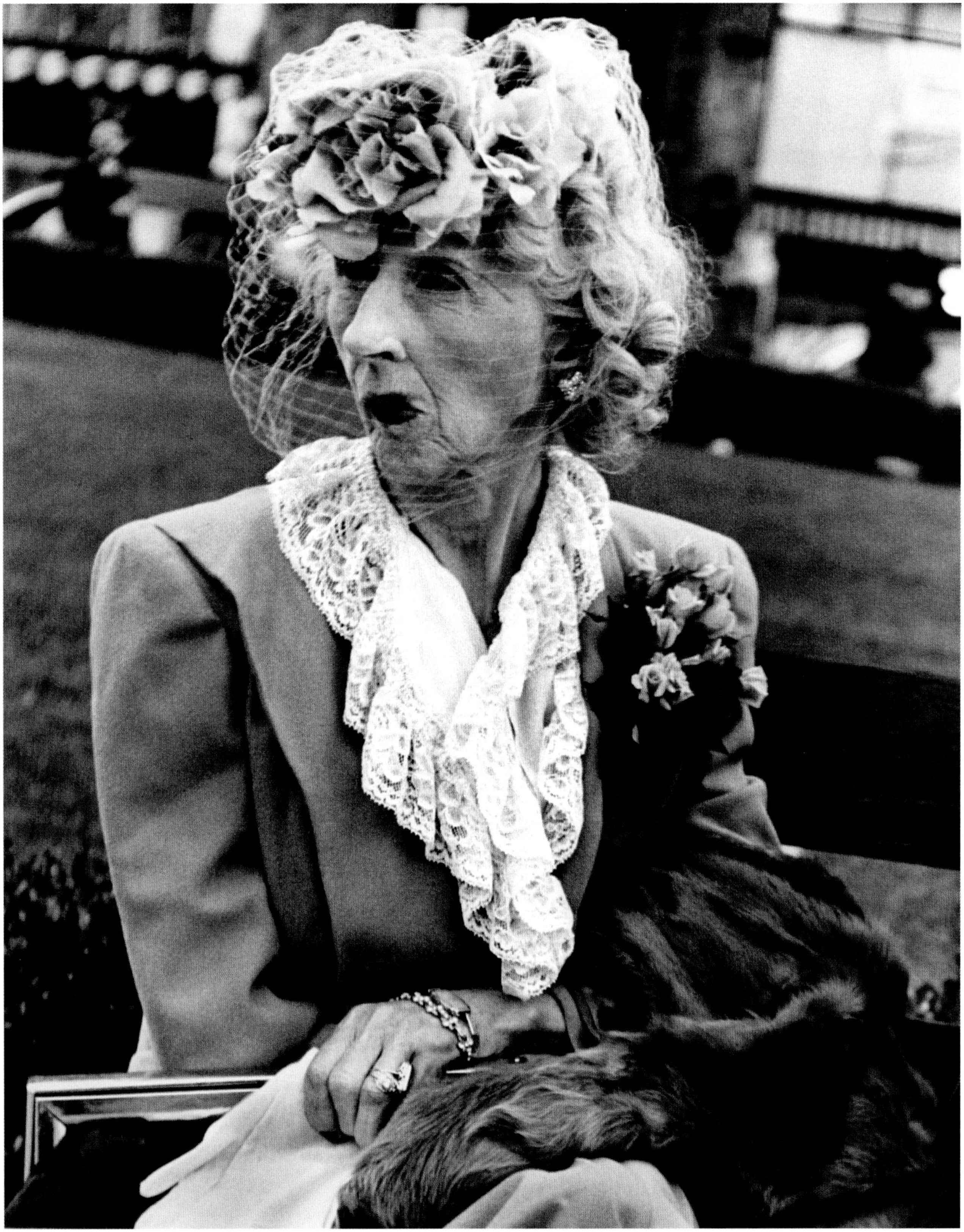

Harry Callahan

Eleanor, Chicago 1949

Harry Callahan photographed constantly, going out almost every day to shoot as he walked through the city, and then spending the afternoons working in the darkroom. Yet, despite his prodigious efforts, he was hypercritical of his work and claimed to make only a handful of good pictures every year. He argued: "I photograph continuously, often without a good idea or strong feelings. During this time the photos are nearly all poor, but I believe they develop my seeing and help later on in other photos."

Callahan photographed his wife, Eleanor, over a period of fifteen years and she was one of his principal subjects. He took pictures of her in every place and format conceivable, continually experimenting with form and technique, effectively using her as a test bed for his ideas and concepts. He kept the constant thread of her face as the common bond in the work and often shot her in the nude. He recalled: "She was innocent and I was innocent. I just try to photograph what I like. I thought she was beautiful. I intuitively photographed her. All my photography is innocent." Stephen White, a photography agent who deals with Callahan's images, says that she was central to his creative process: "Eleanor went beyond being Harry's companion, wife, and the mother of his child. She was an additional f-stop on his lens. Through her, he saw form and structure more clearly, both in nature and in the world. She was present in his photographs even when she wasn't in them. Eleanor was Harry Callahan's collaborator, for she rested inside his psyche." Eleanor herself was more sanguine about posing for Callahan, saying, "He'd photograph me while I was sleeping. Or he'd just sneak up on me. I never protested. Photography was as much a part of our lives as getting up in the morning. I wasn't worried about the pictures. I never had any thought that they would be anything but nice."

> "I am interested in relating the problems that affect me to some set of values that I am trying to discover and establish as being my life. I want to discover and establish them through photography."
>
> Harry Callahan

Harry Callahan (American, 1912–99) was inspired to become a photographer after attending a talk given by Ansel Adams (see p.50) in 1941. By 1946 he had been invited to teach photography at the Institute of Design in Chicago by László Moholy-Nagy (see p.96). In 1961 he moved to the Rhode Island School of Design, teaching there until his retirement in 1977. Callahan was one of the most influential American photographers, tirelessly making photographs and exploring a variety of genres, including portraits, abstracts, and landscapes. He met his lifelong subject and muse, Eleanor Knapp, on a blind date in 1933 when they were both working for Chrysler Motors, and they married three years later. On his death he left behind 100,000 negatives and over 10,000 proof prints, which are archived at the Center for Creative Photography at the University of Arizona.

Creative tips and techniques

Callahan emphasized the sheer grind of being a photographer, stressing that to really understand and control the medium, you need to shoot a lot of pictures. He believed that no amount of book learning could substitute for the simple act of making pictures and that experience is the best teacher of all. This focus on the practice of being a photographer as an almost daily ritual is vital. Set yourself a target of going out every day for thirty days and make a photograph every morning to get into the habit of constantly looking for new images.

Callahan worked constantly, but felt that his success rate was low, claiming that "I guess I've shot about 40,000 negatives and of these I have about 800 pictures I like." Set yourself high standards and really ask yourself whether a picture that you like is as strong as it can possibly be.

Callahan constantly tried out new techniques and formats, including double exposures and sequences, to find new ways of interpreting the subject. He was driven by a strong sense of his own personal, individual vision. He argued that the photographs that excited him were those that say something in a new manner, not for the sake of being different, but "ones that are different because the individual is different and the individual expresses himself." Draw on the influences of others, but always try to maintain your own unique style that identifies you as an image-maker and not simply a derivative copier of others. Weaker pictures in a set often stand out and drag down the stronger ones. Most of the time, less is definitely more and a rigorously tight edit will make the final results more coherent and consistent.

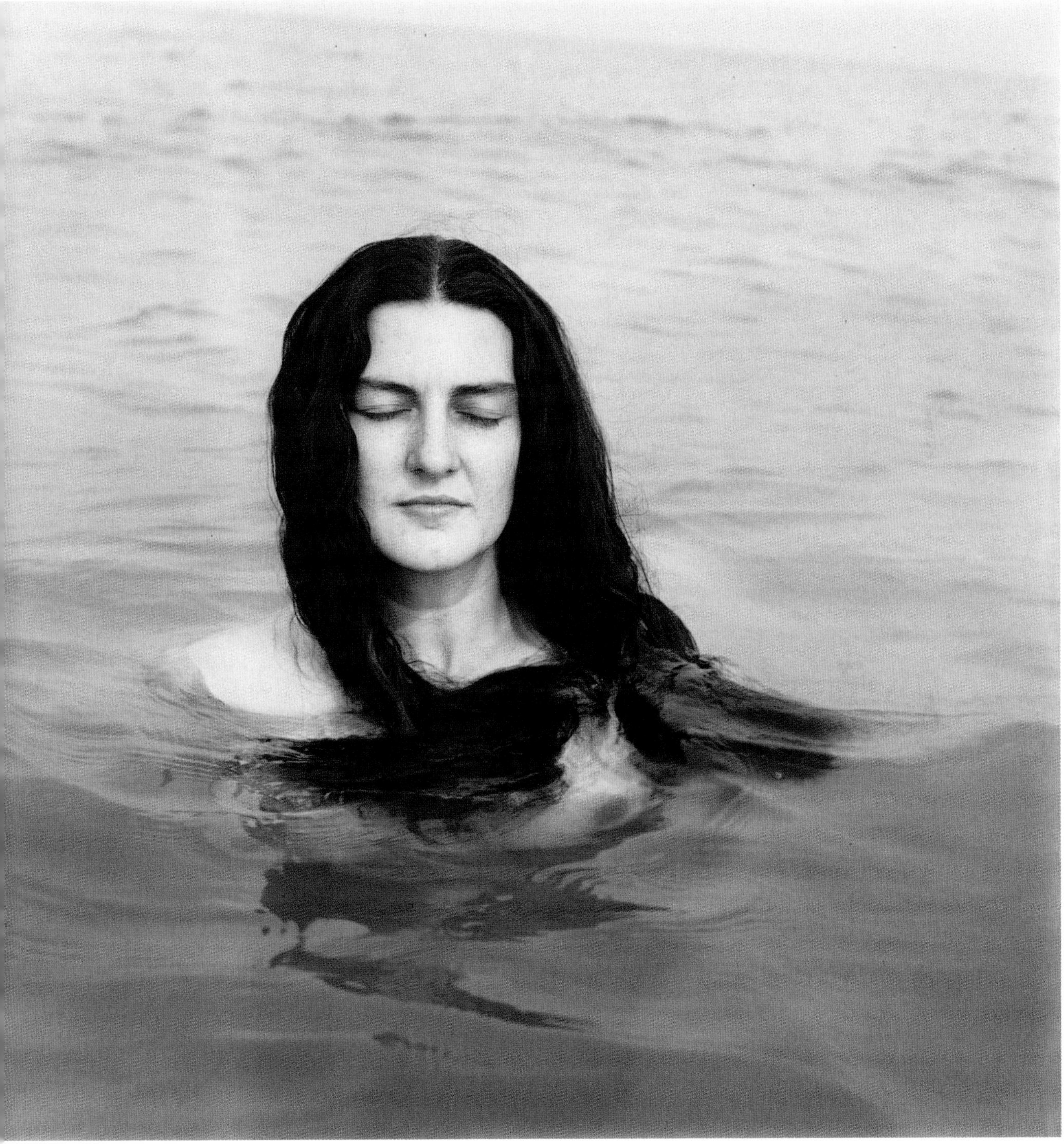

Paul Strand

Young Boy, Gondeville, Charente, France 1951

Paul Strand was a committed documentary photographer and his portraits are often direct and visually arresting. The subjects are presented to the camera in a straightforward way that emphasizes their character without resorting to visual effects of light or position. Strand's subjects were mostly ordinary people and he once remarked: "I like to photograph people who have strength and dignity in their faces; whatever life has done to them." A straight-on shot with the subject's shoulders parallel to the camera often makes a flat, dull image that looks like a passport picture. However, it can be very powerful if used well, as here, where its direct style can be confrontational, demanding the attention of the viewer. The young man's eyes burn out of the frame, staring back at us over the decades as freshly as when the image was taken. The photograph has a strong esthetic impact as a study in texture and tone: the interplay between the skin, clothing, and grain of the wooden door is beautifully rendered in the soft light. Strand recognized the difficulty of making portraits: "It means you must almost bring the presence of that person photographed to other people in such a way that they don't have to know that person personally, but that they are still confronted with a human being that they won't forget. That's a portrait." Strand's powerful character study appeared in a book he collaborated on with writer and poet Claude Roy about life in rural France, entitled *La France de profil*. The book combines Strand's portraits and landscapes with essays, handwritten poems, and notes by Roy in a lyrical, poetic homage to a way of life and a deep meditation on a sense of place.

> **"The decision as to when to photograph, the actual click of the shutter, is partly controlled from the outside, by the flow of life, but it also comes from the mind and heart of the artist. The photograph is his vision of the world and expresses, however subtly, his values and convictions."** Paul Strand

Paul Strand (American, 1890–1976) was a photographer and film-maker who helped establish photography as an art form in the 20th century. His first photography teacher was the renowned documentary photographer Lewis Hine (see p.234), from whom he developed a strong commitment to social issues and the potential for reform in his work. Hine introduced him to Alfred Stieglitz and the other Photo-Secessionists, and Strand produced a series of abstract still lives and views of New York. He also developed a passion for experimental documentary film, collaborating with Charles Sheeler on the short film *Manhattan* (1920), which captured the vibrancy of the metropolis. Strand, although never officially a member of the Communist Party, was arguably a fellow traveler, and many of his friends and associates were Party members and committed socialists. He was closely associated with Frontier Films, which the US Attorney General declared a "subversive" and "un-American" organization, along with twenty other cultural groups. Strand left the United States in 1949 to live in France, where he spent the rest of his life.

Creative tips and techniques

Strand took his inspiration from the world around him, and sought to find circumstances where he could find a way to express his personal political convictions through the formal language of the camera. Although exercises in composition and esthetics are important in developing your vision, they must be allied with a sense of meaning about the world around you.

Strand emphasized the idea of being in the moment and making the image when inspiration strikes. He also noted that Henri Cartier-Bresson's idea of a "decisive moment" does not always mean a split second, but rather demonstrates a deep connection with the intrinsic form of the subject.

Strand posed his subjects in open shade, a location that is not in direct sunlight, but rather in shade—for example, a north-facing wall where the sun is behind the subject but not backlighting it or shining into the lens. This effect can also be obtained on an overcast or cloudy day. The light is soft and diffuse, with a low contrast range between highlights and shadows, and therefore a high level of tonal detail. A useful rule of thumb is that the larger the light source and the closer it is to the subject, the softer the light, and the smaller the light source and the further away it is, the harder the light. For example, on a cloudy day the light source is relatively close to the subject and very large (the whole sky), whereas on a sunny day the light source is very small and very far away, giving hard shadows with a large difference between light and dark. In the studio, using a softbox close to the subject or a spotlight further away creates the same effect.

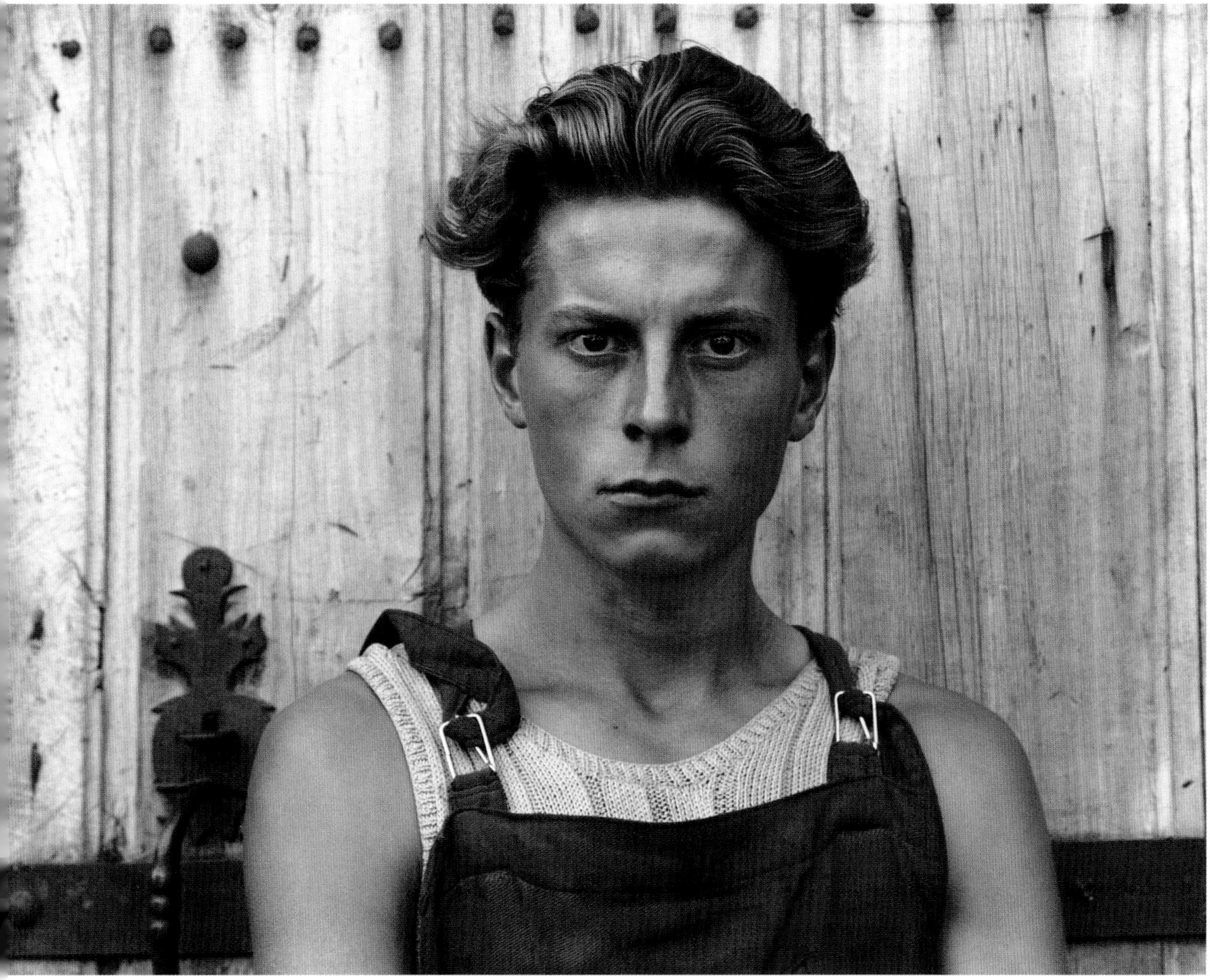

Norman Parkinson

After van Dongen 1959

This striking image is typical of Norman Parkinson's eye for color, dramatic and clean composition, and sense of wit and humor. It also exemplifies his claim that "I like there to be a joke in practically every photo I take. Nobody has the right to make photography boring." The photograph is an object lesson in how to creatively interpret a brief, which here was to show a hat made by celebrated milliner Otto Lucas. The simple shape of the torque is emphasized, as is its dramatic red color, accentuated by the red lips of the model that form the bottom of a compositional triangle with the model's eyes. The way she is looking out of the frame to the left is vital; it gives the image a sense of lightness and dreaminess that would have been destroyed had the model been looking directly at the camera.

The photograph is a homage to a painting by Dutch Fauvist artist Kees van Dongen entitled *The Corn Poppy* (1919), but Parkinson played on the idea by skilful use of depth of field. A similar frame was used in the original *Vogue* magazine spread in 1959, but Parkinson selected this one for the cover of the catalog for his solo exhibition at London's National Portrait Gallery in 1981. Parkinson's compositions make great use of strong, simple shapes, as model Jerry Hall notes: "He had a sense of 'big'—you know, big spaces—he would choose panoramic views and had a great sense of movement across the page. He always enjoyed you moving, doing some kind of a shape, which I really enjoyed, too."

"I like to make people look as good as they'd like to look, and with luck, a shade better."

Norman Parkinson

Norman Parkinson (British, 1913–90) was one of the leading British and international fashion and portrait photographers during his fifty-six-year-long career. Tall, elegantly dressed, and sporting a carefully manicured moustache, "Parks," as he was affectionately known, cut a flamboyant figure and had a larger-than-life personality that was more than a match for that of his celebrity subjects. His approach was to bring out the best in his subjects. He worked extensively for editorial publications, including *Harper's Bazaar* and *Town and Country*, declaring that "a photographer without a magazine behind him is like a farmer without fields." He was especially close to the creative director Grace Coddington at American *Vogue* magazine, who pointed out his humor and freshness, noting that "other photographers didn't have that wit or looseness, they were much more rigid. He was one of the first people to break that whole rigid look in fashion photography." Famously he had a sideline in his cheekily named "Porkinson" sausages, and owned a pig farm on the island of Tobago, his second home.

Creative tips and techniques

This image breaks the rules of focus; to have the background sharp and the subject blurred would conventionally be seen as a mistake. However, in this case, it works brilliantly, creating a powerful effect that makes the model pop out from the elaborate textures of the curtain behind her. The level of blur is carefully controlled, so that the features of the face and the clothing are just visible against the pin-sharp background. A short telephoto lens was used to create this effect, as a wider lens would have had too much depth of field to allow the model to be out of focus against the background, as they are very close together. When you are shooting, don't always focus on the most obvious point in the frame; think carefully about how you might use the focal point more creatively to direct the viewer to key elements in the photograph. Use manual focus, or the focus lock button with autofocus, otherwise the camera will focus on the closest area to the center of the frame. Experiment by lining up a series of subjects in a row, slightly offset from one another. Take a series of images using a wide aperture and focus on each object or person in turn.

Parks was a master at using intense, saturated primary colors in his compositions, often with one color as the dominant theme in a photograph to give it a sense of unity and coherence. He photographed Audrey Hepburn in a pink dress against a luxuriant display of pink flower blossoms, and Jerry Hall in a blue bathing cap, under a blue umbrella and holding a light blue telephone for a *Vogue* cover. Experiment with building a photograph up using a dominant color to tie it together. Then add a complementary or clashing color to see how it affects the result.

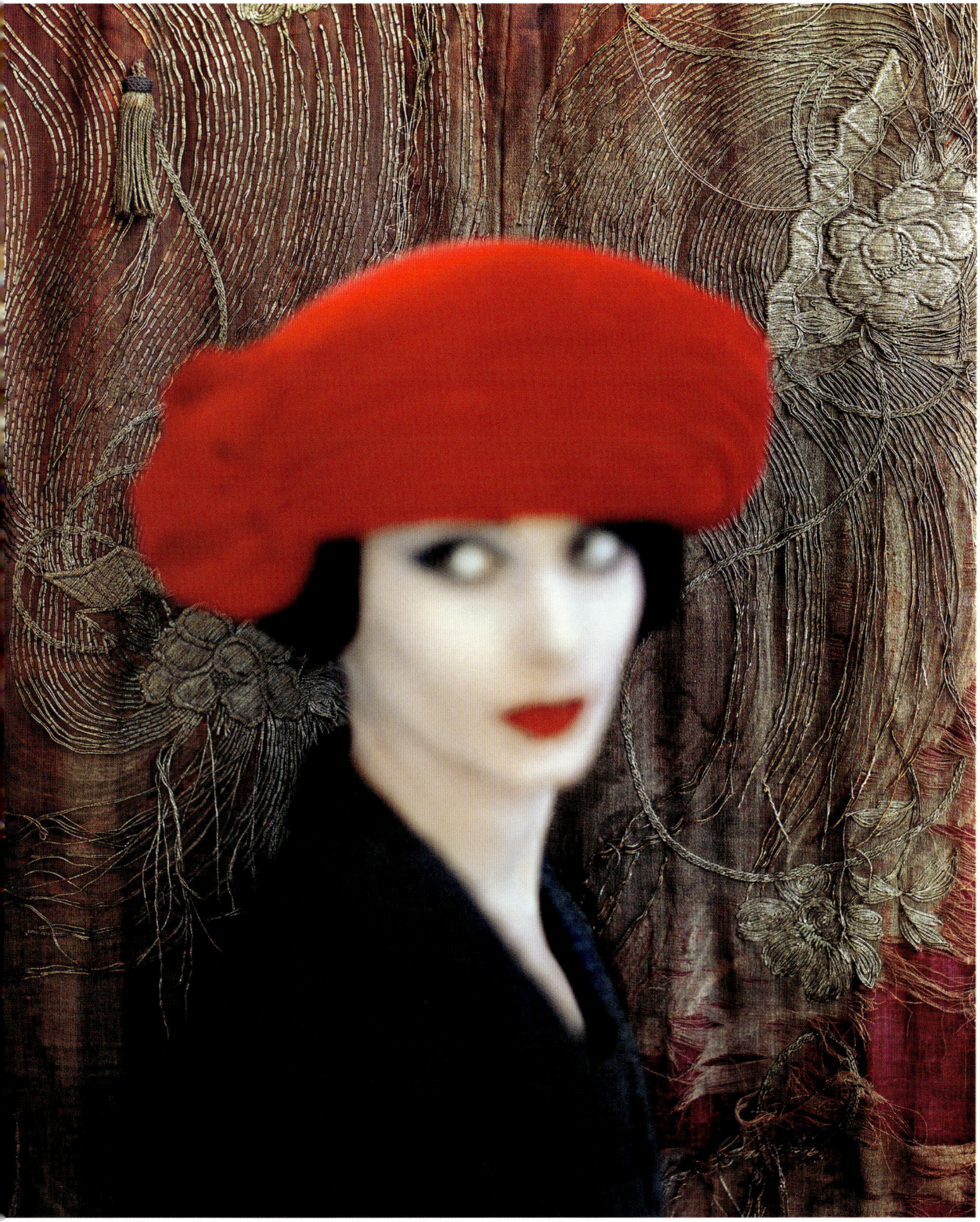

Eve Arnold

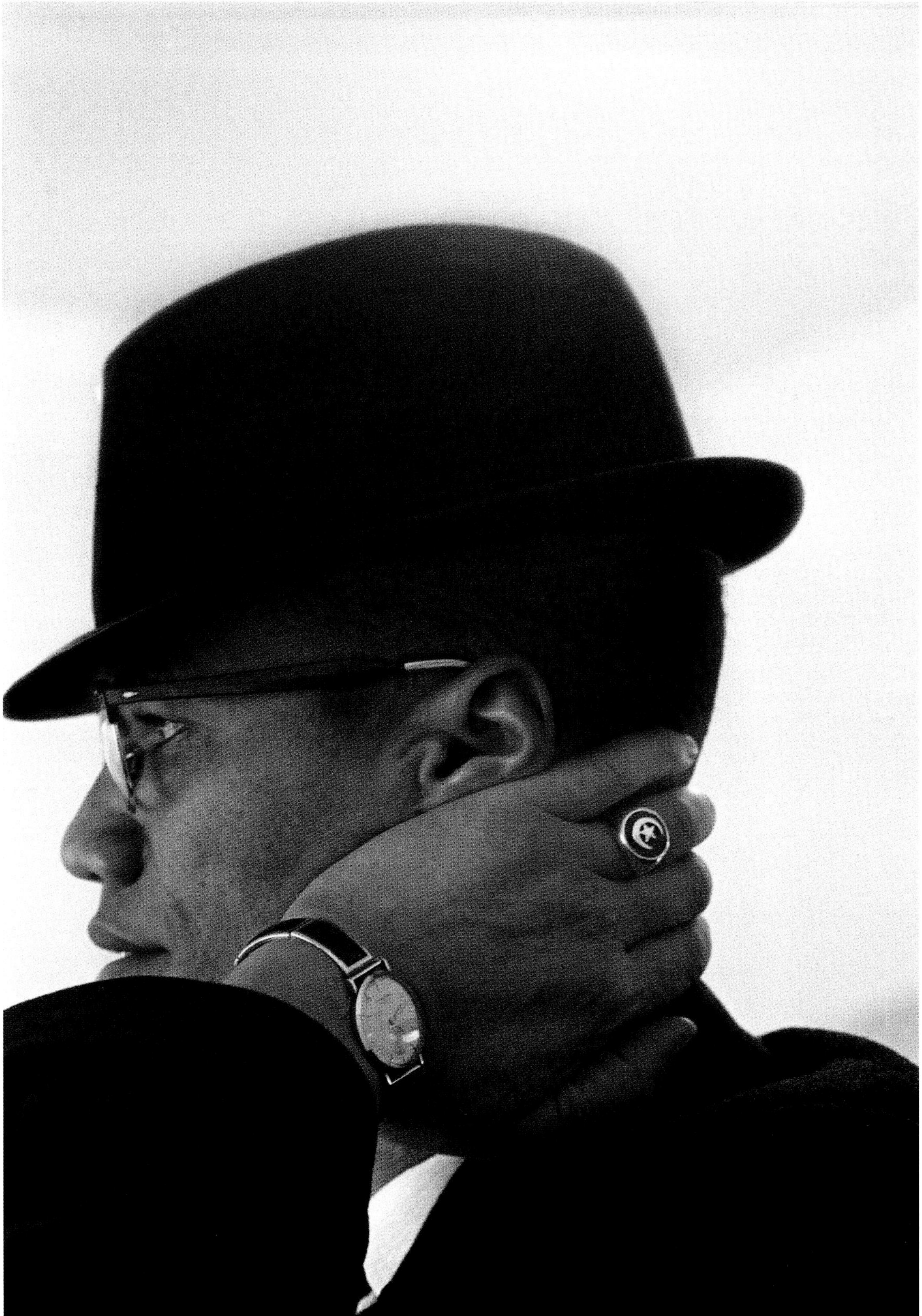

alcolm X during his visit to enterprises owned by ack Muslims 1962

e Arnold was assigned by *Life* magazine to photograph Malcolm n 1961, and she followed him and his Nation of Islam for a year. e remembered him as a "really clever showman, apparently owledgeable about how he could use pictures and the press tell his story." Arnold was frequently the only white person at e rallies she attended, and recounted how after one she found zens of cigarette burns on the back of her sweater where men the crowd had pushed against her. At one rally, in Chicago, d jointly with the American Nazi Party, she photographed leader, George Lincoln Rockwell, who had forged an unlikely ance with the Nation of Islam (and who, like Malcolm X, would assassinated before the decade was over). She recalled that as e took a picture of Rockwell and his supporters, he whispered at r, "I'll make a bar of soap out of you." She retorted, "As long as sn't a lampshade," and kept on shooting.

Arnold's photographs show Malcolm X sympathetically, ming him as a leader and orator who was hugely popular with supporters. She observed how media-literate he was: "I am vays delighted by the manipulation that goes on between a oject and photographer when the subject knows about the nera and how it can best be used to his advantage. Malcolm s brilliant in this silent collaboration." This is an important point, seen in her alliance with Marilyn Monroe: the access given by ubject to his or her life is often offered on the basis that the otographer will in turn be able to present the images in the blic domain. This was typical of Arnold's approach: "What I ve tried to do is involve the people I was photographing. To ve them realize without saying so, that it was up to them to e me whatever they wanted to give me... if they were willing to e, I was willing to photograph."

idn't want to be a woman photographer. That would limit e. I wanted to be a photographer who was a woman, with the world open to my camera." Eve Arnold

Arnold (American, 1912–2012) appeared irst sight an unlikely photojournalist, but she d an incredible tenacity and ability to enter the intimate lives of others. After working at erica's first automated film processing plant Hoboken, New Jersey, in 1946 she took a six-ek photography class with *Harper's Bazaar* art ector Alexey Brodovitch at the New School for cial Research in New York. She joined Magnum otos in 1951; her colleague and friend at the agency, Elliott Erwitt (see p.196), described her as a "tiny, unaggressive kind of person who you wanted to pick up and be nice to, although that was the surface. She had steel and integrity and a work ethic." One of her most celebrated subjects was actress Marilyn Monroe. Arnold wrote in 1987, "I never knew anyone who came close to Marilyn in a natural ability to use both photographer and still camera. She was special in this, and for me there has been no one like her before or after."

Creative tips and techniques

Arnold has placed her subject slightly off-center in the frame, which is unusual for a vertical profile shot. The composition leads the eye from the bottom left corner along the line of the hand, with the ring acting as a full point that directs the eye back again toward the eyes, using the arms of the eyeglasses to direct the viewer. The off-center framing allows Arnold to fractionally slice into the edge of the hat, which has the effect of anchoring the composition, and takes the viewer's journey back down Malcolm X's profile and thence back to his eye again. If the hat did not touch the edge of the frame, the viewer would follow Malcolm X's gaze out of the composition entirely.

Arnold used a telephoto lens for this shot so as to frame Malcolm X's head tightly against a clean background. This is not a posed photograph, but rather the result of the photographer being keenly aware of those moments when the character of a person is visible and focusing in on it. The profile works extremely well as the subject is well known, and Arnold has included the trademark hat and Islamic ring to add extra information to define the subject's character.

A strong vertical image such as this is useful, as it can be published as a single page in a magazine or newspaper story, or even potentially as a cover shot. Arnold framed the image with plenty of white space above Malcolm X's head, allowing room for a magazine masthead. When shooting for editorial publications, make sure you shoot a range of verticals as well as horizontals, and look for potential cover shots that sum up the story in a single strong vertical frame.

Brian Griffin

Siouxsie Sioux 1984

This photograph was made by Brian Griffin for the cover of "Dazzle," a single by British post-punk band Siouxsie and the Banshees. It typifies Griffin's ability to creatively control the studio or location environment, but also his willingness to allow for the serendipity of "mistakes" in his image-making. Griffin is an expert at creating effects in camera; having worked with film in an age before Photoshop, he had to learn how to use light, props and multiple exposures to generate the image he wanted. He is a great improvizer, making one-off, home-made solutions to visual problems—for example, running water down sheets of Plexiglas held in front of the subject to create a rippling effect that makes the subject's face look as if it is melting.

For this image, Griffin used a triple exposure to create the larger-than-life effect of Sioux's eyes against the blackness of her head. Using tungsten lights, Griffin first made an exposure with only the background lit to give a pale gray, with the subject in darkness, creating the dramatic shadow of Sioux's hair. He then wound back the Hasselblad camera film manually, and made a second exposure on the same frame of film, but this time lit the eyes with a spotlight made from a piece of black matt foil to create the complex shape of the beam of light. He also asked Sioux to lean forward from her original position to make her eyes appear bigger in the frame than would be natural. He then accidentally made another exposure, which added the second eye, again in an unnatural position. He acknowledges that this seeming failure in fact made the picture, saying "it ended up being the finest picture in the series." Griffin has useful advice on how to work with a subject and advises: "If you're not a good actor, you'll never make a good portrait photographer. You have to create an atmosphere about yourself that's appropriate to the subject and the environment, so you have to be a bit of a chameleon and a very good manipulator."

Creative tips and techniques

Griffin works with lenses mostly in the range of 80mm to 150mm on a Hasselblad, medium-format, square camera, usually with the camera on a tripod. This puts him at a comfortable distance from the subject where he can fill the frame and compose the image very precisely. He uses the telephoto for its ability to compress the image and bring different elements of the frame together, rather than simply standing further away from the subject. Different focal lengths can give different perspectives to the final photograph, as well as simply allowing you to shoot a subject that is further away. Although he favors fixed lenses, he also likes using zooms. He is very aware of the subtle differences between the optics of different camera systems, and how he can exploit this to get the feel in the final image, suggesting that "a Mamiya lens is more like a woman and a Hasselblad lens is more like a man."

Griffin has a strong personal vision in the way he illuminates his photographs. After leaving college, he created a mini studio in his bedroom, which was lit by a skylight facing north, the classic painter's light. He endlessly experimented with friends as models, posing them with simple props, dressed in suits, mastering how to use light to sculpt and shape the image. Understand how light works inside and you can also apply the same understanding outside.

Although Griffin is a master at creating in-camera effects without using Photoshop, he does use digital as well. He often uses it to get to the point where he is happy with the set-up, then switches to film for the final exposures.

> "At the point of absolute failure arrives success."
> Brian Griffin

Brian Griffin (British, 1948–) is one of Britain's most influential portrait photographers, whose subjects have included Margaret Thatcher, Iggy Pop, and Vivienne Westwood. He redefined the genre of business and industrial portraiture while working for the magazine *Management Today* in the 1980s. Born in Birmingham in 1948, he has shot over 200 album covers, directed dozens of music videos and television commercials, and published eighteen books, including the seminal *Power* (1981). *Life* magazine used his image *A Broken Frame* on the front of a supplement, "The Greatest Photographs of the 80s." Griffin's latest work, *Himmelstrasse* (2015), documents the remains of the railway network that transported Jews to the concentration camps during the Holocaust. Griffin is a master of both light and composition, using precise control of exposure and framing to produce often surreal and complex images. He cites art and music as major influences, and recalls, "I was inspired from my raw beginnings as an editorial photographer to make my photographs powerful and arresting, so I did turn not to photography, but to the art of propaganda…Not necessarily in the content, but in the strength in image construction."

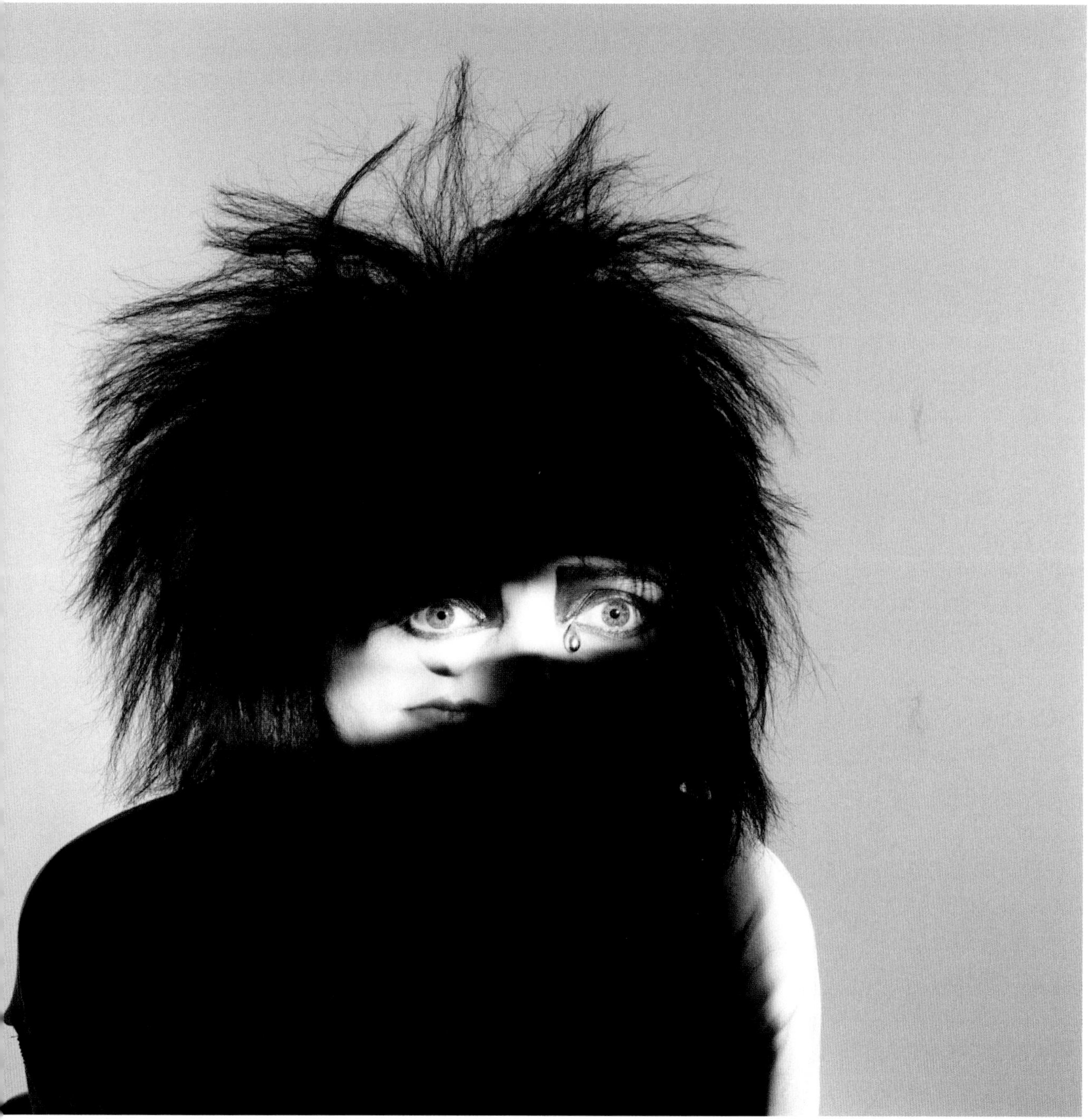

Mary Ellen Mark

Homeless Damm family, for *Life*, Los Angeles area 1987

This poignant portrait was shot while Mary Ellen Mark was on assignment for *Life* magazine. It formed part of a story covering a week in the life of the homeless Damm family, and illustrated the family's day-to-day struggle to keep themselves together. Mark's photograph has echoes of Dorothea Lange's famous migrant mother image from the 1930s (see p.140). Here the couple hold each other tenderly whereas the children gaze out of the car with a seeming look of apprehension about their uncertain future. The magazine article written by Anne Fadiman opened with a description of the family's temporary home, a 1971 Buick Skylark, missing its hood and all the windows on the driver's side: "Most of the upholstery on both seats is gone; when the Damms wear shorts, their legs are indented with red impressions from the springs. The car smells. The interior damage is the work of a pit bull terrier named Runtley, who spends most of his time chained to the right front neck rest. Runtley is a status symbol, a potential weapon, a love object and a form of proof that the Damms, as Dean puts it, 'are something, even if everyone thinks we're nothing'."

When the story was published, *Life* readers donated thousands of dollars, toys, food, and two cars to the family, but sadly when Mark returned to photograph them again in 1995 they had slipped even further into despair. Mark worked in a variety of formats, including color, but chose black and white for most projects. She explored the square format in the 1980s and used it to great effect, especially in her portraits, where she used the balanced shape of the square to give them a more solid, monumental feel than that of the 35mm rectangular format.

> "Photographs can be enigmatic. They sometimes work because of what is included in the frame; and sometimes because of what is not. There's no formula… It's a mysterious process, an endless challenge."
>
> Mary Ellen Mark

Mary Ellen Mark (American, 1940–2015) was a committed documentary photographer. She possessed the ability to enter into the most intimate moments of people's lives and shared a strong affinity with her subjects, who were frequently from among the less fortunate in society. As she explained, she was interested in "people on the edges. I feel an affinity for people who haven't had the best breaks in society. I'm always on their side. I find them more human, maybe. What I want to do more than anything is acknowledge their existence." Mark produced eighteen books during her lifetime, notably *Ward 81* (1979), a series on a women's psychiatric unit at Oregon State Hospital that she encountered while working as a stills photographer on the movie *One Flew Over the Cuckoo's Nest* (1975); *Falkland Road* (1981), on the prostitutes of Bombay; and *Streetwise* (1988), on the homeless youth of Seattle. She was a member of Magnum Photos from 1977 to 1981. Her work has been exhibited in galleries and museums worldwide and widely published in *Rolling Stone*, *The New Yorker*, the *New York Times*, and *Vanity Fair*.

Creative tips and techniques

Mark was adept at gaining her subjects' trust and then being able to work with them over extended periods to document their lives. Her approach was direct and straightforward, with no subterfuge or pretence: "You instantly have to start to work, to let them know that you're there to take pictures." She also noted that you have to be clear to yourself about why you are photographing; any doubt will be recognized by your subject, who will only trust you if you are confident.

For Mark, the formal qualities of the image were only relevant in as far as they added to the emotional content. She always asked herself, "What does this picture mean? What's the best place to put my camera? Do I have anything extra in the picture, things in the background that will distract? Am I in the basic position that will give the essential things for this picture, but not too much?" Her photographs are immediate and simply but powerfully composed without any obvious artifice. Try to refine your vision so that the esthetics you use are there to convey meaning, and not simply a game of visual gymnastics.

Mark recalled how for one trip to India she packed four Nikon FM2s with seven lenses; four Leicas with five lenses; four Hasselblads with six lenses; a Polaroid SX70; six light meters and assorted flashes; and 1,000 rolls of black-and-white Kodak TriX film. To explain this apparent excess, she argued that she always brought backups. Relying on only one camera body and one lens could be potentially catastrophic if you are shooting on an extended trip away. Always try to have a backup body and lens when you travel.

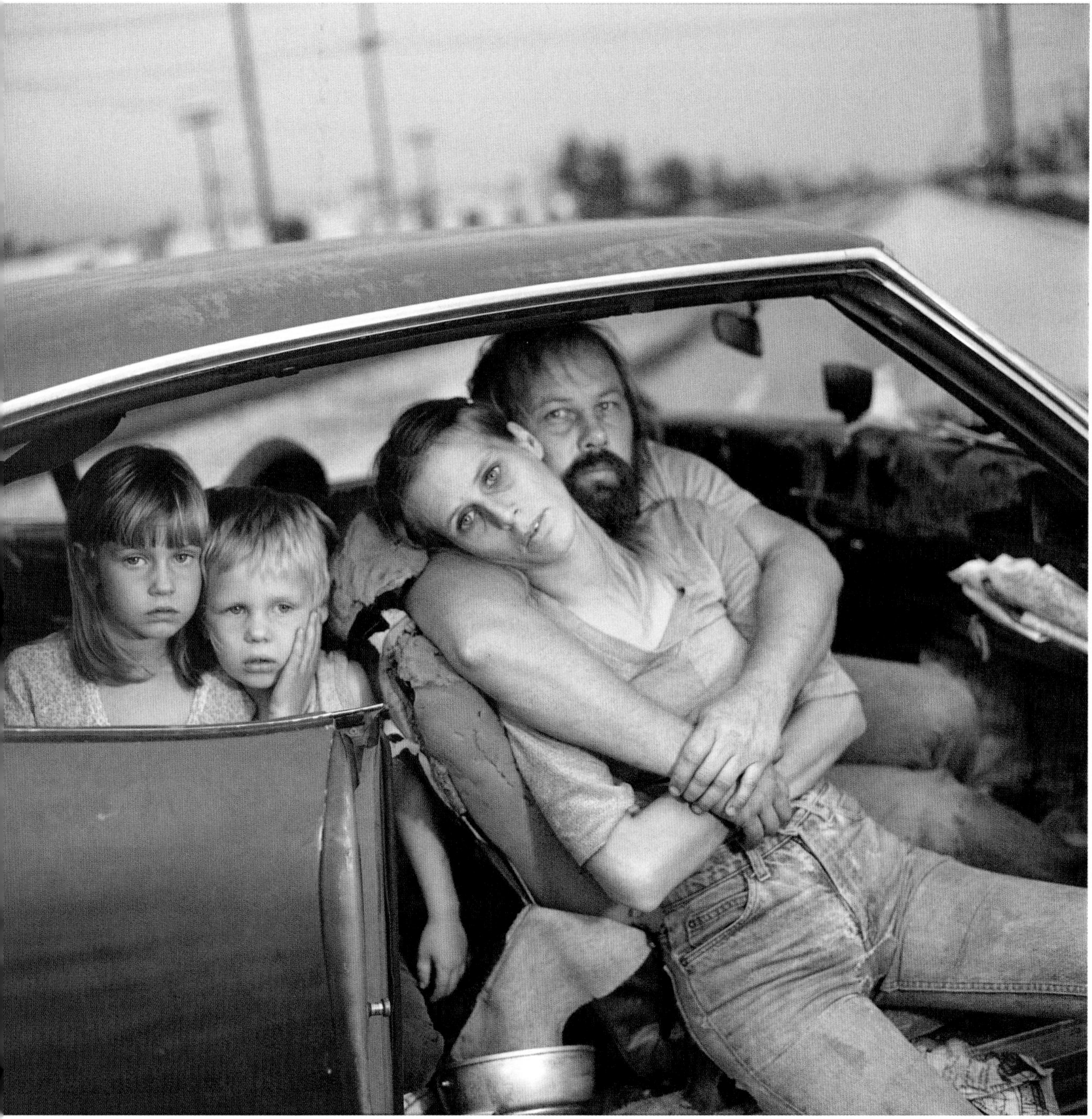

Bruce Gilden

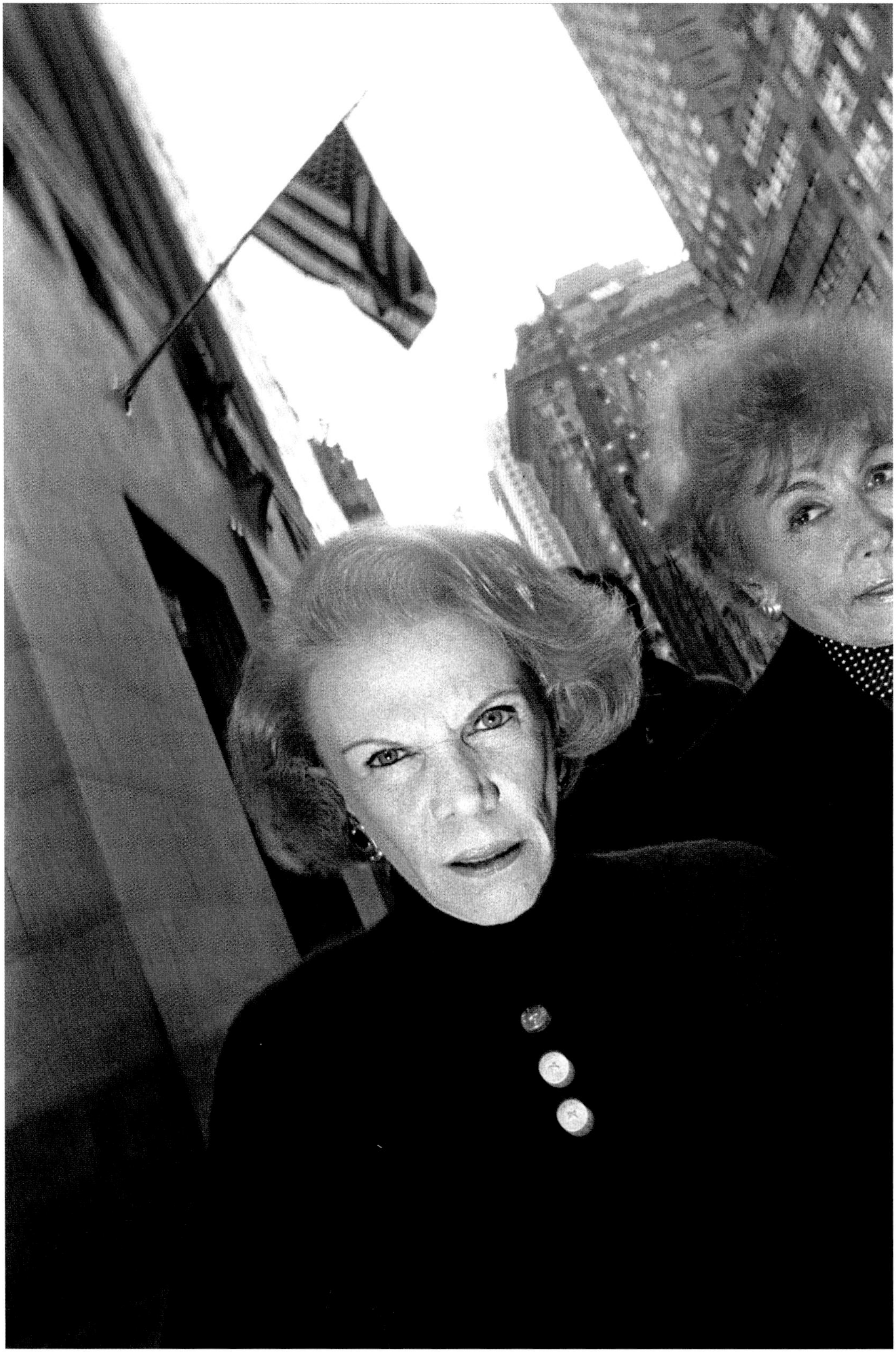

›w York City. Woman walking on Fifth Avenue
92, from "Facing New York"

ıce Gilden's "Facing New York," from which this image is taken, ıs the result of his endless prowling of the streets of Manhattan ›king for distinctive characters that summed up the energy and › of the teeming metropolis. He works instinctively, constantly in ›tion, dancing in and around the crowds until he spots a face that connects with. He notes: "I am showing a slice of life in New York y that in several years won't be there any longer…people are ıding to look more alike, dress more alike…and it's making it ıgher to find people to photograph.'"

As Gilden's work has evolved, the physical proximity between n and his subject has become narrower: "I'm known for taking :tures very close, and the older I get, the closer I get." His rlier work in Coney Island represented more conventional street otography, shot from a middle distance and choreographing veral elements in the frame, whereas his most recent work ›ws portraits in which the frame is completely filled with faces. he puts it, "My old photographs I would say were like stage :s: the viewer looks at it and it's like looking at something on › stage, from outside. Whereas now, I put the viewer at the nter. He becomes part of the picture." Gilden accepts that no ıtter how in tune with his surroundings he is, there is always ıt serendipitous quality of the image that can reveal hidden ths and make or break a photograph. He explains: "I don't look because I'm busy looking for people to photograph…I hand ld the flash in my left hand and when I see something, I take it. nerally, I notice things in my pictures that I didn't notice when I s taking [them]. I describe those things as lucky accidents that ıke a picture into a good photograph."

ove the people I photograph. I mean, they're my friends. ve never met most of them or I don't know them at all, yet rough my images I live with them." Bruce Gilden

ıce Gilden (American, 1946–) spent his early ırs in Brooklyn, New York, where he developed longstanding love affair with the streets, ing them his "second home." He maintains t he "always liked the dark side of life." His rk has revolved around the chaotic energy of street ever since, searching for that magic ›ting interaction with a passerby, a face in the wd, that sparks a connection. He describes y he was attracted to the streets: "as a child I looked out of my second storey window at a very active street life in Brooklyn [. . .] I am more comfortable going to areas where there are crowds of people and I do not need permission; in other words I can just start photographing." Gilden's first major work centered on Coney Island, which he began photographing in 1969. He has since produced books on Haiti, the Japanese *yakuza,* and horseracing in Ireland. His latest work shows close-up faces of the underprivileged.

Creative tips and techniques

For his street photography, Gilden works mostly with a 28 mm wide-angle lens on a Leica rangefinder. This forces him to work in very close proximity to his subjects, often shooting from less than 3 feet (1 meter) from their faces as he moves through the street. Working this close can feel uncomfortable, but the wide angle can allow you to look as if you are photographing something else further away. To learn how to shoot in crowded situations, pick a busy shopping street and walk up and down it, looking out for characters as you go. Try to keep constantly in motion, raising your camera quickly to shoot only at the last possible moment. This will help develop your visual reflexes. A good tip is to use a wide-angle lens and a small aperture of ,say, f11 or f16. This will give you depth of field so that you can set your camera to manual focus at a distance of around 3–6 feet (1–2 meters) and then shoot without focusing the camera every time. This will speed up your shooting and you will not have to worry about losing time to focus every shot. Be aware that many digital cameras have a time lag between pressing the shutter and actually making the exposure, and build this into timing your shots.

Gilden usually uses a flash, even in daylight, to pick out his subjects. He balances the light from the flash with the available light in the scene, normally setting it so that the power of the flash either matches the correct aperture for the ambient light or overpowers it, making the background darker so that the subject stands out more, as the power from the flash falls off quickly and therefore does not light the background. The flash freezes any motion, giving a dramatic effect that can make features appear exaggerated.

Harry Borden

Richard E. Grant 1997

This striking portrait was commissioned for an article about British cult film *Withnail and I* (1987), in which Grant starred. Harry Borden set up a temporary studio in the actor's house, using a black backdrop mounted on telescopic poles, and began by shooting with a ring flash mounted around the lens of the camera. However, he tried a variation on this and placed the flash below the lens to light the face. Normally, such a position would be unflattering for the subject, as it creates a very unnatural direction for the light to come from, giving a spooky, Halloween-like effect. With Grant, however, it was a perfect way to use the light expressively to reveal his character. Borden recalls it "was perfect because he has such an electric smile and great teeth, and it brought out the devilment and mischief in his face, like a gothic gargoyle."

Borden has developed his own distinctive visual style in which he responds to the environment in which he and the sitter find themselves. Visually, he looks for a way to use the physicality of the location to help determine the nature of the image. As he puts it, "any space has a visual tension and it is just a question of being open to it." Borden's ability to put his sitters at ease has resulted in numerous beautifully composed and insightful portraits. He has become more spontaneous as his career and confidence have grown, noting that "I don't like doing big production numbers with lots of stylists, I much prefer going to someone's house to do a shoot on my own."

"The qualities that you bring to a portrait are multi-faceted. It is about observing people, composition, and light: these are all the things that make a great photograph as well as creating a rapport with the individual." Harry Borden

Harry Borden (American, 1965–) has established himself as one of Britain's most sought-after portrait photographers, shooting up to 150 commissioned works a year for editorial clients. Borden has a wonderful ability to connect with something in the character of his subjects and relate that to the environment and spaces in which they are photographed. He explains: "What I do is photograph spaces I find interesting and put people in them, and they then become little stages for people to be themselves and explore what happens. Rather than hammering away at one idea, I will always try and keep things loose." His longer-term personal work includes a project on single-parent fathers and portraits of survivors of the Holocaust.

Creative tips and techniques

Borden regards his work as an interactive process; both he and his subject need to collaborate to make the best possible image for both of them. He feels that the relationship with subjects is crucial to the making of a great image. He says the portraitist needs to create an atmosphere in which sitters are more open to the camera and he is happy for them to have an input. An interesting technique he uses with celebrities is to ask them to think of nothing at all; he explains that for famous people "absence of thought" is interesting, because suddenly they are not giving you anything and it is a betrayal of the celebrity world they are locked into.

He carries a small portfolio of his portraits with him on shoots and uses this at the start of the session to help break the ice and introduce his work. This usually helps convince the sitter to collaborate with him on his ideas. The folio almost always wins the person over, but he does also say that he will not make sitters do something they don't want to. This is excellent advice. Even keeping a selection of images on your phone or iPad is a fantastic way to show your work at a moment's notice.

Borden keeps his equipment simple, mostly using the standard 50mm lens and occasionally a wider angle 35mm. He feels that this is a more authentic way to work, as telephoto and wide lenses can overwhelm the scene.

Borden switched to digital for most of his work, replacing the medium-format cameras he had used previously. He relishes the fluidity and ease of movement that the 35mm digital gives him.

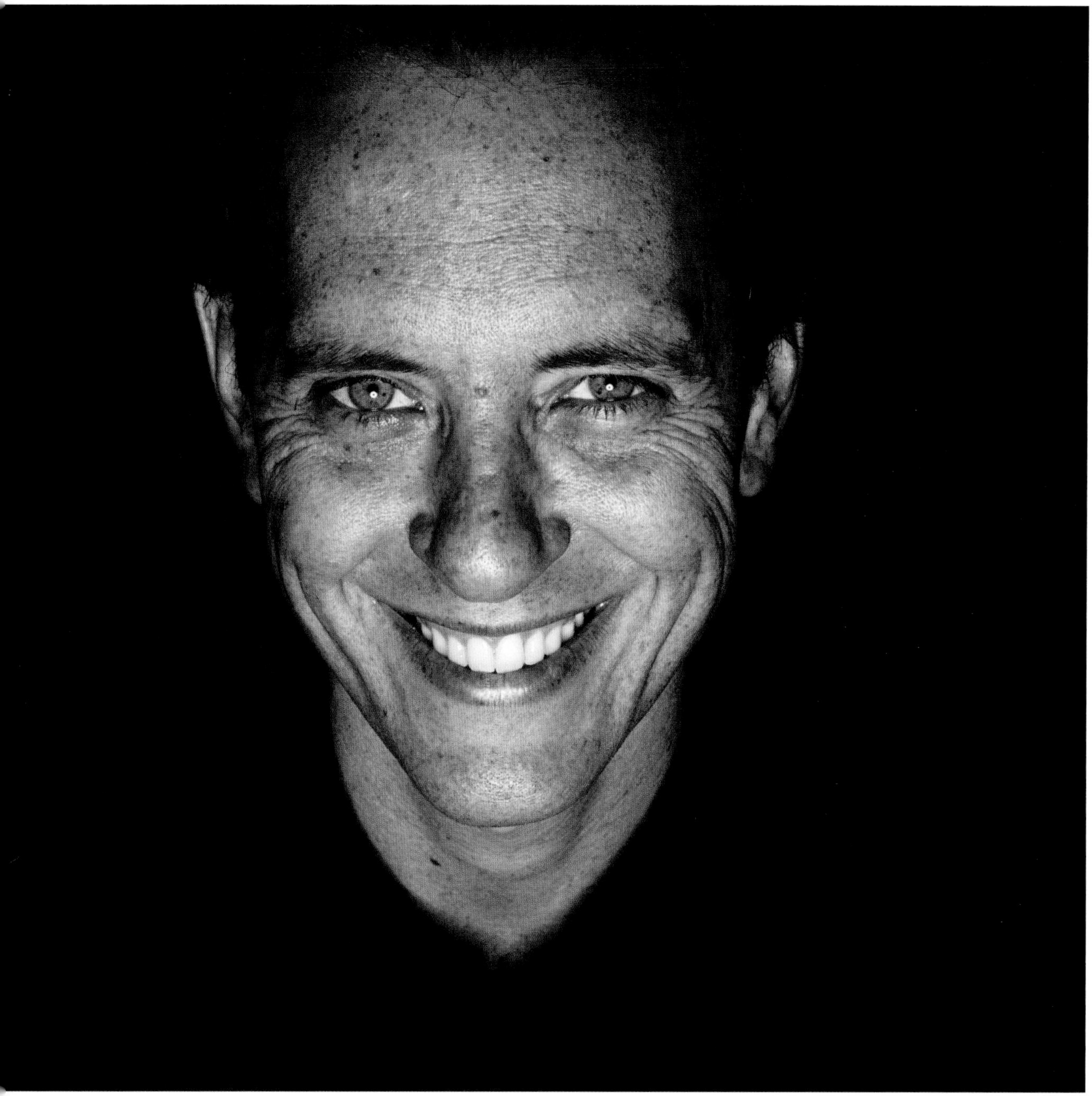

Bodie

S

The human figure is perhaps one of the most fluid sites of photography. It can be a clothes horse, an exercise in esthetic form, an ethnographic document, a celebratory portrait, a character study, or the location of social concerns. The relationship of the body to its environment has provided one of the essential enquiries of photography: how can the physical context and surroundings of an image help us to understand its human subject? Although the face on its own can provide a psychological study, the addition of the body brings a new set of associations to help the viewer determine who the person is and why they are worthy of attention. The sculptural form of the body—its pose, posture, and bearing—represents a rich realm of visual opportunities: it adapts itself to location, at times emphasizing the awkwardness of the human form, at others accentuating its beauty. The human body also offers the potential for comparative study: aligning people of a similar ethnic, social, or professional background will highlight similarities and discrepancies between them; alternatively, a gallery of archetypes can suggest common traits that are shared across a section of society. The direct confrontation between the viewer and the person photographed—presented full length and related to their surroundings—is arguably the most potent way in which a photograph can bridge the gap between audience and subject. The act of photography preserves the image of the person depicted from the past and projects their presence into the present and the future. The body is a site of experience, containing a personal history that also describes broader social forces.

August Sander

Young farmers 1914, from "Face of our Time"

It is hard to look at August Sander's photograph and not read into it the knowledge of German history and imagine what role the subjects might have played in it. Research now suggests that the three men were in fact workers at a coalmine rather than farmers. They came from the rural area of the Westerwald on the borders of the federal states of Rhineland-Palatinate, Hesse, and North Rhine-Westphalia, the region where Sander was himself born, and it seems that he knew the families of these men and had photographed them previously. As such, they typify his sense of connection with his subjects. The three youths encountered Sander on their way to a dance when he asked them to pose for him. The incongruity of their slightly ill-fitting suits, canes, and hats against the muddy track highlights the urbanization of the countryside, as such fine attire would not have been available to them perhaps a generation earlier. The similarity of their stances and clothing marks them as a unified group, but each has unique traits, discernible in the jaunt of a hat, the angle of a cane, or an individual gaze. The two men on the right are brothers, Ewald and August Klein, whereas the young man on the left with the cigarette is Otto Krieger. All three are from the generation that would fight in World War I; August Klein was killed on the Western Front and Otto Krieger was wounded twice.

Sander once explained how the photograph emerged from the act of looking, "People often ask me how I came up with the idea of creating this work. Seeing, observing, and thinking—that answers the question. Nothing seemed more appropriate to me than to use photography to produce an absolutely true-to-nature picture of our age." *Young farmers* was the sixth plate in Sander's "Face of our Time" series in 1929, and appeared again in the first volume of his epic but incomplete "People of the 20th century."

> **"Pure photography allows us to create portraits which render their subjects with absolute truth . . . if we can create portraits of subjects that are true, we thereby in effect create a mirror of the times."** August Sander

August Sander (German, 1876–1964) is one of the most important portrait photographers in the history of the medium. Originally a studio photographer, he advertised his services in 1907 by promising to "produce expressive, characteristic likenesses that completely represent the nature of the subject." His monumental project "People of the 20th Century" documented the German people in the interwar years. His philosophy was that "[w]e know that people are formed by the light and air, by their inherited traits, and their actions. We can tell from appearance the work someone does or does not do; we can read in his face whether he is happy or troubled." Sander created a typological catalog of hundreds of his fellow Germans, categorizing them into seven groups: "The Farmer", "The Skilled Tradesman", "The Woman", "Classes and Professions", "Artists", "The City", and "The Last People". Sander was criticized by the Nazi regime as being un-Aryan and the plates from his book were destroyed in 1936. Sander saved his negatives; however, his studio was destroyed in a bombing raid in 1944.

Creative tips and techniques

Many of Sander's photographs have the appearance of chance encounters, with subjects posed on the road. Street portraiture can be an excellent way of building up a portfolio of portraits, and can help you to develop a keen eye for what makes a person photogenic and worthy of documenting. When shooting portraits outdoors avoid having the subject looking into the sun, as they often squint and close their eyes, which is unflattering. It is better to have the sun over their shoulder or to the side, and use flash or a reflector to fill the shadows, or find a location where the light is more diffuse.

Apart from the headshot, the environmental portrait is one in which the subject is placed in a scene that says something about their life or job. It generally involves using props or objects to tell us about the person, or using a location that explains who they are. Sander's work exemplifies this genre; he depicted a pastry chef in his kitchen with a mixing bowl, a bricklayer with his hod, and a Wehrmacht (German army) soldier in his uniform. It can be difficult if the person you have to photograph works in an office, but look for interesting light or furniture, or an unusual angle, or frame them in a doorway or window.

Choosing a theme for a series of portraits is an excellent way to produce work that has coherence and meaning. Pick a connecting them—for example, an occupation, hobby, or physical characteristic—and make a series of portraits across which the viewer can begin to make connections and contrasts between the different subjects. Keeping a consistent formal strategy—say close-up head shots—will give the work a coherent look.

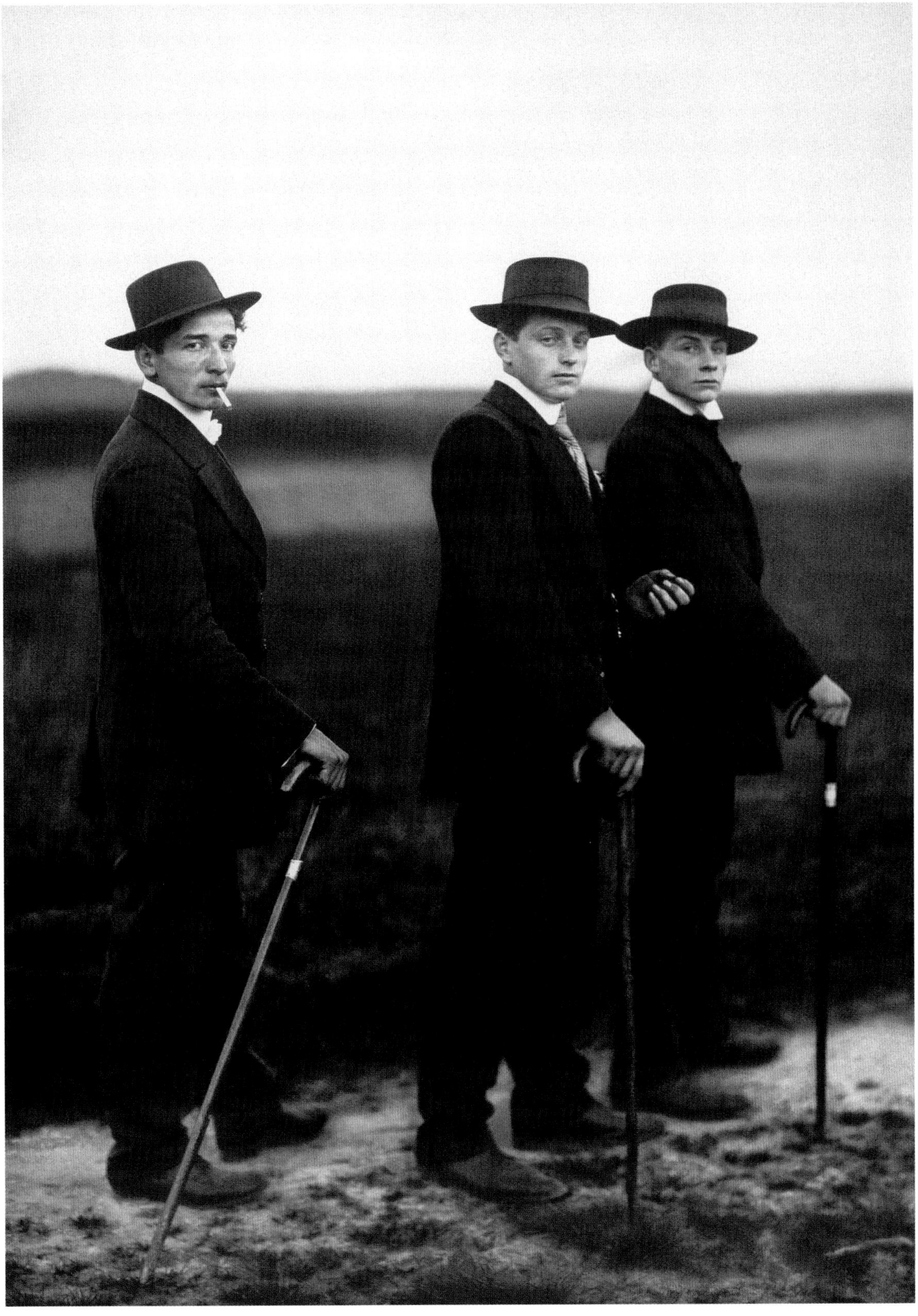

Dorothea Lange

Dorothea Lange (American, 1895–1965) had a difficult childhood; at the age of seven she contracted polio, which left her with a permanent limp, and her father abandoned the family when she was twelve years old. Yet, she used these experiences to strengthen her character, and said that her illness "formed me, guided me, instructed me, helped me, and humiliated me." She began working as a portrait photographer in San Francisco, and in 1933 made a powerful study of poverty with *White Angel Breadline*, which showed a solitary figure turned away from the crowd at a soup kitchen. Soon after, she was invited to join the Resettlement Administration, later called the Farm Security Administration (FSA), which documented poverty across the United States. In 1945, Lange was invited by Ansel Adams (p.50) to join the first fine art photography department at the California School of Fine Arts. In 1952, she cofounded the influential magazine *Aperture*.

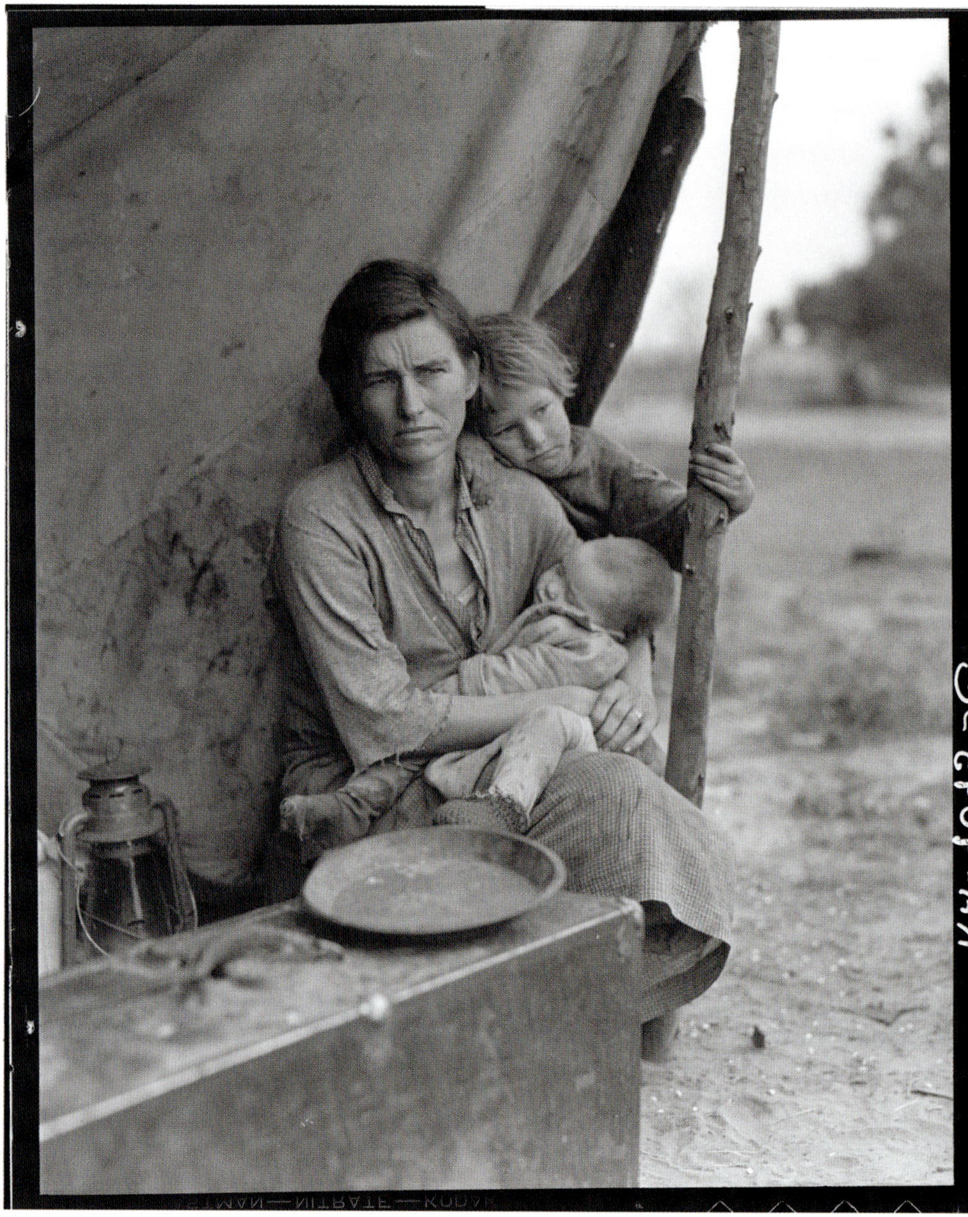

Creative tips and techniques

Lange's images were taken during the Great Depression. She described how she was able to produce such intimate images of people in difficult situations and her words highlight her patient approach: "so often it's just sticking around and being there, remaining there, not swooping out in a cloud of dust: sitting down on the ground with people, letting children look at your camera with their dirty, grimy little hands, and putting their fingers on the lens, and you just let them, because you know that if you will behave in a generous manner, you are apt to receive it." Lange also believed that some photographers tended to give up too easily, and argued that you should "pick a theme and work it to exhaustion . . . the subject must be something you truly love or truly hate."

Lange worked the situation depicted in these images using her 4 x 5 inch large-format camera. She shot from a variety of distances; firstly framing the family in a wide shot that showed the whole tent and their surroundings; she then moved in closer and closer, intensifying the composition each time until she made the image on the right, known as *Migrant Mother*, which has become an iconic photograph. She cropped in tightly on

Migrant agricultural worker's family 1936

These images are from a series Dorothea Lange made of a poor sharecropper family who were living at the side of the road in a makeshift tent in Nipomo, California. Lange was working for the Farm Security Administration (FSA) at the time and described how she approached the woman, Florence Thompson: "I saw and approached the hungry and desperate mother, as if drawn by a magnet. I do not remember how I explained my presence or my camera to her, but I do remember she asked me no questions. I made five exposures, working closer and closer from the same direction. I did not ask her name or her history. She told me her age, that she was thirty-two. She said that they had been living on frozen vegetables from the surrounding fields, and birds that the children killed. She had just sold the tires from her car to buy food. There she sat in that lean-to tent with her children huddled around her, and seemed to know that my pictures might help her, and so she helped me. There was a sort of equality about it." Lange recognized the gravity of the situation and showed her images to a San Francisco newspaper, which published an article about the migrant workers' conditions. This led to federal authorities sending immediate aid to prevent starvation and further distress. These photographs sum up Lange's approach. She strove to make images that would provoke deep engagement with her subjects, and argued that "this benefit of seeing . . . can come only if you pause a while, extricate yourself from the maddening mob of quick impressions ceaselessly battering our lives, and look thoughtfully at a quiet image . . . the viewer must be willing to pause, to look again, to meditate."

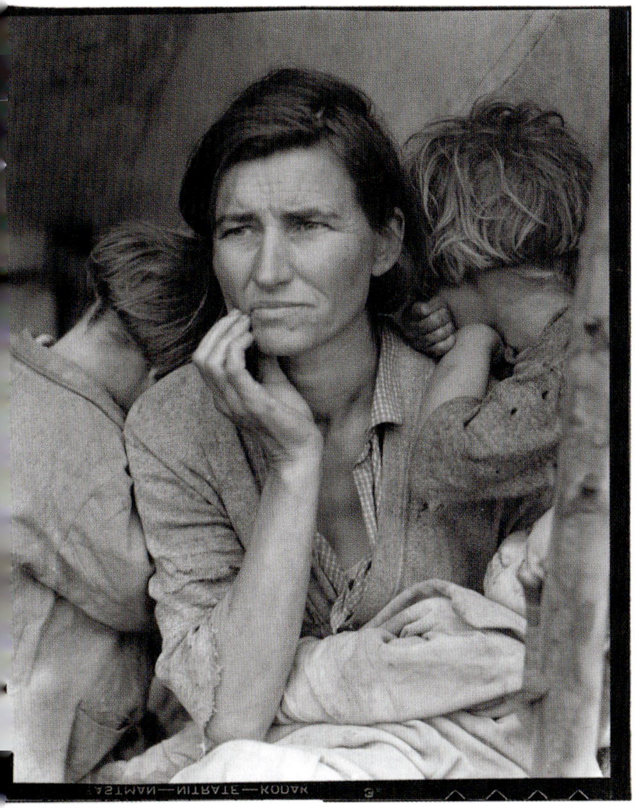

ɔrence Thompson's face with the faces of r children obscured and concentrated the ɿotional power of the photograph on the ɔther's mournful expression. Arguably, wever, the composition of the image on ɘ left is also very intense, as it contains ɔre informational content about the plight the family. The lines of the suitcase in ɘ foreground and the plate balanced top of it lead the viewer's eye into the me and signify the transient nature of the family's life. However, the child's gaze in this particular image leads the eye out of the frame, and suggests the wider world beyond the camp and its lack of empathy. What makes one image more successful than another has often been the subject of fierce debate, but Lange's series demonstrates how the final image that becomes most famous is in reality simply one of a set that are all equally worthy of attention.

"A camera is a tool for learning how to see without a camera."

Dorothea Lange

Horst P. Horst

Irina Baronova, ballerina star of the movie *Florian*, wearing a striped Brigance bathing suit with separate long skirt 1940

Horst P. Horst's sensibilities as a modernist architect are apparent in his compositions, which skilfully use light and shade in an almost physical way. In this image, the deep, black shadows have a tangible weight and solidity, creating substantial blocks contrasting with the triangular highlights. His images are esthetic constructions that create glamor and structure, and he claimed: "I don't think photography has anything remotely to do with the brain. It has to do with eye appeal." Horst has constructed this image almost entirely from light, with the careful use of spotlights to selectively highlight certain areas and throw others into silhouette. To build up an image such as this demands a high level of precise control over the direction and quality of the light. The set is carefully constructed to accentuate the composition, and Horst worked with a team of set builders and technicians for days on many of his shoots. Like many of the *Vogue* photographers of the time, he worked with a large-format view camera, as the magazine's owner Condé Montrose Nast insisted on the highest image quality for the publication. Working with an assistant to load the film sheets, Horst would usually stand by the camera directing the shoot rather than looking through the ground glass screen. However, his dramatic style did have its detractors, as obscuring the model's faces and the clothes in dark shadow made it problematic to display the clothes clearly. Indeed, Edna Chase, then editor-in-chief at *Vogue*, seemingly hated Horst's signature *chiaroscuro* lighting, writing in a memo in 1937 that "I have been lecturing Horst about the lack of light in his photography. We have simply got to overcome this desire on the part of our photographers to shroud everything in deepest mystery."

> "Fashion is an expression of the times. Elegance is something else again."
>
> Horst P. Horst

Horst P. Horst (German-American, 1906–99) had an extraordinary career spanning six decades, during which he worked for *Vogue* magazine, in both its French and American incarnations. Along with Richard Avedon and Irving Penn, he was one of the 20th century's greatest fashion photographers. Having originally trained as an architect, after leaving Germany he worked at the studio of the master of modernist architecture, Le Corbusier, in Paris. However, a meeting with Charles Hoyningen-Huene took his life in a new direction toward photography, and he was introduced to Cecil Beaton (see p.144), and then to Coco Chanel, whom he dubbed "the queen of the whole thing." Fleeing the rise of Nazism in Europe, he moved to New York in 1939. He took one of his most famous images, the Mainbocher Corset, just before he left; he recalled: "It was the last photograph I took in Paris before the war. While I was taking it, I was thinking of all that I was leaving behind." The photograph later became the inspiration for the video for Madonna's song "Vogue." He became a naturalized US citizen in 1943, adopting his signature credit—"Horst."

Creative tips and techniques

Horst meticulously prepared his shoots. He built up images using a mix of structural elements and carefully directed lighting to generate a sense of plasticity and three dimensionality. He worked with "hot lights" rather than flash, which allowed him to see exactly where the light was falling and make minute changes to the position of his models and props. The drawback to hot lights is that exposure times are long and it is hard to capture movement, which is why, in most of Horst's work, the models are posed like statues. He used multiple spotlights and floodlights, precisely controlling the light falling from them with snoots (a tube-like object fitted over a studio light to direct the beam of light) and flags, and often mounted the lights from the ceiling to create pools of light coming down on the model. If you have access to a studio or can set up a temporary space, experiment with spotlights to light the subject, using them to sculpt the light to create dramatic shapes made from the contrast between light and dark. You can make a snoot from a camera flash by either setting the zoom function on the flash head to telephoto but shooting with a wider lens or by making a tube from card or metal foil to put over the flash head.

Horst planned out his shots in advance, making extensive drawings in his sketchbooks. This allowed him to direct set builders and assistants to work in advance of the model coming into the studio. This can be a useful exercise to develop your ability to previsualize a shot. Try to sketch out the composition and work out where to position your lighting in advance, then modify it once it is set up. This will save time in the studio and increase your confidence when working with a model.

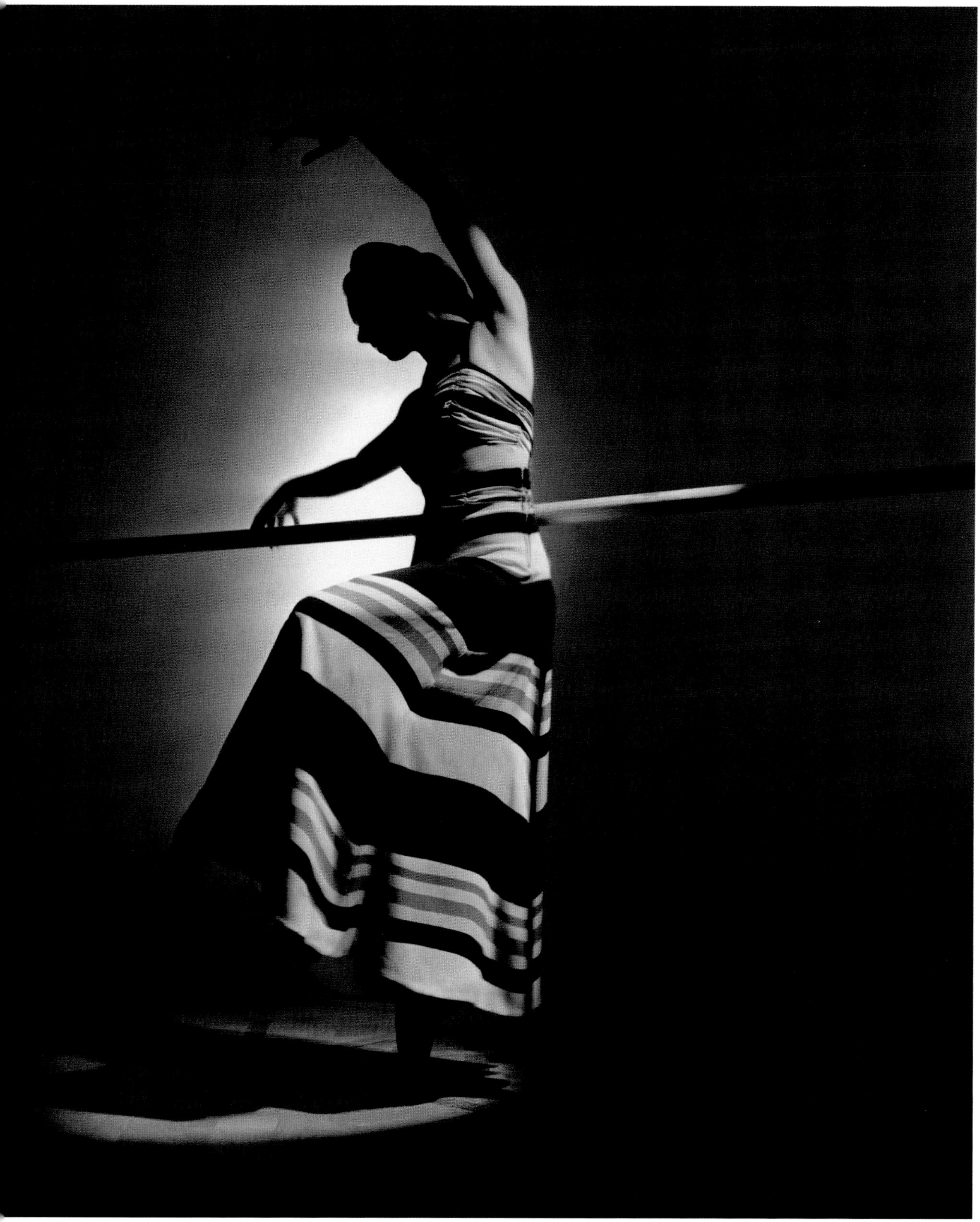

Cecil Beaton

A Royal Navy sailor on board HMS *Alcantara* uses a portable sewing machine to repair a signal flag during a voyage to Sierra Leone 1941

In 1940, Cecil Beaton was commissioned by the British Ministry of Information as a war artist to help produce propaganda to raise morale. His orders were clear: to create the most dramatic images possible to help the war effort. Beaton was regarded as a popular public figure whose photographs carried the cachet of his society connections and the fashion magazines he worked for. Frustrated with his inability to contribute more directly to the war effort, he leapt at the chance. Beaton shared an affinity with the servicemen he was tasked to portray, and he felt compelled to record their faces in the most heroic way possible, with style and visual flair.

Beaton took this eye-catching image when he was en route to Sierra Leone in 1941 to document fighting in the Middle East. It resonates with the acerbic humor for which he was renowned. The idea of a handsome, muscular sailor working a sewing machine must have appealed greatly to Beaton's sense of style as well to as his appreciation of the absurd nature of war. He took his role as a propagandist seriously, seeking to create heroic images of the men and women who were fighting the war and poignant ones of the civilians who were affected by it. One of his most successful images in this context was that of Eileen Dunne, a three-year-old victim of the German bombing of London, whom he depicted with head bandaged, cuddling a doll. It made the cover of *Life* magazine in September 1940 and raised considerable support for the British war effort across the then-neutral United States.

"Be daring, be different, be impractical, be anything that will assert integrity of purpose and imaginative vision against the play-it-safers, the creatures of the commonplace, the slaves of the ordinary." Cecil Beaton

Cecil Beaton (British, 1904–80) is best known for his fashion photography and society portraits, and for his work as an award-winning set and costume designer for film and theater. From the 1930s he worked as a staff photographer for *Vanity Fair* and *Vogue* magazines, shooting many Hollywood stars. During World War II he became a war photographer, renowned for his pictures of the Blitz. Beaton was the unofficial court photographer of the British royal family; he shot the wedding of the Duke and Duchess of Windsor in 1937, the Queen Mother's portrait in 1939, and Queen Elizabeth II's coronation portrait against the backdrop of Westminster Abbey in 1953.

Creative tips and techniques

Beaton was famously sharp in his observations of his portrait subjects and recorded his cutting analysis of them in his candid diaries. However, this often cruel feel for the contours of the human face and body served him well in understanding how to depict his subjects in the most photogenic way, to bring out the best in them and, in the process, often make them appear more graceful than in reality. Detailed observation of the human form is essential for any portrait or fashion photographer; paying concentrated attention to how someone moves and looks through the camera, as well as in life, is crucial.

Beaton had a strong sense of the strange esthetics of the destructive power of modern weaponry on buildings. He used his Rolleiflex camera to record the damage of the Blitz and the battlefields of North Africa during World War II. He noted that Surrealists had anticipated the battleground of war in their work, by acknowledging the incongruities. During the Blitz Beaton shot the dismembered head of a shop mannequin lying on top of a mound of smashed and fractured wood from the ruins of the hairdressers' shop it had been displayed in. The image created a disturbing and harrowing comment on the frailty of human life.

Beaton's experience as a fashion photographer is evident in this image, as he has instinctively spotted the humor and style of this bare-chested sailor with his hat jauntily perched on his head. Eye contact with the subject here is vital; it gives the photograph a wit and playfulness that epitomize the British spirit. Look for juxtapositions and incongruities in your images that can lift a mundane subject into something entertaining.

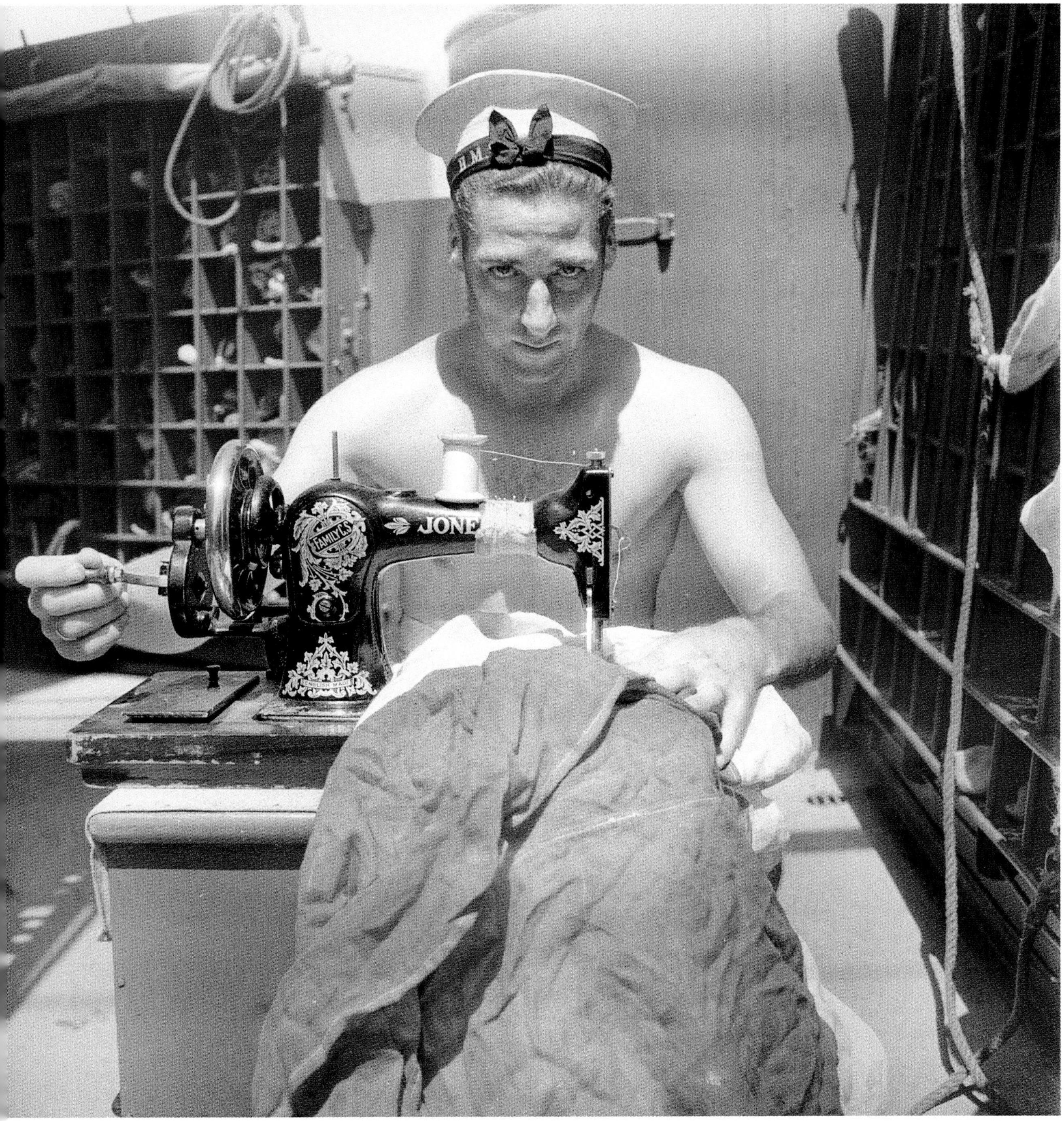
JONE
FAMILY C.S

Malick Sidibé

A moi seul 1978

The extraordinary parade of sharply dressed characters represented by Malick Sidibé's photographic studio is a fascinating contrast to the stereotype of Africa as famine-ridden, desperate, and dispossessed. Instead, in graphically powerful and energetic compositions, the citizens of Bamako, Mali, display themselves in all their finery, showing off the latest trophies of consumer culture, and standing proudly with friends and families. In this striking portrait, Sidibé used the rhythms and patterns of the backdrop to create a dazzling contrast to the man's suit, producing an extraordinary, performative space within the studio. His studio became a destination for people from all walks of life from Bamako, but especially for the youth, who wanted to be photographed with the latest fashions or the newest symbol of material wealth. As he explained, "For people in my country, it's important to have photographs of themselves to be able to show them to their family, their friends... It's a kind of social gesture." Sidibé's approach allowed people to feel at ease and to be happy to show off their latest acquisitions: "More than anyone else, young people enjoyed having their photo taken in their best attire, with their new earrings, curled hair, showing off their best watch, their bracelets... Everyone likes to be beautiful in photographs." The atmosphere was more like a dance club than a commercial premises, as he recalled: "The studio was like no other... relaxed. I did formal family shots, too, but often it was like a party. People would drop by, stay, eat. I slept in the developing room. They'd pose on their Vespas, show off their new hats and trousers and jewels and sunglasses. Looking beautiful was everything. Everyone had to have the latest Paris style." Sidibé was an institution in Bamako, and he forms part of the cultural memory of the country.

"Too often is Africa's image linked to pain, poverty, misery. Denying this reality would be foolish, but Africa is not only that, and this is what I have always wanted to depict in my images." Malick Sidibé

Malick Sidibé (Malian, *c.* 1935–2016) grew up in a village where his family worked the land and herded animals. Their lives were very simple and remote; he recalled that his father only ever saw his own image reflected in water. The young Sidibé was selected for school, however, where his talents for art and drawing meant that he was chosen to go to the School of Sudanese Craftsmen in the capital, Bamako. He joined a photographic studio as a junior in 1955 and brought his first camera, a Brownie flash, in 1956. In 1957 he became a full-time photographer. He opened his own Studio Malick in 1958, describing it as a "place of make-believe." Sidibé is renowned for the black-and-white studies he made of popular culture in Mali during the 1960s, and for his studio portraits. His work is infused with the energy and vibrancy of its cultural life. He maintained that "the country where I work is characterized by a great joy, a great deep-seated joy that pervades everything and that existed even in colonial times. That is something that comes through in the work, because there is a very rich culture."

Creative tips and techniques

Sidibé's compositions were heavily influenced by his early sketching, which he said helped him at the outset because he understood how light and shadow worked in an image. His strong use of contrast and pattern created a dynamic space in which his subjects placed themselves. He created a relaxed atmosphere for the shoot, believing that the ambience of parties and dances meant that he could produce the best images of their faces. He believed that the traditional formal poses of studio portraiture did not suit the energy of the African city. His images have a sense of stilled motion, as if you are seeing a photo that seems to move before your eyes.

Sidibé only ever shot on film and he continued to resist the lure of digital photography. He stuck to black and white, and did his own developing and printing. He felt that the process of working with film remained worthwhile in the development of a photographer, as you had to focus the image, go to the lab, develop and work at it. He felt that analog photography showed all of reality.

Sidibé argued that a sense of the esthetic should be combined with a feeling for the emotions of people to make the ideal portrait photographer. He maintained that you need a talent for observation and to know what you want. He advised choosing the shapes and movements that please you and look beautiful. However, he also emphasized the importance of being friendly and sympathetic to your subjects. He believed that it is extremely important to put people at their ease. Luckily, he noted, this was in his nature.

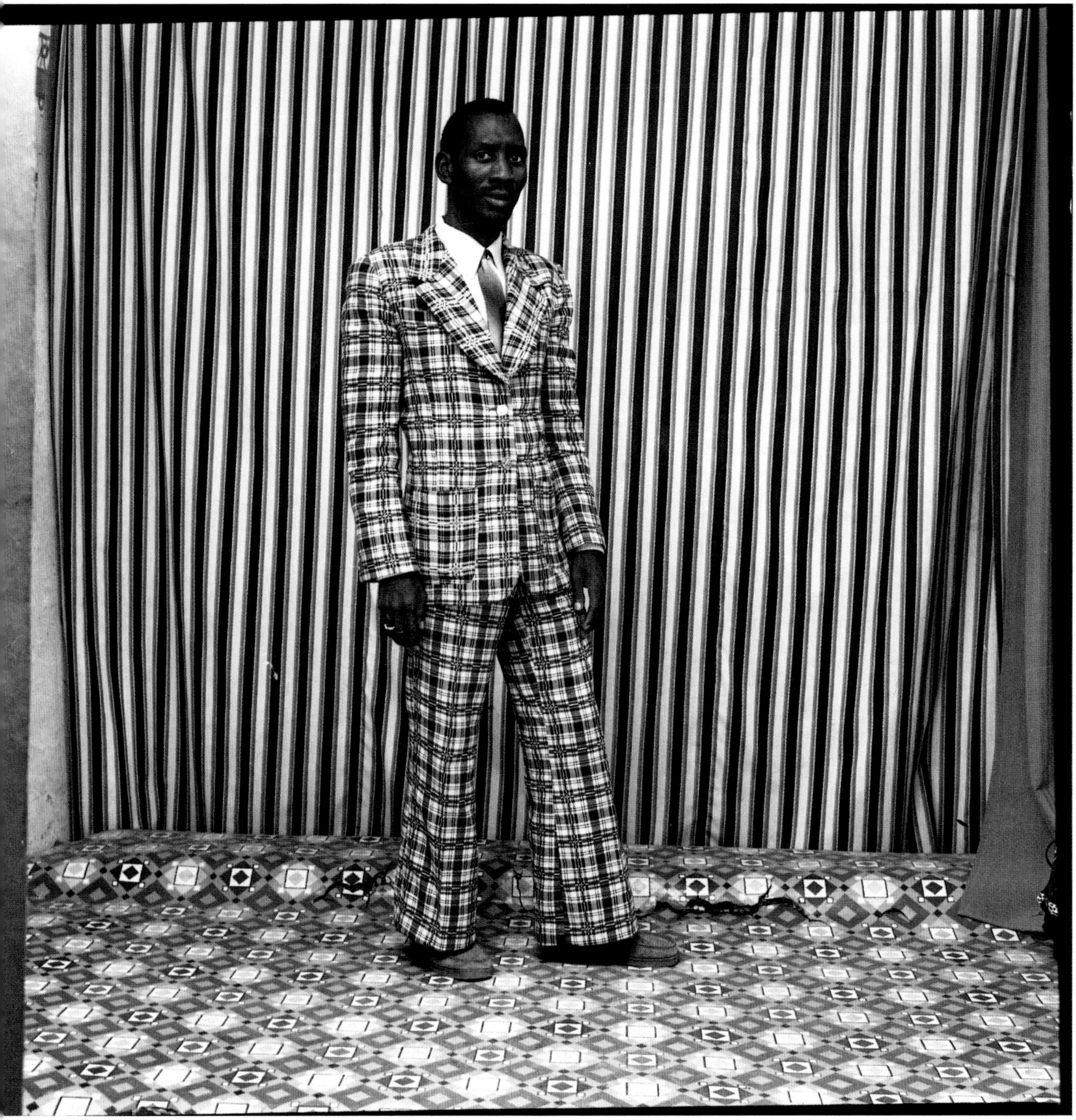

Nan Goldin

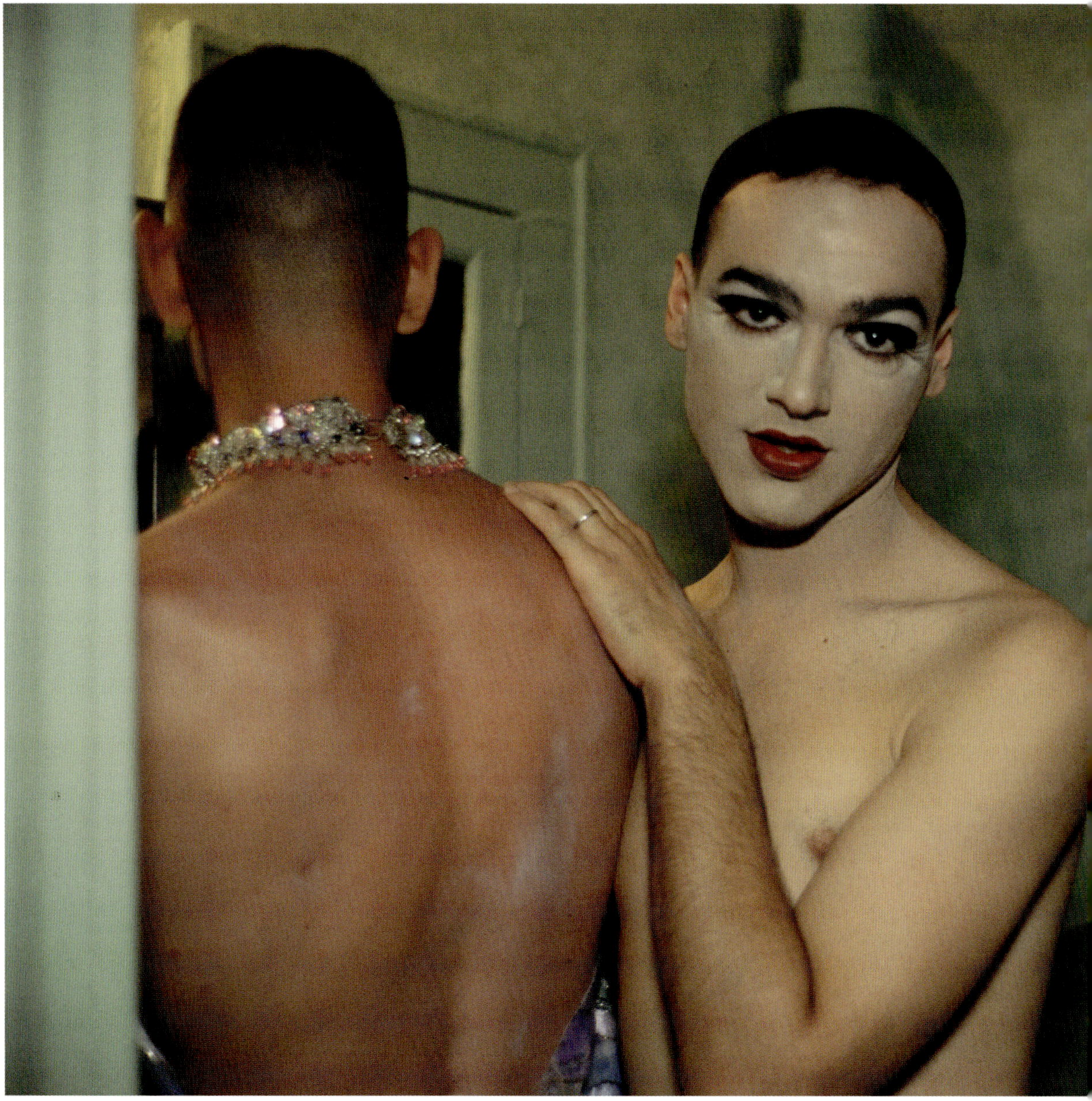

Nan Goldin (American, 1953–) began photography while attending Setya Community School in Lincoln, Massachusetts, where "I didn't get a formal education, but I did get a voice and I learned to relate to other people." She was also introduced to the films of Andy Warhol and Federico Fellini, and the fashion photography of Guy Bourdin and Helmut Newton. She began to photograph the drag queen culture of Boston in the early 1970s, recalling that "I lived with them; it was my whole focus. It was my whole context." After moving to New York she used her camera as a way of relating to friends and acquaintances on the post-punk scene, often fuelled by drink and drugs. Out of this work emerged her performance slideshow, which became a book in 1986, *The Ballad of Sexual Dependency*. Goldin has produced other books including *Eden and After* (2014).

Creative tips and techniques

Goldin began to combine her photographs as slides with musi experimenting with presenting the wor live as a performance, often for the subjects of the photographs themselve This developed into her slideshow, *The Ballad of Sexual Dependency*, which wa an organic, living piece that was edited ar re-edited, sequenced and re-sequenced,

Jimmy Paulette and Taboo! in the bathroom, NYC 1991

This image occupies an interesting space; it is not a formal, posed portrait nor does it assume the illusion of the "fly on the wall" documentary, being seemingly invisible to the protagonists and hence the viewer. Instead, the returned gaze challenges the viewer to relate to the pair, as one of them stares back at the photographer, and therefore at the viewer too, while the other remains hidden, their head turned away, suggesting the complexities of personality and identity. As Nan Goldin acknowledges, "When you set up pictures you're not at any risk. Reality involves chance and risk and diving for pearls." The ambiguous nature of the image reflects Goldin's identification with her subjects and their identities as neither/nor. She says her connection with drag queens was born of a deep respect for their challenge to the accepted norms of sexuality: "I wanted to pay homage, to show them how beautiful they were. I never saw them as men dressing up as women, but as something entirely different—a third gender that made more sense than either of the other two. I accepted them as they saw themselves; I had no desire to unmask them with my camera." Goldin defends her work against accusations of exploitation, arguing that her connection and friendships with her subjects mean that she and they accept the process of making pictures together. She argues: "I am not a voyeur, as voyeurs photograph through closed windows and with me the window is always wide open."

> "There is a popular notion that the photographer is by nature a voyeur, the last one to be invited to the party. But I'm not crashing; this is my party. This is my family, my friends."
>
> Nan Goldin

'er many years in response to each new ›rformance. Goldin sees the slideshow as way of expanding beyond the photograph d not being limited by a single image. ne is interested in the sequence of images d how they cumulatively affect one other. The combination between sound d music is also vital, and *The Ballad of* *xual Dependency* used tracks from a riety of sources that reflected the music her life, including The Velvet Underground and Nina Simone. The narrative voice of the soundtrack gives the work larger context, allowing her to comment on sexual politics, gender, and relationships. *The Ballad of Sexual Dependency* is an epic work, but the lessons of how music and images can be combined in a non-linear narrative can be absorbed by anyone. Experiment in creating a slideshow with music to see how different images and tracks can create radically divergent responses in an audience.

Goldin uses the camera as an extension of her life, initially believing that by recording the people around her she could somehow preserve them, although she now acknowledges that this was perhaps a forlorn hope. Goldin totally integrates photography into her daily existence and this total integration of the photographic process into life creates, fundamentally, moments of connection rather than abstraction.

Rineke Dijkstra

Kolobrzeg, Poland, July 26, 1992 1992

This image is one of a series of portraits of young bathers taken in the United States, Britain, Belgium, Ukraine, Croatia and Poland. The adolescents in Rineke Dijkstra's *Beach Portraits* stand alone, the ocean rolling behind them. Clad in little more than bathing suits, these young people are striking to behold. Dijkstra uses the beach as a liminal space, in terms of both the transition from sea to land and also from youth to adolescent to adulthood; her subjects are caught as if on the edge of something, in transit from one zone to another. The openness of the beach and the semi-clothed state of a bather allow her to examine this key moment in life in a comparative way, seeking a range of children and teenagers and asking the viewer to look across the survey to find clues as to the state of mind of youth.

She uses the singular pose, isolated against a plain background, to emphasize the space between people, accentuating the gap between viewer and subject that the portrait is traditionally meant to close down. She encourages the audience to work harder at interpreting the image by not giving them too many visual clues as to the person's history. She also allows her subjects to find their own physical stance in the images, feeling that this, too, reveals something of their character. However, she believes that this must come naturally from the subject, not from her direction; as she says, she was "interested in photographing people at moments when they had dropped all pretence of a pose... I've never explicitly sought vulnerability; it's more a search for something roughly present but still barely defined in their personalities."

"A photograph works best when the formal aspects such as light, color, and composition, as well as the informal aspects like someone's gaze or gesture, come together. In my pictures I also look for a sense of stillness and serenity." Rineke Dijkstra

Rineke Dijkstra (Dutch, 1959–) has produced a series of portrait projects that isolate single figures but are also related to others in the series. These series have variously depicted bathers on beaches, Israeli soldiers, and adolescent girls and boys in Berlin's Tiergarten park. Dijkstra finds deep significance in the everyday lives of others, arguing that the "importance of photography is that you can point to something, that you can let other people see things. Ultimately, it is a matter of the specialness of the ordinary." Her ongoing series centers on a Bosnian girl, Almerisa, who she initially met in 1994 as a six-year-old and whose family had relocated to Amsterdam as refugees. Since then Dijkstra has continued to photograph Almerisa at one- or two-year intervals, recording her development from child to woman to mother, as well as her cultural transition from eastern to western European.

Creative tips and techniques

Dijkstra works with a 5 x 4 field camera with a standard lens and a tripod, which gives negatives the size of postcards and allows very sharp detail and contrast. This enables her to print large-scale images, ideal for the museum setting. She feels that photography is related to three-dimensional art and sculpture.

Finding the right concept, subject, and location to make the series is central to Dijkstra's methodology. Once she has also found the right person, the relationship between them becomes quite intense, as she tries to search for an uninhibited moment. The result she is looking for is not too forced or posed.

Dijkstra uses flash outdoors to accentuate the figure and make it stand out more against the background. Mostly it is about finding the right balance between the daylight and the flash. She now keeps the set-up simple, having experimented with more complex lighting techniques. This technique works well for highlighting the main subject of a portrait. To master it, take a photographic model and shoot a series of exposures in which you bracket the exposure for the daylight and the flash output to find the balance between them that you like the best. A heavily underexposed background with flash as the main light for the subject will look most dramatic, whereas setting the correct daylight exposure and adding the flash set one or two stops less than the main exposure will give a more subtle effect, just filling in the shadows so that the flash is hardly noticeable. Work with your subject to find a pose they feel comfortable with and that looks natural. If you direct them too much, the image may appear stiff and forced.

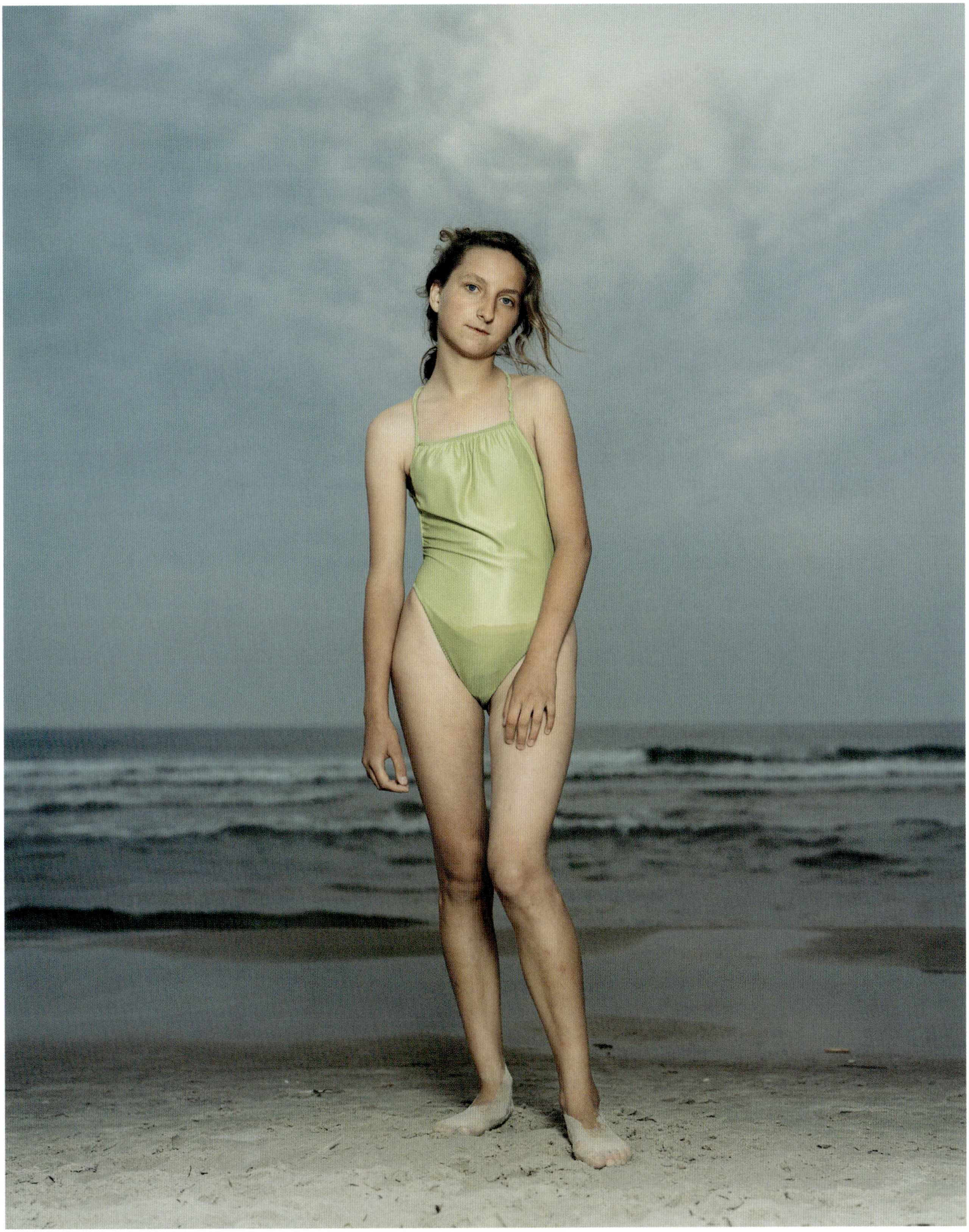

Wolfgang Tillmans

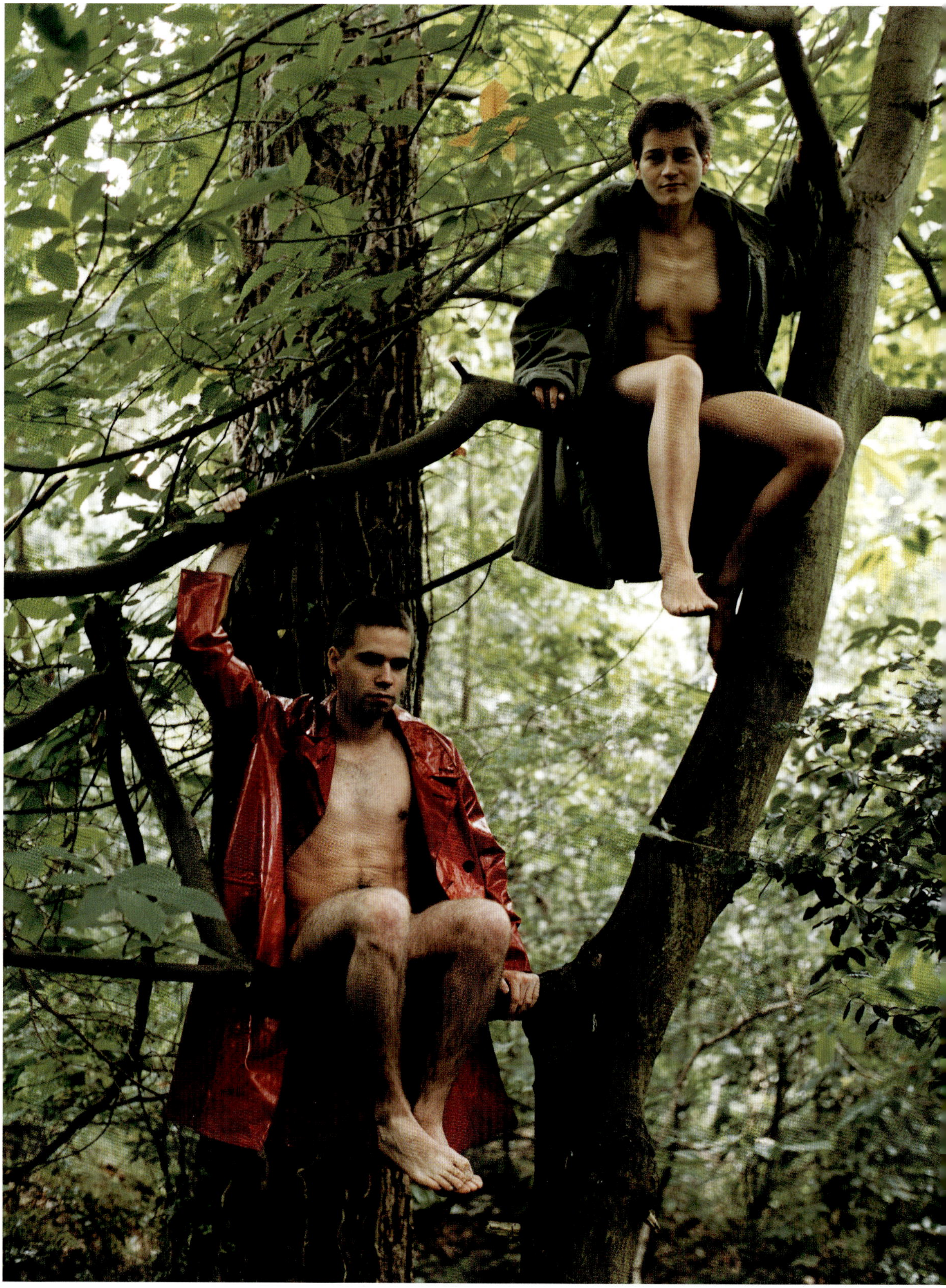

ıtz and Alex sitting in the trees 1992

ıis couple appear like feral animals, children of the forest, ərched on a sculptural tree, surrounded by verdant greenery that ɛems to infuse their bodies. Almost like a contemporary Adam ıd Eve, they are naked apart from raincoats, but Lutz wears s red one and Alex her green, ill-fitting one. The forest has an ;sociation with wildness and release, but also with childhood ars and fantasies, and it connects to a long tradition—especially Germany—in art. Their expressions differ: his is harder edged, ore confrontational; hers softer, more welcoming.

The image typifies Wolfgang Tillmans's ability to work on the dges of genres; it has a feel of a "real" documentary moment, ut also seems otherworldly and performative. As he explains, ɛ is interested in exploring the space between genres: "I found ıotography to be a very powerful tool because as long as it oks real, it is perceived as real. That was the foundation for ıe style that I developed. I made extraordinary things look not ərticularly staged or extraordinary. Two people sitting naked a tree is hardly a documentary picture, but it was somehow stantly seen as a picture of the zeitgeist, of the reality." He escribes further how this strategy developed: "I started to use eople as actors of ideas or actors of their own ideas, like a kind collaboration, or a way for me to see what I would like to ɛe." The fact that this image was for a fashion magazine spread lowed him to play with the expectations of what a photograph ıould be and in what context it should be viewed. It proved to be pivotal image in Tillmans's career. After being exhibited by the ırator Maureen Paley at the Cologne unofficial art fair, the Unfair, 1992, it led to his first major exhibition in 1993.

Vhat intrigues me is the tension of the two key qualities of photograph: the promise of it being a perfect, controlled bject, and the reality of a photographic image being ıechanically quite unsophisticated."

olfgang Tillmans

olfgang Tillmans (German, 1968–) was born Remscheid, Germany, and studied at the ɔurnemouth and Poole College of Art and esign in southern England. During the 1990s chronicled the essence of the decade's club ılture, publishing his photographs in *The Face* ıd *iD* magazines. He used them as a vehicle to esent his work unburdened by the expectations more conventional documentary or fine art ıtlets. He works eclectically across genres and styles, moving seamlessly from magazines, to aerial shots and landscapes, to the gallery wall, where his installations work cumulatively on the viewer with connections and rhythms being made across his entire body of work. He uses a range of devices to produce his images, from photocopied collages to abstracts made in the darkroom. In 2000, he became the first photographer—and also the first non-English person—to win the Turner Prize.

Creative tips and techniques

Tillmans argues that the act of taking a portrait is such a fundamental human act, as well as an artistic one. He believes that the process is a very direct human exchange, and this is what interests him about it. Fleeting expression is central to his work with people. He explains that the moment he puts a camera between his eye and the sitter something happens in the sitter's cheeks—and that's what he observes.

Tillmans creates complex installations for his work that play with the materiality of the image. They generate resonances and interactions between sets and series of photographs, inviting the viewer to respond to them to create their own narrative. He explains that at the most basic level he works with pieces of paper, shaping colors and dyes, and those objects are not the reality they represent. He asks "Why does this paper carry a charge? It's the brain, it's our humanity that brings life to it." He discovered this approach early on, when he worked with a black-and-white photocopier to make enlargements of found images. He recalls that it was a very radical thing at the time, to show magazine pages alongside original photographs and to leave the photographs unframed. Producing these installations is a site-specific activity, with them growing organically in response to the exhibition space he works in. The final product invites the audience to bring their own interpretations of the work.

Tillmans believes in taking risks as an artist, and responding to each individual moment without preconceived ideas. He acknowledges the discomfort this can bring, but maintains that this unpredictability is central to his experience of the world.

Steve Pyke

Last foot on the moon (Gene Cernan), Houston 1998

Steve Pyke had always been fascinated by the idea of astronauts, recalling that: "In 1968, I was just a kid who loved the notion of going into space." In the late 1990s, he eventually embarked on a mission to photograph the surviving Apollo astronauts thirty years after the flight of Apollo 8. He explains that he was "after a very specific experience. What is it actually like to walk on the moon?" Pyke's journey to photograph the Apollo space pioneers was documented in the 2010 documentary film, *Moonbug*.

Most of the images are taken in Pyke's signature style, isolating the sitter's face against a black backdrop lit by natural light. However, for this one, the nature of his subject suggested a different approach because Gene Cernan was the last man to ever set foot on the Moon, having been the last of the crew to board the Apollo 17 Lunar Module in December 1972. The light falling across the lines of Cernan's left foot is suggestive of the surface of the cresent moon seen from a satellite, with its craters and striations mapped across the surface of the skin. Although Pyke is best known for his portraits, he has also shot still lives, and he treats Cernan's foot like a sculptural object, almost as if it were carved in stone. He feels that this sense of immobility is a common thread in his work, which connects him to early photographers such as Octavius Hill, who took portraits and still lives in the 1840s. This carries through to his portraits, as he explains: "In the portraits there is 'stillness' as well, I agree. I like to photograph people in this very still way, but what I strive to do and what I really like is trying to capture those spontaneous eighths of a second that come every so often."

"I like sometimes to do away with environment in portraiture. It seems to me that often it's irrelevant; a lot of the time there's no context between the sitter and the space I'm photographing them in." Steve Pyke

Steve Pyke (British, 1957–) has remained true to a strong personal vision throughout his career, shooting close-up portraits, concentrating on the "person I'm photographing, concentrating on the physiognomy." Pyke has photographed countless celebrities, musicians, actors, and film directors. However, he also works on long-term projects of his own and has produced portrait series of philosophers, children in uniform, and astronauts. Pyke initially pursued a career in music but on a motorcyle tour of the United States in 1976 he took a collection of images with an Instamatic camera that led him to buy a Rolleiflex camera. He abandoned music for photography and from 1981 to 1984 worked for popular culture publications including *The Face* and *New Musical Express*. He became a staff photographer and contributor for *The New Yorker* magazine in 2004. In that year Steve received an MBE in the Queen's New Year's Honors list for his services to the arts. Pyke considers himself a "collector" of faces and maintains that "Photographers essentially become ontologists; they become these people that collect."

Creative tips and techniques

Pyke has used the same camera, a Rolleiflex medium-format film camera with a 80mm 2.8 Planar lens, throughout his career. He finds that today, in the digital age, the twin lens reflex is a rarity that contributes to the performative nature of the exchange with his subjects. The 80mm is the equivalent of a standard 50mm lens on 35mm, but Pyke uses additional Rolleinar close-up lenses on it to allow him to come incredibly close to his subjects' faces, usually only inches away from them. He discovered this technique early in his career when he found the lenses in a camera shop on his way to photograph the film director Sam Fuller. He typically shoots against a sheet of black velvet that he can quickly gaffer tape to a wall or other support, although he has also used a plain white background at times. He shoots mostly with available natural light, mounting the camera on a tripod with an exposure that is typically f8 at 1/8th of a second, on 400 ASA Kodak TriX film. The consistency of his approach means that he is now able to make photographs seamlessly while interacting with his subjects. "Most of my frames are made looking at and interacting with my sitters."

Pyke likes to work slowly, establishing a relationship with his sitter before making any exposures. He describes how a typical session lasts an hour, of which forty-five minutes is talking and getting to know each other. The actual photography can take as little as ten minutes. He maintains a consistent approach, no matter who the subject or client is. His reputation and his methodology now mean that his subjects often come prepared for the session, ready to enter into his intimate world.

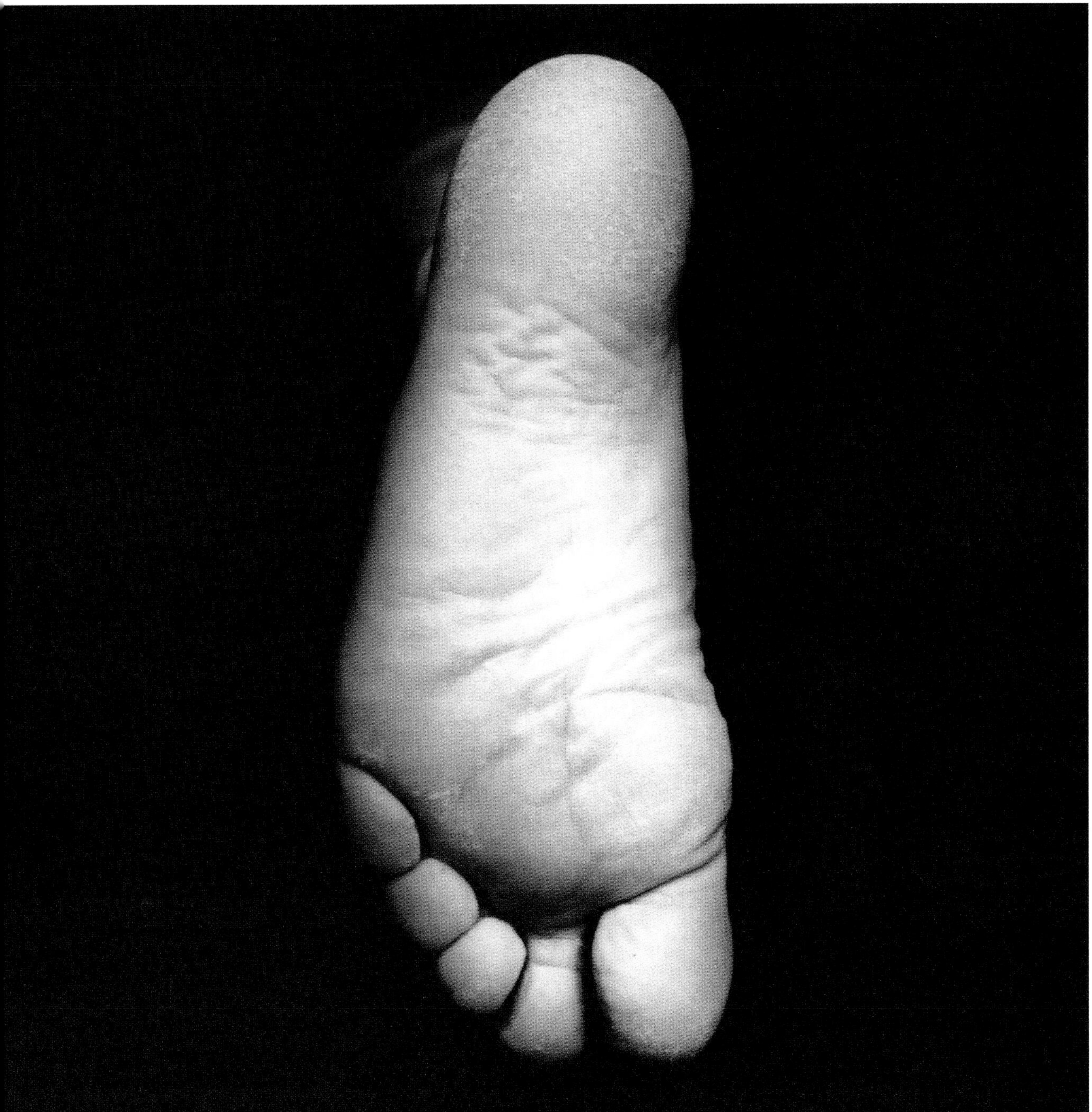

Laura Pannack

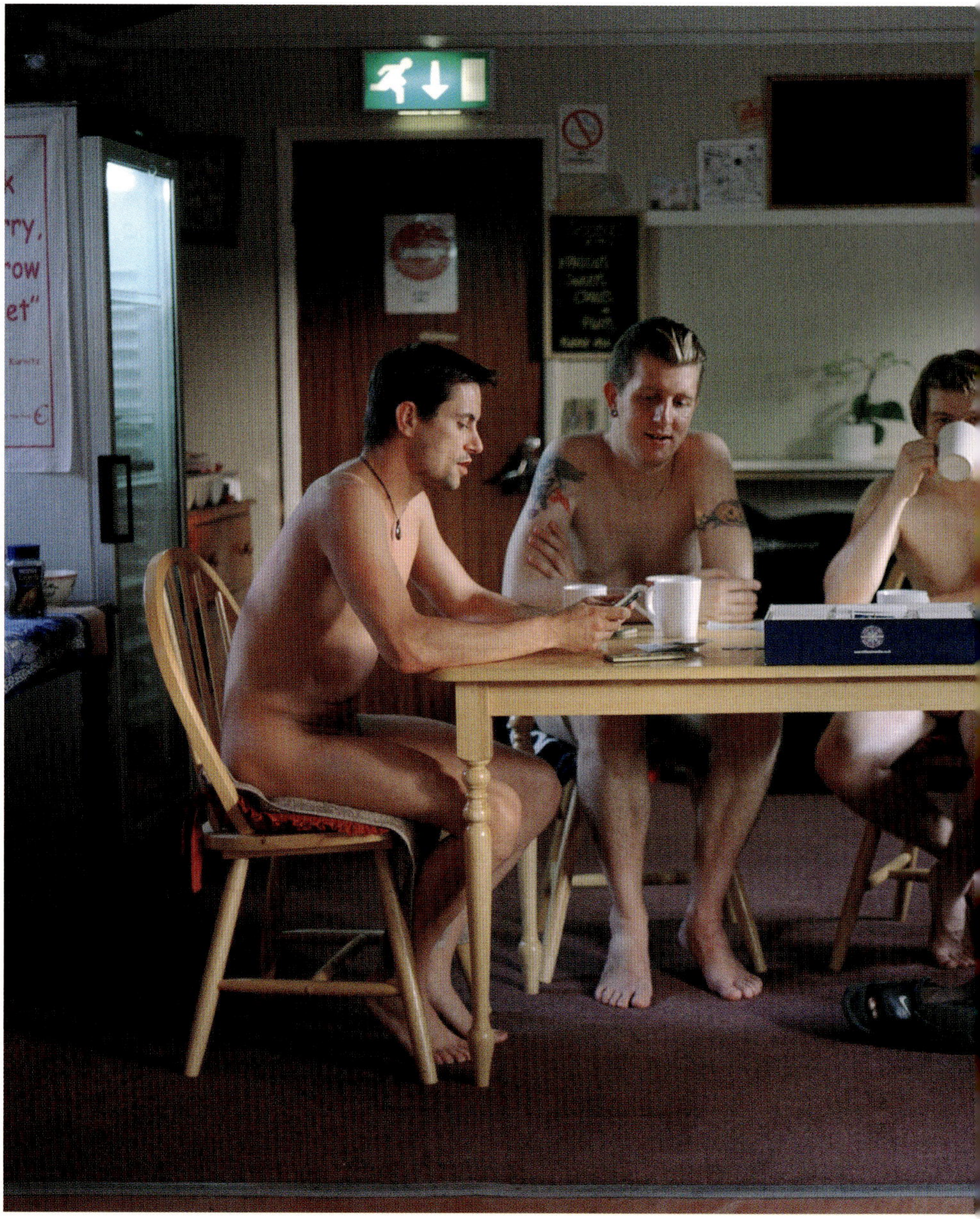

Laura Pannack (British, 1985–) has emerged as one of the most interesting of Britain's documentary portraitists. She works on extended projects focusing on adolescent youth and for editorial clients. She won a World Press Photo award in 2010. She aims to "capture our generation now. I want us to consider who these youngsters will grow up to become. There always needs to be an element of mystery to my imagery. Giving an audience too much information limits the potential of their imaginations."

Creative tips and techniques

Pannack spends a significant amount of time researching her projects and finding the right people to collaborate with. She uses social media initially and scouts around trying to get access and referrals. However, in the end she concludes that simply going out into the world is often the wisest approach. As she explains, "often I just head out and find people. You just have to ask people. What's the worst they can say? I always give the reason I want to photograph them. The main thing to remember is empathy; you have to understand why someone might not want to be photographed."

Pannack feels that spending time first with the people she is going to photograph is important: "I like to spend a day with the subjects. I have ideas of how I want a shot to look, but I don't like to plan The spontaneity is crucial. This is what portraiture is about." This allows her to engage with her prospective subjects and form a connection that will hopefully continue through to the viewer in the resulting image. She highlights the importance of trying to empathize with an respect her subjects to make sure that the feel comfortable during the shoot. Pannac tries to explain to them what she intends

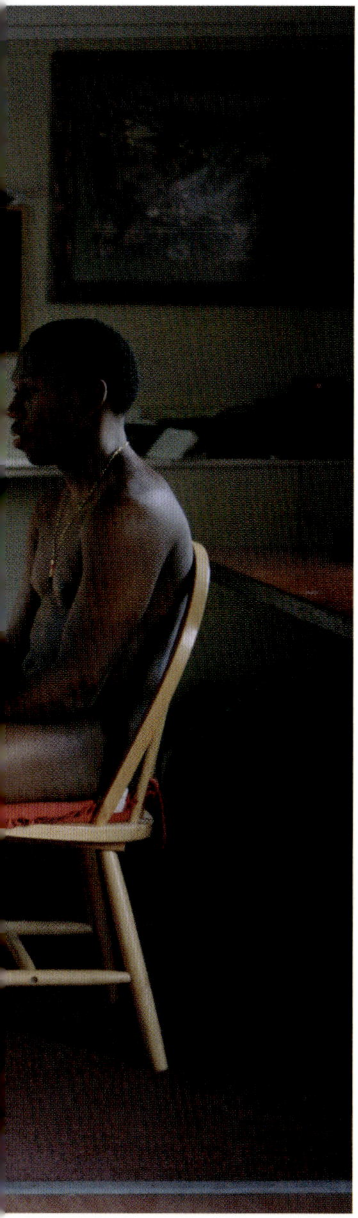

Young British naturists 2011

To make her series on young British naturists, Laura Pannack felt that she herself had to be naked in order to identify with her subjects. She wanted them to relax and be natural, as she explains: "I wanted to show that these people weren't just naked. They were people; I didn't want to photograph their nudity. I wanted to photograph them." This image from the series takes the nudity of the people shown for granted; it becomes a seamless part of their lives and everything else in the frame seems perfectly normal and mundane. However, subtle details of body language and the soft cushions on the chair reveal something of the minutiae of how they respond to their situation.

Pannack wants to counter prevailing views of young people that are stereotyped. She explains: "The media tends to not only influence young people in a negative way, but also present them in a generalized light. I wanted to challenge the thoughts of my viewers and ask them to consider how they view young people and look at the subjects as individuals, unique in their own way regardless of their background." Pannack wants to interact with her subjects, feeling that there has to be a mutual bond between them, no matter how long or short their connection lasts. She also poignantly notes that sometimes the images that are taken only with the eye, not the camera, are the most memorable: "It sounds strange to say this, but I truly believe that the pictures I don't take are just as important than the ones I do. It reminds me why I choose to capture a moment and not just snap." She further adds why she does not carry a camera every day: "Sometimes I feel it is more important to breathe, feel, and see life, and then choose what it is I want to capture and create."

do so that everyone understands the ocess: "when I have a pre-conceived a, I will demonstrate my idea before king my sitter to replicate it. I want ensure that those I photograph feel powered and safe." She thinks that e has an innate sense of who will make owerful portrait. As she puts it, "some bjects have a special gaze or look out them. I can't explain why I am wn to capture or photograph certain people." Pannack describes how when shooting she often finds herself homing in on particular individuals and characters who somehow have a specific appeal: "sometimes I can instantly identify what it is that has seduced me: bright green eyes, gangly awkward limbs or a certain emotional shyness or intensity... other times I can't—a punctum and one that niggles me even after I've developed the film."

"There's a unique relationship between adolescent and photographer. My work is emotional and teenagers have heightened emotions. They are forming their identity and it's exciting to witness that."

Laura Pannack

Ideas

The nature of the photographic medium itself is an intriguing subject for photographers. The formal esthetic qualities of the camera, combined with the technology that it is built upon, creates a rich space of contradictions and questions for the photographer to explore. The contrast between the subjectivity of the photographer and the seeming objectivity of the camera is a key issue. Selective framing and composition can create connections or juxtapositions that perhaps reveal a deeper meaning. The exploration of how the camera converts three-dimensional space to two-dimensional space, and then seemingly brings three-dimensional depth back into the image, is also a recurring theme in the work of those who explore the boundaries of photography. The question of what is a subject worthy of photography is a complex one; the camera has the power to transmute the ordinary into the extraordinary by virtue of the artist choosing to do so. Even the role of the auteur photographer can be questioned; some artists use found images or satellite surveillance, which challenge the idea that the photographer has to take the image in the first place. Applying an artistic or scientific methodology to the world, with a set of predetermined parameters, can shape a project, giving it an underlying coherence and vision that would otherwise be lacking. Applying a conceptual model of thinking based on fine-art practice or a philosophical position can give a project depth and resonance. The medium of photography is relatively young; it continues to draw on more established art forms as well as from its younger sibling, film. Yet the development of a truly photographic language still leaves much to be explored.

Eadweard Muybridge

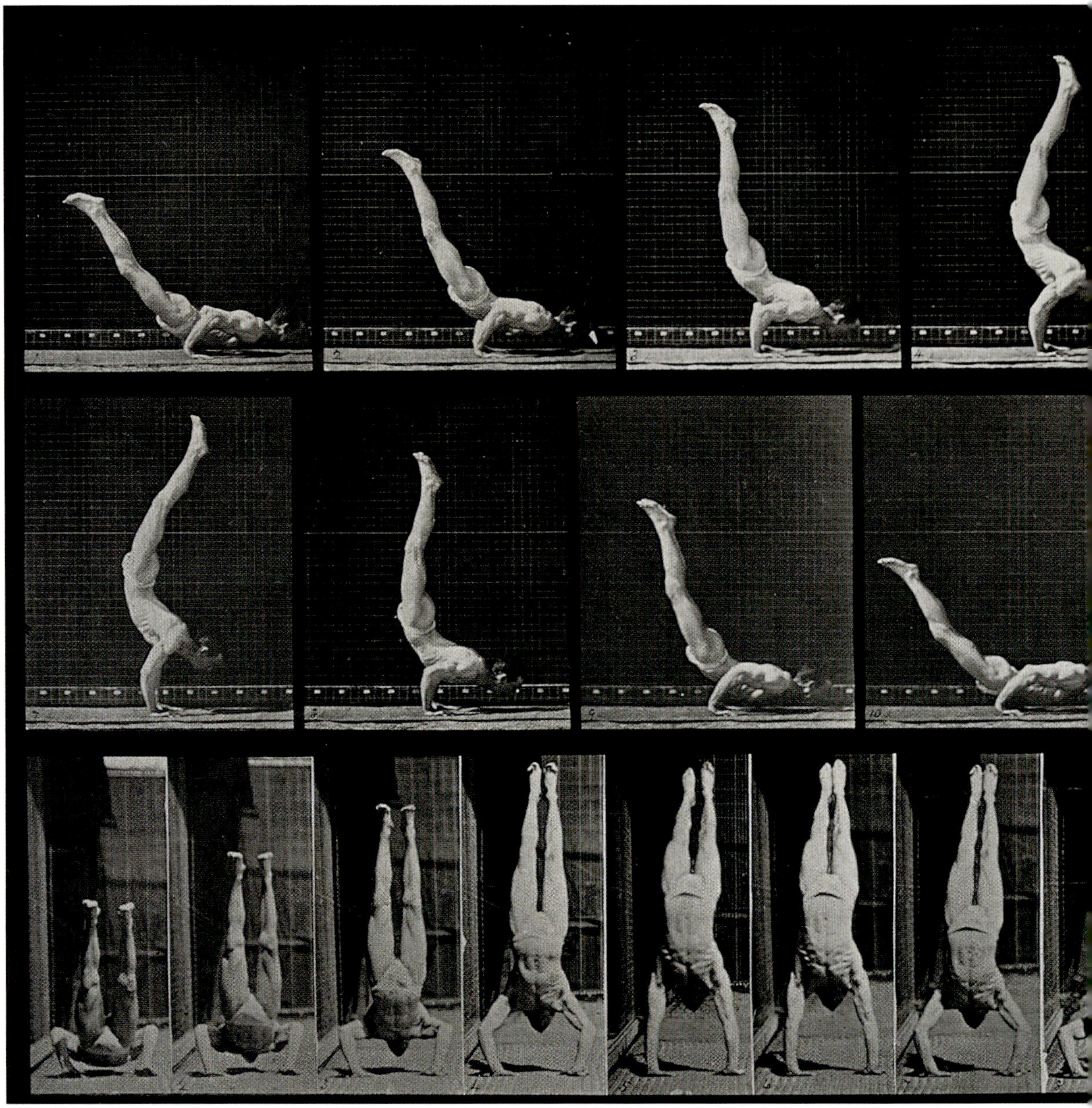

"Only photography has been able to divide human life into a series of moments; each of them has the value of a complete existence." Eadweard Muybridge

Eadweard Muybridge (British, 1830–1904) was born Edward Muggeridge in Kingston, Surrey, but emigrated to the United States in 1850. He returned to England in 1861 when he began experimenting with photography, and then in 1867 went back to California where his landscapes of Yosemite Valley made him famous. In a bizarre incident in 1874, he killed his wife's lover but was acquitted in a jury trial on the grounds of justifiable homicide. In the 1880s Muybridge collaborated with the University of Pennsylvania in Philadelphia to produce thousands of images studying locomotion, capturing what the human eye could not distinguish as separate movements.

Creative tips and techniques

Muybridge was concerned with t passage of time as described by the camera. He was an experimenter ar pioneer, who created numerous patents for equipment to help him overcome the limitations of his era. He developed a shade for the camera that allowed hir to use different exposures for the land and the sky, and often printed clouds ar

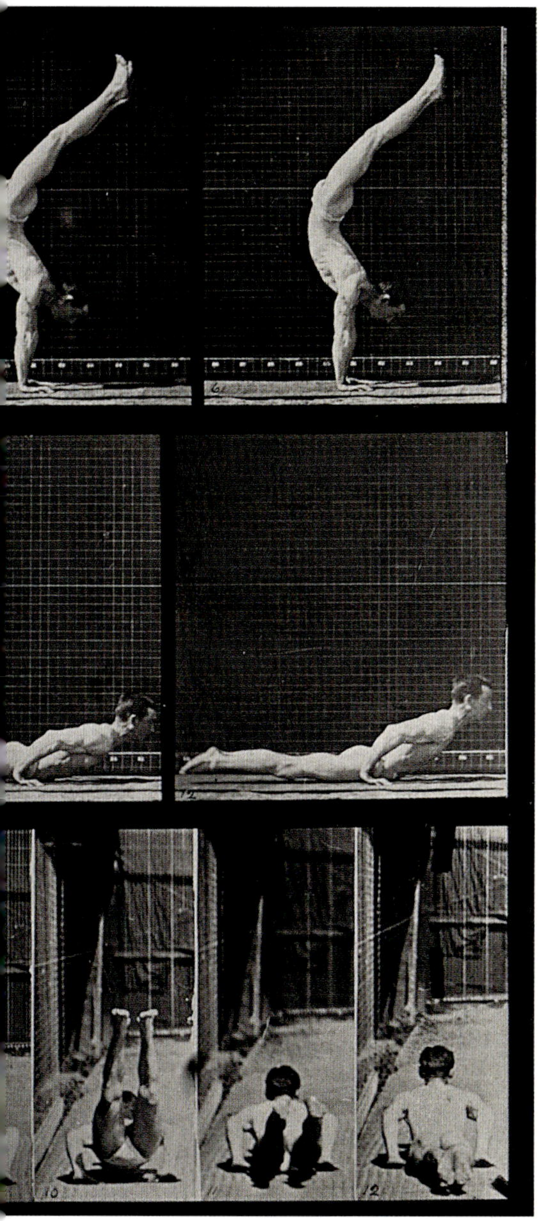

A man standing on his hands from a lying down position 1887

Eadweard Muybridge's achievements in other fields of photography would perhaps have made him famous, but in his studies of human and animal movements he achieved an extraordinary breakthrough in human perception. As in this striking image of a gymnast, he literally slowed time down to make it visible in space, atomizing moments into their individual component parts and then reassembling them into fluid studies of motion. He used multiple cameras so that he could record the subject from several angles, allowing the motion of the body through space and time to be precisely documented in fractional increments. He first began to explore how movement could be captured in sequence in 1872 after being commissioned by Leland Stanford, a businessman and racehorse owner, who had made a bet as to whether all four feet of a trotting horse were off the ground at the same time. Until this point, the majority of artists portrayed trotting horses with one foot always on the ground; only at full gallop were they depicted as having all four hooves in the air. After considerable experimentation, Muybridge resolved the issue with an image that showed Stanford's horse Occident airborne at the trot. Based on this, Muybridge expanded his subject matter to people and a whole range of other animals. In the 1880s Muybridge worked at the University of Pennsylvania on an even more ambitious documentation of motion, eventually published as the monumental work *Animal Locomotion: an Electro-Photographic Investigation of Connective Phases of Animal Movements*. It contained 781 plates comprising 20,000 photographs. The book was hugely influential and has been used as a reference source by artists and animators, with Marcel Duchamp acknowledging it as an influence on his 1912 painting, *Nude Descending a Staircase, No. 2.*

en the moon onto his photographs as the ulsions of the time would not allow all scene to be exposed correctly on the ne negative. He used the stereoscopic mat extensively. For his motion studies, he ated a range of timing devices, automatic utters, and multiple lenses. His final images re made with up to thirty-six lenses with elve to twenty-four cameras, placed at -, 60- and 90-degree angles to the main ject, creating up to thirty-six frames from a variety of fixed angles for each session. His use of the zoopraxiscope, which rapidly projected images from rotating glass disks to give the impression of motion, was a major precursor to motion pictures. With modern digital cameras, motordrives, and strobes, exploring detailed sequences of motion becomes much easier, but no less revealing.

Another of Muybridge's visual achievements was his 360-degree panorama of San Francisco, made from the viewpoint at Nob Hill in 1878. Over five hours he made thirteen separate exposures on huge vertical glass plates, with the sun moving across the landscape like a sundial. The final image was printed as an 18-foot (5-meter) long continuous strip, and the effect turns time and the description of space into a work of art that overwhelms the eye's capacity to take in all the detail.

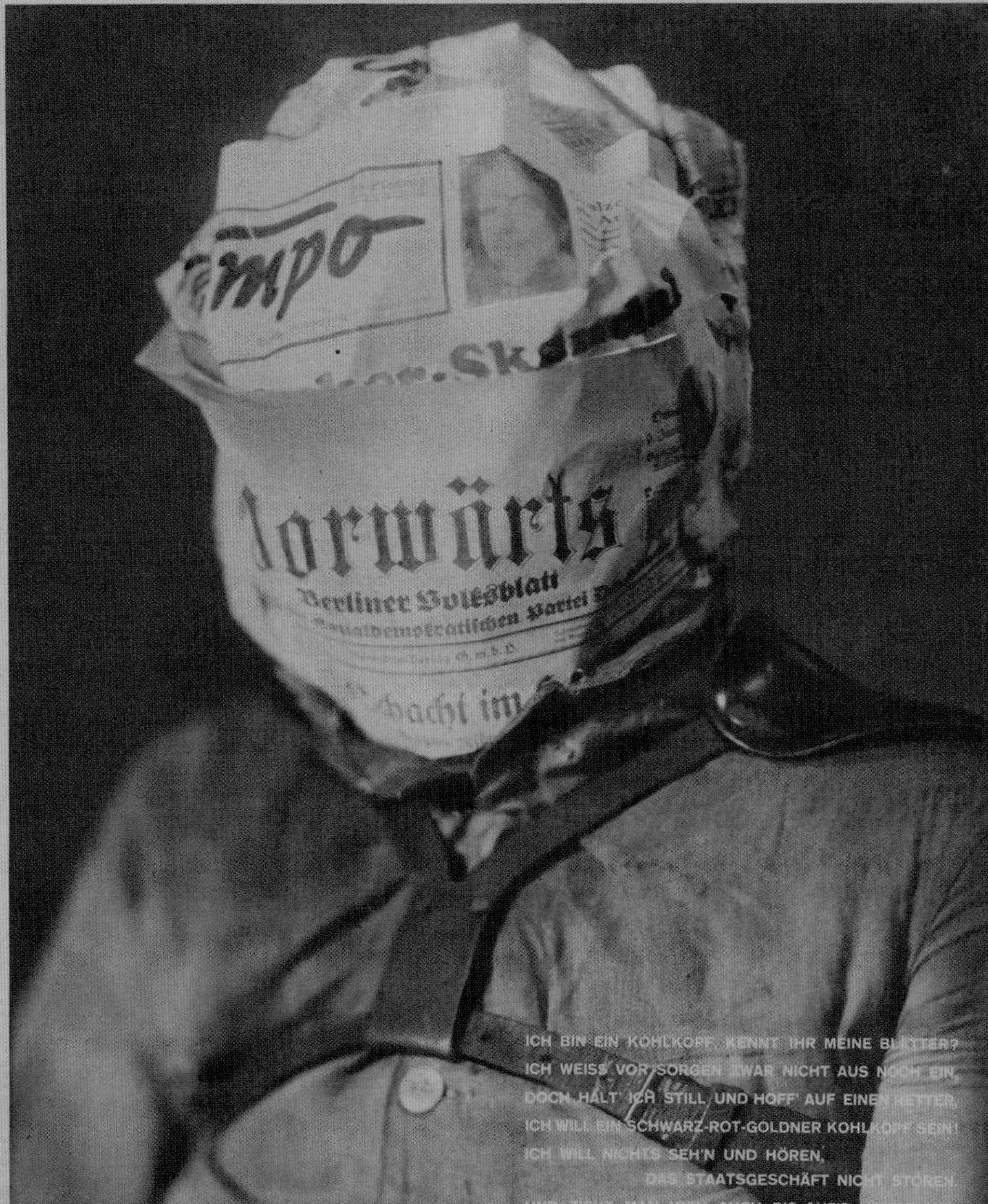

**WER BÜRGERBLÄTTER LIEST WIRD BLIND UND TAUB.
WEG MIT DEN VERDUMMUNGSBANDAGEN!**

103

hoever reads bourgeois newspapers becomes nd and deaf: away with these stultifying bandages!
otomontage 1930

's compelling image marked the beginning of John Heartfield's laboration with the *Arbeiter-Illustrierte-Zeitung* or *AIZ* (The *orkers' Pictorial Newspaper*). Founded in 1924, this anti-fascist, tist weekly was aimed at the working class and had a circulation over 350,000 in its heyday in 1930, giving Heartfield a powerful tform from which to counter the virulent propaganda of the zis. This photomontage was directed at rival publications *rwärts* (*Forward*) and *Tempo*, and its caption implied that ey were misinforming and literally blinding their readers to the lities of the situation. Heartfield made clever use of language d text, not only as a visual device but also to convey meaning, h the titles of the newspapers as the mouth and eye of the ure, and the extended "o" of *Tempo* almost like an eyebrow.

However, the image also stands the test of time as a more neral statement on media bias. It calls to mind Heartfield's ial reasons for using photomontage, as he explained: "I saw th what was being said and not being said with photos in the wspapers... I found out how you can fool people with photos, lly fool them... You can lie and tell the truth by putting the ong title or wrong captions under them, and that's roughly at was being done." Heartfield's image also resonates with the st-war sensibility of German society, still devastated by the unds of the Great War with the head "bandaged" in newspaper ges recalling the casualties suffered.

I assemble documents and juxtapose them with intelligence d skill, the effect of agitation and propaganda on the asses will be enormous."

n Heartfield

n Heartfield (German, 1891–1968) was one he most intelligent and satirical proponents he art of photomontage. He used it as a apon to initially critique the establishment d then to undermine the rise of Hitler and the zi Party. He anglicized his name in 1917 from mut Herzfeld in protest against the anti-British toric in Germany during World War I, and came a member of the German Communist ty (KPD) in 1918. He and his brother Wieland were part of the Dada art movement, along with George Grosz, with whom he founded the satirical magazine *Die Pleite*. He was forced to flee Berlin in 1933 when paramilitary SS troops burst into his apartment looking for him and he only escaped by hiding in a rubbish bin. He fled to England but was declared an enemy alien because of his links to communism. He returned to East Germany after the war, where he was investigated by the Stasi because of his time spent in Britain.

Creative tips and techniques

Heartfield recognized that photomontage could act as a potent vehicle to make political statements that could not be made in other media. He recognized its potential as a powerful form of mass communication. In the 1920s, photomontage became a popular tool for dissent with other Dadaists such as Hannah Hoch, who used it to critique bourgeois society. It was also popular in Soviet Russia, where Constructivist artists including El Lissitzky and Alexander Rodchenko used it to produce propaganda. The word "photomontage" has associations with manual labor, acknowledging photography's mechanical nature, and suggests that a photomontage was "built" from existing components just as an industrial factory worker assembled a product. Heartfield identified with the working classes and often wore overalls rather than a suit.

Heartfield was a perfectionist who worked to deadlines, usually only having about a week to respond to the news of the day before a journal was published. He made an initial detailed sketch of the overall layout, then searched other publications and archives for suitable images to use. He normally hired a photographer to copy, enlarge, or reduce his found pictures and take any additional images needed. After cutting out and assembling the components, he then employed a retoucher to paint out areas and merge the edges of the cut-outs together to create a seamless result. The finished photomontage was then photographed and type added to the negative where necessary. Finally, the printing plate was made; *AIZ* was printed using the copper photogravure process, which gave an excellent result with a wide tonal range and high-quality printing.

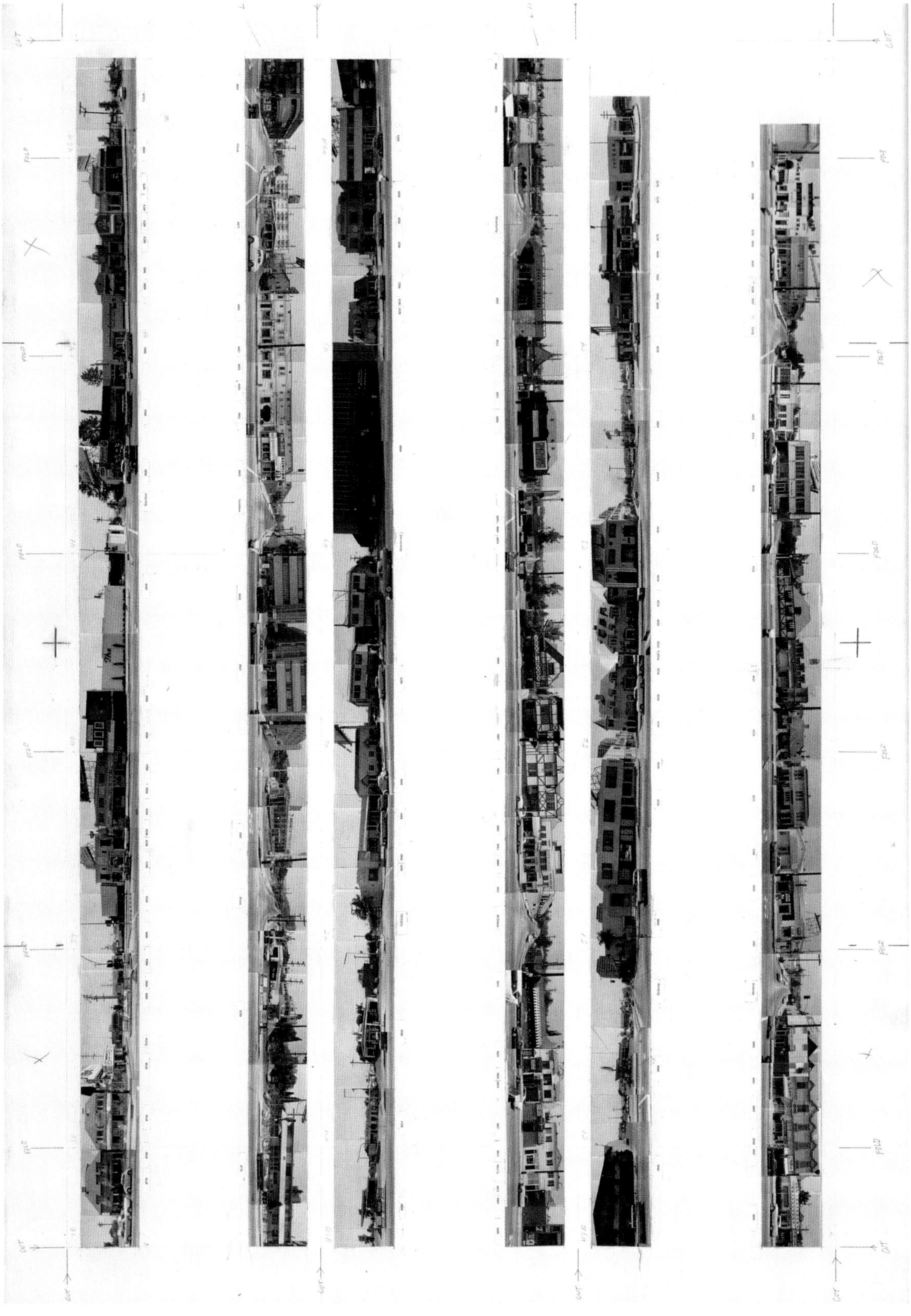

aquette for *Every Building on the Sunset Strip* 1966

ery Building on the Sunset Strip was one of a series of books Ruscha made in the 1960s and 1970s that explored how a oology of everyday objects or nondescript buildings could nerate a meaningful statement about vernacular America. the same time, it questioned what the subject of art and otography could be. Simple in format and cheaply printed, scha's books challenged the idea of the artist book. Walker ans's *American Photographs* (1938) was a clear antecedent, t Ruscha's topographical approach gave his works a conceptual her than a documentary thrust. Sunset Strip is the incarnation Los Angeles, but Ruscha undermines its iconic status by scribing its totality as a continuous façade of unremarkable mmercial buildings. The book's format is innovative; it opens t into an accordion-fold page measuring 27 feet (8 meters) ng, with the south side of the street running along the top d the north side upside down along the bottom. To make the ok, Ruscha fixed his 35mm motor-driven camera on a car and ove along the strip each way, exposing a continuous sequence around 250 black-and-white pictures. The work exposes the n façade of the Hollywood myth: "It's like a Western town, in way. A store-front plane of a Western town is just paper, and erything behind it is just nothing."

never take pictures just for the taking of pictures... I want ne end product; that's what I'm really interested in... I use to do a job, which is to make a book." Ed Ruscha

Ruscha (American, 1937–) is an artist who rks across a range of media. He has been sociated with the Pop art movement of the 60s, but his work also draws on the ideas of daism, Surrealism, and Abstract Expressionism. ords and phrases play a central role in his rk, along with a low-key deadpan humor. tween 1963 and 1978, Ruscha produced teen photographic books, exploring the nality and mundanity of American life through serial explorations of themes of advertising, commercialization, and suburbanism, publishing most of them himself. Ruscha lives and works in Los Angeles. His work is playful, and explores the conventions of what is a subtle subject for art, challenging the notion that it has to be an elevated sense of the sublime. Much of his work concerns vernacular, commercial culture. He says that, for him, "Good art should elicit a response of 'Huh? Wow!' as opposed to 'Wow! Huh?'".

Creative tips and techniques

The construction of Ruscha's book was complex, because of its unusual concertina format. To make the dummy, or maquette, each photograph had to be printed at the correct size for the final book, and then cut to line up with the next frame and hand pasted onto a board. Finally, the street numbers had to be carefully positioned under the appropriate facades. In the final book, the length of continuous images were actually nine glued-together sheets of about six folded pages each. Making a dummy like this is a very useful process, as the final result is a tangible physical object and gives a better sense of the feel of the final book than a digital file can ever achieve. It is a very useful process to go through with a set of images, and restores something of the craft element of photography.

Ruscha starts his projects with a concept or idea, often triggered by a specific word or phrase that ntrigues him. He explains how this developed through his first book using the topographic approach. He began with the phrase "twenty-six gasoline stations" until the idea of the images of the gas stations came to him. He recalls how the book caused consternation among its initial viewers, which was exactly as he had hoped: "I was after the head scratching."

As an artist using photography, Ruscha is less concerned with the traditional markers of photographic quality and esthetics, but more interested in how the unique process of the camera described the world: "Other artists translate the three dimensions of the real world into a two-dimensional image. The photograph did that for me." In this way, for Ruscha, the camera is a tool to achieve a final concept.

Duane Michals

The fallen angel 1968

Duane Michals describes his sequences as "fictionettes." They are like short stories or visual haikus, expressing an idea or a feeling in a cinematic flow of narrative. Many of his sequences have the feel of a moral fable or aphorism; here, Michals examines temptation and shows an angel succumbing to lust. Yet there is often also a sense of mystery in his work. He believes that more should be left to the viewer's imagination: "I don't think photographs should tell you too much. Photographs should make you come to them. They shouldn't spill the beans." His work connects on an emotional level, which he argues can be attuned to the nature of the image: "The best part of us is not what we see; it's what we feel." He began to add text to his images because he felt "frustrated by the silence of the still photograph." He feels that combining words and images generates deeper meaning: "I write with this photograph not to tell you what you can see, rather to express what is invisible. I write to express these feelings. We are our feelings."

> "I always said I want my photographs to whisper. Whereas a lot of photographs shout to get attention."
>
> Duane Michals

Duane Michals (American, 1932–) initially worked commercially, shooting portraits in people's environments rather than in the studio. He developed this approach into photo series, expanding the single image into short stories, often using handwritten text to expand the narrative. He claims "everything is a subject for photography, especially the difficult things of ou lives: anxiety, childhood hurts, lust, nightmares. T things that cannot be seen are the most significa They cannot be photographed, only suggested."

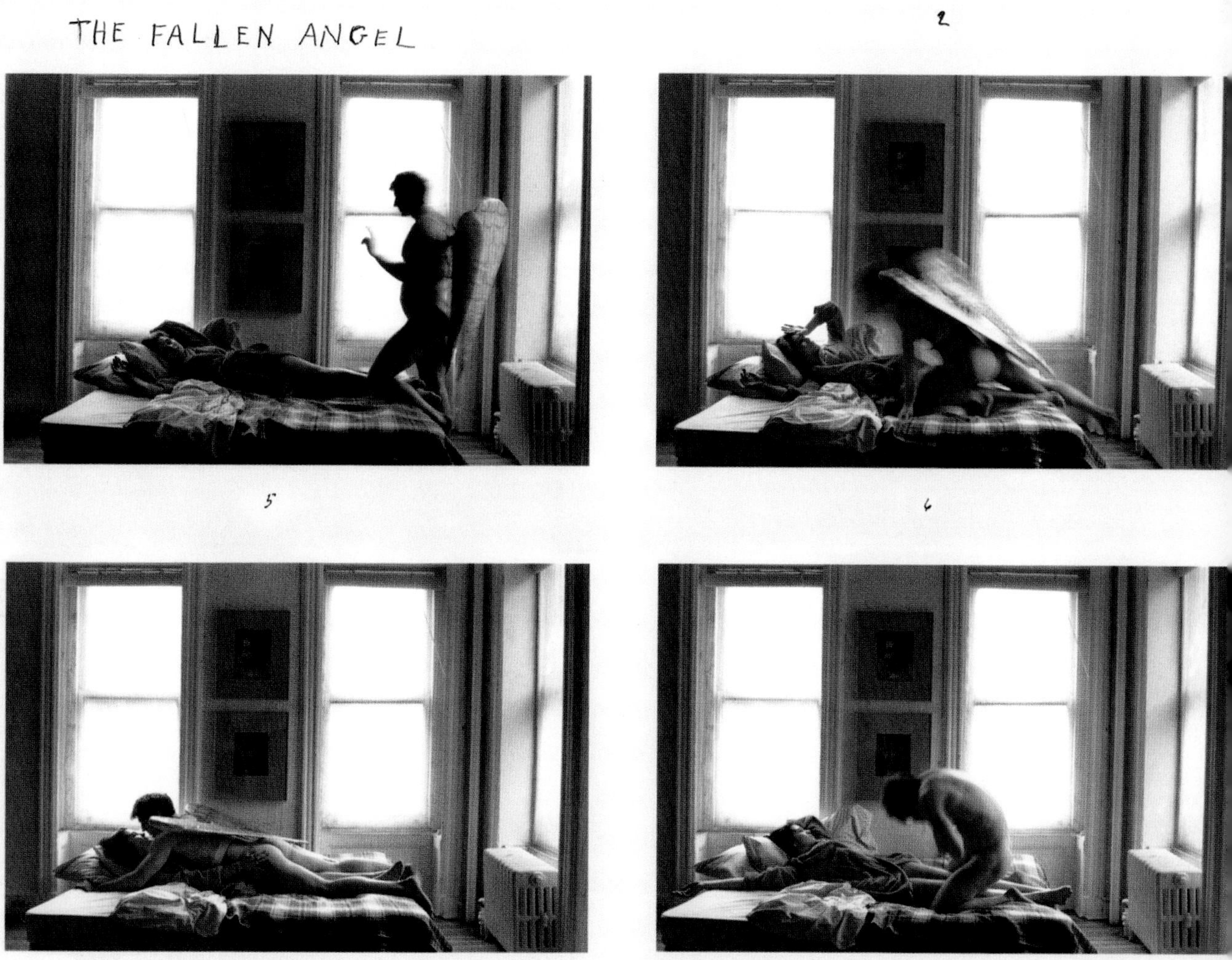

Creative tips and techniques

Michals has been a prolific photographer for many years, and can reflect on a long career of image-making. His advice on the perspective of ageing is touching; he noted that, at the age of eighty-two, he could do things that he would not have felt confident enough to do at the age of twenty-eight. Age has given him a greater sense of emotional and psychological maturity and a heightened sense of perspective on the nuances of life, which enhances his work. He elaborates on this theme by speaking of the subtlety that comes with perspective, noting that "what poetry is all about is paying attention to subtle details. Great art is paying attention to the things that are lost. When you are young, emotions are much broader; there's that 'anywhere you go, I will go with you' mentality. As you get older, it becomes more like tea that steeps for a long time and gets richer. That's the sublime quality of life."

Michals is skeptical of the idea that a single portrait image can truly capture the character of a subject. He believes that people are rarely what they appear to be, especially in front of a camera. As an alternative, his photo series expand the idea of the photographic moment into a longer temporal continuum, and he feels that this can be applied to portrait photographs, too. He describes his approach as making a "prose portrait," which does not necessarily show you what someone looks like. A prose portrait tells you about the nature of the person. A variation on this would be to make a series of different images of the same person, and present them together as a way of describing their character more fully than in a single image. You could work with your subject to collaboratively come up with a short shooting script for a sequence that explores an aspect of their lives, with them acting out a role that reflects an aspect of their character.

3

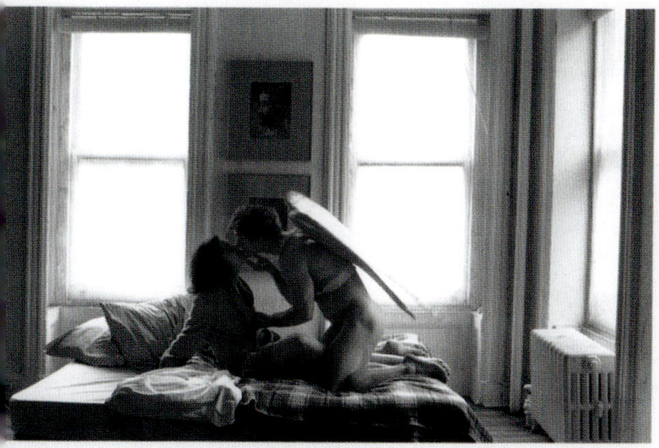

4

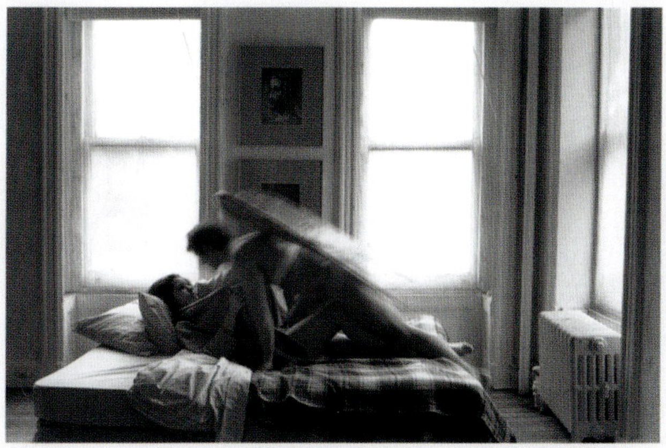

7

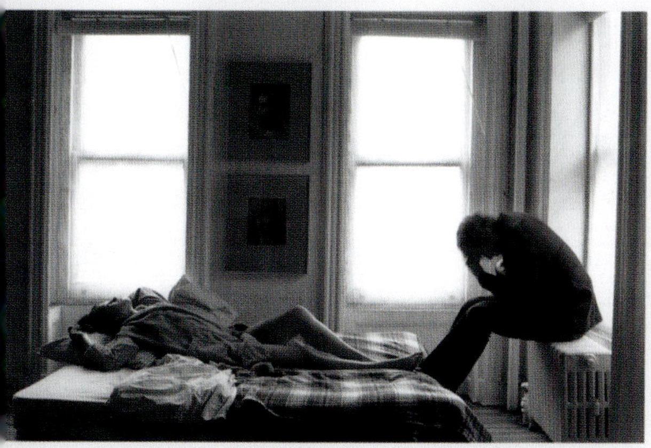

8

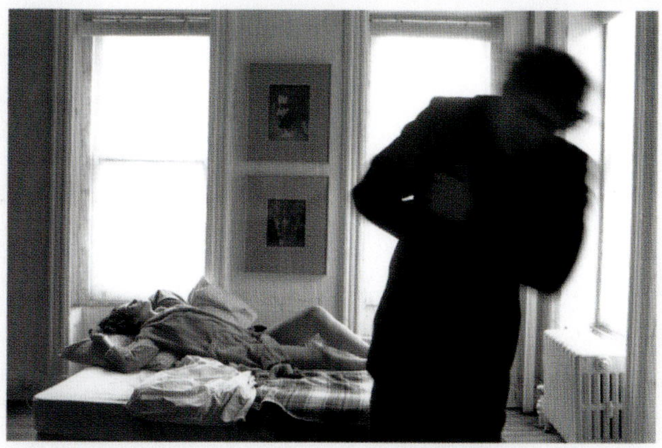

Nicholas Nixon

The Brown sisters 1975/2015

These two photographs are the first and most recent in an ongoing series documenting the gradual changes that each passing year brings to the same group of women. The series is an extraordinary meditation on the ageing process and on family relationships; however, it began almost by accident, as photographer Nicholas Nixon—husband of the eldest sister, Bebe—recalls: "We'd go down to visit Bebe's parents on weekends. It was kind of boring, a lot of socializing, we were expected to show up for dinner every day... Out of a friendly desperation, I said: 'Let's take a picture.'" Each year since then, he has brought the four Brown sisters together to make a new group portrait, always in the same order from left to right. When he took the first image in 1975, Heather was twenty-three, Mimi was fifteen, Bebe was twenty-five, and Laurie was twenty-one. "We joke about it," he says, "but everybody knows that certainly my intention would be that we would go on forever, no matter what. To just take three, and then two, and then one. The joke question is: what happens if I go in the middle. I think we'll figure that out when the time comes." The images are haunting, as the passage of time etches new experiences on each face, with subtle differences in posture and body language suggesting how each character has changed over an extended period. Viewing all the images together is an emotional experience and audiences have been known to cry openly at exhibitions of the work.

"Physically, looking through a giant ground glass and seeing how the world looks is amazing. When composing a shot, I see a combination of the real facts of my subject and the camera's transformation of their image at the same time."

Nicholas Nixon

Nicholas Nixon (American, 1947–) first came to prominence when his large-format images of Boston and New York were included in the influential "New Topographics" show curated by John Szarkowski in 1975. Nixon has continued to document the changing urban landscape of Boston, where he lives, but he expanded his repertoire into portraiture. He is an expert at choreographing groups of people in fluid compositions, despite using the slow and cumbersome 10 x 8 camera mounted on a tripod. He says: "I never get tired of photographing people, because they are all very different. They smell different, they look different, I engage with them differently. My interest is intense and changing, one slice of the life cycle at a time." He has also worked on issues of health and ageing, including a series on his own dying father and one on people living with AIDS. Originally a literature student, he cites writers William Faulkner, Henry Green, Marcel Proust, Charles Dickens, and Ernest Hemingway as major influences. He has been a professor at Massachusetts College of Art and Design since 1975.

Creative tips and techniques

Nixon describes how the encounter with the subject is a collaboration, in which the photographer, the subject, and the technical process of using the view camera come together to create the final image. He notes that people are self-conscious at first, but this situation improves "as we kind of dance with each other" and become more comfortable together. He adds, "The best pictures are usually the last ones."

Nixon is able to compose complex images using the large-format camera, as he has become adept at setting it up quickly. He notes that understanding how the reversed image is seen through the camera can actually help in making compositions, remarking how it shows "if there is any magic happening—it shows the moment intensified." The quality of the final image is paramount, and the ability to make contact prints directly from the negative gives Nixon the ability to make this as high as possible, with no loss of detail or tonal value through enlargement. He maintains that the biggest possible negative has the most clarity and impact.

Nixon has interesting ideas for the assignments he sets his students. He suggests tasks such as "photograph five men you would like to sleep with without them knowing," or themes such as "flesh," "details," or "people with animals." Try some of his ideas or set briefs of your own; working to a theme is an excellent way of helping you to delve more deeply into both the technical and esthetic aspects of photography, as it will concentrate your efforts. Use this approach to develop areas of your practice that you feel are underdeveloped, rather than trying to push forward a range of abilities simultaneously.

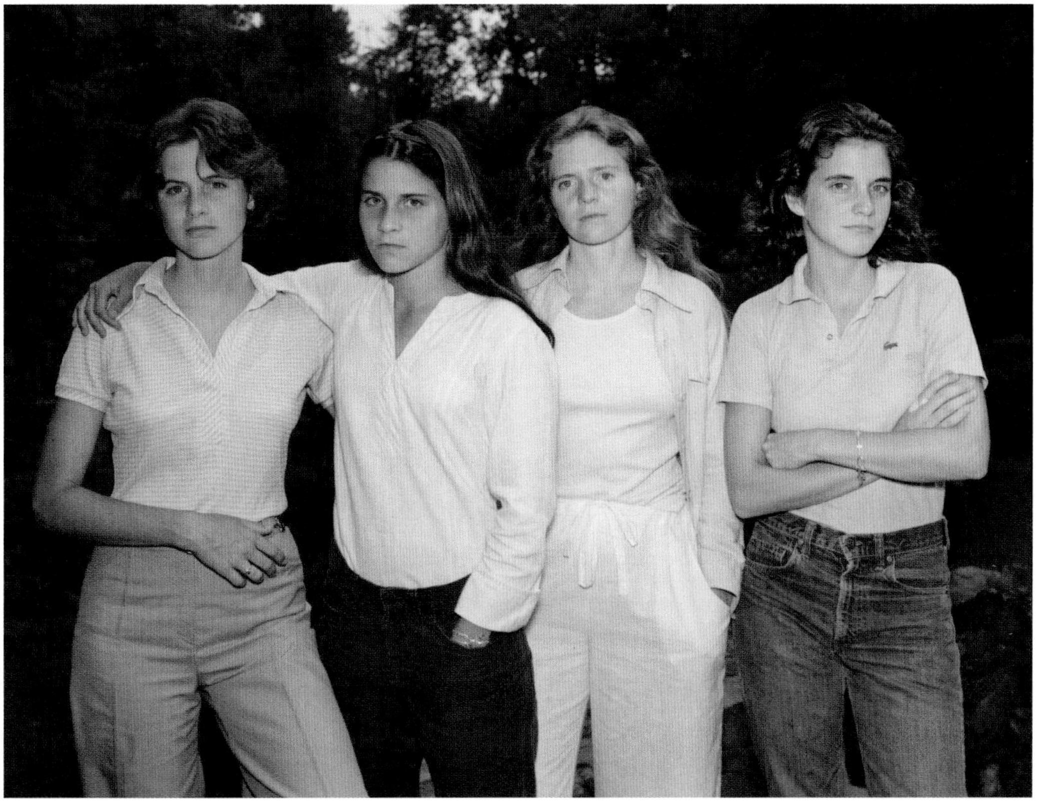

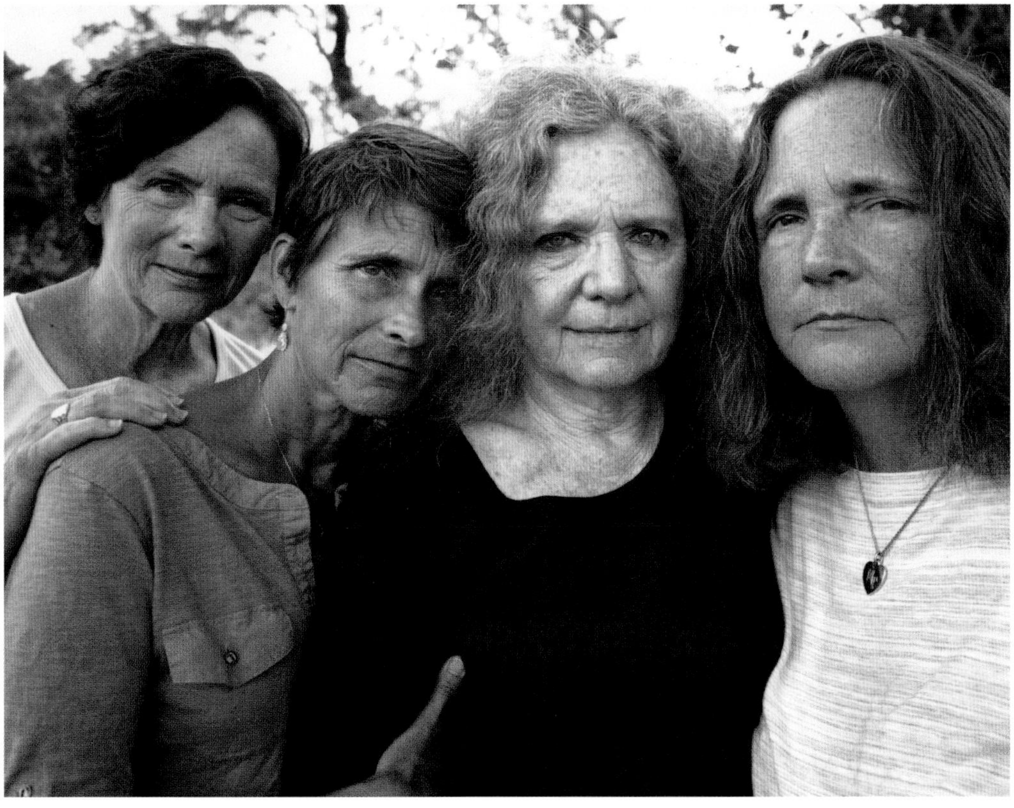

Cindy Sherman

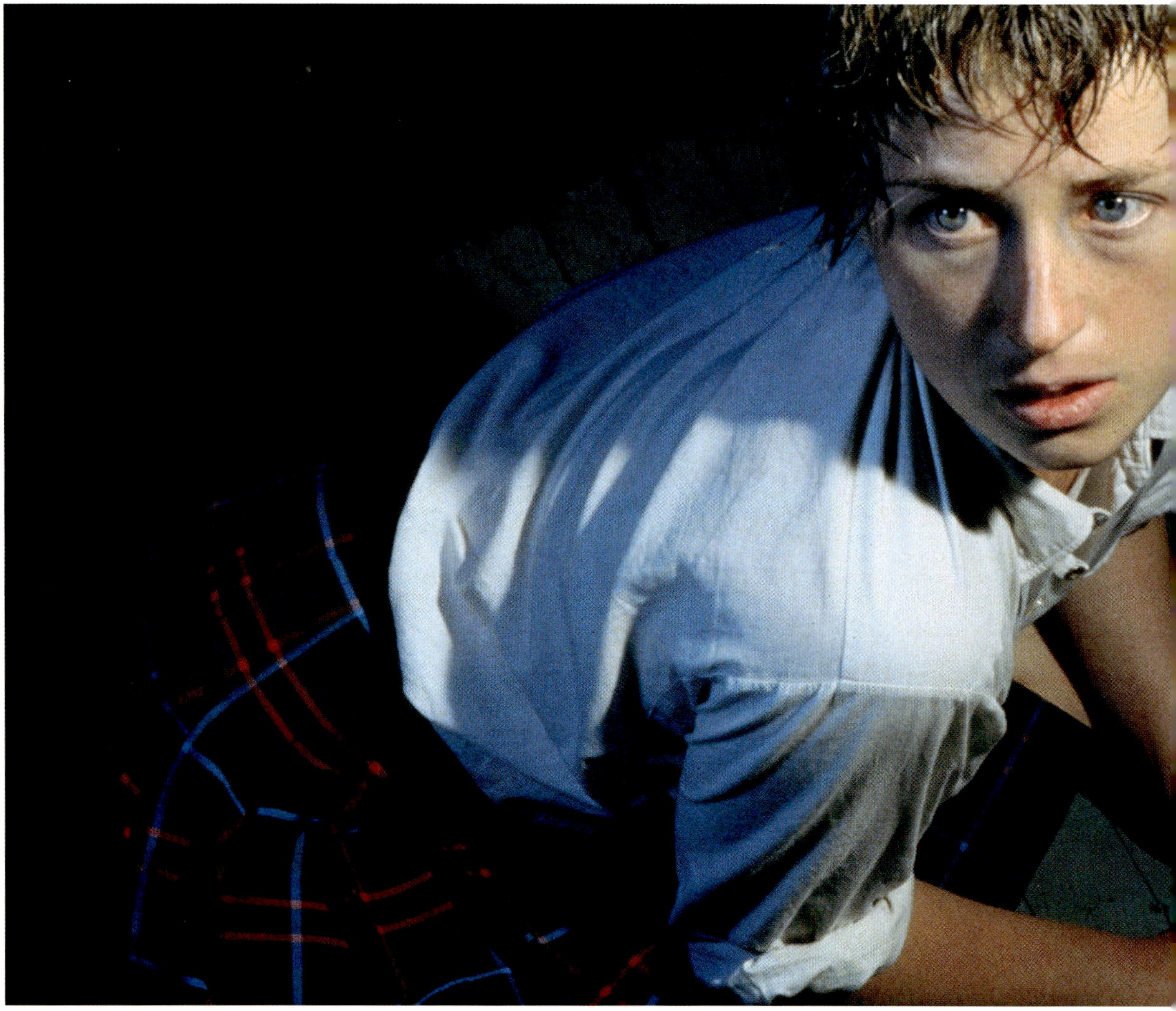

Untitled #92 1981, from the series "Centerfolds"

This photograph was a development from Cindy Sherman's breakthrough series "Untitled Film Stills" (1977–80), in which she adopted the imagined persona of a young actress playing multiple roles in a fictional environment. The work was initially commissioned by *Artforum* magazine, and Sherman developed the idea of making the images in a way that resembled the center pages of a pornographic magazine, but also referenced the widescreen format of the movies; she also switched to color. Critic Peter Schjeldahl explained that "this is photography as one-frame movie making. The pictures feature wide-screen proportions 2 x 4 feet (0.5 x 1 meter), high-angle mid-shot compositions, 'classy' cinematographic lighting, punched-up color, and the look of Method acting." The sense of the hyperreality of cinema, combined with a fictional fantasy representation of something that does exist in the real world, is at the heart of Sherman's practice. The woman in this shot appears afraid, as if she is about to be attacked, perhaps, which Sherman regarded as a conscious reference to the dangers inherent in the exploitation of women. As she explains, "in horror stories or in fairy tales, the fascination with the morbid is also, at least for me, a way to prepare for the unthinkable... That's why it's very important for me to shov the artificiality of it all, because the real horrors of the worl are unmatchable, and they're too profound." Although the photographs have a cinematic sensibility, Sherman is carefu not to be too precise about her inspiration, noting that "some people have told me they remember the film that one of my images is derived from, but in fact I had no film in mind at all." The work is, however, about self image, and how we create a face for the world that may or may not truly represent how we feel.

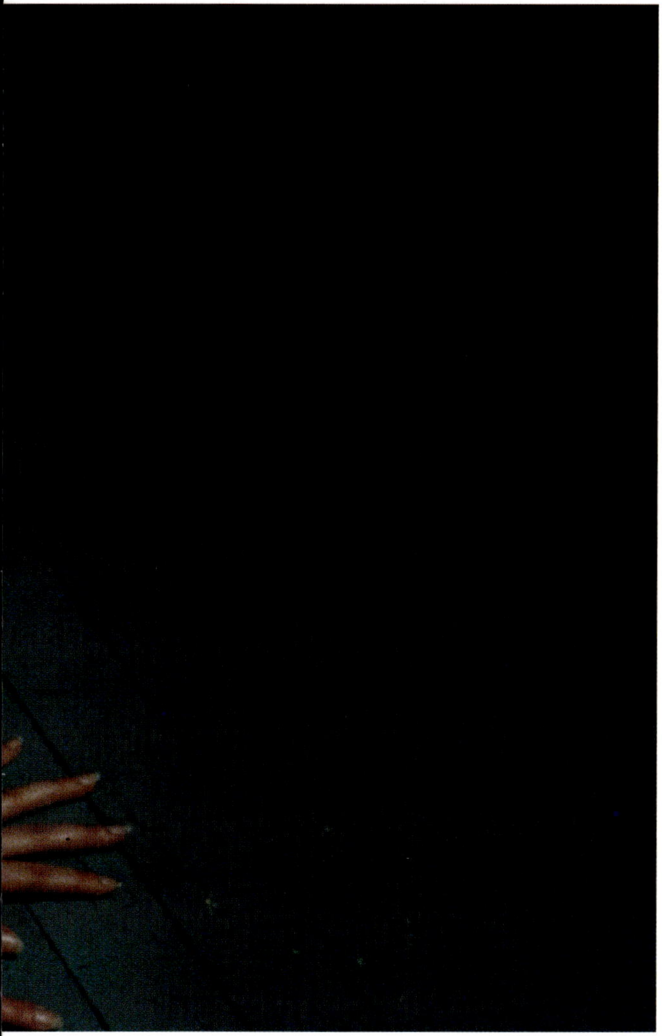

veryone thinks [my photographs] are self-portraits, but they
re not meant to be. If I photograph myself it's because I can
ush my own limits to the extreme." Cindy Sherman

ndy Sherman (American, 1954–) initially
orked as a painter, but realized that the camera
uld provide her with a more effective way to
plore the issues of identity and persona that
erested her. She recognized that she was
ood at using my face as a canvas…I'll see a
otograph of a character and try to copy them
to my face. I think I'm really observant, and
inking how a person is put together, seeing them
the street and noticing subtle things about
them that make them who they are." Sherman graduated from State University College, Buffalo, New York in 1976. She began her "Untitled Film Stills" series after moving to New York City in 1971. "Centerfolds," which explores ideas of voyeurism and fantasy, exhibited at the Skarstedt Gallery, New York in 1981. "Fairy Tales and Disasters" (1985–89) looked at the grotesque aspect of fairy tales. New York's Museum of Modern Art showed "The Complete Untitled Film Stills" series in 1997.

Creative tips and techniques

Sherman worked intuitively on these series, allowing the character of each photograph to emerge in the process of making the image. Yet, she stresses that she was not making a self-portrait or adopting the persona of someone else, but rather creating a character purely for the camera. She draws on recognizable traits so that the viewer can make connections with the idealized subjects she creates. She does not view herself as an actress; she saw the taking on of a persona as a necessary result of the feel she was seeking in the work. She found using herself as a model was more effective than working with others, as she could adopt more extreme positions.

Sherman's work has investigated how she can use herself as the transformational model through a range of different strategies and genres, but this in itself has difficulties inherent within it, of avoiding repetition. As she has matured as an artist, she is more comfortable with the consistent themes that run through her work.

The self-portrait has a long history in photography; many artists have used themselves as models to explore their own psyche. Using yourself as a subject allows you to push the image further than you might with a model; as Sherman's work shows, you can make significant statements about the social world through careful staging and construction of an image. Sherman often uses a mirror to help her build up the image, so that she can, in a sense, perform for herself. Photographers such as Lee Friedlander have used other reflective surfaces (for example, a window in the frame itself) to embed themselves into a scene.

Jeff Wall

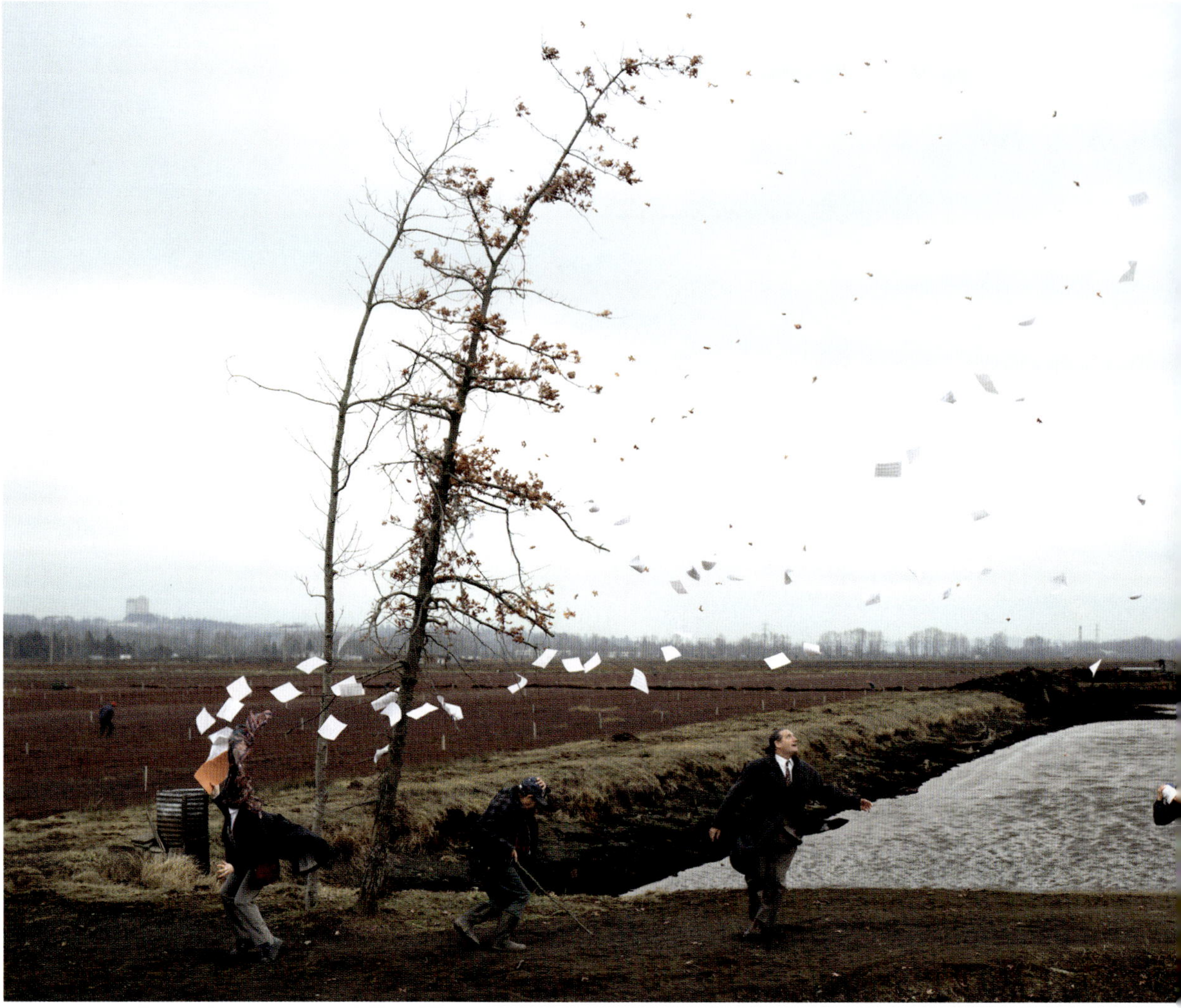

A sudden gust of wind (after Hokusai) 1993

One of the most famous works by Jeff Wall, this image references a 19th-century Japanese woodcut by Katsushika Hokusai (above right). Wall's image is full of movement and drama, with the trees bending in the wind and the figures struggling to catch the flying papers. Despite its apparent veracity, the image is actually made up of a digital composite of over 100 photographs, made over two years, and then combined together to make the huge final montage. Wall explains that the ability to slowly construct his photographs step by step is extraordinarily liberating: "When I began working on the computer, I realized you don't have to do it all at once. Of course it's exciting trying to get everything in one shot, but working digitally slowed things down. It made the process more complicated and, I hope, deeper." Freed from the need to capture everything at the same moment, Wall says that this process has been highly creative for him: "Not photographing gives me imaginative freedom that is crucial to the making of art." Wall's images typically show an interrupted moment, giving the sense that something has happened before the moment of the photograph, and that something will happen afterward, too. He describes how "photography is supposed to be instantaneous, and I have nothing against that. But for me, the plasticity of the process, where things turn into something else, comes from the time I spend on it." Describing them as "prose poems"—phrase borrowed from the French poet Charles Baudelaire—the final images are meant to suggest rather than confirm a predetermined idea. He emphasizes that the formal qualities of the work are key to the experience of viewing it, stating that a picture is "also the color ensemble, the textural nature of things, the patina or lack of patina. All these things are themselves beautiful, regardless of what the thing is about."

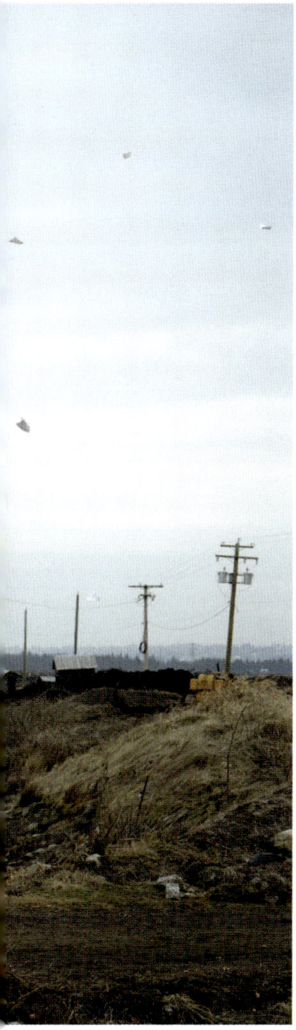

Katsushika Hokusai
Yejiri Station, Province of Suruga, c. 1832

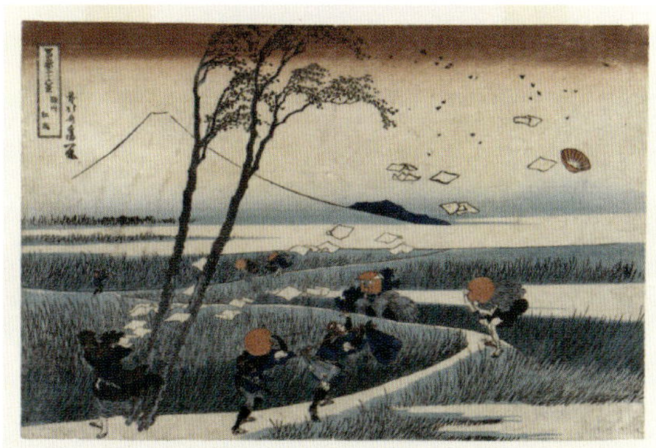

earned a lot from the scale of painting when trying to work photography, not to be like painting, but to please group of people standing in front of a wall in a way that's lated to what people like in a painting." Jeff Wall

f **Wall** (Canadian, 1946–) studied fine art and history, and his understanding of the heritage he Old Masters as well as the challenges of nceptual art equipped him with the vision develop his large-scale constructed images. ll was inspired by seeing the grand paintings Velázquez and Goya during a visit to the Museo del Prado in Madrid in 1977, and combined this with a realization that the backlit displays of advertising hoardings could be an effective form of display. His large-scale images have been hugely influential, and he has had numerous solo exhibitions. He was awarded the Hasselblad Award in 2002.

Creative tips and techniques

Wall's work questions one of the basic tenets of the art of photography, that it somehow offers a window on reality. He argues that this is often merely a matter of convention and that he prefers photographs that do not look the way they are supposed to. As he goes on to explain: "We don't really know how photographs are 'supposed to look.' The existing conventions make it seem that we do, because they are authentic and central to photography, but they cannot predict what the next interesting photograph is going to look like. Nobody claims to be able to predict what the next good painting will look like."

Wall makes large light boxes and prints of his complex montages for display in exhibition. This particular image is 8 x 13 feet (2.5 x 4 meters) in dimension. Wall's use of this large-scale format—together with his embracing of the techniques, composition, and subject matter used in the great history paintings of 19th-century artists—gives his images a grandeur and presence that allow the viewer to immerse themselves in the world he has created. He expresses how his training in art history gave him the sense of scale necessary for his photography. He finds this pictorial structure suggestive and rich, because it transforms the thing it depicts in the process of depicting and recording it. He explains: "The 'motif,' the thing depicted, comes to life not because of its own liveliness—even though it has that, too—but because of the way it almost vanishes into the tableau. The tableau-form, like a magic substance, both records with great fidelity and transforms the thing to which it is being true into another thing: a picture."

Adam Broomberg & Oliver Chanarin

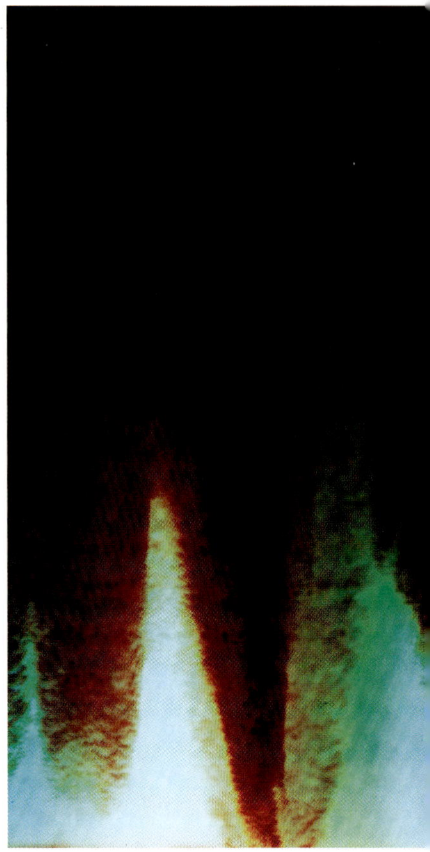

The Day Nobody Died 2008

Adam Broomberg and Oliver Chanarin's work is concerned with the imbalance of power between subject and photographer. They are interested in how the media relies on stereotypes of suffering and bravery in the depiction of war. This photograph challenges the limitations of the way in which access to military operations was controlled by the British Ministry of Defence and the restrictions applied to journalists and photographers in Iraq and Afghanistan.

This work was a development of an earlier project, *Chicago*, a fake Arab town built by the Israeli military as a secret training base. They explain how journalists had developed a bond with troops that led to a more "heroic" depiction of their actions: "So they invented the embedding system, which on the surface promises the photographer unprecedented access to the frontline (but less apparent was the access it granted the defence ministries to the photographer's movement and material). It was a deal with the devil." They applied for permission to go to Afghanistan under the guise of journalism, but with a different agenda: "In order to get embedded, we signed a form effectively banning us from taking any images that showed evidence of conflict (no dead bodies, no wounded bodies, no evidence of enemy fire... the list is endless). So our only option was to make a performative act of resistance." They took a roll photographic paper, encased in a large box, all the way fro their London studio to the British military base in Helmanc province, arriving during the most violent month of the wa On their first day, a BBC fixer was dragged from his car an executed, and nine Afghan soldiers were killed in a suicide attack. The next day, three British troops were killed. The fighting continued until the fifth day, when nobody died.

As a response to these happenings, and to more prosaic events such as a visit by the Duke of York, they unfurled the photographic paper and exposed 19½-foot (6-meter) sections of it to the light for twenty seconds. The entire process was filmed, following the box of paper as it was transported from one military base to another, on aircraft, tanks, and jeeps, producing a piece of performance art tha challenges the "objective reality" of conventional reporting These abstract images, with their random swathes of color cannot help but be seen as violent expressions of the natu of warfare, despite their being made entirely by the action of the sun without human interference. Broomberg and Chanarin describe them as "in a sense, real witnesses."

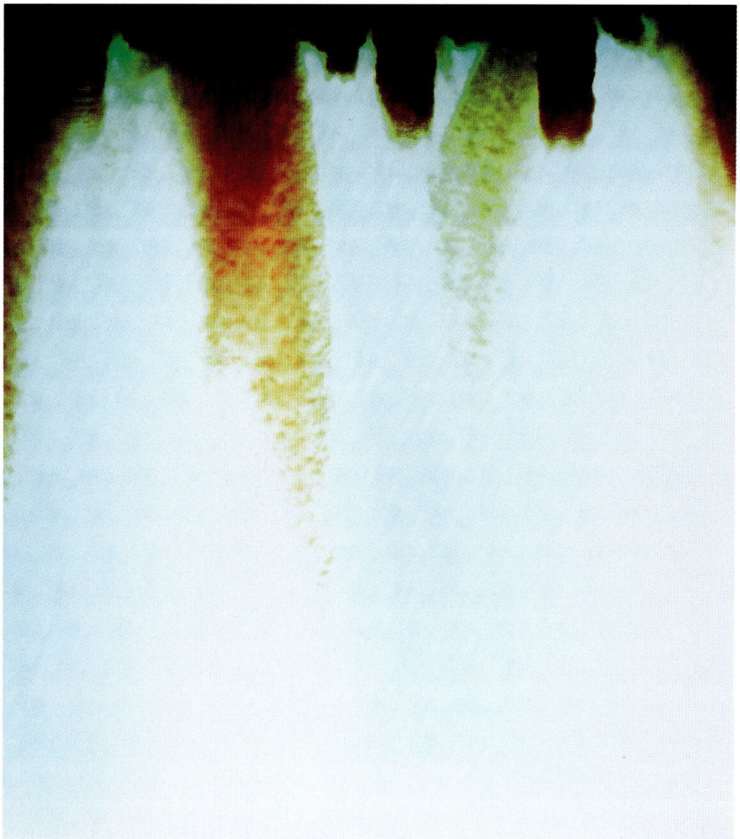

"The moral, political, and financial world that images work in began to interest us more than the individual images. So our work began to look at revealing the mechanisms at work around image making, distribution, and consumption."

Adam Broomberg & Oliver Chanarin

am Broomberg (South African, 1970–) and **ver Chanarin** (British, 1971–) have worked ether since they met at the influential gazine *Colors*. Together they have produced eries of projects and publications that lore the limits of documentary photography, mining how a variety of formal strategies, uding portraiture, landscape, and hival work, can interrogate the ethics of resentation. They explain that: "We began eel uncomfortable about how naive our jects were about the power of an image, that hotograph is a piece of currency that has an erlife. We wanted to make work that critiqued t." Broomberg and Chanarin were awarded Deutsche Börse Photography Prize for their ok *War Primer 2*, a reinterpretation of Bertolt cht's initial 1955 publication. They established opped Liver Press to publish and sell their own oks as well as those by other artists.

Creative tips and techniques

Broomberg and Chanarin are unusual in that they produce all their work under one banner, not claiming any distinction over who actually "pressed the shutter." The large format they work with allows them both to play a part in framing the subject. They usually use a plate camera, so that both can look and frame. They explain that because they have grown together as artists and worked together for so long, their artistic thinking has become enmeshed. They describe their working process as organic.

The pair work with a variety of techniques, from formal portraits and landscapes to abstracts and still lifes, adapting their formal approach to the demands of a particular project rather than having a rigid style. They work extensively with archives, mining them for hidden meanings and revealing connections between images that create new interpretations of past events. Working with found or archival images can be very rewarding. Try to find an archive to work in; the sheer pleasure of opening boxes of vintage prints and bringing new life to them is an engaging process.

Mishka Henner

Coronado feeders, Dalhart, Texas 2013, from "Feedlots"

Seen from an aerial view, this extraordinary pattern, looking like a huge stain on the landscape, is in fact a feedlot, known as a Concentrated Animal Feeding Operation (CAFO). Taken from Mishka Henner's series "Feedlots," it houses thousands of animals in tiny, confined spaces before they are slaughtered. Access to such sites on the ground is virtually impossible, as they are protected by so-called "ag-gag" laws that prevent the photographing of farming operations. In fact, as Henner explains, such images do exist: "Many of them are from satellite images taken by the farming administration themselves." He came across feedlots while working on another series on oilfields, and recalls that at first he had no idea what he was seeing: "The mass and density of the black and white dots seemed almost microbial. To understand what they were I had to learn about the meat industry and its methods for maximizing yield in the minimum amount of time for the highest profit." The epic scale and the disturbing chemical outflow of waste in the image carry a powerful message about the industrialization and commodification of the food industry, as well as human life generally. Henner warns: "These images reflect a blueprint and a horror that lie at the heart of the way we live."

Henner is one of a growing number of artists who use satellite imaging and Google Street View in their work. He argues that the artistic credibility of the work lies in his vision and curation of such images, not in the fact of whether he himself took the photographs: "A social reality has been captured by a remote device taking billions of pictures no one else ever looked at or collected in this way before."

"My motivation isn't to make you feel or to care—it's to make you think." Mishka Henner

Mishka Henner (Belgian, 1976–) initially worked as a photojournalist, but gradually became disillusioned with conventional documentary methodology, explaining that, "I no longer really trusted the camera in my hands. I don't think subjects trusted it. It seemed to get in the way of an interaction, an encounter, and change it dramatically. I would be performing and the person in front of it would be performing. It was all a performance. That made the idea of objective truth redundant, so that all that was left was a kind of stylistic exercise that could be applied to any subject: a tow-bar factory, a war in Syria. I started to really distrust that. The world is so much richer than my stylistic cloaking of it." Since then he has explored a wide variety of strategies to interrogate the world around him, mostly involving digital technology to uncover material that would otherwise be difficult, if not impossible, to photograph by traditional means, including *Fifty-one US Military Outposts* (2010) and *Dutch Landscapes* (2011), both on secret military sites. Henner lives and works in Manchester, United Kingdom.

Creative tips and techniques

Henner's work raises interesting questions about the role of the photographer in the digital age and what constitutes the act of photography. He describes his practice as an amalgamation of intelligence gathering, data aggregation, image-making, and packaging. His projects involve an immense amount of research, thought, and planning, together with a methodical, systematic approach. His final images have a clear and powerful esthetic, but are also rich in content. Although digital composites, they are initially made with a camera, even if he is not the initial operator. He argues that the mark of his authorship is in the composition, framing, color, and contrast.

Henner spends hours scouring satellite images looking for his subjects. As most of them are not marked directly on maps, he has to search for them visually by painstakingly mapping vast swathes of the US landscape on Google Maps in satellite view. Once he locates a feedlot or oilfield, he works out its dimensions and then zooms in to the maximum resolution of Google Maps and makes a screen grab of each sector of the site. He takes hundreds of screenshots and then stitches them together manually to get fantastic detail. He elevates what is essentially a dull image in post-production.

Henner realized that the advent of digital on demand publishers such as Blurb allows an artist to produce books that can generate as much impact as a book produced by a mainstream publisher, but without the cost. This makes books—for example, his extraordinary work *Astronomical* (2011)—that would be uneconomic to produce conventionally completely viable for these platforms.

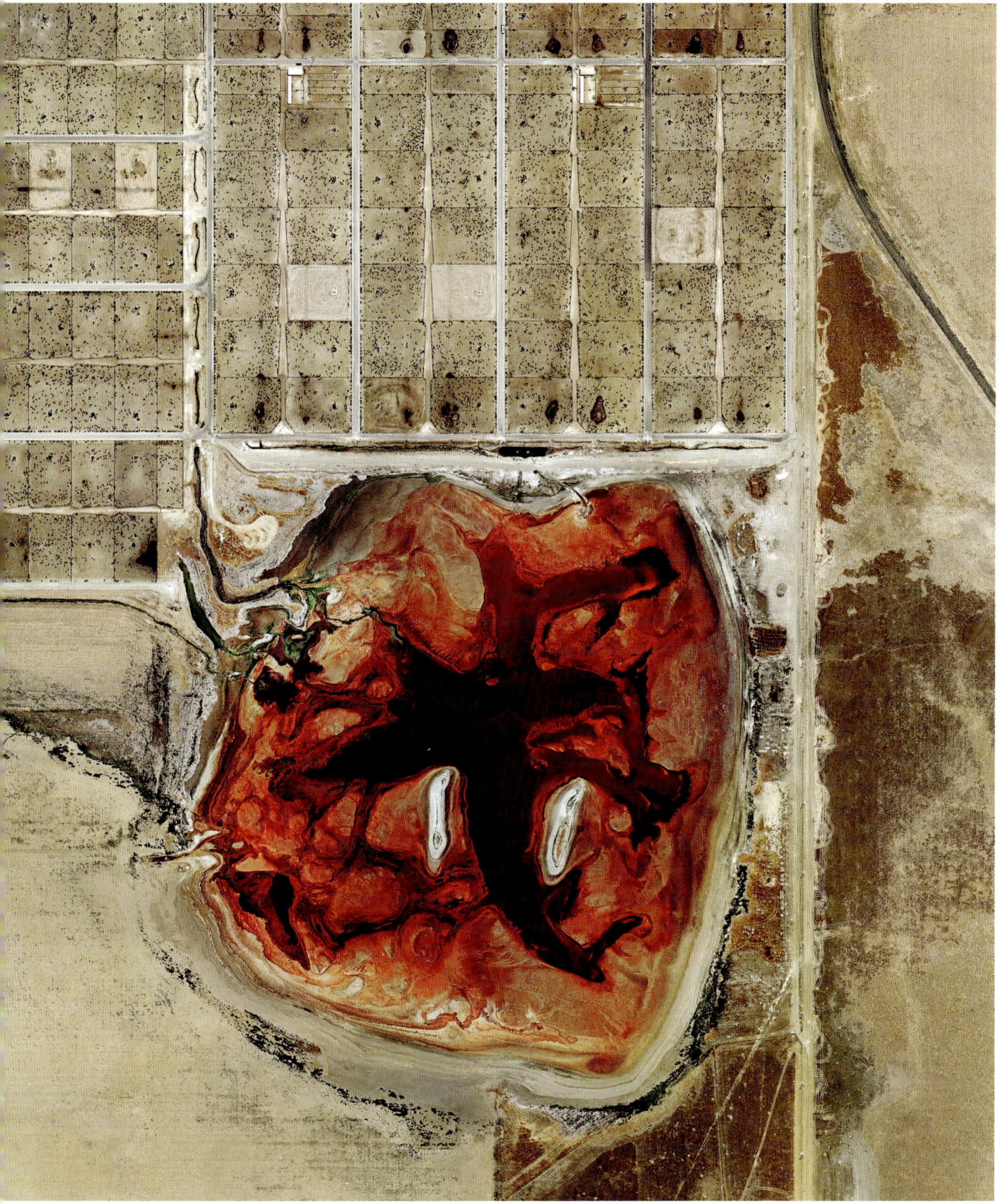

Mom

nts

Many of the greatest photographs capture a moment, that split second in time, in which everything comes together to make a perfect image. Such moments can be encountered anywhere—on the street, in sport, at a family celebration, or at a news event. These “moment” pictures give life to a scene, elevating it from the everyday into something more profound. They look effortless, but they require consummate patience and quick reflexes. The street has been a focal point for photographers from the earliest beginnings of the medium in the 19th century. This public space provides the stage for much of everyday life—business, entertainment, getting from one place to another, relationships, and every manner of human activity. Time spent on one’s feet—walking endlessly, hunting for visual prey—is fundamental to street photography. That patience always pays off, however; the possibility of the serendipitous chance encounter is rare, but the more time spent searching for it, the more likely it is to be found. Mistakes are common and moments fleeting, but the instinctive control of the camera can visually explore the lively movement and organization of the street. The street can be a chaotic, crazy place, full of life, or it can be a tranquil and quiet environment. The scene is constantly changing, as the light moves through the day, casting shadows and creating reflections that can transform an apparently dull scene into one loaded with life, vibrancy, and meaning. The street is a site of performance, both of the people existing on it and in terms of the photographer's relationship to it. It is truly a theatrical space in which the photographic choreographer can orchestrate the world around himself or herself in a dizzying display of visual gymnastics.

Manuel Álvarez Bravo

Daughter of the dancers 1933

Manuel Álvarez Bravo's work occupies the space between reality and dreams. His images of ordinary life are imbued with a heightened sense of magic and fantasy, and invite the viewer into an imaginative engagement with the moment. His photographs are ingrained with a sense of the Mexican theater of life, which he described as "down here, everything is symbol and mystery." In the street, Álvarez Bravo found a stage set full of signs, cafés, shop windows, and street vendors that delivered aesthetic and formal opportunities. In this haunting image, a girl looks through an aperture in a wall that resembles some deep eye socket through which she can travel to another world, perhaps losing her innocence in the process. Her right foot is balanced on her left to lift her slightly, showing her desire to see more, but also recalling the poses of classical statues. Her clothes and hat reference Mexican peasantry and traditional life, which are challenged by the possibilities of modernity that lie beyond the dark hole. This image typifies Álvarez Bravo's ability to transform the mundane into the magical, and explains his attraction to European Surrealism. He encouraged photographers to "Shoot what you see, not what you think." He explained how he did not set out with a specific idea in mind, but rather allowed the situation to reveal its deeper meaning: "When one takes a photograph, one doesn't think about saying anything in particular...but rather of creating something visual which later can bear a meaning that one didn't intend to transmit—depending on the viewer's interpretation but not necessarily on the photographer's."

> "A photographer's main instrument is his eyes. Strange as it may seem, many photographers choose to use the eyes of another photographer, past or present, instead of their own. Those photographers are blind."
>
> Manuel Álvarez Bravo

Manuel Álvarez Bravo (Mexican, 1902–2002) is one of the major forces in photography to have emerged from Latin America. His work embodied the surrealism and magic realism found in Mexican life. Both his grandfather and father were amateur photographers, and he studied painting at the Academy of San Carlos but was a self-taught photographer. Early in his career he met Tina Modotti and Edward Weston (see p.98), who gave him great encouragement. His work developed in the period after the Mexican Revolution, known as the Mexican Renaissance, when the forces of modernization combined with a search for national identity. European Surrealists such as Henri Cartier-Bresson (see p.260) and André Breton were drawn to Mexico, and became friends with Álvarez Bravo. He also worked as a film stills photographer and taught successive generations of Mexican photographers.

Creative tips and techniques

This image is also a study in patterns and shapes, with the repeated circular forms of the hat, the frame of the window and the black form of the shadowed aperture forming a tunnel-like series of structures leading the eye into the image. These are contrasted with the rectangular shapes of the tiled wall, which gives the image great energy but also a stillness at the center, cleverly juxtaposing the visual movement of the different lines in the image to create a visually compelling series of contrasting forces. Look out for patterns in everday life; the repetition of similar shapes can give your images great structure and form.

Álvarez Bravo was a master of using light and shade in his compositions; in this image the darkness of the hole is compared to the white of the girl's dress and hat. The shadows too are skillfully used to create extra definition to the composition. Understanding how the color world will translate into photographic tones is a skill you need to really work at. Learning to see in black and white takes practice as well as trial and error.

This photograph is a study of texture as well as pattern. The scuffs and scratches on the wall add a sense of the "real" to the image, with the smooth paint scraped away by the passage of time, especially in the ring around the hole in the wall, suggesting that hundreds of people have peered though it over the years. The drapery of the girl's dress contrasts with the smooth wall, and with the flatness of the brim of the hat. All these elements add to the three dimensionality of the image. Look out for how you can use similar textures to give extra sensual richness to a photograph.

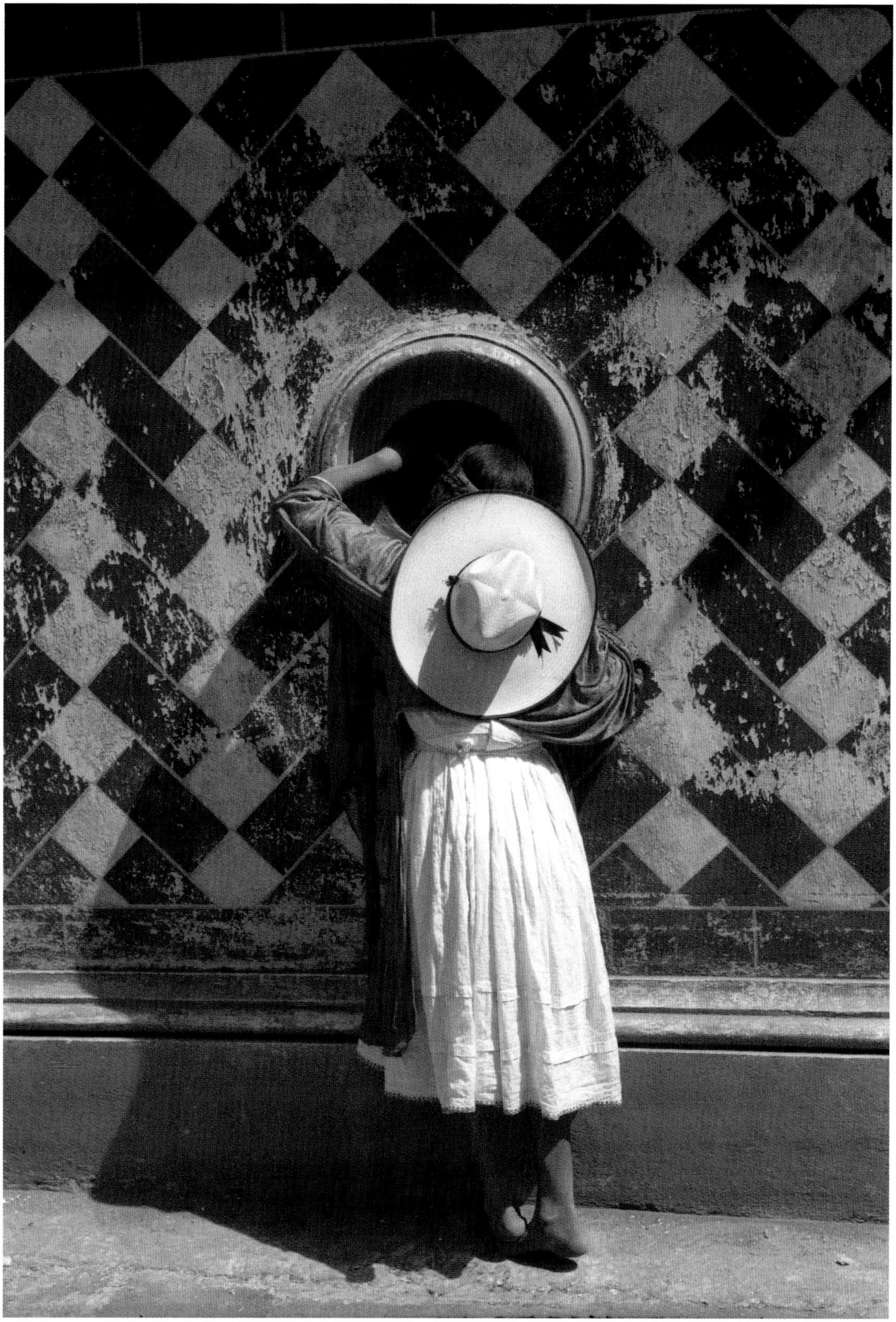

Robert Frank

Trolley, New Orleans 1955

This photograph of an everyday scene in New Orleans deals with the complexity of the racial situation in the American South. Each window of the trolleybus segregates an individual who is emblematic of the divisions in US society, from the middle-class woman looking sternly and disapprovingly at the photographer to the two African Americans who represent the stereotypes of the black housemaid and the reliable "Uncle Tom" worker. In the center, the young boy in his bow tie symbolizes the gulf between rich and poor. As well as being full of meaning, the image is also formally complex and rich, with the different textures of metal, cloth, skin, and glass. The side of the bus is a flat, two-dimensional screen, out of which the figures project. Along the top of the frame, the reflections in the windows are like a self-contained film strip, blurry cinema stills carrying their own internal narrative.

Robert Frank is a master at transforming an everyday situation into one laden with mystery, drama, and unease. This image perfectly illustrates his idea that photographs must contain "the humanity of the moment," and it featured prominently in his landmark book, *The Americans* (1958). To make the book, he traveled more than 10,000 miles during a -year trip that took him to 30 states, and shot 767 rolls of film. On his return to New York, he spent a year editing the images down to 1,000 prints, from which he created the sequence and final edit for the book. Frank refused to compromise his work, even to the point of commercial failure, believing that his personal statement was more important than financial success if it meant abandoning his unique vision.

> "Black and white are the colors of photography. To me they symbolize the alternatives of hope and despair to which mankind is forever subjected."
>
> Robert Frank

Robert Frank (American, 1924–) produced one of the most significant books in the history of photography with *The Americans* (1958). Funded by grants from the Guggenheim Foundation, the Swiss-born photographer traveled across the United States for two years in the mid-1950s. Frank examined the flip side of the American dream, photographing the dark corners and hidden places, the racism and segregation, the poor and the rich, and the fear of the outsider that was prevalent in the Cold War-obsessed 1950s. He focused on the icons of American life—jukeboxes, cowboys, cars, the road—but instead of celebrating them, he used them as metaphors for the alienation of modern life. The book remains one of the most influential photography books of the 20th century. Frank has also worked as an avant-garde film-maker and co-directed *Pull My Daisy* in 1959. He had his first solo show at the Art Institute of Chicago in 1961, and he published his autobiography, *The Lines of My Hand*, in 1972. In 2009 the exhibition "Looking In: Robert Frank's 'The Americans'" celebrated the fiftieth anniversary of his iconic book.

Creative tips and techniques

Frank's work should not be seen in isolation. He was influenced by Walker Evans (see p.78), who was his mentor and one of his sponsors for the Guggenheim grant that funded the work. In turn, Frank's style has been much copied since, giving rise to the "snapshot" esthetic used by Garry Winogrand (see p.192) and others in the 1960s.

For *The Americans*, Frank worked with a Leica rangefinder and a wide-angle lens, and although the images appear casually framed, he was fully aware of the esthetics of how to make compelling images that challenged the contemporary approach of clean, formally perfect photographs. He worked quickly and many of his images are out of focus, off-center, grainy, underexposed, and blurred. Yet these elements, normally seen as mistakes, in Frank's expert hands only serve to add to his message, giving atmosphere and drama to his images. Frank broke many of the then accepted rules of documentary and reportage photography, and was heavily criticized at the time for making photographs that appeared technically flawed. Yet he was highly skilled and consciously sought to make his photographs more ambiguous, intense, and metaphoric.

The Americans lacks the linear narrative of a magazine story, but it does have a complex, nuanced structure that takes the viewer on a visual journey that is sequenced and controlled. The combination of free-form text written by Jack Kerouac and rhythmic patterns of the book, with images one to a page with a white facing page, creates a visual poem. *The Americans* has a strong point of view and a message that is relevant today.

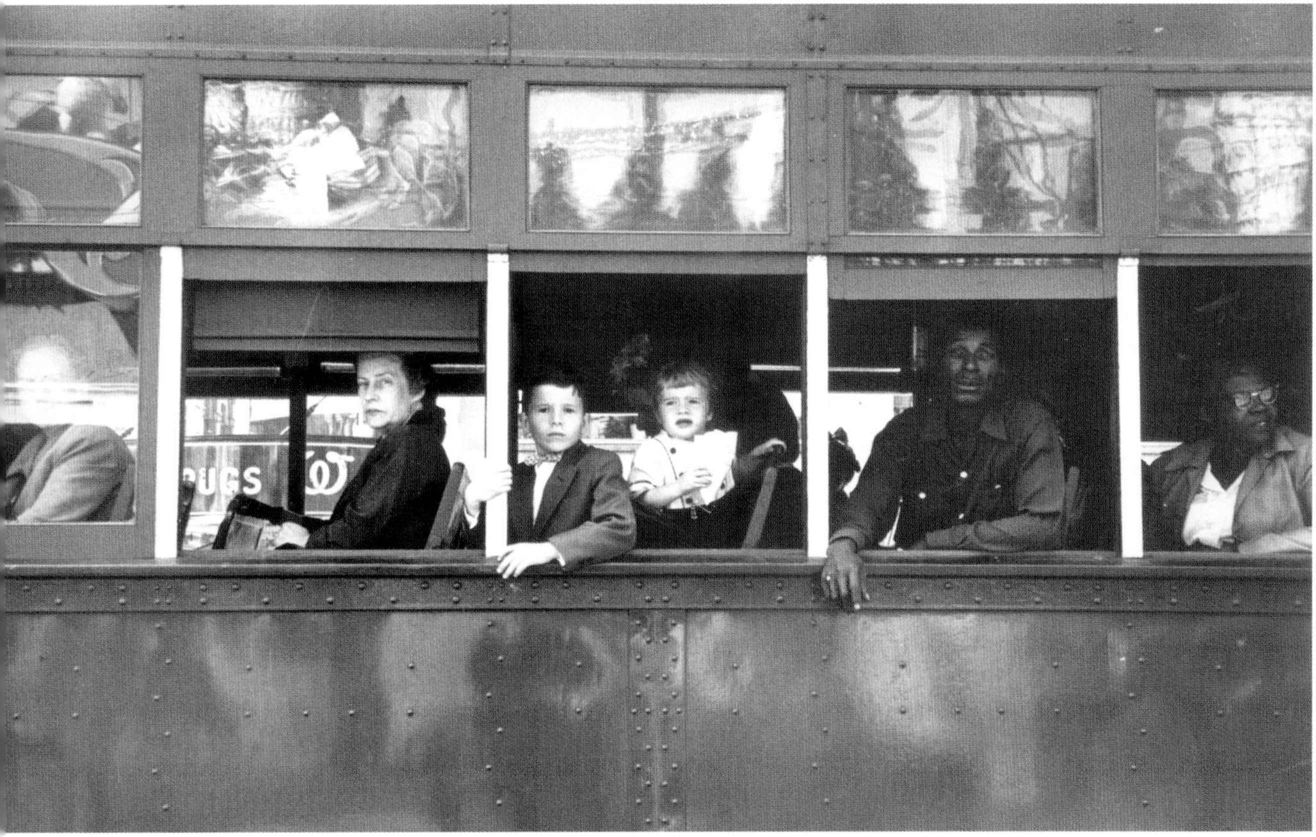

William Klein

Four heads, Thanksgiving day, New York 1955

This densely framed photograph was the opening image in William Klein's photo book on New York City in 1956, and it displays his hallmark use of wide-angle lenses to get extremely close to the subjects, with the faces of the four characters stretched at the edges. He captured in one frame the multicultural life of the city, bringing together a range of ethnicities and types all assembled by chance on a random street corner during a Thanksgiving Day parade. Shooting on film, he revelled in the process of editing the frames afterward, recalling how "I would look at my contact sheets and my heart would be beating . . . I liked the idea of luck and taking a chance." Despite the close proximity at which he worked, he claimed that most people did not find the encounter uncomfortable or threatening, but rather engaged in a sense of performance for the camera: "Unposed, caught unaware, they might reveal ambiguous expressions, brows creased in vague internal contemplation, illegible, perhaps meaningless." He goes further to claim that the subject unveils something of themselves in the encounter: "Maybe people will reveal themselves as violent or tender, crazed or beautiful. But in some way, they reveal who they are. They'll have taken a self-portrait." The self-taught Klein rejected the conventions of professional photography in favor of a looser, more instinctive approach. Instead he found a style that was more suited to the frantic energy of the city.

"I'd crop, blur, play with the negatives. I didn't see clean technique being right for New York. I could imagine my pictures lying in the gutter like the *New York Daily News*." William Klein

William Klein (American, 1928–) is one of the most iconoclastic and energetic of photographers, whose dynamic use of wide angles, blur, grain, and out-of-focus areas revitalized photography in the 1950s. He enrolled at the Sorbonne in Paris, and later studied with painter Fernand Léger. However, at the opening of an exhibition of his kinetic sculptures he met Alexander Liberman, the *Vogue* art director, who invited him to work for the magazine. He broke all the conventions and rules of fashion photography, shooting on the streets and pushing the camera and film to its limits. He carried this into an intense burst of activity photographing the streets of his native New York, published as *Life is Good and Good For You in New York: Trance Witness Revels* (1956). He describes the book as: "pseudo-ethnography, parody, dada," and says that he set out to "document the proud New Yorkers in the same way a museum expedition would document Kikuyus." He produced similar projects on Paris, Rome, and Tokyo, before abandoning photography for film-making for many years, then returning to it late in life.

Creative tips and techniques

For this work Klein used a 28mm wide-angle lens very close to his subjects, allowing him to include a wide field of view and capture all the energy of the street around him. He felt that the standard lens used by Henri Cartier-Bresson (50mm) was too precise for his vision, and that he needed the fluidity and expansiveness of the wide angle. However, he is aware that neither lens is perfect because in reality we see out of two eyes, compared to the camera's one. Super wide-angle lenses of 28mm and wider do cause distortion, but if used in the way Klein does to give a sense of hyperrealism and visual dynamism to the scene, they can be very effective, as long as you are clear that they are a distortion of the scene. Be careful especially with the edges of the frame, where the distortion will be greatest.

Klein turned his limited experience in photography to his advantage, as it freed him up from the conventions of the technical process. His lack of training opened him to what he describes as: "A technique of no taboos: blur, grain, contrast, cock-eyed framing, accidents, whatever happens." He thinks that blur is not an artificial trick of the camera but inherent in life itself. Experiment with rating your cameras ISO high to get noise and grain, and spend a day shooting at 1/8th and 1/15th of a second on the street to see how blur can add energy and drama to a scene.

Once Klein started to shoot with digital cameras, he found the experience liberating. However, like many photographers who learned their art in the film era, he feels that with the speed of digital capture you get an image without accidents, which is a disadvantage.

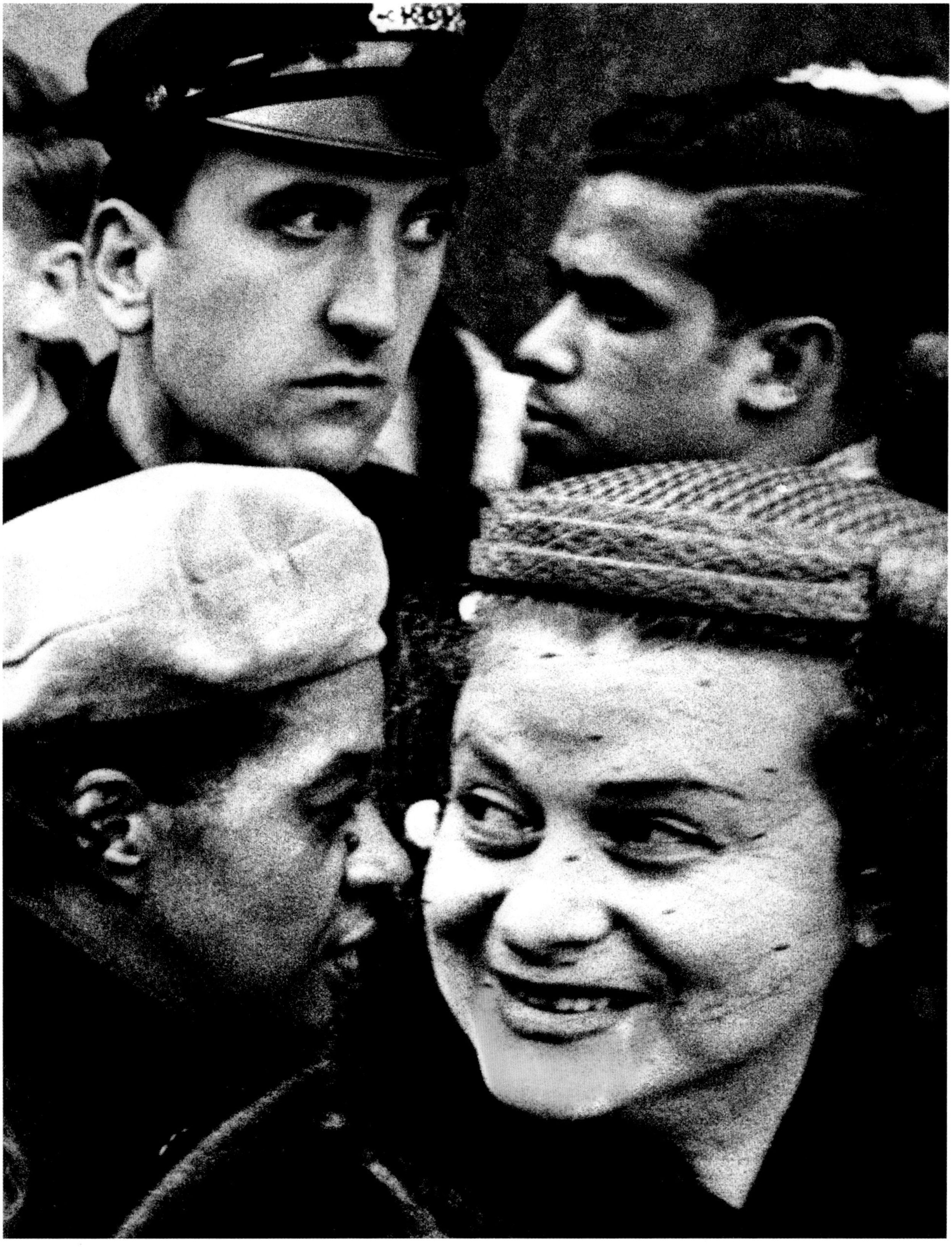

Tony Ray-Jones

Ramsgate 1967

Tony Ray-Jones had a keen eye for the surreal and comic nature of English life. His images combined the energy of US street photography with poetic lyricism in a uniquely British sensibility. This photograph, taken from the beach of a Kent seaside town, demonstrates his exceptional control of the choreography of the moment and his intent to create "slow motion accounts of a brief episode that takes longer to read than it took to happen."

The contact sheet shows him trying first a vertical, then a horizontal, framing with the man in the white shirt and tie anchoring the composition in the bottom left corner. He then moves slightly, and waits for the scene to unfold in front of him, until the little girl skips down the ramp seemingly unobserved by the cast of characters around her. The image can be broken up into a series of vignettes within the composition, each part of the frame potentially succeeding as a self-contained image of its own, from the child contorting on the window sill on the right, to the couple with the pram to the man entering from stage left at the edge of the frame. Covering up parts of the image still leaves an interesting picture in the rest of the frame. The text and street furniture add an important element of description; Ray-Jones was attuned to the language contained within his images and how this could add meaning. Tiny details build on the narrative: the abandoned sandals speak of the liberation of the sand toward which the girl is scampering, and the dog appears to have been formed from the indeterminate black stain below it on the ramp.

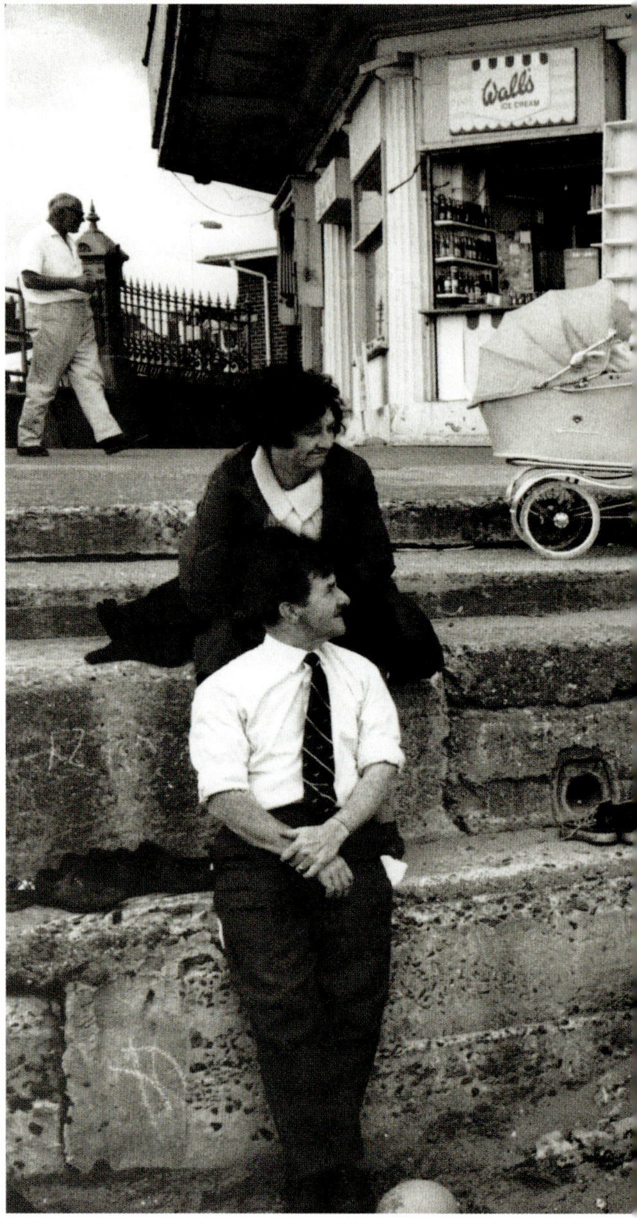

Creative tips and techniques

Tony Ray-Jones kept extensive notes and diaries, and often made himself lists of things to focus on in his work. His list is a perfect aide-memoire for any aspiring street photographer:

- BE MORE AGGRESSIVE
- GET MORE INVOLVED (TALK TO PEOPLE)
- STAY WITH THE SUBJECT MATTER (BE PATIENT)
- TAKE SIMPLER PICTURES
- SEE IF EVERYTHING IN BACKGROUND RELATES TO SUBJECT MATTER
- VARY COMPOSITIONS & ANGLES MORE
- BE MORE AWARE OF COMPOSITION
- DON'T TAKE BORING PICTURES
- GET IN CLOSER (USE 50MM LENS)
- WATCH CAMERA SHAKE (SHOOT 250 SEC OR ABOVE)
- DON'T SHOOT TOO MUCH

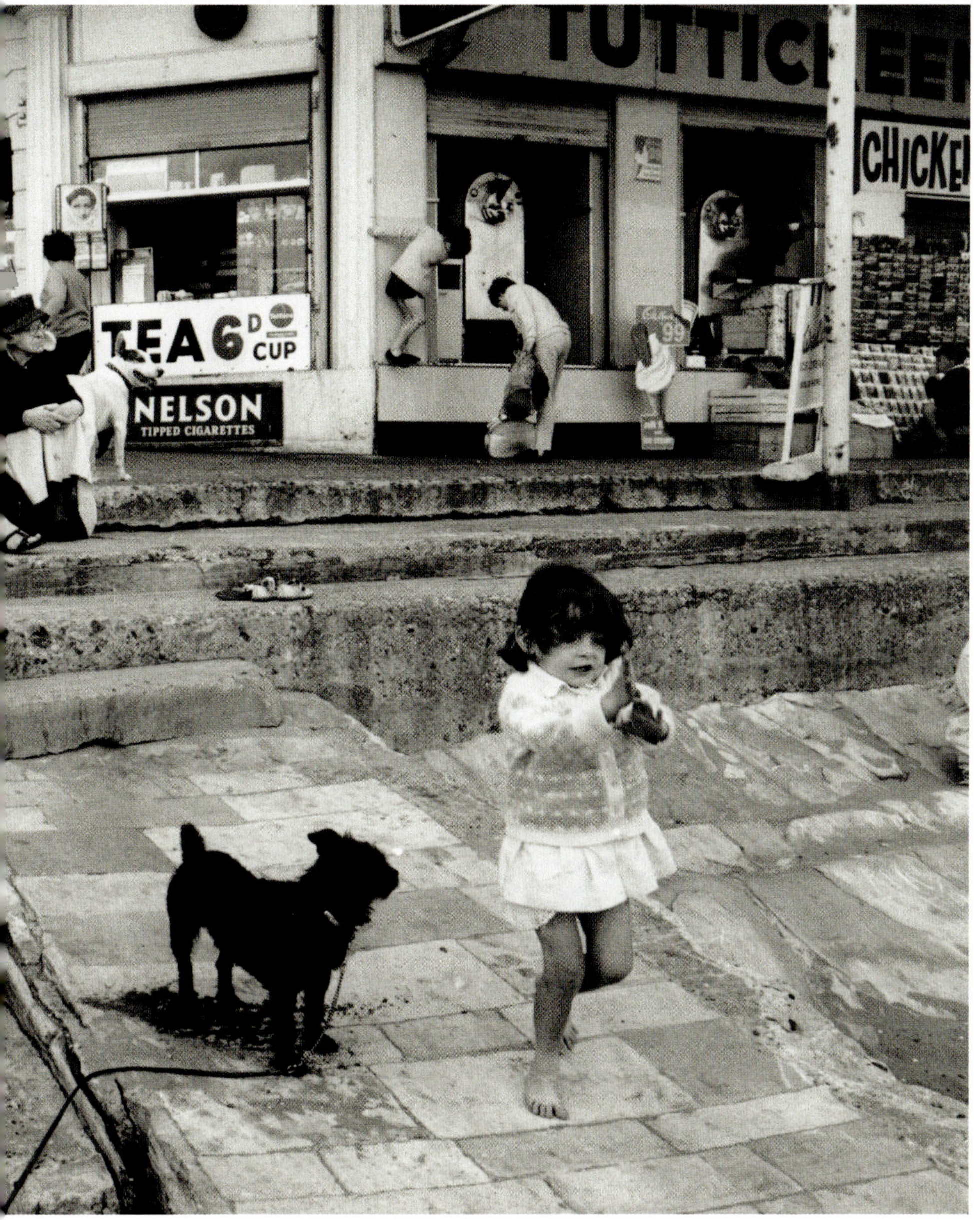

Tony Ray-Jones (British, 1941–72) was one of the most important post-war British photographers. His influence on later practitioners, notably Martin Parr (see p.102), has been profound. Ray-Jones studied graphic design at the London School of Printing (now the London College of Communication), but left England at the age of nineteen to study at Yale University School of Art in the United States. There he was drawn to the teachings of Alexey Brodovitch at the Design Lab and became friends with Joel Meyerowitz (see p.60); together they shot the New York streets. Ray-Jones returned to England in 1965 and began his exploration of the eccentricity of British life. Despite his early death in 1972 from leukemia, his legacy has secured him a position as one of the greatest street photographers. His unfinished book was published posthumously in 1974 as *A Day Off: An English Journal*.

> "Photography can be a mirror and reflect life as it is..."
>
> Tony Ray-Jones

OT ALL EYE LEVEL
O MIDDLE DISTANCE.
y-Jones also prepared this script in vance of shooting a Thanksgiving parade New York in 1964, which again provides excellent set of guidelines for organizing ay of shooting: "Excitement; largeness balloons; smallness of people, simplify; ract elements; overall shots; spectators; k for reflections and through images; cial commentary; powerful commentary."

Street photography is all about orchestrating the image; like a conductor at a concert, the photographer is trying to make sense of the world around them. Look hard at people's body language, how they relate (or don't relate) to each other and to their surroundings. Pay special attention to people's eyes and hands, as they can say a lot about someone's attitude to those around them. Look out for juxtapositions and contrasts. You need to develop a sense of awareness of the ways in which people move, as well as the ability to predict the direction in which someone is moving in order to time your shot perfectly. Try to project yourself visually into the space in front of you, so that you can imagine how a scene would look from that different position. Then work out if that angle can work and will make the final photograph better; if so, move there.

Garry Winogrand

Apollo 11 moon shot, Cape Kennedy, Florida 1969

This witty image captures a group of spectators at the Apollo 11 launch in 1969 and comes from Garry Winogrand's *Public Relations* (1977). The book depicts the absurdities and contradictions of public staged events, and covers political demonstrations, art parties, and sporting occasions. These events provided Winogrand with a rich seam of material, and he shot complex images against the background of American social and political life during the Vietnam era. He once commented that "A still photograph is the illusion of a literal description of how a camera saw a piece of time and space. Understanding this, one can postulate the following theorem: anything and all things are photographable." He explored the conventions of the still image, how it should be framed and composed, pushing it to the limits.

Winogrand was a mercurial force when shooting, always in motion trying to find the moment of collision with the world around him, where the elements would coalesce and then be transformed by the medium into a unique photographic object. There are several accounts of his working methods from photographers who took workshops with him. Mason Resnick recalls that he shot prolifically: "his eyes were always looking for the next shot... like a predator looking for his next meal." He described how "he would literally walk up to the subject and snap the camera up to his eye and instantly freeze long enough to press the shutter. Then he would keep walking past the subject, his head already moving from side to side looking for the next subject, all the while lowering his camera. A 1/1,000th of a second later, he was gone."

> "Photography is about finding out what can happen in the frame. When you put four edges around some facts, you change those facts." Garry Winogrand

Garry Winogrand (American, 1928–84) was the quintessential street photographer, who claimed, "I photograph to see what things look like photographed." He grew up in the Bronx area of New York and initially studied painting, but also took a photojournalism class with Alexey Brodovitch at the New School in 1951. He worked as a commercial and editorial photographer in the 1950s, but along with Lee Friedlander (see p.194), Tod Papageorge, and Joel Sternfeld (see p.54) began to explore New York's vibrant street culture in the 1960s. He was included in the "New Documents" show of 1967, and produced his first book, *Animals*, on the peculiar relationships between people and animals at the zoo, in 1969. From the 1970s onward he supported his work mainly by teaching, moving to Austin, Texas, in 1973 and then on to Los Angeles in 1978. He was a prodigious shooter who went out to photograph almost every day. At the time of his death in 1984, he left 2,500 rolls of undeveloped film, 6,500 rolls of developed but not proofed exposures, and 3,000 rolls that only had contact sheets made, making a total of 300,000 unedited images.

Creative tips and techniques

Winogrand remarked that "the world isn't tidy; it's a mess. I don't try to make it neat." He often positioned the frame of his images at an angle to the horizontal elements of the scene. However, he argued that this was a resistance to the "arbitrary idea that the horizontal edge in a frame has to be the point of reference." Instead, he would use vertical lines as his anchor points, depending on which worked best to get the information into the frame that he wanted. He explained that "it's not tilted. You use the vertical edge as the point of reference, instead of the horizontal edge." Every composition does not have to follow a formula. Go out and shoot for a day and think about building up your image using lines in the scene that do not run straight across or up and down the frame; focus on diagonal lines.

Winogrand famously did not look at his images immediately after he made them; instead he would often leave them for months or even a year until he studied the contact sheets. He felt that distancing himself from the moment of exposure helped him forget the circumstances in which the picture was made and concentrate on a more objective review of it. When developing film, he adjusted the processing time to avoid overly contrasting or flat negatives.

Winogrand worked mostly with a 28mm lens on a Leica rangefinder, but he also experimented with the 35mm and the super wide 21mm, but he found that had too much distortion at the edges of the frame. The lesson here is to go out with one lens only and use it until you are totally familiar with how it describes the world, what field of vision it has, and what level of distortion, if any.

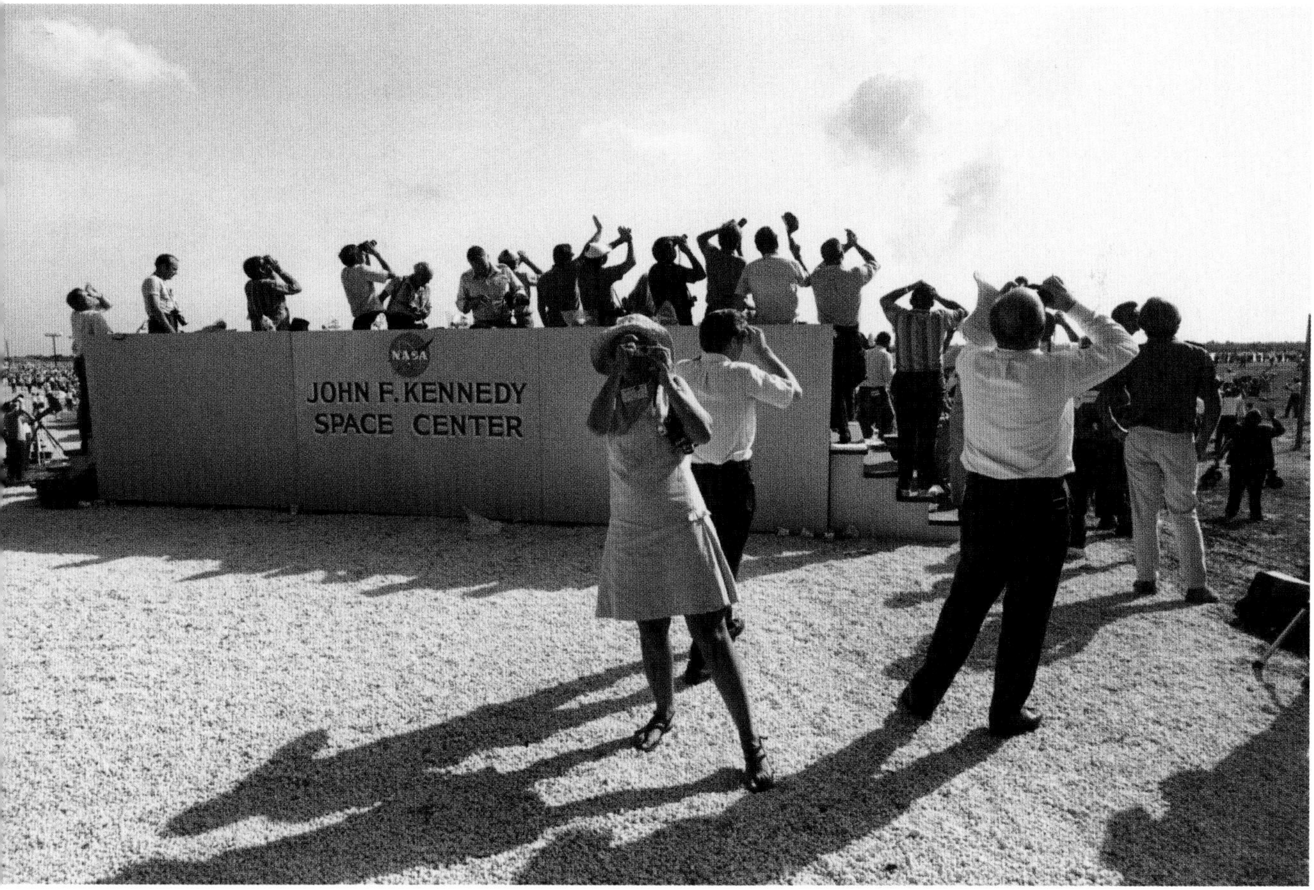
NASA
JOHN F. KENNEDY
SPACE CENTER

Lee Friedlander

Hillcrest, New York 1970

Lee Friedlander is endlessly fascinated with how the camera captures everything before it, rendering every quotidian element of whatever is presented in front of the lens. He has described this extraordinary process whereby "in a snap, or small portion of time, all that the camera can consume in breadth and bite and light is rendered in astonishing detail: all the leaves on a tree, as well as the tree itself and all its surroundings." This image was taken at a point when Friedlander was exploring how he could use screening and reflective devices such as windows and car and truck rearview mirrors to fracture the flat surface of the image, bisecting it with vertical and horizontal elements such as telegraph poles and lampposts. The image becomes like a visual jigsaw, with the same elements of sky, trees, wires, and street furniture repeated throughout; some are in front of the camera and others are behind, yet they all combine to create a seamless view of the world. Friedlander often includes himself in the frame, with the single eye staring back at the world—the reflective bonus of the Leica rangefinder camera, which uses only one eye to view from, leaving the other free to observe the scene. He admits that he finds this visual complexity exciting: "That is an interesting concept to me: how much I can put in and still make it pull together?" He often includes fragments of words and letters in the frame. Note how the tiny figure of the man on the left of the picture is vital to the whole composition; he creates a kind of visual punctuation mark around which the whole image rotates. Cover him up with your finger and see what happens to the energy of the frame.

"Witness is borne and puzzles come together at the photographic moment..." Lee Friedlander

Lee Friedlander (American, 1934–) worked through the 1950s and 1960s as an editorial photographer in New York, where he documented the jazz scene. He was included in the landmark 1967 "New Documents" exhibition, along with Garry Winogrand (see p.192) and Diane Arbus, for which the curator, John Szarkowski, wrote: "Their work betrays sympathy—almost affection—for the imperfections and the frailties of society." Friedlander, perhaps more than almost any other photographer, has mastered the peculiar process by which the frame of the camera translates the three-dimensional world with all its complexity into a two-dimensional flat surface, which in turn generates the visual illusion of depth. He has documented the American social landscape extensively, publishing numerous books, notably *The American Monument* (1976), *Factory Valleys* (1982) and *America by Car* (2010). He often includes fragments of words and isolated letters in his work, and even created an entire book of photographs of the alphabet, *Letters from the People* (1993).

Creative tips and techniques

Friedlander describes how he moved in order to explore how elements that others would ignore or avoid could be used to give his images visual depth. He uses a sporting metaphor to compare the flow of street photography to that of an athlete "in the zone." Getting into this frame of mind when you are photographing takes practice, but it can be liberating when you are totally focused in the moment, yet open to the infinite possibilities of chance. Try to explore the physical world around you, looking for unusual ways to break up the frame and challenge the received wisdom of how a photograph should look. Look at Cubist and Abstract Expressionist artists and see how they control the plane and surface of the image, and try to apply that to your photography.

As a commercial and editorial photographer Friedlander mastered all the camera formats, but for most of his work in the 1960s and 1970s he worked with a Leica rangefinder and a 35mm or 28mm wide-angle lens, as it allowed him to include the field of view he wanted with sufficient depth of field to relate all the elements together on the picture plane. In his later work, he has used a Hasselblad with a super wide-angle lens.

He advises that a photographer should become totally familiar with each piece of equipment and what it does, before expanding his or her range. Go out with only one camera and one lens for a week, and let your eye and brain find the images rather than letting the camera dictate how you will frame the scene. Use your legs and body to modify the composition, rather than changing lens or zooming in and out all the time.

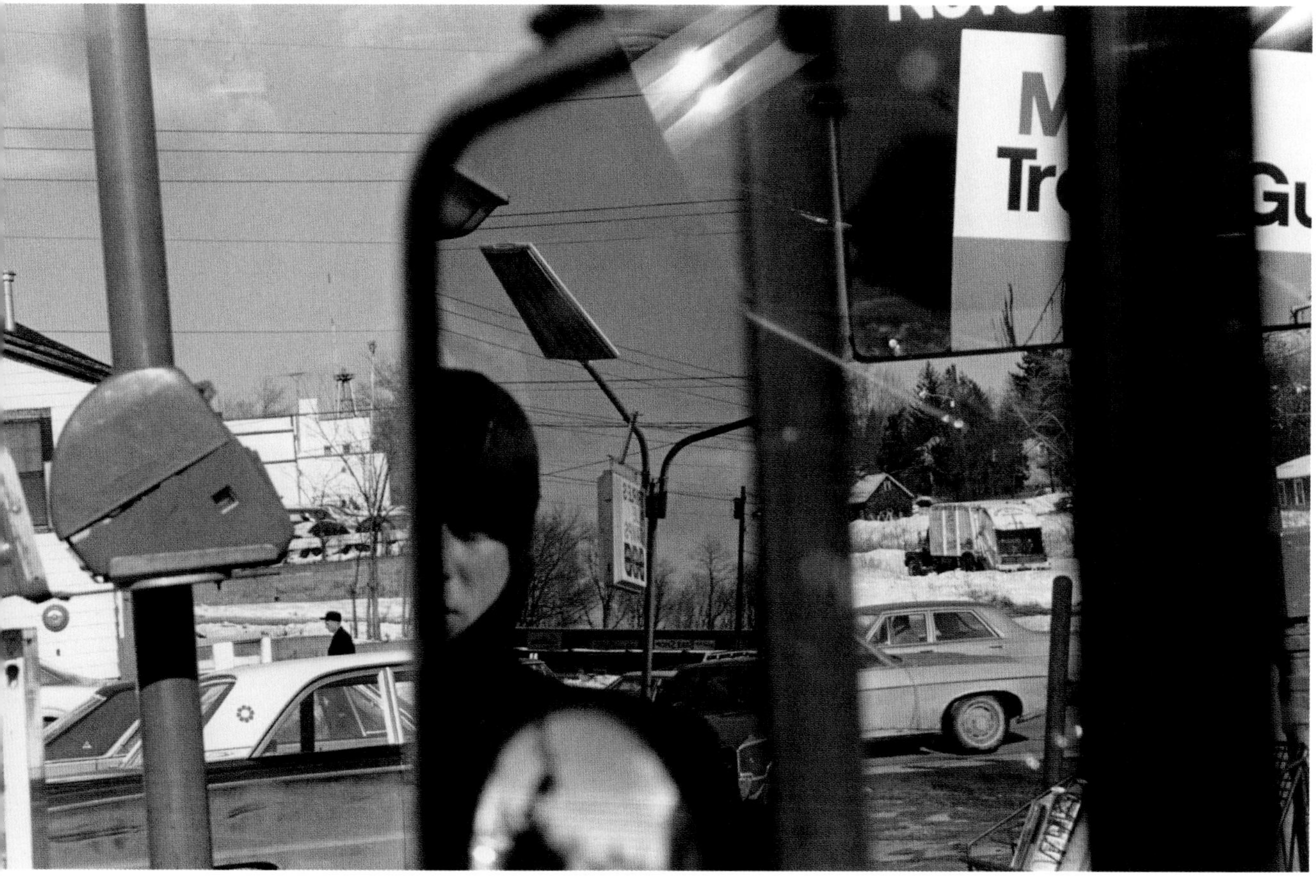

Elliott Erwitt

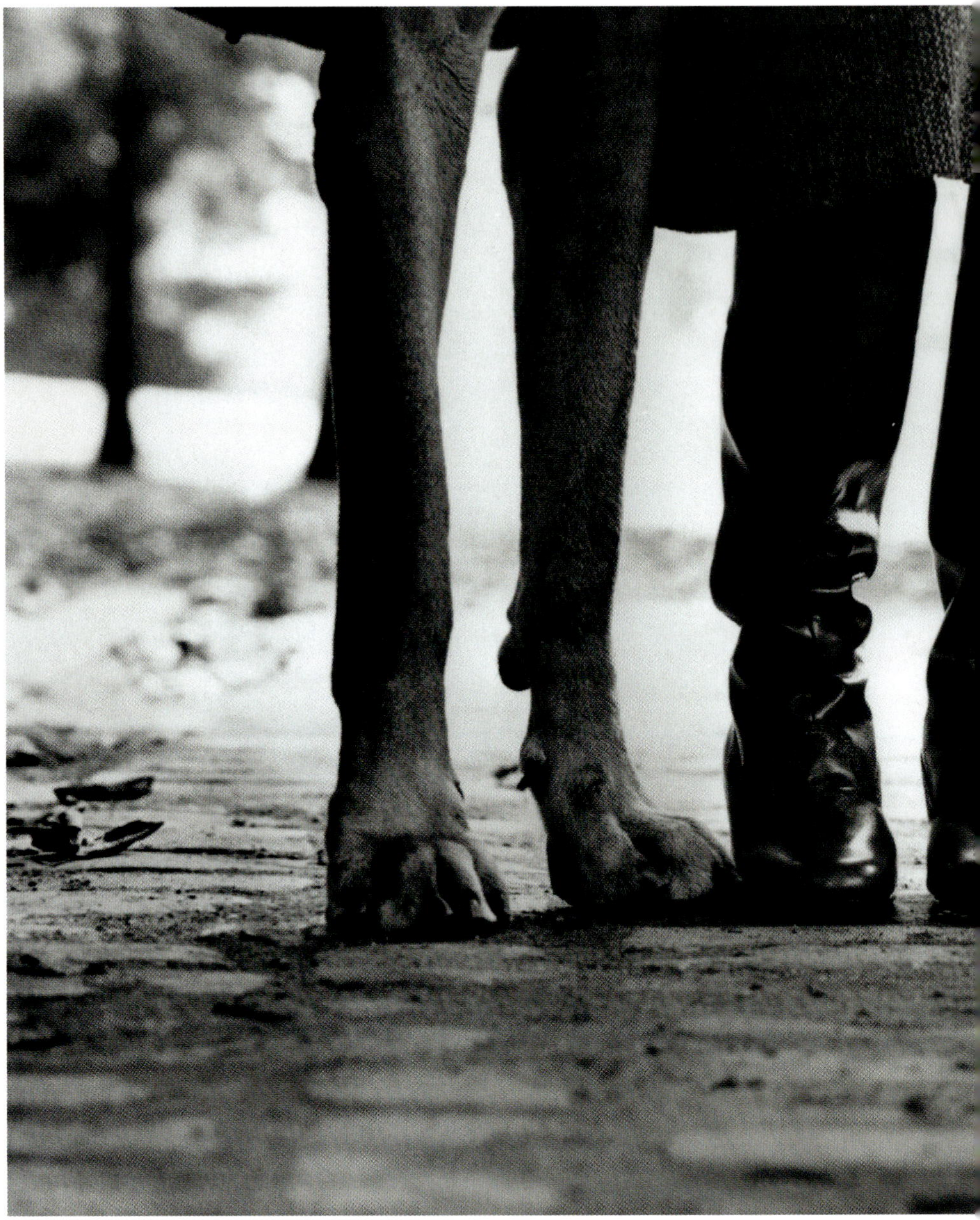

Elliott Erwitt (American, 1928–) was born in Paris to Russian parents, but grew up in Milan until he left for the United States with his family in 1939. In 1951 he was drafted for military service and joined the Army Signal Corps as a photographer, which led to his first editorial publications. In New York, Erwitt met Edward Steichen, Robert Capa (see p.262), and Roy Stryker, the former head of the Farm Security Administration, who encouraged him to develop a career as a photographer. He joined Magnum Photos in 1953, and has served as its President for three terms of office. Known for his wit and dry sense of humor, Erwitt sums up his approach to the medium thus, "Well, I'm not a serious photographer like most of my colleagues. That is to say, I'm serious about not being serious."

Creative tips and techniques

Although Erwitt acknowledges that digital offers many advantages, especially when shooting on assignment, he still tries to be strict and shoot very little. He still prefers to shoot on film for his own work, feeling that the slowing down of the process is actually an advantage. Like many other photographers, he cautions that digital has drawbacks in that it is too forgiving and too easy, and can lead to sloppiness.

Erwitt is a master of balanced compositions that juxtapose the elements in the frame with one another to make a telling point or visual pun. However, this is the result of careful looking, rather than over-determining the scene by setting things up. He also notes that sometimes the photographer is not quick enough to capture everything, and that a certain amount of post-processing is acceptable.

Erwitt is a master of all the camera formats and lenses in his commercial work, but for his personal observational photography he keeps it very simple, working mostly with just one camera and one lens, mostly a 50mm on a 35mm Leica rangefinder. While he acknowledges that exotic equipment can

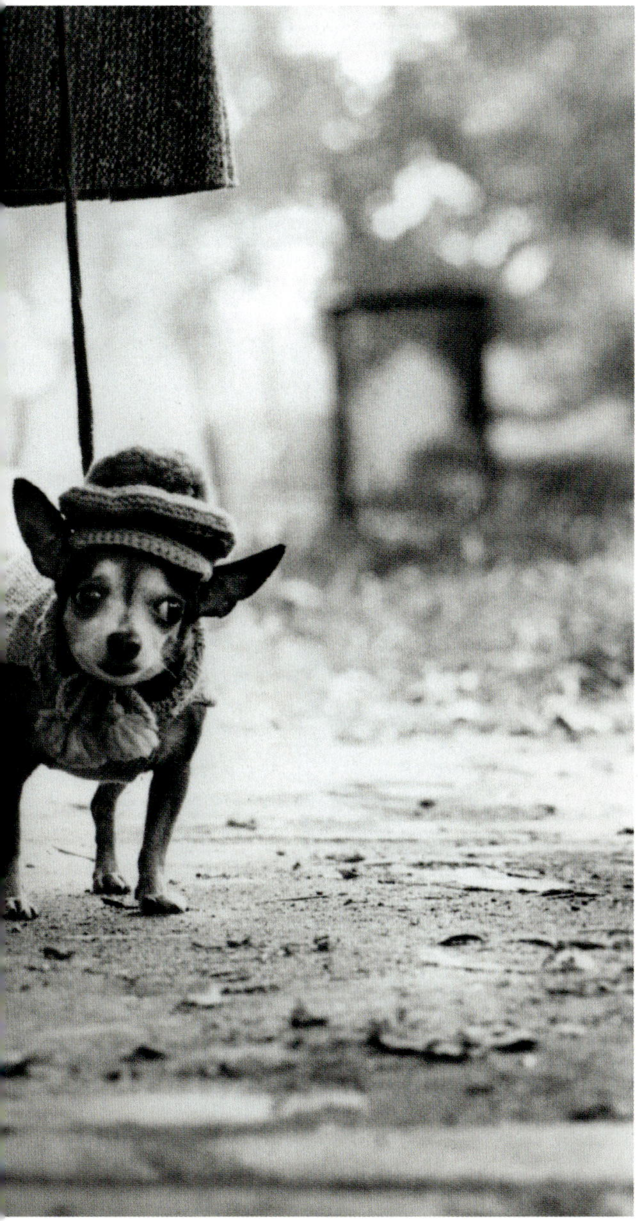

Felix, Gladys, and Rover 1974

Elliott Erwitt is renowned for his humorous and witty juxtapositions and observations, as in this photograph showing a woman's booted feet between that of a Great Dane's legs and a little chihuahua. Dogs have been an enduring theme for Erwitt—"They're people with more hair. They have human qualities"—and he has produced eight books featuring his canine subjects. He is keen to avoid kitschness, however, and maintains that his approach to dogs is not sentimental. He explains why he thinks that they make such good subjects: "dog pictures work on two levels. Dogs are simply funny when you catch them in certain situations, so some people like my pictures just because they like dogs. But dogs have human qualities, and I think my pictures have an anthropomorphic appeal. Essentially, they have nothing to do with dogs... I hope what they're about is the human condition."

Erwitt is a master observer of the everyday and is adept at finding a way of framing it that brings out the essence of human nature in a wide variety of conditions. He expresses his philosophy: "to me, photography is an art of observation. It's about finding something interesting in an ordinary place... I've found it has little to do with the things you see and everything to do with the way you see them." However, he is also highly aware of the serendipity of chance encounters that the photographer has no control over, but must seize and make the most of, arguing that "when photography is good, it's pretty interesting, and when it is very good, it is irrational and even magical... nothing to do with the photographer's conscious will or desire. When the photograph happens, it comes easily, as a gift that should not be questioned or analyzed."

useful for exaggerating a situation that s limited visual appeal, he generally oids it when shooting for himself, eferring a simpler form of direct servation. Super wide angles and long ephotos are useful when you are far ay or have to get very close, but too ten they dominate the final image and ake it appear to be the product of the chnology rather than the creative eye of e photographer. All you really need for the majority of photographic encounters is one camera and a fixed lens.

Erwitt is known for his humorous juxtapositions and observations, but his work is deeply imbued with the full range of human emotions as well; he claims, "some people say my pictures are sad, some think they're funny. Funny and sad, aren't they really the same thing? They add up to normality."

"You can find pictures anywhere. It's simply a matter of noticing things and organizing them. You just have to care about what's around you and have a concern with humanity and the human comedy."

Elliott Erwitt

Josef Koudelka

Portugal 1976

This photograph is taken from Josef Koudelka's book *Exiles* (1988), which represents a meditation on his habitual life on the road as well as part of his ongoing documentation of the gypsy community. The image plays with light and shadow, projecting the double silhouette of the man like a puppet onto the wall. The triangular composition creates a strong sense of diagonal movement around the frame, leading the viewer's attention to the key figures; the mysterious shrouded woman, the angelic child, and the peasant's crook all add to the complexity of the image, leaving the viewer to imagine the narrative of the situation.

Koudelka relates how he has "always sought out pictures that tell a story in themselves, letting each viewer see a story that suits them. For me, a good photograph is one that tells a different story to each person who sees it." Koudelka considers his nomadic lifestyle a natural way to work as a photographer, explaining that his experiences photographing other cultures taught him the insignificance of material goods: "what I gained from working with the gypsies was to learn that I don't need much to be alive." He describes how "for sixteen years I worked for no one. I never took a commission, never took pictures for money. I scraped by, trying not to have any possessions. I didn't pay rent for sixteen years. I didn't want to have a home. I didn't need much, just a sleeping bag, a pair of shoes, two pairs of socks, and one pair of pants per year. A jacket and two shirts would last me three years."

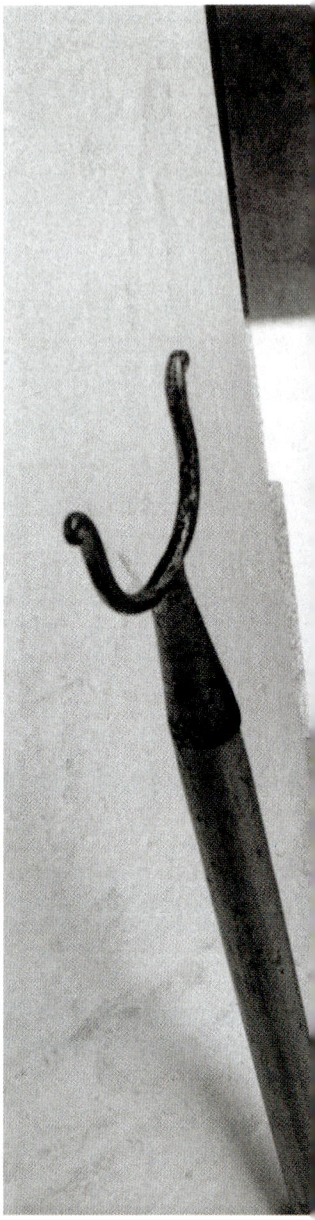

> "I've never stayed anywhere longer than three months. When I couldn't find anything else to photograph, I had to leave." Josef Koudelka

Creative tips and techniques

Koudelka has a unique approach to editing his own work and regards the views of others as essential to deciding on the final selection of photographs. He says that when he travels, he shows his pictures to the people he meets to see what they like and don't like. He explains: "A good photograph speaks to many different people for different sorts of reasons. And it depends what sort of lives these people have. What they've gone through. It happens very rarely that you see something you can't forget. That is a good photograph." Unlike many photographers, he is aware that the photographer is often not the best editor or judge of his or her own work. He says he refers to three individuals to appraise whether a picture is good or not: one who knows something about life, but not much about photograp or composition; a second person who knows about composition; and a third one who knows something about both. If thes three people like a particular image as we as him, then he is more likely to believe th the image is good.

Koudelka considers the book an ideal vehicle for him to express his feelings about the world. In a book you hav

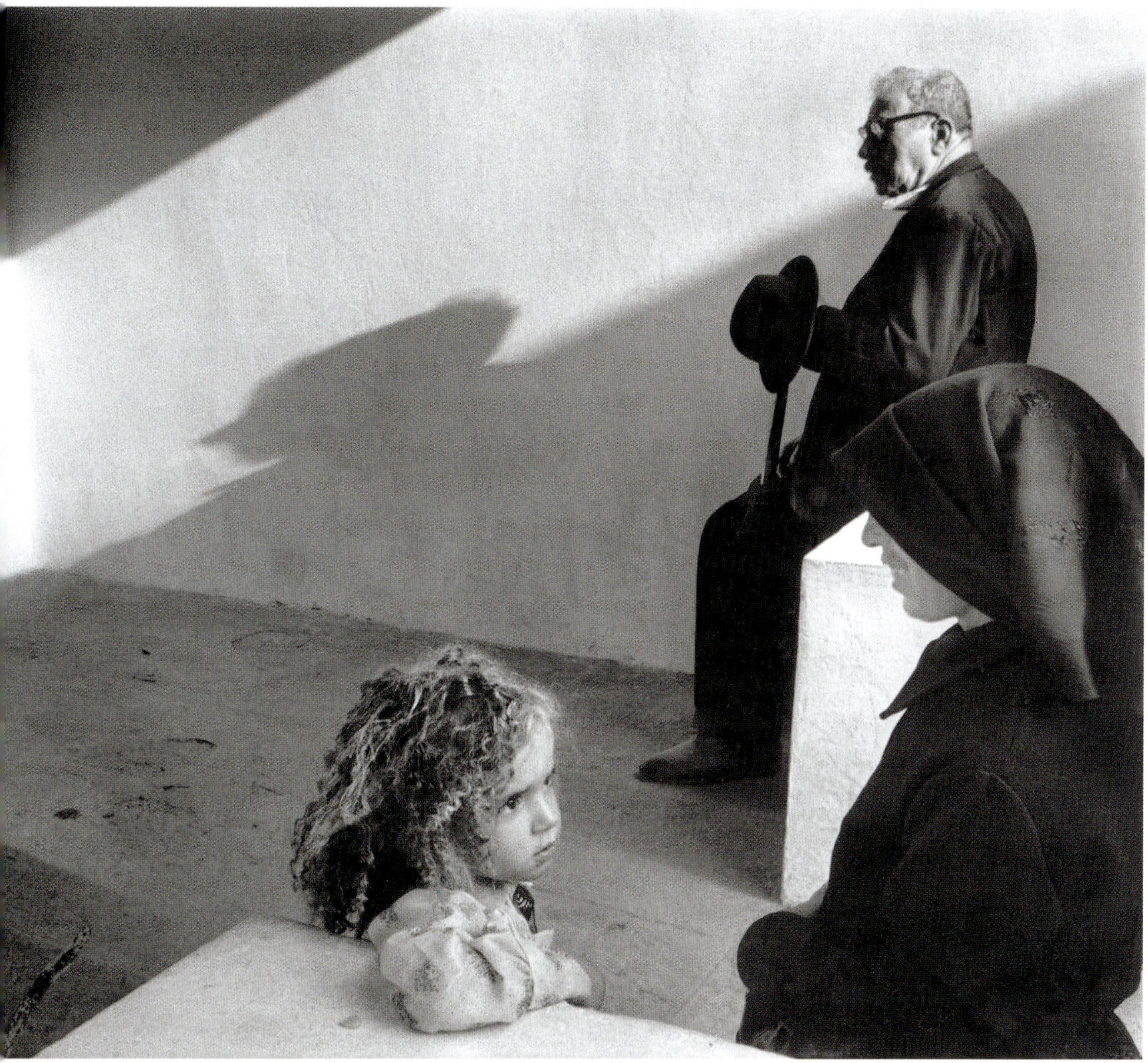

·mething to say (content) and a way say it (a visual story). He describes inging the two together as a complex, uitive process. The act of making a ·ok over a long period of time suits approach, as photography is a slow ocess. He says: "You don't just take ctures, you have to organize and think out them. *Exiles* is built around moments one photograph leads to another, uitively, without there being a 'story'."

Josef Koudelka (Czech, 1938–) was born in Moravia and worked as an aeronautical engineer before becoming a full-time photographer in 1967. His first project was photographing gypsies in Slovakia and Romania. He has lived a nomadic lifestyle since leaving his native Czechoslovakia in 1970 as a political exile, after his powerful photographs of the Soviet invasion of Prague were published anonymously but to acclaim. He joined Magnum Photos shortly afterward. He explains: "Today I feel more European and do not belong to any nationality. When the English gave me my first residence permit, they put me in the category of 'Nationality Doubtful,' for people who cannot provide proof of their birthplace or British nationality. I never considered it to be an insult—on the contrary. There's only one earth, and we're all its citizens."

Alex Webb

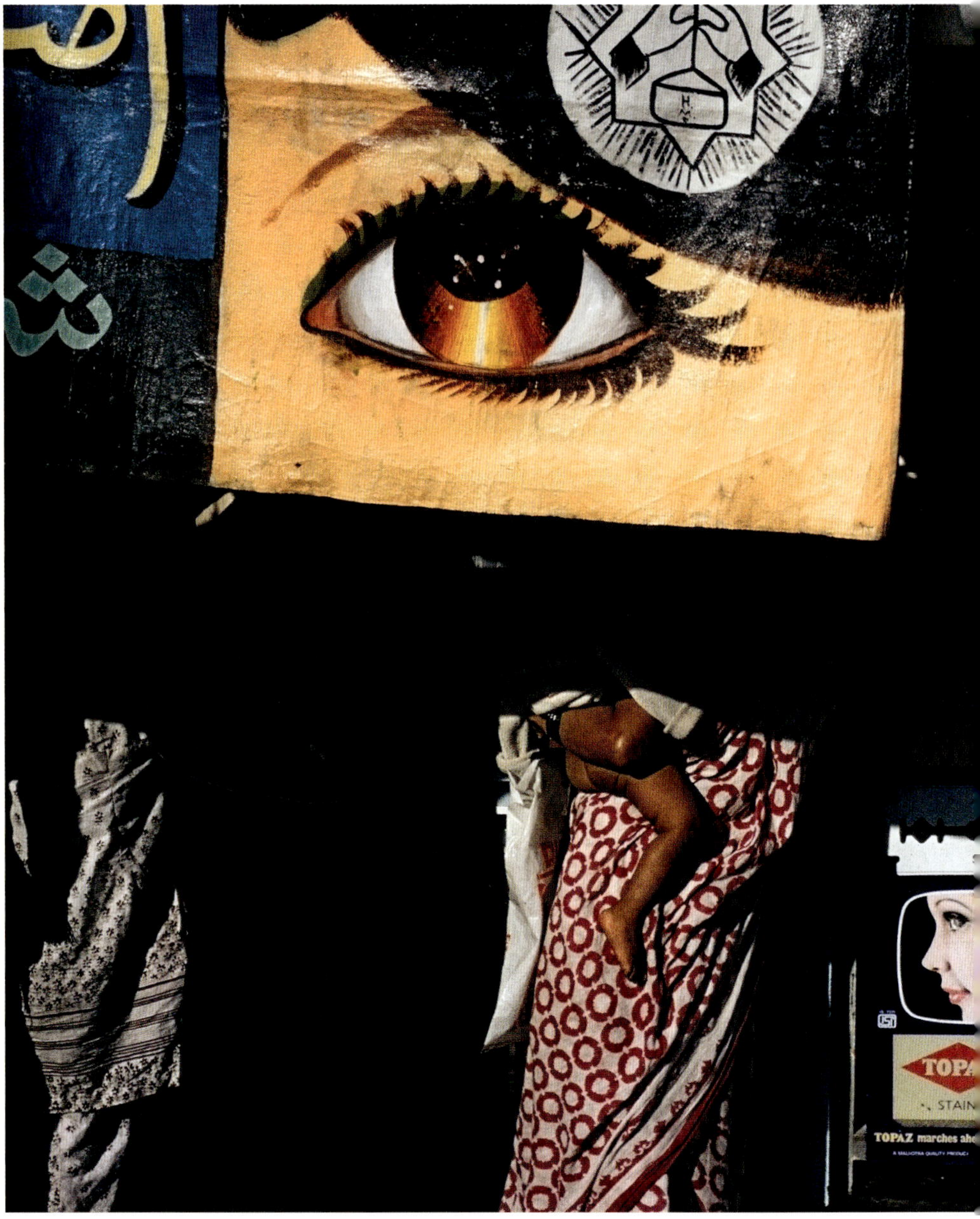

Alex Webb (American, 1952–) studied history and literature at Harvard University, and began working as a photographer in 1974, joining Magnum Photos as one of its youngest-ever nominees in 1976. He initially began working in black and white, but discovered the richness and emotional charge of color in 1978. He has published seven books of his work, including *Hot Light/Half Made Worlds* (1986) and *The Suffering of Light* (2011). Webb is the quintessential color street photographer; his complex images are dense with information as well as being psychologically and emotionally charged. As he describes it, he has "chosen to wander the streets of places where political and social tensions lie more on the surface, places where life often seems lived on the stoop or in the street. It's a different kind of theatre of the street—a rawer one—that I have sought out."

Creative tips and techniques

Webb's methodology is deceptively simple. His working method in the field follows a similar rhythm each day and he is attuned to the quality of light as the sun moves through its phases, which can totally change the look and feel of a location. For example, he notes how in the midday sun everything is bleached white with shadows coming across people's faces, whereas in late afternoon the light is golden. Plan your day in advance, ensuring that you will be at the right location at the right time. When you are in a place, think about how it might look at different times of day, and adjust your schedule to return when the light is perfect.

Webb makes himself open to the chance encounter, but increases the likelihood of that magical moment when everything comes together by a heightene sense of awareness of his surroundings. H likens street photography to gambling—you wander into potentially interesting situations, work when the light is good, and remain alert, but you never know wha is going to happen. What is most exciting is when the unexpected happens and you manage to be at the right place at the right time and push the shutter at the righ

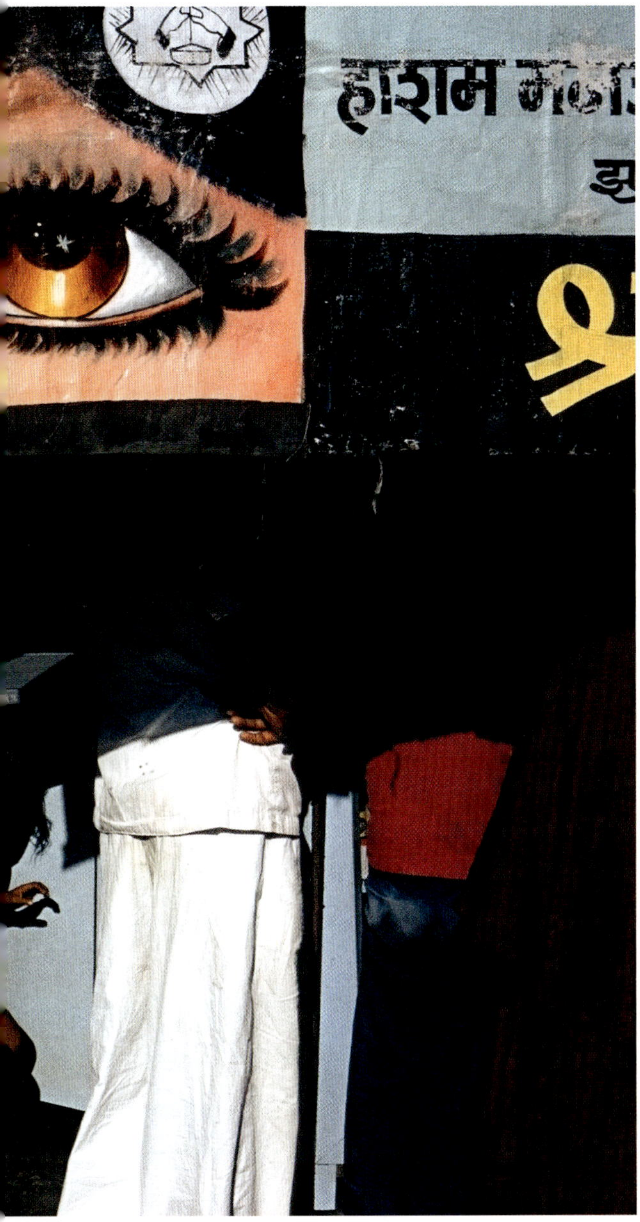

India, Bombay 1981

Alex Webb's images have a visceral feel for the vibrant street life of the tropics. As in this photograph of a Bombay (now Mumbai) street scene, he seeks out its rich, saturated colors and combines them in intriguingly constructed images that resonate with the atmosphere and spirit of place. Webb feels that his work "gravitates toward visual complexity, with multiple layers, paradoxical juxtapositions, and frames within frames." Attracted to the intense directional light found in the tropics, he makes maximum use of dense shadows, intensified by the Kodak film he employed until recently, in his photographs. He elaborates: "the way of working in the tropics was certainly helped by the technical choices I made as a photographer and that I worked with Kodachrome, which is a film that has very intense deep blacks, the kind that punches the emotionality into the pictures. Sometimes blacks are sort of carved out."

He has developed an enhanced sensitivity and feel for how color and light interact, and the impact this has on the viewer. He explains, "when I look at a scene, I am sensing not just what seems to be 'happening' in front of my eyes and the various shapes that fill the frame, but I am also acutely aware of the colors, their relationship, and their emotional and sensory resonances." He is acutely aware of the "color of light, the angle of light: how a shaft of light, or a particular tone of light, can utterly transform a situation." The resulting compositions, such as this one, are visual riddles that reward repeated viewings to explore their complex weaving together of form and content. Webb says that he seeks to combine the maximum number of elements without the image collapsing into itself: "It's not just that that and that exists. It's that that, that, that, and that all exist in the same frame… I'm always playing along that line: adding something more, yet keeping it sort of chaos."

oment. "Most of the time it doesn't work ıt that way. This kind of photography is 9.9% about failure."

Webb combines research and practice in the field, learning about a ace through simultaneously experiencing ıd studying it. He tries not to go to a new ace with too many preconceived ideas. efore he visits a new location he will read ovels set there to get a feel of how another artist perceives the essence of that place. However, he spends most of his time simply walking around the location, looking for those serendipitous moments where the image coalesces with his sense of the place. Once he has worked there for some time, he undertakes further reading and research so that his understanding of the place develops as he experiences it both personally and intellectually.

> "I feel the space, the light, the color, the form, and the scene simultaneously. I'm not thinking, I'm sensing the street… I'm intrigued with the emotional and sensory tenor of these elements."
>
> Alex Webb

Dougie Wallace

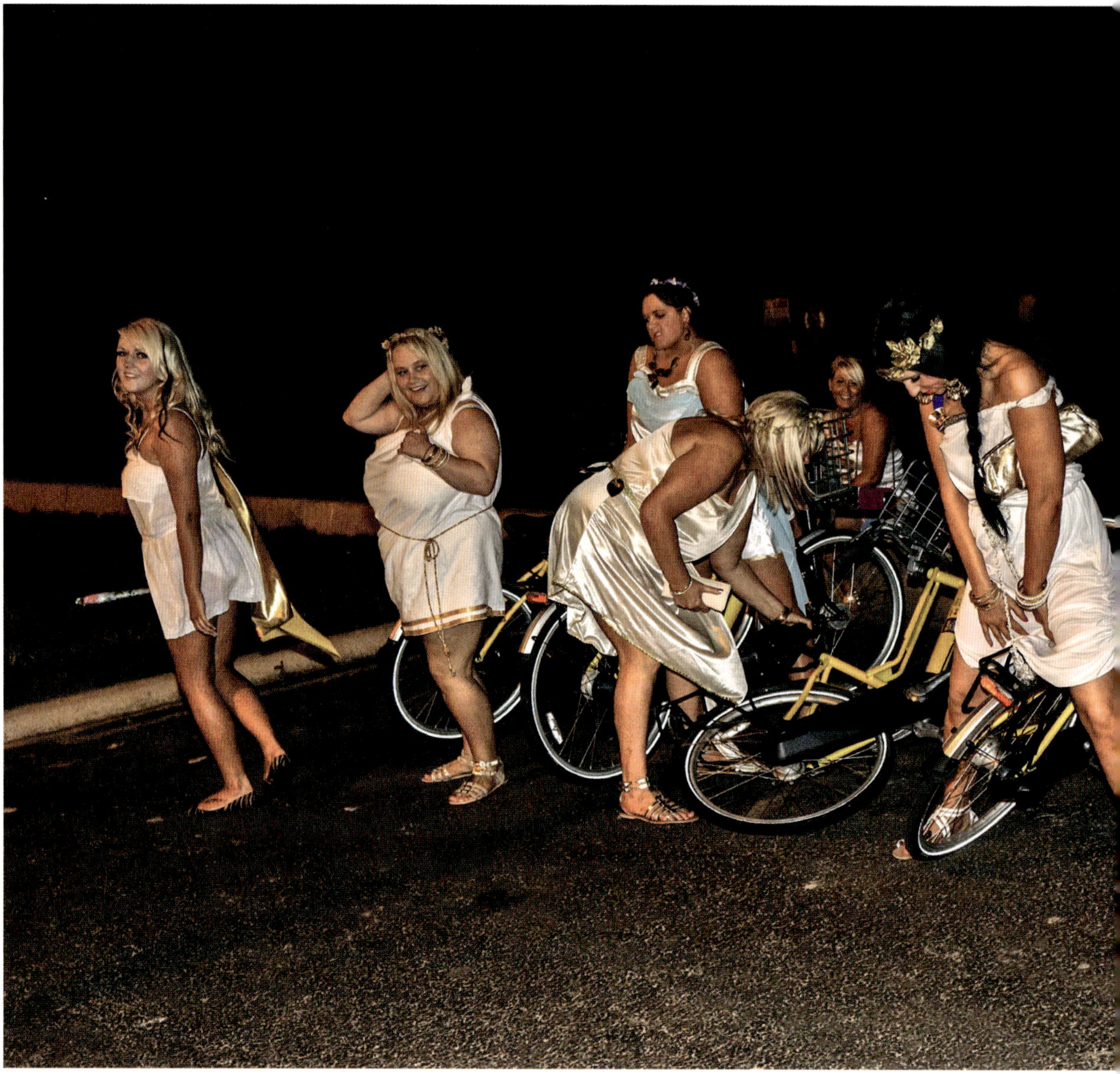

Stags and hens, Blackpool 2011

Street photographer Dougie Wallace describes Blackpool as a "dirty great whorl of debauchery, licentiousness, laughter, vomit, furry handcuffs, fancy dress, and drunken oblivion." He made thirty trips to the northern English seaside resort, now a mecca for rowdy stag and hen parties, over a three-year period and declares: "I didn't set out to be Hogarth depicting modern urban mayhem, but in Blackpool the visual satire staggers up the street to meet you." He defends himself against any suggestion that his images exploit his subjects: "In my youth I'd been a reveller in Blackpool, which is why I could approach the subject as an insider and why I think the shots aren't cruel." He says his experiences living in the town helped him understand his subjects: "my knowledge of the place seemed to give me a sixth sense...Somehow I'd find myself in the right place at the right time." He admits that in the era of the selfie and Facebook, it has become difficult to be accepted as a street photographer: "In our panicky age of social hysteria, it's become harder to take pictures without someone causing a fuss. This, and the anticipation of knowing what might resonate visually, can be frustrating when you're trying to enter into a group's personal space. A social distance has crept into culture nowadays, perhaps a reflection of the celebrity age."

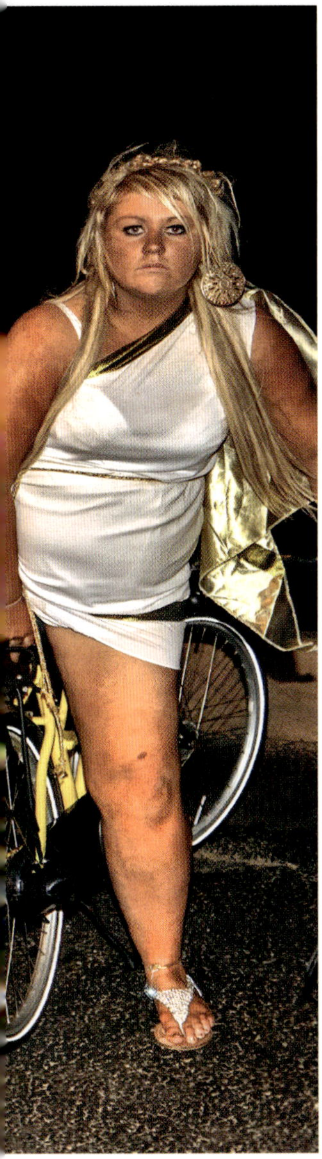

became part of each individual pack's story: the Glaswegian
ith the flashgun fleshing out a heightened reality…"

ugie Wallace

ugie Wallace (British, 1974–), known as lasweegee" because of his home town and use of flash (see p.210), has documented e vibrant street life of the city in hyperreal lor photographs filled with humor and visual ergy. He says, "My work is informed by day's growing culture of commercialization, e effect this has on our leisure time, global urism, and the inescapable consequences of corporate and brand domination that have ensued. Translating this into social wit, criticism, and humorous vignettes through my lens is what stimulates me." He has published three books, *Stags, Hens & Bunnies: a Blackpool Story* (2014), *Shoreditch Wild Life* (2014), from his fifteen years photographing the East End of London, and *Road Wallah* (2016), which captures the disappearing taxi drivers of Premier Padminis in India.

Creative tips and techniques

Unlike many street photographers, who have little real interaction with their subjects, moving on quickly from situations, Wallace tends to work with the people he is shooting, even if only momentarily. He describes how he interacts with his subjects: "My shots come from becoming part of the scene. I take pics with my instincts and intuition, using a bit of psychology and sometimes my physiology and body language." Also, unlike many photographers, he is not afraid of eye contact in his images. He explains that although he does not set shots up, his presence is very much part of the situation; he is not invisible, claiming that he even uses the flash to "provoke" the situation. He remarks that people often ask him if his photographs are staged and responds, "while none of them are staged, a lot of them are a reaction to me. I don't sit and wait for something to happen. I'll run across the street to photograph something I think is interesting and my presence will change the dynamic. I've had groups of girls before where they kind of commandeer you, like you're their official photographer for the night."

Wallace works mostly with a 35mm lens, like many street photographers, and uses multiple flashes to create a miniature studio. He mounts one on the camera and another one either underneath or held out on a cord to create a more directional light, which gives saturation and vibrancy to his images. He explains that the colors result from the flash, although he sometimes takes out saturation in post-production: "Nowadays I don't sharpen or put clarity on them. As soon as you color balance them right, the images just pop."

David Alan Harvey

Havana. 1998. A group of children playing in a playground 1988

David Alan Harvey works simply, with minimal gear, preferring as little as possible to come between him and his subject. This image retains his characteristic approach of engaging with the subject, as he explains: "I really need to get close and then fill the frame. I am often within handshaking distance while shooting some of my subjects! That is my personal style." Compositionally, it is also typical of how he tries to construct his images: "one of my favorite techniques is to keep an important character occupying half the frame in the foreground." He feels that a "photograph must have drama, but not because of the equipment. The 'Aha!' moment should be present because of the timing, the placement of various elements, the expressions or the mood created in the photograph—not because of some unusual lens that is used." Harvey says his projects do not seek to describe every element of a situation: "I am never interested in the hypothetical 'whole story'. When I think of literary authors, they never tell the whole story. Just their own." Harvey has started to use an iPhone extensively, using it spontaneously to document the flow of life around him and then posting the images on his blog and Instagram site, where he has almost 350,000 followers.

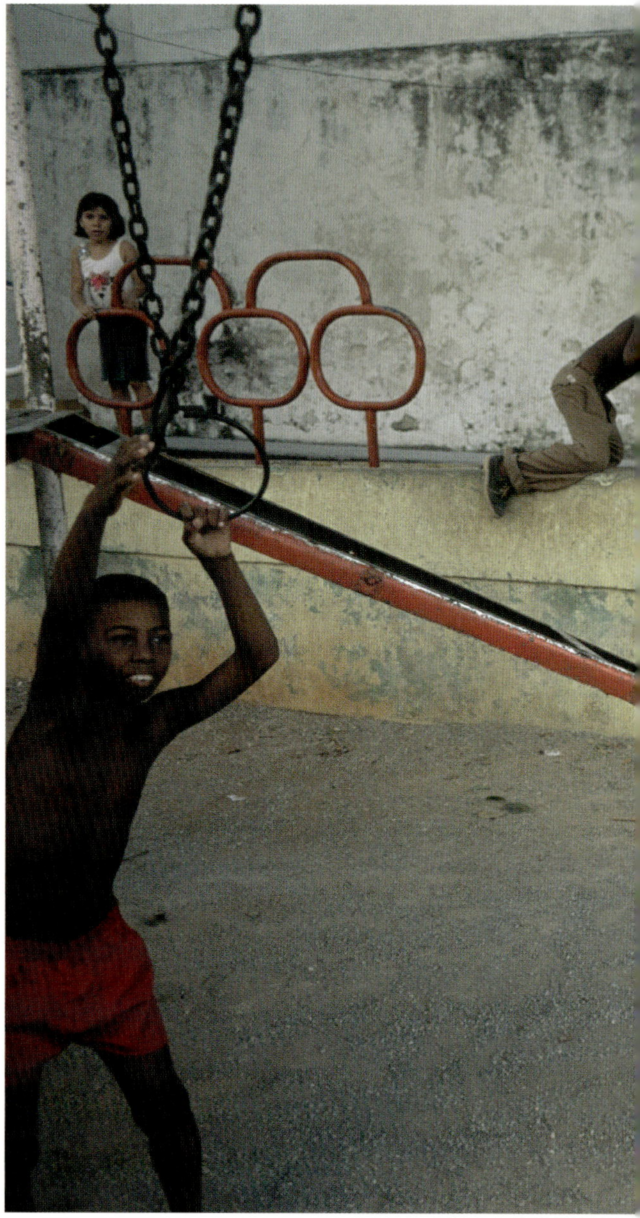

Creative tips and techniques

Harvey has good tips for working on the street in an unfamiliar country: appear confident yet not arrogant; wear solid white, black, or beige; do not carry a camera around your neck with a zoom lens; know where you are going before you go; do not open maps on busy street corners: "a dead giveaway that you are from out of town."

Many of the situations Harvey photographs are on the edges of available light, either early in the morning late in the evening, and he feels that a sma auxiliary flash can be used subtly to great effect to boost the illumination and add extra energy in a scene. He often uses a tir flashgun to add extra fill light. He uses Slo Sync Flash to capture action and energy, although warns that wider lenses cast a shadow while using flash.

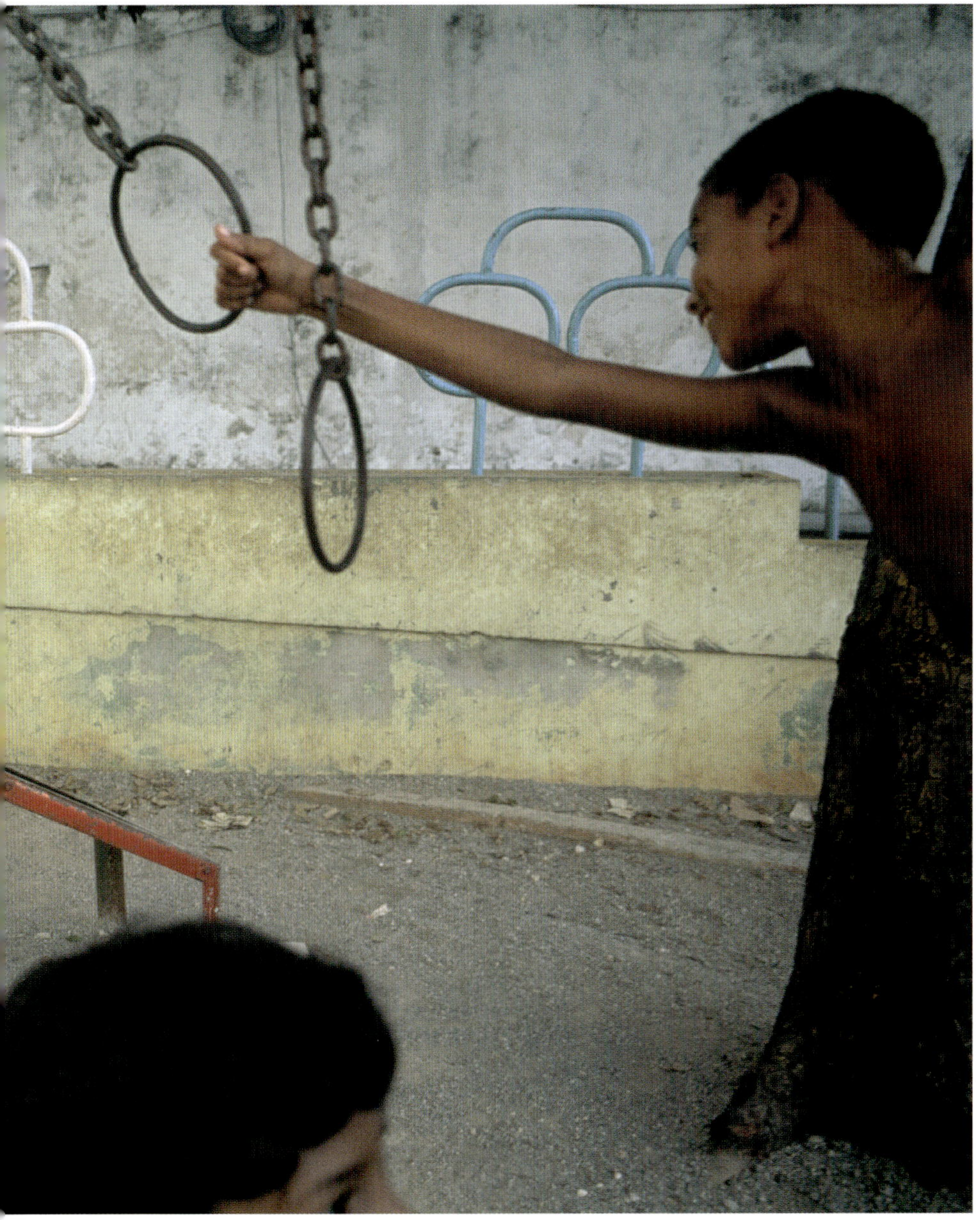

David Alan Harvey (American, 1944–) is a photographer who immerses himself in the situations he documents, putting himself at the center with those he photographs. He has worked extensively for *National Geographic* and examined the legacy of colonialism in the Spanish-speaking world in two books, *Cuba* (2000) and *Divided Soul* (2003). He joined Magnum Photos in 1993. He has embraced technology, exploring the possibilities of camera phones and social media to help promote not only his own work but also that of others, notably through the online magazine *Burn*. Harvey is a passionate teacher who constantly shares advice and ideas through workshops and his online blog.

"Don't shoot what it looks like. Shoot what it feels like."

David Alan Harvey

Harvey works with very minimal equipment, often using only one mera and one lens, or even simply his one. He feels that the 35mm combines vide perspective and a shallow depth field that blurs the background, but still eps it recognizable. The physicality of the s is also important, as it can make people l comfortable and capture an "intimate l." He thinks that the equipment is condary to more vital qualities, such as documenting a great story, and he concludes: "You will need to walk around for hours, days, and even months. Finally, and this is most important—have an open mind, open heart, and a smile."

Harvey has embraced technology, using the iPhone as an extension of his normal way of working, feeling that the immediacy and spontaneity it gives is liberating. He uses the screen on the phone in a manner akin to the ground glass on a large-format camera, saying that even with conventional cameras he doesn't use the viewfinder, preferring live view. He also cautions that the proliferation of images means that you must strive to develop your own unique individual visual signature, arguing that "with everyone being able to make technically perfect photographs with a cell phone, you need to be an 'author'."

Stori

The narrative potential of photography is central to the work of the photojournalist and documentary photographer, whether in a single image or in an extended photo essay. The image itself contains an internal narrative based on interactions and juxtapositions within the frame, but it also invites the viewer to build a narrative for themselves. The viewer is therefore invited to actively participate in generating their own meaning for the image, rather than allowing the meaning to be given to them by its author. Paradoxically, although the still image is a single, discrete, temporal event, it has the ability to transcend time. By playing on the imagination of the viewer, the image can project backward and forward through time, suggesting what has gone before and potentially what will come after the moment of exposure. In a photo essay, the task is to assemble a series of individual elements into a larger, overarching chronicle. The ability to find visual moments that are representative of a situation, and then extract them from the continuum of the action, is a vital skill that can be developed by breaking down the story into its separate elements and then finding the image that best illustrates or explains each of them. In parallel with the historian, the photographer takes these fragmentary pieces of evidence and sequences them in order to construct an argument or a narrative. Each image builds on the others, without unnecessary repetition, until the whole set of images tells us the complete story. Some images will be more important, dramatic, or powerful than others, whereas others may be more informational or descriptive, but all are needed to explain everything.

Weegee

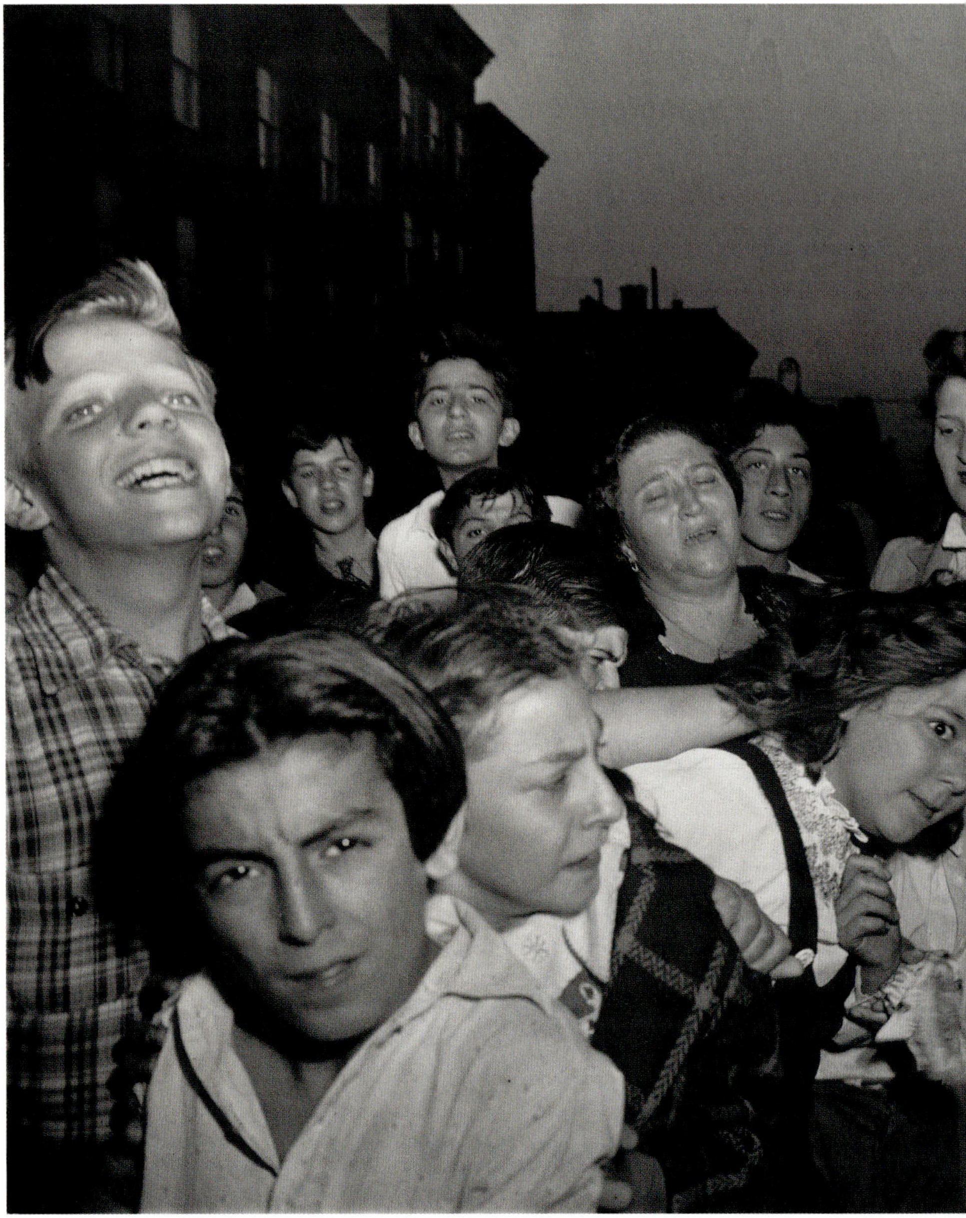

Weegee (American, 1899–1968) was born Usher Fellig in Złoczów, near Lemberg, Austria (now Ukraine). After his family moved to the United States, he became Arthur, and later adopted the soubriquet "Weegee" because of his seemingly supernatural ability to be first at the scene of a crime or disaster, as if he was using an ouija board. He was one of the few photographers licensed to carry a police radio in his car, and spent the nights prowling the streets of the city ready to rush to the scene of a grisly murder, dramatic fire, or daring robbery. When he became a photographer, in 1935, at least a dozen daily papers were being published in New York, with several in the new picture-fronted tabloid format. Weegee sold his shots to any willing buyer, becoming one of the role models for the freelance photojournalist. His direct style and voracious production have influenced generations of photographers, including Diane Arbus.

Creative tips and techniques

Weegee was very precise in describing his equipment and working method in the field. He always shot with a "5 x 4 Speed Graphic camera with a Kodak Ektar lens in a supermatic shutter and Garflex-synchronized flash (flashbulbs). Film—Super Pancro Press Type B." He usually shot everything with flash, whether at nighttime or in daylight, noting the "exposure is always the same, 1/200 part of a second at stop f/16 at a distance of ten feet." He described that when taking pictures he was often in a trance, held in the drama of the moment, and it was only when developing his film that he really saw the pictures he was making. Like a digital news photographer today, Weegee developed his photographs in a makeshift darkroom in the trunk of his car so that he could instantly take them to his clients. Weegee effectively used a zor focusing system, where the lens is preset at a fixed distance, usually between 6 ½– feet (2–3 meters), with a wide-angle lens and a small aperture. This ensures that everything from around 3 feet (1 meter) t infinity will be sharp, so no time needs to lost in focusing. As Weegee worked most at night, he could not even see anything to focus by anyway. This is a useful skill to practice; it works especially well with

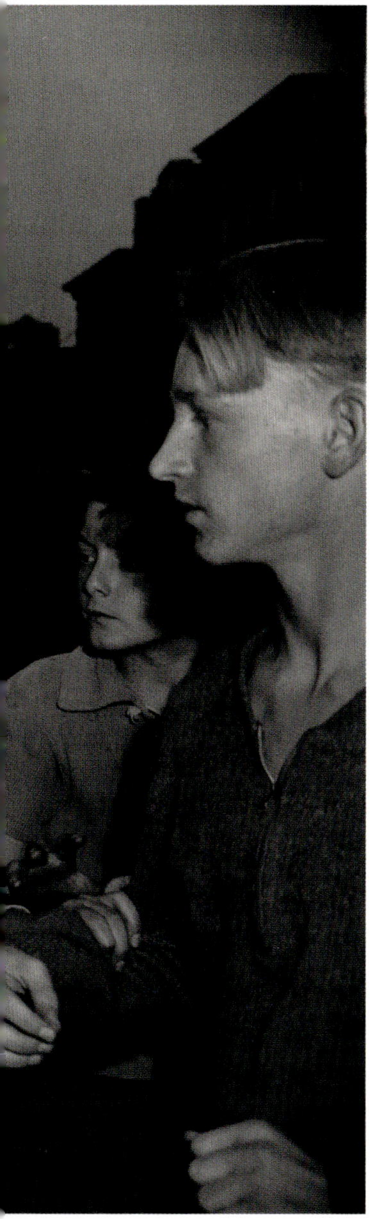

The first murder 1941

Press photographer Weegee published this startling image in the "Murders" chapter of *Naked City*, his 1945 book documenting the afterhours life of New York. The caption read: "A woman relative cried... but neighborhood dead-end kids enjoyed the show when a small-time racketeer was shot and killed." On the opposite page he showed the dead body lying in a pool of blood. It was typical of Weegee's approach: close to the subjects, using direct flash to give an unforgiving yet illuminating light, capturing an unsettling range of emotions from horror to curiosity, suspicion, and even nervous laughter at the encounter with the photographer. In its character study of faces, orchestrated across the frame, it rivals the paintings of Dutch Masters such as Rembrandt.

Weegee constantly pounded the streets in search of such telling moments, but he admitted that he also sometimes reacted with his subjects: "For the pictures in this book I was on the scene; sometimes drawn there by some power I can't explain, and I caught the New Yorkers with their masks off... not afraid to laugh, cry, or make love. What I felt I photographed, laughing and crying with them." *Naked City* is full of extraordinary advice, at once practical but also chilling. Weegee advised that the "easiest kind of a job to cover is a murder, because the stiff will be laying on the ground, he couldn't get up and walk away or get temperamental, and he would be good for at least two hours. So I had plenty of time," whereas at "fires, you had to work very fast." The economics of his trade are fascinating, and he had a knack for maximizing his profits, commenting that "if I had a picture of two handcuffed criminals being booked, I would cut the picture in half and get five bucks for each." He once wrote that he had so many unsold murder pictures lying around his room, "I felt as if I were renting out a wing of the City Morgue."

ıgefinder cameras because of their clear ›ect viewfinders. Prefocus the camera and ɔot on the street for a period of time :hout ever focusing the lens. Look at ır results; you will be surprised that ɔst are sharp, even though you never ɜnged the focus.

Weegee explained how he approached crowds at the scene of an incident, ɡuing that "one just doesn't go up to strange men, women, children, elephants, or giraffes and say, 'Look this way please. Laugh—cry, show some emotion, or go to sleep underneath a funeral canopy'." His advice to a young photographer is still invaluable: "be original and develop your own style, but don't forget above anything and everything else... be human... think... feel... when you laugh and cry with their laughter and tears, you will know you are on the right track."

"Keep your eyes open. If you see anything, take it. Remember—you're as good as your last picture." Weegee

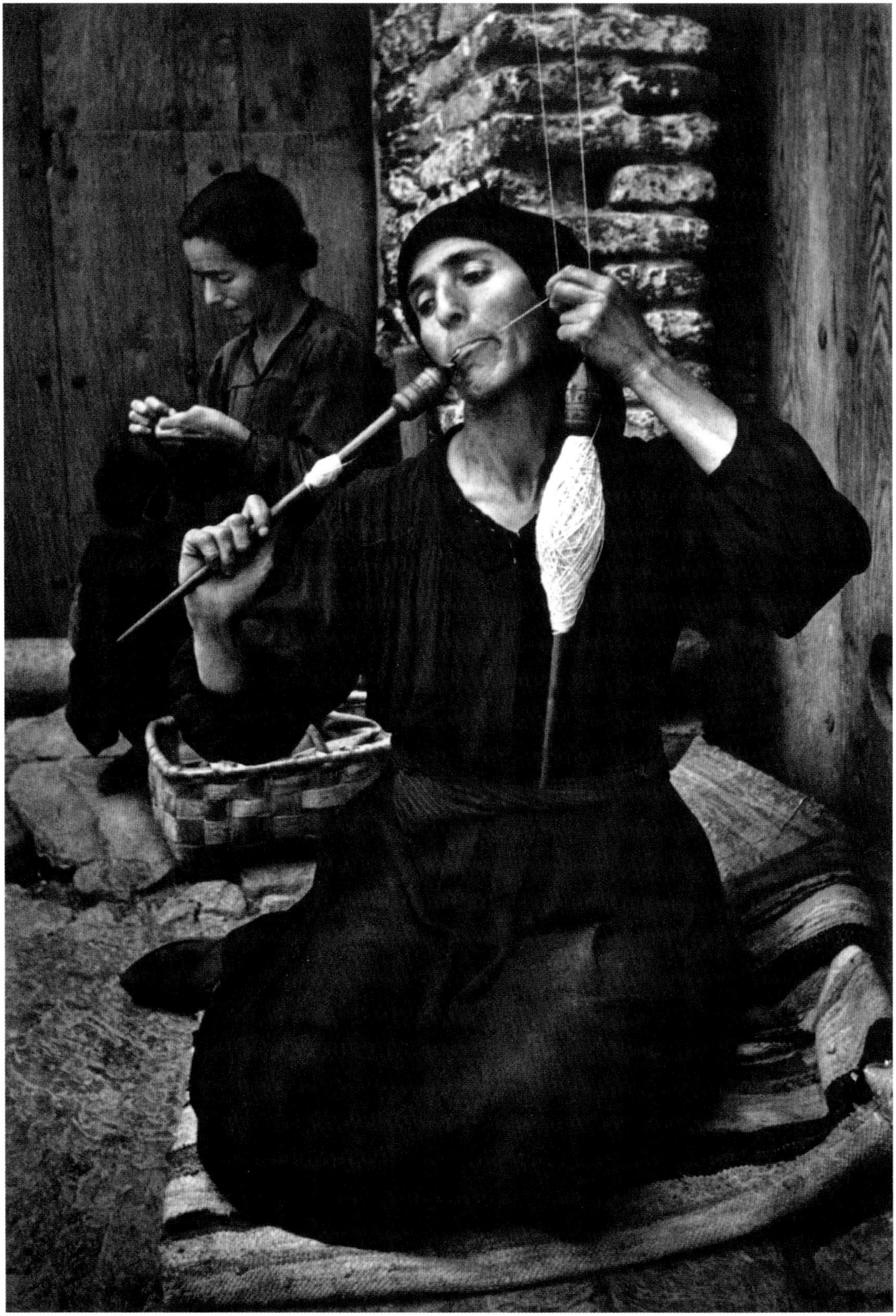

woman spinning 1951, from "Spanish Village," *e magazine*

Eugene Smith spent enormous amounts of time researching stories. For "Spanish Village," the photo essay from which s image is taken, he visited dozens of villages in Spain before ding the ideal one. It appeared in *Life* magazine on 9 April 1951, d is considered by many to be the "perfect" photo essay. e evocative images, such as this one showing two women nning, provide a powerful portrait of daily life in rural Spain ring Franco's dictatorship. The essay opened with the following rds: "The village of Deleitosa, a place of about 2,300 peasant ople, sits on the high, dry, western Spanish tableland called tremadura, about halfway between Madrid and the border of rtugal. Its name means 'delightful,' which it no longer is, and its gins are obscure, though they may go back a thousand years Spain's Moorish period. In any event it is very old and *Life* otographer Eugene Smith, wandering off the main road into the age, found that its ways had advanced little since medieval times." tremadura was then one of the most underdeveloped regions of ain with no water or sewage system and hardly any electricity. Smith's visual style was marked by high-contrast images, with ep blacks and white whites, and he favored *chiaroscuro* lighting: music I still prefer the minor key, and in printing I like the light ming from the dark. I like pictures that surmount the darkness, d many of my photographs are that way. It is the way that I see otographically." Smith worked obsessively; his notebooks show w he planned out each essay in detail, and then photographed ch situation repeatedly until he got the image he wanted, but was a deeply troubled man, torn by his commitment to his aft and the realities of the marketplace.

/hat use is having a great depth of field, if there is not an dequate depth of feeling?" W. Eugene Smith

Eugene Smith (American, 1918–78) began rking as a photographer in New York at a ung age. He covered World War II for *Life* agazine, but was badly injured in combat, calling, "I forgot to duck but I got a wonderful ot of those who did... my policy of standing up en the others are down finally caught up with ." After his recuperation, he returned to work *Life*, and produced a series of photo essays the 1940s and 1950s that are seen as classics of the genre. Smith refused to compromise his vision, but remained committed to the idea of magazine photojournalism as his true vocation. He often battled with his employers and editors about how his pictures should be used, and he resigned from several jobs, including *Life*. After his *Life* resignation, he produced an epic book on the city of Pittsburgh, as well as a monumental essay on the horrific consequences of mercury poisoning on the Japanese town of Minamata.

Creative tips and techniques

Smith felt that the original exposure was only the beginning of the process of producing the final image. He was happy to crop his photographs to get the results he wanted, arguing that the "world just does not fit conveniently into the format of a 35 mm camera." He regarded his original negatives only as part of the drafting process, unlike the final image: "The print—and a proper one—is the only completed photograph, whether it is specifically shaded for reproduction, or for a museum wall." Smith worked obsessively on his prints, burning them to bring out features he wanted to enhance and removing extraneous detail. He would burn in areas to total black, and use ferrocyanide to bleach and lighten highlights such as eyes and hair to make them really pop out.

Smith argued it is impossible for the photojournalist to be completely objective. He believed that an authentic interpretation of the subject was paramount, and even went as far as setting up and orchestrating a scene for maximum impact. He also montaged pictures together to get the exact elements he wanted in the same frame. He maintained: "Whenever this is done for the purpose of a better translation of the spirit of the actuality, then it is completely ethical. If the changes become a perversion of the actuality for the sole purpose of making a 'more dramatic' or 'saleable' picture, the photographer has indulged in 'artistic license' that should not be." This complex issue still causes much debate. TV documentary crews regularly restage events for the camera to get the best angles and interviews, but the general feeling is that in photographic work that is truly "documentary," it is going too far.

Anders Petersen

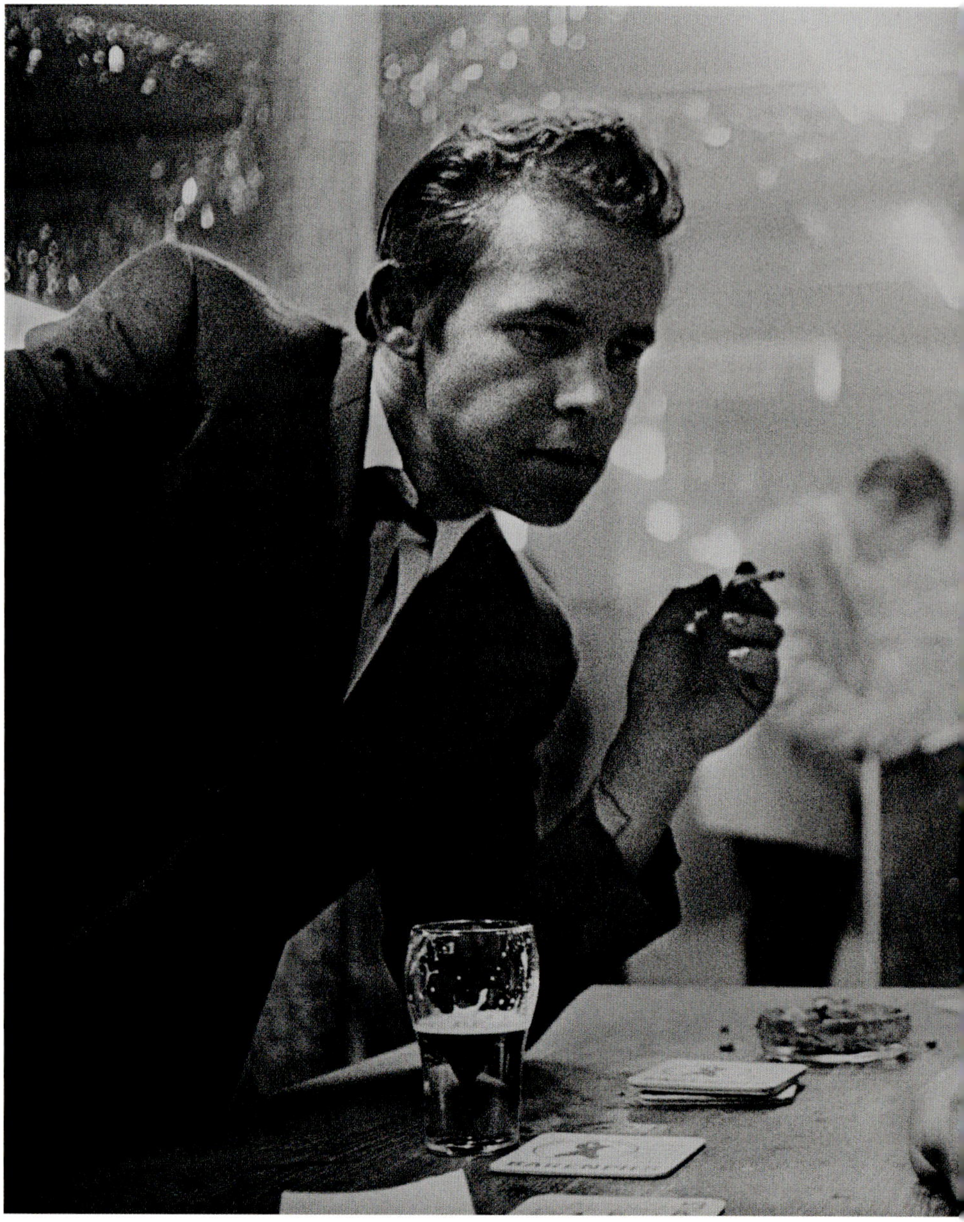

Anders Petersen (Swedish, 1944–) studied photography in 1966 at the Fotoskolan school in Stockholm under the influential photographer Christer Strömholm. Petersen moved to Hamburg, and began frequenting a late-night bar called Café Lehmitz in the Reeperbahn red-light district. He photographed its regular clientele of prostitutes, transvestites, drunks, lovers, and drug addicts, publishing the work as a book of the same name in 1978. He has since explored the intimate lives of inmates in high-security prisons, mental hospitals, and homes for the aged, and published a further twenty books. He describes how close he became to his subjects: "They lived a brutal and tender life that I had never experienced before, but that changed my way of looking at the world. It was a real lesson for me, a young, respectable boy from Sweden. A lesson in how to live."

Creative tips and techniques

Petersen explains how he channels his emotions into his work, and how in a counter-intuitive way you have to reveal your flaws as well as your strengths in order to get close to people. He maintains that you have to open yourself up to risks or you will never make creative breakthroughs. He believes that by channelling longings, dreams, secrets, and nightmares—whatever you are afraid of—you can use feelings creatively. He recommends: "go inside and open up like a sharp knife, like a doctor operating." This is a strong metaphor: connect with your inner feelings to open up your vision. Cut out the extraneous, focusing on the essential experience in front of you.

He also explains how he tries to be as instinctive as possible when he is shooting, letting the moment of experienc[e] be his guide rather than a predetermined idea or attitude, thinking about the work only after it is made, not before. He claims that it is when he is looking at the contact sheets, editing and choosing, that "the responsibility comes in." He sees this as an intensely personal process, revealing as much about himself as about his subject. He maintains that he wants every image t[o] be a kind of self-portrait: "If I take a pictur[e]

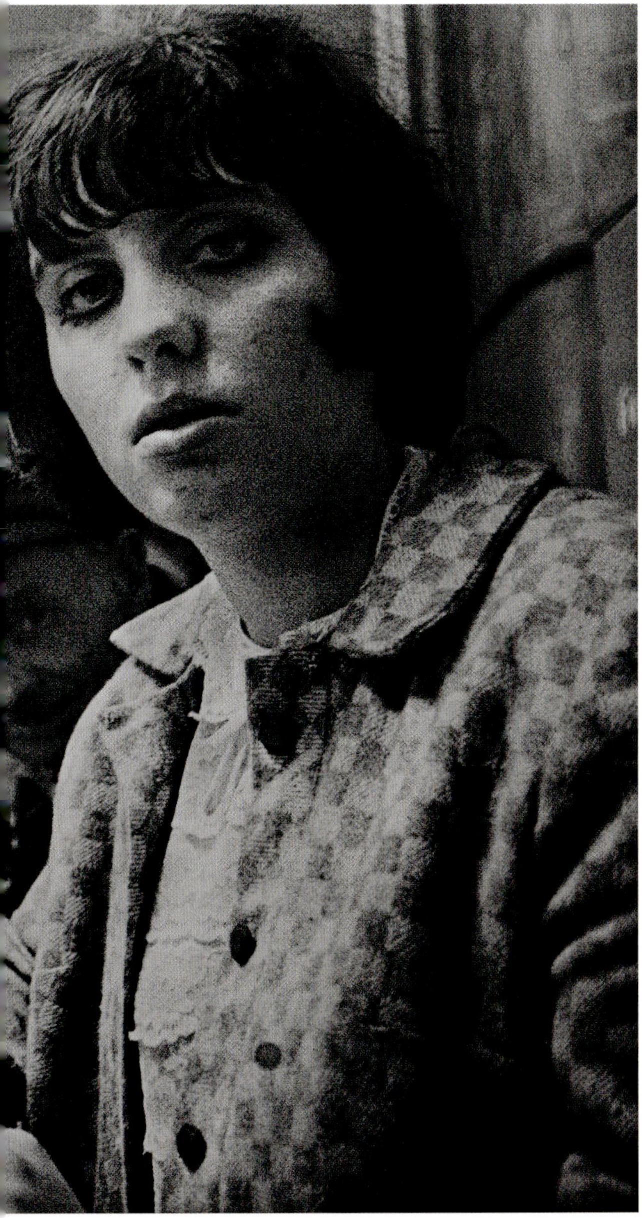

Lilly, Rose, and Scar in Café Lehmitz, Hamburg 1970

Anders Petersen describes how he began to work in Hamburg's Café Lehmitz, after talking to one of the customers about his camera: "Suddenly, across the room, I noticed a group of people were throwing my camera back and forth, taking pictures of each other. I went over and said: 'Please take a picture of me because it's my camera.' OK, they said, then handed it back. So I took some pictures of my own—and that was how I started photographing in Café Lehmitz." He continued to drink and work there, becoming friends with its colorful cast of characters.

He explains how the personalities of the subjects are central to this image: "Lilly was everyone's darling, a charismatic woman—many men were in love with her, and she knew it. The man on the left was known as Rose because of the tattoo on his chest. He was well dressed because he had come from work, a restaurant ten minutes away. Every night, he would come to Café Lehmitz to see his friends, but mostly to see Lilly... Lilly was angry with me when I took this picture because I had been photographing her so much... You see the little guy behind her? That is Scar. He was a very famous sword-swallower."

The image draws the viewer in—its receding series of figures forms a zigzag line that directs the eye deeper into the smoky interior, whereas the darker forms of the foreground faces give the image a sense of depth. The sight lines of the characters are significant, with Scar and Lilly engaged with the viewer while Rose only has eyes for Lilly. After three years photographing in the bar, Petersen held an impromptu exhibition there. He recalls how he "pinned 350 pictures above the bar and said if anyone recognized themselves they could take the picture down and keep it... it only lasted four or five days, until there were no pictures left, just a small one of me. It was still there ten years later."

that apple on the table, it can be a self-ortrait." He suggests not thinking and eing as intuitive as possible, using your erve, heart, and gut. He has dubbed this ersonal process "private documentary."

Petersen now shoots most of his work on a small compact film amera, eschewing bulky SLRs and digital ameras. He says that the camera is only tool and he wants as little as possible to be between himself and his experience. Shooting with minimal equipment, perhaps a camera phone, can be very liberating; you think less about the gear and technical details and more about the lived moment. Try going to the same café, bar, or other social arena every day for a week, with only one camera and one lens, and attempt to capture your instinctive feelings about the people that you engage with.

"In black and white there are more colors than color photography... you can use your experiences, your knowledge, and your fantasy, to... put in your own colors."

Anders Petersen

William Albert Allard

"If you strive for simplicity, you are more likely to reach the viewer."
William Albert Allard

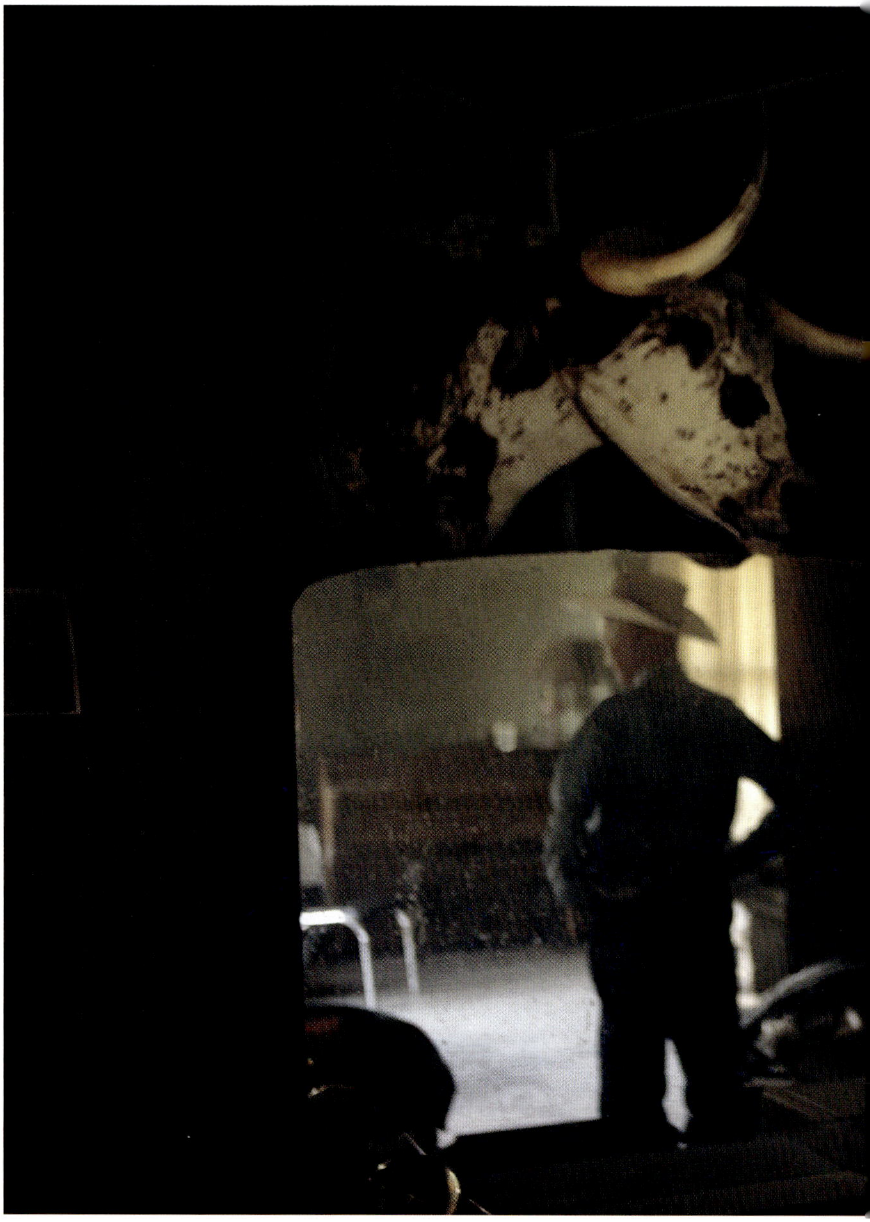

William Albert Allard (American, 1937–) has been a mainstay of *National Geographic* magazine since 1964, when he joined as an intern. Since then he has shot over forty stories for the publication, covering the lives of American cowboys, the Amish community, and the Basque region of Spain. Working entirely in color, his images have a painterly quality, with a rich, dense palette, complex compositions, and a distinctive feel for light. He cites painters such as Henri Matisse, Edward Hopper, the Impressionists, and the Dutch Masters as inspiration for his work, saying, "In my photography, color and composition are inseparable. I see in color." Allard is also one of the few photographers who can really write about his stories, too, feeling that "there are a lot of parallels between good writing and good pictures."

Creative tips and techniques

Allard works with both SLRs and rangefinders, using each for the unique qualities they bring in different situations. He explains that when he looks through an SLR he is more aware of composition and the structure of the image, whereas with a rangefinder camera he is aware of spatial relationships. Allard often shoots in situations where the light levels are low, sc is frequently working at maximum apertur and slow shutter speeds. Learn how to handhold your camera by controlling your breathing and timing, and use objects like tables or a monopod to brace yourself.

Allard has a great sense of how to enter into a situation gently, without drama, until he is accepted by the people he is documenting. Taking one's time is

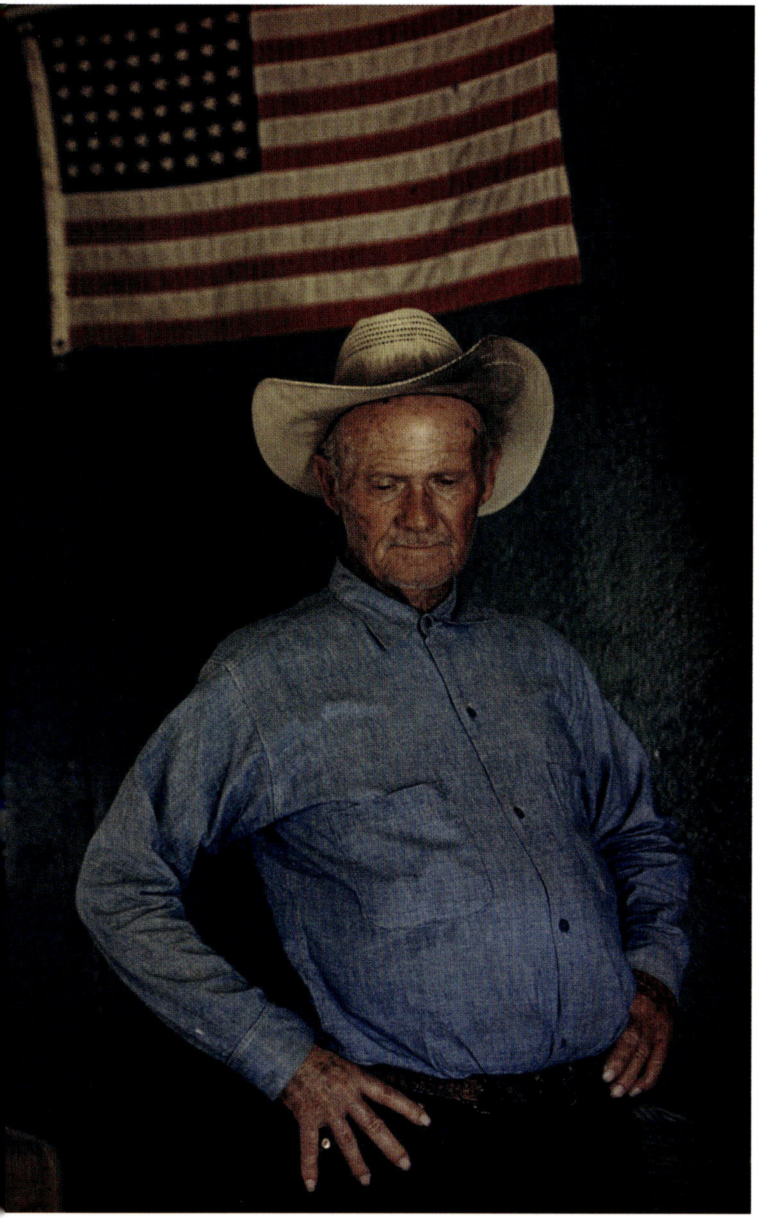

Henry Gray, Arizona 1970

This powerful character study of an ageing cowboy is taken from William Albert Allard's love letter to the last American cowboys, *Vanishing Breed*, published in 1982. He reveals how he felt a strong connection to the subject: "I think I fell in love with the spaciousness of the American West...I grew up in the prairie country of Minnesota. When I first saw those Rocky Mountains beckoning in the distance while driving across the West in my early years of working, it was extremely inspiring as a visual motif. And true westerners have a work ethic and certain cultural ways I was drawn to." The subject, seventy-two-year-old Henry Gray, had been a rancher for fifty years, but the US government wanted his cattle off the land. Allard describes how "as we moved about the house, Henry paused, lost in his thoughts, behind him a 48-star flag." Here, Allard sums up the life of this man in a single frame, combining the flag, the bull's head, his hat, and his reflection into a strong circular composition that suggests both the internal and external world surrounding Gray. His resigned expression speaks of the end of an era.

Allard often includes this type of portrait in his stories; however, they are not staged or set up, but, rather, spontaneous and unplanned. Allard explains his working method and approach to his subjects: "I will say, 'Try to forget I'm here. I won't ask you to pose, I won't ask you to do anything.' It's important that I just be allowed to be around, to be present." Many of his images have a sense of a paused moment like this one, as he believes in the "resonance and staying power of quiet photographs."

portant; ease your way into a situation adually to avoid alienating people. He lvises: "Acceptance is what it always mes down to. If I am accepted to be part the scene, whatever and whoever is my bject area, and I'm allowed to be part of pictures will come. In a sense, they will be ven every bit as much as taken."

Allard is a master at finding the right locations to make his images. He suggests finding a space where the light is doing something: "Watch the light and see how it changes. Change lenses. Do it again. Look at it again...It's very much like rewriting a passage until you get it right." This is a process that cannot be hurried, and patience often leads to that magical moment when the unexpected happens. Allard points out that while serendipity is hugely important to street photographers, "to me it's almost everything. I've seen some wonderful pictures I wasn't able to get on film or on a digital file, but seeing them was great." This sense of not simply looking for the obvious thing to photograph, but exploring around it to find a unique angle, is central to his approach. He believes that "the best pictures are often on the edges of any situation; I don't find photographing the situation nearly as interesting as photographing the edges."

Sebastião Salgado

Guatemala 1978

This image comes from Sebastião Salgado's first photo book, *Other Americas* (1986). From 1977 to 1984 he traveled across Central and South America in search of themes that express the cultural and religious traditions of the region. He captured the everyday lives of poor rural communities during a period of rapid industrial growth, political conflict, and rising inequality. Influenced by the literature of Gabriel García Márquez and Baroque religious art, Salgado's book has a sense of magic realism. The work was also an expression of his own history, as he explains: "This story that I'm photographing is my story also. I am a migrant, too." Born on a farm in the Brazilian state of Minas Gerais, Salgado spent an itinerant childhood moving with his family first to a small town, then a larger one, before eventually settling in the city of São Paulo. There Salgado trained to be an economist, but he finally left Brazil and went to live in France, where he began working as a photographer in 1973.

Salgado admits that his experience in business contributed to his world view as a social documentary photographer. He recalls: "My visual heritage comes from the mountains where I grew up and a lot of my intellectual heritage from having been an economist ...So when I became a photographer, I had a series of instruments for analysis and synthesis." For *Other Americas* it is fitting that Salgado returned to his roots in Latin America, where, as he puts it, "dignity and poverty ride on the same horse." As in this image—which shows a young toffee-apple vendor being watched from a window by an older woman—Salgado's work is marked by a real sense of empathy and respect for his subjects, regardless of their social status. He argues: "Dignity is not an exclusive property of the rich countries of the north, but exists all over the planet. That's what photography was for me, my language, my life, and my way of going about and doing things."

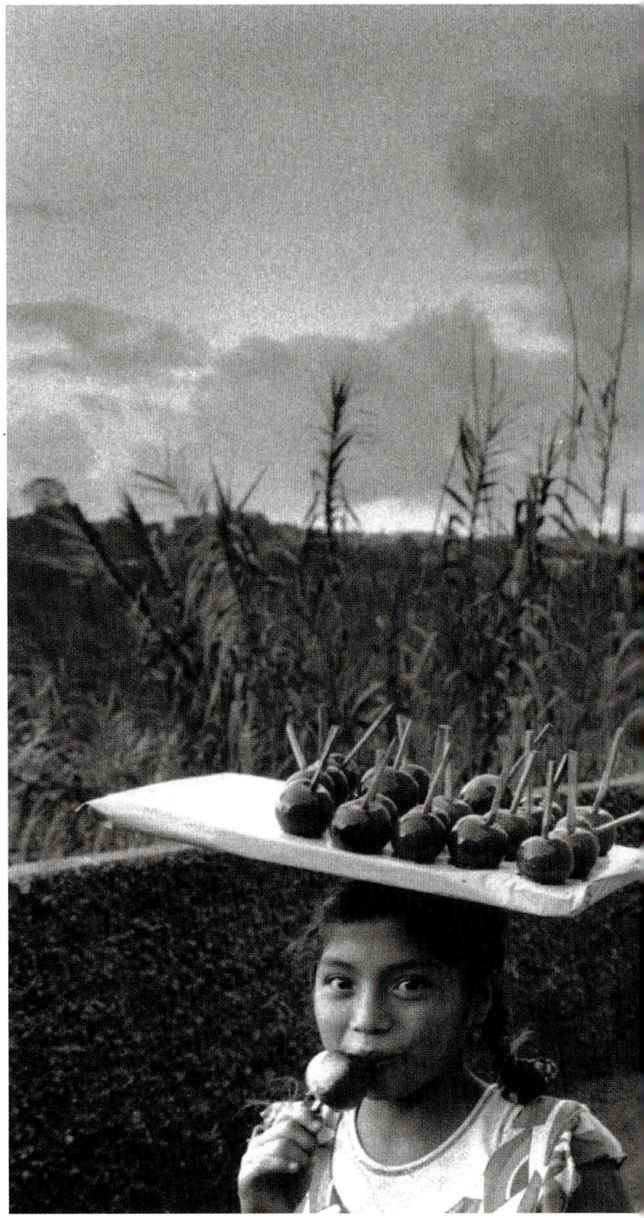

Creative tips and techniques

Salgado identifies global social themes and divides them up into self-contained stories, which he can execute one by one over a period of some years. He often shoots more than forty individual projects before bringing them together in one final publication. This then allows him to fund each project as he is going along, as the photographs from each chapter can be sold individually, helping to support the production of the next. This is an effectiv strategy, as working in the locations he chooses to shoot is often expensive. In hi studio in Paris, he has a team of assistant working on research and post-productior led by his wife, who designs most of the books. However, in the field he works alone, which, he feels, makes people mor receptive to him.

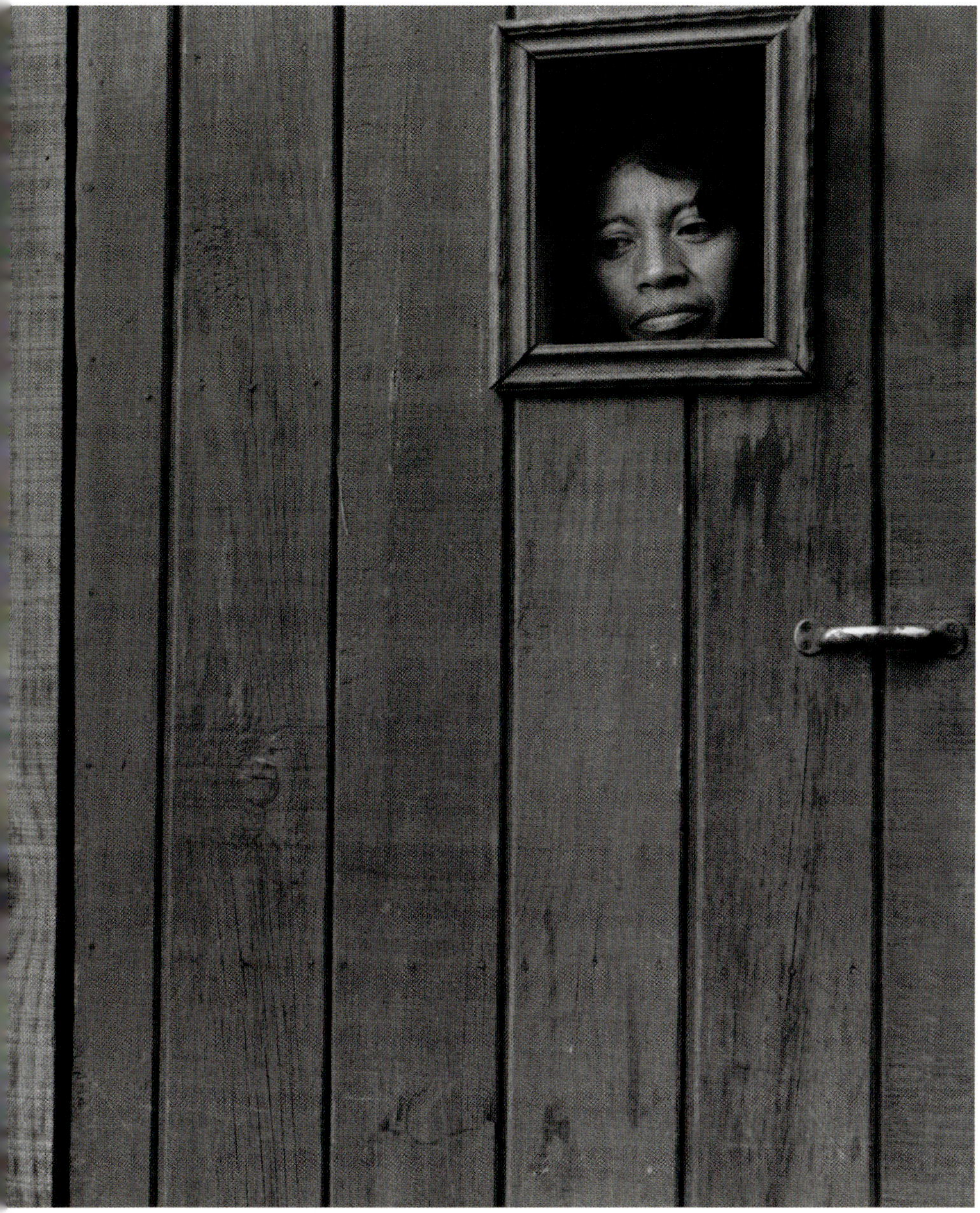

Sebastião Salgado (Brazilian, 1944–) initially worked as an economist for the International Coffee Organization. After his wife, the architect Lélia Wanick, introduced him to photography, he switched careers and has become one of the world's leading documenters of social and economic change. He has produced a series of monumental works that each take many years to complete, including *Workers* (1993), *Terra* (1997), *Migrations* (2000), and *Sahel* (2004). In 1998 he and his wife started the Instituto Terra in his home state in Brazil, an organization aimed at reforestation, conservation, and environmental education. This inspired his work, *Genesis* (2013), on the last unspoilt wildernesses of the world.

"It's not just pictures that are important—it's important that you are in the moment of your society that your pictures show. If you understand this, there is no limit for you."

Sebastião Salgado

Salgado shoots almost entirely in black and white, arguing that color ın be a distraction. His photographs splay a feel for the full range of tonal lues, especially grays. There are tricks to elp develop a feel for how the world looks black and white. Half close your eyes and ok at a scene; this will knock back colors ıd emphasize the tonal values. Or you can e a strong color filter, such as red, which ll take the color out of the situation.

Salgado's work is marked by his mastery of light; he has a great sensitivity to side- and backlight, using them to create depth and a three-dimensional feel. He says that this is a result of growing up in Brazil where he wore a sunhat: "I was raised in the shadows." It is important to learn how to deal with difficult light conditions, as they often produce exceptional images. Try to deliberately shoot against the sun, to control contrast and flare.

Salgado converted to digital for *Genesis*, but he still uses film. After each trip he returns to Paris with around 10,000 pictures. He does not view the images on screen, but instead has contact sheets made from the digital files and edits those in the same way he would with film using a loupe. Around 100 of the best frames from each trip are chosen and then a film negative is made, from which the final prints are developed.

Raghu Rai

Local commuters at Church Gate railway station, Mumbai 1995

In this striking image depicting the rush of energy that is daily life in India, Raghu Rai uses a variety of techniques to accentuate the scale of human activity at the crowded railway station. The use of a slow shutter speed blurs the majority of the commuters as they stream past the camera, split by the group of men in the center who seem oblivious to the crowds around them as they peruse the daily news; their eyeglasses and moustaches add a bourgeois element to their characters. The framing emphasizes the size of the railway station, one of the busiest in the city, with trains arriving at one-minute intervals, disgorging millions of commuters daily. The converging lines of the framing suggest that the platform runs on forever, receding into the burnt-out highlight of the world outside. Rai makes a witty comment, too, with the advertisement on the left referencing both the clockwork precision of the railway timetable and the scale of the country.

Rai uses the technical language of photography to reflect something of what he feels about his native country, which he describes as follows: "India is a multi-religious, multicultural society in which several centuries live together at the same time. The experience of India has to be multi-layered and so a moment in time is not enough. The vision is larger, and what is captured is much more than what a photograph shows." Rai is seeking moments of almost spiritual inspiration and he likens seeing to "Darshan"—the moment of divine revelation in Hindu philosophy: "Photography is about connectivity and presence. Darshan is so much more than seeing, witnessing, or glancing. It brings everything together: the energies, vibrations, physicality, and the visual experience. When everything is put together, it makes a whole." However, he also acknowledges that his role as an observer of his own culture creates a tension, such that "I am the outsider as well as the insider. I am a stranger and I am also part of them. It's a paradox, at once difficult to understand and yet simple to assimilate."

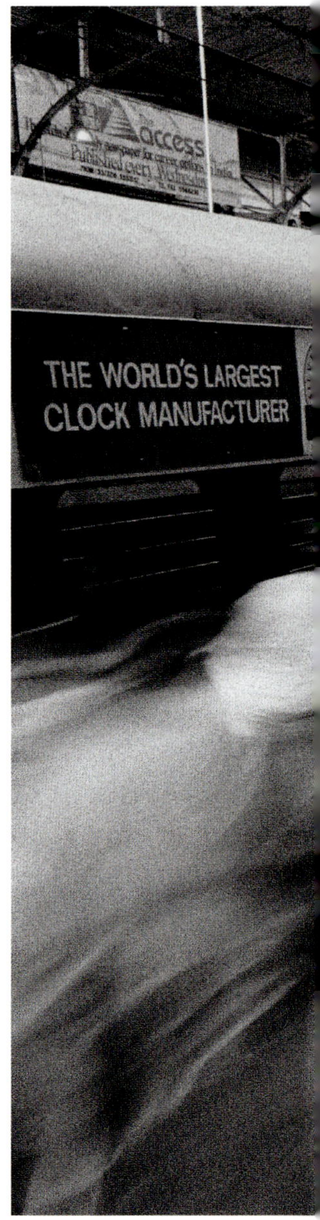

Creative tips and techniques

Rai extends his philosophy of making a spiritual connection with the world around him to the way he constructs his images. He says that he never composes his photographs: "Sometimes I begin with a frame in mind, aim, and suddenly the magic begins... a cloud shifts, a face appears from nowhere, a dog whizzes past, a crow descends among pigeons, an expression changes, and the odhni flies in a gust of wind. It's really God in each of those moments." However, he cautions that such a connection with the world around you only comes as a result of total concentration and hard work, not some magical luck: "You have to be intuitive, instinctive, and wait for that moment where you make a 'connection.' You have to be able to merge with that moment and click."

Rai feels that color is a more demanding medium than black and white, because "each color has its physica response, its emotional response... We see everything in color, so when you put a black-and-white filter on life, it silences the noise of color. It's far easier to make a goo black-and-white picture, and it is far easier to appreciate the black-and-white picture." Thinking of color in this way is important; controlling your use of color

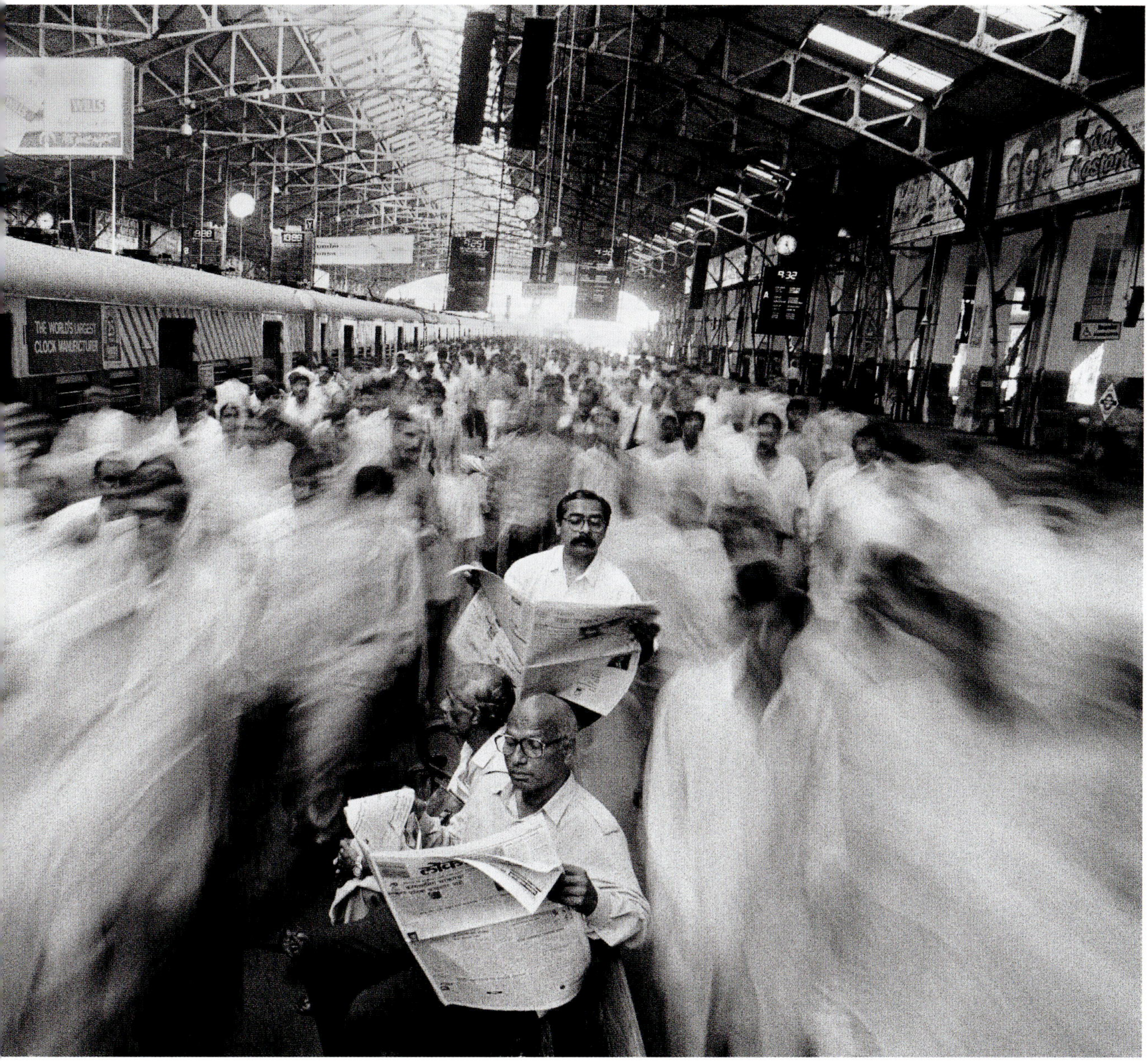

refully to express specific feelings you
ve about a situation in front of you will
eatly enhance the eventual impact of
ur images.

Since converting to shooting with
digital cameras, Rai admits that he
s few regrets. He argues: "Technology
your tool and new technology gives
u greater freedom and greater control
doing your work."

"To me the camera is an instrument of learning... It's a learning of the self and the world." Raghu Rai

Raghu Rai (Indian, 1942–) began working as a photographer in 1965, and a year later joined the staff of *The Statesman* in New Delhi. In 1976, he left the paper and became a freelance photographer, joining *India Today* in 1982 as director of photography. Rai joined Magnum Photos in 1977. He has produced more than eighteen books, including an in-depth portrayal of the aftermath of the Bhopal disaster, *Exposure: Portrait of a Corporate Crime*, in collaboration with Greenpeace. In his documentation of Indian life, he has displayed a powerful sense of the spiritual undercurrents of the country. He sums up his philosophy: "Either you capture the mystery of things or you reveal the mystery. Everything else is just information."

Larry Towell

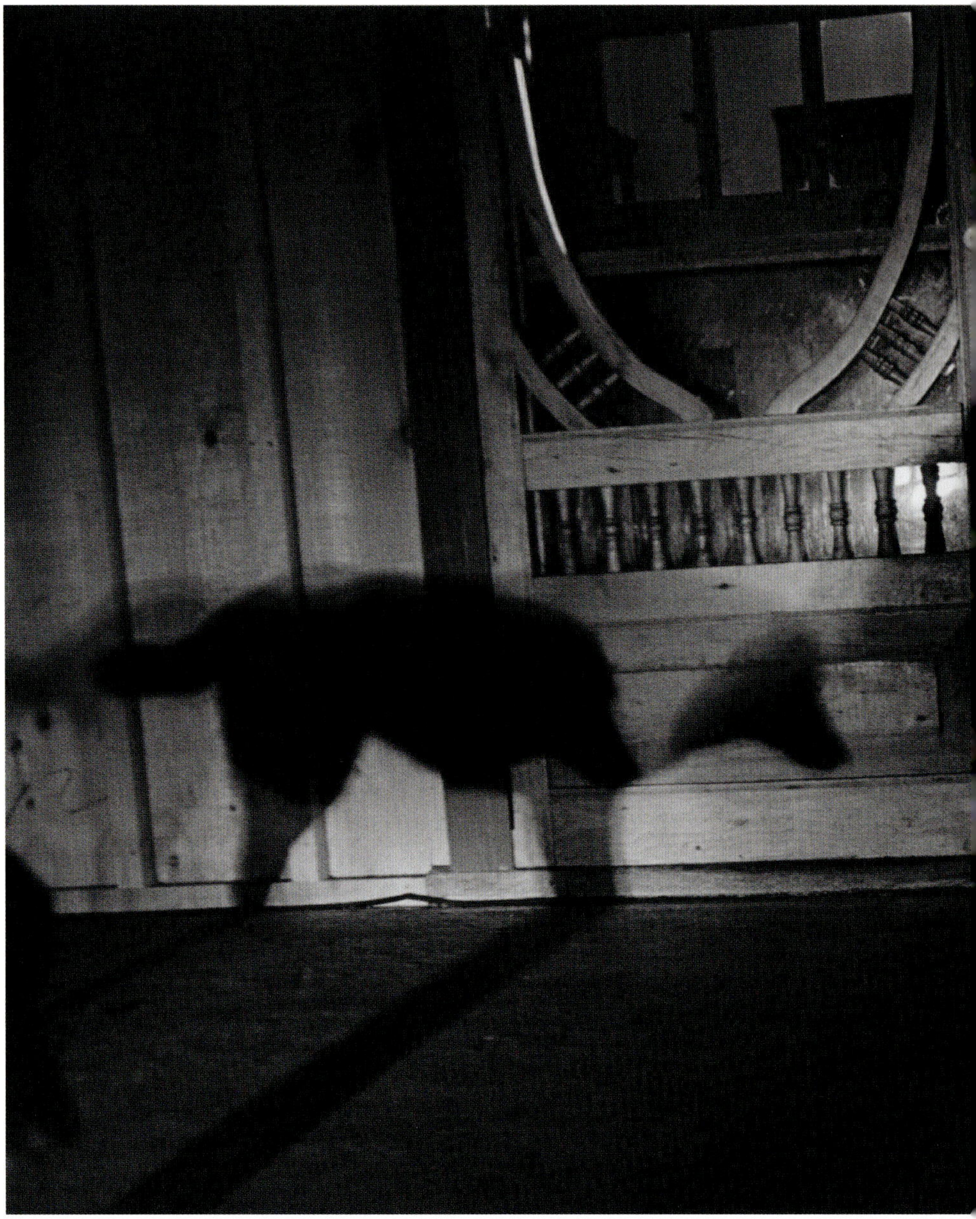

Larry Towell (Canadian, 1953–) combines photography, music, writing, and poetry in his work. It centers on long-term projects that are concerned with the lives of the dispossessed, exiles, and peasant rebellion. He explains: "If there's one theme that connects all my work, I think it's that of land-lessness: how land makes people into who they are and what happens to them when they lose it and thus lose their identities." He became a freelance photographer in 1984 and initially worked in Central and Latin America, documenting the civil wars in Nicaragua and El Salvador. He joined Magnum Photos in 1988. Towell's bibliography includes books of photographs, poetry, and oral history, as well as CDs of original poetry and songs. Towell lives in rural Ontario, where he sharecrops a farm. His business card reads simply, "Larry Towell, Human Being."

Creative tips and techniques

Towell has remained firmly wedded to a simple approach for his photography. He shoots in black and white, but he also carries a digital camera; however, he uses them very differently. He feels that he does not need the speed of digital because he doesn't "accept the deadlines that digital photographers have forced upon them." He explains that black and white is still the poetic form of photography, whereas digital is for the moment.

Towell has always written poetry and text, and is a musician and songwriter, too. He has often combined these with his photographs. He has some useful advice on how to combine the different formats, allowing each to perform its own role within a body of work: "photography can be didactic or it can be more poetic, like music. You have to find t right approach to putting them together otherwise they only complicate each other, or only explain each other, and they shouldn't do that. Both should be a journe on their own."

Towell typically works on several projects simultaneously, with some in the development, research, and plannin

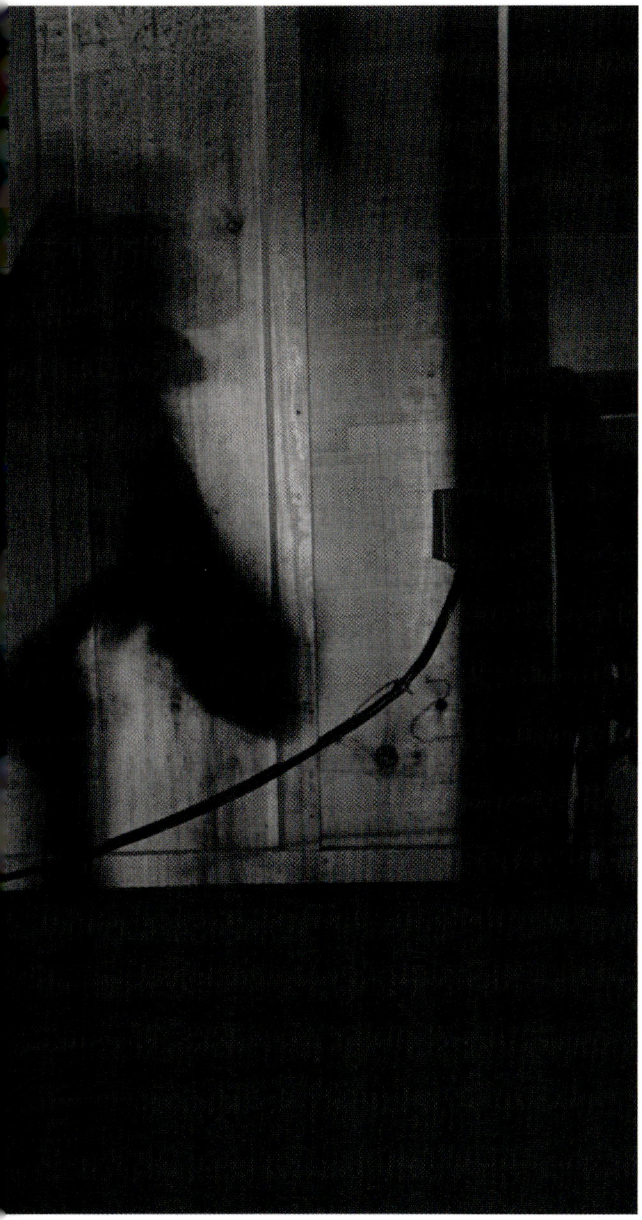

Shadow of the photographer, Lambton County, Ontario 1996

The idea of “home” is central to Larry Towell’s work. He has documented the struggle for land rights in Latin America and the Middle East and among the Mennonite communities of Canada and Mexico. This connection to the land has made recording his own domestic life a natural extension of his work. He observes: “Although I travel extensively, it is usually with a sense of exile. From Hanoi to Managua, from San Salvador to East Jerusalem and the Occupied Territories, the longing for home persists. Although a journalist must work in the arena of international events, when I am not traveling, I turn the camera inward.” This image, with its ghostly form of Towell, wearing his trademark straw hat and standing in the characteristic pose of the photographer, is an evocative moment that explores his relationship with travel and returning home. The double shadow of the dog against the ornate yet homely door suggests the wanderings and journeys to come.

In 2009 Towell published *The World from My Front Porch*, a collection of photographs taken over twenty years of his family and farm in rural Lambton County, Ontario, combined with reportage, poetry, and images of artefacts collected on his travels, including rubber bullets and grenades. He describes it as “a family book, both the history of the land, landlessness, my family, revolutions, insurrections I’d photographed, and what photography meant to me in the context of that.” Towell feels that this connection to his own home is key to his ability to relate to the lives of others, remarking that “once I had my own front porch, I felt positioned in the world.” Towell is committed to telling stories that might otherwise go unnoticed, and feels that it is important they are documented: “You never know what effect you’re going to have... You can’t change the world, but you can be part of the process for change, and sometimes you don’t even know it.’

ages. Others he is actively shooting, d others in post-production and ssemination. He explains that this is effective strategy to keep him fresh d use his energy wisely. Within this, he lvises short, intense periods of working, terspersed with more reflective periods editing and thinking. He tends to work r three-week cycles during which taking otographs is all he thinks about; the st of the time he carefully edits and sequences: “you spend more time editing and looking than shooting.” He tends to organize his year around the rhythms of the story but also of his own life, feeling that “everything has its own period of time that you have to devote to it. So you can travel for two months, or a month, and you can also process that work as a photographer, but then maybe in the summer time, you write, or write music—which is what I do.”

“A photojournalist’s job is to monitor power. That doesn’t mean you have to do it, but if you’re not then you’re not doing your job.” Larry Towell

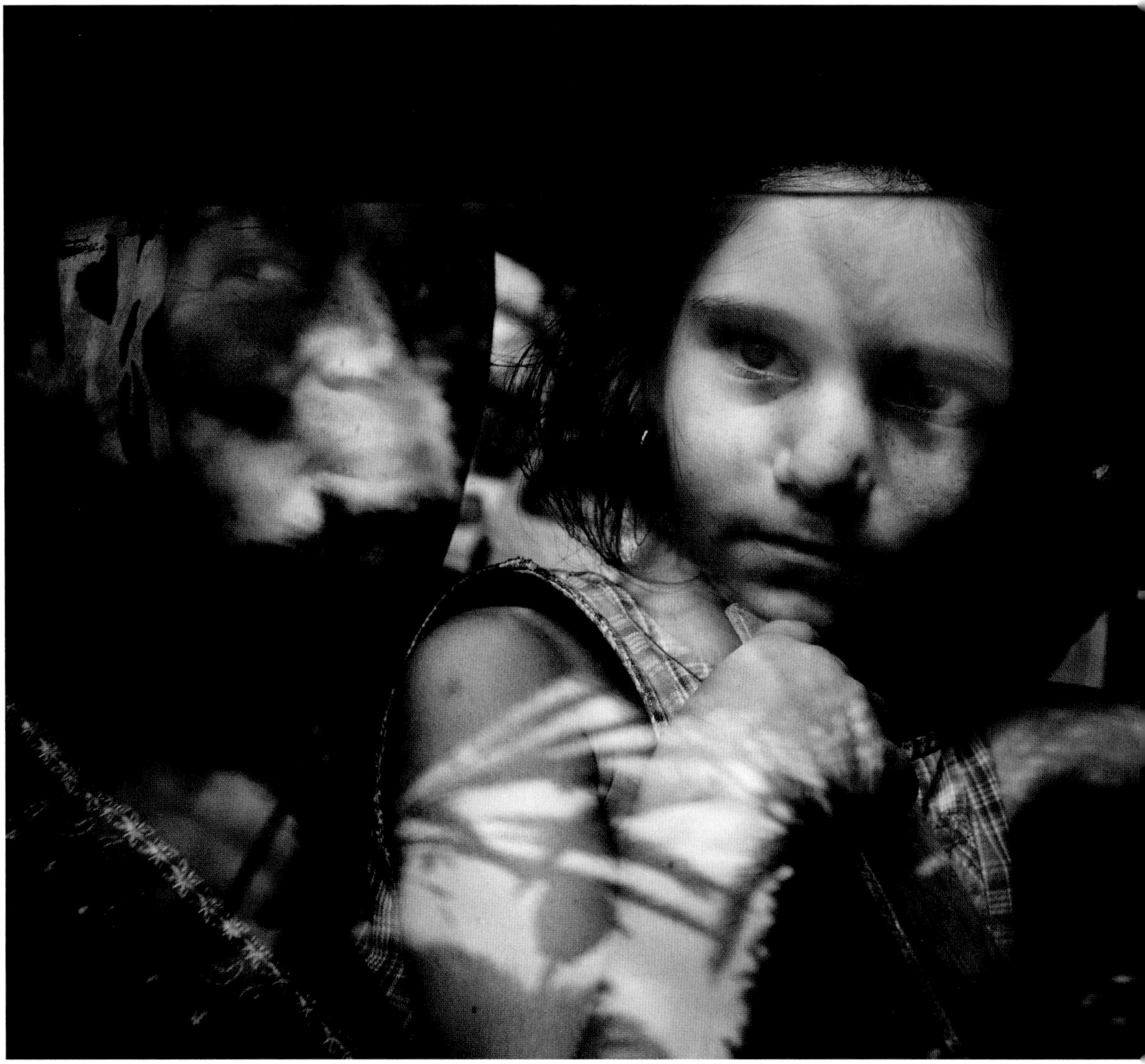

Civilians arrive in Tyre after fleeing their villages in southern Lebanon 2006

Like specimens fossilized in a piece of amber, the figures in this photograph seem trapped by the windows around them. The image suggests dislocation and a journey not yet complete; the reflection of the palm trees in the vehicle's window indicates a tropical location, but this suggestion of paradise contrasts sharply with the girl's troubled expression, which tells us that this journey is not a happy one. The viewer is drawn, empathetically, into imagining what misfortune or tragedy has befallen her. The image typifies Paolo Pellegrin's journalistic strategy: he focuses the viewer's attention on one individual caught up in a wider enterprise. The dark, brooding nature of the *chiaroscuro* lighting, the reflections implying a world outside the photograph, the dislocated framing, the sense of visual depth and, above all, the isolation of the main actor in the image are all characteristic of his photographic approach. Pellegrin's desire to give his images "depth" is exemplified by his use of mirrors and windows, and he often shoots through reflective surfaces. All of these strategies work toward Pellegrin's aim of bridging the gap between viewer and subject, opening up a space where interaction can take place—a "hole in reality," as he puts it—through which the audience can enter the world of the characters in his dramas. He seeks not to answer questions, but rather to allow an arena in which the audience can begin the process of imagining themselves in the lives of others.

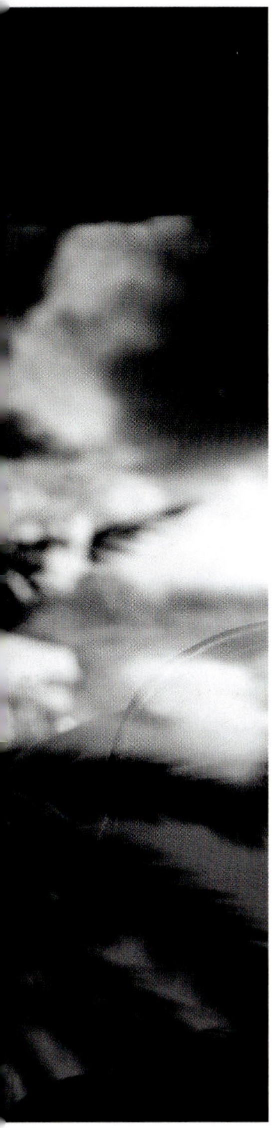

"I go with the eyes of a foreigner...trying to find relationships, to understand, to create a dialog."

Paolo Pellegrin

olo Pellegrin (Italian, 1964–) initially trained as architect, an experience that he draws on in s photography; this "sense of thinking spatially, organizing elements in a given space, [which] very much what we do in photography. We ve a rectangle through which we see the world. e compose and organize things in a way that understandable for us and for the viewer." orking predominantly in black and white, which identifies as "an abstract element that helps to convey meaning and symbols," he has established himself as one of the leading photojournalists of his generation, winning almost every major award. Pellegrin has worked as a contract photographer for *Newsweek* and is a regular contributor to the *New York Times* magazine, positions through which he is able to regularly cover major global news events and stories in his own unique way. He has been with Magnum Photos since 2001.

Creative tips and techniques

"I spent twenty years thinking of how to give a photograph the dimension it doesn't have—depth, layers," says Pellegrin. "It got more and more complex. At some point, the opposite process occurs—deconstructing, subtracting, taking away." This "process of taking away," Pellegrin claims, amounts to "searching for the essence of a story." He tries to make a connection between himself, subject, and audience, describing how "by some alchemical process, you translate who you are and your own experience into the picture."

Pellegrin is, above all, a communicator whose work is published in mainstream news magazines. He seeks to use this platform to make connections between the story and the viewer, to open up a space for dialog. His esthetic is calculated to support this idea of questioning and he maintains his "interest is in using the tool of photography to investigate things."

Pellegrin often seeks out situations that technically other photographers might consider too difficult, shooting at twilight, in darkness, and in adverse weather. A major effect of working in marginal light conditions is that many of his images are blurred and out of focus, due to camera shake caused by long exposures. It creates images that typically would be rejected as technically flawed; however, if used consciously rather than accidentally, this can heighten the drama and expressiveness of the scene. Go out in bad weather and shoot in low light to see how far you can take the technical edge of the medium. Know the limits of your equipment, then you can push them as far as they can go.

Signal: impoverished African migrants crowd the night shore of Djibouti City 2013

Lit by moonlight, this image has a primal glow. It shows a group of migrants on a beach holding their mobile phones in the air as if worshipping the god of technology. It is a stunning photograph that eloquently sums up the complexities of global migration. Photographer John Stanmeyer recounts how he came to take it: "I was walking along the beach at night in Djibouti City and I asked my translator why these people were holding their phones in the air. My translator told me that people, mostly Somalis, come to this spot to 'catch' a sign from a neighboring cell phone tower by using a Somali SIM card in their phones." The image tells a story of modern-day migration and illustrates what is now a universal desire to call home. This vignette also had a poignant significance for Stanmeyer himself; as a photographer who spends long periods away from his own family, he notes: "I have been that man or that woman in that frame countless times as I tried to reach my family back home. I'm thankful and honored that something poetic, that I hope screams loudly, is shared this way now."

Shot on assignment for *National Geographic* magazine, the image featured on the opening spread of the magazine's series "Out of Eden" in December 2013. Stanmeyer recalls how he came to be in Africa—a region often described as the cradle of humanity: "I spent a month driving and walking through Ethiopia and ended up in Djibouti, and I remember talking with my writer Paul Salopek on the beach at the Red Sea where, ironically, 60,000 years ago there was a land bridge that allowed us to continue our path—to connect." Stanmeyer believes that *Signal* is "an image of all of us as we stand at the crossroads of humanity, where we must ask ourselves what is truly important, demanding our collective attention in a global society where the issues of migration, borders, war, poverty, technology, and communication intersect."

Creative tips and techniques

Stanmeyer often works at the edges of what is technically possible, shooting in very low light situations. He favors a fast wide-angle lens, the Canon 35mm f/1.4, which he says is his "eyeball into the dark side ... the dark side being the other twelve hours of our human existence after the sun sets." This time of day is special to him because "people take to the streets in a completely different and illuminated way." The fast maximum aperture of the lens means he can shoot only with available light. This image was shot with the 35mm wide open at f1.4, with a shutter speed of 1/40th of a second and an ASA of 10,000. When working in low light, the rule of thumb is to use a shutter speed higher than the focal length of the lens to avoid camera shake, as Stanmeyer has done here. You can go slower, especial with a wide-angle lens and a rangefinder; an image-stabilized lens will help, too. Practice shooting at slow speeds to find th spot where you can still get a sharp image.

Stanmeyer often distributes his wor on social media, reaching thousands of viewers without needing to wait for a traditional publication to present the work. H is happy to use a camera phone, often usin

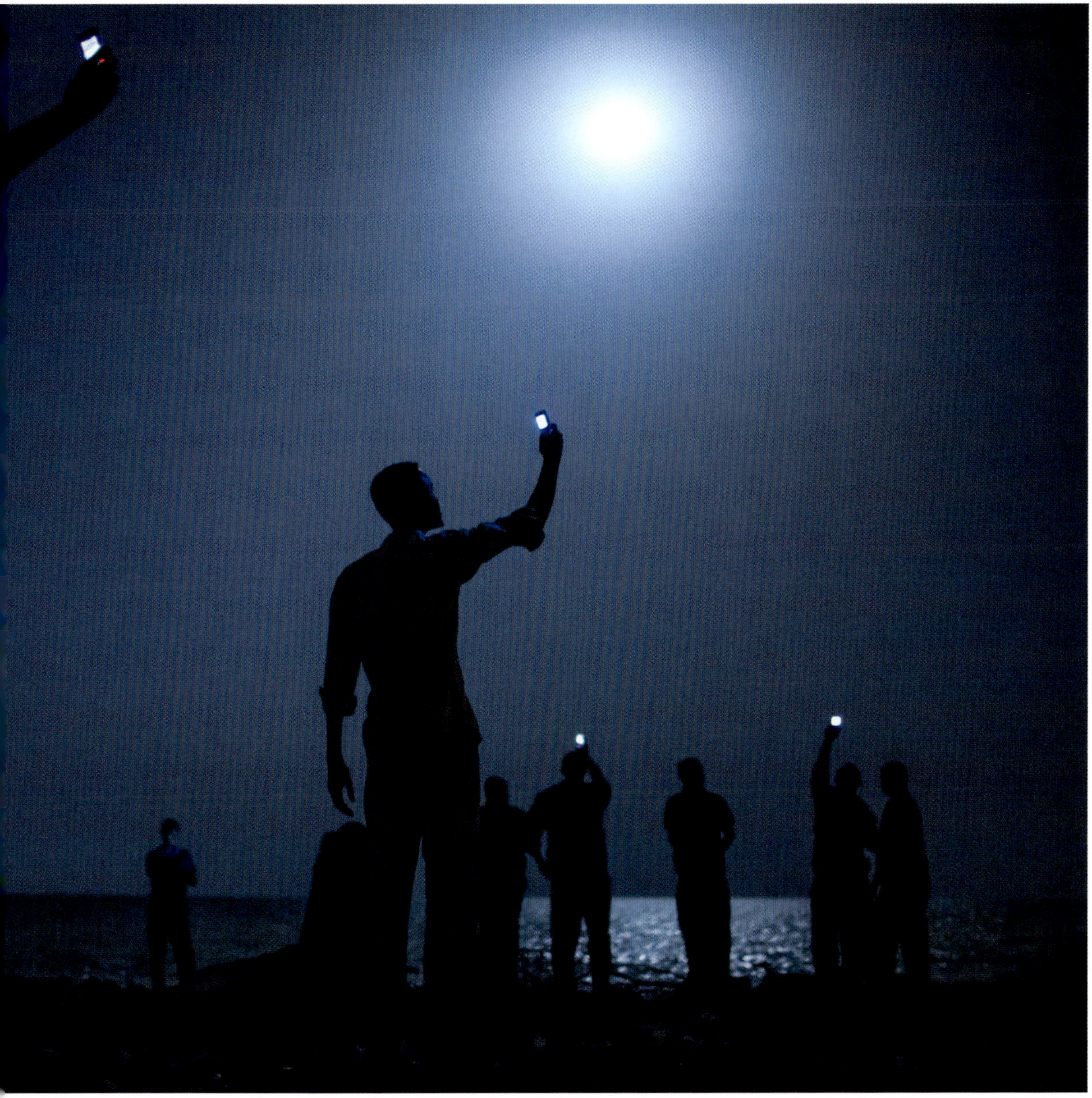

s favourite app, Hipstamatic. As long as e photographer retains an authentic ›nnection with the subject, he is happy use technology to enhance his vision.

Stanmeyer notes that "we now tote a substantial collection of zmos and contraptions, each requiring eir own special cable." He packs 2 Canon)mk111s, with 16–35mm, 24–70mm, 4mm 1.4, 35mm 1.4, and 50mm 1.2 lenses.

"Do this work not for yourself . . . Do it for the greater purpose of others, our collective humanity." John Stanmeyer

John Stanmeyer (American, 1964–) is a photojournalist who has shot eighteen covers for *Time* magazine, for whom he worked covering the war in Afghanistan, the fight for independence in East Timor, the fall of Suharto in Indonesia, and other major global news stories. In 2001 he co-founded the VII Photo Agency. Since 2004 he has shot more than fourteen stories for *National Geographic*. He has received many awards, including the Robert Capa Gold Medal, Magazine Photographer of the Year, World Press Photo of the Year—for *Signal*—and an Emmy nomination for the VII documentary film series, *Starved for Attention*. He is based in Massachusetts where he runs a joint gallery and coffee house, through which he combines ethical, direct-trade coffee and the social issues represented in his photography.

Docu

nents

Photography has an evidentiary force. The seeming verisimilitude of the camera, combined with its ability to identify social, political, or economic trends, presents a powerful tool to document issues. The documentary photographer's prime concern is a long-term interaction with the subject. This often involves repeated visits over substantial periods of time, during which an account of the subject is slowly and incrementally developed. Research is a significant component of the process; detailed accounts of the background to an issue are frequently combined with first-person narratives from subjects themselves. By identifying key social issues and exploring them in depth through the camera, documentary photographers provide us with a rich source of knowledge about humanity. The photographer performs a vital role in describing fundamental societal shifts and revealing the underlying forces that make up the social fabric of the world we live in. The documentary photographer works behind the major historical event or short-term news story, digging out structural elements that reflect these significant events, operating both underneath and in parallel with them. Intimacy and affinity to the subject are crucial features of this documentary work, which can sometimes border on an obsessive engagement with a particular theme that would otherwise pass by undocumented. The photographer's unique eye and the active process of paying careful attention to the world around him or her mean that images are generated that would not otherwise exist in the public domain. This category of photographic work provides an essential social function for understanding the complex world around us.

Lodgers in Bayard Street tenement, five cents a spot 1889

Jacob Riis used the images he took to generate public awareness of the terrible conditions in New York City's slums, combining them with vivid accounts of the lives of slum dwellers in *How the Other Half Lives: Studies Among the Tenements of New York* (1890). Riis made no claims to be a photographer; he had no desire to create esthetic objects, but used the camera as a recording device to gain evidence of the appalling conditions he witnessed. Alongside this image he described the sobering scene he was confronted with at a particularly bad slum on Mulberry Street on the Lower East Side: "In a room not thirteen feet either way slept twelve men and women, two or three in bunks set in a sort of alcove, the rest on the floor. A kerosene lamp burned dimly in the fearful atmosphere, probably to guide other and later arrivals to their 'beds,' for it was only just past midnight. A baby's fretful wail came from an adjoining hall-room, where, in the semi-darkness, three recumbent figures could be made out. The 'apartment' was one of three in two adjoining buildings we had found, within half an hour, similarly crowded. Most of the men were lodgers, who slept there for five cents a spot." Riis's work had a significant impact; as well as providing a unique documentation of a key period in US history, it also led to limited reform of the conditions in the tenements.

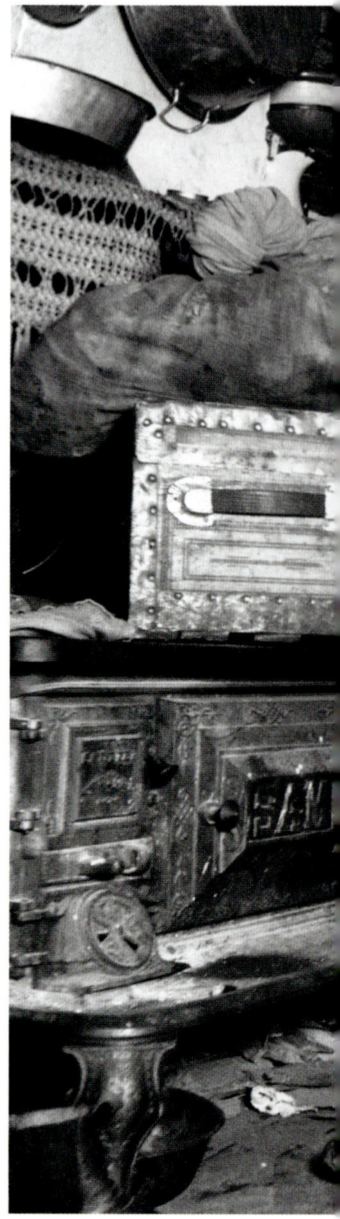

Creative tips and techniques

The key breakthrough for Riis in his work was his adoption of the recent invention of flash photography. Much of his reportage was conducted at night, when light levels were too low to be able to photograph effectively. However, once he discovered that he could use flash to illuminate the gloom, he literally turned a spotlight onto the darkness and was able to reveal the truly miserable nature of the living conditions. To illuminate dimly lit interiors, he used magnesium powder mixed with potassium chlorate, which created a bright light and clouds of acrid smoke. He evocatively described how his visits were the cause of much consternation among the slum dwellers: "it is not too much to say that our party carried terror wherever it went. The flashlight of those days was contained in

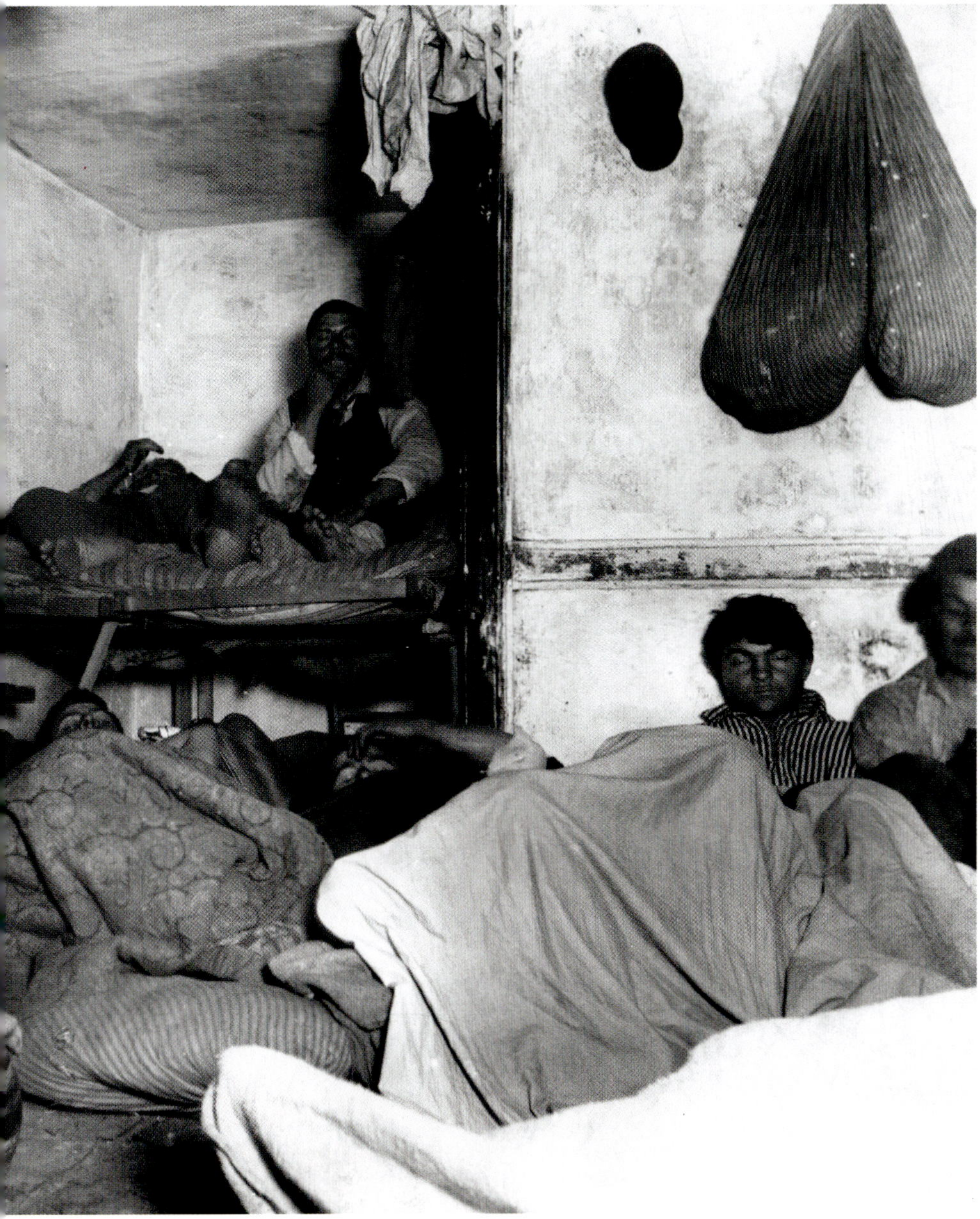

Jacob Riis (American, 1849–1914) was born in Denmark and was himself an immigrant to the United States, where he worked as a carpenter and laborer before becoming a journalist. He joined the *New York Tribune* as a police reporter on the infamous Mulberry Street, nicknamed "Death's Thoroughfare," in the heart of the city's slum tenements. Frustrated at the lack of impact his words were having and determined to further the causes of social reform, Riis turned to the camera to provide visual documentation of impoverished New Yorkers.

"When the report was submitted to the Health Board the next day, it did not make much of an impression... until my negatives, still dripping from the dark-room, came to reinforce them. From them there was no appeal." Jacob Riis

ırtridges fired from a revolver. The spectacle half a dozen strange men invading a ›use in the midnight hour armed with g pistols, which they shot off recklessly, as hardly reassuring, however sugary our ›eech, and it was not to be wondered at the tenants bolted through windows and ›wn fire-escapes wherever we went."

Before he published his books, Riis gave talks, which he illustrated using a magic lantern with glass slides. He showed his original, larger-than-life photographs, and gave an extraordinarily vivid and dramatic vocal accompaniment in his own words that virtually led his audiences through the streets and basements of the city's darkest corners. Riis's performances had a powerful impact on audiences, who reportedly fainted, moaned, and shuddered at the sights and sounds of his show. He was effectively heralding the rise of documentary film and contemporary multimedia production. Experiment with making your own multimedia slideshows, and record a narrative to accompany the images. You could use an interview with the subject or write a script that takes the viewer on a journey with the images. The combination of the spoken word and the photograph can enhance the emotional content of your work.

Lewis Hine

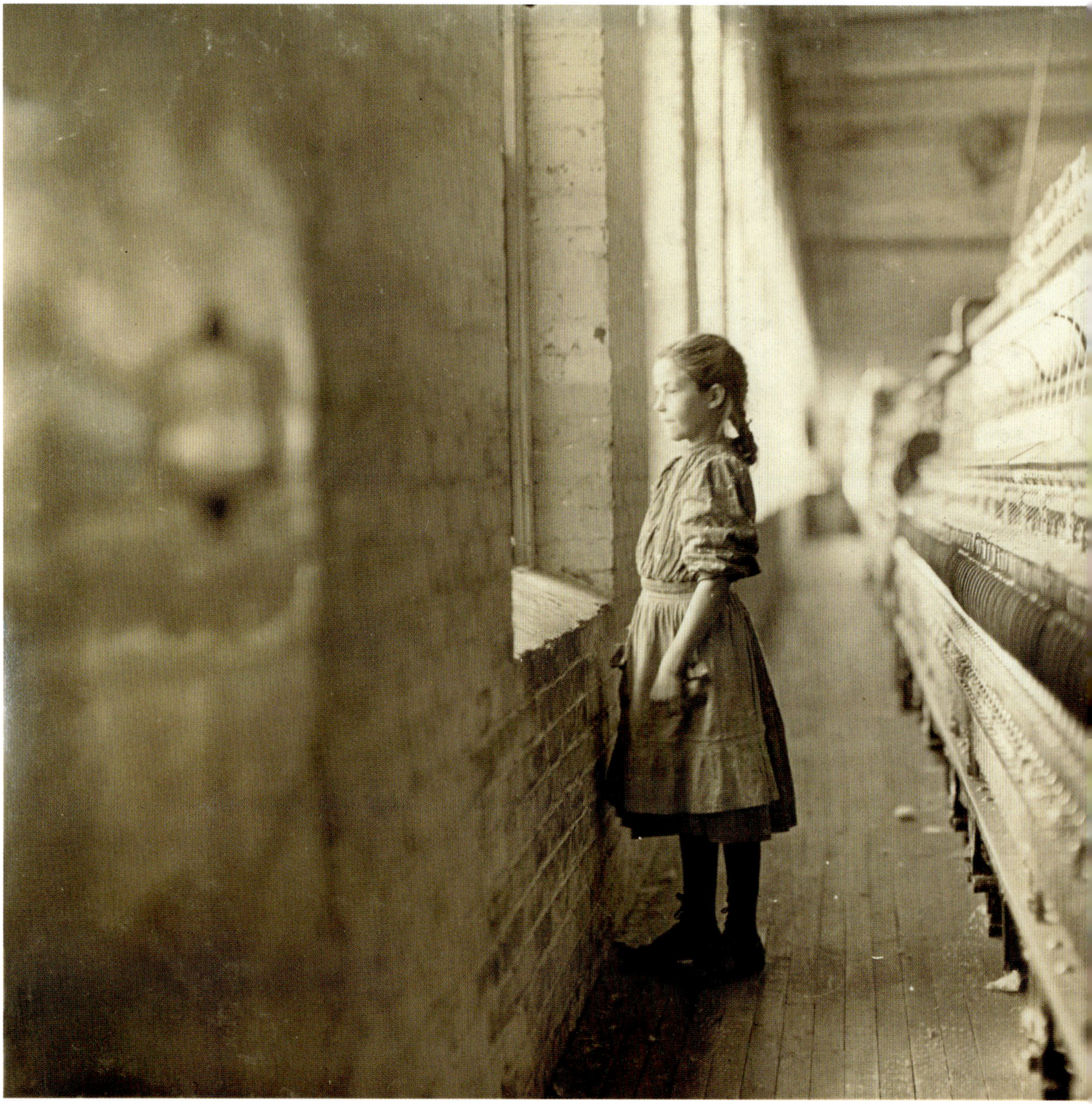

"Photography can light up darkness and expose ignorance." Lewis Hine

Lewis Hine (American, 1874–1940) was one of the leading proponents of using the camera as a tool to advocate for social reform, and he campaigned in particular for the rights of child laborers. He began taking photographs for the Ethical Culture School in New York City where he worked as a teacher, and in 1907 he became the staff photographer of the Russell Sage Foundation, for whom he conducted a study of steel making in Pittsburgh. He joined the NCLC (National Child Labor Committee) in 1908 as a reporter and photographer. He argued that "the dictum, then, of the social worker is 'Let there be light;' and in this campaign for light we have for our advance agent the light writer—the photograph."

Creative tips and techniques

Hine often portrayed single figure within their environments. This emphasized their isolation and presente them as individuals that the viewer cou empathize with. He often named his subjects, and gave details of their heigh weight, and age to add to the emotiona force of his images. In this photograph he uses the converging lines and patter

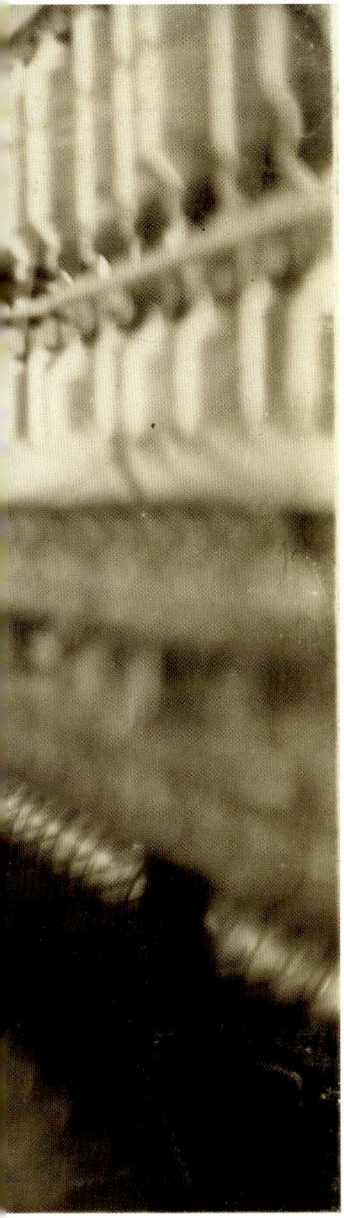

A moment's glimpse of the outer world. Said she was 11 years old. Been working over a year. Rhodes Mfg. Co. Lincolnton, North Carolina 1908

Lewis Hine's work for the National Child Labor Committee (NCLC) was frequently risky, because factory owners did not want the working conditions of their employees exposed, especially if they were illegally employing children. North Carolina, where this powerful study of a child working in a cotton mill was made, had one of the worst reputations for abuse of child labor in the whole country. Hine described his activity as "detective work;" he was threatened by factory police and foremen, and often resorted to subterfuge to gain entry, posing as a fire inspector, bible salesman, and industrial photographer making studies of machinery. He traveled extensively, often up to 30,000 miles in one year, photographing factories, strawberry fields, tobacco plantations, and slum tenement housing. Initially he felt that words were the most important part of his work, but came to believe that it was in fact his images that could have the most impact, claiming: "In my early days of my child-labor activities I was an investigator with a camera attachment. . .but the emphasis became reversed until the camera stole the whole show."

Hine once proclaimed to his audience: "Perhaps you are weary of child-labor pictures. Well, so are the rest of us, but we propose to make you and the whole country so sick and tired of the whole business that when the time for action comes, child-labor pictures will be records of the past." Hine also designed exhibitions, posters, and publications for the NCLC during the decade he worked there. Conditions did improve somewhat, but remained difficult for child workers throughout the period.

the walls and the cotton mill machinery frame the child, whose wistful gaze ıt of the window suggests that she is eaming of a better life outside the factory.

Here Hine used a wide aperture on the lens to create a shallow depth of ɜld, placing all attention on the girl. Imagine ɔw different the image would be if he had opped down the lens to make everything sharp focus. Think about the combination of shutter and aperture you need to create the desired effect; don't shoot everything with a medium depth of field.

In the later part of his career, Hine specialized in making photographs of industrial workers, often portraying them as heroic figures, their muscles straining against the machinery they serviced and operated. He typically used the shapes and forms of industrial machinery to contrast with the skin and clothing of the workers. In 1930 Hine began to document the construction of New York's Empire State Building, during which he was lifted up in a cherry picker and swung out in a basket 1,000 feet (30 meters) above Fifth Avenue. His now iconic images show the workers almost like dancers or circus artists floating epically above the city, and even a group seemingly asleep on a girder suspended in mid-air.

David Goldblatt

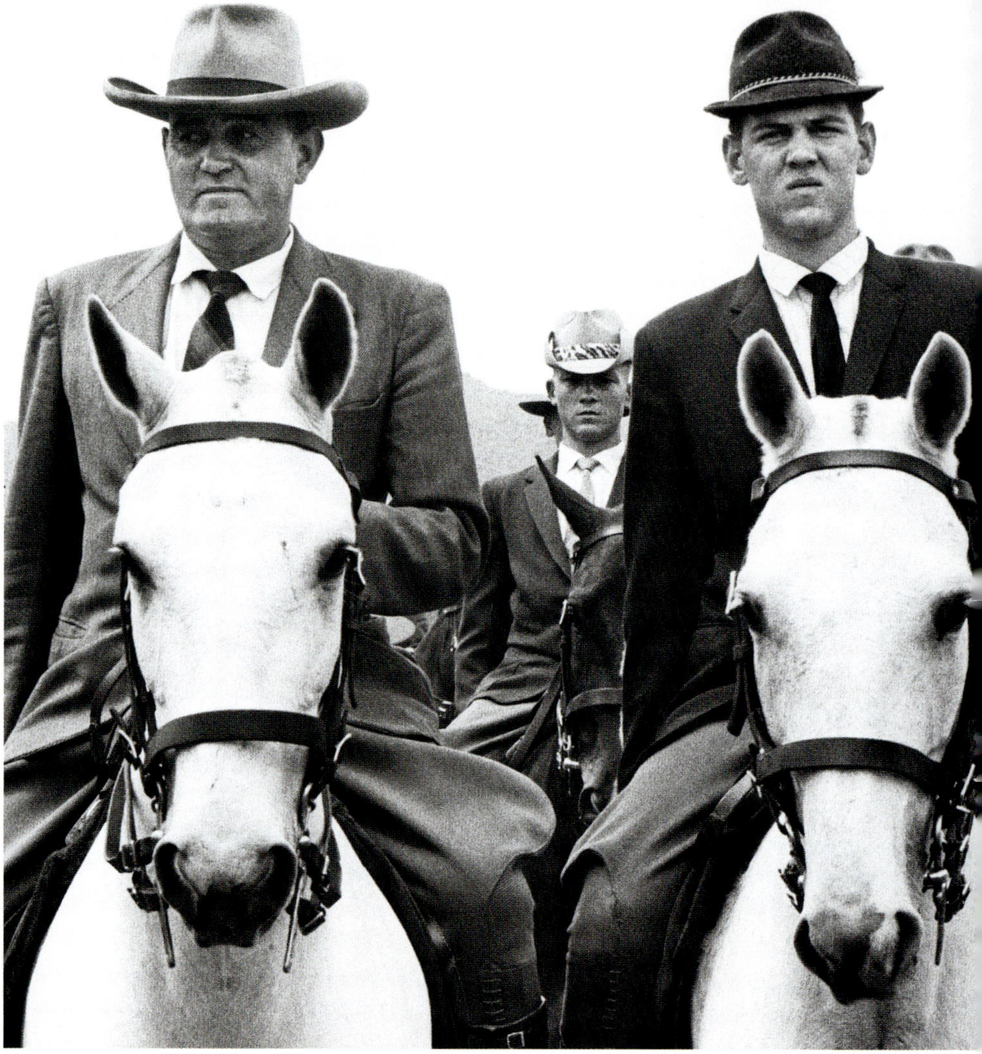

David Goldblatt (South African, 1930–) has spent his photographic life documenting the tensions in South African society, both during the years of white rule and in the post-apartheid era. He decided to commit himself to staying in the country rather than traveling abroad to work, stating, "I have a sense of belonging here, an intimacy with the place that I doubt I could have anywhere else. It was often uncomfortable, but it was undeniable. My viscera and my involvement are here." Goldblatt founded the Market Photography Workshop in 1989 in Johannesburg. In 1998 he was the first South African to be given a one-man exhibition at the Museum of Modern Art in New York. He is the recipient of the 2006 Hasselblad Award, the 2009 Henri Cartier-Bresson Award, and the 2013 ICP Infinity Award.

Creative tips and techniques

Goldblatt gave this advice on how the development of a photographic sensibility is necessary but problematic: "When you are new to photography, what you see in your early prints or slides is often unexpectedly and mysteriously different from what you saw at the moment of exposure. Some things in the photograph are uncannily real—they are just as you remember them only more so. Others are unaccountably changed. The big seems ridiculously small and the insignificant becomes overwhelming. Emotional values that you did not see in the original are present in the photograph, and what you thought beautiful seems now devoid of interest. As you gain experience, you learn to anticipate some of the things that happen in the photographic process so that there are fewer surprises."

He also gave effective direction on how to previsualize the final image: by simply "screwing up your eyes and making your fingers into a frame you are able... to see the world as a neatly sliced two-dimensional picture... You learn to visualize color and light and shade in term of grey and white and black."

The harsh light of Africa was initially a challenge to Goldblatt. However, a

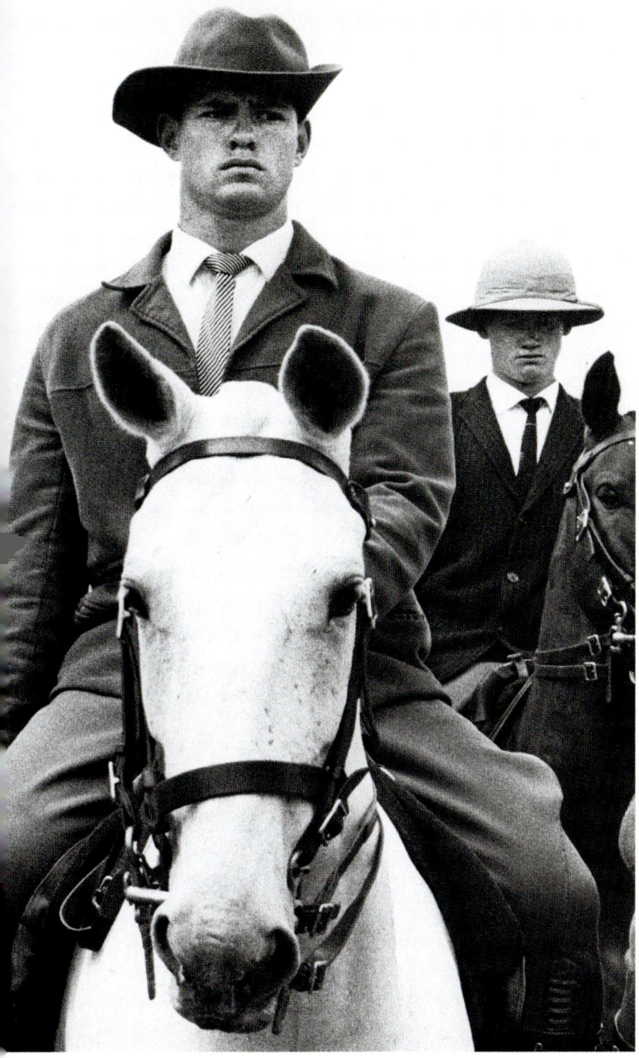

The commando of the National Party stalwarts, which escorted Prime Minister and National Party leader Hendrik Verwoerd and his wife, Betsie, to the party's fiftieth anniversary celebrations at De Wild 1964

This photograph comes from a series David Goldblatt made during the 1960s on the Afrikaners who then ruled South Africa. It explores how the values of a group can be embodied in the faces, clothes, and bearing of its members. The repetition of dress, with subtle colonial variations of headgear, gives the feel of a paramilitary unit, whereas the faces of the white horses reflect the Afrikaners' belief in their right to power and supremacy. In the introduction to the book he published from the work, *Some Afrikaners Photographed* (1975), Goldblatt stated that he could not make a definitive survey of their lives, but instead could offer only a partial and personal viewpoint.

Goldblatt was acutely aware that he did not want to cover the news events that wracked his native South Africa, feeling that he was "far more engaged by the states of being that led to events, by the conditions of society rather than the climactic outcomes of those conditions." Instead, he explored the deeper undercurrents that permeated the social structures of the contested country, as he explained: "I sought out irony and tried to impregnate pictures with a sense of it, for it often revealed the nuances and complexities of our life in South Africa." He describes himself as a "self-appointed observer and critic of the society into which I was born, with a tendency to doing honor or giving recognition to what is often overlooked or unseen." Goldblatt has always been careful to distance himself from the politicization of his work, claiming that the "camera was not a machine gun and that photographers shouldn't confuse their response to the politics of the country with their role as photographers." His images are full of subtle detail and observation, demonstrating that he sought the "quiet moments that contained in them everything that emerged later."

explains, he eventually learned to work
th the essential quality of the continent
:her than against it: "Long ago I tried to
ake pictures that were like those that
me from Europe, soft and beautifully
odulated. It used to break my heart—I
uld never get my pictures to look like
at. Then, in 1961, I realized that it had to
with light. We have a lot of it in South
rica, and it is often sharp and harsh. So
stead of fighting our light, I began to enjoy it and to work with it. I photographed from within rather than as if I were visiting from somewhere else." This is excellent advice. Light is the single most important element of photography. Learning how to use any lighting situation to best advantage is an essential skill, and can be developed by challenging oneself to shoot in difficult situations—for example in the middle of the day when shadows can be harsh and unforgiving.

"I would like to imbue these pale, two-dimensional rubbings of reality . . . with something of the subtlety and ambiguity of our shifting and frequently contradictory perceptions of reality."

David Goldblatt

Danny Lyon

Elkhorn, Wisconsin 1966, from *The Bikeriders* (1968)

Danny Lyon immersed himself in the life and culture of the Chicago Outlaw Motorcycle Club, an outlaw gang of bikers. On his own Triumph TR6 motorbike, he followed them on road trips and to gatherings and races. He recalls: "I wanted adventure and I wanted dirt—all the things my parents didn't want. I wanted freedom for myself. I had a huge sense of adventure and I wanted to experience it." Lyon claimed he was "a bike rider, a photographer, and a history student, probably in that order", and that he was seeking to capture "the spirit of the hand that twists open the throttle on the crackling engines of big bikes and rides them on racetracks or through traffic or, on occasion, into oblivion."

In the Chicago Outlaws, Lyon found a powerful subject that resonated with the cultural mythology of Americana and the heritage of the West. He argues that "photographers show character through how people look and the bikers were a perfect subject because they were what they looked like. They had leather jackets, they were dirty, they had weapons and boots." Shot with a Nikon F camera, this complex image draws the eye into the scene, dividing the frame into sections, with the windshield framing the chopper in front of it, whereas the reflection of Elkhorn in the mirror positions the viewer in the saddle of the bike, ready to ride away with the gang. Lyon's subsequent book of the project, *The Bikeriders*, captures the spirit of the road, even if the characters of its subjects are questionable. It is a theme that Lyon feels inescapably drawn to: "none of my films are about Chicanos, or poverty or prison, or the border, all of which I deal with. They are about the existential struggle to be free. That is what unites everything I have done. And the first person that has to be free, is me." Lyon forms a deep connection to his subjects and argues: "We have tremendous emotion as humans. If I can bring some of that to my work and get it out on ink and paper and pass it to others and have that then resonate with their own latent emotions, that's great. We all have these turbulent emotions."

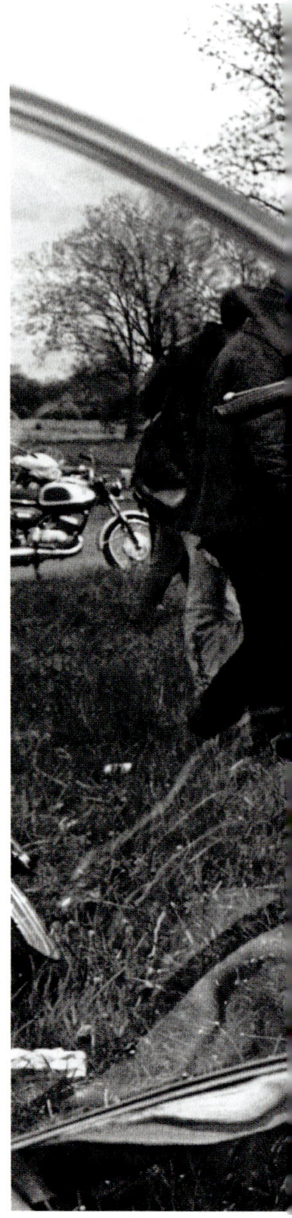

Creative tips and techniques

Lyon is aware of the transience of photography, yet also senses its power to connect with the viewer, stating that "pictures have no mortality to them. The moment they're made, they go into the future. I deal with that and I love it." For Lyon making photographs about people existing on the edges of society is an important personal one, and he maintains that "photography is a lonely journey... you really have to be by yourself, because you're trying to interact with reality. I put myself through an ordeal in order to create something." He channels his emotions into his work, recalling how as a child he was afraid of many things, but "as soon as I held a camera in my hand, I began to expose myself to the very things that were foreign to me and that I had always feared." This bond between him and his subject is central to his practice: when he has a camera in his hands he says that he wants to get emotionally, rather than physically, close to his subjects. Lyon is no[t] seeking intervention from his audience, bu[t] something potentially more profound. He feels that "the pictures do not ask you to 'help' these people, but something much more difficult; to be briefly, intensely awar[e] of their existence, an existence as real and significant as your own."

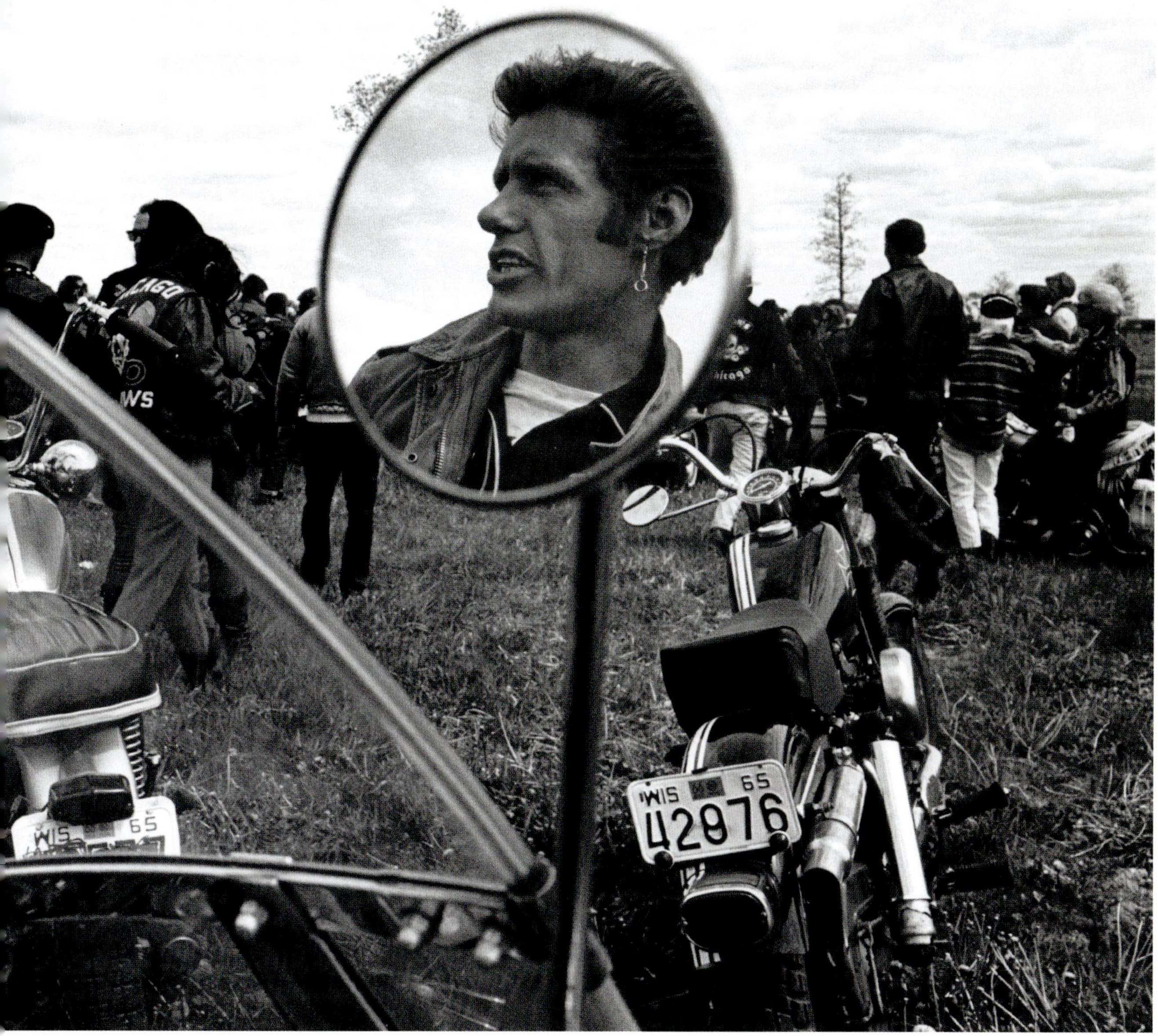

"The use of the camera has always been for me a tool of investigation." Danny Lyon

Lyon uses text extensively in his work. In *The Bikeriders* there e long first-person monologs and nversations from the main characters, plaining their lives and experiences. He gards this expanded documentation as sential to his projects: "The works I do e works of dreams and vision, and in at sense the only reality I actually listen is the reality inside my head. Reality, to e, is made up. I make it up."

Danny Lyon's (American, 1942–) first major body of work was documenting the southern US civil rights movement in 1963. Encouraged by Hugh Edwards, curator of the Art Institute of Chicago, he committed himself to documentary storytelling, later publishing *The Bikeriders* (1968). In the powerful series "Conversations with the Dead" (1971) he explored the harsh prison system of Texas, claiming that "I entered the Texas prisons determined to destroy them." Lyon once said: "My greatest strength has been my empathy with others different from myself." He later wrote about his advice to photographers: "One, to change society, change the media. Two, to change the media, change yourself. Three, personalize the media, personalize yourself." In addition to photography, Lyon has produced documentary films and a book of non-fiction writing.

Bernd & Hilla Becher

Gas tanks 1973–2009

The Bechers' approach of creating a visual typology of categories of industrial architecture sprang from a desire to catalog features that were disappearing from the Western landscape. In spite of a seemingly clinical and distanced visual strategy, it was a rather romantic endeavor to preserve the evidence of a moment in history before it was destroyed forever. Bernd expressed this eloquently: "We are documenting the sacred buildings of Calvinism. Calvinism rejects all forms of art, and therefore never developed its own architecture. The buildings we photograph originate directly from this purely economical thinking." Initially they approached their vast project more as ethnographers than artists, using the methods of natural history. Adopting a common methodology and using a large-format camera and black-and-white film, they systematically photographed the architecture from a set position that allowed comparisons across the series.

Their comparative studies, such as this one of gas tanks, gave an intriguing insight into the national characteristics of each country as expressed in the form of the buildings. Hilla observed that: "English people are pragmatic. They don't mind when there is a wheel in the landscape;" whereas the Germans were similar to the French: "they often added some features so they looked like castle towers." Ultimately these images convey the beauty and dignity of structures that once defined the Western industrial landscape. As Hilla concluded: "these objects are not made to be beautiful, but they still possess a beauty. Like a hammer or pliers, things that are honest and perfect, things you can't improve any further."

> "We want to offer the audience a point of view, or rather a grammar, to understand and compare the different structures…To do so, the objects must be isolated from their context and freed from all association." Bernd & Hilla Becher

Bernd (German, 1931–2007) and **Hilla Becher** (German, 1934–2015) first collaborated on documenting German industrial architecture after meeting as students at the Kunstakademie Düsseldorf in 1957. They married in 1961 and continued their systematic cataloging of a variety of structures, many of which were about to be demolished as the nature of heavy industry shifted. As Bernd expressed it: "I became aware that these buildings [blast furnaces] were a kind of nomadic architecture which had a comparatively short life—maybe 100 years, often less, then they disappear. It seemed important to keep them in some way and photography seemed the most appropriate way to do that." The Bechers traveled first across Germany, France, and Italy, and then England and South Wales in 1966. They took hundreds of photographs of the coal industry around Liverpool, Manchester, Sheffield, Nottingham, and the Rhondda Valley. In 1976 Bernd joined the faculty at the Kunstakademie Düsseldorf,where he taught and influenced a generation of photographers who became known as the Düsseldorf School.

Creative tips and techniques

The Bechers spent their entire careers working together. As Hilla recalls, this was an effective way to divide their labors given the constraints they were working under: "We always worked as a team. One of us would entertain spectators or watch out, the other one would fix the tripod at the railing or cut away weeds. We had to help each other. It's very tiring to climb over ladders and stairs onto a blast furnace when you have to carry heavy equipment. When possible, we also worked with two cameras. We often had to work under time pressure, because we were only allowed to be in those areas for a limited amount of time, and the weather had to be right, too." Hilla acted as a foil to Bernd's precise nature, explaining that he was obsessed with details and often repeated everything until it was perfect.

The Bechers favored cloudy days when the light was diffuse and flat. They worked mostly in the morning during the seasons of spring and fall, feeling that this gave a more consistent and predictable final result than working in direct sunlight. As Hilla explained, "you can see the details more easily when it's overcast. Contours don't double because of shadows. We didn't want a mood in the photos, we wanted universality." This even illumination allowed them to compare objects more easily. By taking out the emotional charge that a more dramatic light would have brought, the final result was for them more effective. As Hilla explained, "When you take a photo of a lake behind which the sun is setting, then the sunset is the most important element of the photo. But we were only interested in the lake. Except that, for us, the lake was a coal storage tank or a blast furnace."

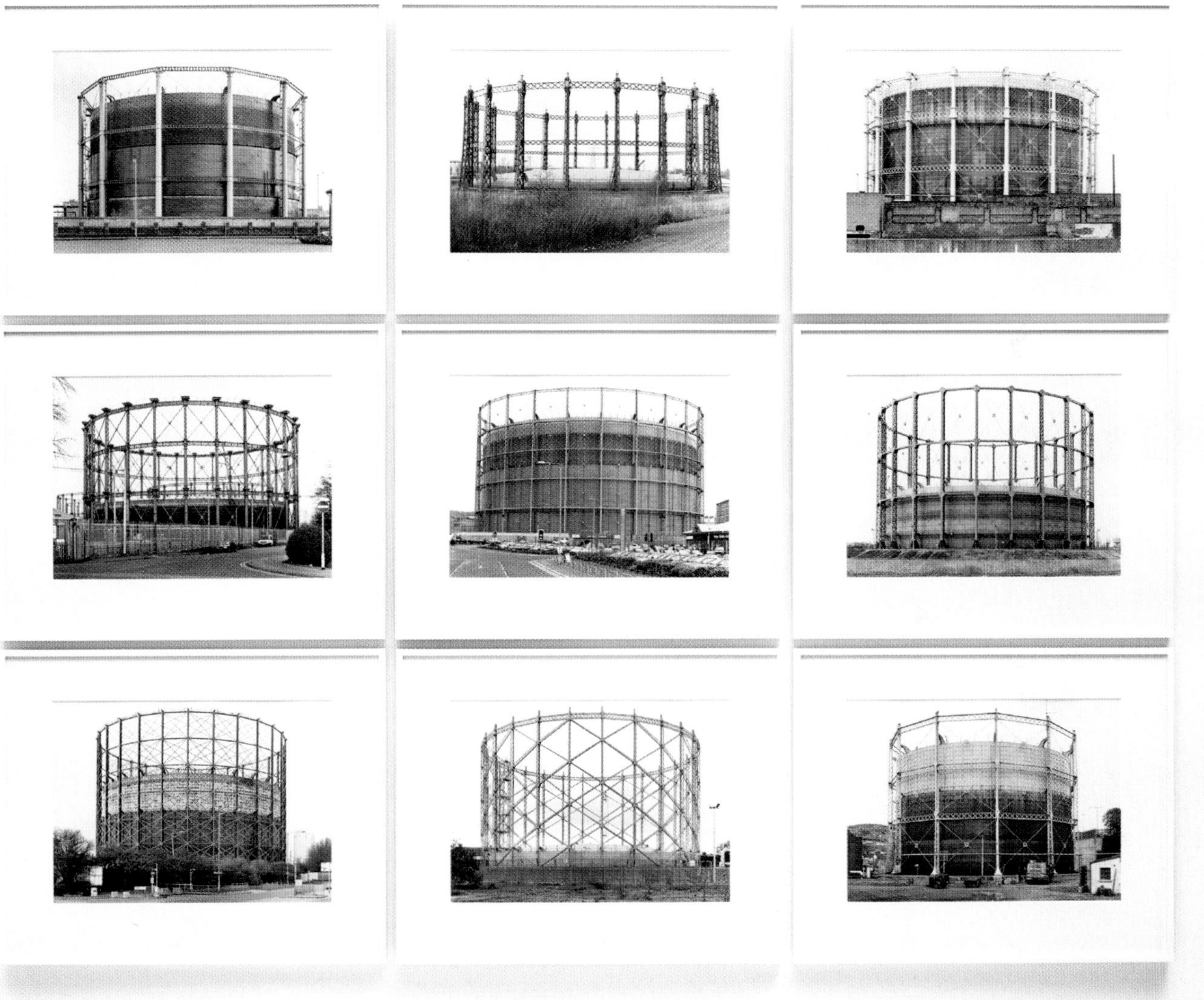

Chris Killip

Youth on wall, Jarrow, Tyneside 1976

This powerful study of coiled and caged emotion was a defining image of Chris Killip's 1988 photobook *In Flagrante*. The boy, wearing oversized Doc Marten boots, seemed to encapsulate the frustration and anger of a lost generation of working-class northerners whose economic prospects had been laid waste by the collapse of Britain's industrial base. The book continued the approach that Killip had developed for an earlier work, *Isle of Man* (1980), which combined portraits, landscapes, and more fluid moments to describe the complexities of life. Killip used a large-format 5 x 4 view camera to make both bodies of work; his ability to create complex and choreographed images of people is remarkable, given the cumbersome nature of the camera.

A section of *In Flagrante* concerned the sea-coalers, a community of travelers and former miners who lived on the beach, collecting scraps of coal washed ashore from the spoil of a mine further up the coast. It took Killip almost eight years to overcome the community's initial resistance to his presence, but he finally lived with them for over a year. He later wrote that "the place confounded time; here the Middle Ages and the twentieth century intertwined;" his images depict what seems more like a medieval or post-apocalyptic vision of hard labor rather than one of the world's wealthiest nations. The book had a simple, unadorned format, as Killip explains: "It had become very important to me to let the images speak without interference, as I believe that they have their own eloquence and in some cases a degree of ambiguity—a mixture that leaves the work open to interpretation by the viewer."

"This is a subjective book about my time in England. I take what isn't mine and I covet other people's lives. The photographs can tell you more about me than about what they describe." Chris Killip

Chris Killip (British, 1946–) was born in Douglas on the Isle of Man. He trained as a hotel manager, but in 1964 decided to pursue photography full time and became a beach photographer in order to earn enough money to leave the island. In 1975 he was awarded a fellowship as the Northern Arts Photography Fellow. He moved to live in Newcastle-upon-Tyne, where he became a founding member of Side Gallery, committed to documentary photography, as well as its director, from 1977 to 1979. In 1994 he became a tenured professor at Harvard University in the United States.

Creative tips and techniques

Killip's work is intimately connected with a sense of place, but it is concerned with time. He describes photography as a "mechanical description of time, which is realized through the action of light on a sensitized surface." He is fully aware that the photographic image is intimately bound up in the process of historical memory, claiming that the "moment you make a photograph you consign whatever you photograph to the past, as that specific moment no longer exists; it is history. The photography that I practice takes place in a specific time and place, depicting real moments in people's lives. In some ways I think of myself as a historian, but not of the word. History is most often written from a distance, and rarely from the viewpoint of those who endured it."

Killip has committed himself to long-term projects during which he spends considerable time with his subjects, feeling that he wants the photograph "to be more than a document, to be something that is as close as you could possibly be to the subject." He recalls advice given to him by photographer Josef Koudelka, who told him that if six photographers worked in the same place for six weeks, "inevitably their photographs would have a sort of similarity." However, if "you stayed for two years, your pictures would be different, and if you stayed for three years they would be different again. You could get under the skin of a place and do something different, because you were then photographing from the inside. I understood what he was talking about. I stayed in Newcastle for fifteen years. I mean, to get the access to photograph the sea-coal workers took eight years. You do get embroiled in a place."

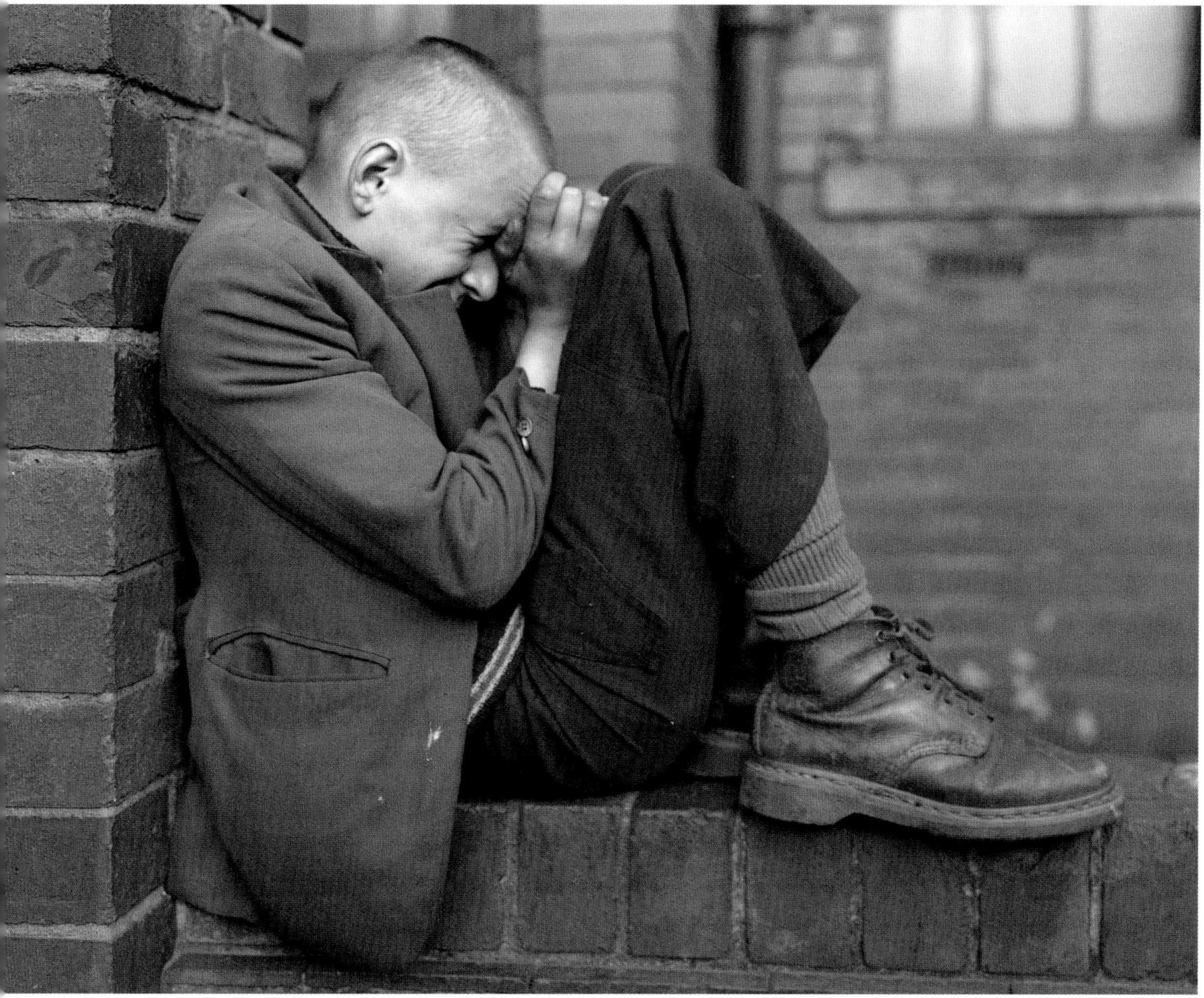

Larry Sultan

"I realize that beyond the rolls of film and the few good pictures, the demands of my project and my confusion about its meaning, is the wish to take photography literally. To stop time. I want my parents to live forever."

Larry Sultan

Larry Sultan (American, 1946–2009) began working as a conceptual photographer in the 1970s. He collaborated with fellow photographer Mike Mandel on the seminal book *Evidence* (1977), which sourced images from corporate and government archives. The pair discovered in these obscure archives extraordinary images that resonated with developing trends in fine-art photography. From 1982 Sultan explored the complexities of his own family and his relationship to his parents, published as *Pictures from Home* (1992). *The Valley* (2004) investigated the residences used by the Californian porn industry. Sultan was also an exceptional educator, and was a professor at California College of the Arts in San Francisco.

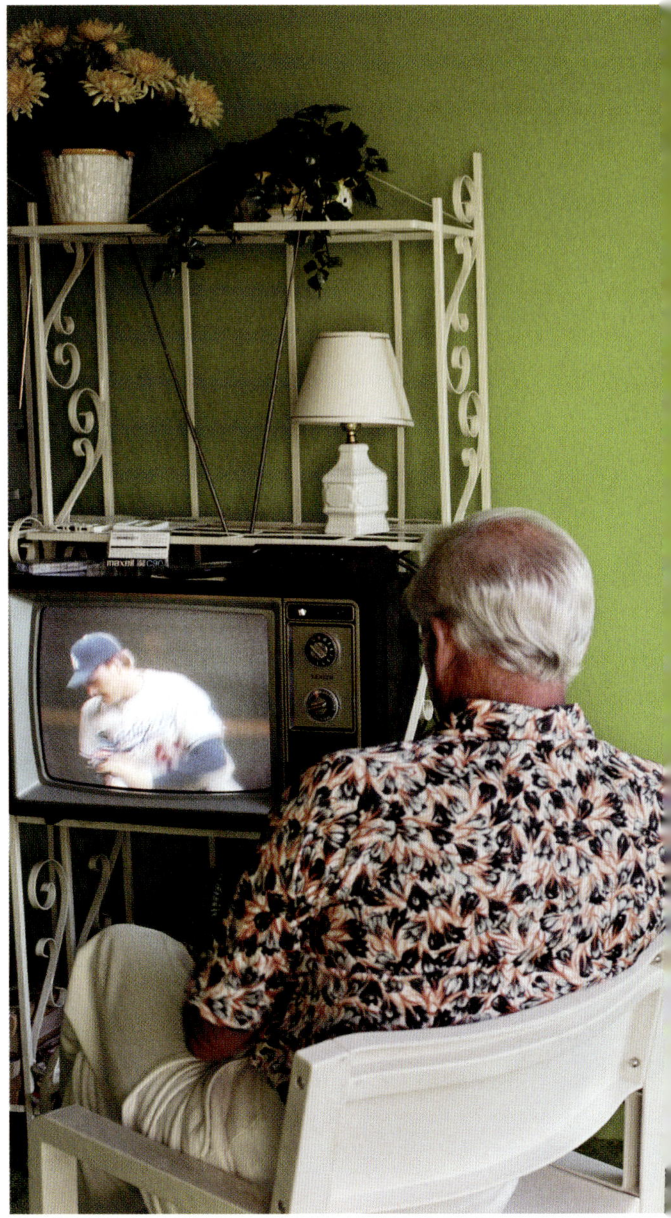

Creative tips and techniques

Sultan often worked in everyday situations, yet showed himself able to make highly emotionally and psychologically charged photographs, where being sensitive to details of body language, posture, and expression is paramount. Try to be hyper-aware of the smallest detail in a scene. Follow Sultan's advice of finding "that room to make pictures that don't jump off the wall, or detonate as dramatic, either in lighting or i form or in composition or in subject matte but more ordinary, that's the challenge."

Sultan was methodical in his photographic work, and wrote lists planning what to capture rather than simp hoping that a good picture would emerge spontaneously. Make a list of potential situations you could photograph, rather

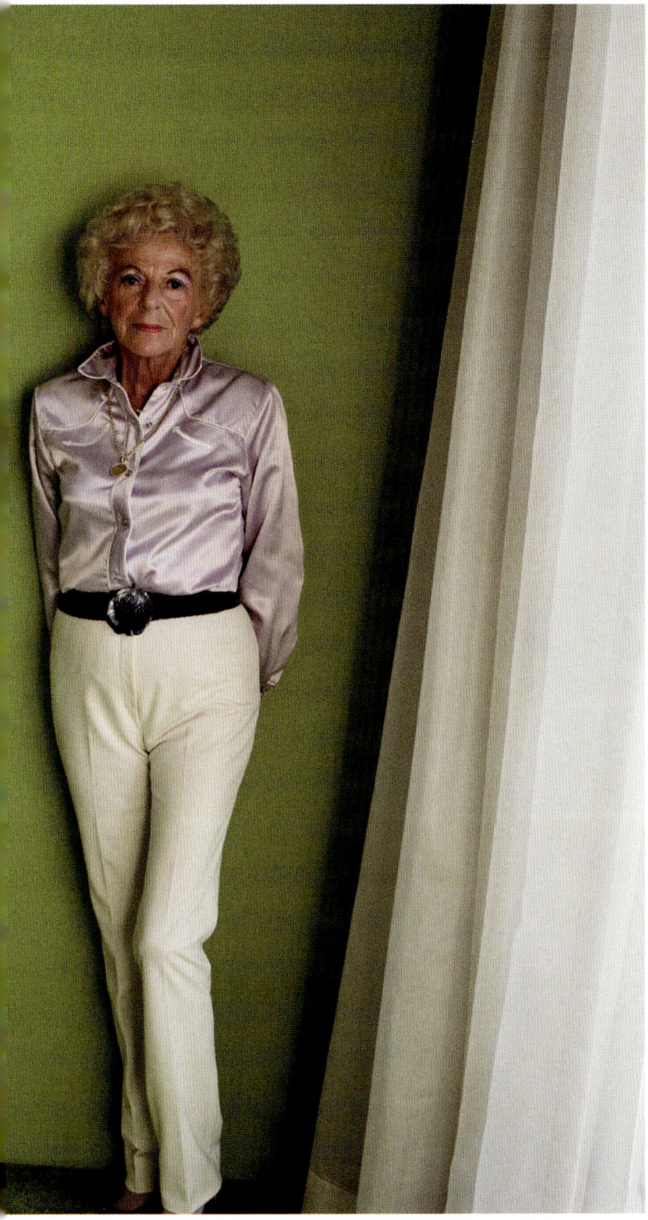

My mother posing for me 1984, from *Pictures from Home* (1992)

Larry Sultan created an intense, complex body of work in collaboration with his parents that is a poignant and moving examination of the relationship of an artist to his own family. The photographs chart their lives over more than a decade, engaging subtly with their relationships to one another, as well as to the social mores of US society. Although intensely personal and private, the work, with its universal themes of parenthood, ageing, and gender, also resonates with a wider audience.

This photograph has the appearance of simplicity, but it is in fact very complex and operates on a variety of levels, not only in content and meaning but also in its formal elements. Sultan commented that he was interested in "making the photographs look real, but a lot of them are highly synthetic. They're hybrids, located somewhere between the found and the constructed." The triangle formed by the head of the baseball player on the television screen and the mother's vertical stance gives the photograph a strong internal structure that leads the eye around key elements of the frame, passing unsentimentally across the bald patch on his father's head. The color palette is harmonious, which along with the texture and patterns of the clothing is representative of a particular social class in the United States. Sultan wrote movingly about the experience of documenting his parents' lives: "What drives me to continue this work is difficult to name. It has more to do with love than with sociology, with being a subject in the drama rather than a witness. And in the odd and jumbled process of working, everything shifts; the boundaries blur, my distance slips, the arrogance and illusion of immunity falters. I wake up in the middle of the night, stunned and anguished. These are my parents. From that simple fact, everything follows."

‹e a shooting script, as in this example ›om *Pictures from Home*: "Dad looking ‹e Johnny Carson; Mom looking up—hotographed from high vantage point (like movie still); Walking the dog at night; lom at work, at the office or at an open ouse; Where are pictures of them with ıeir kids?; Still-life of dresser or desk; Dad ›oking to the side with sloppy background, ıaybe car; Shaking hands; Project the Dale 'arnegie photograph and do portrait of dad standing in front of it; Close-up, looking to the side; Mom opening up curtain; At the water, fishing; Pictures of me?"

Sultan wrote a series of questions for his graduate students, which serve as a superb analysis of how to develop any creative practice: "What do I need to sustain my practice? Economically, psychologically, philosophically? What does that mean in terms of my relationship to the art world and the art market? Does art need to have a social/political value? How do I make a contribution? How do I know if any of this is worthwhile to anyone other than me? How important is it to be innovative? Are innovations primarily formal in nature? What does it mean to critically defend my work? How much do I need to say? To write? To explain? Do I need to have a developed theoretical back-story to what I do? If so—where do I get one???"

Jim Goldberg

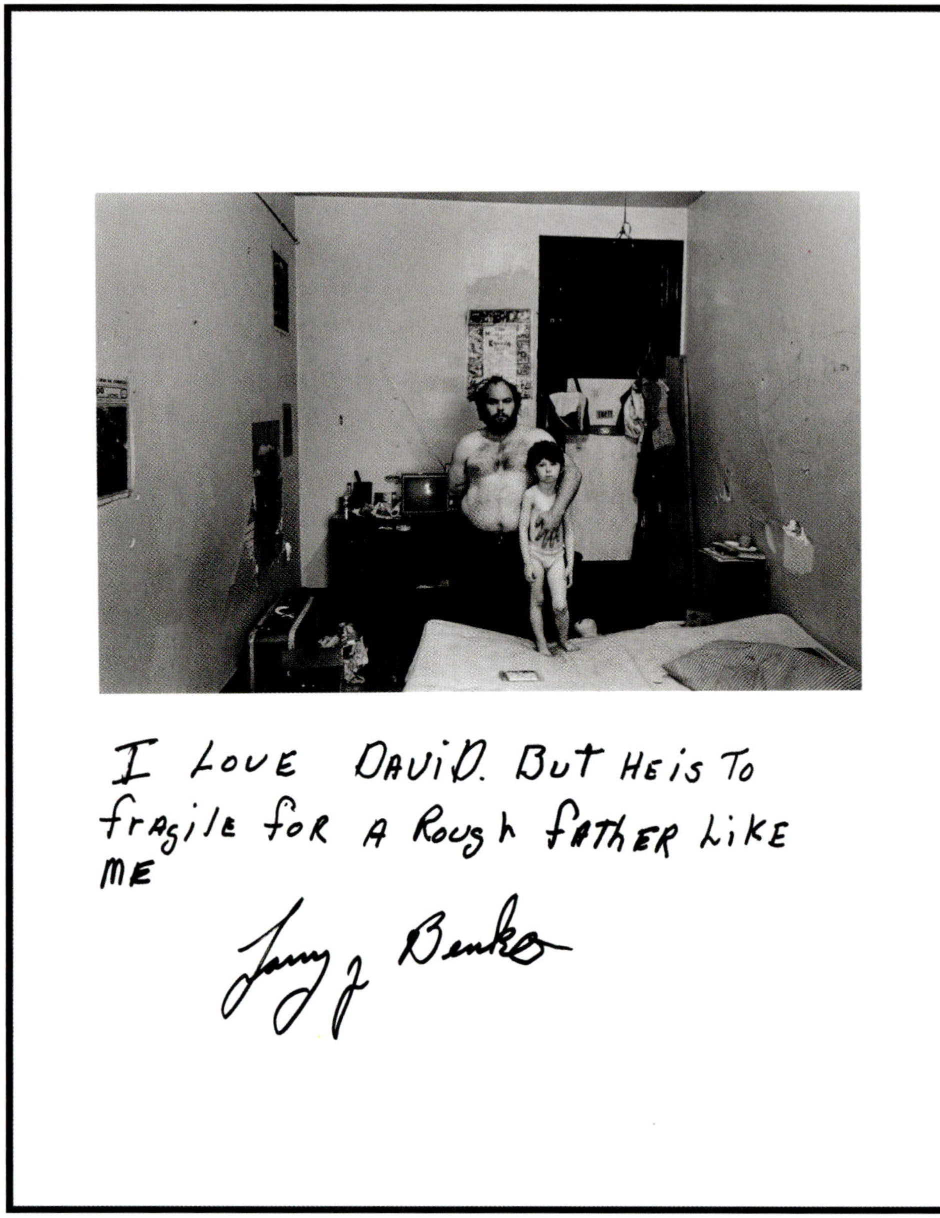

Jim Goldberg (American, 1953–) has developed an approach to documenting the lives of those affected by the social and economic crisis by expanding beyond the photograph to include text, handwriting, home movies, video, audio, drawings, diaries, and found objects. He states that he is "obsessed with this idea of total documentation." For *Raised by Wolves* (1995), he followed runaway teenagers in San Francisco and Los Angeles and immersed himself in their lives. He has recently worked in Europe on issues around migration. Goldberg has been a full-time member of Magnum Photos since 2006, and was formerly Professor of Art at the California College of Arts and Crafts.

Creative tips and techniques

Goldberg feels that his approach allows for a more expansive view of the complexities of the lives of his subjects. He believes that "everyone has more than one life story, depending on who's telling it, and where that person stands. So it's not only about what he thinks, but it's also about the audience and how they take it. So the interaction between the subject and viewer is really personal." He also believes that the viewer should be left to do some of the interpretative work themselves: "sometimes I think it's okay not to be told everything, to not have the answers to everything. There's sometimes a reason not to give all the answers. So I don't know if I'm so much telling stories as witnessing personal histories as they unfold. . .The multi-layered quality of life—of people's motives and actions—is what fascinates me, rather than having answers." He sees the photograph as a "kind of a proof—a proof that I actually met these people, that they actually have lives, and that they're worth considering." However, he is sensitive to the ethical issue of working with those on the edges of society and reveals that he sometimes misses images on purpose: "I've done too many of them before and photographing them again doesn't change the world, or me."

Rich and poor 1985

From 1977 to 1985 Jim Goldberg worked with the extremes of US society to produce his book *Rich and Poor* (1985). He photographed in a hotel for transients, where whole families were living in poverty, as well as in the homes of the wealthy trustees of his own art college. He questioned them about their lives, hopes, and fears, initially asking: "If you were going to die or leave this room tomorrow, and this picture were going to be hung up on the door as a remembrance of you, what would you say?" As the work progressed, Goldberg expanded his questions to explore their lives in more depth. The book contrasted the language and emotions expressed by different classes; the rich often appeared self-absorbed and detached, whereas the poor expressed more fundamental human emotions. The poignant, brutally honest quote from the father about his son on the left contrasts with the self-absorption of the wealthy woman on the right. The juxtaposition of handwritten text and image makes the connection with the subjects feel tangible and visceral: it exploits the space between what can be seen and what is being said.

Goldberg was attempting to tell the stories of these people from within their lives, rather than as an observer, explaining that "I wanted to open up the discussion, to highlight the complexities of each person's situation and crack into the (sometimes contradictory) discussions that journalism, economics, and sociology sometimes do not allow." In this, he was seeking to question the narratives that debates about poverty and wealth normally engender, and who controls the discourse, hoping that his work "raises questions about how poverty or youth homelessness are framed." Goldberg produced a new edition of the book in 2014 when he sadly acknowledged that "conditions for the 'rich' and the 'poor' haven't changed much since this book was first published. But I can't let go of the desire, the impulse, to want to believe in a society where things really will get better."

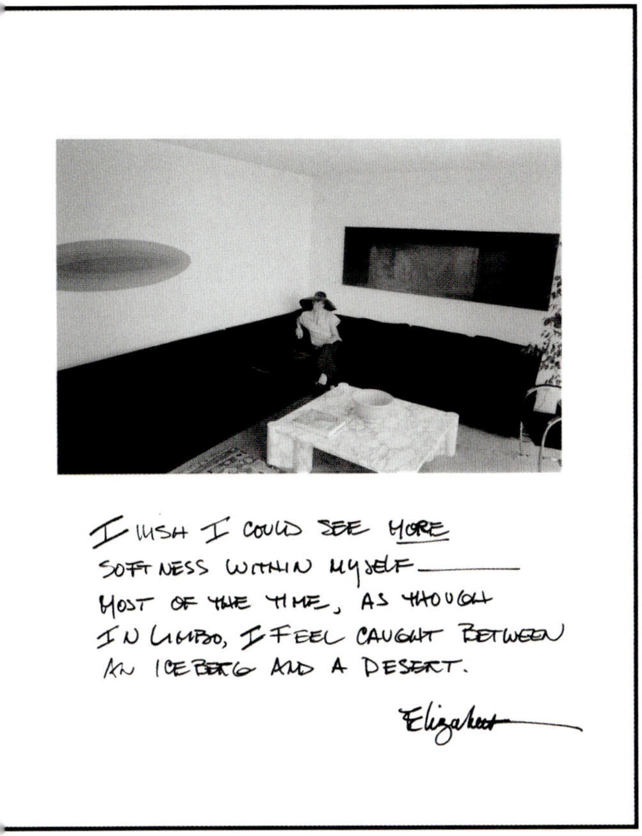

When Goldberg was approached to reprint *Rich and Poor,* it gave him unique opportunity to revisit the work nd rethink its original presentation. He ent back to his archive to see what he ould "reinvent." He says that the process rovided him with a way to experience his d work with a fresh mind, and he found mself excited about seeing things that e had passed over years before during his riginal edit. He modified the structure of the book, so that he could relate the past to the present, explaining that the accordion fold-out "is intended to bring the present day into dialog with the past." He explains that the idea for the covers of the insert was to show two portraits, one of a rich person and one of a poor person from the original book. "Between their two faces, as you unfold the book, are the current streets of San Francisco where the poor and rich live."

> "There's a thread that runs through all the work that is to do with bearing witness. The photographs are about asking questions, though, not answering them." Jim Goldberg

Anna Fox

"The most interesting photography… observes what most of the world ignores and dismisses as dull or 'too ordinary'."

Anna Fox

Anna Fox (British, 1961–) is one of the second generation of British color documentary photographers that emerged after Martin Parr (see p.102) and Paul Graham (see p.58). She was taught by both of them, as well as by Karen Knorr, at West Surrey College of Art and Design in the early 1980s. Fox recalls how Graham "tended to be interested in the less predictable images; his editing (when he looked at our pictures) was always highly complex, intelligent and informed by his interest in politics/social conditions—his vision of what was interesting really made me question my beliefs all the time." After a series of projects including *Work Stations* (1988), *Friendly Fire* (1995), which examines the culture of paintballing, and *The Village* (1993), which looks at the fantasy of rural life, her work has become more autobiographical, but still focuses a critical eye on the mores of English social discourse. She is Professor of Photography at the University of the Creative Arts at Farnham, Surrey.

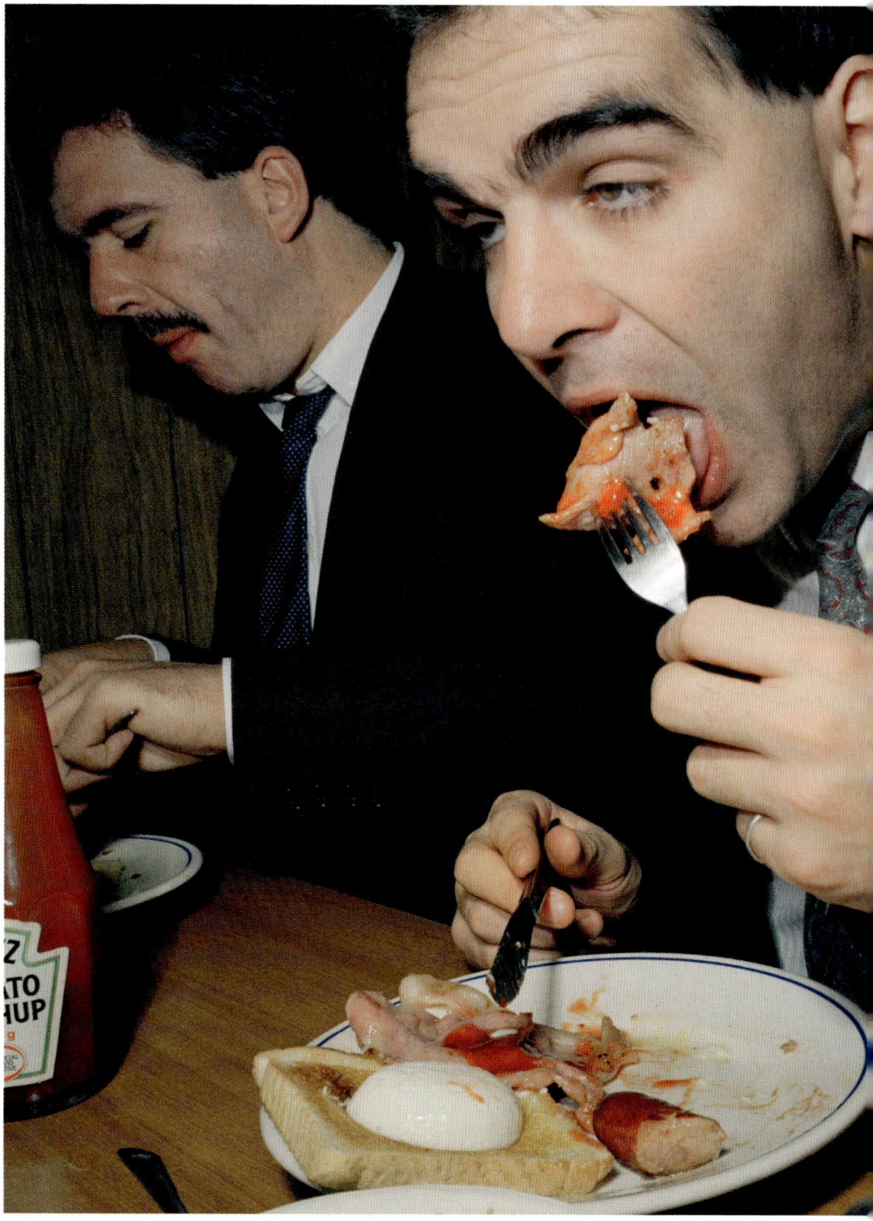

Creative tips and techniques

Fox's combination of texts and photographs acts as a commentary to the images, rather than simply as captions. For *Work Stations,* she wanted to tell a story that reflected the social conditions of Margaret Thatcher's Britain and her infamous statement: "There is no such thing as society; just individuals." Fox spent time researching the texts and collecting captions through essays, magazines, and interviewing people. She collected a huge amount of material and then slowly edited it before starting to put it with the images that she had edited in the same way. She played with the combinations of texts and images, but "in the end most of them were obvious in terms of what went with what—liked the idea of creating a filmic narrative—or a short story about office life."

Workstations, Cafe, the City. Salesperson (9) "Fortunes are being made that are in line with the dreams of avarice." Business 1987 1988, from *Work Stations*

Anna Fox's acerbic critique of office life in Thatcher's Britain used a variety of visual strategies to enhance the sense of alienation and avarice prevalent in the competitive business culture of the 1980s. Using a medium-format Plaubel Makina camera with a Metz flash and bounce card, Fox often isolated figures through framing and cropping; by screening figures behind their desks and office furniture, she made them appear engulfed by their environments. With a wry and witty sense of the absurdities of office life, she created a surreal and satirical commentary on the mores of a certain set of values prevalent at the time. This image speaks to the excess of consumption of the period; the flash transfixes the worker as he forces food into his mouth, his eyes caught as if drunk with the rush of the business world.

Fox was interested in power structures within the working office environment in Thatcher's Britain, an experience that she had personal experience of: "All my family worked in offices at the time, from the paper trade to the banking industry to a design office. I had worked in insurance prior to studying photography. *Work Stations* was a bit like *The Office* (that brilliant comedy that came out in the 1990s), but with less comedy."

Work Stations was commissioned by Camerawork Gallery and the Museum of London, and Fox spent a year and a half gaining access to around sixty London offices. Belonging to the new wave of color photographers who were exploiting the medium's descriptive powers to exaggerate the world they saw, and to challenge the traditional documentary mode of black-and-white reportage, Fox felt that she "wanted to use color and flash because of the very immediate feel that they give to the work—you really feel like it is happening here and now rather than in the distant past."

In her later work Fox has explored her own life, but she relates her autobiographical projects to broader social issues such as the family, the mythology of rural life, parenting, and even the tribulations of sharing a house with friends. She explains that she has explored using projects and the camera to "exorcise difficult issues," including the tension within her own family, between her father and mother. Much of this work she produces only for her own eyes, and she reveals that she always has a project like this on the go although she does not tend to show them in public and sometimes destroys them. She confesses: "I think autobiography is insanely difficult and one has to be absolutely sure that it is necessary to do before making the work public." Even some of her earlier work has this sense of connection to her own life, such as her project *The Village*, which focused on the West Sussex village where her grandmother lived and her mother grew up. She was particularly interested in women's lives and how they operate in a patriarchal society. She reveals: "photography helped me to articulate things I thought or felt but definitely couldn't say—it gave me the confidence to speak and was incredibly liberating. I had not realized how sinister a scene I would set in what looked like a twee English village."

Richard Billingham

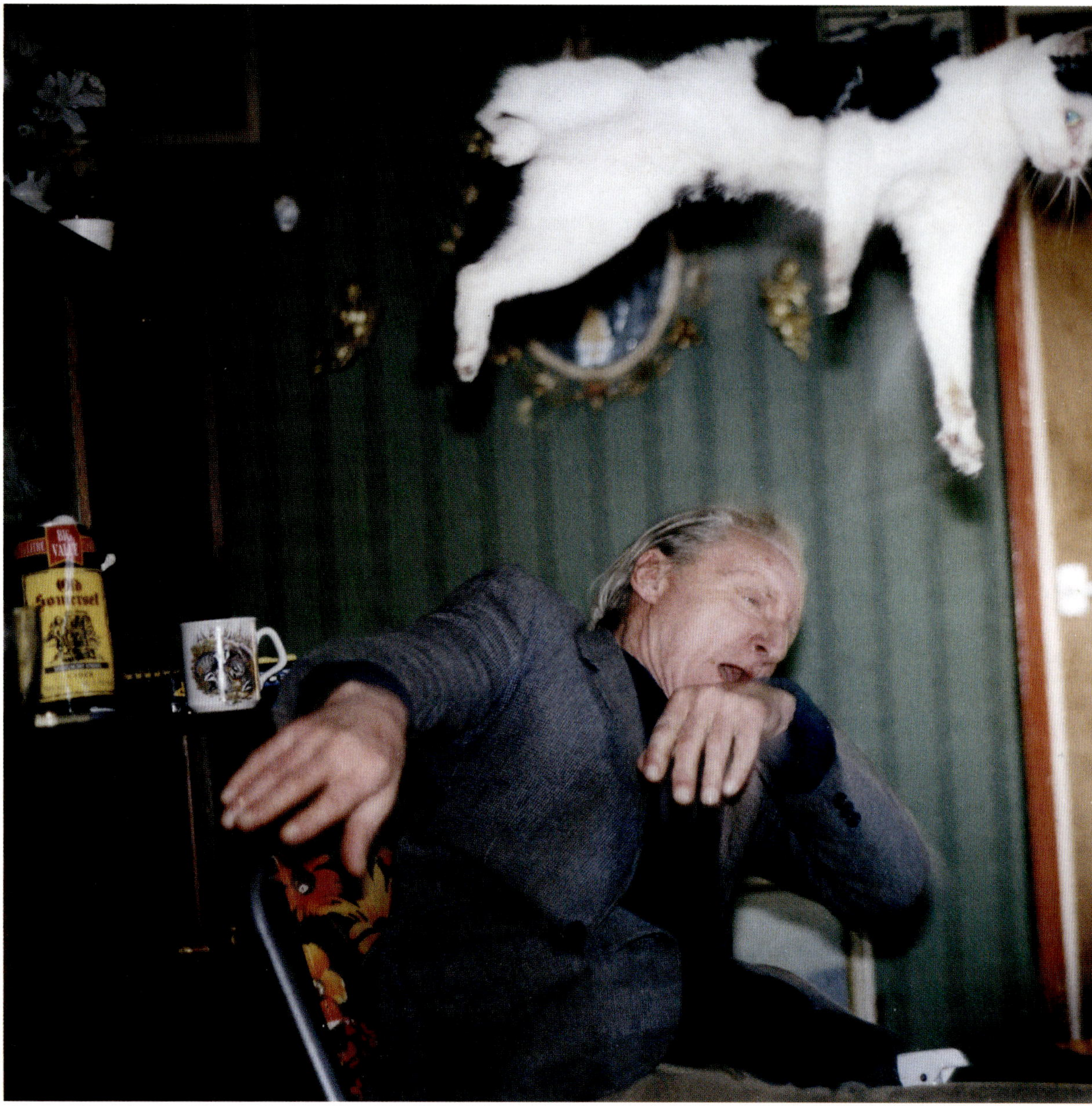

"My father, Raymond, is a chronic alcoholic. He doesn't like going outside; my mother, Elizabeth, hardly drinks, but she does smoke a lot." Richard Billingham

Richard Billingham (British, 1970–) studied fine art and initially wanted to be a painter. However, after the extraordinary impact images of his family made on the photographic scene when published as the book *Ray's a Laugh* (1996), he began to concentrate on photography instead. He worked on a series of large-format landscapes of the West Midlands area he grew up in, published as *Black Country* (2003), followed by *Landscapes, 2001–2003* (2008). In 1997 Billingham was part of the "Sensation" exhibition at the Royal Academy of Arts, which included many of the Young British Artists. In the same year he won the Citigroup Photography Prize.

Creative tips and techniques

Billingham did not want to portray his family negatively, stating that, "It's not my intention to shock, to offend, sensationalize, be political or whatever, only to make work that is as spiritually meaningful as I can make it." However, he admits that the reception of the work was not how he had intended the images to be viewed. The focus was on his family's

Ray's a Laugh 1996

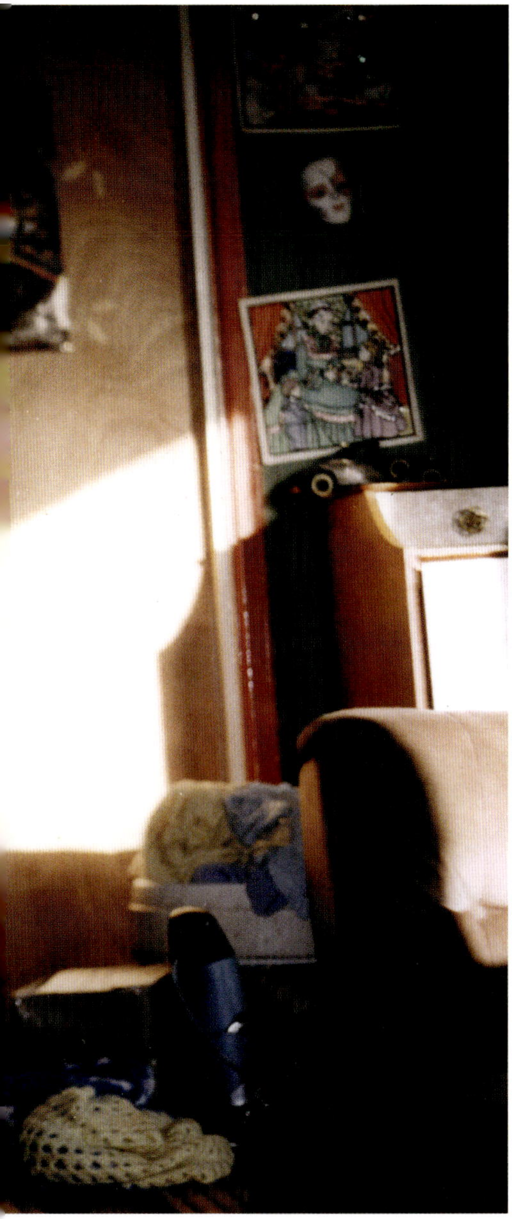

A cat flies through the air, caught in mid-jump by the blinding light of a flash, which also freezes the man in a theatrical pose against the backdrop of a cluttered and discordant room. The image is at once comic and disturbing, the narrative of the situation unclear. What makes this body of work extraordinary is that it was made by the son of the subject; it is a painfully personal exploration of the relationships inside the photographer's own family, with Billingham acting as a kind of participant observer of his own environment. *Ray's a Laugh* (1996) is a challenging book; the photographs are presented full bleed with no captions, filling the page with a vivid and unsettling portrait of what appears to be a dysfunctional family. The family members are often seemingly drunk and unaware of the camera, and the depiction seems to veer dangerously toward the exploitative, but the knowledge that these are Billingham's own relatives creates a tension in the ethics of representation.

Billingham initially started to take photographs of his father as references for his paintings. He explains: "I was living in this tower block; there was just me and him. He was an alcoholic, he would lie in the bed, drink, get to sleep, wake up, get to sleep, didn't know if it was day or night. But it was difficult to get him to stay still for more than, say, twenty minutes at a time so I thought that if I could take photographs of him that would act as source material for these paintings and then I could make more detailed paintings later on." The lives of his family are chaotic, but also full of color and often emotion, which Billingham tuned into, recalling that "my dad had moved into my mum's place by this time and I could not believe how it looked. She'd had two years away from my dad, so she had created her own psychological space around herself that was very 'carnivalesque' and decorative. There were dolls, jigsaws everywhere. She'd got a load of pets by this time; she had about ten cats... two, three dogs."

ing conditions rather than the underlying thetic: "they caught the general public's e because they were looking at the bject matter. . .I was shocked when ealized it, that people can't read otographs. It was 'Oh, look at those stains the wall, look at his mum's tattoos. . .' d I never saw none of that, honestly, that st happened to be there. People weren't eing any beauty underneath, none of the mposition, none of the pattern."

On a superficial level Billingham's images appear amateurish; the camera is simple with direct flash, saturated colors, under- and overexposure, and extreme grain. Billingham acknowledges that he cared little about technical quality, "I just used the cheapest film and took them to be processed at the cheapest place. I was just trying to make order out of chaos." However, this disguises a strong formal element to the work, with its spontaneous compositions and framing of movement far surpassing that of the usual family album. This lack of finesse serves to accentuate the honesty of the work. By removing conventional standards of quality, it is rawer and perhaps more convincing. This is an approach that has become more relevant in the digital age, as photographers use the snapshot to give their images a feeling of authentic "reality" as opposed to polished professionalism.

Histo

ies

The idea of the photographer as a witness to history is deeply embedded in the nature of the medium. The apparent veracity of the camera's lens seemingly gives the viewer a ringside seat at significant moments of human activity. The camera acts as a kind of visual prosthesis; extending our ability to see spatially and temporally, it allows distant events to be brought to our attention and for representations of the world to be recorded, stored, transmitted, distributed, archived and interpreted after the image has been made. The condensing of important historical moments into iconic photographs performs a vital role in humanizing complex issues and creating a space in which audiences can identify with the protagonists of the events depicted. Photographs personalize historical events and help an audience connect to the subject and their situation.

The photograph as a discrete object is often viewed in private; it can compress the distance between viewer and event, bringing the faraway into the domestic space of the audience. Complex events are thus made manageable by the operation of the frame, and history is miniaturized into a palpable object that can be intimately viewed at close range. This forms a chain of links between the recorded subject, the media and the viewer, and this chain establishes a relationship of interaction between the parties. After their initial appearance as rallying points for public awareness of an event or issue, iconic images become part of the process of establishing that moment as a historical one. Following careful editing, when images are sifted in preference to others, and over time, these iconic images become markers of our collective memory.

Roger Fenton

Valley of the shadow of death 1855

When Roger Fenton traveled to the Crimea, he had only been taking photographs for three years. The trip was financed by publisher and print dealer Thomas Agnew and by Britain's secretary of state for war, Henry Pelham-Clinton, who tasked Fenton with making images to encourage support for the war against Russia. He landed at Balaklava on 8 March 1855 with two assistants, a converted horse-drawn carriage to act as a mobile darkroom, five cameras, and 700 glass slides. He worked with a large-format camera and the wet-plate collodion process, which limited him to shooting static subjects. Most of the 360 images he produced were portraits of troops or landscapes of the camps. He deliberately avoided scenes of death and refrained from photographing dead bodies even though he saw them. Fenton made this image in a valley near to the one made famous by Tennyson's poem "The Charge of the Light Brigade," which led to the epithet "the valley of death." According to his diary, Fenton had visited the same location previously, without his camera. Some controversy, however, surrounds this image as another negative exists in which the road is cleared of cannonballs. Recent research suggests that this photograph was made before the more famous one, and that Fenton or someone else moved them back onto the path, potentially to simulate the scene that he had observed days earlier.

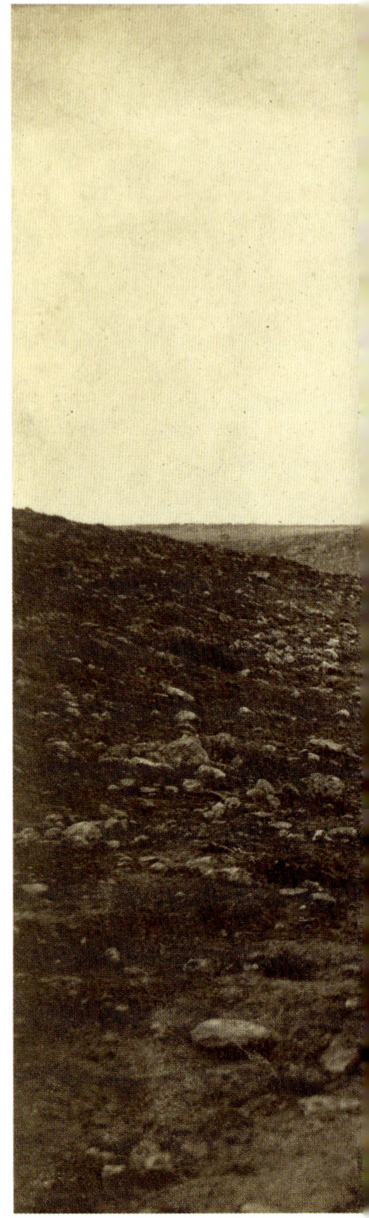

Creative tips and techniques

Fenton's photograph is composed following the classical form of the golden mean, also known as the rule of thirds. It is widely regarded as an efficient way to create a balanced composition, and is a good starting point from which to construct an image if you are seeking to create a harmonious frame. The pictorial space or subject is divided up into thirds—horizontally and vertically—with the main points of interest aligned along them and at the intersectior where they meet. In this image, the horizo line is approximately two-thirds of the way up the photograph and the lines of the trail and the stream bed all run toward a vanishing point on the horizon, again one-third of the way across the frame. This creates a strong sense of movement within the frame.

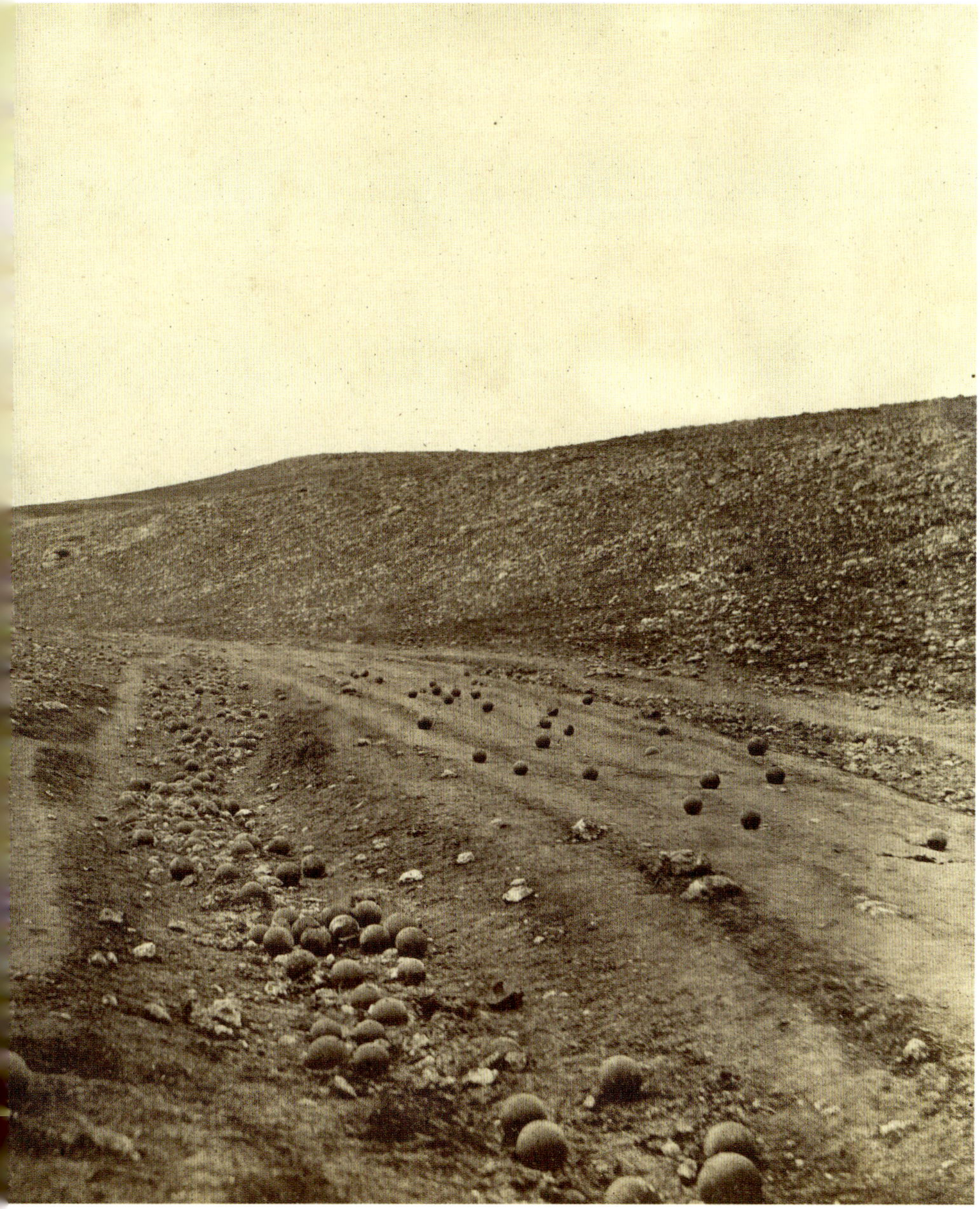

Roger Fenton (British, 1819–69) had a relatively short career, working for only eleven years, but in that time he established himself as one of the most important practitioners of the medium. Originally trained as a lawyer, he also studied painting in Paris. He excelled across a range of genres, from landscape and portraiture to architecture and still life. In 1854, Queen Victoria invited him to photograph the private life of the royal family. The same year, he became the first official photographer of the British Museum, London.

"In coming to a ravine called the valley of death, the sight passed all imagination. Round shot and shell lay in a stream at the bottom of the hollow all the way down; you could not walk for treading upon them." Roger Fenton

Despite not showing the direct impact of warfare on soldiers or the eat of the action, Fenton's image still akes a powerful statement about the pact of modern technology on the fragile dies of soldiers; it helps the viewer to agine the human experience of being rced to march up a hill under a rain of nnonballs. The visual space of the image closed down, narrowing the field of view the close terrain of the path up the slope. This accentuates the claustrophobic feeling of moving under heavy artillery fire, as the troops advance toward the objective of the action lying unseen over the rise. Fenton's image is one of the earliest examples of what is now called "aftermath" photography, where the artist revisits the scene of a traumatic event to explore how the traces of the past are still visible in the landscape. This approach invites the viewer to think about how the topography of a place can contain meaning, and to project themselves back in time to imagine how the scene would have looked. Often the scene looks empty and banal, but then the caption provides information about what happened on that spot that completely changes the perception of the image. This sense that past events still haunt the landscape, and that it can be read as a kind of map of the past, is a powerful conceptual tool.

Erich Salomon

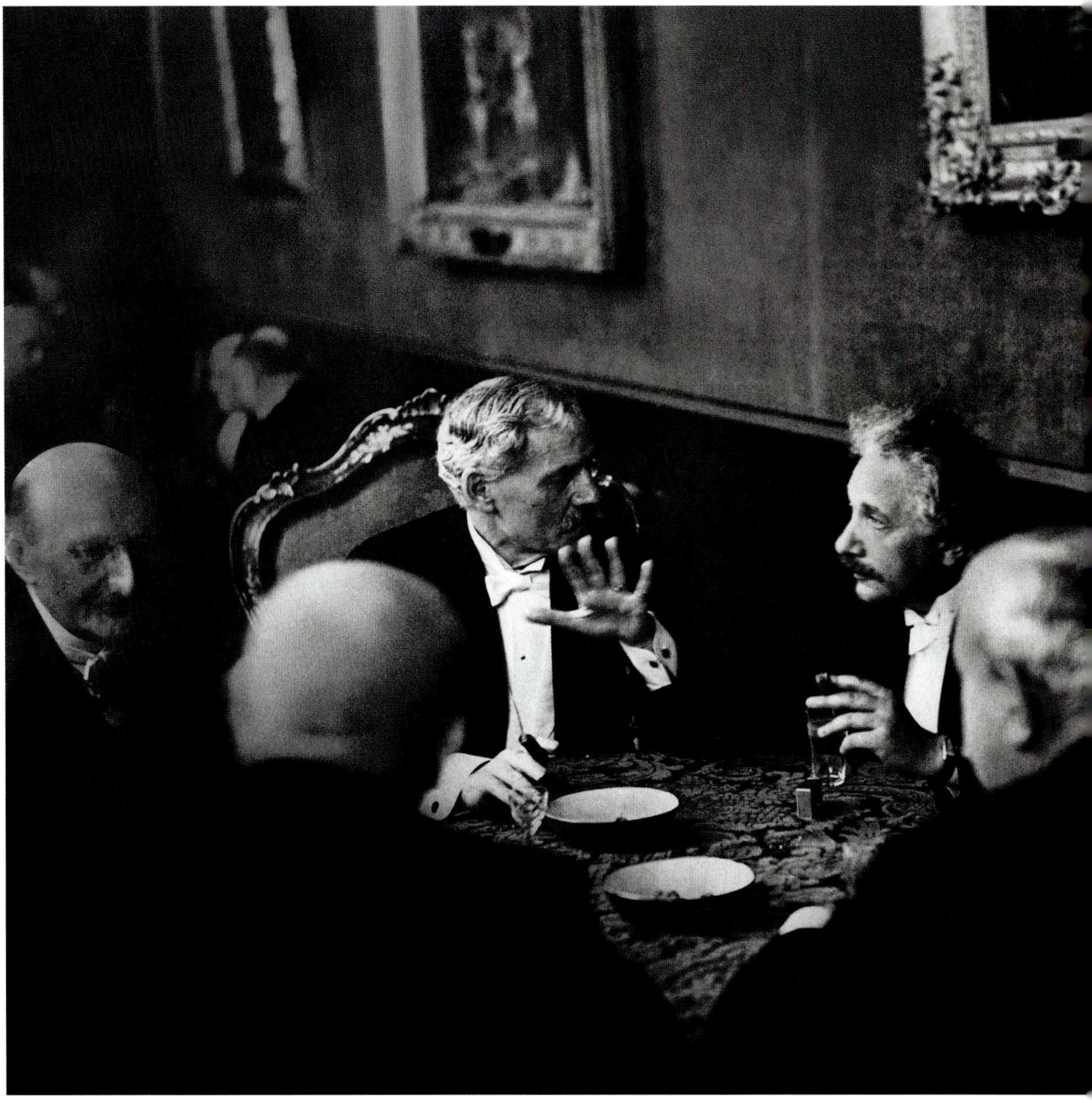

Erich Salomon (German, 1886–1944) was born in Berlin. He was multilingual and initially studied law, engineering, and zoology. He did not pick up a camera until he was forty-one, but soon mastered the art of "fly-on-the-wall" news photography and was dubbed the "Houdini of photography," in reference to his ingenious methods of concealing the camera. In 1928 he began working at *Berliner Illustrirte Zeitung*, fast achieving a reputation for being able to gain access to the highest levels of social, diplomatic, and political life, and documenting the delicate negotiations over Europe's future. In 1929 the *London Graphic* coined the phrase "candid camera" to refer to his work, but he described himself as a *bildjournalist*—still the German word for photojournalist. After the Nazis seized power, Salomon fled to the Netherlands, but he was arrested in 1943 and sent to Auschwitz where he died on 7 July 1944.

Creative tips and techniques

Salomon initially used the compact plate Ermanox camera which allowed shooting in low light because of its fast f2 lens. He later switched to the 35mm Leica in 1932. He was one of the first photographers to exploit the potential of smaller cameras recognizing that they allowed him to work discreetly without flash. He still

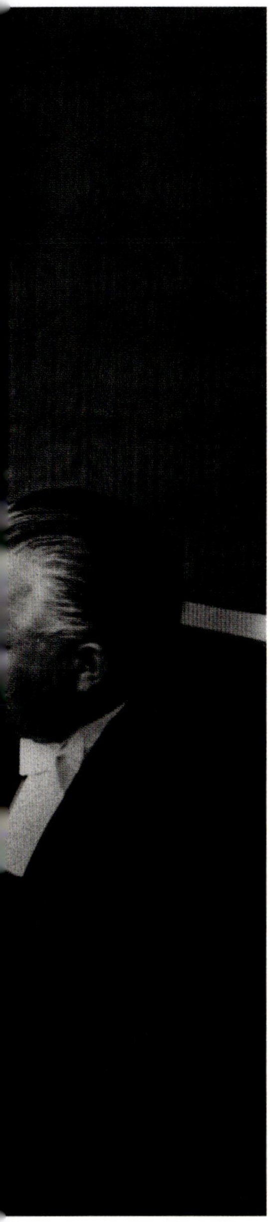

British Prime Minister Ramsay MacDonald and Albert Einstein 1931

Erich Salomon's photographs of the machinations of power were a revelation compared to the stiff, posed images of world leaders that the media was then used to. Using small cameras that he could conceal and no flash, he captured the ebb and flow of political intrigue as it was happening. His appearance belied his skill; he was unassuming, bespectacled, and balding, but he turned this to his advantage. Dressed in black tie and tails, he merged into the background of events and was able to work as if invisible to the participants. At the signing of the Kellogg–Briand Pact in 1928, Salomon boldly walked into the room and sat in the empty place for the Polish delegate to shoot his pictures. His clever advice was that "if you stand before the doors of a meeting room and ask the man in charge to be let in, it is not hard for that man to tell you all the reasons he can't let you in. If, however, before the meeting begins you are already in the room—this requires a far greater psychological effort on his part." Salomon was expert at blending into the entourages of politicians, often arriving in a limousine along with the delegates. His presence became such an accepted part of events that, when asked if Salomon should be allowed onto a boat to shoot a secret meeting with the British Labour government, the Prussian Prime minister remarked "Surely it's inevitable. Nowadays, you can hold a conference without ministers, but not without Dr. Salomon." This particular image shows the British prime minister and Albert Einstein in animated conversation at a reception in 1931.

"The work of a press photographer who wants to be more than a journeyman is a continual struggle for his picture." Erich Salomon

eeded to use a tripod, however, as the lm speeds were very slow. His ability to isappear into the background, combined ith using a long cable release, meant that ne politicians were often unaware of his resence, despite him having to change lates for every shot. His sense of timing as immaculate; given that his exposures ere long, and he was able to capture ne gestures of the political theater with emarkably little blur.

Salomon was crafty and used various tricks to get his candid shots. On an assignment to cover a murder trial, he hid a camera inside his bowler hat, cutting a hole in it for the lens. When he was discovered, he handed over several blank unexposed plates to the court attendant, keeping the real images in his pocket. On another occasion, he concealed his camera in an attaché case, with a complex set of levers to trigger the shutter. To photograph President Hoover he hid behind a floral display, to get into the US Supreme Court he placed his camera in an arm sling, and to shoot the famously secretive Casino at Monte Carlo he hollowed out a mathematics textbook. However, his subterfuge was not always successful. When he tried to infiltrate a gathering of Scottish nobility, with his camera hidden in bagpipes, he made the mistake of wearing the tartan kilt of a rival clan and was swiftly ejected.

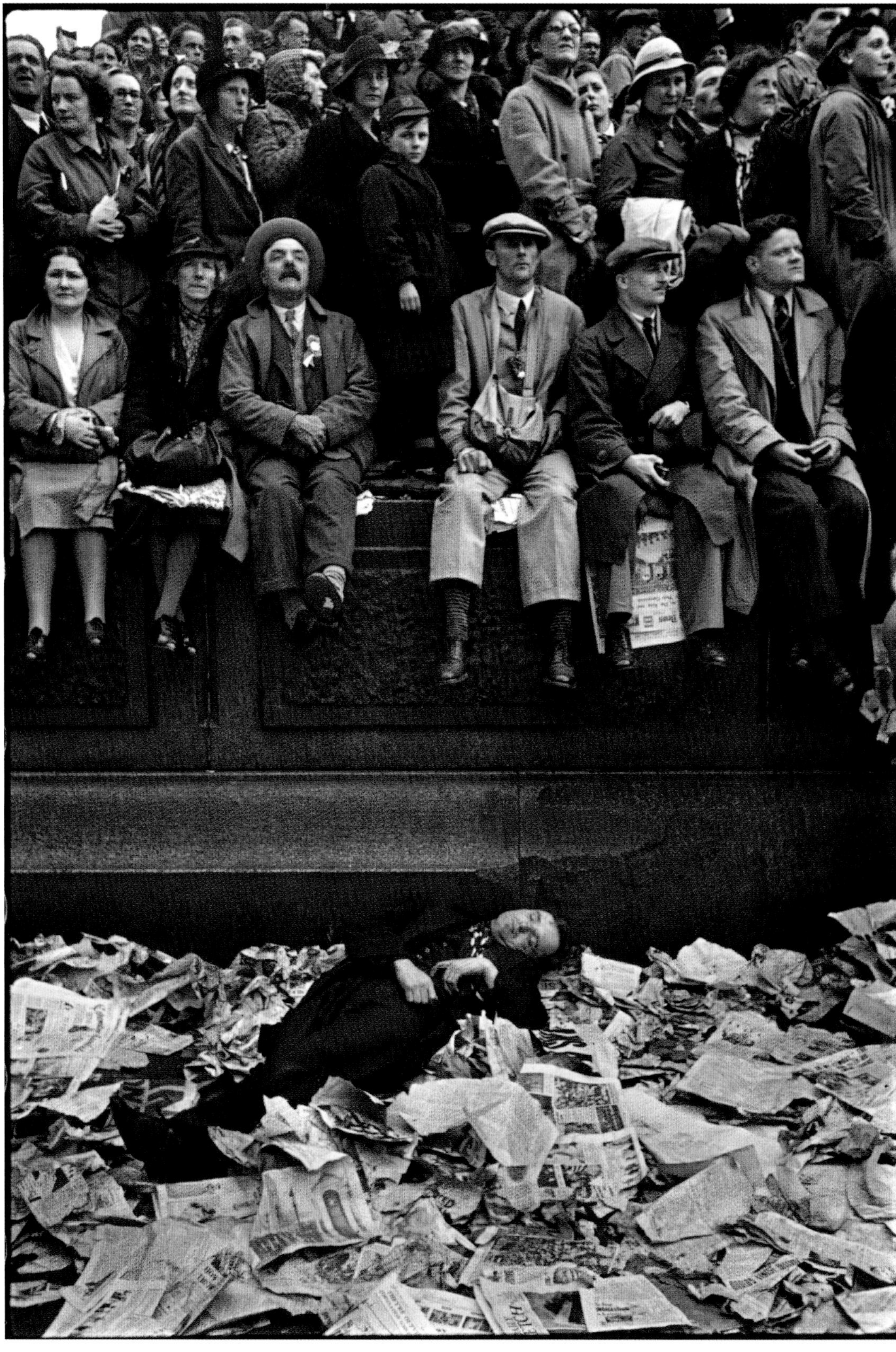

oronation of King George VI. London, 12th May 1937

ıis photograph came from Henri Cartier-Bresson's first real ssignment as a photojournalist, covering the coronation of King eorge VI and Queen Elizabeth for the French weekly *Regards*. ather than following the other photographers and focusing ı the pomp and circumstance of the occasion, he instead oncentrated on the crowds lining the London streets and took o pictures of the new king. He shot instinctively, but was always ware that the esthetics of the image were inseparable from its eaning. The image is a delightful interpretation of the grandeur f the event, with the sharp contrast between the excited onlookers ıd the recumbent man, and the piles of newspapers making a ry comment on the nature of the news, discarded so quickly. his was typical of Cartier-Bresson's approach: he sought to ustrate the essence of a situation by engaging with the elements f everyday life, noting that the "smallest thing can become a g subject; an insignificant human detail can become a leitmotif. /e see and we make seen as a witness to the world around us; ıe event, in its natural activity, generates an organic rhythm f forms." Cartier-Bresson was a master of the fly-on-the-wall oproach: unobtrusive but alert, always looking and finding in the veryday an extraordinary beauty and truth that still resonates ears after the images were made.

Creative tips and techniques

Cartier-Bresson used a very limited range of equipment, shooting almost everything with only a 50mm standard lens. It is vital to truly get to know your equipment and to understand instinctively the field of view of the range of focal lengths you work with, so that you can frame the image almost without thinking. As an exercise, go out for the day with only one focal length lens (if you have a zoom, use it on only one setting) and see how limiting the choice of lens can, in fact, be very liberating.

Cartier-Bresson emphasized knowing how to estimate the correct exposure for a situation. He noted how during the day, he did not need a light meter; he would guess first, then check. Follow his advice and switch your camera to manual exposure. Try to estimate the correct setting by eye and then check it in camera and on the screen. As a guideline, on a sunny day the exposure will be around 1/250th of a second at f16 at 400ASA. On a dull, cloudy day it will be around 1/250th of a second at f8.

Many people do not use the vertical format other than for portraits. However, it can be excellent for organizing the frame in other situations. The 50mm lens is perfect for this kind of shot, as it allows a precise structuring of the frame without the distortion of a wide angle or the compression of a telephoto. In this image, Cartier-Bresson created five layers to the composition, with the two lines of people, the stone wall, the sleeping man, and the newspapers. The eye is drawn to the young boy in the center, who breaks the line between the two rows of people. The body of the sleeping man runs at an angle to the rest of the image, drawing the eye back up again into the frame.

> ?eality offers us such wealth that we must cut some of t out on the spot, simplify. The question is, do we always :ut out what we should?" Henri Cartier-Bresson

enri Cartier-Bresson (French, 1908–2004) is egarded as the father of photojournalism. In ıe 1930s he was one of the first photographers) use the new Leica Rangefinder cameras with 5mm film, which liberated photographers from eavy, cumbersome plate cameras. Cartier-resson's early ambition, however, was to be ı artist, and he spent the 1920s in Paris, where e was introduced to Surrealism. In a highly reative period in the early 1930s Cartier-Bresson produced many masterpieces of street photography that remain poetic celebrations of everyday life. In 1947 he co-founded Magnum Photos—the model creative photo-agency. His book *The Decisive Moment* (originally titled *Images à la Sauvette*, published in 1952) established his visual philosophy: "What the eye does is to find and focus on the particular subject within the mass of reality; what the camera does is simply to register upon film the decision made by the eye."

Robert Capa

Crowds running for shelter after an air-raid alarm sounded, Bilbao 1937

Robert Capa reported extensively on the Spanish Civil War from 1936 to 1939, and made repeated trips there during the conflict. He covered fighting on the front lines with an urgency and drama that were rare in news reporting until then. However, he also focused his correspondent's eye on the suffering of the civilian population, as witnessed in this powerful image depicting fear on the streets of the Basque city of Bilbao. He described the scene as follows: "Nowhere is there safety for anyone in this war. The women stay behind, but the death, the ingenious death from the skies finds them out. There is little protection in the cities. The bombs break through the shelters. In Valencia, in Madrid, there is a daily toll. Always the same: the sirens, the panic rush, the fracas of the bombs and then, as the dust settles, people go off to the morgue to wait, to see if by chance the son, the father, the mother who did not come home is on the list." During the Spanish Civil War, the Nationalists under Francisco Franco made extensive use of aerial bombing on civilian targets. Capa stood on this street corner taking a sequence of shots of civilians hurrying past him to get to air-raid shelters. His keen eye for honing in on the details of the situation spotted that the little girl buttoned her coat up wrongly in the rush to get to safety.

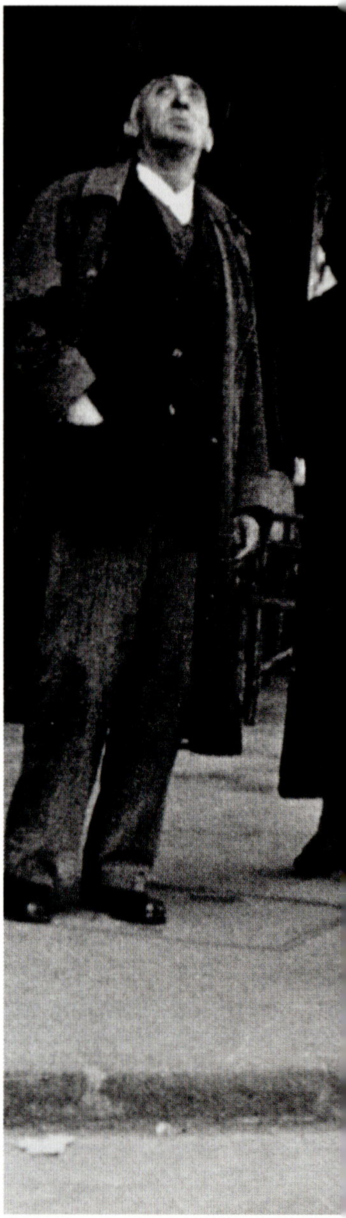

Creative tips and techniques

Capa's famous quote "if your pictures are not good enough, you're not close enough" is usually interpreted as an exhortation to photographers to be physically close to the subject. While this was certainly true of Capa's approach, arguably he also meant that you should be emotionally, psychologically, and even perhaps politically close to the subject, too. He also recommended that you should "like the people you shoot and let them know it." He was partisan and did take sides, clearly aligning himself with the values of the Republicans against the fascist Franco regime during the Spanish Civil War. He explained that: "in a war, you must hate somebody or love somebody; you must have a position or you cannot stand what goes on."

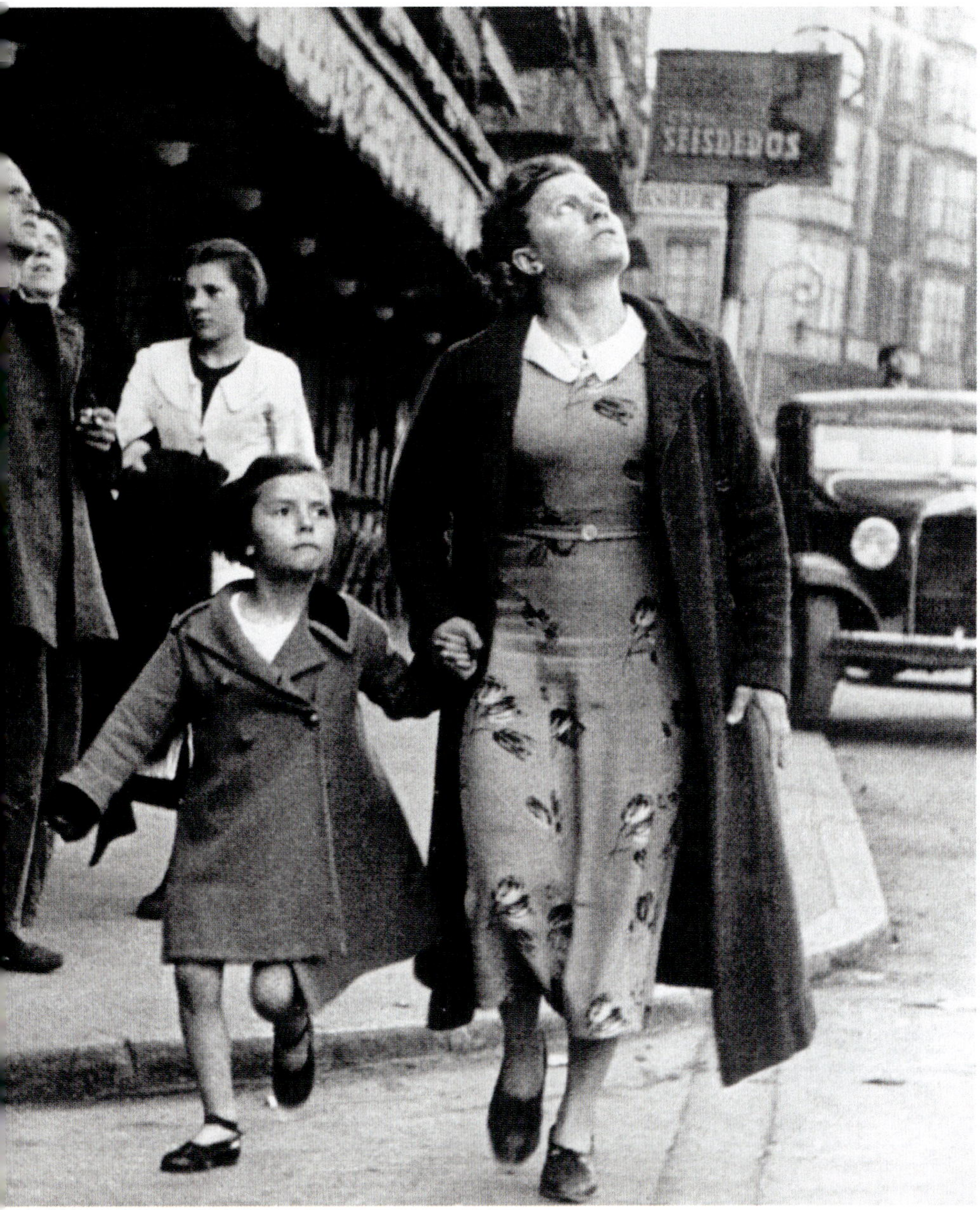

Robert Capa (Hungarian, 1913–54) was born Endre Friedmann in Budapest and wanted to be a writer but took up photography after moving to Berlin in 1931. He adopted the name Capa after he and his girlfriend, Gerda Taró, invented the "great American photographer, Robert Capa" as a way to get his work published when they moved to Paris in the 1930s. Capa was heralded by *Picture Post* as the "greatest war photographer in the world" for his coverage of the Spanish Civil War. In 1944 he made iconic images of the D-Day landings in France. After the war he co-founded Magnum Photos, saying "I hope to stay unemployed as a war photographer till the end of my life." Drawn back to the combat zone, he was killed by a landmine in Indochina in 1954.

"The truth is the best picture, the best propaganda."

Robert Capa

Capa was a master at the business of being a war correspondent. He 'as proficient at organizing logistics and etting the necessary paperwork to allow im to operate at the crucial moments of attles. During World War II, despite his atus as an "enemy alien," he was able to ain permission to accompany the troops the front lines, including parachute rops into Germany. His wit and humor ere reflected in his statement that "for a war correspondent to miss an invasion is like refusing a date with Lana Turner." He also famously recommended to friend and fellow photographer Henri Cartier-Bresson to be wary of labels: "Somebody's going to stick one on you that you'll never get rid of—'the little surrealist photographer'. You'll be lostyou'll get precious and mannered. Take instead the label of 'photojournalist' and keep the other thing for yourself, in your heart of hearts." He also told Cartier-Bresson that "if you call yourself an artist, you won't get anything published. Call yourself a photojournalist, and then you can do whatever you want." The lesson here is to be creative and think laterally about how to position yourself to get access to situations. Be persistent and patient, and don't be afraid to push a situation that bit harder than you think people are comfortable with: that is often when the best images happen.

Larry Burrows

"I will do what is required to show what is happening. I have a sense of the ultimate death. And sometimes I must say 'To hell with that.'"

Larry Burrows

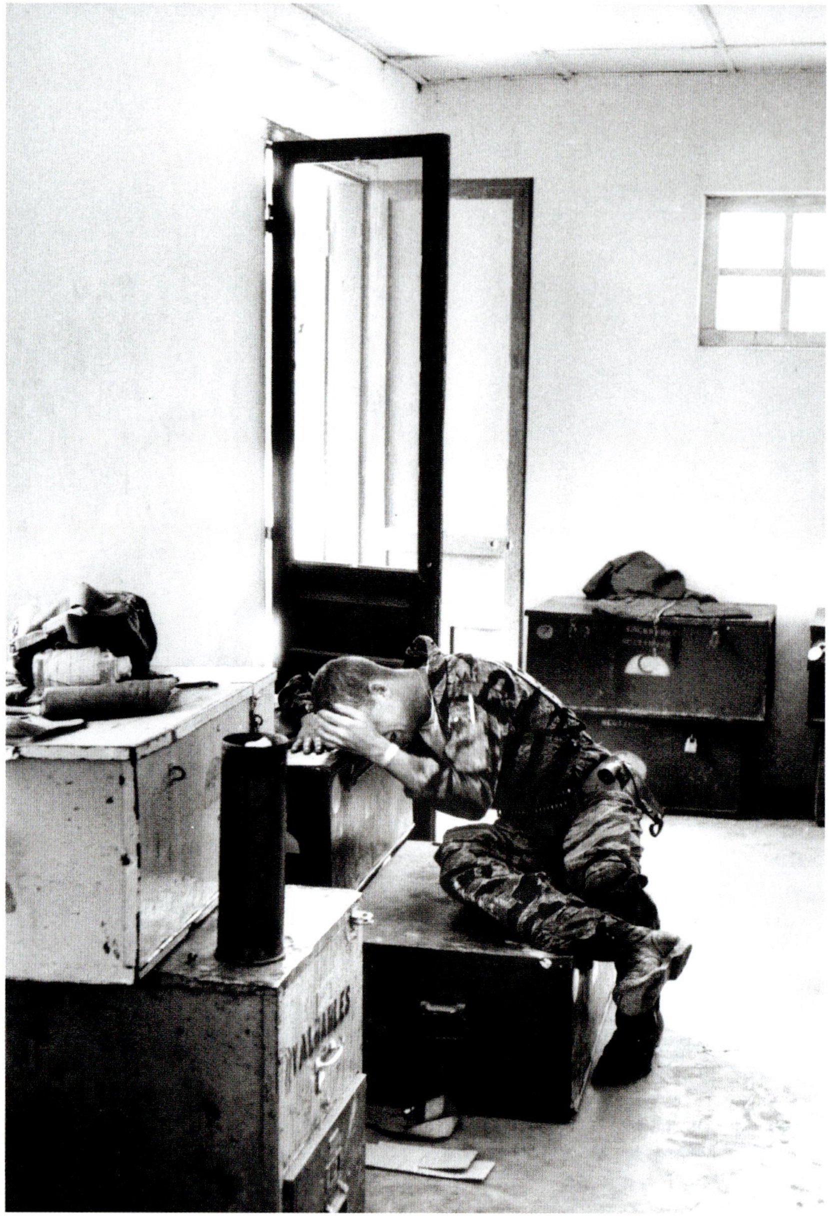

Larry Burrows (British, 1926–71) was one of the greatest chroniclers of the Vietnam War. He spent nine years documenting the conflict from before the US intervention up until his death in February 1971, when the helicopter he was traveling in with fellow photographers Henri Huet, Kent Potter, and Keisaburo Shimamoto was shot down over Laos. Burrows served his photographic apprenticeship at *Life* magazine during World War II. After the war, he honed his technical craft shooting reproductions of Europe's great artworks and his journalistic skills covering conflicts in the Middle East and the Congo. He realized that the Vietnam War would be the defining story of his generation and created a series of iconic stories, including his account of the US Marines' battle for Hill 484, for which he shot the famous image *Reaching Out*.

Creative tips and techniques

Burrows saw his work very much as a storyteller. His colleague at *Life*, Milton Orshefsky, recalled how Larry "saw not only in single pictures, but also how a set of pictures could be developed logically into a story line." "Yankee Papa 13" is a classic day-in-the-life feature, albeit with a more violent outcome than most. However, in its structure and narrative drive it offers a case study in how to use horizontal and vertical shots, and a mix of wide and close-ups, to give visual pace and energy. Burrows was aware that the story was always driven by human relationships. If you are shooting a similar story, try not to take every image from the same camera position and viewpoint, vary the distance from the subject, and shoot at least 10–20 percent of the images as verticals—the format for a magazine cover.

In a supply shack, hands covering his face, an exhausted, worn James Farley gives way to grief 1965

In the spring of 1965, shortly after the arrival of 3,500 US Marines in Vietnam—marking a major escalation of the war with the commitment of US ground troops—Larry Burrows joined the US Marines' Helicopter Squadron 163 with the plan to follow one of its crew on a mission to document the life of a typical marine. He chose Lance Corporal James Farley as his subject, the door gunner of a UH-34D helicopter codenamed YP13, for which the call sign was Yankee Papa 13. Neither man was aware of how dramatic the day would turn out to be nor of the impact that the story Burrows shot would have. When it ran across the cover and fourteen pages of *Life* magazine two weeks later, the story began: "On this day [Burrows] would be riding in Farley's machine and both were wondering whether the mission would be a no-contact milk run or whether, as had been increasingly the case in recent weeks, the Vietcong would be ready and waiting with 30-caliber machine guns." The unit came under sustained ground fire from the Vietcong; Burrows wrote in his text: "We were all like sitting ducks and their raking crossfire was murderous." Another of the unit's helicopters had crash landed under fire and the crew of YP13 landed close by to try to evacuate casualties. Bullet holes had ripped both left and right of his seat.

Burrows described the scene as they tried to take off after picking up two badly wounded crew: "The plexiglas had been shot out of the cockpit and one V.C. bullet had nicked our pilot's neck. Our radio and instruments were out of commission. We climbed and climbed fast the hell out of there." Burrows kept photographing as the troops desperately battled to save the life of the co-pilot of the other chopper: "Farley began bandaging Magel's wound. The wind from the doorway kept whipping the bandages across his face. Then blood started to come from his nose and mouth and a glazed look came into his eyes. Farley tried mouth-to-mouth resuscitation, but Magel was dead. Nobody said a word." After they landed back at base, Burrows photographed Farley as he finally broke down, overcome with the emotion and stress of losing his comrade.

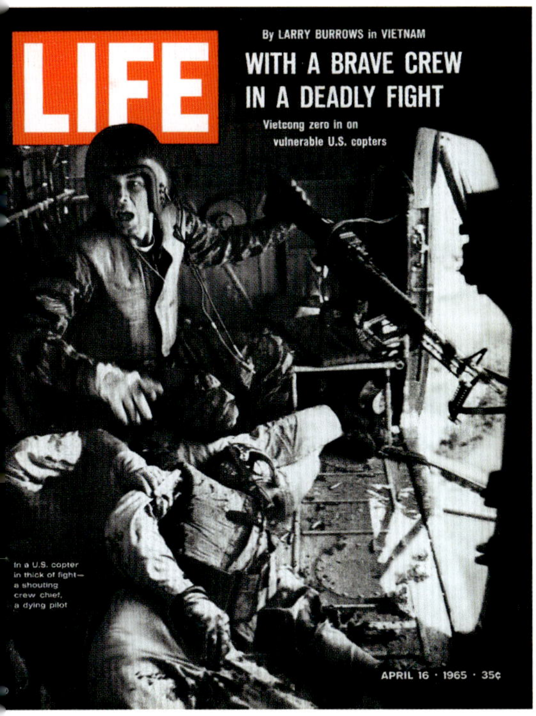

Burrows was a master craftsman, who was obsessed with having exactly the right equipment for the job. He typically worked with four cameras—two Leica rangefinders with wide-angle lenses and two Nikons with telephotos. For the story on YP13, he mounted the 21mm wide-angle lens of a Nikon onto the outside of the helicopter in advance, so that he could show Farley behind his machine gun and relate him to the terrain below. Burrows even had his own special combat jacket made, with multiple pockets so that he could store his equipment. He invented a system of straps and webbing that meant he could lift his camera out of the way with only one hand when crossing rivers.

Learning how to shoot strong verticals is important for reportage. Often, a telephoto lens is used to isolate a figure or face in a scene. However, as in these images by Burrows, a wider lens can also be used to relate the foreground and background together; the open door in the image on the left suggests the world outside that Farley must return to. In the cover image on the right, the framing makes the viewer feel as if they are in the helicopter with the crew, with the body of the wounded soldier leading the eye to Farley's face; the machine gun then leads the eye out of the door.

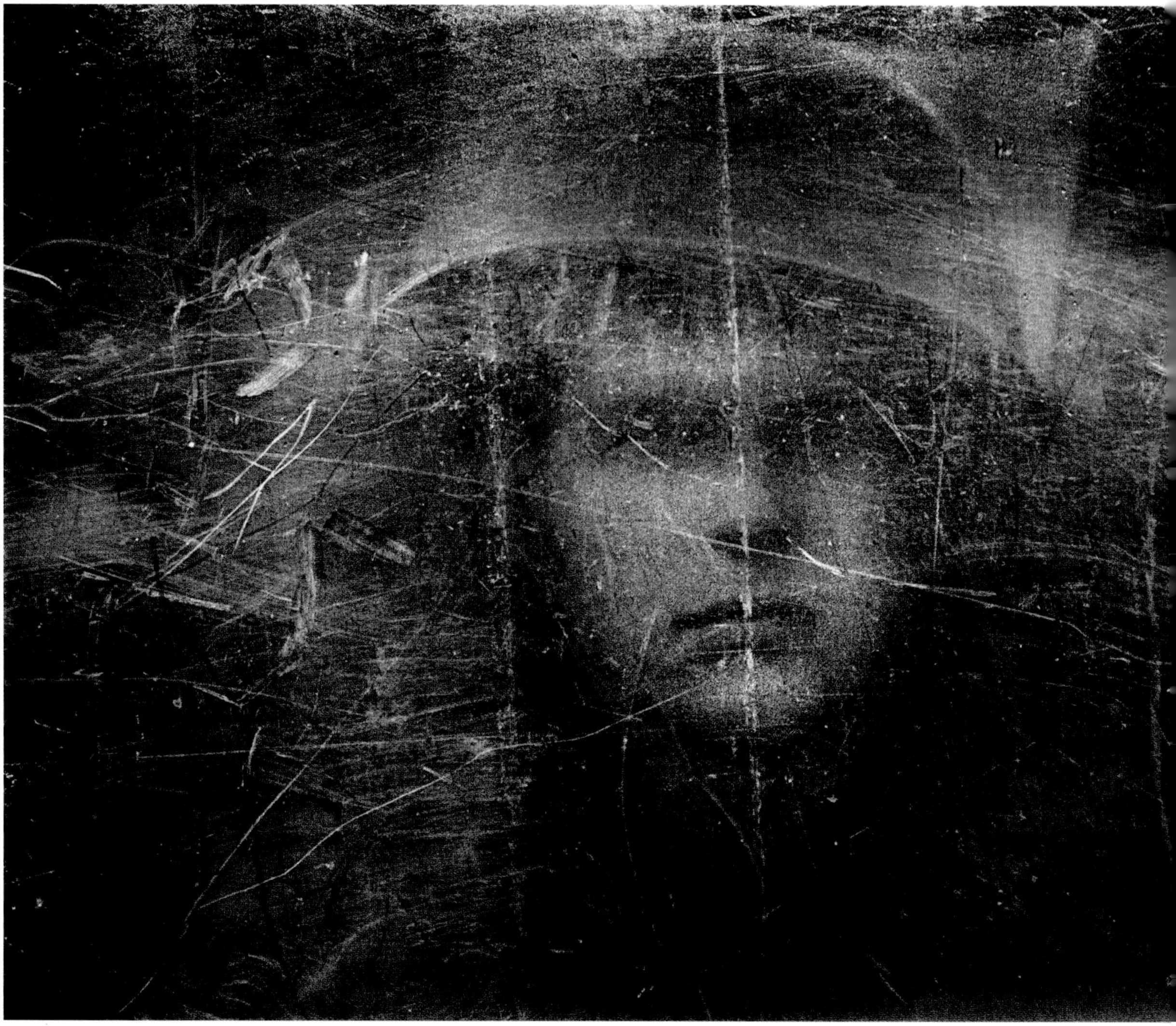

Soldier with bulletproof shield, Northern Ireland 1973

This powerful image was selected by Philip Jones Griffiths as the cover for his retrospective monograph on war, *Dark Odyssey* (1996). The original caption demonstrates his dry wit and intelligence: "Since ancient times, the shield has presented a challenge to military designs—how to see the enemy without sacrificing protection. The latest development is one made of Plexiglas. Unfortunately, it affords a dimmed visibility after repeated blows." Griffiths sought to convey the impact that conflict has on all those who are affected by it, civilians and soldiers alike, commenting that, "All wars depend on de-humanizing the 'enemy'—the foreign 'other.' I've tried to concentrate on showing the human face of conflict."

Griffiths spent a lot of time with soldiers, and although he usually disagreed vehemently with their presence in the countries he worked in, he was aware of the complexity of young men who go to war. He wrote: "I've spent lots of time with soldiers and my attitude, to quote a pulpitism, was to: 'Love the sinner, hate the sin.' I never underestimated their capacity for violence, but by being honest I was always treated fairly. Sometimes I had to work at winning them ove and some became friends. My objective was not to allow my positive feelings toward them as individuals to cloud the fact that they were prosecuting a genocidal war." Griffiths strongly believed that the role of the photojournalist was to effect change and to point attention to the misdeeds of governments, maintaining: "To me, there is no point in pressing the shutter unless you are making some caustic comment on the incongruities of life. That is what photography is all about. It is the only reason for doing it."

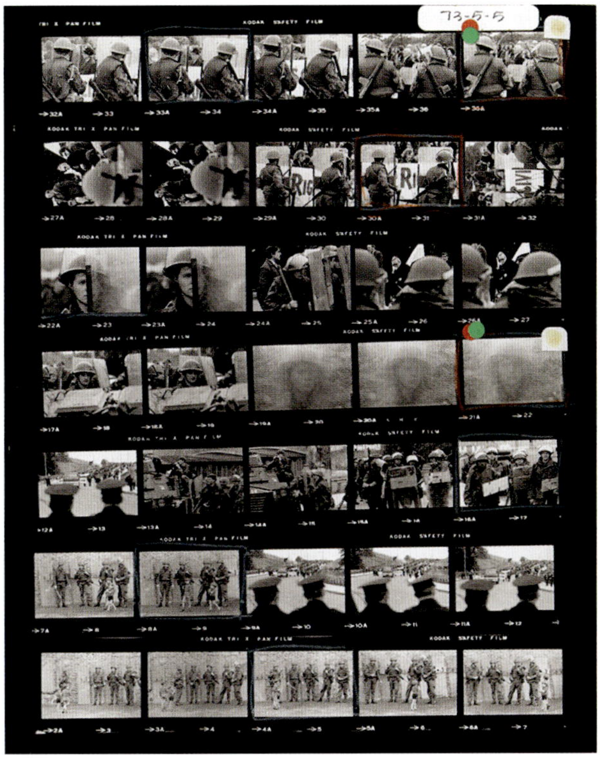

attempt to channel my anger into the tip of my orefinger as I press the shutter." Philip Jones Griffiths

hilip Jones Griffiths (British, 1936–2008) was great chronicler of conflict. He brought a keen ense of politics and a penetrating, often humorous nalysis of the situation to his work, supporting is images with dense captions that revealed ne context of the situation. He initially trained s a chemist, and the rigor of that profession emained with him. He noted: "Pharmacy teaches ou a lot about rationality, about logic and cause and effect. Of course you respond emotionally—all Welshmen respond emotionally—but at the same time there is an overlay, a sort of explanation of why you feel the way you feel." His Welsh heritage was key to his identity, and gave him an affinity with other small nations. He had a long relationship with the people of South East Asia and made a series of books that dealt with the conflict there, including *Vietnam Inc.* (1971).

Creative tips and techniques

Griffiths was passionately committed to journalism, but felt that acting as a witness to history was also an important function; he believed that "Even if not a single picture is ever published, they exist. And that means that we are recording the history of the human race." He acknowledged that one has to be able to moderate one's emotions in order to work in difficult situations as a journalist, emphasizing that the ability to keep things in perspective is very important.

The contact sheet for this photograph (near left) shows how Griffiths explored his subject, finding a theme in the soldiers with their shields and figuring out how he might make the strongest image. He claimed he never held the camera to his eye for more than three seconds to take a picture and sought that moment when story and aesthetics come together. You can see how he worked the situation, initially shooting from behind the line of troops, but then moving in front of them.

Griffiths shot through Plexiglas and, when the young man looked toward him, he made the final shot of a short sequence, producing the image here. He then played with juxtaposing the RUC (Royal Ulster Constabulary) officers against the distant crowd, using their hats as a framing device. He switches between this shot and one of the soldiers lined up against the wall with the children in front of them, probably standing in one spot and turning from side to side to shoot the two situations, keeping an eye on each as the scene changes. This shows how totally different images can be made from exactly the same physical position.

Gilles Peress

Gilles Peress (French, 1946–) began working in photography in 1970, after studying political science and philosophy in Paris. He joined Magnum Photos in 1971, and along with Susan Meiselas (see p.272) was regarded as one of the "new photojournalists" who emerged in the 1970s with a more personal, subjective viewpoint. He identifies that his "subject has always had to do with a struggle of individuals in a historical context. And about how individual memories interact with history, how individual perceptions interact with the larger landscape of history. And, if I'm being candid with myself, I bring to all this my own historical baggage." His long-term project "Hate Thy Brother" has explored the experience of societies riven by internal conflict and violence. He maintains that "war is about dislocation, fragmentation—dislocation of communities, of families—fragmentation of bodies, which means that somebody next to you one minute is gone the next."

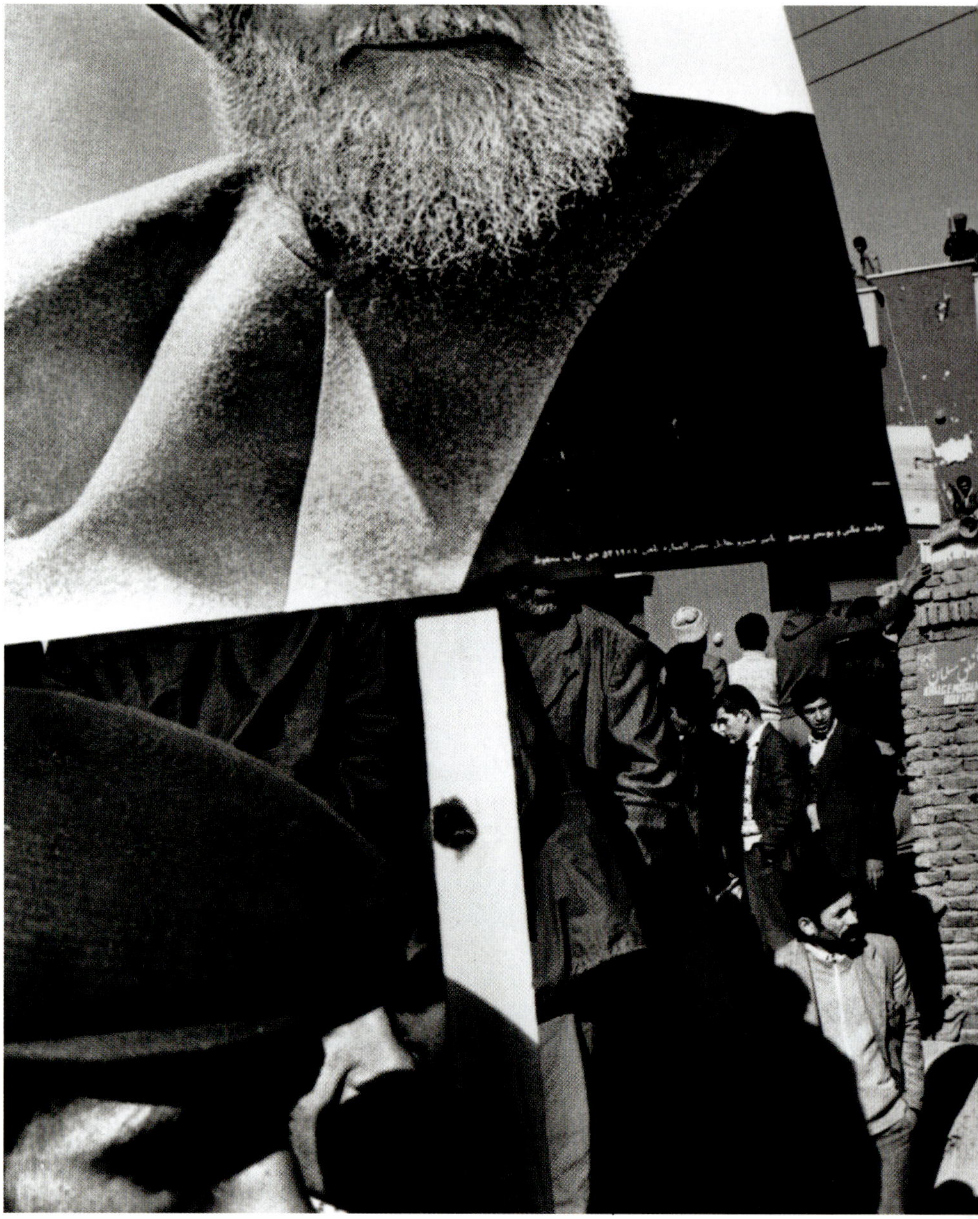

Creative tips and techniques

Peress explains that he approaches a new subject by feeling his way into the situation experientially. He tries to avoid beginning with preconceived ideas of the end result. He explains that for him the whole process involves going on an assignment, spending time trying to understand his subject and then doubting his own understanding, but through doubting himself he reaches a kind of objectivity. He then returns, edits his pictures, lives with them, and puts his books together. He notes that it is only at the end, once the book is made, that he has a sense of what it is he went through, externally and internally. He describes it as a "painful" process.

Peress is very eloquent in describing the relationship between photographer and subject and how this is mediated by the camera. He maintains that a "photograph has a multiplicity of authors the photographer, the camera, each has a different voice, a Leica with 28mm, a Nikon with a 24mm, everything speaks, cameras speak. Then there is reality and reality always speaks with a vengeance, with a very forceful voice." He is also extremely aware that photography operates in relatio to other forms of expression, and that it is

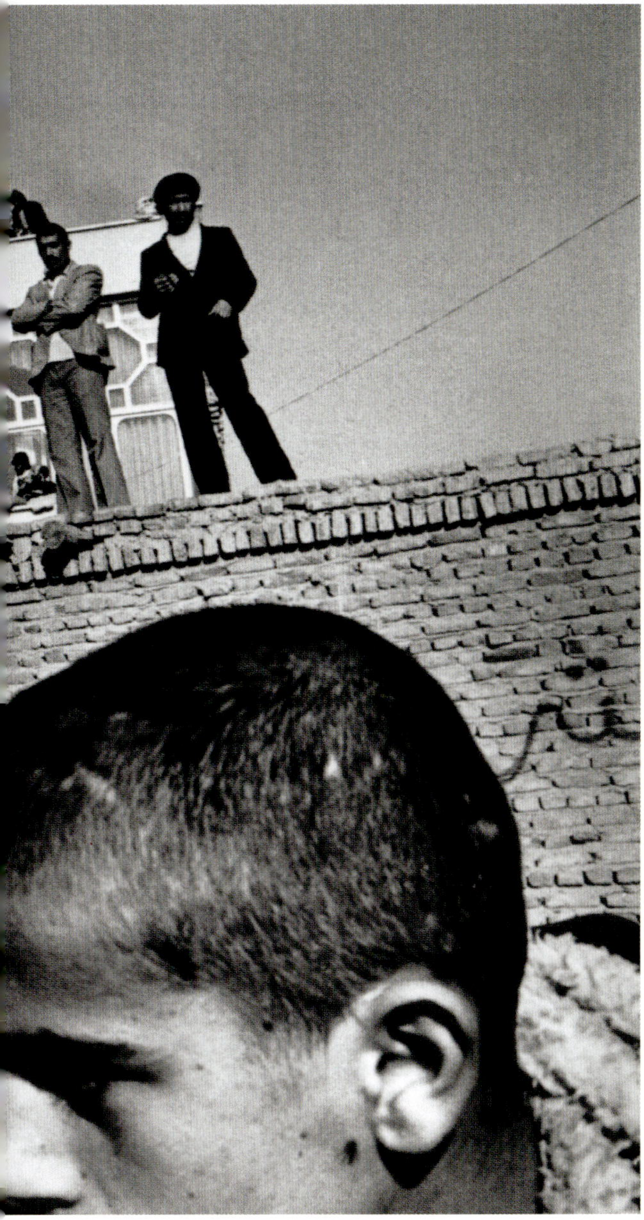

Tabriz, Iran—A demonstration in favour of the leading opposition figure, Ayatollah Kazem Shariatmadari 1980

This complex image appeared on the cover of Gilles Peress's seminal work *Telex Iran* (1978), for which he used radical cropping and framing to emphasize his sense of uncertainty about the events unfolding before him during the Iranian Revolution. The frame is broken up into four quarters; each contains its own internal visual narrative, with the mouth and chin of the cropped head of the boy on the right and the beard of the cleric on the left forming a visual puzzle to be solved by the viewer. This complexity has meaning, however; it is not simply a formal exercise in visual gymnastics. Peress acknowledges that major political and social events cannot be reduced to the simplistic narratives of mainstream news, and instead he tries to visualize the intricacies of such monumental events. He argues: "When I looked at reality, I saw contradictions, confrontations between different meanings, different processes, different individual histories, all occurring at the same time. At a practical level, I've always tried to break the frame in little, physical ways, to reflect those contradictions."

Peress sees the photographic image as a unique form of communication, and he argues that a complex image can encourage the audience to try to decipher its meaning: "Photography, because of its stillness, provides a private moment in which people can sort out their own feelings from within, without the headlines of magazines, without the captions, without the univocalness of news images that have one meaning only." Peress's method is to experience the story at first hand, observing every element of it and trying to make sense of what he sees and feels, no matter how small or grand the narrative.

the boundaries between genres and art rms that the most interesting and citing moments occur. He argues: "What's teresting about photography is when it cates itself at the convergence of various rms of expression and reality. I was never terested in what was happening within e defined territory of the medium, but stead, in the no-man's land between otography and other genres—literature, nema, painting."

Peress argues that any pretence at objectivity as a starting position is flawed, but that through an ongoing process of self-questioning, a form of authenticity in the situation can be established. Essentially this means that you should find your own perspective on events, constantly question the world around you, including sources of news and information, and not accept things at face value.

"I don't care so much anymore about "good photography"; I am gathering evidence for history." Gilles Peress

Anthony Suau

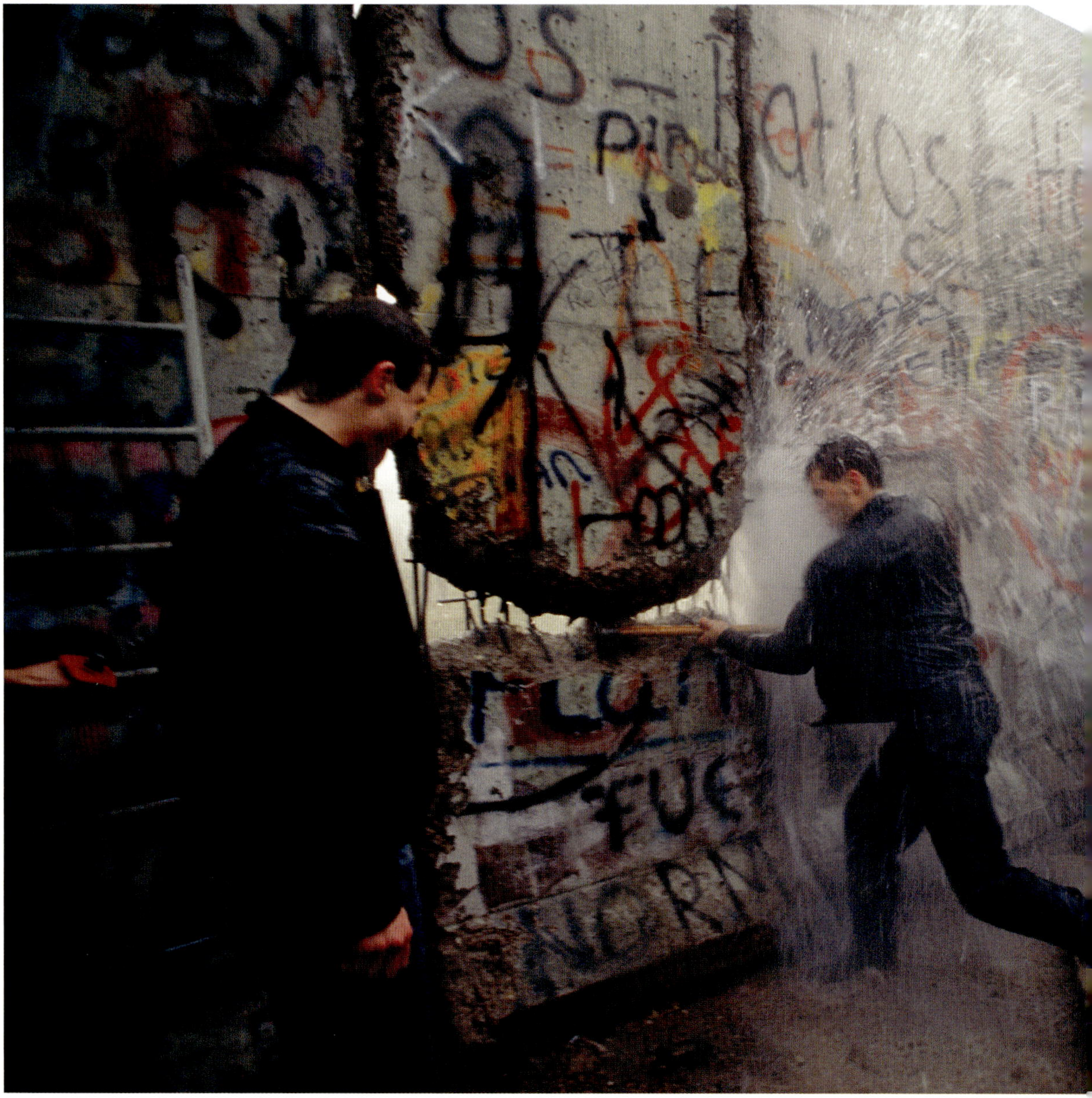

"I think a picture shows what words fail to describe... [photography] has the tendency to be more honest, especially for depicting history." Anthony Suau

Antony Suau (American, 1956–) has won many awards, including two World Press Photo of the Year awards, a Pulitzer Prize for his images of the famine in Ethiopia, and the Robert Capa Gold Medal for his coverage of the war in Chechnya. Suau was one of the co-founders of the collective project "Facing Change: Documenting America," established in 2009 to document the impact of the economic recession on the lives of Americans. In 2013 he produced a documentary film about the crisis in food production in the United States, entitled *Organic Rising* (2013).

Creative tips and techniques

Suau has developed a series of large-scale projects, spanning years of work and covering major social, economic, and political issues. This process involves a huge amount of behind-the-scenes work, but also brings substantial benefits for the photographer. He admits that big projects are literally about fundraising

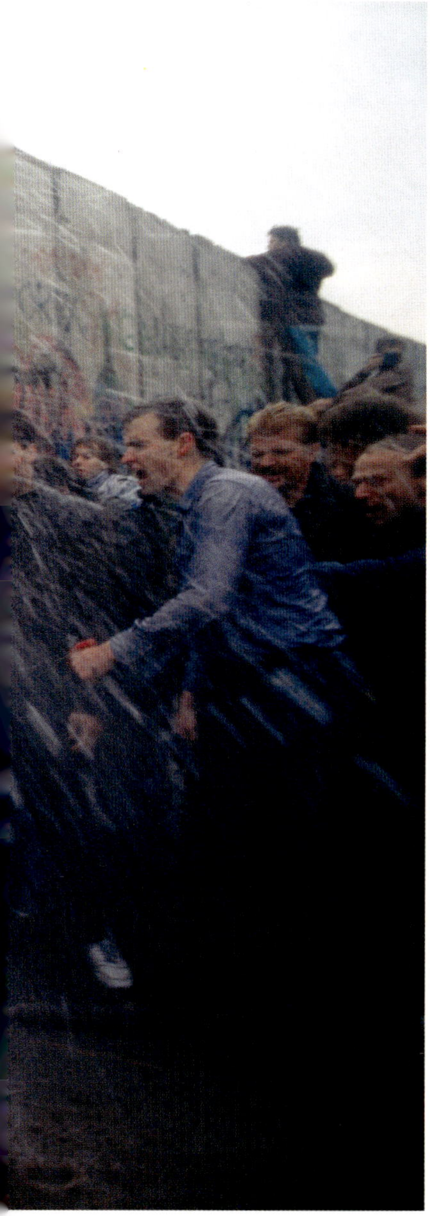

Fall of the Berlin Wall 1989

This photograph by Anthony Suau encapsulates the essence of a historical moment, capturing its drama and energy. The wide-angle lens brings us right into the action, as does the water spraying over the camera lens, as citizens of Berlin destroy the hated symbol of division. Suau was aware of the monumental event that was unfolding before him in November 1989, recalling that "there was definitely a sense that the fall of the Berlin Wall was something special, an enormous event in history that was going to change the world." He was conscious also, however, of the immense effect it would have on the ordinary people living through it, and acknowledges that the event had a deep impact on him, too. He recalls how such events are always very emotional: "it's not like you can separate yourself from these on a human level, you are living through those moments too, you are looking at it through a camera but you are human, they affect you, they have a profound effect on how you see the world going forward... emotionally it was so powerful that I was having a very hard time on the first day because I was crying so much."

After photographing the unification of Germany in 1989 Suau embarked on a ten-year project, "Beyond the Fall," exploring the transformation of the former Soviet bloc across Eastern Europe. Looking back, he recognizes how valuable this documentation of historical change can be to the generations that follow. He explains that when he exhibited the work in Moscow he was "completely surprised by the response. I did not even consider the fact that the work I had done ten or fifteen years ago would have such a big impact on a young audience. The Russia that I photographed has literally disappeared for these young people, and they have not seen the Russia of the past. I think when you originally take the photograph you do not think what will happen to this image ten or twenty years down the line."

nd finding the right backers to support iem. However, he relishes the artistic eedom this then gives him to make work ee from the constraints of magazines.

Suau has also begun to work in documentary film, and feels that is medium greatly expands his ability to ddress the issues he feels passionately bout. He describes how he can "use sound nd motion, to bring all of those elements together. I make my photographs in the same way but I can add sound, music, motion, I fly a drone, use a Go-pro. I'm collecting these amazing images and then bringing that together with a great story that you can tell." Suau says that he feels great excitement at the possibilities of film, with its "huge white canvas to build and build and build the story, using these timelines to create the most important way of communicating in our culture."

Using a wide-angle lens allows you to work very close to the subject and fill the frame with action, making the viewer feel as if they are a part of the event. A 28 or 24mm lens is ideal; anything wider risks distortion, especially at the edges. In eventful situations, photographers need to be aware of their safety, as it is easy to become so absorbed in what is in front of the lens that you forget what is around you.

Susan Meiselas

"For me the essence of documentary photography has always had to do with evidence..." Susan Meiselas

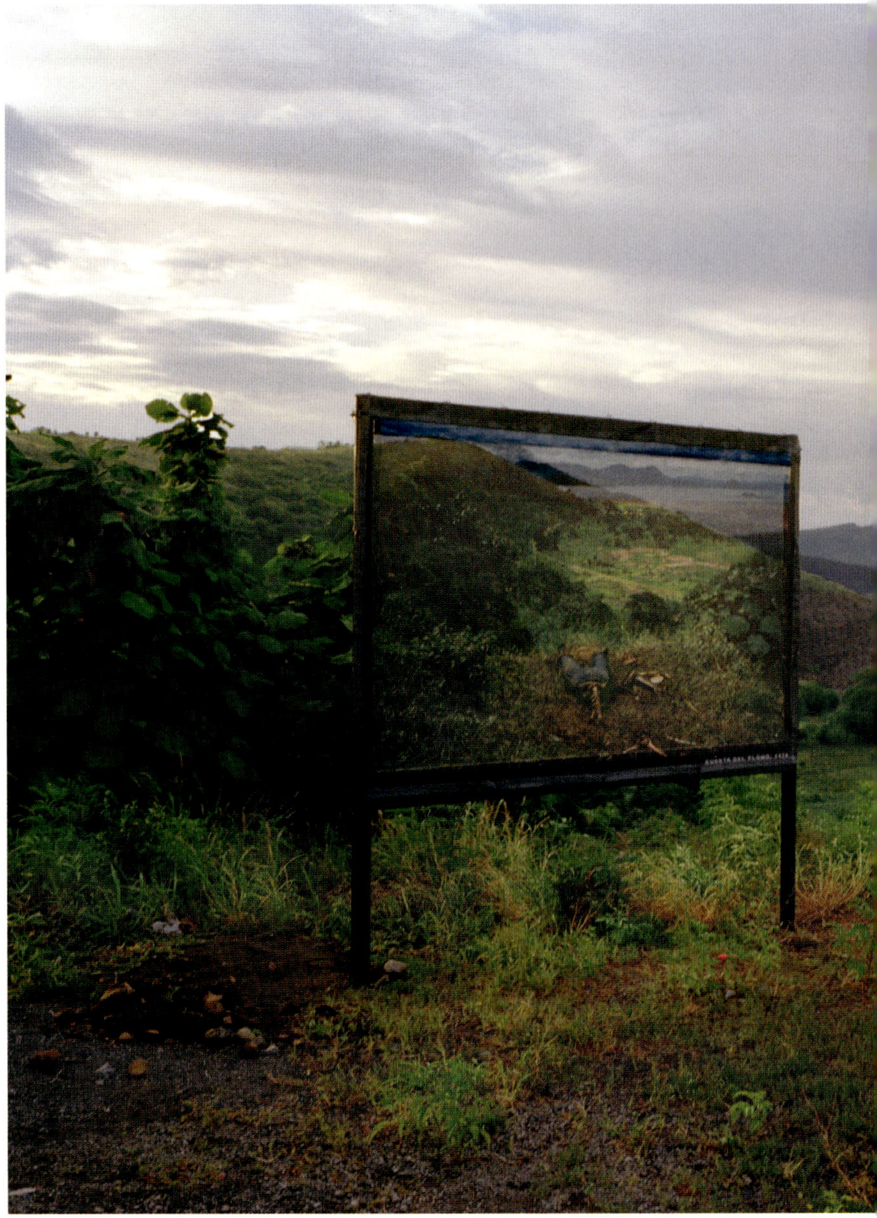

Susan Meiselas's (American, 1948–) first major project was *Carnival Strippers* (1976), which explored the lives of women working in striptease at New England country fairs. She joined Magnum Photos in 1976 and, along with Gilles Peress (see p.268), was identified as one of the new breed of "concerned" photojournalists in the late 1970s and early 1980s. Critic Andy Grundberg described them as "more interested in the complexity of issues and events, and in conveying the flavor of their experience of them, than in producing easily digested, simple-to-understand images." Much of Meiselas's work has focused on human rights issues, especially in Latin America, and on the relationship between photography and the history of communities, which she explored in *Kurdistan: In the Shadow of History* (1997). She was awarded a MacArthur Fellowship in 1992.

Creative tips and techniques

Meiselas sees herself as one voice among many, but argues that such a perspective is a necessary one, maintaining that she enjoys putting herself "in a timeline of image-makers, alongside other travelers, such as anthropologists, colonists, missionaries, even tourists. . .I see myself as only one of many storytellers." She is aware that one single image cannot tell the whole story, but that it can be linked to a series to generate greater understanding. When working, she does not enter into it with a predetermined sense of what the story should be. Instead, she allows her personal response to the situation to determine its significant features. At times, rather than going on assignment, she chooses to go to a place simply because she feels that whatever is happening there is important.

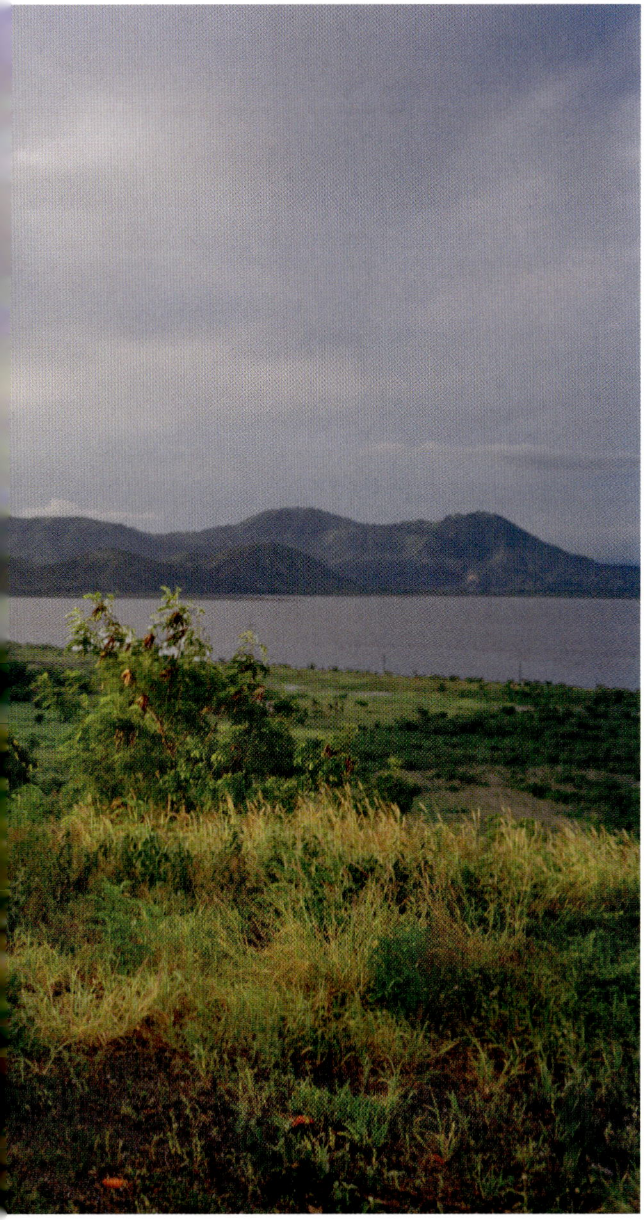

Managua, Nicaragua 2004, from "Re-framing History"

Susan Meiselas is fascinated by the process of history and how images play a part in shaping perceptions of the past in the present. The photograph inside the frame in this image originally featured in the groundbreaking book *Nicaragua* (1981), in which she documented the Sandinista Revolution. Meiselas identifies the moment of taking the original photograph in 1978 as a key one in her understanding of events. While driving around Cuesta del Plomo, a hillside outside Managua, she spotted a corpse, half-eaten by vultures. She explains: "the images I made of the body were powerful partly because of the contrast with the beauty of the landscape. For me [the photo] was the link to understanding why the people of Nicaragua were so outraged. . .the American public could not relate their reality to this image. They simply could not account for what they saw." Her use of color and her subjective approach brought a new energy to photojournalism.

Meiselas returned to Nicaragua in 2004 for the twenty-fifth anniversary of the revolution to mount an outdoor installation of images from her book, presented as giant, poster-sized murals situated at the exact locations where the original images were made. One example is the final photograph of the original image re-embedded into the landscape shown here. The "Reframing History" project involved working with local communities to create sites for collective memory. Meiselas is aware that her motivations for making images and disseminating them also change with time, as the function of the photograph shifts from its value as a newsworthy commodity to one that is linked to the historical process. She feels that it was significant to bring the photographs back to Nicaragua twenty-five years after she first took them but adds: "I wasn't prescient enough to be aware of that while I was making them; it only made sense when I'd lived that history in some sense."

Meiselas explains how the process of editing can reveal the essence of the [si]tuation. She describes looking at contact [sh]eets as "a great set of footprints" from [w]hich to assess whether you found the [ri]ght frame. She notes: "suddenly you find [the] frame and it just seems to be there, it just [se]ems to know itself and sort of reveal itself."

Meiselas feels part of a tradition of encounter and witness in her documentary photography, which is often based on a concern about human rights violations. She articulates the self-reflexivity necessary in this role in her understanding of the limitations in the act of witnessing, claiming that the "other side of 'witness' is that we do intervene, and we intervene by the fact of our presence in a particular place. We change how people see themselves sometimes and how others may come to see them. I'm also concerned about how we see ourselves in the process of our role as witnesses.'" Meiselas believes in the role of the camera as a passport to engage with the world, observing that "it gives me both a point of connection and a point of separation." However, she is also highly aware that the final photograph is only part of the equation, and that it needs to be related to broader social and political contexts in order for it to make sense.

David Burnett

Alistair Brownlee winning the triathlon, London Olympics 2012

In this iconic image of sporting prowess, David Burnett emphasizes the theatricality of the sporting arena by making it look like a model. The use of differential focus transforms the scene into a spectacular celebration of the moment of victory, placing all attention on the victorious athlete as he breaks the tape to win the gold medal. Although Burnett is not a specialist sports photographer, he has covered eight summer Olympics since 1984 as a feature photographer. Sport, with its drama, characters, and visual impact, has rich potential for "behind the scenes" shots that go beyond the action. Burnett has this advice: "Sport photography can be very challenging; it is easy to take interesting action pictures, but taking the picture to the next level gets to be very complicated. It requires a certain understanding of what is going to happen so that you can anticipate." He explains that the Olympics is the pinnacle of sport not only for athletes but also for photographers, remarking that there is "something addictive about the Olympics that we photographers share with the rest of the world. The collection of the best athletes in one place provides an opportunity for us to try and do our best—the Photographers' Olympics, too, it seems."

When working, Burnett tries to find a point of view from which he can interpret events in his own way. Rather than positioning himself down at the track in the middle of the action, he looks instead for a different vantage point from which he can get a more interpretative image that will make his photographs stand out from the rest. He feels that "the hardest thing, no matter the gear, is to force yourself to see things in a slightly different way. And don't go to the finish line, go to the third turn where nothing ever happens and try to make a picture there." Part of his approach is to use a Graflex Speed Graphic camera, which he argues "forces me to see things differently, and taking into account the difficulties which accompany a big camera (lack of stealth, slow operation, remembering to do all the right things in a particular order) that kind of painting yourself into a corner can have some advantages. You see things you might have missed."

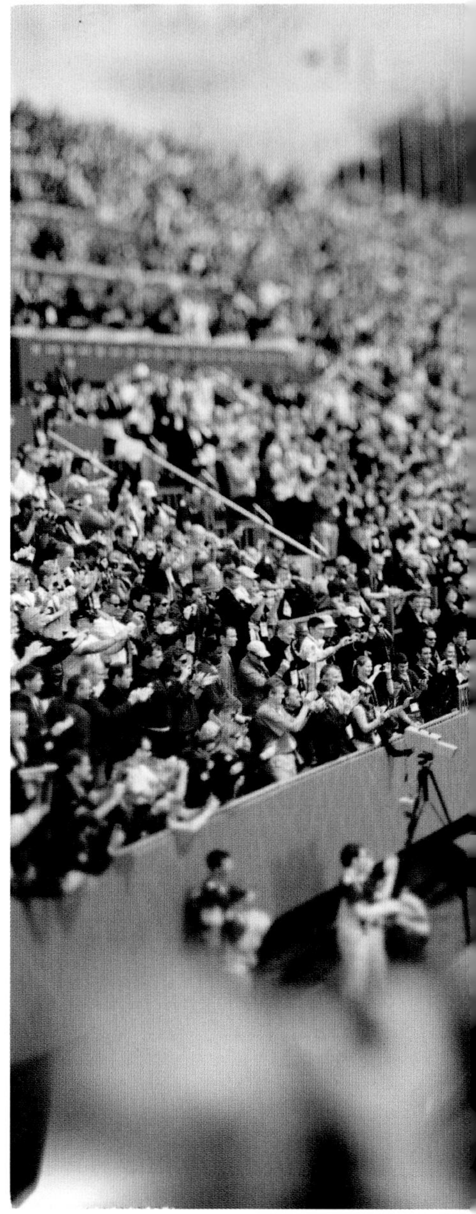

"I don't do a lot of sports coverage in between the Olympics. For me, it's more than a sports event. I'm always trying to make some bigger contextual view of it." David Burnett

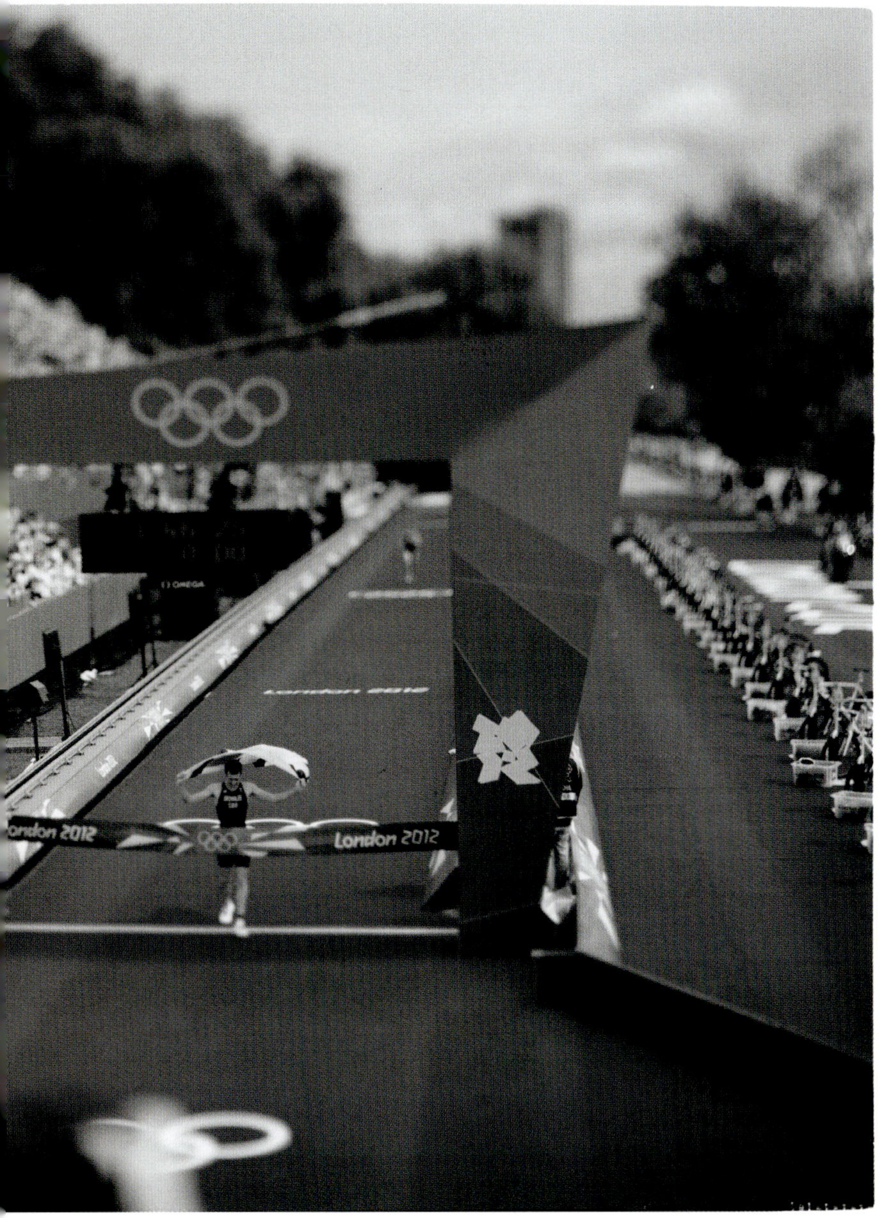

avid Burnett (American, 1946–) is one of ıe most experienced photojournalists in the usiness. He has covered news and feature stories om the Vietnam War onward and has won ımerous awards, including the Robert Capa old Medal and the World Press Photo of the ear. In 1975 he co-founded Contact Press Images ith Robert Pledge, in New York City. For the st three decades he has traveled extensively, orking for most of the major magazines in ıe United States and Europe. He is constantly esponding to technical changes in the industry, always looking forward not back, as he jokes: "When you've lived through the golden age of photojournalism, there's no point in being nostalgic." He has photographed eight winter and summer Olympics since 1984, when he made an iconic shot of US track athlete Mary Decker falling during the final of the women's 3,000 metres. Latterly Burnett has used large-format cameras to give a different perspective to his coverage, seeking the "satisfaction that comes from working next to 500 photographers and coming away with something different."

Creative tips and techniques

While Burnett celebrates the speed and ease of use of digital cameras, he also feels that some of the craft of photography has been lost, especially because of the downside of being able to see the image immediately on the screen on the back of the camera. He recommends the experience of shooting film as you "will benefit from having a lack of assurance and embracing the lack of certitude, which film necessarily delivers." He has an excellent suggestion to help develop your vision: "put a piece of gaffer tape over the screen on your camera, and shoot like a film photographer for a day or a week. You'll be angry, you'll be frustrated, but if you live through it for a week, watch how much better your pictures start to become. And in the end, that is what it's all about."

Burnett uses the camera movement of his field camera to create this tilt shift effect, where only a shallow plane of the image is in focus, creating the effect of isolating the main subject and making the image look almost like a model miniature. He works with his Speed Graphic wide open, as he explains: "I have usually f2.8 or 4. I tend to like the way the wide apertures isolate the subject; it gives you a little bit of technical advantage in terms of trying to cut the subject out from everything around it." The same effect can be obtained on a film or digital SLR by using a tilt shift lens or in post-processing using the new tilt shift focus filter in Photoshop. Several iPhone apps also offer this filter, and the results can be visually arresting. This approach works well when the initial photograph is taken from a high vantage point looking down on the subject, as in this image.

Bibliography

Adams, Ansel, *Examples: The Making of 40 Photographs*, Little, Brown, 1989

Adams, Ansel, *Ansel Adams: 400 Photographs*, Little, Brown, 2013

Adams, Robert, *Why People Photograph: Selected Essays and Reviews*, Aperture, 2005

Adams, Robert, *The New West*, Joshua Chang (ed.), Steidl Verlag, 2016

Allard, William Albert, *William Albert Allard: Five Decades*, National Geographic Society, 2010

Arbaïzar, Philippe, *Henri Cartier-Bresson: The Man, the Image and the World: A Retrospective*, Thames & Hudson, 2003

Arnold, Eve, *All About Eve*, teNeues Verlag GmbH + Co KG, 2012

Barnard, Lisa, *Hyenas of the Battlefield, Machines In the Garden*, GOST Books, 2015

Beaton, Cecil, *Beaton: Photographs*, Jonathan Cape, 2015

Becher, Bernd and Hilla, *Typologies of Industrial Buildings*, MIT Press, 2004

Benedict-Jones, Linda, *Storyteller: The Photographs of Duane Michals*, Prestel, 2014

Billingham, Richard, *Ray's a Laugh*, Errata Editions, 2014

Brothers, Caroline, *War and Photography: A Cultural History*, Routledge, 1997

Brookman, Philip, *Helios: Eadweard Muybridge in a Time of Change*, Steidl Verlag, 2010

Burrows, Larry, *Vietnam*, Knopf, 2002

Callahan, Harry, *Harry Callahan*, Kehrer Verlag, 2013

Campany, David (ed.), *Art and Photography*, Phaidon, 2012

Capa, Cornell (ed.), *The Concerned Photographer 1 and 2*, International Center of Photography, 1968 and 1972

Capa, Robert, *Slightly Out of Focus*, Modern Library, 1999

Crewdson, Gregory and Lethem, Jonathan, *Gregory Crewdson*, Rizzoli, 2013

Davies, John, *The British Landscape*, Chris Boot, 2006

Dijkstra, Rineke, *Portraits*, Schirmer/Mosel, 2005

Eggleston, William, *William Eggleston's Guide*, The Museum of Modern Art, New York, 2002

Erwitt, Elliott, *Elliott Erwitt's Dogs*, teNeues Media GmbH + Co., 2008

Erwitt, Elliott, *Personal Best*, teNeues Media GmbH + Co., 2014 (Mul edition)

Evans, Walker, *American Photographs*, Museum of Modern Art, New York, 1989

Frank, Robert, *The Americans*, Secker & Warburg, 1989

Fraser, Peter, *Peter Fraser*, Tate Publishing, 2013

Fulton, Marianne, *Eyes of Time: Photojournalism in America*, Little, Brown, 1988

Gernsheim, Helmut and Alison, *Roger Fenton: Photographer of the Crimean War*, Secker & Warburg, 1954

Gilden, Bruce, *Facing New York*, Dewi Lewis Publishing, 2002

Goldberg, Vicki, *The Power of Photography: How Photographs Changed Our Lives*, Abbeville Press, 1991

Goldin, Nan, *The Ballad of Sexual Dependency*, Aperture, 2014

Graham, Paul, *Troubled Land*, Cornerhouse Publications, 1990

Griffin, Brian, *Work*, Central Books Ltd, 1989

Gursky Andreas, *Andreas Gursky*, The Museum of Modern Art, New York, 2002

Harvey, David Alan, *Divided Soul: A Journey Through the Hispanic Diaspora*, Phaidon, 2003

Heron, Liz and Williams, Val (eds), *Illuminations: Women Writing on Photography from the 1850s to the Present*, Tauris, 1996

Hurn, David and Jay, Bill, *On Being a Photographer*, LensWork Publishing, 2001

Jeffrey, Ian, *Photography: A Concise History*, Thames & Hudson, 1981

Jones Griffiths, Philip, *Vietnam Inc.*, Macmillan, 1971

Jones Griffiths, Philip, *Dark Odyssey*, Aperture, 1996

Jurovics, Toby, *Framing the West: The Survey Photographs of Timothy H. O'Sullivan*, Yale University Press, 2010

Kander, Nadav, *Bodies 6 Women 1 Man: Inner Condition*, Hatje Cantz, 2012

Killip, Chris, *In Flagrante Two*, Steidl Verlag, 2016

Klein, William, *William Klein, ABC*, Tate Publishing, 2012

Klett, Mark, *Third Views, Second Sights: A Rephotographic Survey of the American West*, Museum of New Mexico Press, 2004

Koetzle, Hans-Michael, *Eyes Wide Open! 100 Years of Leica Photography*, Kehrer Verlag, 2015

Koudelka, Josef, *Gypsies*, Thames & Hudson, 2011

Koudelka, Josef, *Exiles*, Thames & Hudson, 2014

Leo, Patric and Stahel, Urs, *Anders Petersen*, Max Strom, 2013

Light, Ken (ed.), *Witness in Our Time, Working Lives of Documentary Photographers*, Smithsonian Institution Press, 2000

Linfield, Susan, *The Cruel Radiance: Photography and Political Violence*, University of Chicago Press, 2010

Lyon, Danny, *The Bikeriders*, Aperture, 2014

Mark, Mary Ellen, *25 Years*, Bulfinch Press, 1991

Mark, Mary Ellen, *Mary Ellen Mark: On the Portrait and the Moment* (The Photography Workshop Series), Aperture, 2015

Meiselas, Susan, *Nicaragua*, Random House Inc., 1981

Meiselas, Susan, *In History: Susan Meiselas and Documentary Photography*, Steidl Verlag, 2008

Meyerowitz, Joel, *Joel Meyerowitz: Retrospective*, D.A.P./Verlag Der Buchhandlung Walther König, 2014

Meyerowitz, Joel, *Cape Light*, Aperture, 2015
Meyerowitz, Joel and Westerbeck, Colin, *Bystander: A History of Street Photography*, Bulfinch Press, 1994
Miller, Russell, *Magnum: Fifty Years at the Front Line of History*, Pimlico, 1999
Misrach, Richard, *Violent Legacies*, Cornerhouse Publications, 1992
Model, Lisette, *Lisette Model*, Aperture, 2007
Morse, Rebecca, *Larry Sultan: Here and Home*, Prestel, 2014
Muir, Robin, *Norman Parkinson: Portraits in Fashion*, Palazzo Editions Ltd, 2015
Nachtwey, James, *Deeds of War*, Thames & Hudson, 1989
Nachtwey, James, *Inferno*, Phaidon, 2000
Nixon, Nicholas, *Nicholas Nixon: The Brown Sisters: Forty Years*, The Museum of Modern Art, New York, 2014
Nixon, Nicholas, *Nicholas Nixon: About Forty Years*, Fraenkel Gallery, 2015
Nordstrom, Alison, *Lewis Hine*, Distributed Art Publishers, 2012
Norfolk, Simon, *For Most of it I Have No Words*, Dewi Lewis, 1996
Norfolk, Simon, *Afghanistan: Chronotopia*, Dewi Lewis Publishing, 2002
Norfolk, Simon, *Bleed*, Dewi Lewis Publishing, 2005
Parr, Martin, *The Photobook: A History Volumes I, II, III*, Phaidon, 2004, 2009, 2014
Pellegrin, Paolo, *Kosovo: The Flight of Reason*, Trolley Books, 2002
Pellegrin, Paolo, *As I Was Dying*, Dewi Lewis Publishing, 2008
Peress, Gilles, *Farewell to Bosnia*, Scalo, 1994
Peress, Gilles, *The Silence – Rwanda*, Scalo, 1996
Peress, Gilles, *Telex Iran: In the Name of Revolution*, Scalo, 1998
Peress, Gilles, *The Graves: Srebrenica and Vukovar*, Scalo, 1998
Polidori, Robert, *Havana*, Steidl Verlag, 2001
Pyke, Steve, *Philosophers*, Oxford University Press, 2011
Rai, Raghu, *Raghu Rai's India: Reflections in Colour*, Haus Publishing, 2008
Ristelhueber, Sophie, *Operations*, Thames & Hudson, 2009
Rowell, Margit and Weinberg, Adam, *Ed Ruscha, Photographer*, Steidl Verlag, 2006
Rubinfien, Leo, *Garry Winogrand*, San Francisco Museum of Modern Art, 2013
Salgado, Sebastião, *Other Americas*, Pantheon, 1986
Salgado, Sebastião, *An Uncertain Grace*, Aperture, 1990
Sander, Gerd, *August Sander: People of the 20th Century*, Schirmer/Mosel Verlag GmbH, 2013
Sherman, Cindy, *The Complete Untitled Film Stills*, The Museum of Modern Art, New York, 2003
Sidibè, Malick, *The Portrait of Mali*, Skira Editore, 2012
Smith, W. Eugene, *Let Truth Be the Predujice*, Aperture, 1985
Soth, Alec, *Sleeping by the Mississippi*, Steidl Verlag, 2004
Soth, Alec, *Niagara*, Steidl Verlag, 2006
Southam, Jem, *Shape of Time: Rockfalls, Rivermouths, Ponds*, Photoworks, 1999
Sternfeld, Joel, *On This Site: Landscape in Memoriam*, Chronicle Books, 1996
Sternfeld, Joel, *American Prospects*, Distributed Art Publishers, 2004
Strand, Paul, *Paul Strand: Aperture Masters of Photography*, Aperture, 2014
Suau, Anthony, *Beyond the Fall: The Former Soviet Bloc in Transition, 1989–99*, Network Photographers, 2000
Sugimoto, Hiroshi, *Hiroshi Sugimoto*, Hatje Cantz, 2010
Sussman, Elisabeth, Doon Arbus et al, *Diane Arbus: Revelations*, Jonathan Cape, 2003
Szarkowski, John, *Atget*, The Museum of Modern Art, New York, 2004
Tillmans, Wolfgang, *Wolfgang Tillmans*, Taschen, 2011
Towell, Larry, *The World from My Front Porch*, Chris Boot, 2008
Wagstaff, Sheena, *Jeff Wall: Photographs 1978–2004*, Tate Publishing, 2005
Wallis, Brian, *Weegee: Murder is My Business*, Prestel, 2013
Wallace, Dougie, *Shoreditch Wild Life*, Hoxton Mini Press, 2014
Wallace, Dougie, *Stags Hens and Bunnies*, Dewi Lewis Publishing, 2014
Webb, Alex, *Hot Light/Half-made Worlds: Photographs from the Tropics*, Thames & Hudson, 1986
Webb, Alex, *Under a Grudging Sun: Photographs from Haiti Libere 1986–1988*, Thames & Hudson, 1989
Webb, Alex and Norris Webb, Rebecca, *On Street Photography and the Poetic Image* (The Photography Workshop Series), Aperture, 2014
Weiss, Marta (ed.), *Julia Margaret Cameron*, Mack, 2015
Wells, Liz (ed.), *The Photography Reader*, Routledge, 2003
Weston, Edward, *The Flame of Recognition*, Aperture, 2015
Weston, Edward, *The Daybooks of Edward Weston: Two Volumes in One I. Mexico II. California*, Aperture, 1990 (2nd edition)
Whelan, Richard and Capa, Cornell, *Robert Capa: The Definitive Collection*, Phaidon, 2001
Williams, Val, *Anna Fox: Photographs 1983–2007*, Photoworks, 2007
Williams, Val, *Martin Parr*, Phaidon, 2014
Wintour, Anna and Brown, Susanna, *Horst: Photographer of Style*, V & A Publishing, 2014

Glossary

35mm format
Introduced originally for cinema film in 1909, 35mm was soon adopted for still cameras and became the most widely used format, producing a negative or transparency measuring 35 x 24 mm. This format continues in "full frame" digital cameras.

Albumen print
A process of producing photographic prints by using paper coated in albumen from egg whites. It was first used in 1848 for coating glass plates.

Aperture
The opening through which light passes to expose sensitized material or a sensor. It is usually located behind or within a lens mount, originally as removable "stops" and later as an iris diaphragm. The size of the aperture is defined in f-numbers.

Backlighting
Describes lighting from a source behind the subject. It is usually used with other lights, but by itself it can separate the subject from a dark background or create a halo effect around it.

Calotype
A photographic process patented by William Henry Fox Talbot in England and Wales on 8 February 1841; also known as Talbotype. The process was a significant enhancement of Talbot's photogenic drawing process and used silver iodide combined with gallic acid to enhance its sensitivity. After exposure the paper was developed to produce a negative and then chemically fixed to make it permanent. The calotype was the first negative/positive process and it provided the basis of modern photography.

Chronophotography
A method of analysing movement by taking a series of still pictures at regular intervals. It was pioneered separately by Étienne-Jules Marey and Eadweard Muybridge, among others, from the early 1870s. In 1877, Muybridge was able to confirm by chronophotography Marey's assertion that a horse lifted all four hooves off the ground at once when trotting.

Close-up lens
A supplementary lens fitted to a camera lens that changes the focal length. For close-up work, a positive lens effectively shortens the focal length so that with a given lens-to-subject distance the near focusing limit is reduced.

Collodion process
A dry—or more commonly—a wet process using collodion as a medium to support a light-sensitive emulsion. The wet-collodion process was described by Frederick Scott Archer in 1851 and, after refinement, came into widespread use from around 1854. It remained dominant until the mid 1870s. Collodion was also used to produce direct positives on glass (ambrotypes) and tin (tintypes).

Collotype
A screenless printing process invented by Alphonse Poitevin in 1856 and commercially popular from the 1870s to the 1920s.

Combination printing
A technique using two or more photographic negatives or prints to make a single image. It was initially suggested by Hippolyte Bayard in 1852 for improving the appearance of skies. It was first shown by William Lake Price in 1855. O. G. Rejlander's *Two Ways of Life* of 1857 and Henry Peach Robinson's *Fading Away* of 1858 are the best-known examples. The technique was revived in the 1920s and 1930s when it was often employed to produce surreal work. Digital techniques have made it obsolete.

Cropping
Altering the boundaries of a photograph, negative or digital image to improve the composition, remove unwanted elements or to fit a method of display.

Darkroom
A space in which there is total darkness or limited illumination by red or orange safelights so that light-sensitive materials such as film or paper can be handled, processed or printed without being affected by unwanted light.

Depth of field
The zone of sharp focus seen in the camera. Manipulation of this zone by extending or reducing it is an important aspect of creative control and view cameras have evolved to facilitate this.

Digital print
This refers to a photograph produced from either a conventional negative or a digital file by a digital printer. It includes various fine art digital printing techniques, inkjet, and laser printing.

Documentary photography
A photographic depiction of the real world intended to show the subject in a literal and objective way. Early examples include the work of Maxime Du Camp in recording the Near East, Roger Fenton in the Crimea, and Mathew Brady in the American Civil War. An important sub-genre is social documentary photography, which records the human condition within a wider context. Examples range from Thomas Annan in Glasgow in the 1860s to Jacob Riis in the 1890s and the Farm Security Administration photographers of the 1930s in the United States.

Double exposure
The recording of two superimposed images on the same piece of photo-sensitive material. This may be through error or as part of the creative process.

Düsseldorf School
A group of students who studied at the Kunstakademie Düsseldorf in the mid 1970s under influential photographers Bernd and Hilla Becher, who produced clear, objective, black-and-white images of industrial structures. Among its best-known students are Thomas Struth and Andreas Gursky.

Dye-transfer print
This is a subtractive process for making color prints from color positives or negatives. There were processes from 1875 but Eastman Kodak's wash-off relief process of 1935—which was improved and reintroduced in 1946 as the dye-transfer process—was the most successful. Although complex it produced attractive permanent prints with strong colors.

Emulsion
A light-sensitive colloid usually of silver halide grains in a thin gelatin layer, and coated onto glass, film, or a paper base.

Exposure
The process of allowing light to act on a sensitive material. Within the camera this is controlled by the shutter and aperture.

Field camera
Usually refers to a large-format camera that can be folded to reduce its size, therefore making it easier to transport.

Fill flash
This is a technique used to reduce the contrast in a subject in harsh lighting or when the subject is backlit. Flash is combined with the main exposure, usually balanced to be one or two stops below the overall exposure to fill in the shadows.

Filter
An optical colored or neutral glass or plastic usually mounted in front of the camera lens. Most remove or reduce particular parts of the light spectrum; others such as neutral density or polarizing filters affect light absorption in other ways.

Fine art photography
Photographs that are made by a photographer as art work and usually intended to be offered for sale.

Flash
An electronic light source that adds light in very short bursts, typically 1/1000th to 1/200th of a second to help illuminate a scene. Many cameras have built-in flashes, but an accessory flash can be mounted on the camera or hot shoe or used off camera in a studio or location setting.

Focal length
The focal length of the lens is the distance between the lens and the image plane when the subject is in focus. It is usually described in millimetres, for example, 20mm, 50mm, 135mm. Zoom lenses are described by giving their minimum and maximum focal lengths, for example, 24–70mm.

Frame
A term that has a number of different meanings within photography. It can refer to a single image within a series on a length of film or a single digital image; a border made from one of a number of materials to enclose and protect a photograph; or the boundaries of a subject seen through a camera viewfinder.

F-stop
The f-stop, or relative aperture of a lens, is the ratio of the lens' focal length to the diameter of the aperture. It is a quantitative measure of lens speed and is an important concept in photography. For example, a fast lens suitable for shooting in low light would have a maximum f-stop of f1.4.

HDR
High-dynamic-range imaging (HDR or HDRI) reproduces a greater dynamic range of luminosity than is possible with standard digital imaging or photographic techniques. It is particularly useful in difficult lighting situations with high levels of contrast.

High-key image
The use of bright lighting to overexpose most or all the harsh shadows, giving a light feel to the final photograph.

Ink-jet print
A print made up from tiny droplets of ink being expelled onto paper using electromagnetic fields to guide charged ink streams. The technology was developed from the 1950s and for digital photographic printing from the 1970s.

JPEG file
A file format for digital images, where the degree of compression can be adjusted, allowing a choice between storage size and image quality. JPEG typically achieves 10:1 compression with little perceptible loss in image quality.

Kodachrome
A color transparency film introduced by Eastman Kodak in 1935 in 35mm, sheet and motion picture film formats. For many photographers it was the standard by which all other films were judged. Manufacture ceased in 2009.

Low-key image
A low-key photograph is structured predominantly from dark tones and colors, with reduced lighting and underexposure. Shadows and dark areas become the central element of the composition. Like high-key images, low-key photographs convey mood and atmosphere.

Macro lens
A macro lens focuses very close to the subject allowing extreme enlargements to be made, often more than life size.

Mammoth plate
An outsize plate format approximately 18 x 21 inches and used by some nineteenth-century outdoor photographers, notably Carleton E. Watkins and William Henry Jackson when working in the American West. Some contemporary photographers continue to use very large formats.

Medium-format camera
The medium-format camera takes 6 cm roll film, creating negatives or either 6 x 4.5 cm, 6 x 6 square or 6 x 7 format. The Hasselblad is one of the most famous 6 x 6 cameras.

New Topographics
The landmark exhibition "New Topographics: Photographs of a Man-Altered Landscape" encapsulated a significant moment in the development of American landscape photography. The show was curated by William Jenkins at the International Museum of Photography at George Eastman House (Rochester, New York) in 1975. The term was used to describe a group of photographers including Robert Adams, Nicholas Nixon, Lewis Baltz, and Stephen Shore, who used a detached style, which echoed that of nineteenth-century topographic photographers such as Timothy H. O'Sullivan.

Overexposure
The exposure of light-sensitive material with too much light. With negative film this has the effect of increasing shadow contrast and the total density range. Overexposed images require longer printing times and appear grainier.

Photobook

Traditionally referred to as photographically illustrated books and then illustrated books, the term photobook has become popular since the 1980s to refer to a book in which the photographs make a significant contribution to the content. Significant examples include Henri Cartier-Bresson's *The Decisive Moment* (1952; see p.260) and Martin Parr's *The Last Resort* (1986; see p.102). The term "photobook" is also a commercial one applied to single or very short-run, digitally printed books.

Photogram

An image produced without a camera or lens by placing an opaque, translucent or transparent object between—often directly onto—a piece of photographic paper or film and a light source. These were among the earliest photographic images produced by Thomas Wedgwood, Humphry Davy, and William Henry Fox Talbot, who described them as photogenic drawings. Photograms had renewed popularity as a creative technique in the 1920s with Man Ray, who called them rayographs.

Photogravure

A photomechanical, intaglio ink-printing process capable of rapid, high-quality reproduction of photographs that preserve detail and tone on paper.

Photojournalism

The term was coined in 1924 (possibly by Frank Luther Mott) to designate a sequence of photographs that emphasized photographic reportage, requiring the skills of both photographer and journalist. This distinguishes it from press or news photography. It thrived with the rise of illustrated news magazines, such as *Picture Post* and *Life* from the 1920s to 1960s, and is now best seen in newspaper color supplements.

Photomontage

A composite image created by assembling a number of different images, sometimes in other media, by cutting and pasting, projection, or digital techniques.

Pictorialism

A term that was used generally by photographers from the late nineteenth century and was popular until World War I to define an artistic approach to photography. Pictorialism was part of a larger debate around art and photography that had preoccupied photographers since the 1850s and it was, in part, a reaction against the ease of taking photographs from the mid 1880s. In the 1920s Pictorialism gave way to realism and objectivity in photography, although it never quite disappeared and interest in it continues today.

Polaroid

The Polaroid Corporation was founded by Edwin Land in the United States in 1937 to produce polarizing glasses for three-dimensional applications. In 1948 Land launched the Polaroid Model 95 camera, which offered almost instant photography. In 1963 instant color film was introduced and in 1972 the iconic Polaroid SX70 camera was launched, which introduced true instant photographs that developed without the need for peeling or the subsequent coating of the photograph. The launch of Polavision instant movie camera system in 1978 failed as video proved more attractive to consumers. In 2001 the corporation filed for Chapter 11 bankruptcy protection as digital photography had eroded its traditional markets.

Post-processing

A term that refers to the work traditionally done on a negative or print after the normal process has been completed. With the digital era, the term is more usually associated with adjustments made to the RAW image file using software such as Photoshop.

Rangefinder

A camera that is fitted with a range-finder, whereby the photographer views the scene through a window mounted to the side of the camera rather than through the lens itself. Rangefinder cameras are typically smaller and quieter than SLRs and take photographs that are sharp in focus.

RAW file

A camera RAW image file contains minimally processed data from the image sensor of a digital camera. RAW files are so called because they are not yet processed, however, they contain the maximum level of information and can therefore be considered the equivalent of a digital negative. The photographer then has the choice of how to process the file in order to obtain the highest-quality results.

Resin-coated (RC) paper

A paper that has been sealed on both sides with a pigmented polyethylene resin and has the light-sensitive emulsion coated onto one side. RC paper does not absorb water or chemicals, which makes it quick to process and dry. It was widely introduced from around 1968. With traditional fiber-based papers the emulsion is absorbed into the paper, which gives more depth to the image. Fibre-based papers are considered more archivally stable than RC paper and are generally preferred by photographic artists.

Retouching

In terms of film and paper this referred to work done with a brush or knife to the emulsion of a negative or print to either remove parts or add to it. The advent of digital working has added these and other tools via software, of which Photoshop is the best known. Photoshop has become a verb in its own right.

Roll film

A length of light-sensitive film rolled on a spool usually with a backing paper and able to be loaded into a camera in daylight. Cellulose nitrate roll film was commercially introduced in 1889, daylight-loading film cartridges in 1891 and paper-backed film, which remains in production today, in 1892. A large number of roll film formats and lengths have appeared since 1889 with the most common being 120, 620, and 127 sizes. The safer film base cellulose acetate was increasingly used from 1934; in the late 1940s, cellulose triacetate was introduced, and in the 1980s polyester bases became the norm.

Salted paper print
The earliest form of silver halide printing paper developed by William Henry Fox Talbot around 1834. Talbot used paper soaked in salt; this was dried and then brushed with silver nitrate before being exposed and subsequently fixed with a concentrated salt solution or, later, sodium thiosulphate ("hypo").

Saturation
A setting on a digital camera or in image editing software that adjusts the intensity of color relative to its own brightness. A desaturated image will appear with gray tones.

Shutter
A device that allows light to pass for a preset period, exposing the film or sensor to light to capture a permanent image of a scene. Shutter speeds are typically expressed as fractions of a second, for example, 1/250ths.

Silver print
Also known as gelatin silver print, this refers to photographs mainly produced since the early 1870s using gelatin as a colloid. More recently the term has been applied in the photographic art market to differentiate images produced using traditional silver-based techniques from digital printing.

Single-lens reflex (SLR) camera
SLR cameras (SLRs) use a mirror and prism, which therefore allows the photographer to view directly through the lens and see exactly what will be captured for any particular focal length.

Solarization
A photographic effect achieved in the darkroom or digitally whereby an image on a negative or photographic print is wholly or partially reversed in tone. Dark areas appear light or light areas appear dark. It can be created in error but it is also used for creative effect.

Staged photography
A posed scene or performance enacted before the camera similar to *tableaux vivants* (living pictures). It can include studio portraiture and scenarios involving people that are directed or manipulated by the photographer.

Stereograph
A pair of photographs mounted together that are designed to be viewed with a stereoscope. The term applies to any medium used to create the pair of images, but can be refined to be process specific, for example, stereo-daguerreotype.

Stereoscope
An optical instrument with two viewing lenses, which fuses two images so that a single three-dimensional image is perceived. The three principal designs have been the Wheatstone (1838); the Brewster lenticular (1838, but popular from around 1849) and the Holmes pattern (*c.* 1895).

Straight photography
Photography that attempts to depict a scene or object as realistically and objectively as possible. The term first emerged in the 1880s as a reaction against manipulated photography. In 1932 Group f/64 defined it as: "possessing no qualities of technique, composition or idea, derivative of any other art form."

Street photography
A style of documentary photography that features subjects in public spaces. It became popular from the 1890s with the introduction of hand cameras. The genre has attracted renewed interest since the early 2000s.

Telephoto lens
A type of long-focus lens in which the physical length of the lens is shorter than the focal length, and which magnifies the image, making it appear closer. They also produce a foreshortening effect, compressing the final image. Typical focal lengths are from 85mm (suitable for portraits) up to 600mm (suitable for sports and wildlife).

TTL flash
Through-the-lens or TTL flash meters the light from a flashgun reflected back from the subject through the camera lens and is therefore a very accurate way to control the exposure of the image, allowing the flash to be fine tuned creatively, for example, in using fill flash.

Underexposed
The exposure of light-sensitive materials with too little light or light that is insufficient to produce normal image contrast. In negative film this reduces density with a resultant loss of contrast and detail in the darker subject areas. In transparent film it results in an increase in density.

Vernacular photography
Refers to images usually created by amateur or "unknown" photographers and often depicts family or people in everyday and domestic situations. Their frequent banality, humor, or photographic errors and occasional artistic merit can give them an unintentional artistic quality or charm. They have attracted increasing interest from collectors and galleries. Walker Evans in particular was influenced by vernacular photography.

View camera
Also known as a technical camera. The term refers to a large-format camera usually with lateral and vertical movements plus swing or tilt adjustment on the camera back and/or front lens standard. Traditionally, the image was viewed on a ground glass screen on the camera back. Increasingly this has been replaced with a digital back with the subject viewed on a monitor.

Wide-angle lens
A lens of shorter than normal focal length, which gives a larger angle of view.

Zone System
A technique designed to bridge the gap between sensitometry and creative photography. The Zone System was developed by photographers Ansel Adams and Fred Archer around 1939–40 at the Art Center School in Los Angeles, United States. The system relied on empirical testing by the photographer of film and paper to provide information about the characteristics of the materials to support the photographer in defining the relationship between the way a subject was visualized and the end result.

Index

M

N

O

P

T

U

V

W

Y

Z

Picture credits

8–41 Paul Lowe **46–47** © The Francis Frith Collection **49 top** Timothy O'Sullivan (U.S. Geological Survey), courtesy Rephotographic Survey Project **49 below** Mark Klett and Gordon Bushaw for the Rephotographic Survey Project, courtesy Rephotographic Survey Project **51** © Ansel Adams Publishing Rights Trust / Corbis **53** © Robert Adams, courtesy Fraenkel Gallery, San Francisco **54–55** © Joel Sternfeld, courtesy of the artist and Luhring Augustine, New York **56–57** © John Davies **60–61** © Joel Meyerowitz, courtesy Howard Greenberg Gallery **63** © Richard Misrach, courtesy Fraenkel Gallery, San Francisco **64–65** Courtesy Jem Southam **66–67** Simon Norfolk / INSTITUTE **73** Photo by National Media Museum / Royal Photographic Society / SSPL / Getty Images **75** The Metropolitan Museum of Art / Art Resource / Scala, Florence **77** Berenice Abbott / Getty Images **79** Gilman Collection, Purchase, Alfred Stieglitz Society Gifts, 2005 (2005.100.593) © Walker Evans Archive, The Metropolitan Museum of Art, The Metropolitan Museum of Art / Art Resource / Scala, Florence **80–81**© Hiroshi Sugimoto, courtesy Fraenkel Gallery, San Francisco **82–83** © Andreas Gursky, courtesy Sprüth Magers Berlin London / DACS 2016 **84–85** courtesy of the artist and Paul Kasmin Gallery **86–87** © Gregory Crewdson, courtesy of the artist Gagosian Gallery **89** Courtesy Lisa Barnard **94–95** The Metropolitan Museum of Art / Art Resource / Scala, Florence © Man Ray Trust / ADAGP, Paris and DACS, London 2016 **97** The Metropolitan Museum of Art / Art Resource / Scala, Florence © Hattula Moholy-Nagy / DACS 2016 **99** The Museum of Modern Art, New York / Scala, Florence © Center for Creative Photography, The University of Arizona Foundation / DACS, 2016 **100–101** © Eggleston Artistic Trust, courtesy Cheim & Read, New York **102–103** © Martin Parr / Magnum Photos **104–105** © Alec Soth / Magnum Photos **106–107** Courtesy Peter Fraser **112** Photo by SSPL / Getty Images **114** The J. Paul Getty Museum, Los Angeles, digital image courtesy of the Getty's Open Content Program **115** Charenton-le-Pont, Médiathèque de l'Architecture et du Patrimoine, photo © Ministère de la Culture – Médiathèque du Patrimoine, Dist. RMN-Grand Palais / Atelier de Nadar **116** © The Lisette Model Foundation, Inc. (1983) Used by permission, courtesy of Bruce Silverstein Gallery **119** © The Estate of Harry Callahan; courtesy Pace / MacGill Gallery, New York **121** © Aperture Foundation Inc., Paul Strand Archive **123** © Norman Parkinson Ltd. / Courtesy Norman Parkinson Archive **124** © Eve Arnold / Magnum Photos **127** Courtesy Brian Griffin **129** Courtesy Mary Ellen Mark **130** © Bruce Gilden / Magnum Photos **133** Courtesy Harry Borden **139** © Photograph Samml. / SK Stiftung Kultur – A. Sander Archiv, Köln / VG Bild-Kunst, Bonn and DACS, London 2016 **140** Library of Congress, LC-USF34- 009058-C 141 Library of Congress, LC-USF34- 009095-C 143 Photo by Horst P. Horst / Condé Nast via Getty Images **145** © Imperial War Museums (CBM 1049) **147** © Malick Sidibé, courtesy Galerie MAGNIN-A, Paris. INV Nbr. MS.8088 **148–149** Courtesy Nan Goldin and Matthew Marks Galle **151** Courtesy of the artist and Marian Goodman Gallery **152** © Wolfgar Tillmans, courtesy Maureen Paley, London **155** Courtesy Steve Pyk **156–157** Courtesy Laura Pannack **162–163** Wellcome Library, Londo Wellcome Images, copyrighted work available under Creative Commo Attribution only licence CC BY 4.0 creativecommons.org/licenses/by/4.(**164** The Metropolitan Museum of Art / Art Resource / Scala, Florenc © The Heartfield Community of Heirs / VG Bild-Kunst, Bonn and DAC London 2016 **166** Getty Research Institute, Los Angeles (2012.M. © Ed Ruscha **168–169** © Duane Michals, courtesy of DC Moore Galler New York **171** © Nicholas Nixon, courtesy Fraenkel Gallery, San Francisc **172–173** Courtesy Cindy Sherman and Metro Pictures, New Yor **174–175** Courtesy Jeff Wall **175** right Brooklyn Museum, Gift of Frederic Pratt, 42.74 **176–177** Courtesy Adam Broomberg & Oliver Chanarin and Lissc Gallery, London **179** Courtesy Mishka Henner **185** © Colette Urbajtel / Archiv Manuel Álvarez Bravo SC **187** © Robert Frank from The Americar **189** Courtesy William Klein **190–191** SSPL / Getty Images **193** © The Esta of Garry Winogrand, courtesy Fraenkel Gallery, San Francisc **195** © Lee Friedlander, courtesy Fraenkel Gallery, San Francisc **196–197** © Elliott Erwitt / Magnum Photos **198–199** © Josef Koudelka Magnum Photos **200–201** © Alex Webb / Magnum Photos **202–203** Doug Wallace / INSTITUTE **204–205** © David Alan Harvey / Magnum Photo **210–211** Photo by Weegee (Arthur Fellig) / International Center c Photography / Getty Images **212** © W. Eugene Smith / Magnum Photo **214–215** Courtesy Anders Petersen **216–217** William Albert Allard National Geographic Creative **218–219** Sebastião Salgado / Amazonas nbpictures **220–221** © Raghu Rai / Magnum Photos **222–223** © Larr Towell / Magnum Photos **224–225** © Paolo Pellegrin / Magnum Photo **226–227** John Stanmeyer / National Geographic Creative **232–234** Bettmann Getty Images **234–235** Library of Congress, LC-USZ62-3845 **236–237** Courtesy David Goldblatt and Goodman Gallery **241** © Bern and Hilla Becher **243** Courtesy Chris Killip **244–245** The Estate c Larry Sultan **246–247** © Jim Goldberg / Magnum Photos **248–249** © Ann Fox, courtesy James Hyman Photography, London **250–251** © Richar Billingham, courtesy Anthony Reynolds Gallery, London **256–257** Digit image courtesy of the Getty's Open Content Program **258–259** Photo b bpk / Salomon / ullstein bild via Getty Images **260** © Henri Cartier-Bresson Magnum Photos **262–263** © Robert Capa © International Center c Photography / Magnum Photos **264** Photo by Larry Burrows / The LIF Premium Collection / Getty Images **265** Photo by Larry Burrows / Th LIFE Picture Collection / Getty Images **266–267** © Philip Jones Griffiths Magnum Photos **268–269** © Gilles Peress / Magnum Photo **270–271** Courtesy Anthony Suau **272–273** © Susan Meiselas Magnum Photos **274–275** © David Burnett / Contact – IOC